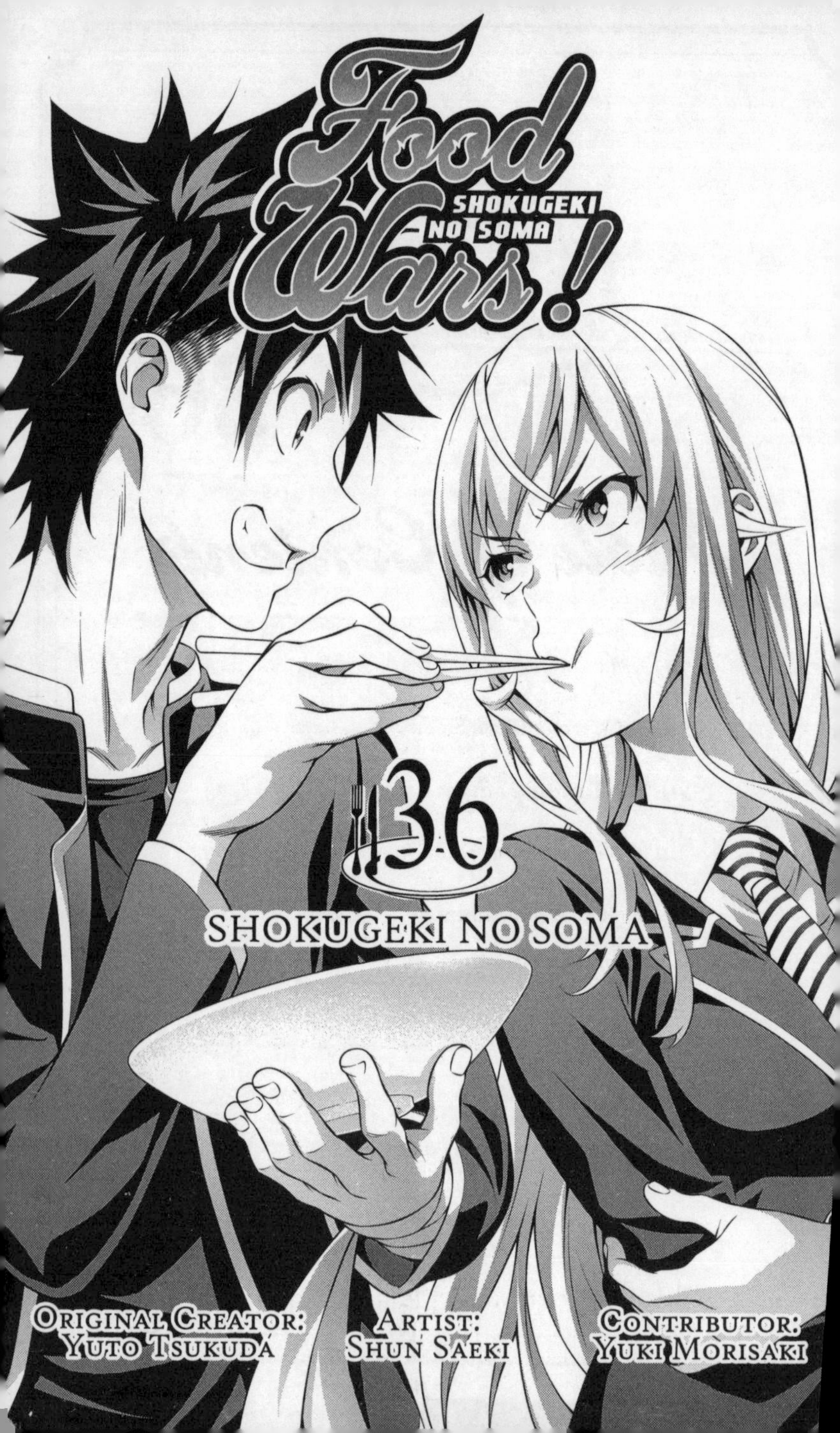
Food Wars!
SHOKUGEKI NO SOMA
36
SHOKUGEKI NO SOMA
ORIGINAL CREATOR: YUTO TSUKUDA
ARTIST: SHUN SAEKI
CONTRIBUTOR: YUKI MORISAKI

Food Wars! SHOKUGEKI NO SOMA 36

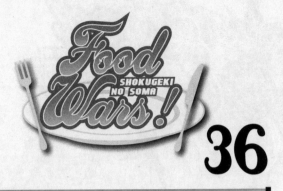

Table of Contents

309 TRUE INTENTIONS

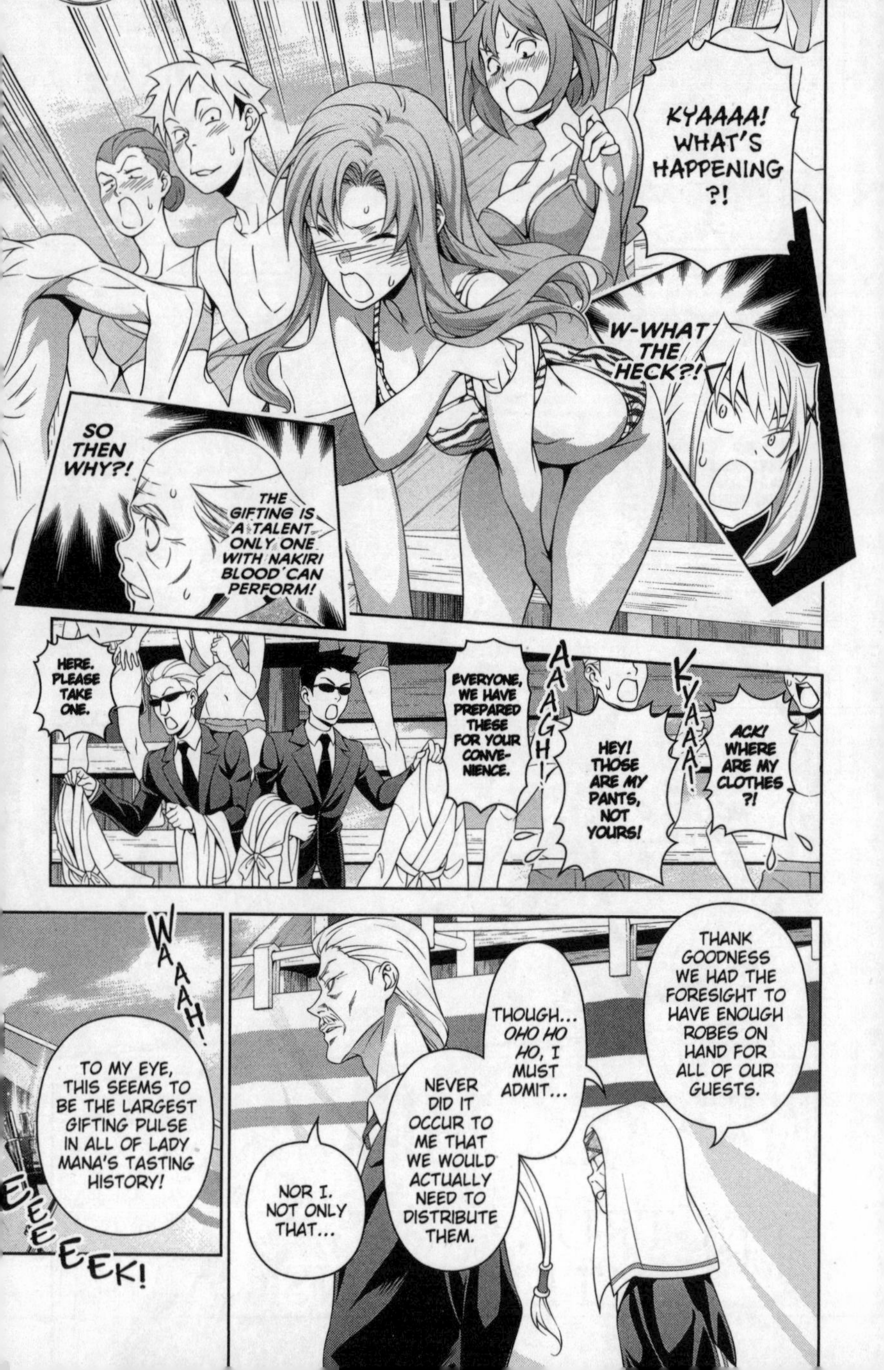
KYAAAA! WHAT'S HAPPENING ?!
W-WHAT THE HECK?!
SO THEN WHY?!
THE GIFTING IS A TALENT ONLY ONE WITH NAKIRI BLOOD CAN PERFORM!
ACK! WHERE ARE MY CLOTHES ?!
KYAAA!
HEY! THOSE ARE MY PANTS, NOT YOURS!
AAAGH!
EVERYONE, WE HAVE PREPARED THESE FOR YOUR CONVE-NIENCE.
HERE. PLEASE TAKE ONE.
THANK GOODNESS WE HAD THE FORESIGHT TO HAVE ENOUGH ROBES ON HAND FOR ALL OF OUR GUESTS.
THOUGH... OHO HO HO, I MUST ADMIT...
NEVER DID IT OCCUR TO ME THAT WE WOULD ACTUALLY NEED TO DISTRIBUTE THEM.
NOR I. NOT ONLY THAT...
WAAAH!
TO MY EYE, THIS SEEMS TO BE THE LARGEST GIFTING PULSE IN ALL OF LADY MANA'S TASTING HISTORY!
EEEEEK!

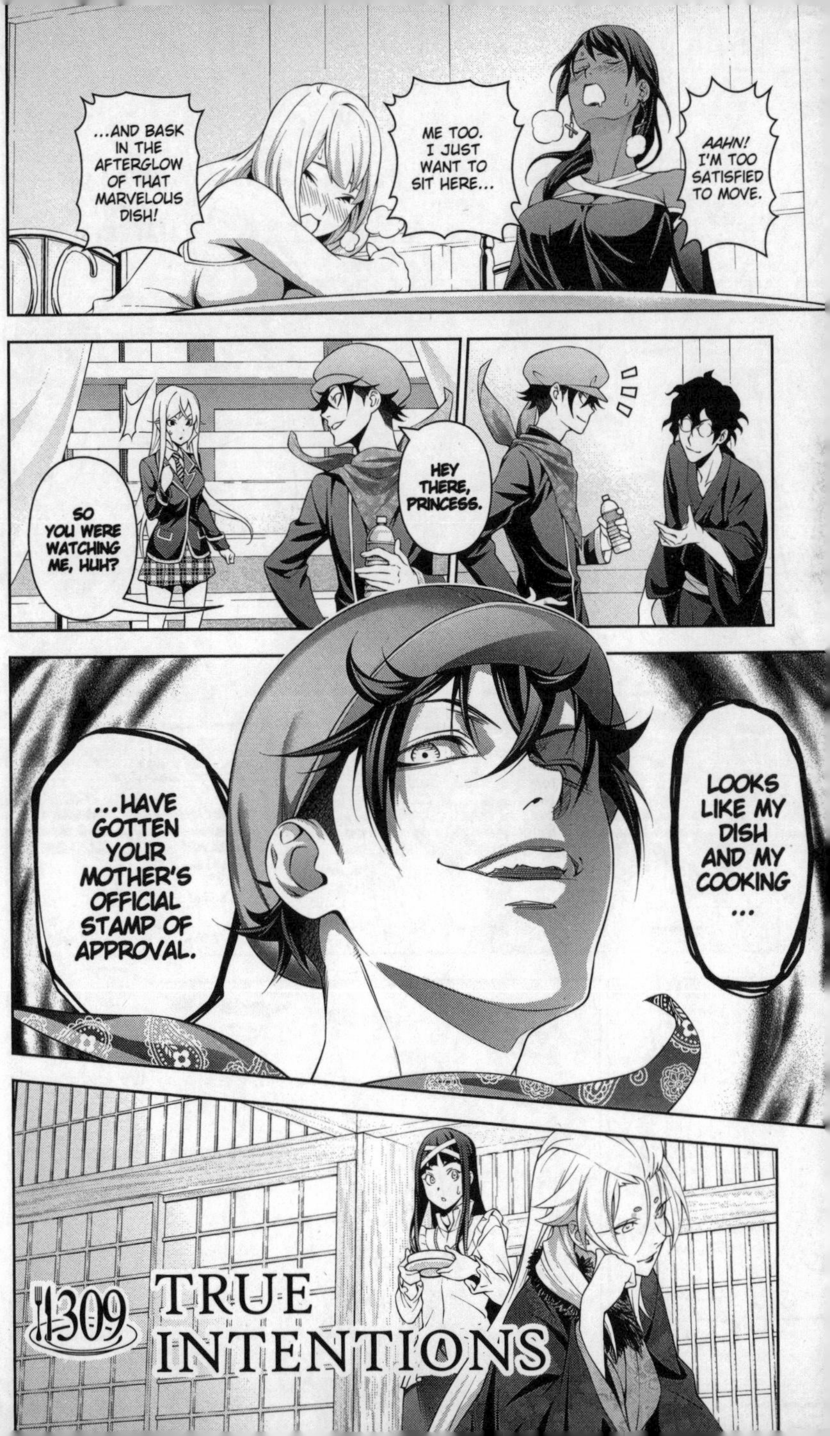
AAHN! I'M TOO SATISFIED TO MOVE.
ME TOO. I JUST WANT TO SIT HERE...
...AND BASK IN THE AFTERGLOW OF THAT MARVELOUS DISH!
HEY THERE, PRINCESS.
SO YOU WERE WATCHING ME, HUH?
LOOKS LIKE MY DISH AND MY COOKING ...
...HAVE GOTTEN YOUR MOTHER'S OFFICIAL STAMP OF APPROVAL.
309 TRUE INTENTIONS

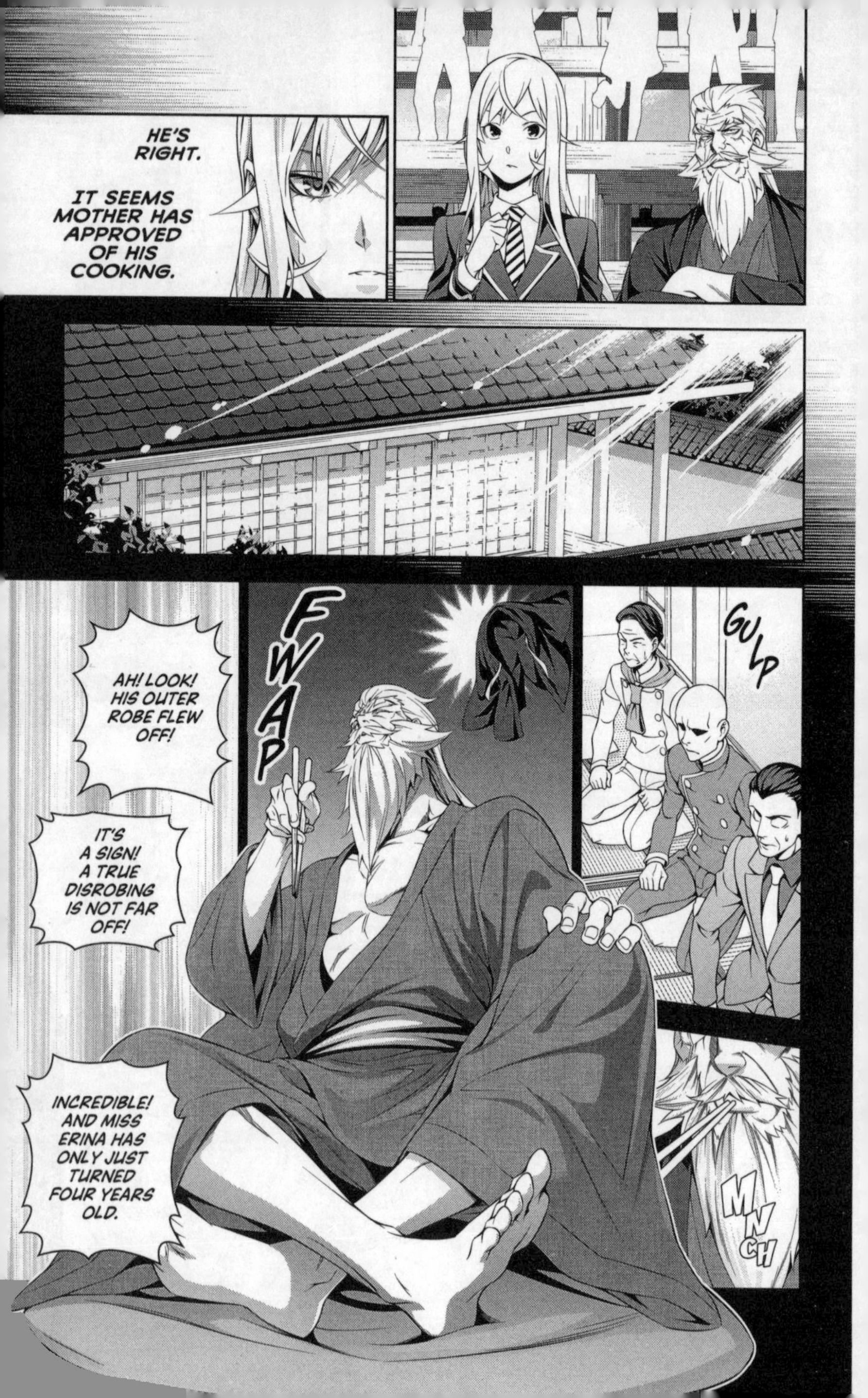
HE'S RIGHT.
IT SEEMS MOTHER HAS APPROVED OF HIS COOKING.
GULP
FWAP
AH! LOOK! HIS OUTER ROBE FLEW OFF!
IT'S A SIGN! A TRUE DISROBING IS NOT FAR OFF!
MNCH
INCREDIBLE! AND MISS ERINA HAS ONLY JUST TURNED FOUR YEARS OLD.

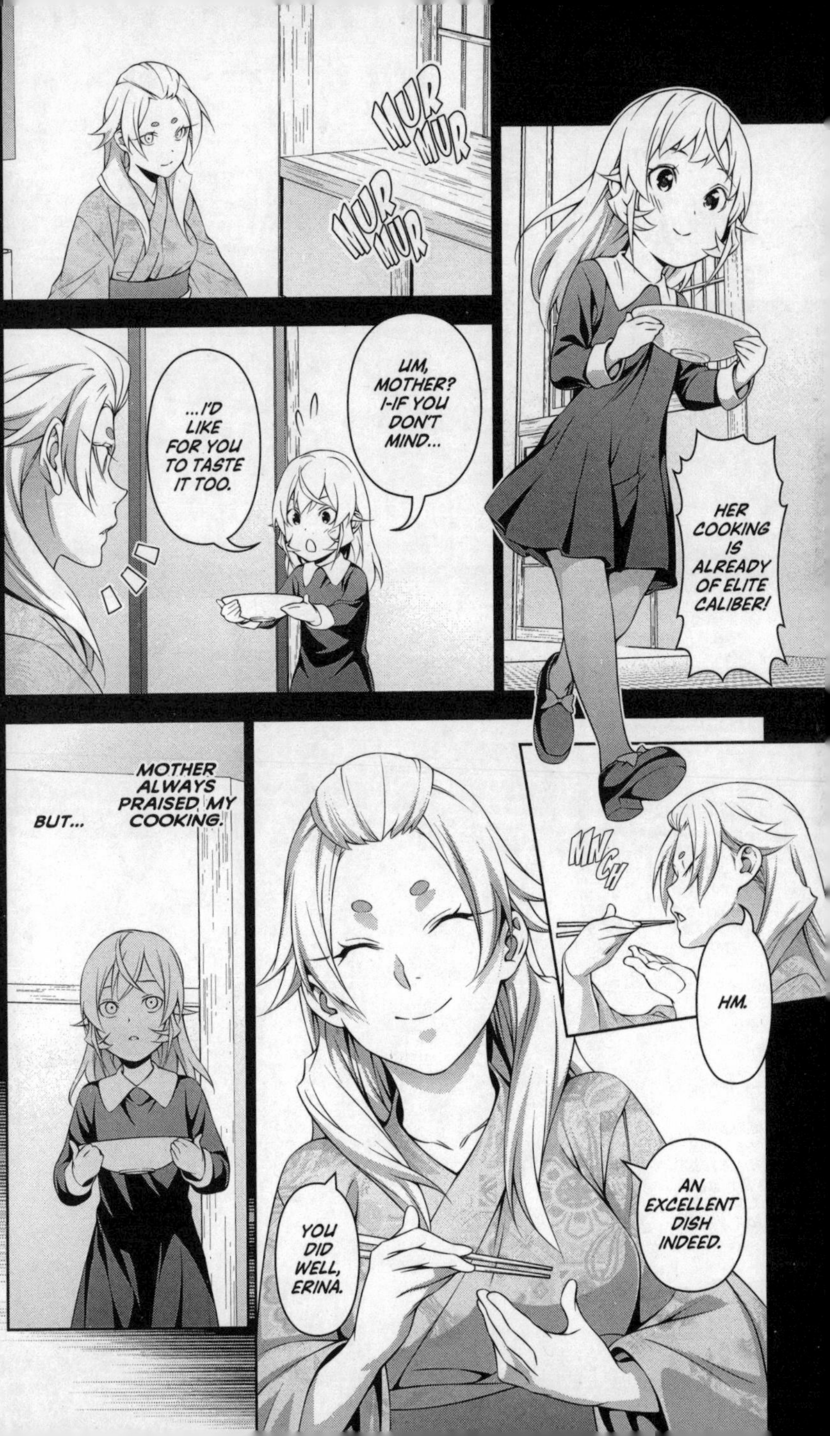
HER COOKING IS ALREADY OF ELITE CALIBER!
MUR MUR
MUR MUR
UM, MOTHER? I-IF YOU DON'T MIND...
...I'D LIKE FOR YOU TO TASTE IT TOO.
MNCH
HM.
AN EXCELLENT DISH INDEED.
YOU DID WELL, ERINA.
MOTHER ALWAYS PRAISED MY COOKING.
BUT...

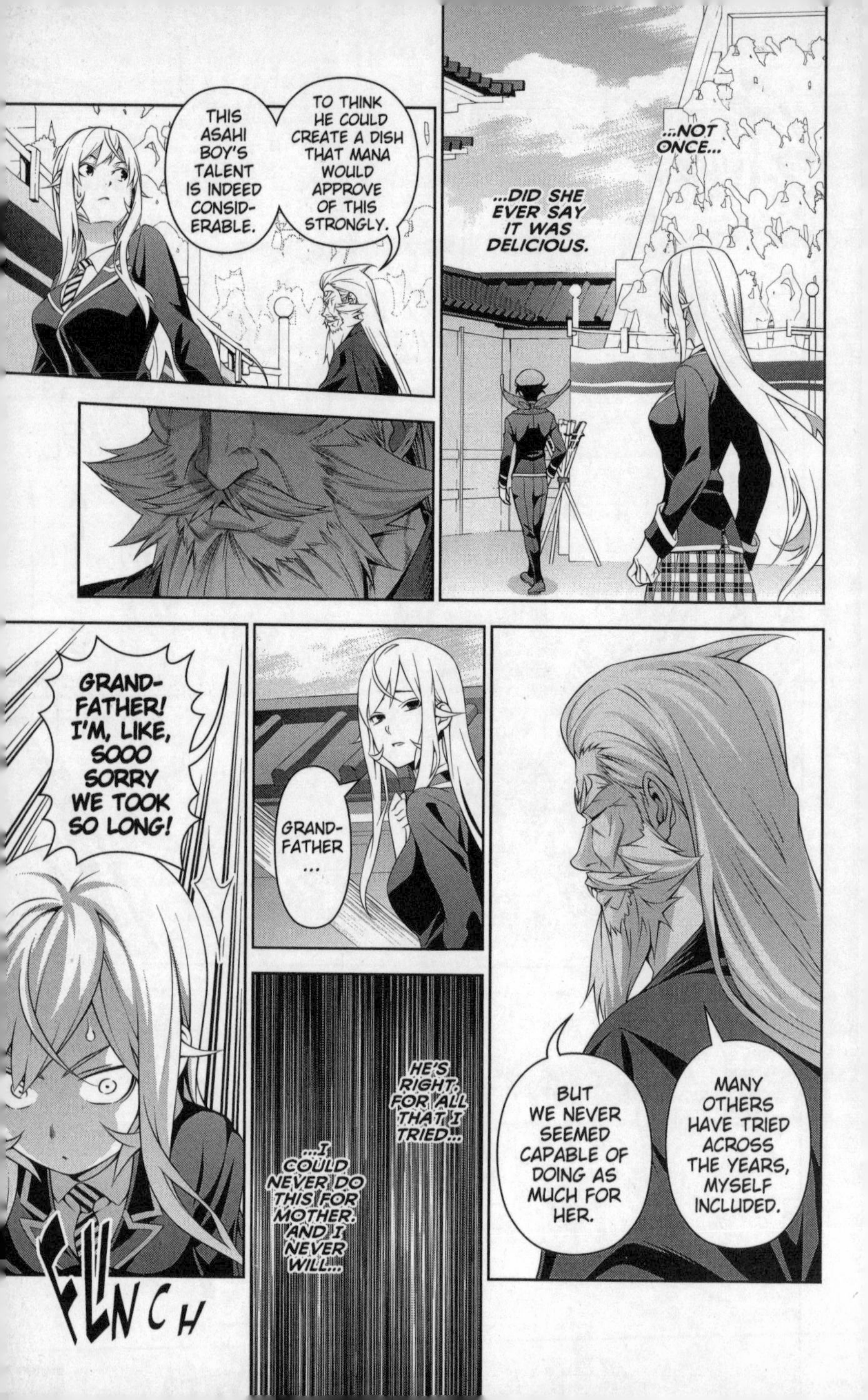
...NOT ONCE...
...DID SHE EVER SAY IT WAS DELICIOUS.
TO THINK HE COULD CREATE A DISH THAT MANA WOULD APPROVE OF THIS STRONGLY.
THIS ASAHI BOY'S TALENT IS INDEED CONSID-ERABLE.
MANY OTHERS HAVE TRIED ACROSS THE YEARS, MYSELF INCLUDED.
BUT WE NEVER SEEMED CAPABLE OF DOING AS MUCH FOR HER.
GRAND-FATHER...
HE'S RIGHT. FOR ALL THAT I TRIED...
...I COULD NEVER DO THIS FOR MOTHER. AND I NEVER WILL...
GRAND-FATHER! I'M, LIKE, SOOO SORRY WE TOOK SO LONG!
FLINCH

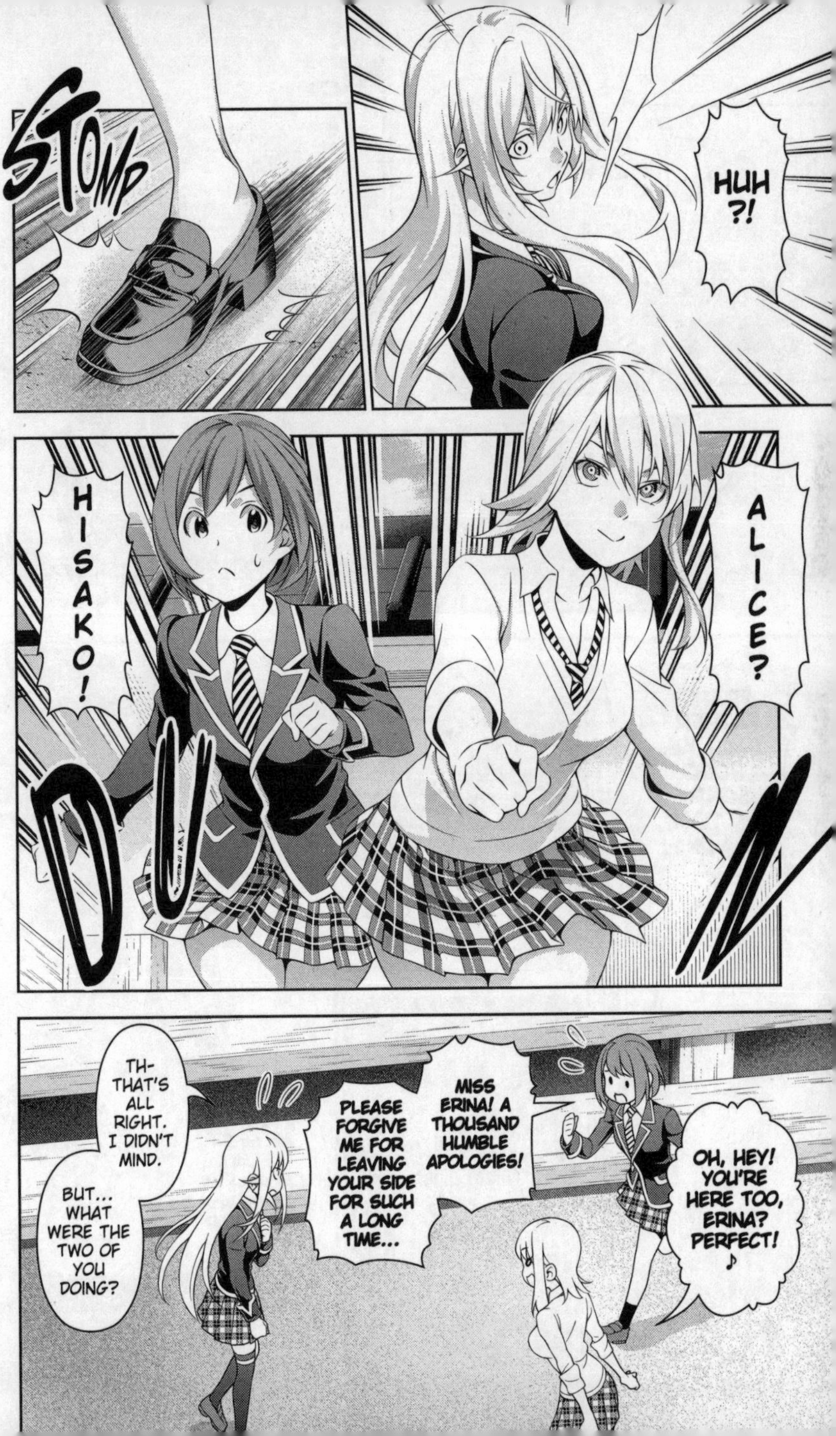
HUH ?!
STOMP
ALICE?
HISAKO!
DU
N
OH, HEY! YOU'RE HERE TOO, ERINA? PERFECT! ♪
MISS ERINA! A THOUSAND HUMBLE APOLOGIES!
PLEASE FORGIVE ME FOR LEAVING YOUR SIDE FOR SUCH A LONG TIME...
TH-THAT'S ALL RIGHT. I DIDN'T MIND.
BUT... WHAT WERE THE TWO OF YOU DOING?

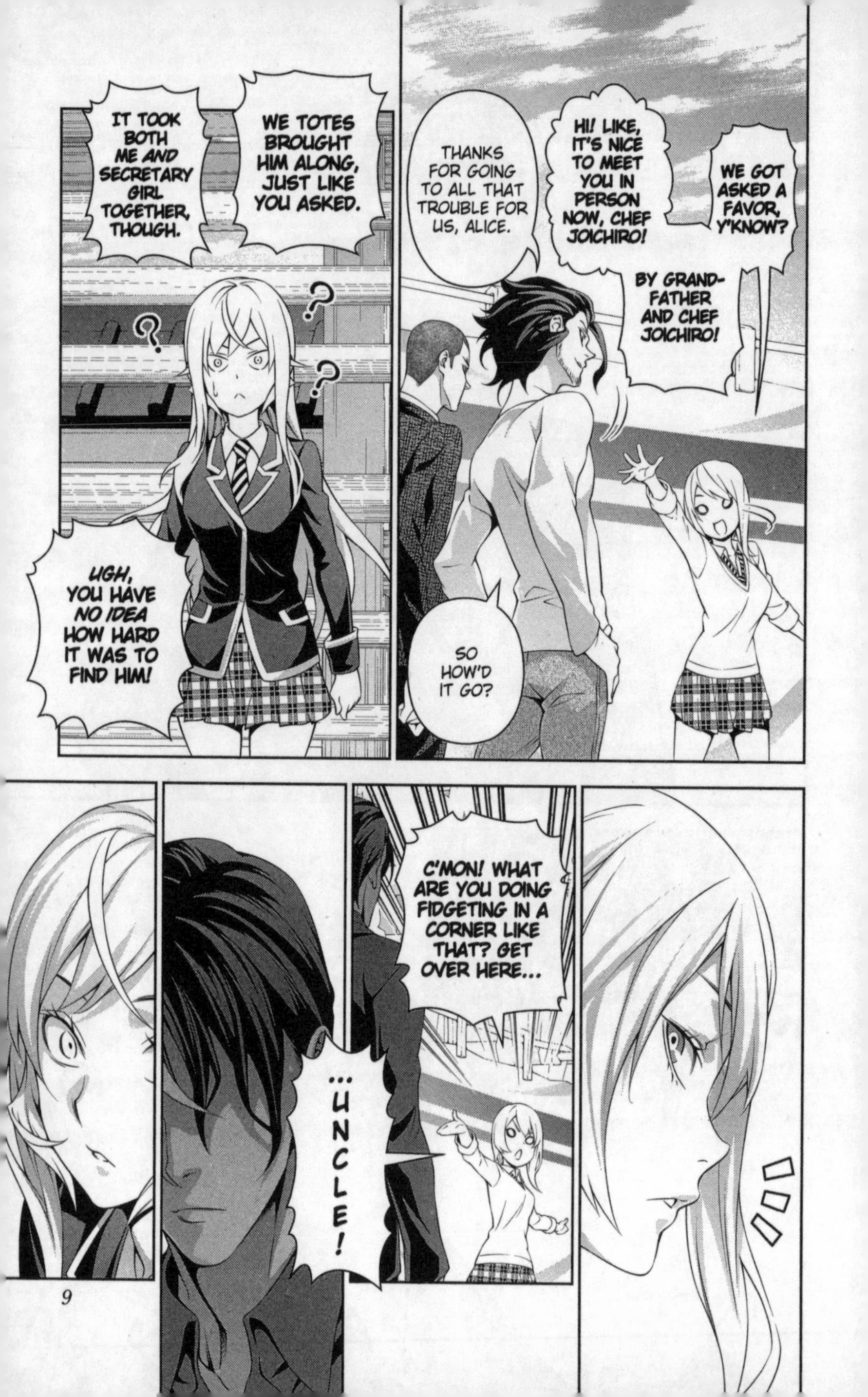
WE GOT ASKED A FAVOR, Y'KNOW?
BY GRAND-FATHER AND CHEF JOICHIRO!
HI! LIKE, IT'S NICE TO MEET YOU IN PERSON NOW, CHEF JOICHIRO!
THANKS FOR GOING TO ALL THAT TROUBLE FOR US, ALICE.
SO HOW'D IT GO?
WE TOTES BROUGHT HIM ALONG, JUST LIKE YOU ASKED.
IT TOOK BOTH ME AND SECRETARY GIRL TOGETHER, THOUGH.
UGH, YOU HAVE NO IDEA HOW HARD IT WAS TO FIND HIM!
C'MON! WHAT ARE YOU DOING FIDGETING IN A CORNER LIKE THAT? GET OVER HERE...
...UNCLE!

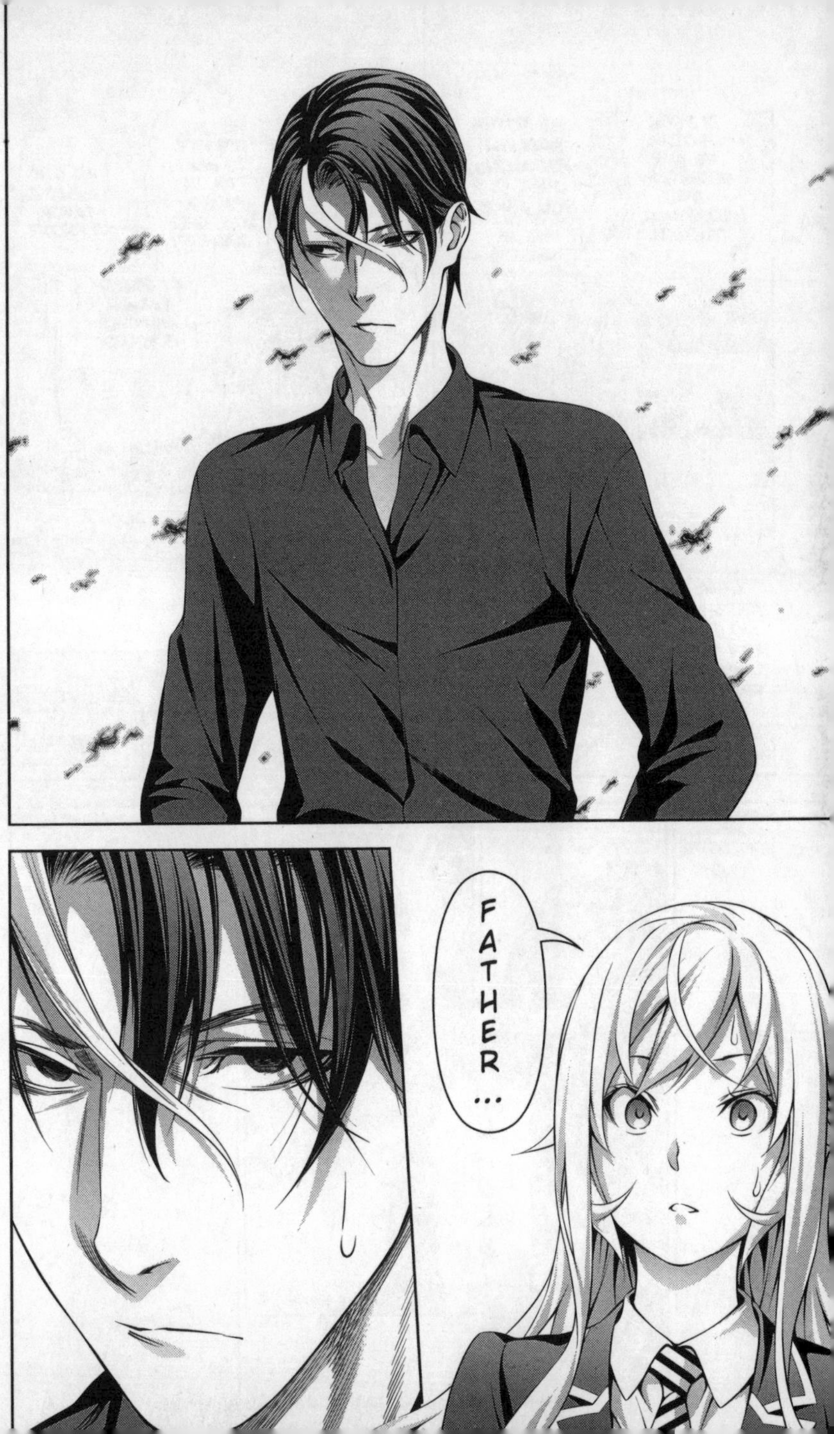
FATHER...

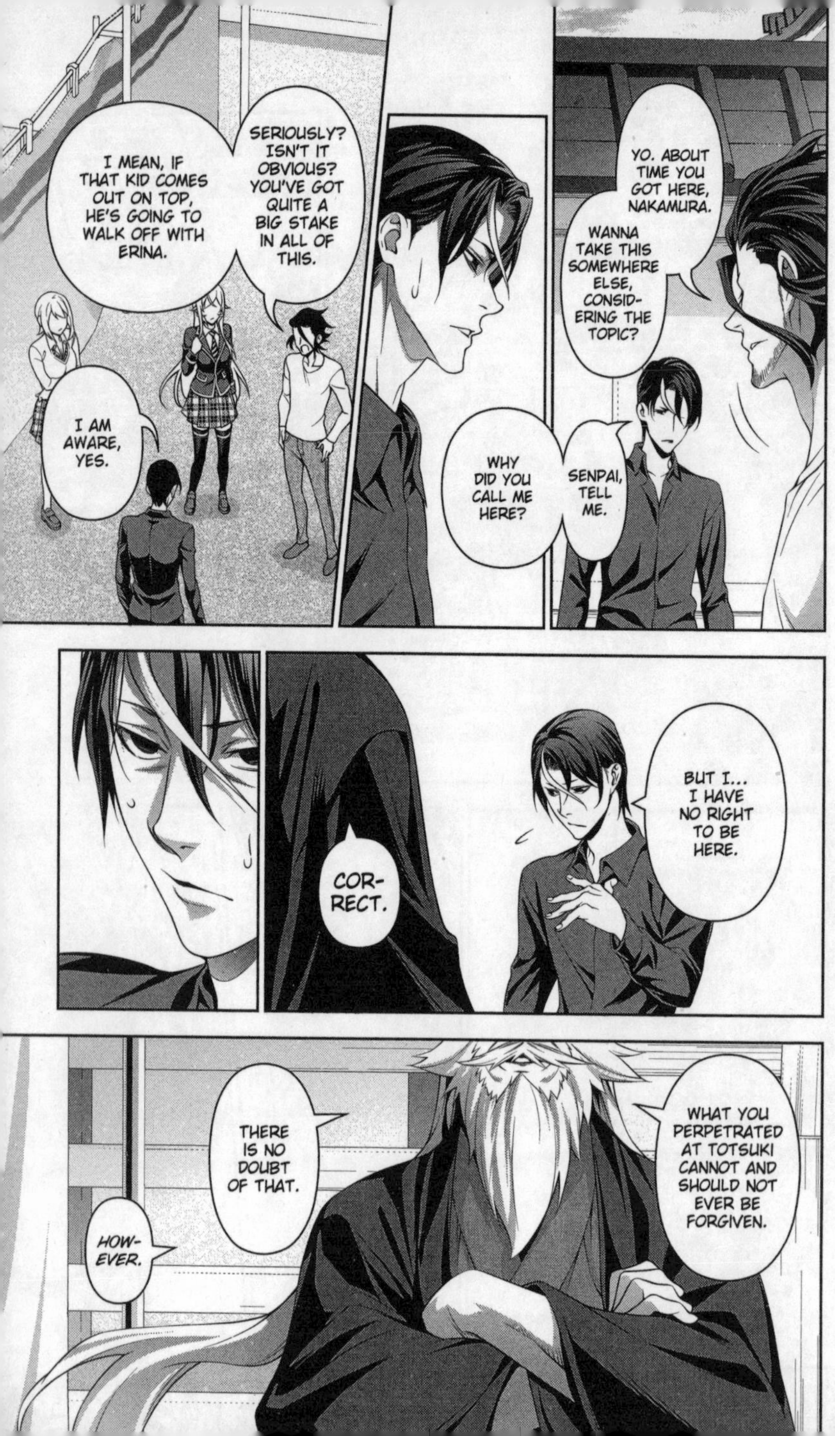
YO. ABOUT TIME YOU GOT HERE, NAKAMURA.
WANNA TAKE THIS SOMEWHERE ELSE, CONSIDERING THE TOPIC?
SENPAI, TELL ME.
WHY DID YOU CALL ME HERE?
SERIOUSLY? ISN'T IT OBVIOUS? YOU'VE GOT QUITE A BIG STAKE IN ALL OF THIS.
I MEAN, IF THAT KID COMES OUT ON TOP, HE'S GOING TO WALK OFF WITH ERINA.
I AM AWARE, YES.
BUT I... I HAVE NO RIGHT TO BE HERE.
CORRECT.
WHAT YOU PERPETRATED AT TOTSUKI CANNOT AND SHOULD NOT EVER BE FORGIVEN.
THERE IS NO DOUBT OF THAT.
HOWEVER.

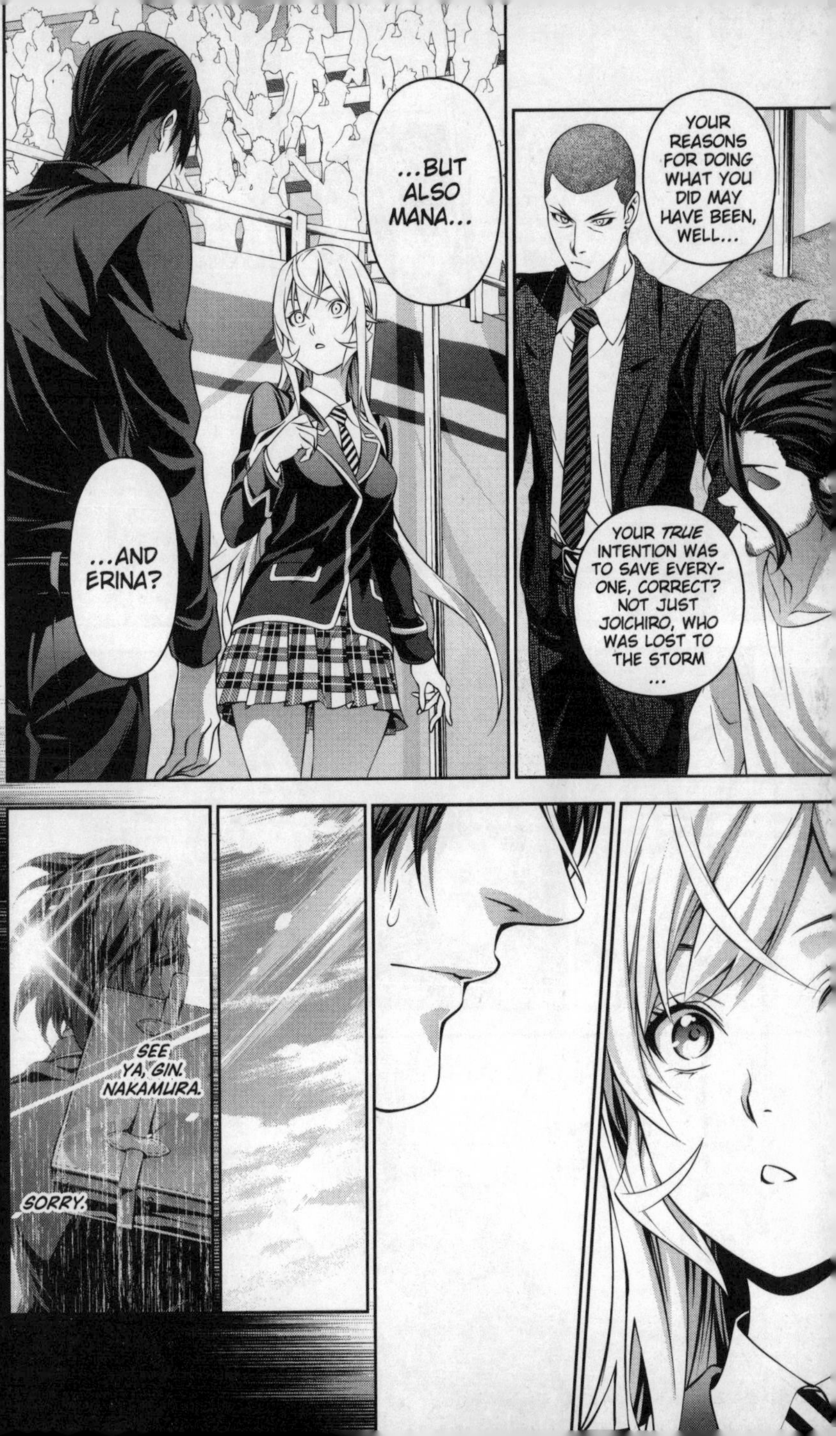
YOUR REASONS FOR DOING WHAT YOU DID MAY HAVE BEEN, WELL...
YOUR *TRUE* INTENTION WAS TO SAVE EVERY-ONE, CORRECT? NOT JUST JOICHIRO, WHO WAS LOST TO THE STORM ...
...BUT ALSO MANA...
...AND ERINA?
SEE YA, GIN. NAKAMURA.
SORRY.

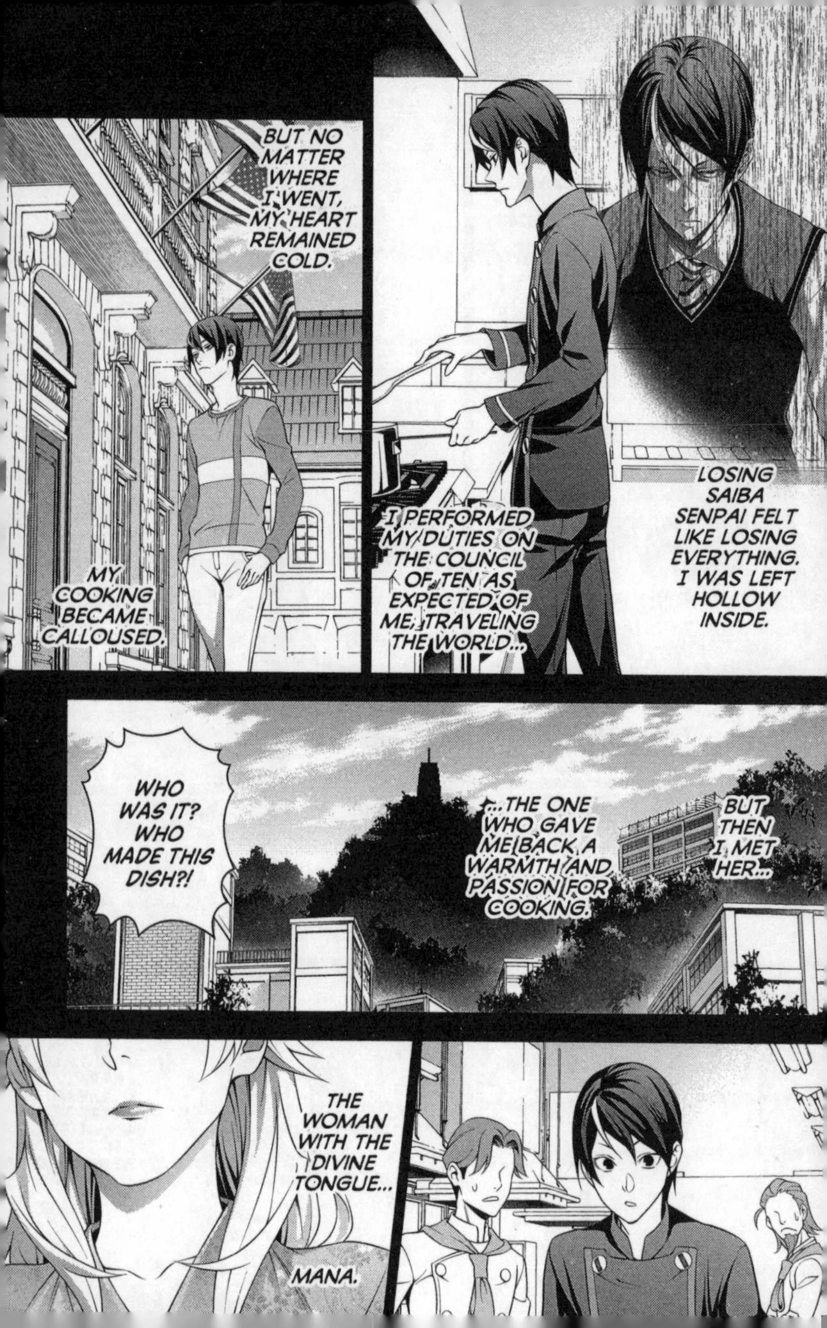
LOSING SAIBA SENPAI FELT LIKE LOSING EVERYTHING. I WAS LEFT HOLLOW INSIDE.
I PERFORMED MY DUTIES ON THE COUNCIL OF TEN AS EXPECTED OF ME, TRAVELING THE WORLD...
BUT NO MATTER WHERE I WENT, MY HEART REMAINED COLD.
MY COOKING BECAME CALLOUSED.
BUT THEN I MET HER...
...THE ONE WHO GAVE ME BACK A WARMTH AND PASSION FOR COOKING.
WHO WAS IT? WHO MADE THIS DISH?!
THE WOMAN WITH THE DIVINE TONGUE...
MANA.

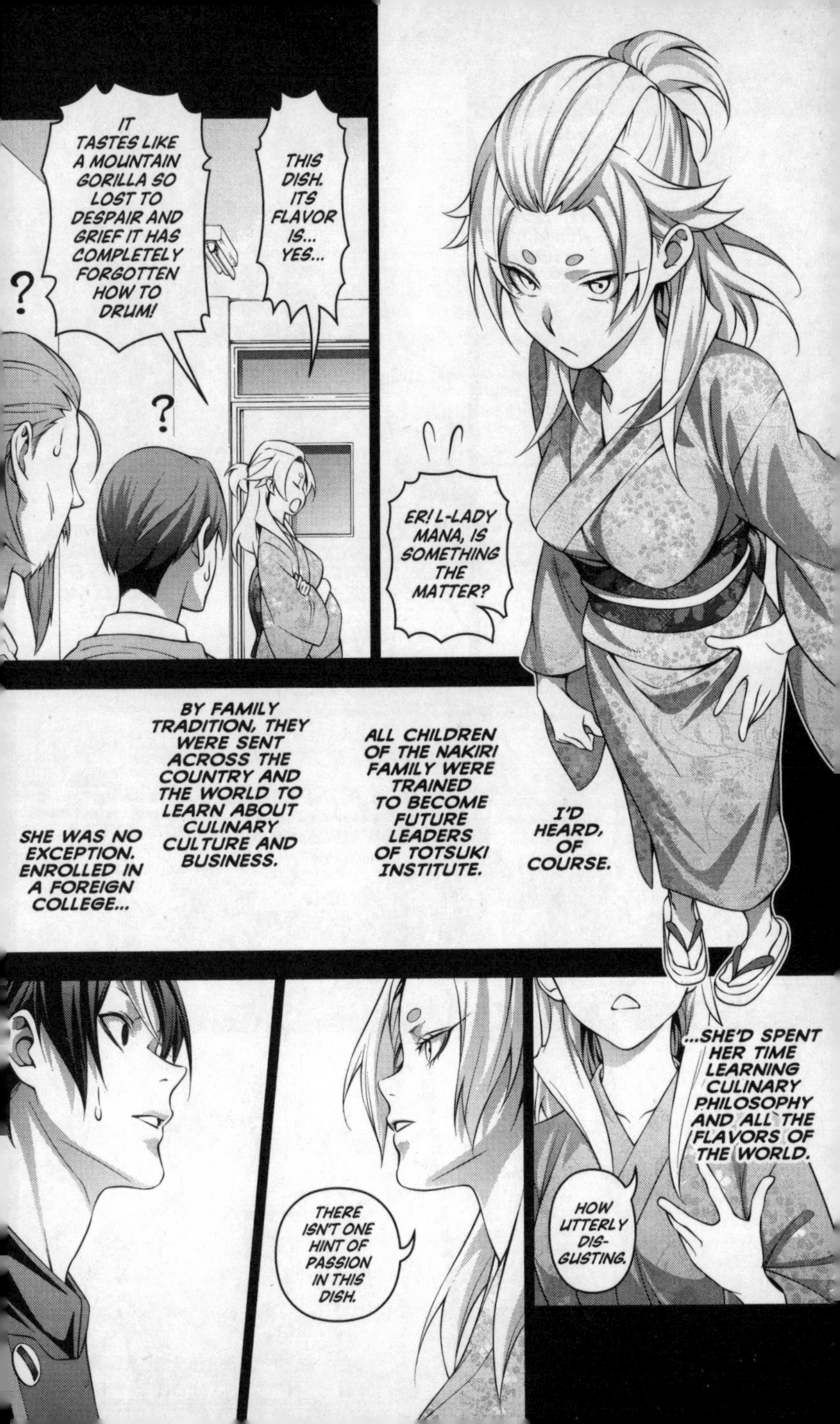
ER! L-LADY MANA, IS SOMETHING THE MATTER?
THIS DISH. ITS FLAVOR IS... YES...
IT TASTES LIKE A MOUNTAIN GORILLA SO LOST TO DESPAIR AND GRIEF IT HAS COMPLETELY FORGOTTEN HOW TO DRUM!
?
?
I'D HEARD, OF COURSE.
ALL CHILDREN OF THE NAKIRI FAMILY WERE TRAINED TO BECOME FUTURE LEADERS OF TOTSUKI INSTITUTE.
BY FAMILY TRADITION, THEY WERE SENT ACROSS THE COUNTRY AND THE WORLD TO LEARN ABOUT CULINARY CULTURE AND BUSINESS.
SHE WAS NO EXCEPTION. ENROLLED IN A FOREIGN COLLEGE...
...SHE'D SPENT HER TIME LEARNING CULINARY PHILOSOPHY AND ALL THE FLAVORS OF THE WORLD.
HOW UTTERLY DIS-GUSTING.
THERE ISN'T ONE HINT OF PASSION IN THIS DISH.

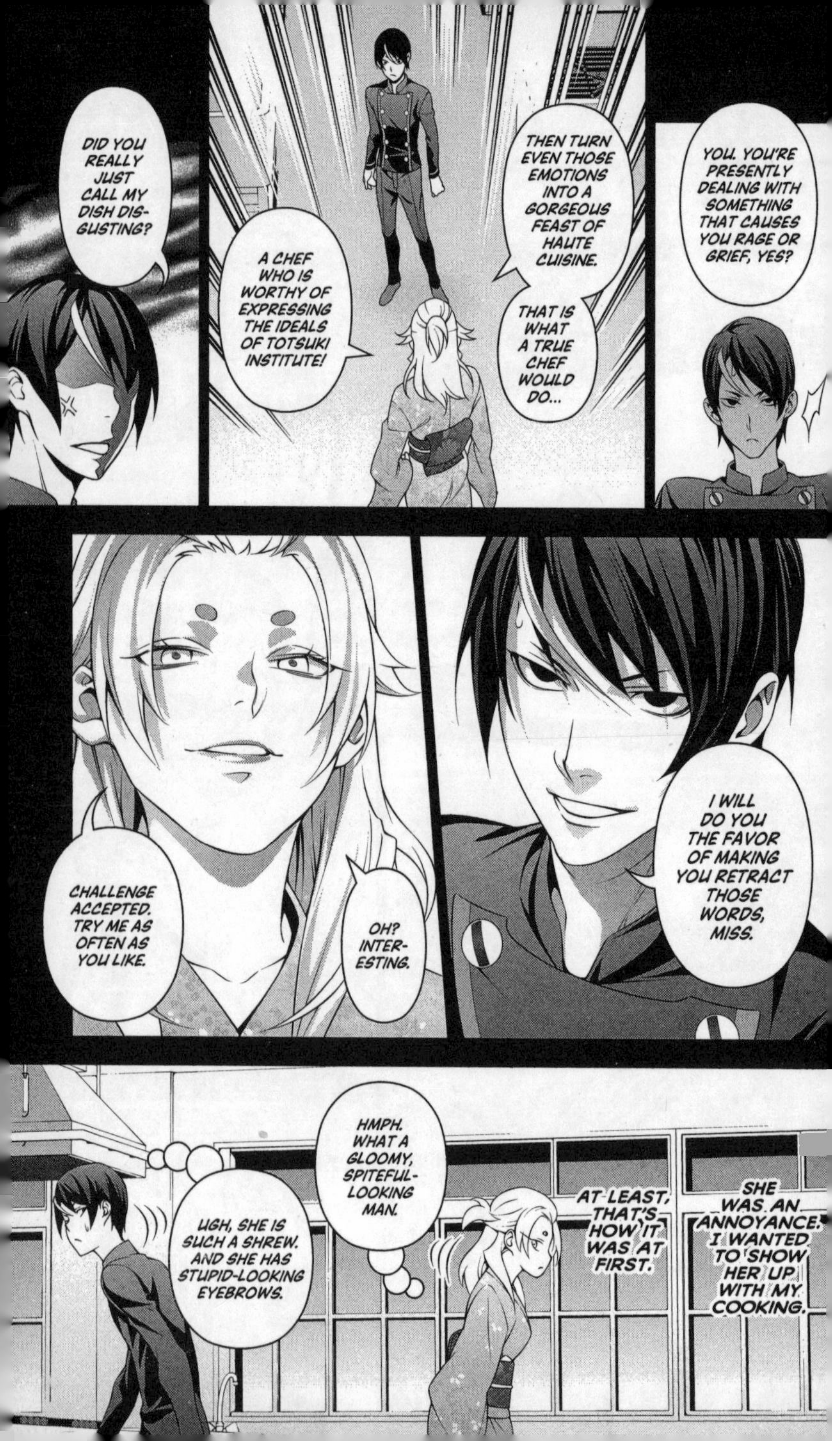
YOU. YOU'RE PRESENTLY DEALING WITH SOMETHING THAT CAUSES YOU RAGE OR GRIEF, YES?
THEN TURN EVEN THOSE EMOTIONS INTO A GORGEOUS FEAST OF HAUTE CUISINE.
THAT IS WHAT A TRUE CHEF WOULD DO...
A CHEF WHO IS WORTHY OF EXPRESSING THE IDEALS OF TOTSUKI INSTITUTE!
DID YOU REALLY JUST CALL MY DISH DIS-GUSTING?
I WILL DO YOU THE FAVOR OF MAKING YOU RETRACT THOSE WORDS, MISS.
OH? INTER-ESTING.
CHALLENGE ACCEPTED. TRY ME AS OFTEN AS YOU LIKE.
SHE WAS AN ANNOYANCE. I WANTED TO SHOW HER UP WITH MY COOKING.
AT LEAST, THAT'S HOW IT WAS AT FIRST.
HMPH. WHAT A GLOOMY, SPITEFUL-LOOKING MAN.
UGH, SHE IS SUCH A SHREW. AND SHE HAS STUPID-LOOKING EYEBROWS.

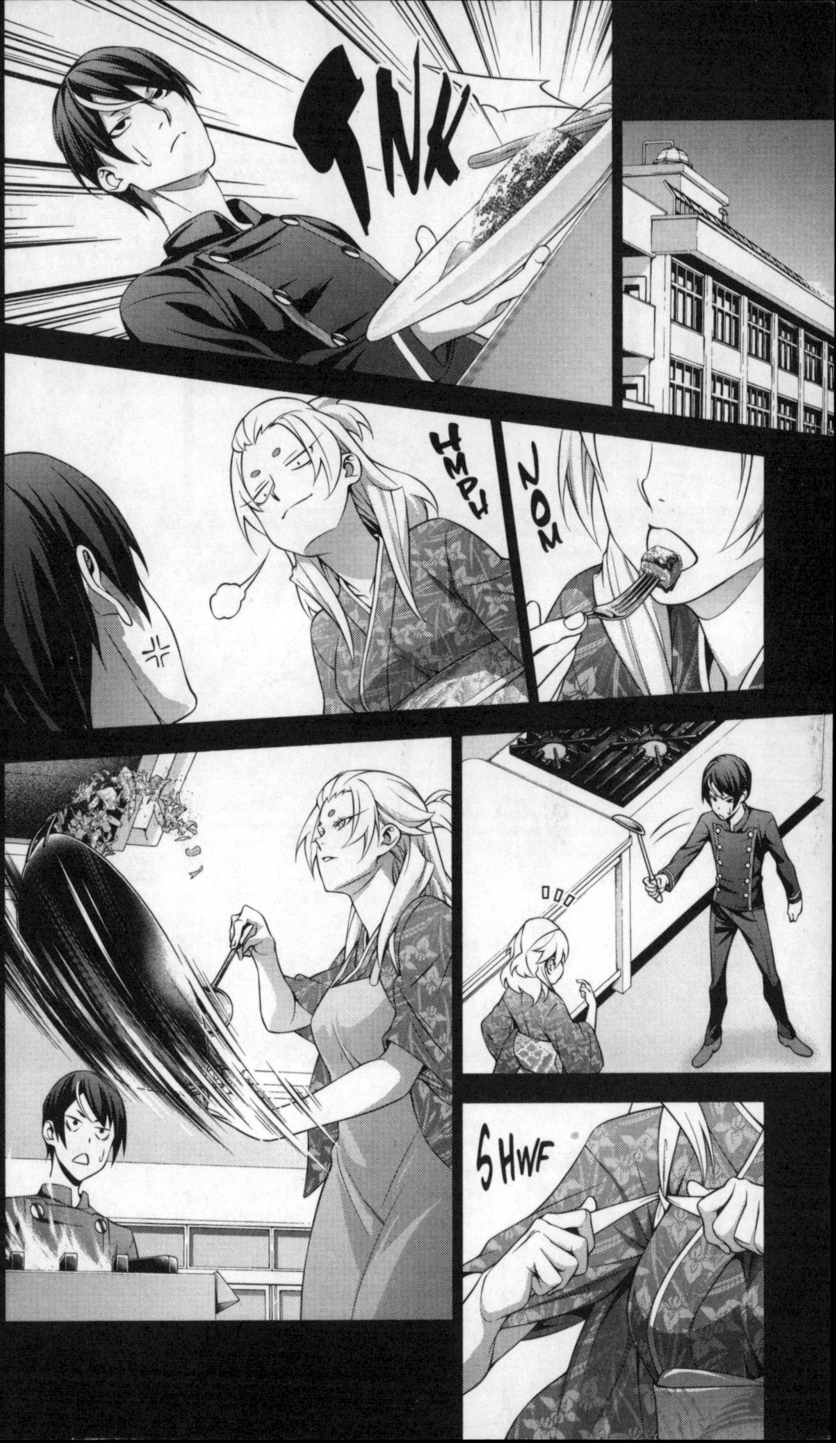
TNK
HMPH
NOM
SHWF

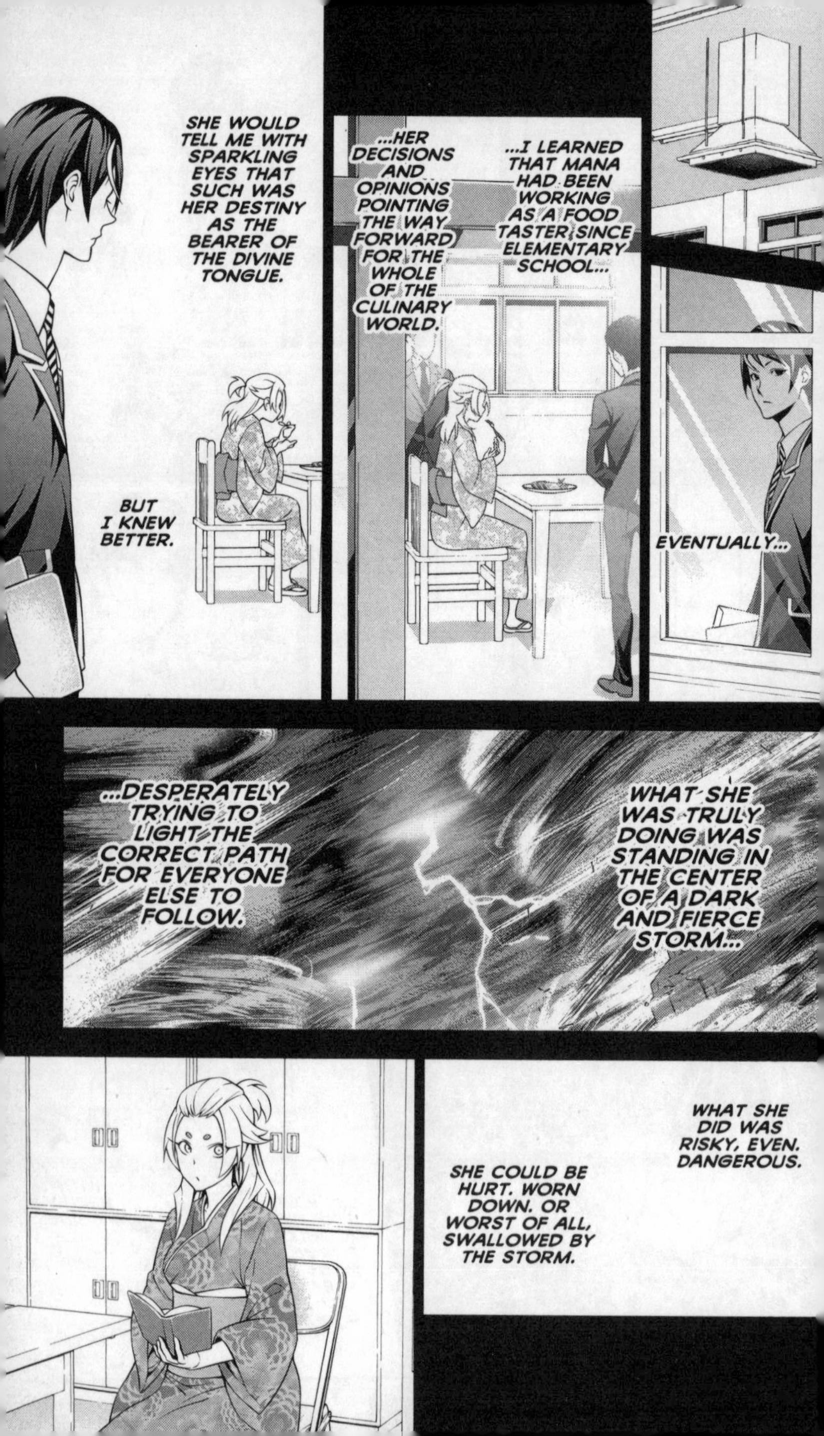
EVENTUALLY...
...I LEARNED THAT MANA HAD BEEN WORKING AS A FOOD TASTER SINCE ELEMENTARY SCHOOL...
...HER DECISIONS AND OPINIONS POINTING THE WAY FORWARD FOR THE WHOLE OF THE CULINARY WORLD.
SHE WOULD TELL ME WITH SPARKLING EYES THAT SUCH WAS HER DESTINY AS THE BEARER OF THE DIVINE TONGUE.
BUT I KNEW BETTER.
WHAT SHE WAS TRULY DOING WAS STANDING IN THE CENTER OF A DARK AND FIERCE STORM...
...DESPERATELY TRYING TO LIGHT THE CORRECT PATH FOR EVERYONE ELSE TO FOLLOW.
WHAT SHE DID WAS RISKY, EVEN. DANGEROUS.
SHE COULD BE HURT. WORN DOWN. OR WORST OF ALL, SWALLOWED BY THE STORM.

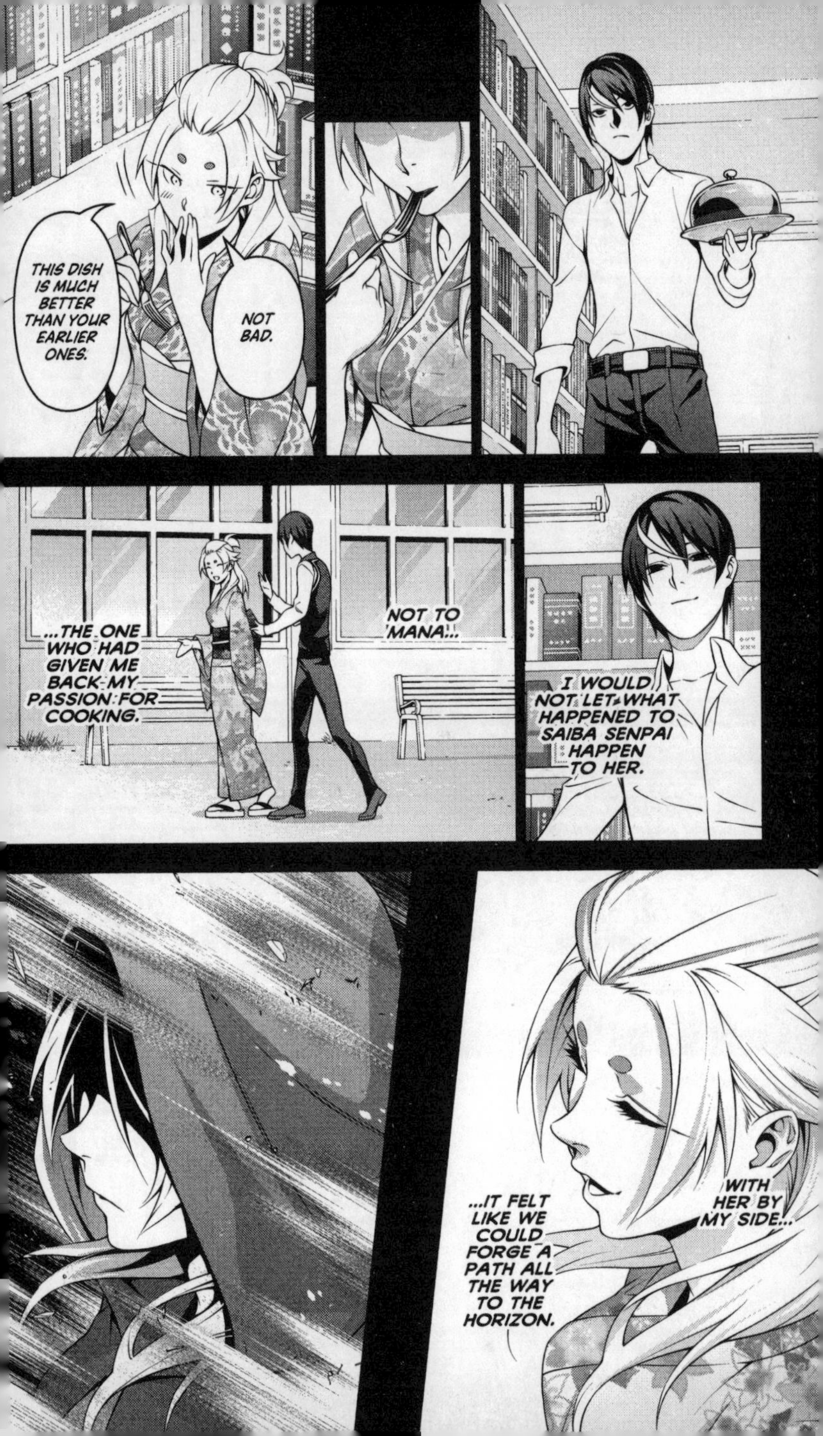
NOT BAD.
THIS DISH IS MUCH BETTER THAN YOUR EARLIER ONES.
I WOULD NOT LET WHAT HAPPENED TO SAIBA SENPAI HAPPEN TO HER.
NOT TO MANA...
...THE ONE WHO HAD GIVEN ME BACK MY PASSION FOR COOKING.
WITH HER BY MY SIDE...
...IT FELT LIKE WE COULD FORGE A PATH ALL THE WAY TO THE HORIZON.

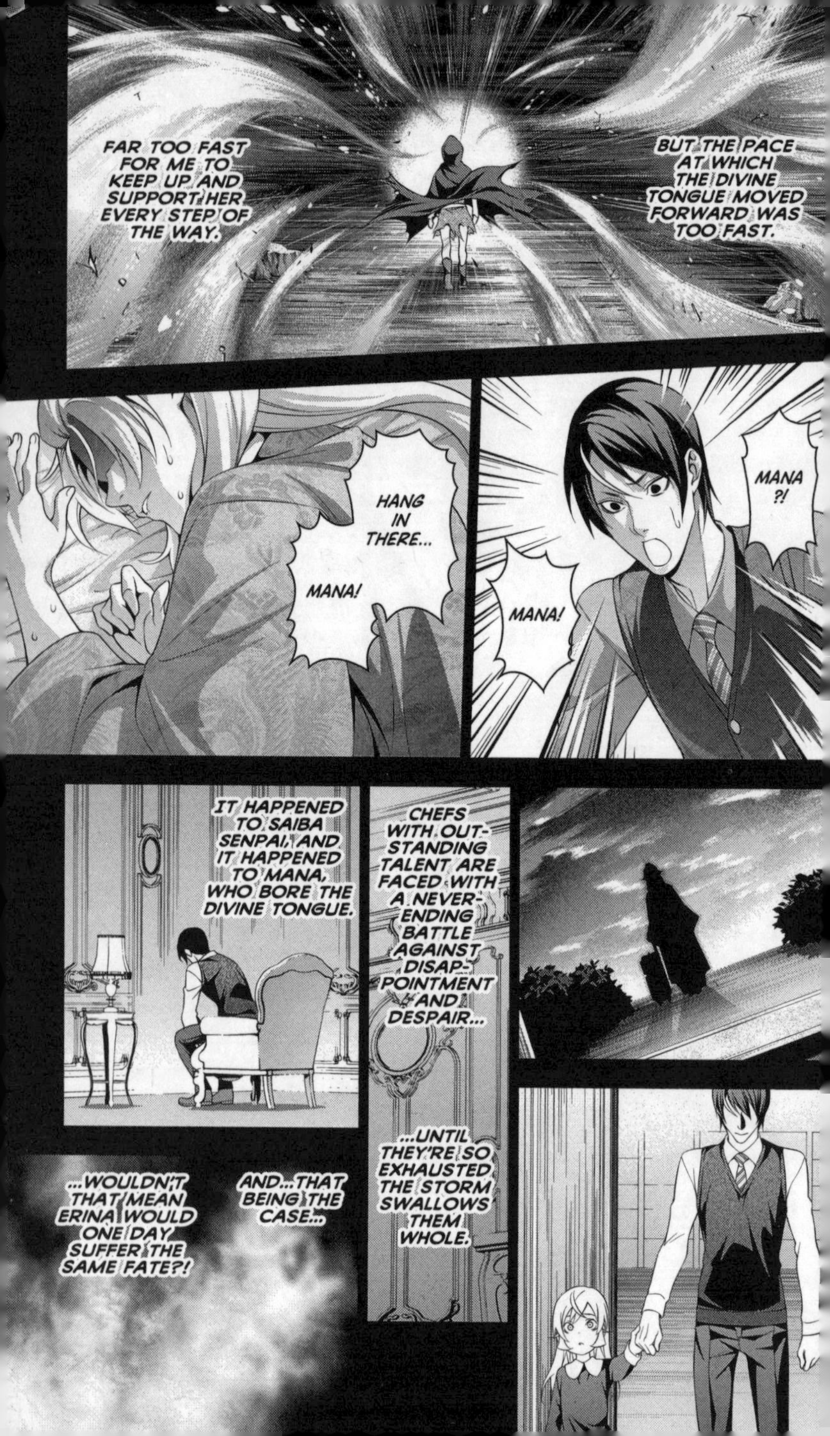
BUT THE PACE AT WHICH THE DIVINE TONGUE MOVED FORWARD WAS TOO FAST.
FAR TOO FAST FOR ME TO KEEP UP AND SUPPORT HER EVERY STEP OF THE WAY.
MANA ?!
MANA!
HANG IN THERE...
MANA!
CHEFS WITH OUT-STANDING TALENT ARE FACED WITH A NEVER-ENDING BATTLE AGAINST DISAP-POINTMENT AND DESPAIR...
...UNTIL THEY'RE SO EXHAUSTED THE STORM SWALLOWS THEM WHOLE.
IT HAPPENED TO SAIBA SENPAI, AND IT HAPPENED TO MANA, WHO BORE THE DIVINE TONGUE.
AND...THAT BEING THE CASE...
...WOULDN'T THAT MEAN ERINA WOULD ONE DAY SUFFER THE SAME FATE?!

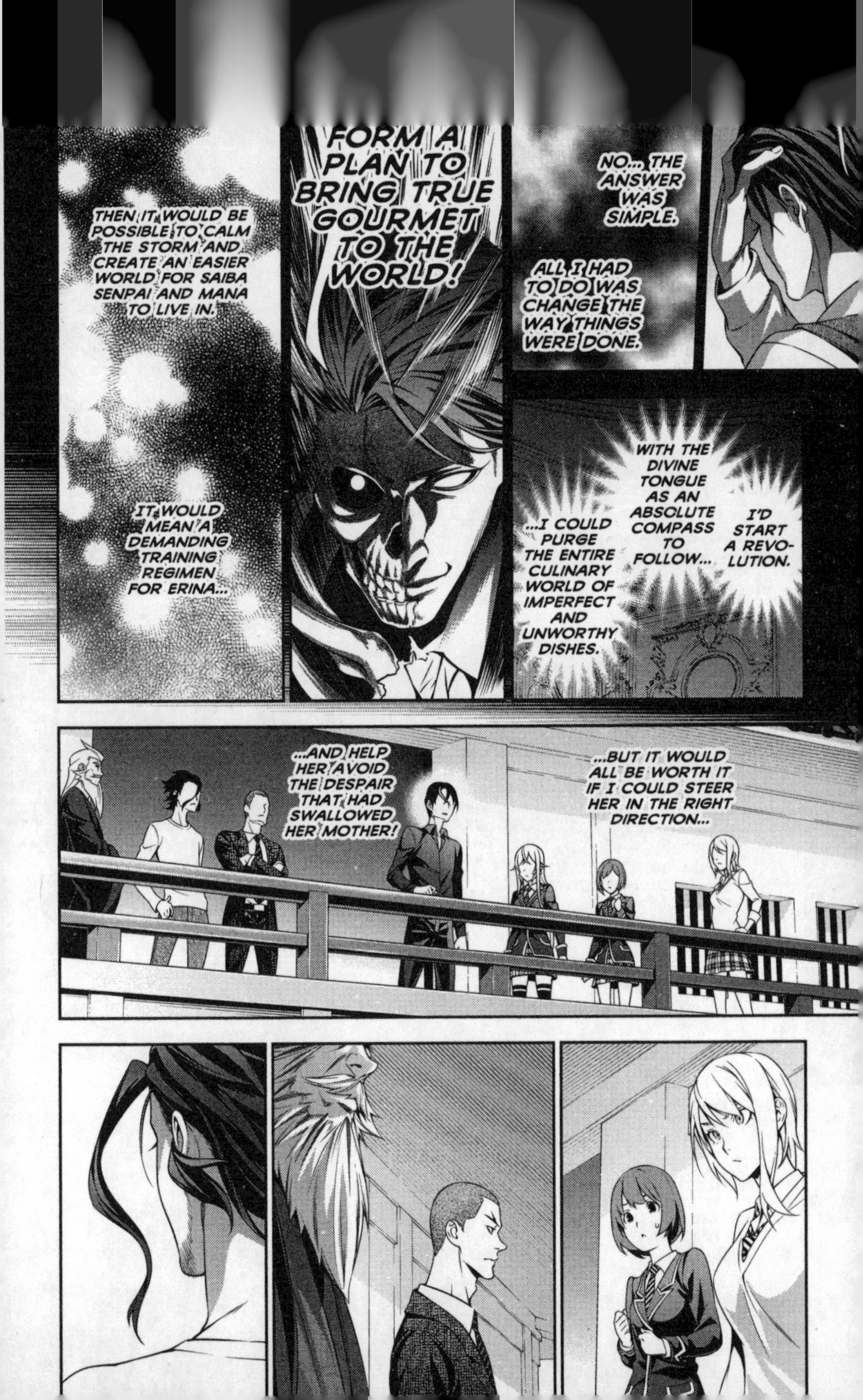
NO... THE ANSWER WAS SIMPLE.
ALL I HAD TO DO WAS CHANGE THE WAY THINGS WERE DONE.
I'D START A REVOLUTION.
WITH THE DIVINE TONGUE AS AN ABSOLUTE COMPASS TO FOLLOW...
...I COULD PURGE THE ENTIRE CULINARY WORLD OF IMPERFECT AND UNWORTHY DISHES.
FORM A PLAN TO BRING TRUE GOURMET TO THE WORLD!
THEN IT WOULD BE POSSIBLE TO CALM THE STORM AND CREATE AN EASIER WORLD FOR SAIBA SENPAI AND MANA TO LIVE IN.
IT WOULD MEAN A DEMANDING TRAINING REGIMEN FOR ERINA...
...BUT IT WOULD ALL BE WORTH IT IF I COULD STEER HER IN THE RIGHT DIRECTION...
...AND HELP HER AVOID THE DESPAIR THAT HAD SWALLOWED HER MOTHER!

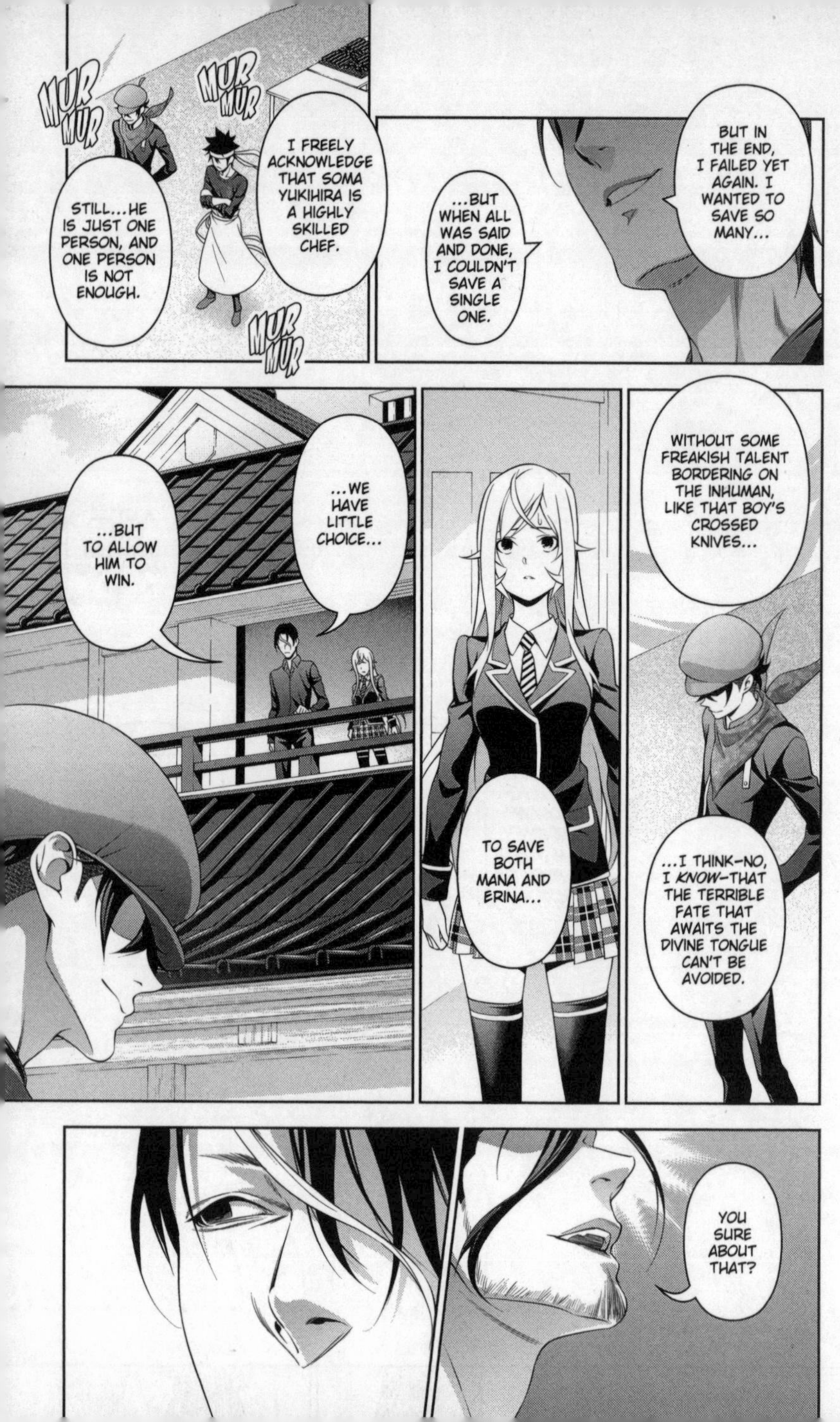
BUT IN THE END, I FAILED YET AGAIN. I WANTED TO SAVE SO MANY...
...BUT WHEN ALL WAS SAID AND DONE, I COULDN'T SAVE A SINGLE ONE.
MUR MUR
MUR MUR
I FREELY ACKNOWLEDGE THAT SOMA YUKIHIRA IS A HIGHLY SKILLED CHEF.
STILL... HE IS JUST ONE PERSON, AND ONE PERSON IS NOT ENOUGH.
MUR MUR
WITHOUT SOME FREAKISH TALENT BORDERING ON THE INHUMAN, LIKE THAT BOY'S CROSSED KNIVES...
...I THINK—NO, I *KNOW*—THAT THE TERRIBLE FATE THAT AWAITS THE DIVINE TONGUE CAN'T BE AVOIDED.
TO SAVE BOTH MANA AND ERINA...
...WE HAVE LITTLE CHOICE...
...BUT TO ALLOW HIM TO WIN.
YOU SURE ABOUT THAT?

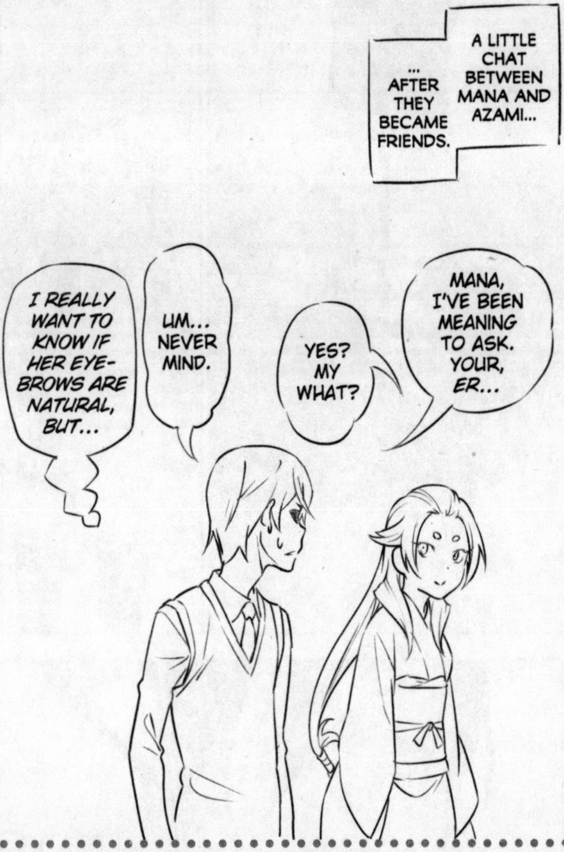
A LITTLE CHAT BETWEEN MANA AND AZAMI...
... AFTER THEY BECAME FRIENDS.
MANA, I'VE BEEN MEANING TO ASK. YOUR, ER...
YES? MY WHAT?
UM... NEVER MIND.
I REALLY WANT TO KNOW IF HER EYE-BROWS ARE NATURAL, BUT...

310 A GOURMET CLASH

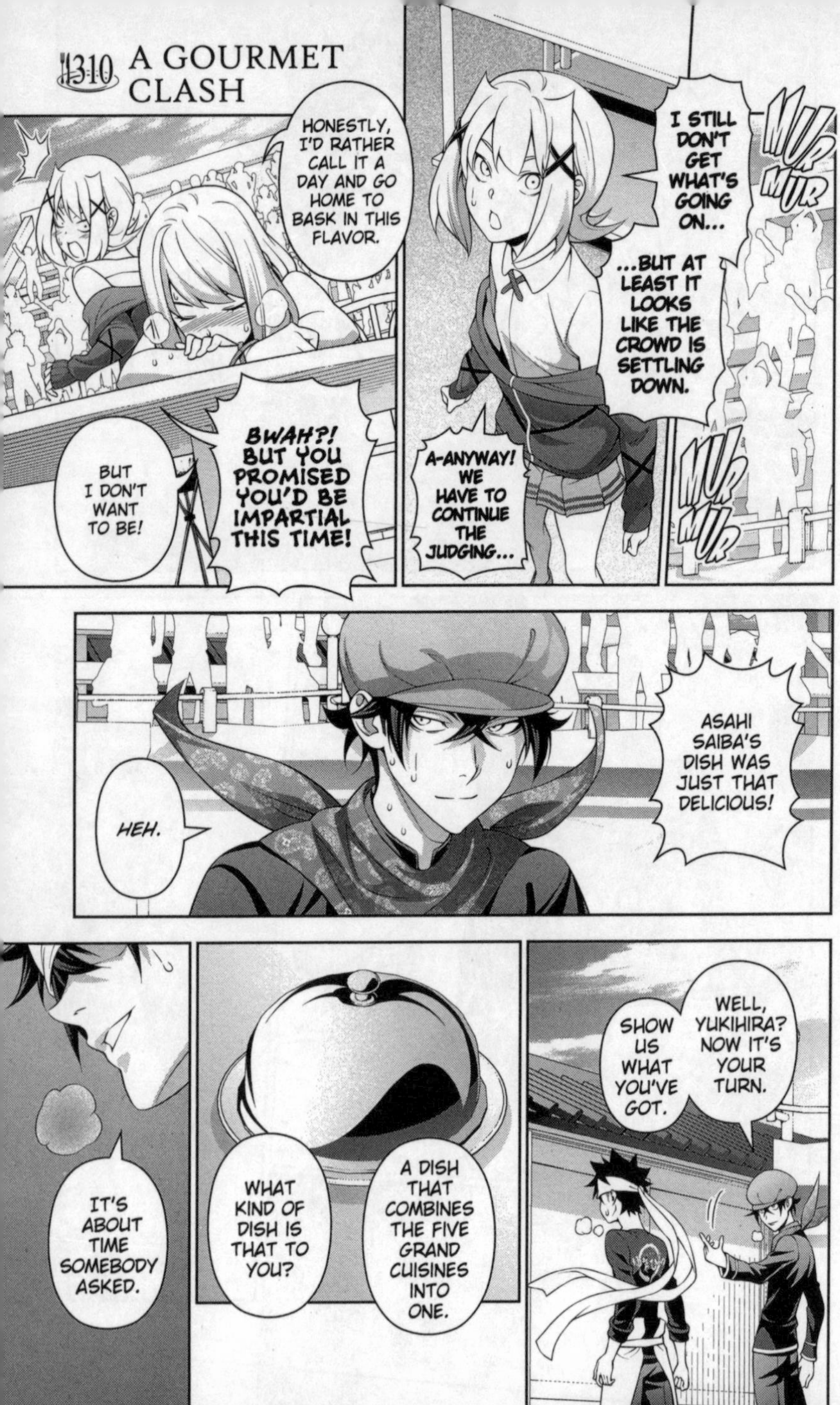
MUR MUR
I STILL DON'T GET WHAT'S GOING ON...
...BUT AT LEAST IT LOOKS LIKE THE CROWD IS SETTLING DOWN.
MUR MUR
A-ANYWAY! WE HAVE TO CONTINUE THE JUDGING...
HONESTLY, I'D RATHER CALL IT A DAY AND GO HOME TO BASK IN THIS FLAVOR.
BWAH?! BUT YOU PROMISED YOU'D BE IMPARTIAL THIS TIME!
BUT I DON'T WANT TO BE!
ASAHI SAIBA'S DISH WAS JUST THAT DELICIOUS!
HEH.
WELL, YUKIHIRA? NOW IT'S YOUR TURN.
SHOW US WHAT YOU'VE GOT.
A DISH THAT COMBINES THE FIVE GRAND CUISINES INTO ONE.
WHAT KIND OF DISH IS THAT TO YOU?
IT'S ABOUT TIME SOMEBODY ASKED.

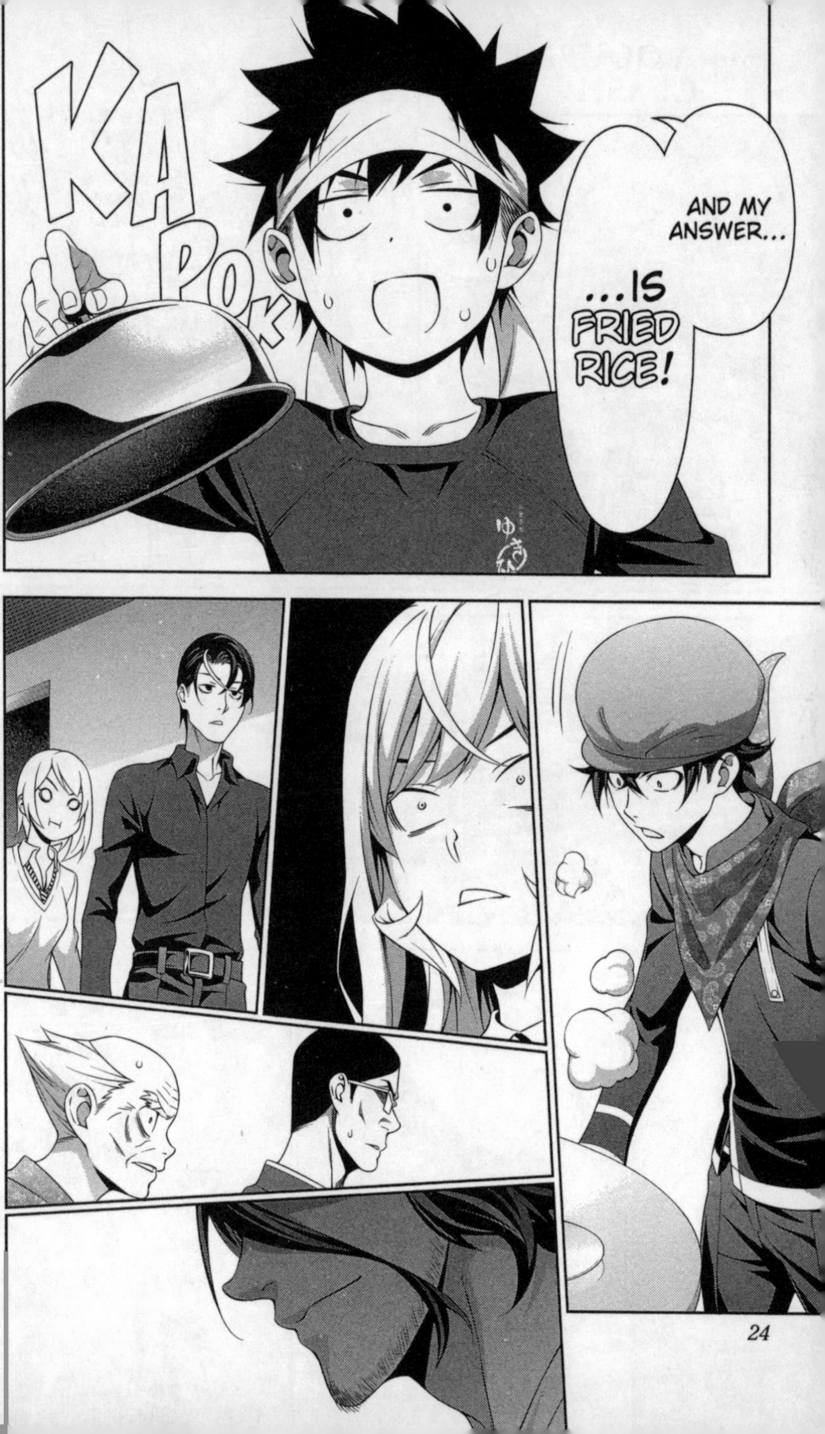
AND MY ANSWER...
...IS FRIED RICE!
KA POK
ゆきひら

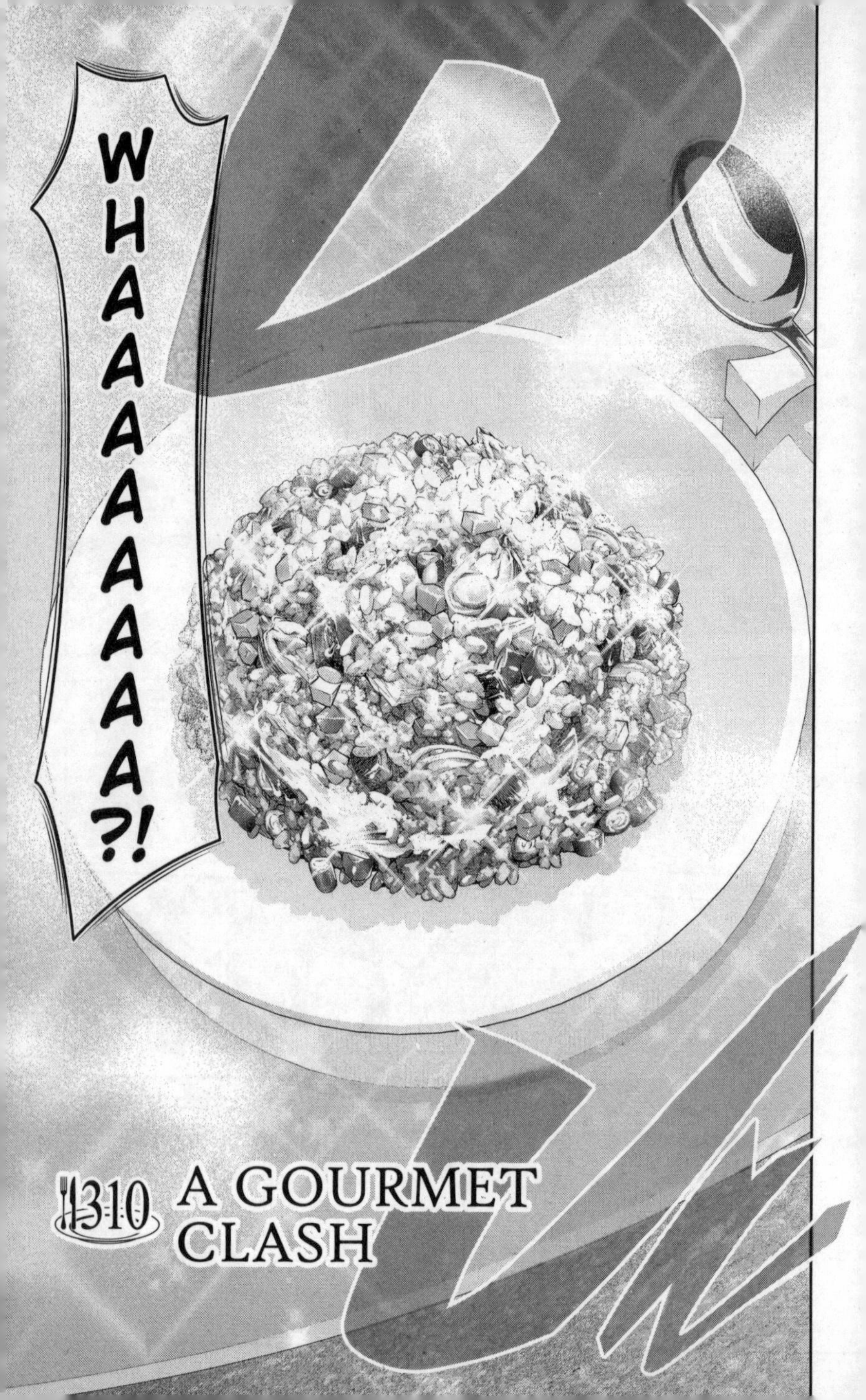
WHAAAAAAAAA?!
310 A GOURMET CLASH

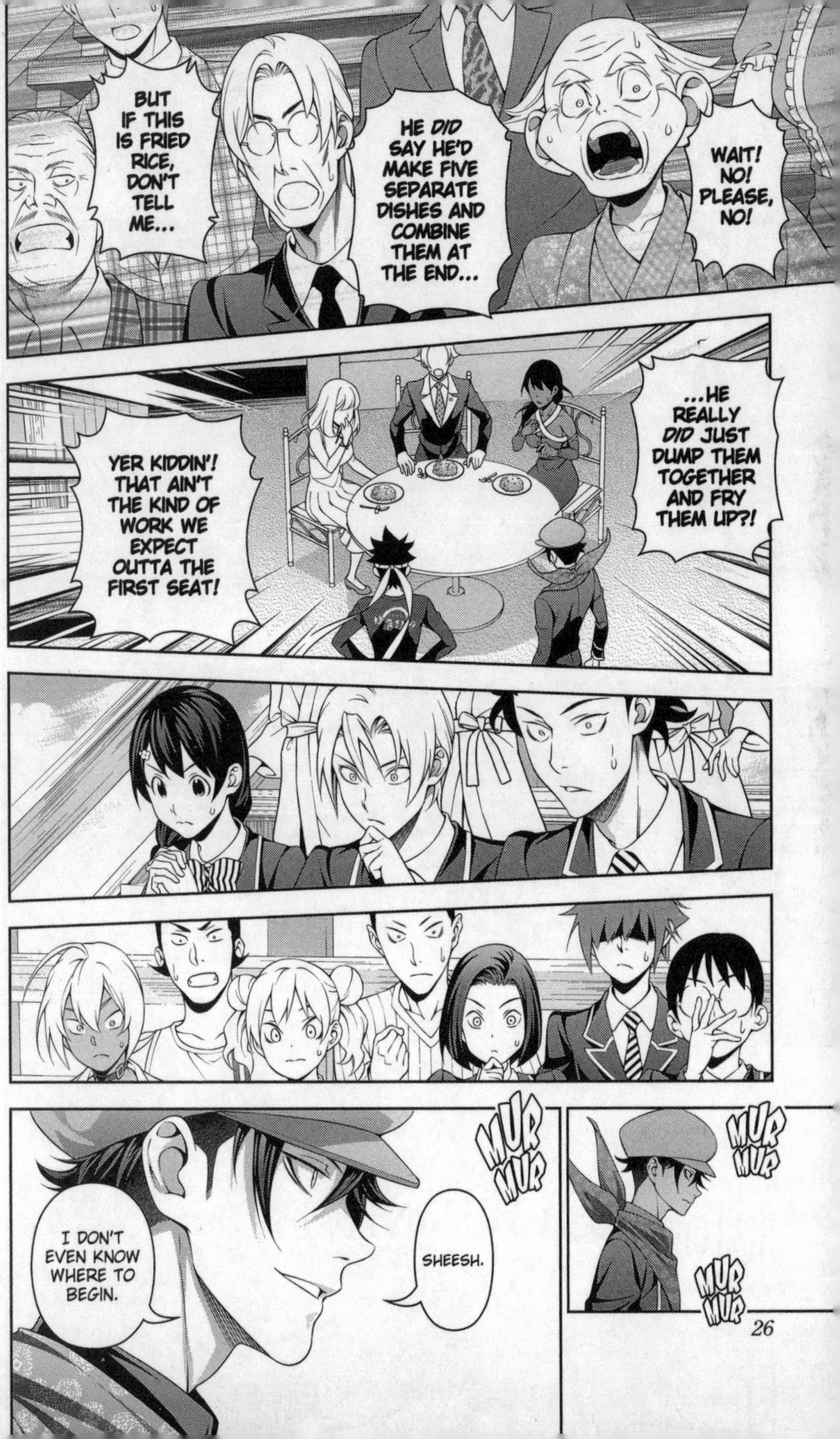
WAIT! NO! PLEASE, NO!
HE *DID* SAY HE'D MAKE FIVE SEPARATE DISHES AND COMBINE THEM AT THE END...
BUT IF THIS IS FRIED RICE, DON'T TELL ME...
...HE REALLY *DID* JUST DUMP THEM TOGETHER AND FRY THEM UP?!
YER KIDDIN'! THAT AIN'T THE KIND OF WORK WE EXPECT OUTTA THE FIRST SEAT!
MUR MUR
MUR MUR
MUR MUR
SHEESH.
I DON'T EVEN KNOW WHERE TO BEGIN.

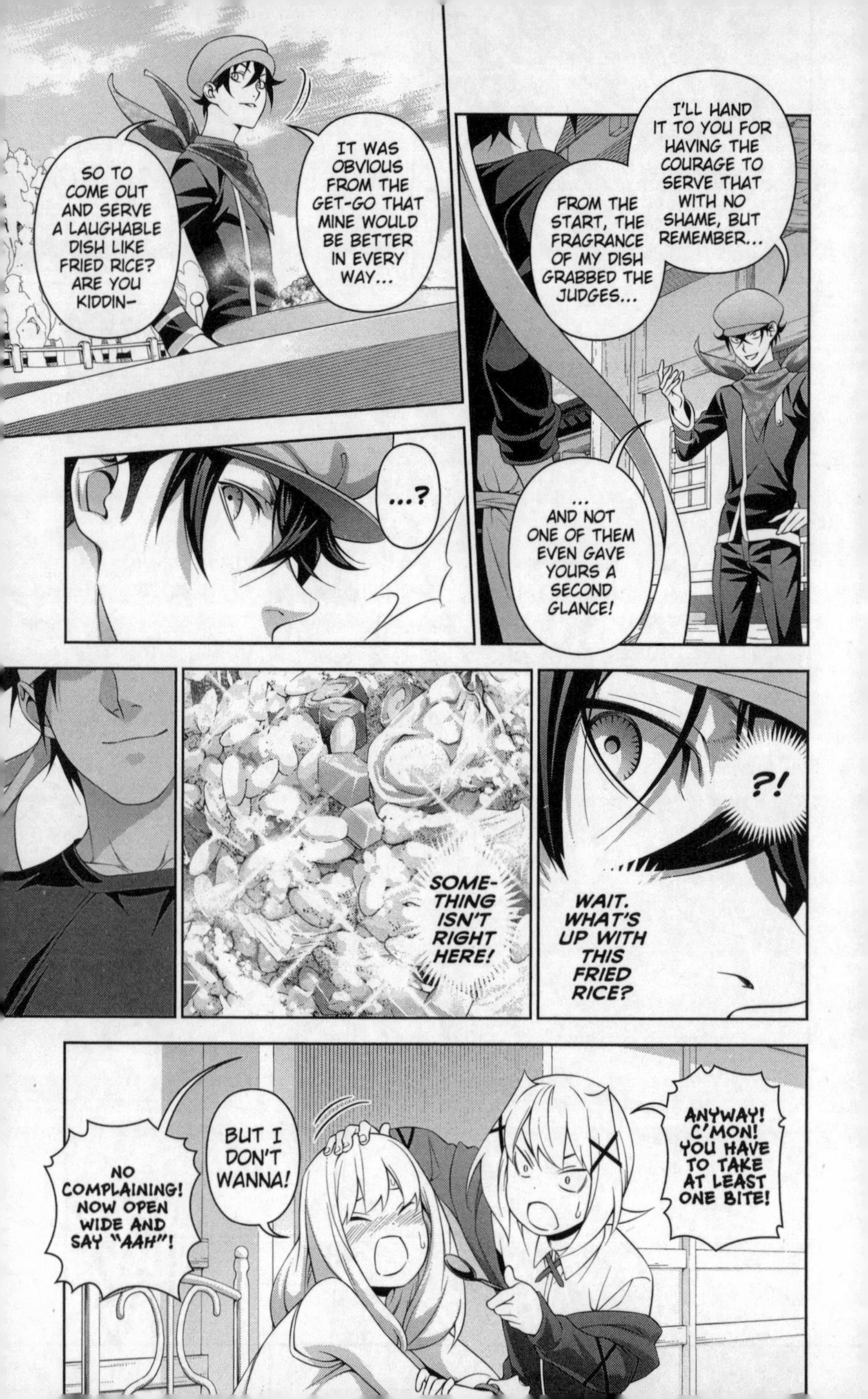
I'LL HAND IT TO YOU FOR HAVING THE COURAGE TO SERVE THAT WITH NO SHAME, BUT REMEMBER...
FROM THE START, THE FRAGRANCE OF MY DISH GRABBED THE JUDGES...
...AND NOT ONE OF THEM EVEN GAVE YOURS A SECOND GLANCE!
IT WAS OBVIOUS FROM THE GET-GO THAT MINE WOULD BE BETTER IN EVERY WAY...
SO TO COME OUT AND SERVE A LAUGHABLE DISH LIKE FRIED RICE? ARE YOU KIDDIN–
...?
?!
WAIT. WHAT'S UP WITH THIS FRIED RICE?
SOMETHING ISN'T RIGHT HERE!
ANYWAY! C'MON! YOU HAVE TO TAKE AT LEAST ONE BITE!
BUT I DON'T WANNA!
NO COMPLAINING! NOW OPEN WIDE AND SAY "AAH"!

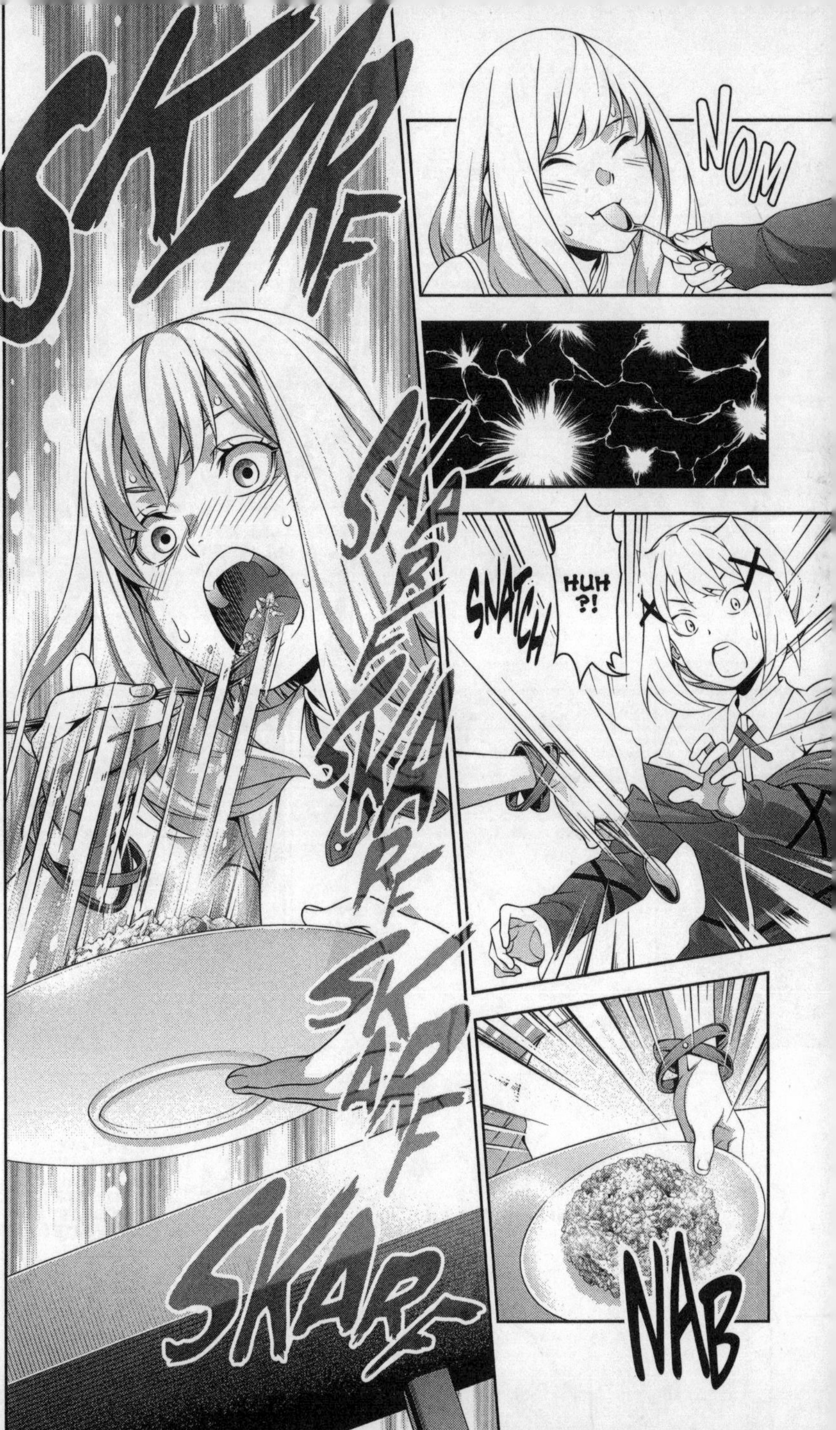
NOM
HUH ?!
SNATCH
NAB
SKAF
SKAF
SKAF
SKAF

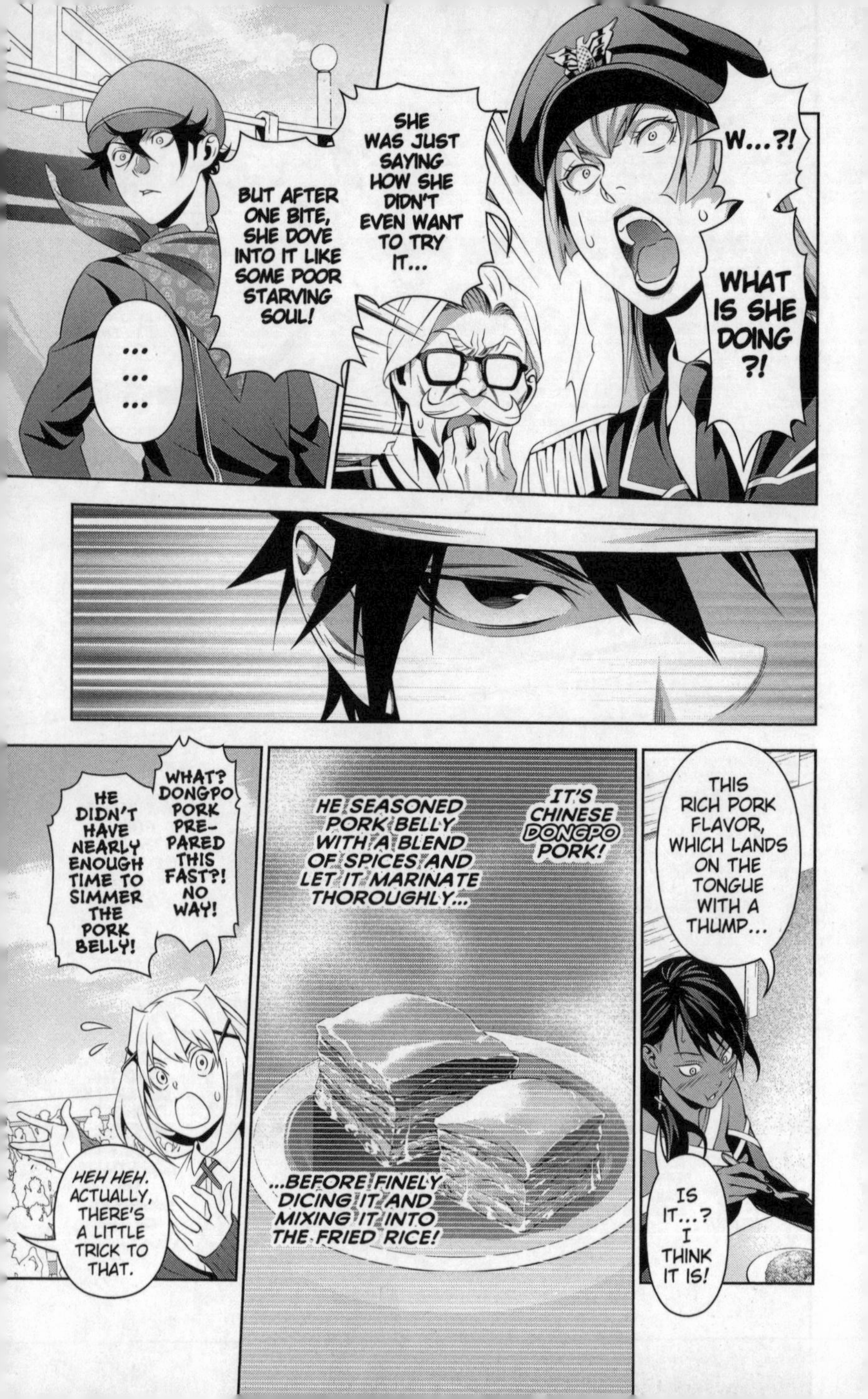
W...?!
WHAT IS SHE DOING ?!
SHE WAS JUST SAYING HOW SHE DIDN'T EVEN WANT TO TRY IT...
BUT AFTER ONE BITE, SHE DOVE INTO IT LIKE SOME POOR STARVING SOUL!
... ...
THIS RICH PORK FLAVOR, WHICH LANDS ON THE TONGUE WITH A THUMP...
IS IT...? I THINK IT IS!
IT'S CHINESE DONGPO PORK!
HE SEASONED PORK BELLY WITH A BLEND OF SPICES AND LET IT MARINATE THOROUGHLY...
...BEFORE FINELY DICING IT AND MIXING IT INTO THE FRIED RICE!
WHAT? DONGPO PORK PRE-PARED THIS FAST?! NO WAY!
HE DIDN'T HAVE NEARLY ENOUGH TIME TO SIMMER THE PORK BELLY!
HEH HEH. ACTUALLY, THERE'S A LITTLE TRICK TO THAT.

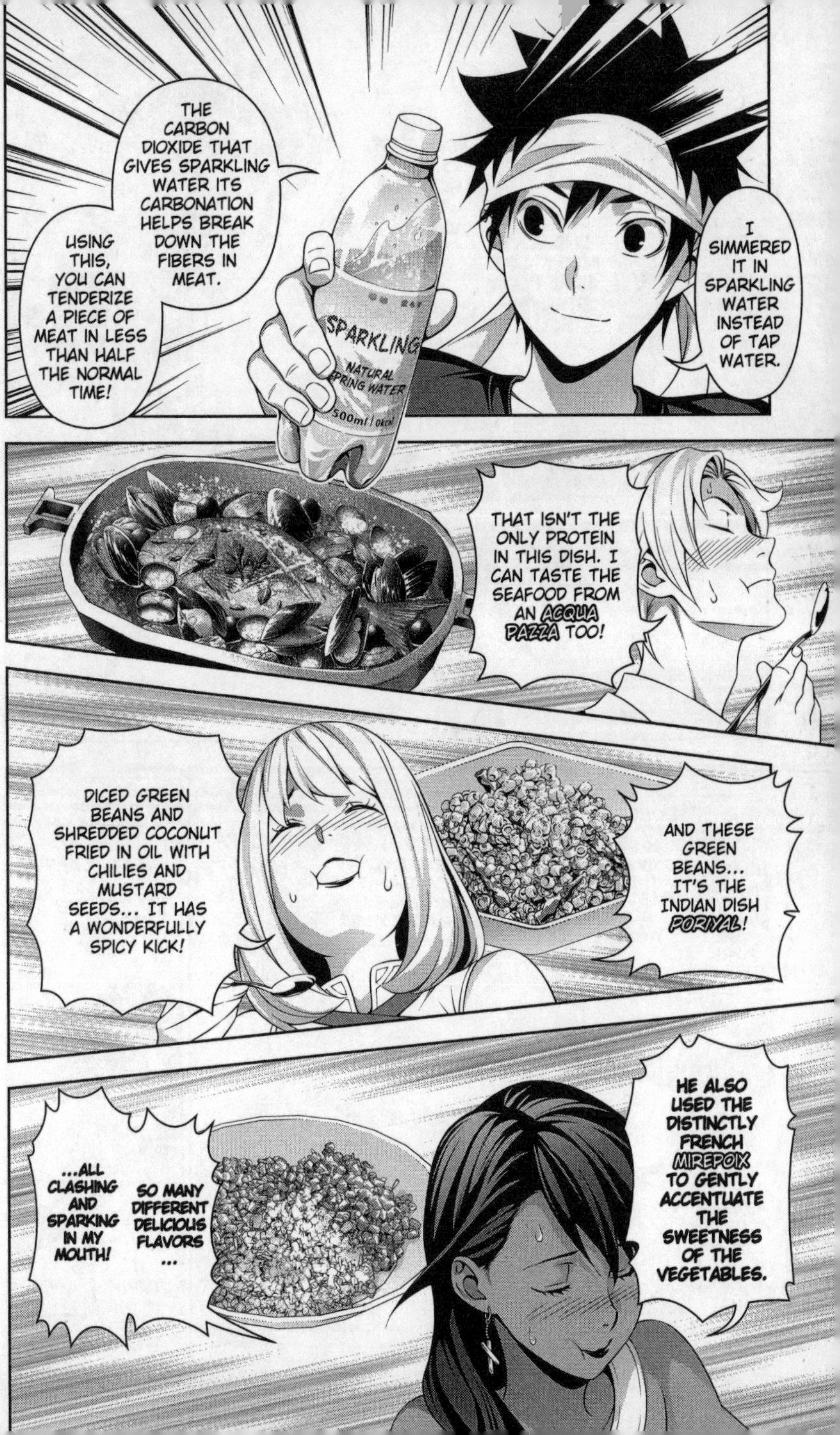
I SIMMERED IT IN SPARKLING WATER INSTEAD OF TAP WATER.
THE CARBON DIOXIDE THAT GIVES SPARKLING WATER ITS CARBONATION HELPS BREAK DOWN THE FIBERS IN MEAT.
USING THIS, YOU CAN TENDERIZE A PIECE OF MEAT IN LESS THAN HALF THE NORMAL TIME!
SPARKLING
NATURAL SPRING WATER
500ml | 0kcal
THAT ISN'T THE ONLY PROTEIN IN THIS DISH. I CAN TASTE THE SEAFOOD FROM AN ACQUA PAZZA TOO!
AND THESE GREEN BEANS... IT'S THE INDIAN DISH PORIYAL!
DICED GREEN BEANS AND SHREDDED COCONUT FRIED IN OIL WITH CHILIES AND MUSTARD SEEDS... IT HAS A WONDERFULLY SPICY KICK!
HE ALSO USED THE DISTINCTLY FRENCH MIREPOIX TO GENTLY ACCENTUATE THE SWEETNESS OF THE VEGETABLES.
SO MANY DIFFERENT DELICIOUS FLAVORS ...
...ALL CLASHING AND SPARKING IN MY MOUTH!

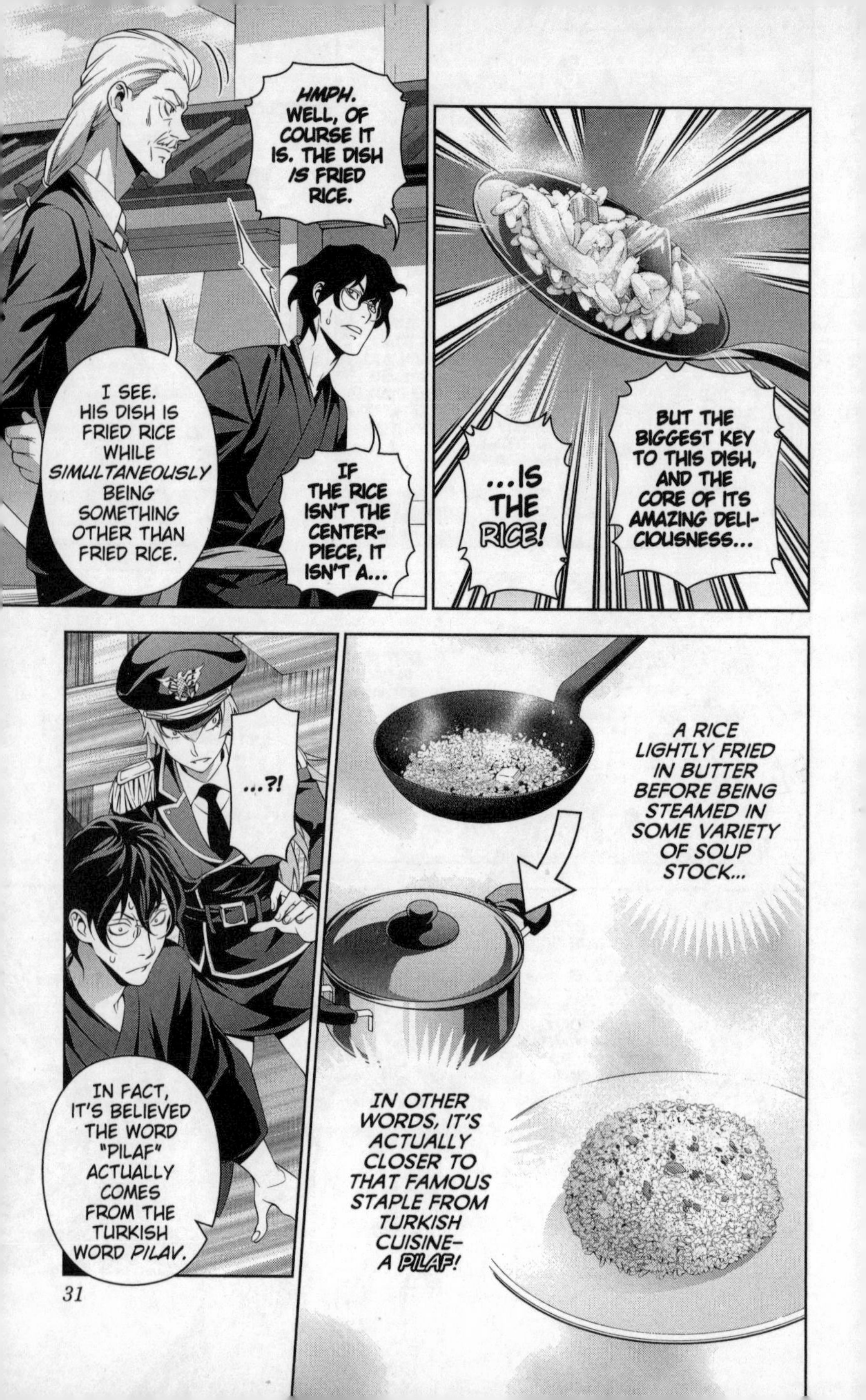
BUT THE BIGGEST KEY TO THIS DISH, AND THE CORE OF ITS AMAZING DELI-CIOUSNESS...
...IS THE RICE!
HMPH. WELL, OF COURSE IT IS. THE DISH *IS* FRIED RICE.
I SEE. HIS DISH IS FRIED RICE WHILE *SIMULTANEOUSLY* BEING SOMETHING OTHER THAN FRIED RICE.
IF THE RICE ISN'T THE CENTER-PIECE, IT ISN'T A...
A RICE LIGHTLY FRIED IN BUTTER BEFORE BEING STEAMED IN SOME VARIETY OF SOUP STOCK...
IN OTHER WORDS, IT'S ACTUALLY CLOSER TO THAT FAMOUS STAPLE FROM TURKISH CUISINE– A PILAF!
...?!
IN FACT, IT'S BELIEVED THE WORD "PILAF" ACTUALLY COMES FROM THE TURKISH WORD *PILAV*.

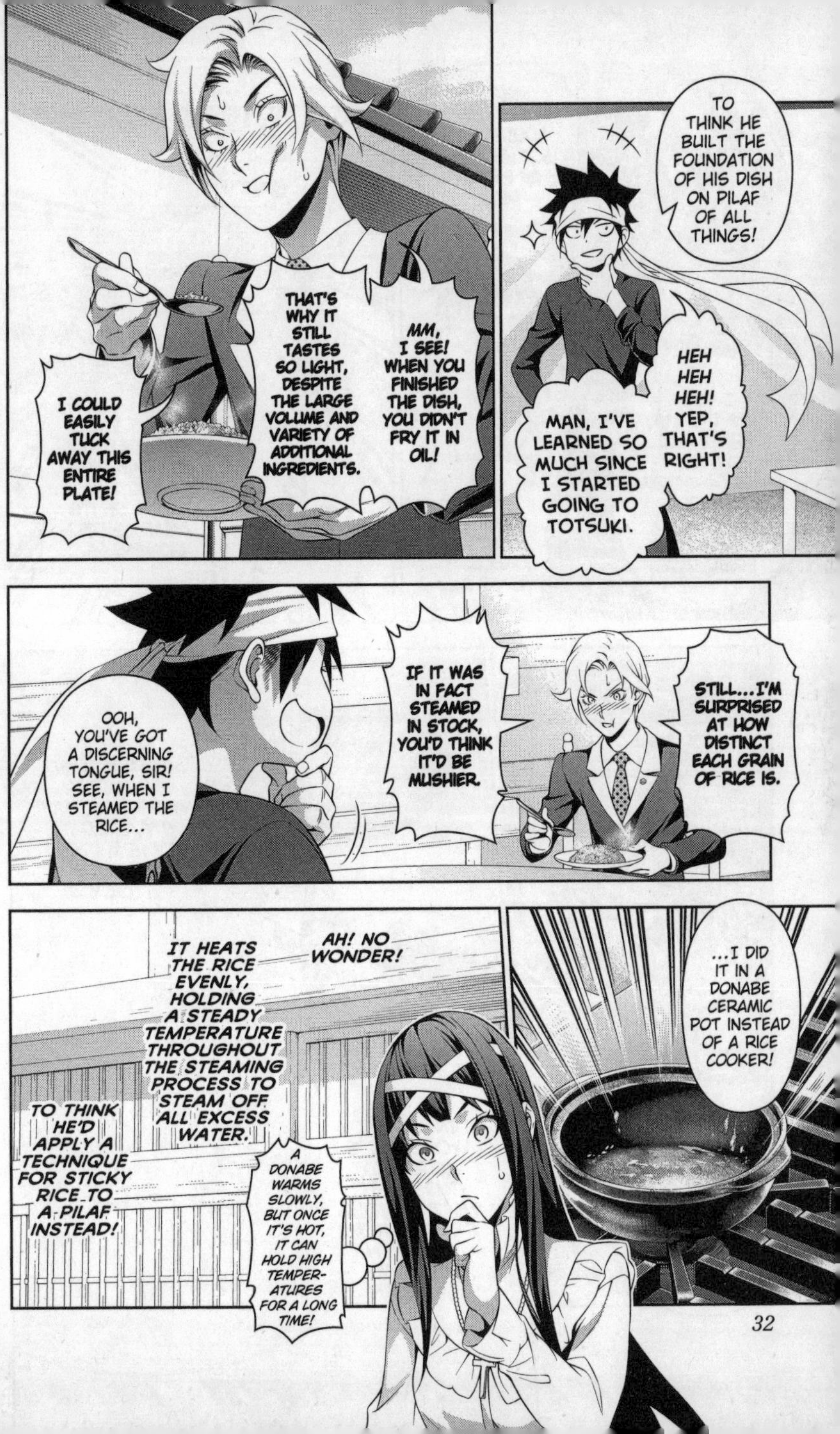
TO THINK HE BUILT THE FOUNDATION OF HIS DISH ON PILAF OF ALL THINGS!
HEH HEH HEH! YEP, THAT'S RIGHT!
MAN, I'VE LEARNED SO MUCH SINCE I STARTED GOING TO TOTSUKI.
MM, I SEE! WHEN YOU FINISHED THE DISH, YOU DIDN'T FRY IT IN OIL!
THAT'S WHY IT STILL TASTES SO LIGHT, DESPITE THE LARGE VOLUME AND VARIETY OF ADDITIONAL INGREDIENTS.
I COULD EASILY TUCK AWAY THIS ENTIRE PLATE!
STILL...I'M SURPRISED AT HOW DISTINCT EACH GRAIN OF RICE IS.
IF IT WAS IN FACT STEAMED IN STOCK, YOU'D THINK IT'D BE MUSHIER.
OOH, YOU'VE GOT A DISCERNING TONGUE, SIR! SEE, WHEN I STEAMED THE RICE...
...I DID IT IN A DONABE CERAMIC POT INSTEAD OF A RICE COOKER!
AH! NO WONDER!
IT HEATS THE RICE EVENLY, HOLDING A STEADY TEMPERATURE THROUGHOUT THE STEAMING PROCESS TO STEAM OFF ALL EXCESS WATER.
A DONABE WARMS SLOWLY, BUT ONCE IT'S HOT, IT CAN HOLD HIGH TEMPER-ATURES FOR A LONG TIME!
TO THINK HE'D APPLY A TECHNIQUE FOR STICKY RICE TO A PILAF INSTEAD!

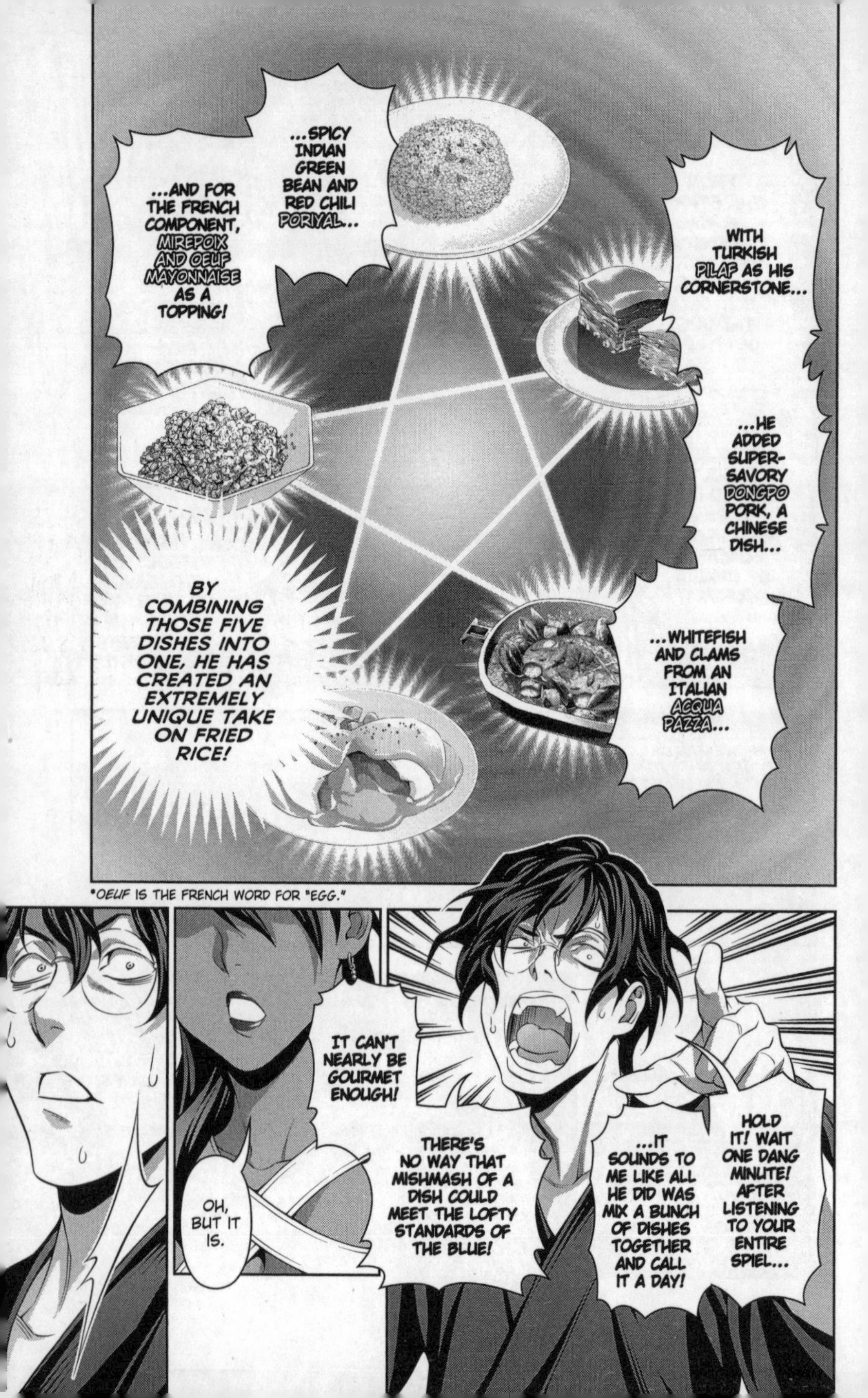
WITH TURKISH PILAF AS HIS CORNERSTONE...
...HE ADDED SUPER-SAVORY DONGPO PORK, A CHINESE DISH...
...WHITEFISH AND CLAMS FROM AN ITALIAN ACQUA PAZZA...
...SPICY INDIAN GREEN BEAN AND RED CHILI PORIYAL...
...AND FOR THE FRENCH COMPONENT, MIREPOIX AND OEUF MAYONNAISE AS A TOPPING!
BY COMBINING THOSE FIVE DISHES INTO ONE, HE HAS CREATED AN EXTREMELY UNIQUE TAKE ON FRIED RICE!
HOLD IT! WAIT ONE DANG MINUTE! AFTER LISTENING TO YOUR ENTIRE SPIEL...
...IT SOUNDS TO ME LIKE ALL HE DID WAS MIX A BUNCH OF DISHES TOGETHER AND CALL IT A DAY!
THERE'S NO WAY THAT MISHMASH OF A DISH COULD MEET THE LOFTY STANDARDS OF THE BLUE!
IT CAN'T NEARLY BE GOURMET ENOUGH!
OH, BUT IT IS.
*OEUF IS THE FRENCH WORD FOR "EGG."

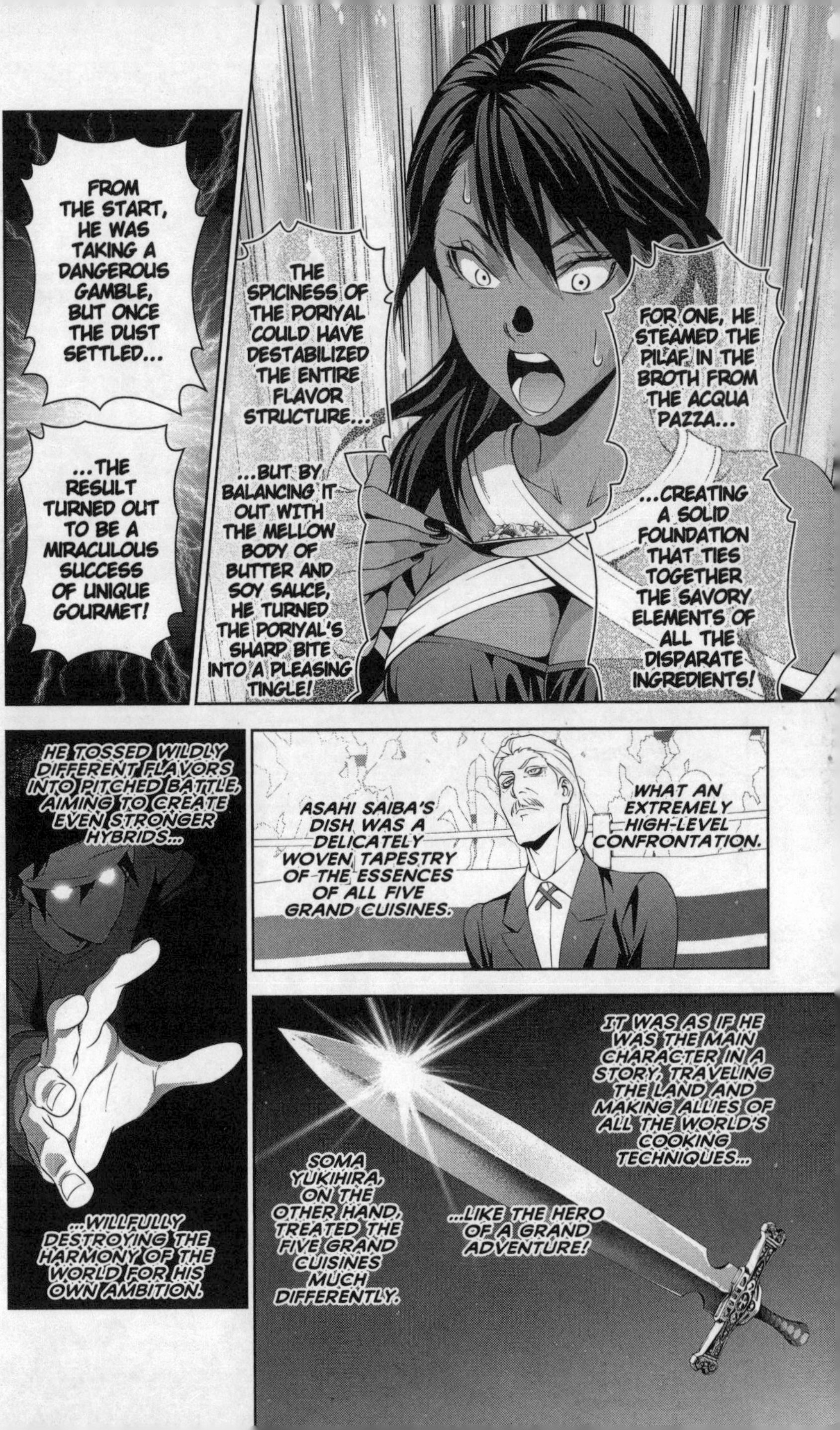
FOR ONE, HE STEAMED THE PILAF IN THE BROTH FROM THE ACQUA PAZZA...
...CREATING A SOLID FOUNDATION THAT TIES TOGETHER THE SAVORY ELEMENTS OF ALL THE DISPARATE INGREDIENTS!
THE SPICINESS OF THE PORIYAL COULD HAVE DESTABILIZED THE ENTIRE FLAVOR STRUCTURE...
...BUT BY BALANCING IT OUT WITH THE MELLOW BODY OF BUTTER AND SOY SAUCE, HE TURNED THE PORIYAL'S SHARP BITE INTO A PLEASING TINGLE!
FROM THE START, HE WAS TAKING A DANGEROUS GAMBLE, BUT ONCE THE DUST SETTLED...
...THE RESULT TURNED OUT TO BE A MIRACULOUS SUCCESS OF UNIQUE GOURMET!
WHAT AN EXTREMELY HIGH-LEVEL CONFRONTATION.
ASAHI SAIBA'S DISH WAS A DELICATELY WOVEN TAPESTRY OF THE ESSENCES OF ALL FIVE GRAND CUISINES.
IT WAS AS IF HE WAS THE MAIN CHARACTER IN A STORY, TRAVELING THE LAND AND MAKING ALLIES OF ALL THE WORLD'S COOKING TECHNIQUES...
SOMA YUKIHIRA, ON THE OTHER HAND, TREATED THE FIVE GRAND CUISINES MUCH DIFFERENTLY.
...LIKE THE HERO OF A GRAND ADVENTURE!
HE TOSSED WILDLY DIFFERENT FLAVORS INTO PITCHED BATTLE, AIMING TO CREATE EVEN STRONGER HYBRIDS...
...WILLFULLY DESTROYING THE HARMONY OF THE WORLD FOR HIS OWN AMBITION.

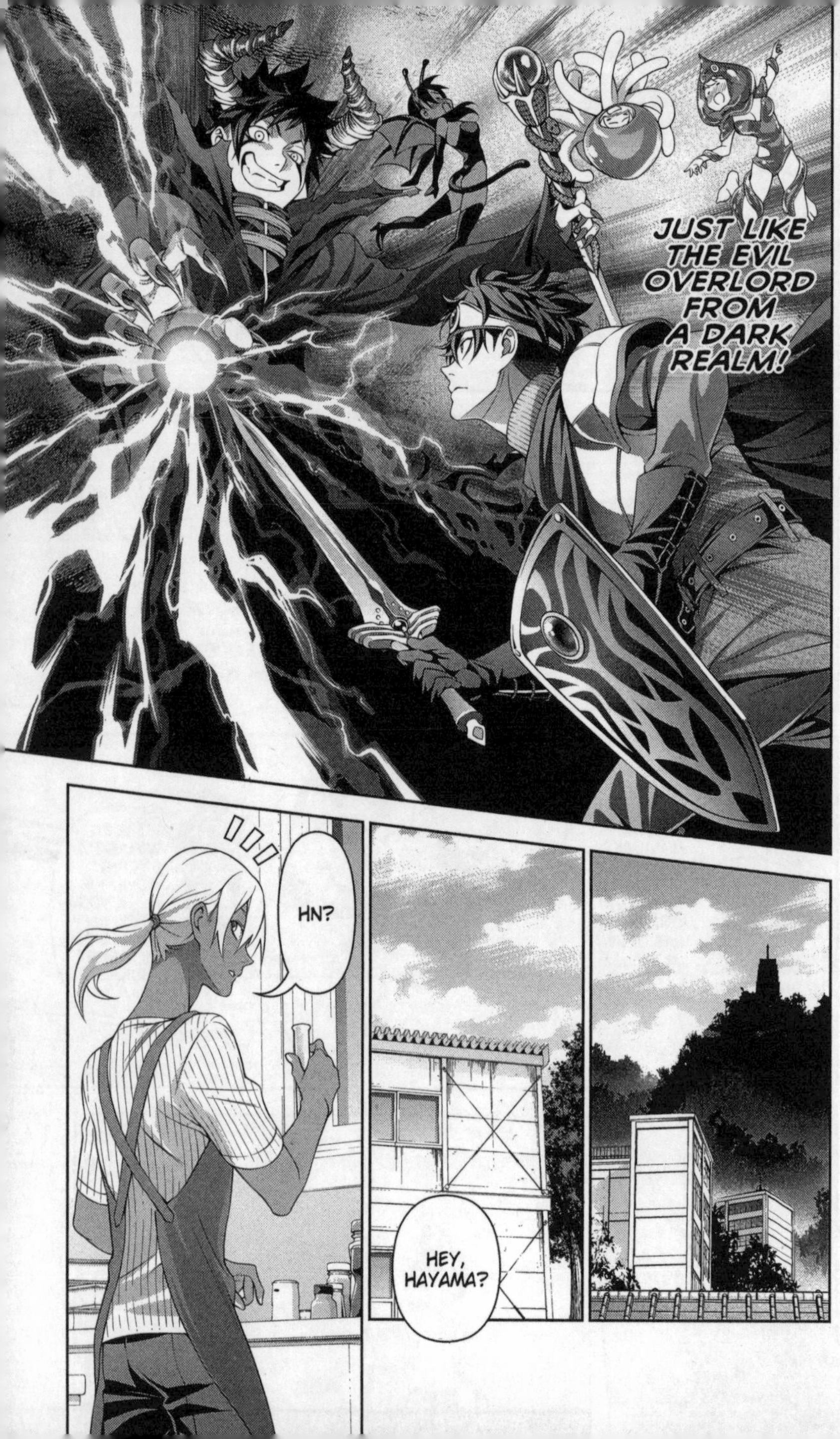
JUST LIKE THE EVIL OVERLORD FROM A DARK REALM!
HEY, HAYAMA?
HN?

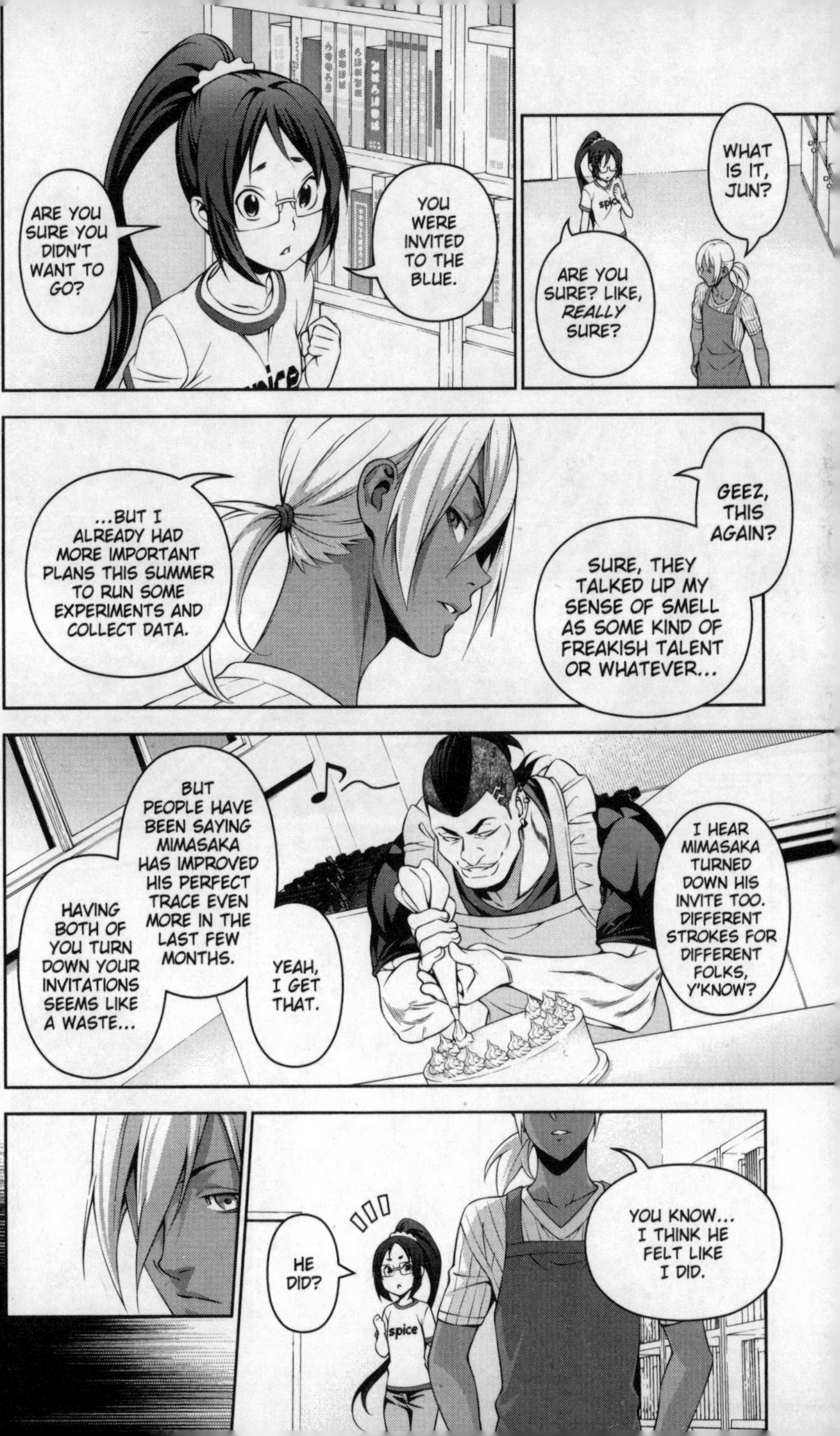
WHAT IS IT, JUN?
ARE YOU SURE? LIKE, *REALLY* SURE?
YOU WERE INVITED TO THE BLUE.
ARE YOU SURE YOU DIDN'T WANT TO GO?
GEEZ, THIS AGAIN?
SURE, THEY TALKED UP MY SENSE OF SMELL AS SOME KIND OF FREAKISH TALENT OR WHATEVER...
...BUT I ALREADY HAD MORE IMPORTANT PLANS THIS SUMMER TO RUN SOME EXPERIMENTS AND COLLECT DATA.
I HEAR MIMASAKA TURNED DOWN HIS INVITE TOO. DIFFERENT STROKES FOR DIFFERENT FOLKS, Y'KNOW?
YEAH, I GET THAT.
BUT PEOPLE HAVE BEEN SAYING MIMASAKA HAS IMPROVED HIS PERFECT TRACE EVEN MORE IN THE LAST FEW MONTHS.
HAVING BOTH OF YOU TURN DOWN YOUR INVITATIONS SEEMS LIKE A WASTE...
YOU KNOW... I THINK HE FELT LIKE I DID.
HE DID?

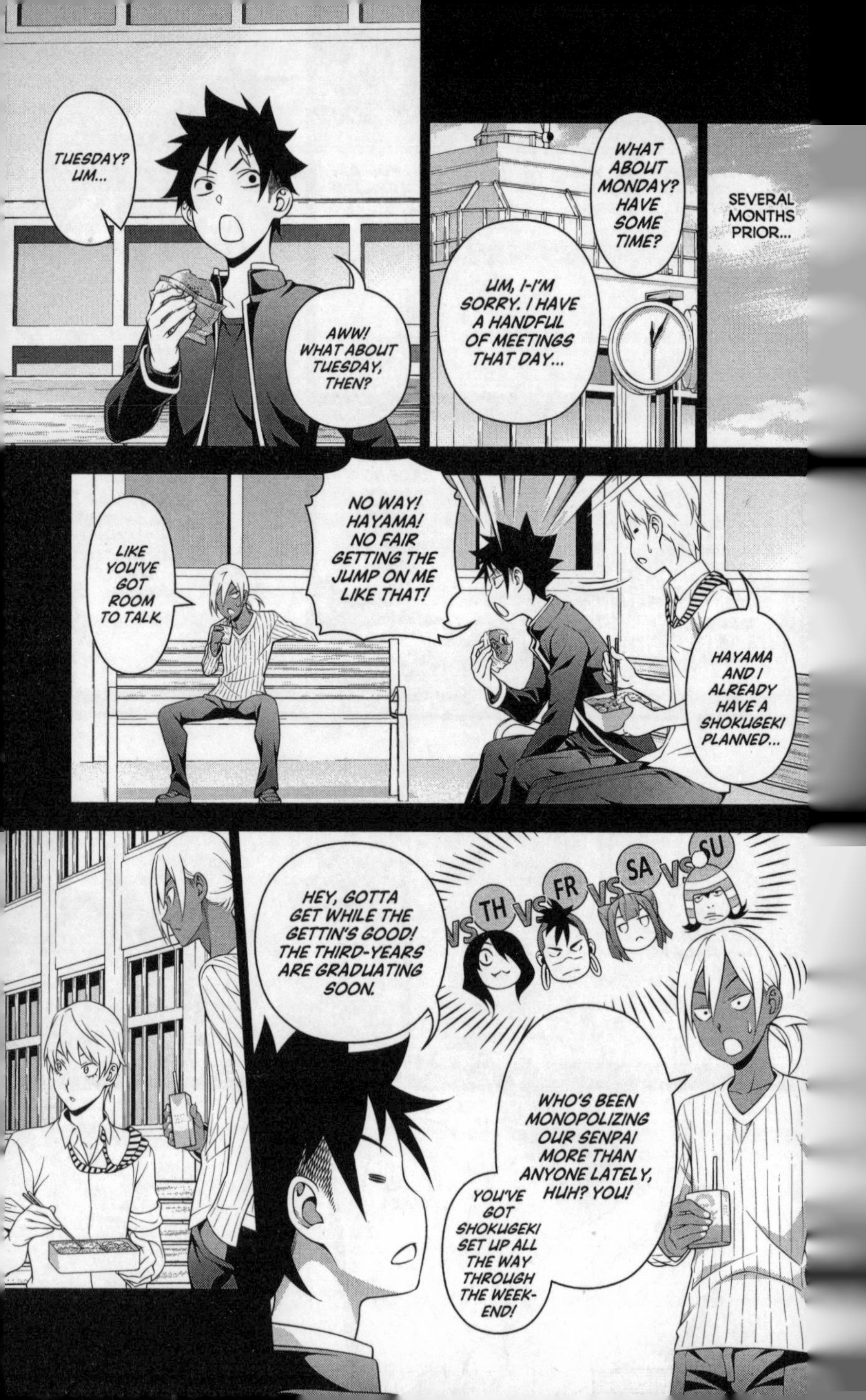
SEVERAL MONTHS PRIOR...
WHAT ABOUT MONDAY? HAVE SOME TIME?
UM, I-I'M SORRY. I HAVE A HANDFUL OF MEETINGS THAT DAY...
AWW! WHAT ABOUT TUESDAY, THEN?
TUESDAY? UM...
HAYAMA AND I ALREADY HAVE A SHOKUGEKI PLANNED...
NO WAY! HAYAMA! NO FAIR GETTING THE JUMP ON ME LIKE THAT!
LIKE YOU'VE GOT ROOM TO TALK.
TH VS FR VS SA VS SU
VS
WHO'S BEEN MONOPOLIZING OUR SENPAI MORE THAN ANYONE LATELY, HUH? YOU!
YOU'VE GOT SHOKUGEKI SET UP ALL THE WAY THROUGH THE WEEK-END!
HEY, GOTTA GET WHILE THE GETTIN'S GOOD! THE THIRD-YEARS ARE GRADUATING SOON.

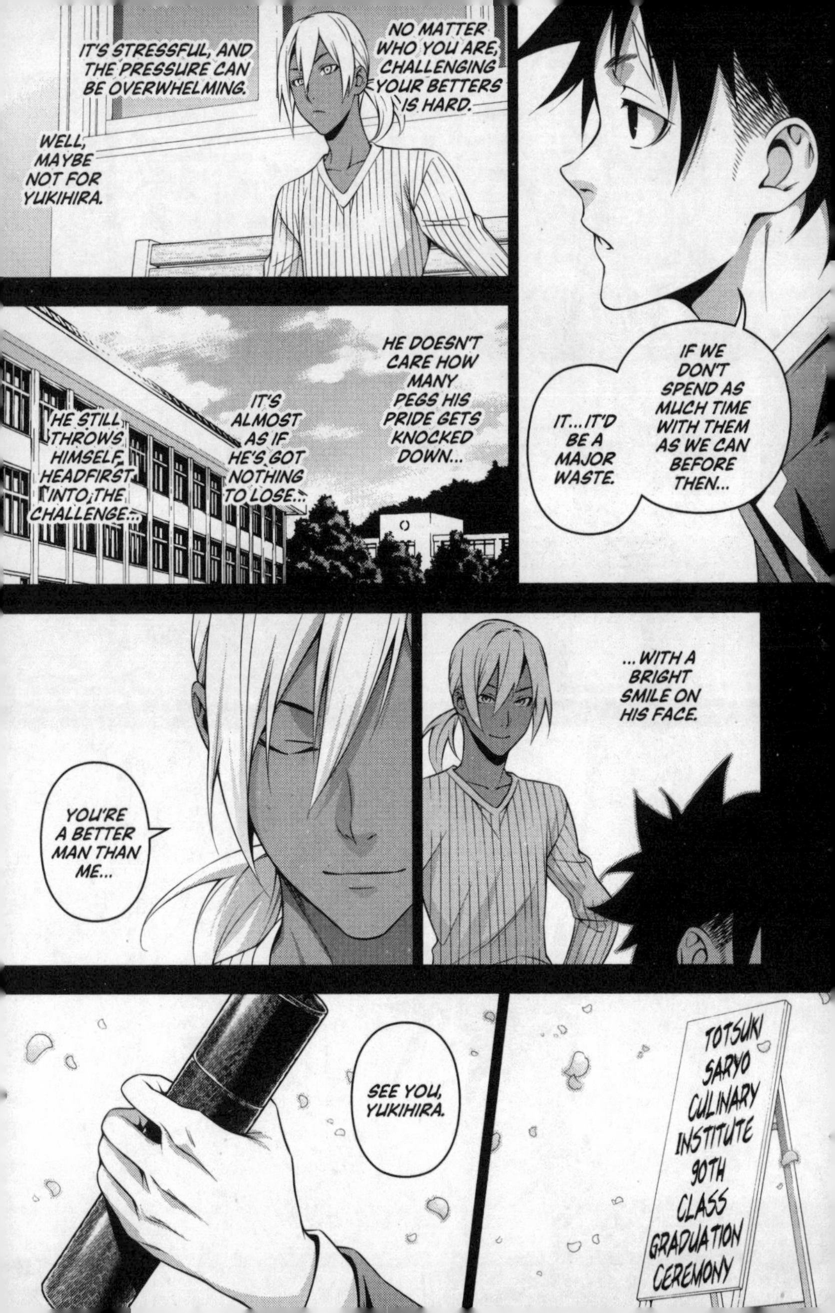
IF WE DON'T SPEND AS MUCH TIME WITH THEM AS WE CAN BEFORE THEN...
IT... IT'D BE A MAJOR WASTE.
NO MATTER WHO YOU ARE, CHALLENGING YOUR BETTERS IS HARD.
IT'S STRESSFUL, AND THE PRESSURE CAN BE OVERWHELMING.
WELL, MAYBE NOT FOR YUKIHIRA.
HE DOESN'T CARE HOW MANY PEGS HIS PRIDE GETS KNOCKED DOWN...
IT'S ALMOST AS IF HE'S GOT NOTHING TO LOSE...
HE STILL THROWS HIMSELF HEADFIRST INTO THE CHALLENGE...
...WITH A BRIGHT SMILE ON HIS FACE.
YOU'RE A BETTER MAN THAN ME...
TOTSUKI SARYO CULINARY INSTITUTE 90TH CLASS GRADUATION CEREMONY
SEE YOU, YUKIHIRA.

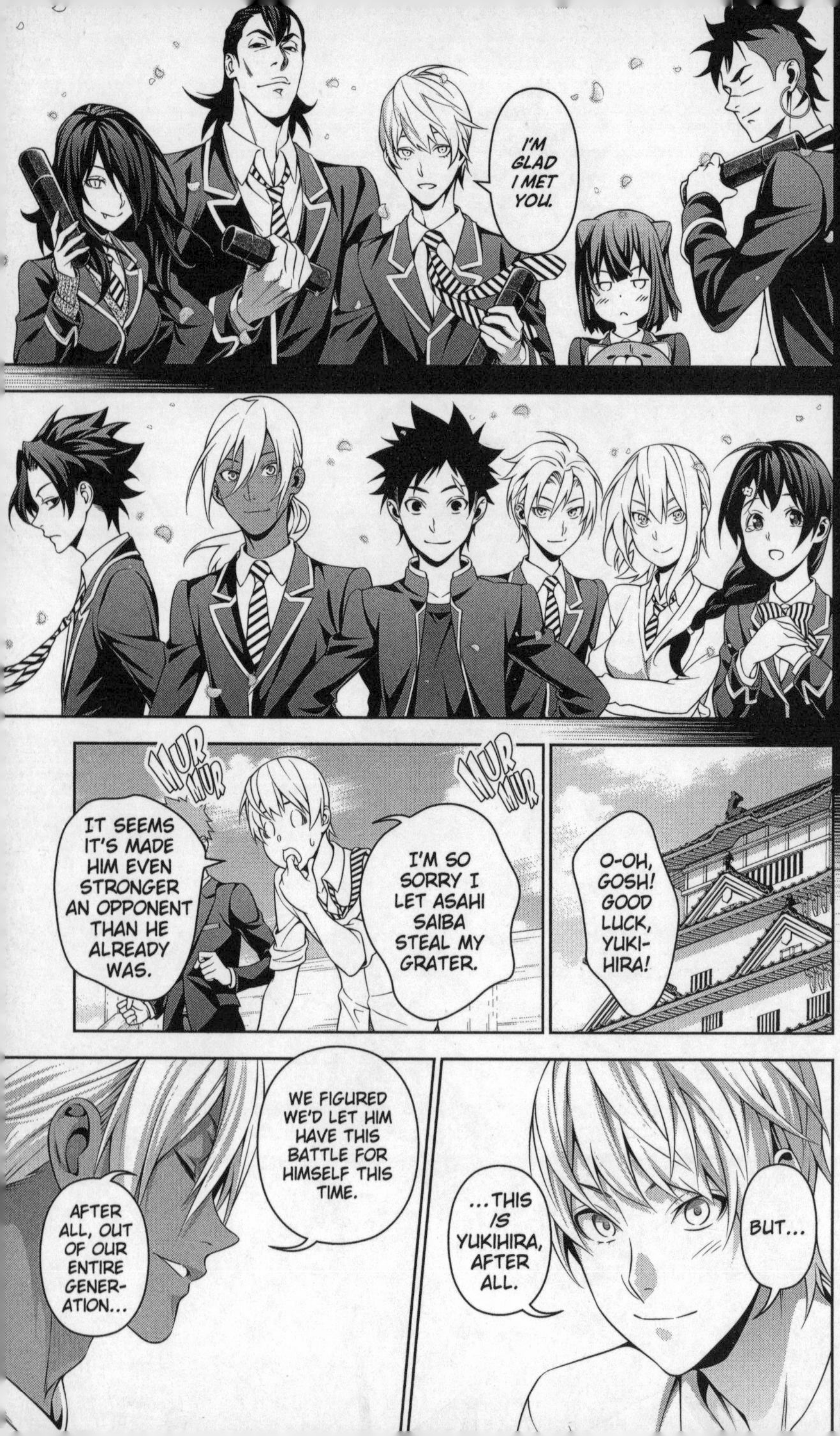
I'M GLAD I MET YOU.
O-OH, GOSH! GOOD LUCK, YUKI-HIRA!
MUR MUR
I'M SO SORRY I LET ASAHI SAIBA STEAL MY GRATER.
MUR MUR
IT SEEMS IT'S MADE HIM EVEN STRONGER AN OPPONENT THAN HE ALREADY WAS.
BUT...
...THIS IS YUKIHIRA, AFTER ALL.
WE FIGURED WE'D LET HIM HAVE THIS BATTLE FOR HIMSELF THIS TIME.
AFTER ALL, OUT OF OUR ENTIRE GENER-ATION...

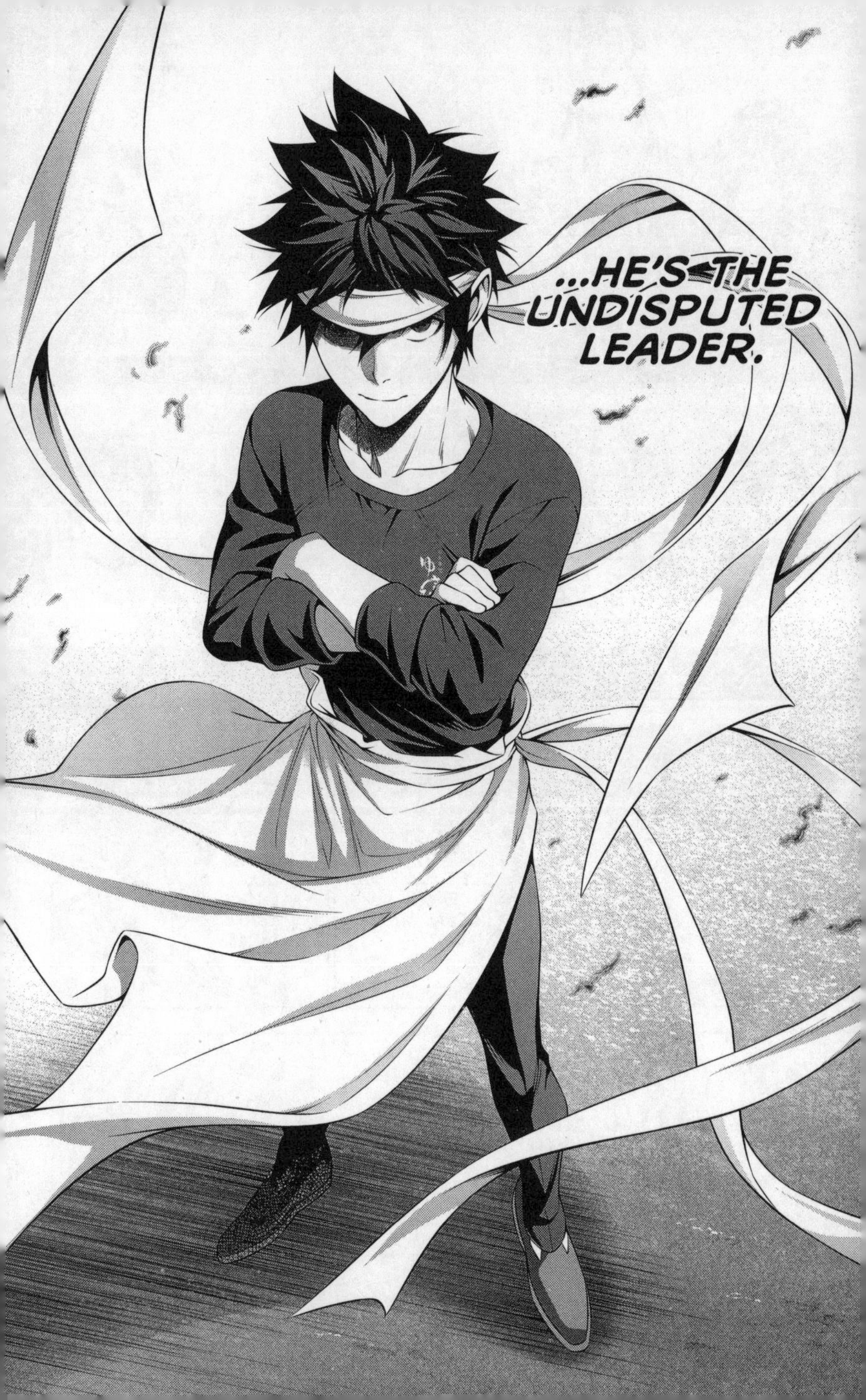
...HE'S THE UNDISPUTED LEADER.

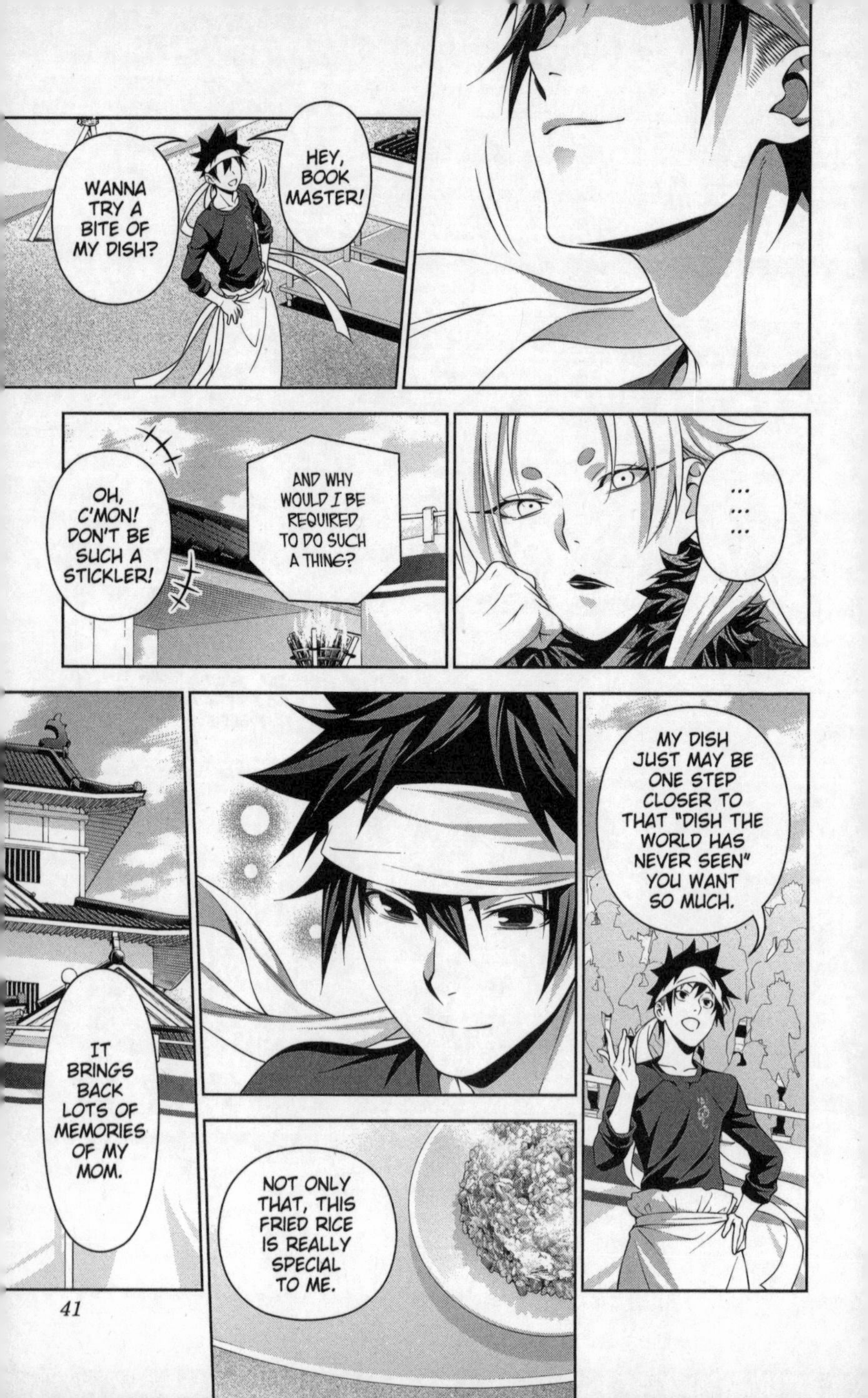
HEY, BOOK MASTER!
WANNA TRY A BITE OF MY DISH?
... ...
AND WHY WOULD I BE REQUIRED TO DO SUCH A THING?
OH, C'MON! DON'T BE SUCH A STICKLER!
MY DISH JUST MAY BE ONE STEP CLOSER TO THAT "DISH THE WORLD HAS NEVER SEEN" YOU WANT SO MUCH.
NOT ONLY THAT, THIS FRIED RICE IS REALLY SPECIAL TO ME.
IT BRINGS BACK LOTS OF MEMORIES OF MY MOM.

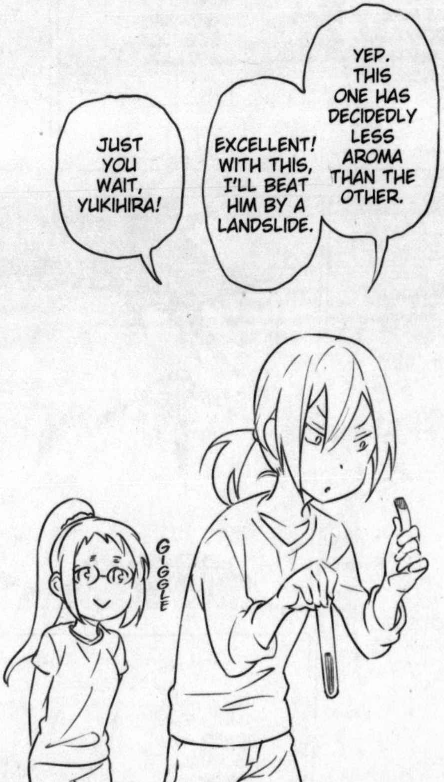
YEP. THIS ONE HAS DECIDEDLY LESS AROMA THAN THE OTHER.
EXCELLENT! WITH THIS, I'LL BEAT HIM BY A LANDSLIDE.
JUST YOU WAIT, YUKIHIRA!
GIGGLE

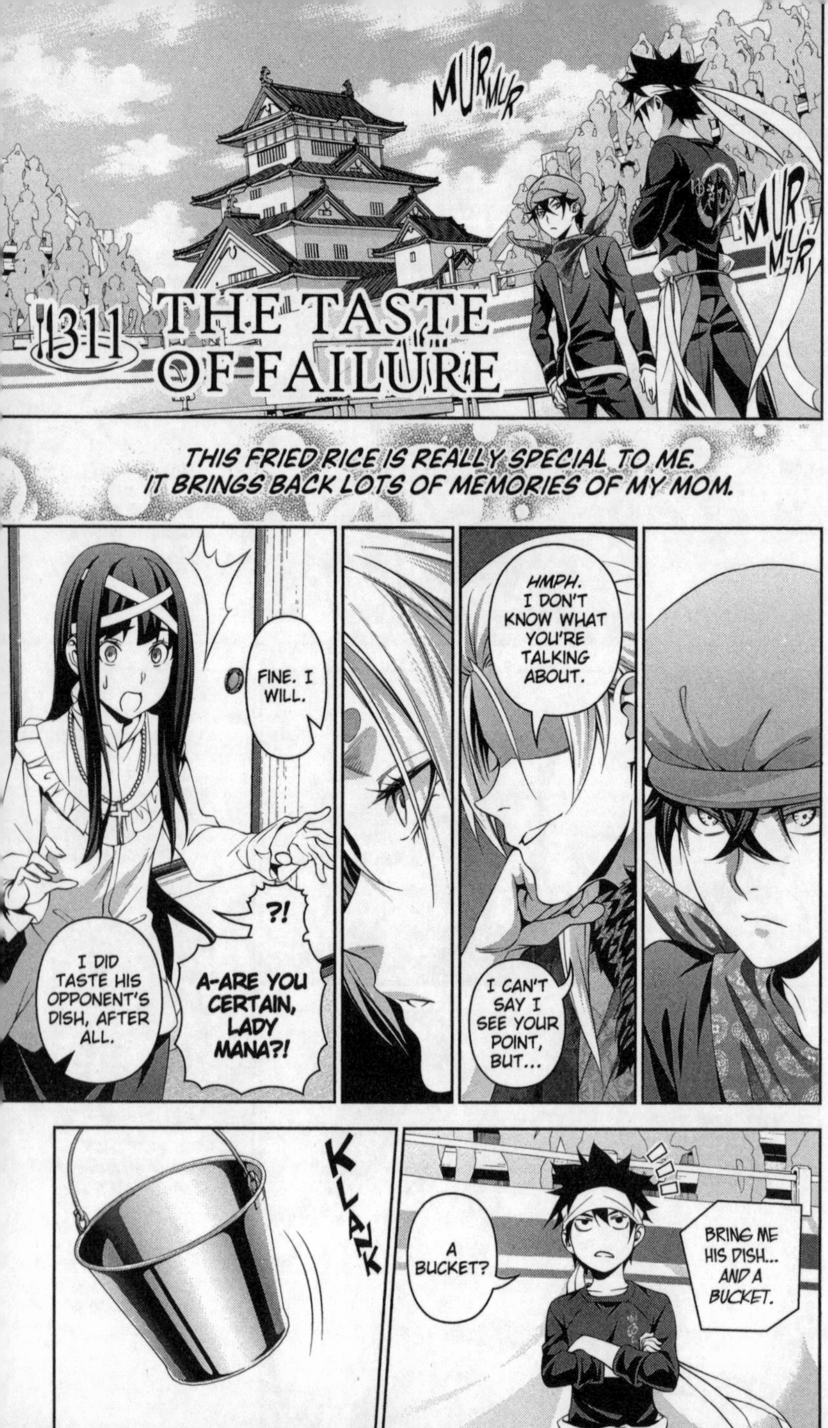
MUR MUR
MUR MUR
311 THE TASTE OF FAILURE
THIS FRIED RICE IS REALLY SPECIAL TO ME.
IT BRINGS BACK LOTS OF MEMORIES OF MY MOM.
HMPH. I DON'T KNOW WHAT YOU'RE TALKING ABOUT.
I CAN'T SAY I SEE YOUR POINT, BUT...
FINE. I WILL.
?!
A-ARE YOU CERTAIN, LADY MANA?!
I DID TASTE HIS OPPONENT'S DISH, AFTER ALL.
BRING ME HIS DISH... AND A BUCKET.
A BUCKET?
KLANK

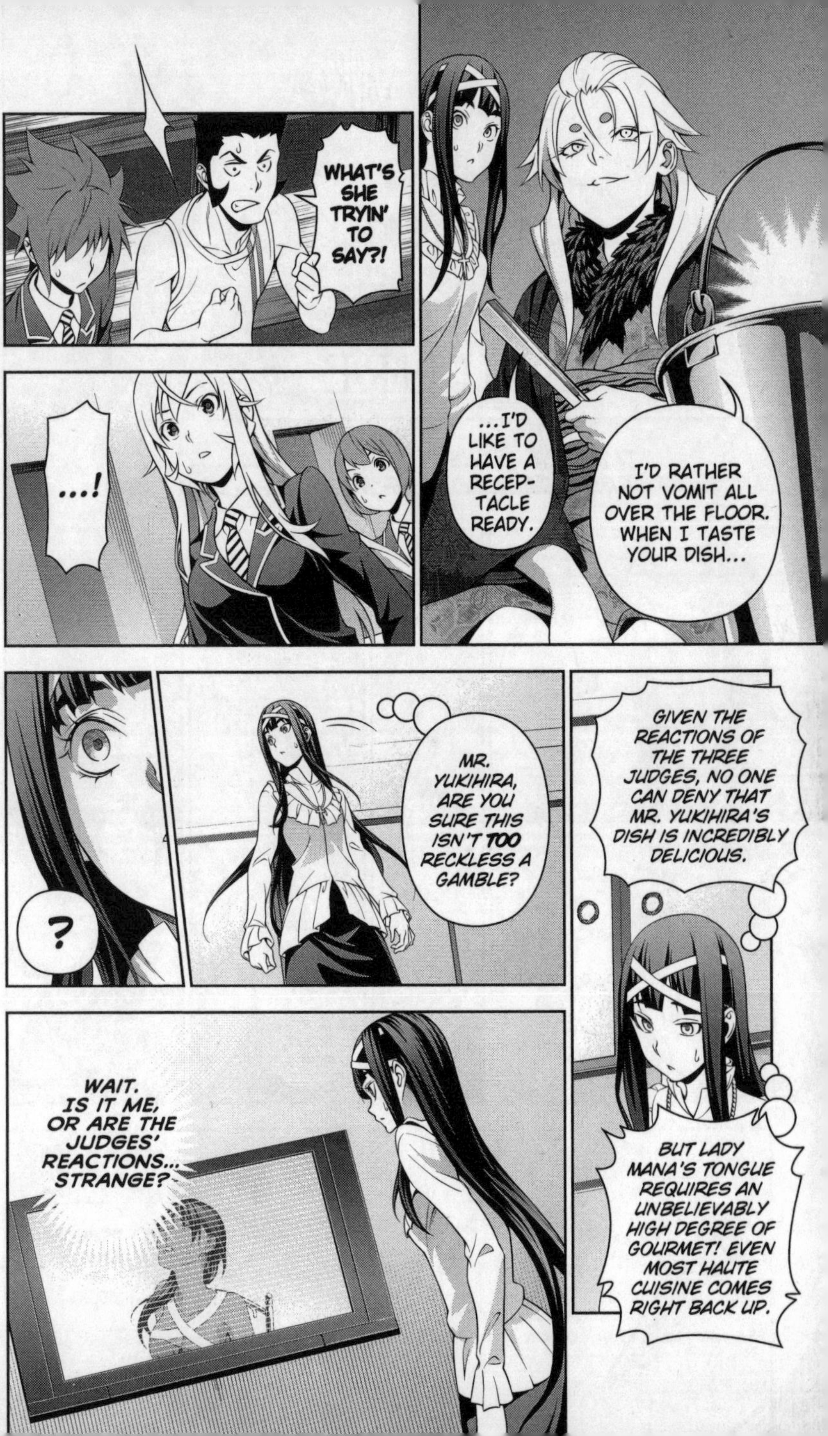
I'D RATHER NOT VOMIT ALL OVER THE FLOOR. WHEN I TASTE YOUR DISH...
...I'D LIKE TO HAVE A RECEPTACLE READY.
WHAT'S SHE TRYIN' TO SAY?!
...!
GIVEN THE REACTIONS OF THE THREE JUDGES, NO ONE CAN DENY THAT MR. YUKIHIRA'S DISH IS INCREDIBLY DELICIOUS.
BUT LADY MANA'S TONGUE REQUIRES AN UNBELIEVABLY HIGH DEGREE OF GOURMET! EVEN MOST HAUTE CUISINE COMES RIGHT BACK UP.
MR. YUKIHIRA, ARE YOU SURE THIS ISN'T **TOO** RECKLESS A GAMBLE?
?
WAIT. IS IT ME, OR ARE THE JUDGES' REACTIONS... STRANGE?

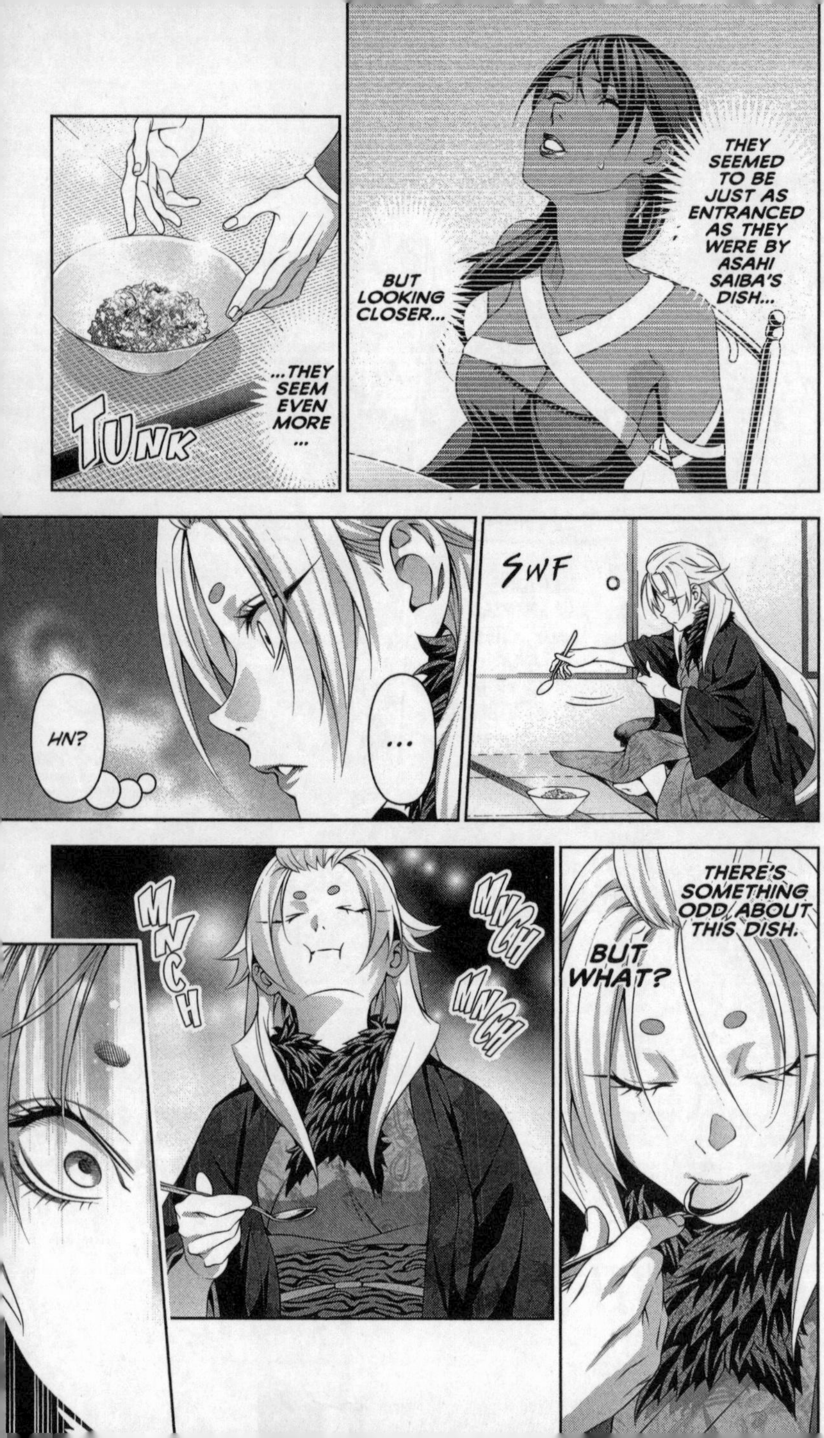
THEY SEEMED TO BE JUST AS ENTRANCED AS THEY WERE BY ASAHI SAIBA'S DISH...
BUT LOOKING CLOSER...
...THEY SEEM EVEN MORE ...
TUNK
SWF
...
HN?
THERE'S SOMETHING ODD ABOUT THIS DISH.
BUT WHAT?
MNCH
MNCH
MNCH

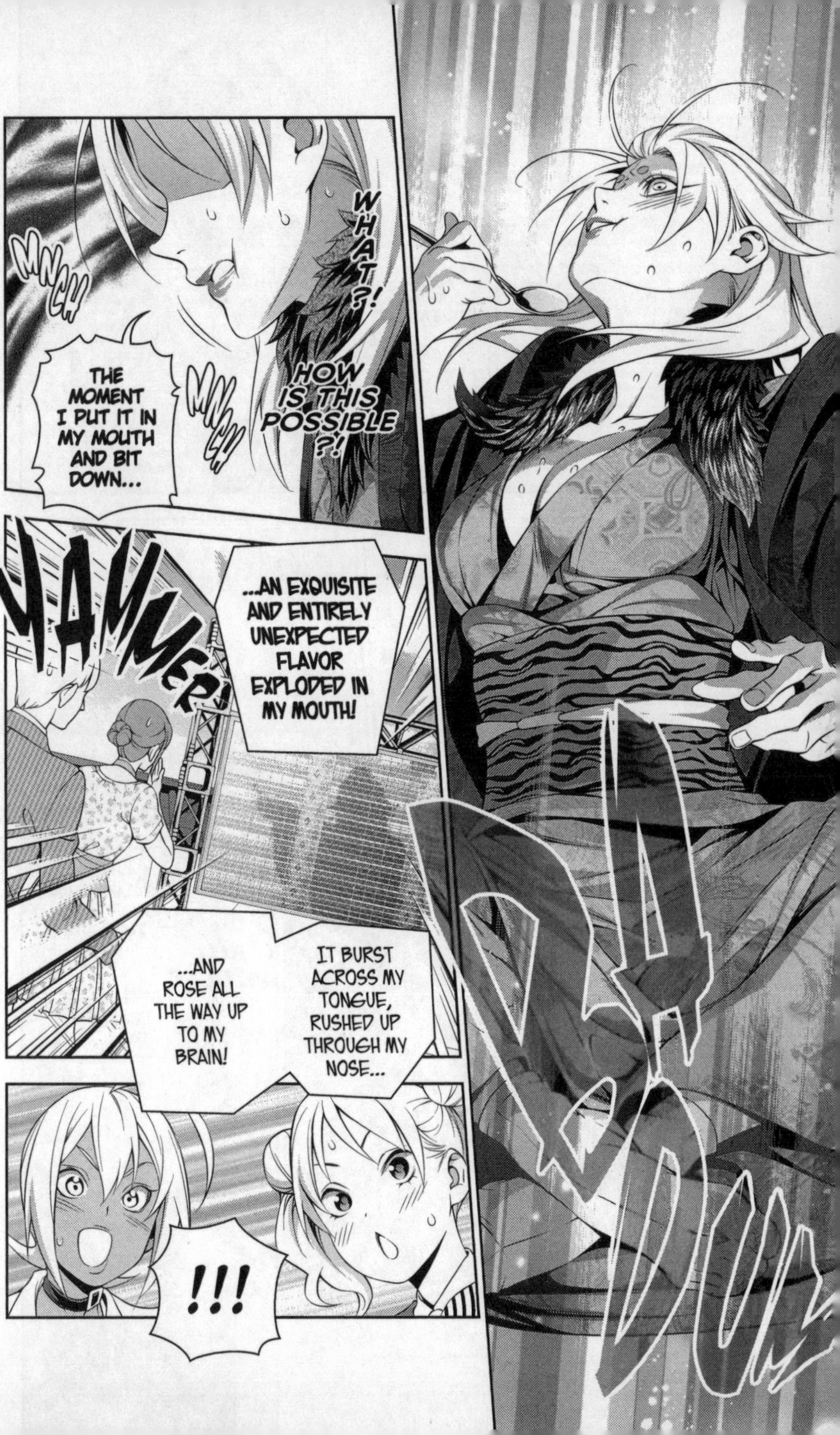
WHAT?!
HOW IS THIS POSSIBLE?!
MNCH
THE MOMENT I PUT IT IN MY MOUTH AND BIT DOWN...
MNCH
...AN EXQUISITE AND ENTIRELY UNEXPECTED FLAVOR EXPLODED IN MY MOUTH!
HAMMER!
IT BURST ACROSS MY TONGUE, RUSHED UP THROUGH MY NOSE...
...AND ROSE ALL THE WAY UP TO MY BRAIN!
!!!

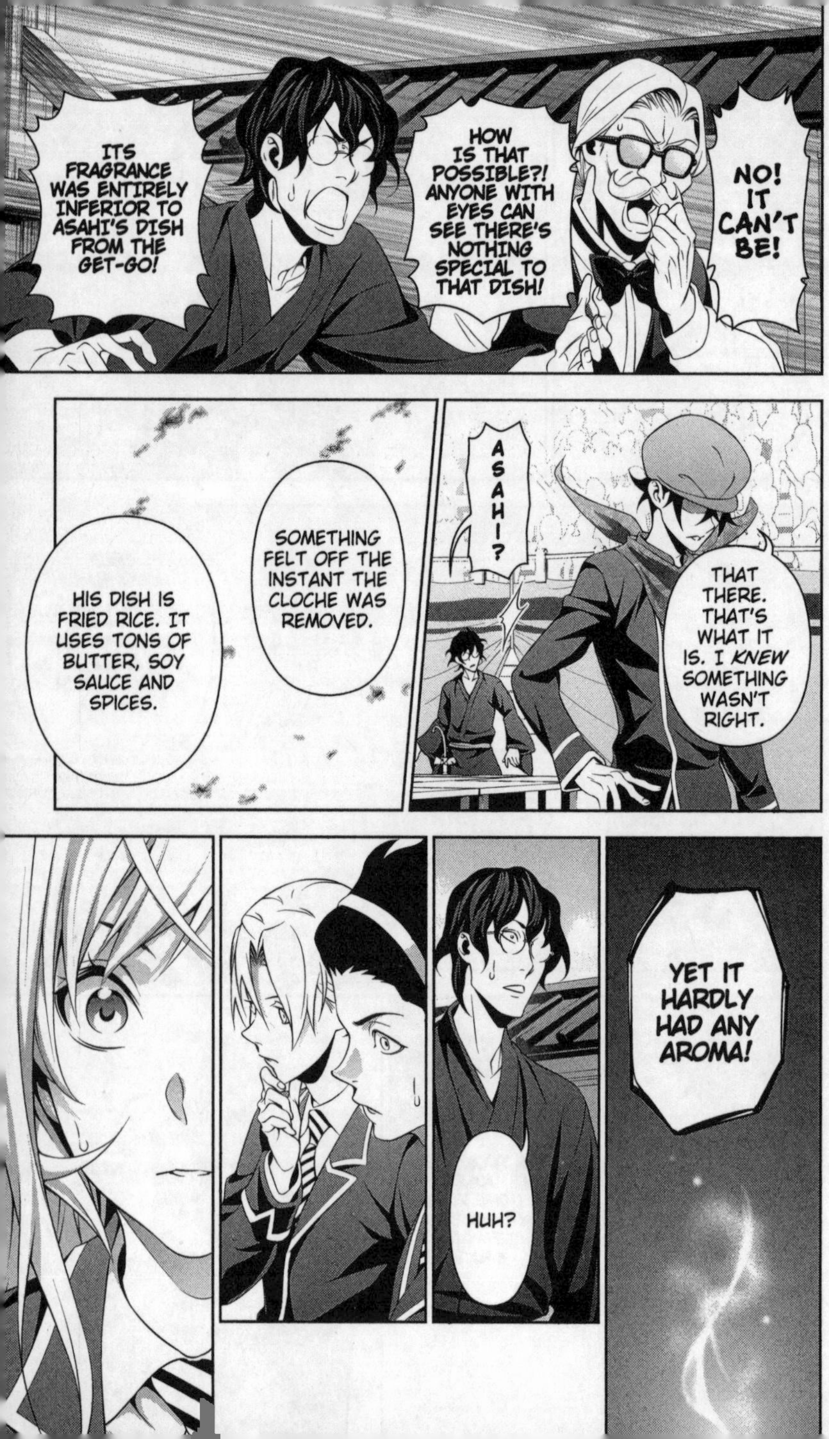
NO! IT CAN'T BE!
HOW IS THAT POSSIBLE?! ANYONE WITH EYES CAN SEE THERE'S NOTHING SPECIAL TO THAT DISH!
ITS FRAGRANCE WAS ENTIRELY INFERIOR TO ASAHI'S DISH FROM THE GET-GO!
ASAHI?
THAT THERE. THAT'S WHAT IT IS. I *KNEW* SOMETHING WASN'T RIGHT.
SOMETHING FELT OFF THE INSTANT THE CLOCHE WAS REMOVED.
HIS DISH IS FRIED RICE. IT USES TONS OF BUTTER, SOY SAUCE AND SPICES.
YET IT HARDLY HAD ANY AROMA!
HUH?

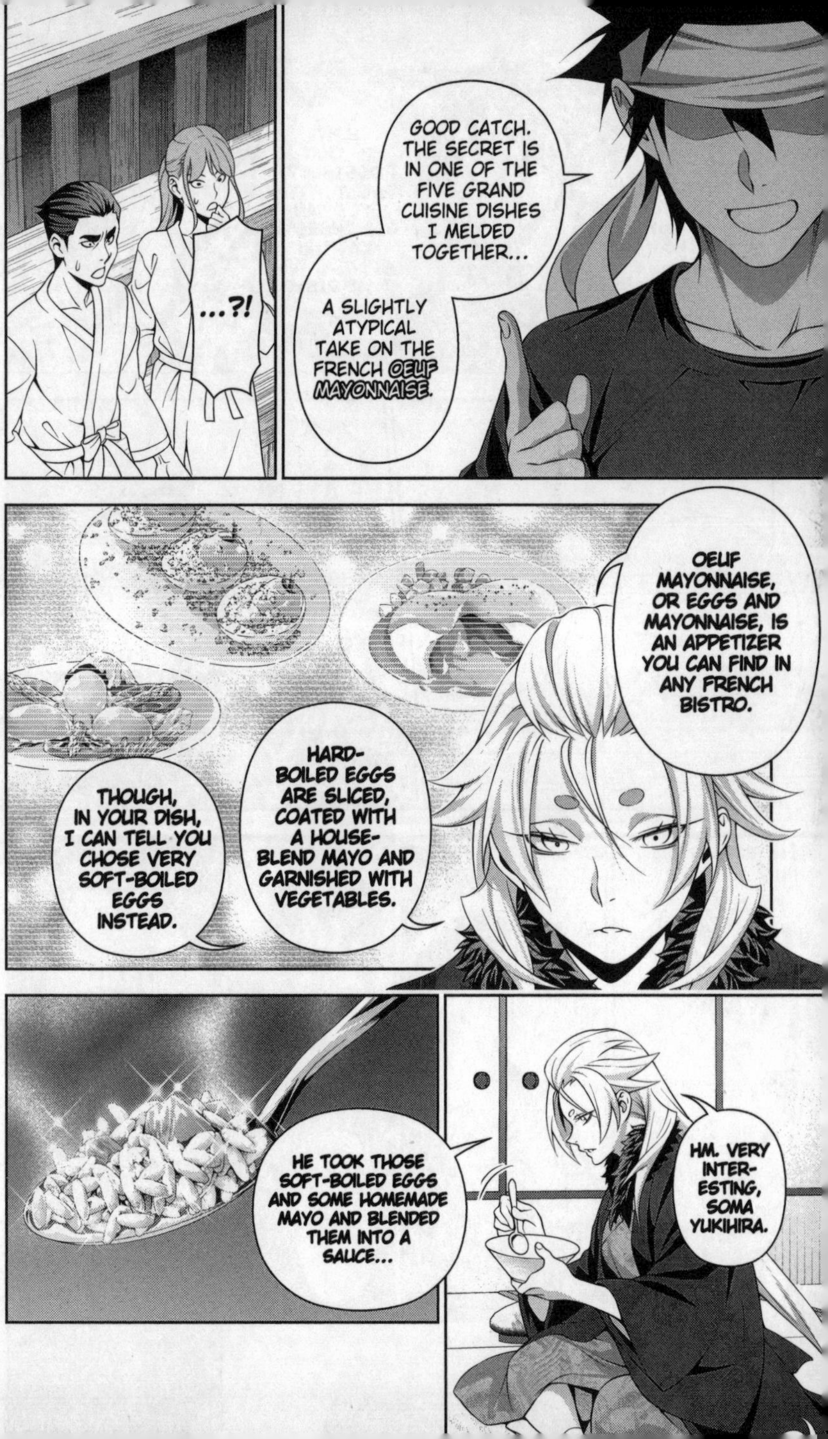
GOOD CATCH. THE SECRET IS IN ONE OF THE FIVE GRAND CUISINE DISHES I MELDED TOGETHER...
A SLIGHTLY ATYPICAL TAKE ON THE FRENCH OEUF MAYONNAISE.
...?!
OEUF MAYONNAISE, OR EGGS AND MAYONNAISE, IS AN APPETIZER YOU CAN FIND IN ANY FRENCH BISTRO.
HARD-BOILED EGGS ARE SLICED, COATED WITH A HOUSE-BLEND MAYO AND GARNISHED WITH VEGETABLES.
THOUGH, IN YOUR DISH, I CAN TELL YOU CHOSE VERY SOFT-BOILED EGGS INSTEAD.
HM. VERY INTERESTING, SOMA YUKIHIRA.
HE TOOK THOSE SOFT-BOILED EGGS AND SOME HOMEMADE MAYO AND BLENDED THEM INTO A SAUCE...

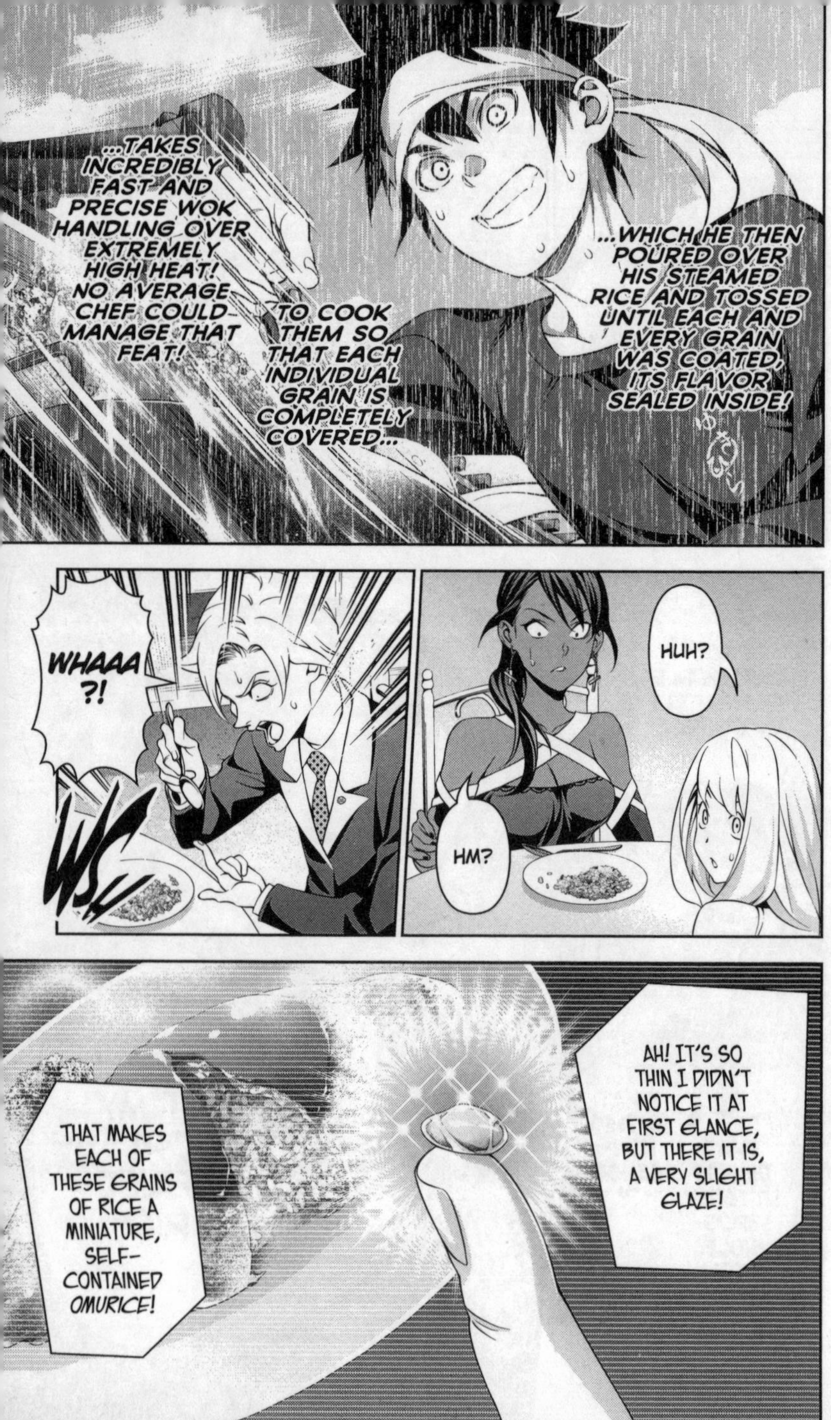
...WHICH HE THEN POURED OVER HIS STEAMED RICE AND TOSSED UNTIL EACH AND EVERY GRAIN WAS COATED, ITS FLAVOR SEALED INSIDE!
TO COOK THEM SO THAT EACH INDIVIDUAL GRAIN IS COMPLETELY COVERED...
...TAKES INCREDIBLY FAST AND PRECISE WOK HANDLING OVER EXTREMELY HIGH HEAT! NO AVERAGE CHEF COULD MANAGE THAT FEAT!
HUH?
HM?
WHAAA?!
WSH
AH! IT'S SO THIN I DIDN'T NOTICE IT AT FIRST GLANCE, BUT THERE IT IS, A VERY SLIGHT GLAZE!
THAT MAKES EACH OF THESE GRAINS OF RICE A MINIATURE, SELF-CONTAINED OMURICE!

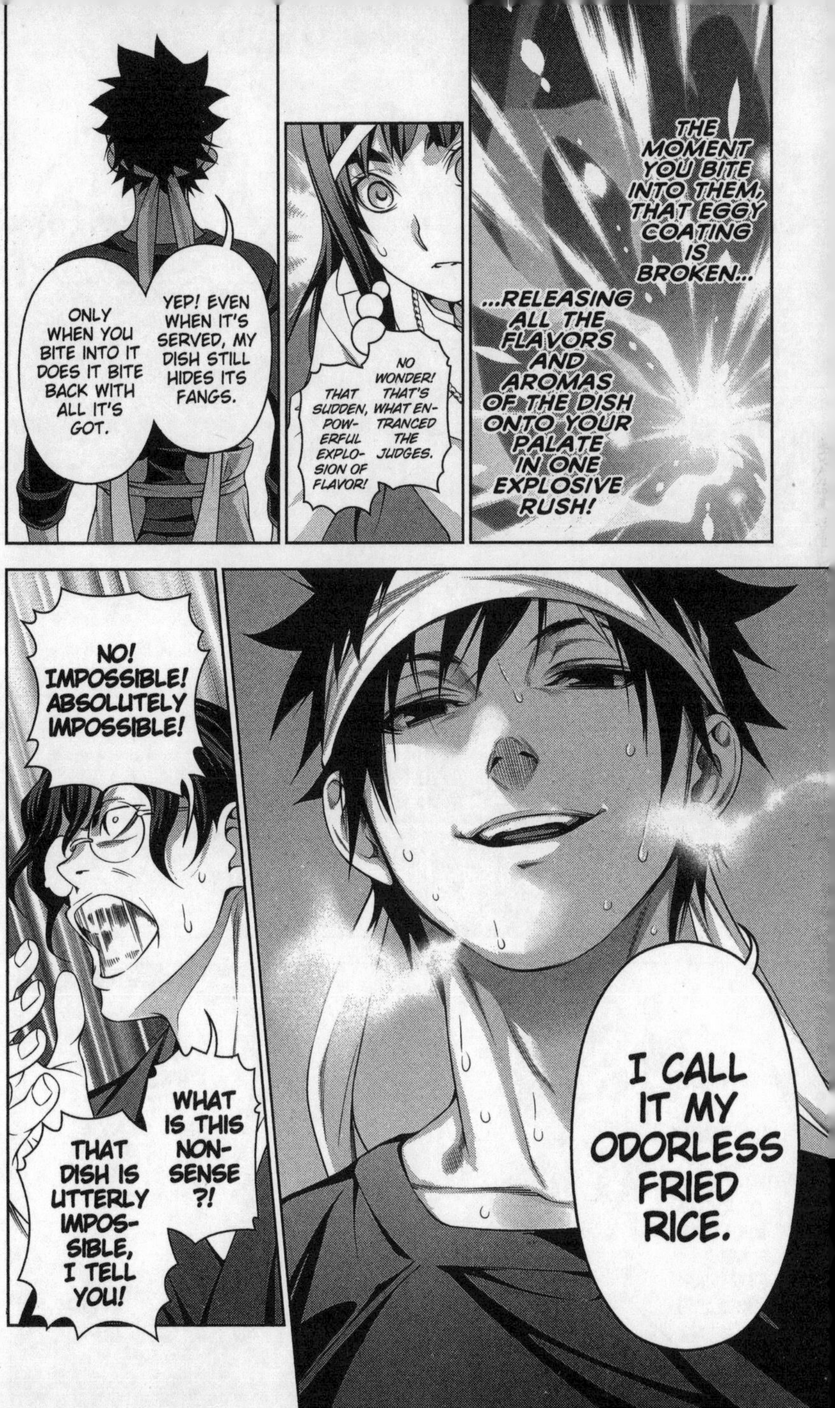
THE MOMENT YOU BITE INTO THEM, THAT EGGY COATING IS BROKEN...
...RELEASING ALL THE FLAVORS AND AROMAS OF THE DISH ONTO YOUR PALATE IN ONE EXPLOSIVE RUSH!
NO WONDER! THAT'S WHAT ENTRANCED THE JUDGES.
THAT SUDDEN, POWERFUL EXPLOSION OF FLAVOR!
YEP! EVEN WHEN IT'S SERVED, MY DISH STILL HIDES ITS FANGS.
ONLY WHEN YOU BITE INTO IT DOES IT BITE BACK WITH ALL IT'S GOT.
I CALL IT MY ODORLESS FRIED RICE.
NO! IMPOSSIBLE! ABSOLUTELY IMPOSSIBLE!
WHAT IS THIS NONSENSE?!
THAT DISH IS UTTERLY IMPOSSIBLE, I TELL YOU!

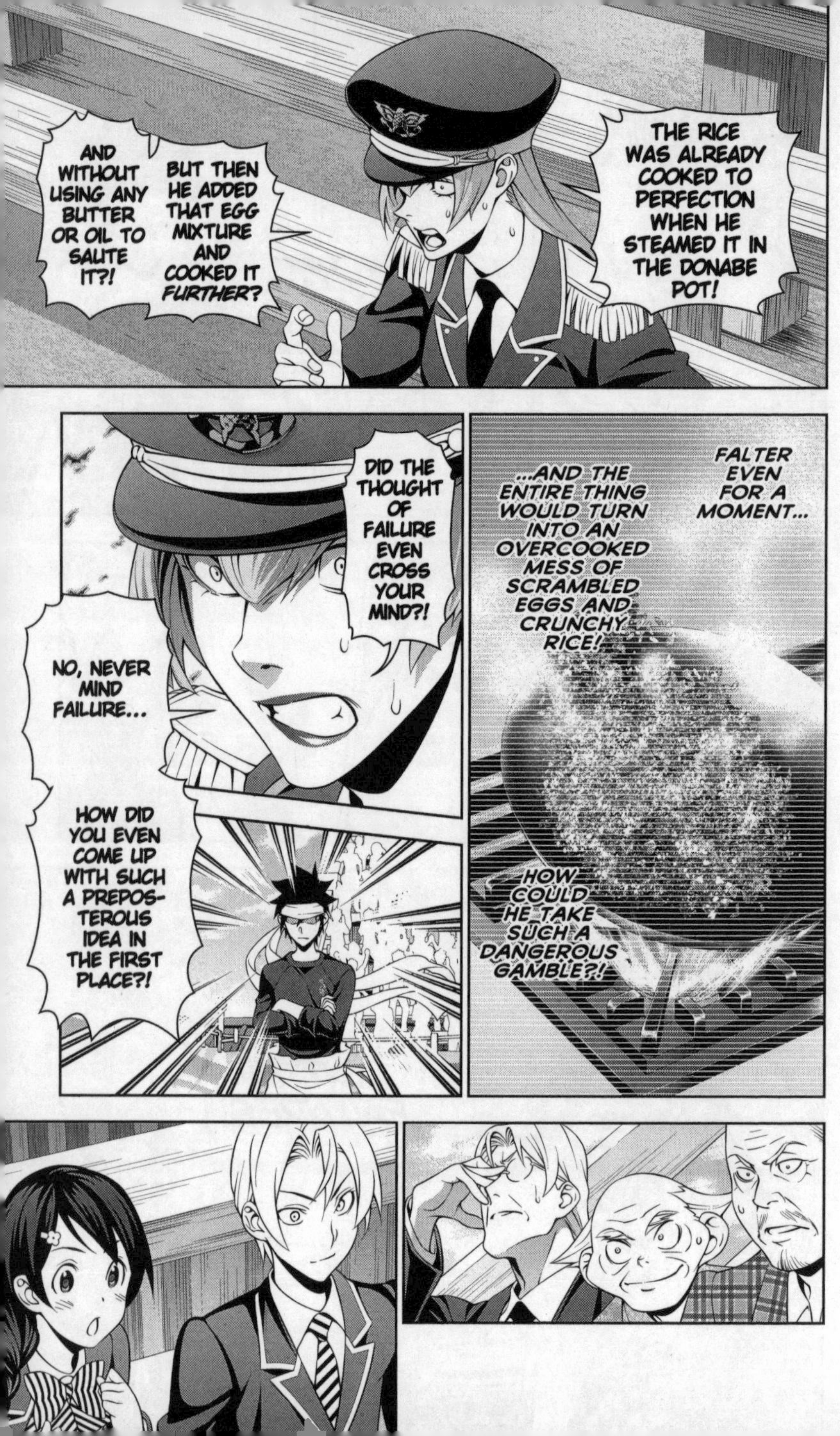
THE RICE WAS ALREADY COOKED TO PERFECTION WHEN HE STEAMED IT IN THE DONABE POT!
BUT THEN HE ADDED THAT EGG MIXTURE AND COOKED IT *FURTHER*?
AND WITHOUT USING ANY BUTTER OR OIL TO SAUTE IT?!
FALTER EVEN FOR A MOMENT...
...AND THE ENTIRE THING WOULD TURN INTO AN OVERCOOKED MESS OF SCRAMBLED EGGS AND CRUNCHY RICE!
HOW COULD HE TAKE SUCH A DANGEROUS GAMBLE?!
DID THE THOUGHT OF FAILURE EVEN CROSS YOUR MIND?!
NO, NEVER MIND FAILURE...
HOW DID YOU EVEN COME UP WITH SUCH A PREPOSTEROUS IDEA IN THE FIRST PLACE?!

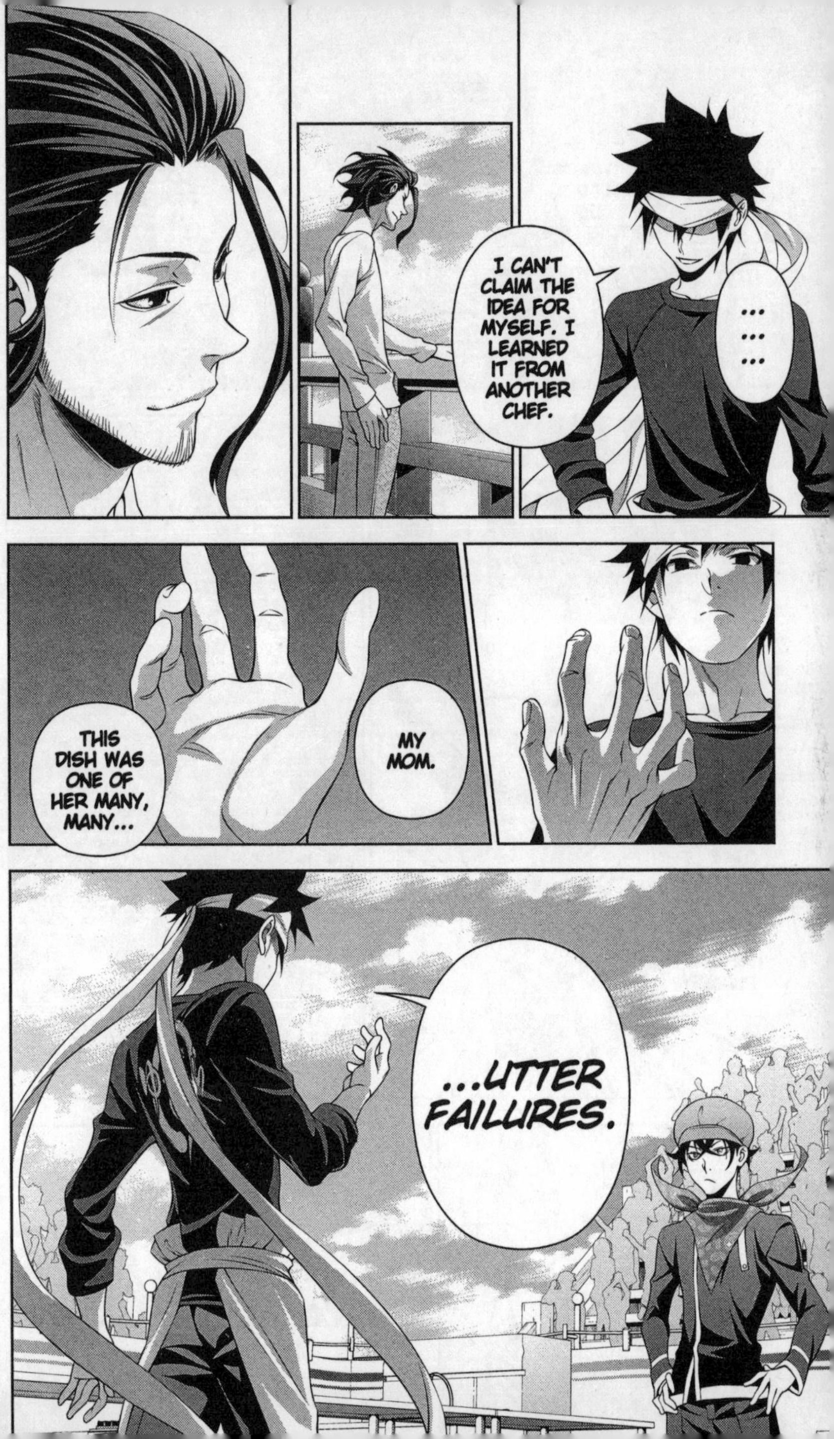
...
...
...
I CAN'T CLAIM THE IDEA FOR MYSELF. I LEARNED IT FROM ANOTHER CHEF.
MY MOM.
THIS DISH WAS ONE OF HER MANY, MANY...
...UTTER FAILURES.

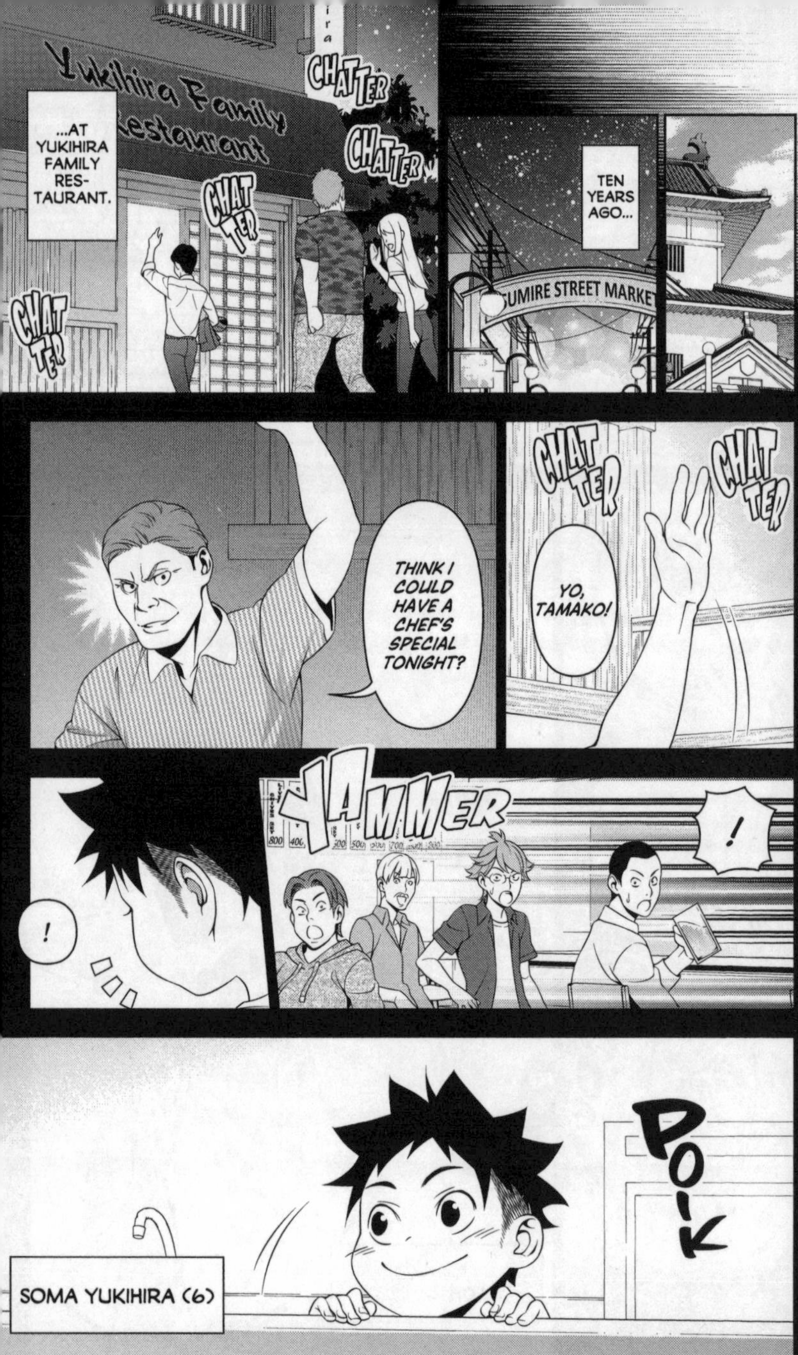
TEN YEARS AGO...
UMIRE STREET MARKET
...AT YUKIHIRA FAMILY RES-TAURANT.
Yukihira Family Restaurant
CHATTER
CHATTER
CHATTER
CHATTER
CHATTER
YO, TAMAKO!
CHATTER
THINK I COULD HAVE A CHEF'S SPECIAL TONIGHT?
YAMMER
!
!
POIK
SOMA YUKIHIRA (6)

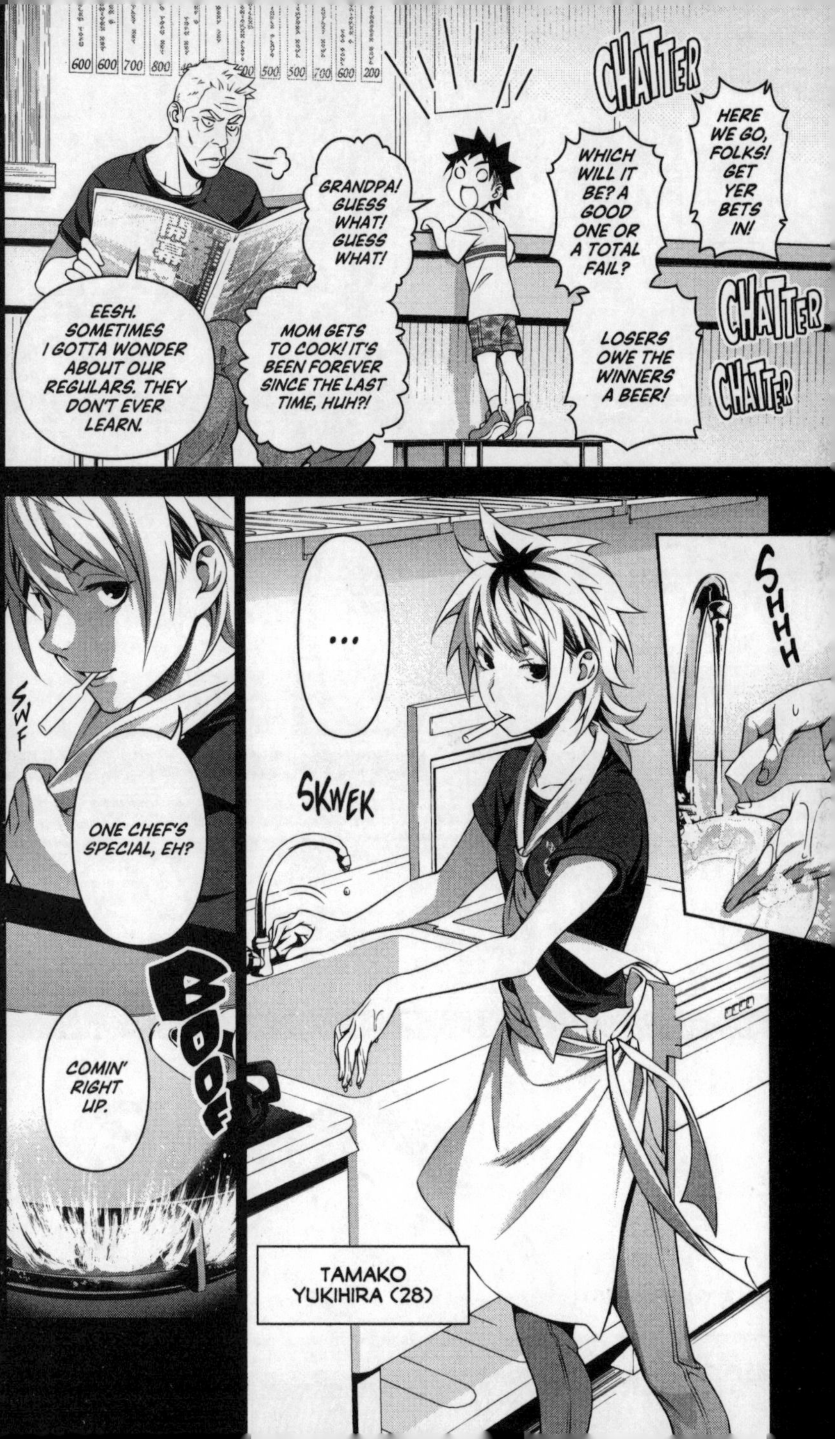

CHATTER
HERE WE GO, FOLKS! GET YER BETS IN!
WHICH WILL IT BE? A GOOD ONE OR A TOTAL FAIL?
CHATTER CHATTER
LOSERS OWE THE WINNERS A BEER!
GRANDPA! GUESS WHAT! GUESS WHAT!
MOM GETS TO COOK! IT'S BEEN FOREVER SINCE THE LAST TIME, HUH?!
EESH. SOMETIMES I GOTTA WONDER ABOUT OUR REGULARS. THEY DON'T EVER LEARN.
SHHH
...
SKWEK
TAMAKO YUKIHIRA (28)
SWF
ONE CHEF'S SPECIAL, EH?
BOOF
COMIN' RIGHT UP.

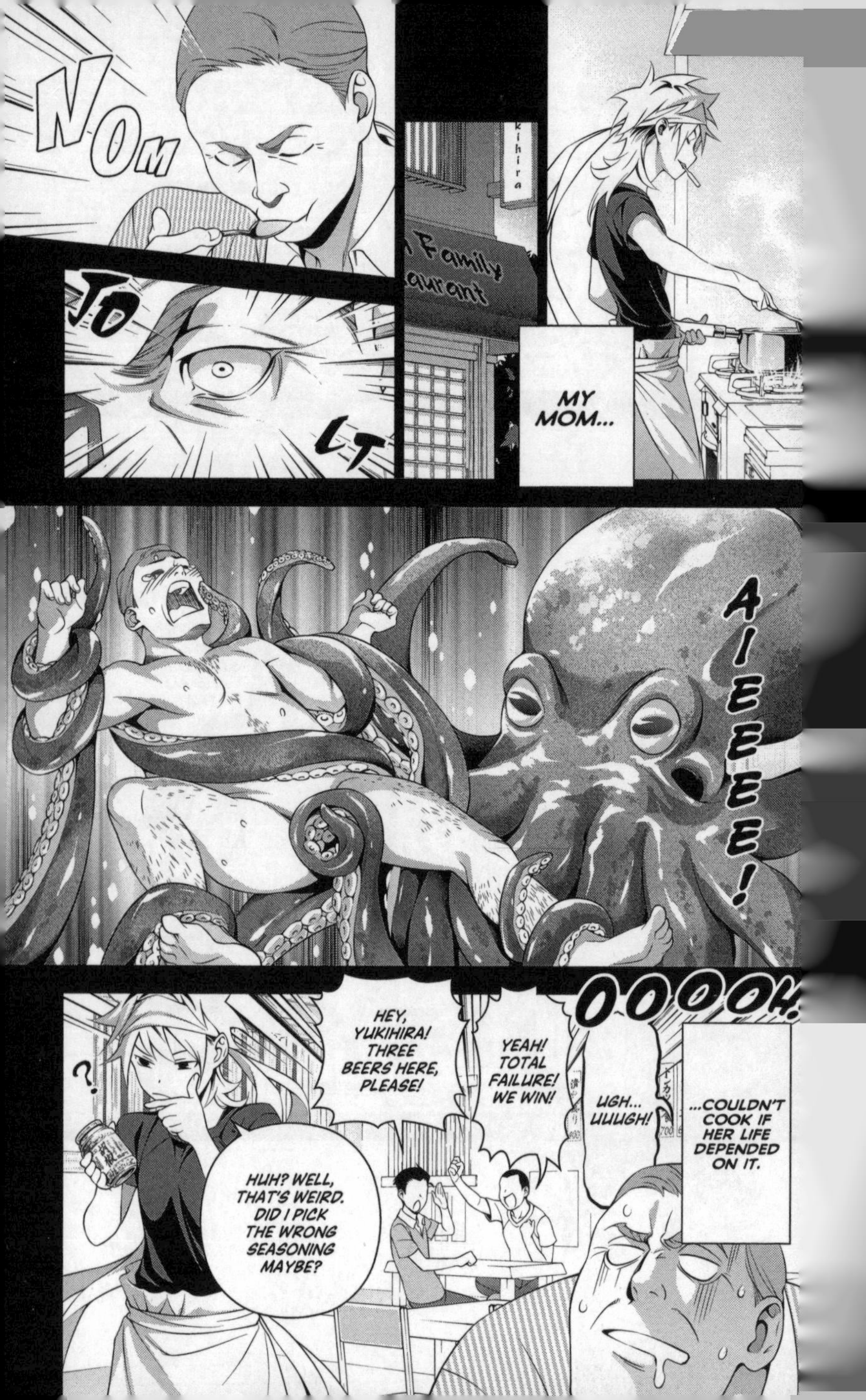
NOM
JOLT
Yukihira Family Restaurant
MY MOM...
AIEEEEE!
O-O-O-OH!
...COULDN'T COOK IF HER LIFE DEPENDED ON IT.
UGH... UUUGH!
YEAH! TOTAL FAILURE! WE WIN!
HEY, YUKIHIRA! THREE BEERS HERE, PLEASE!
?
HUH? WELL, THAT'S WEIRD. DID I PICK THE WRONG SEASONING MAYBE?

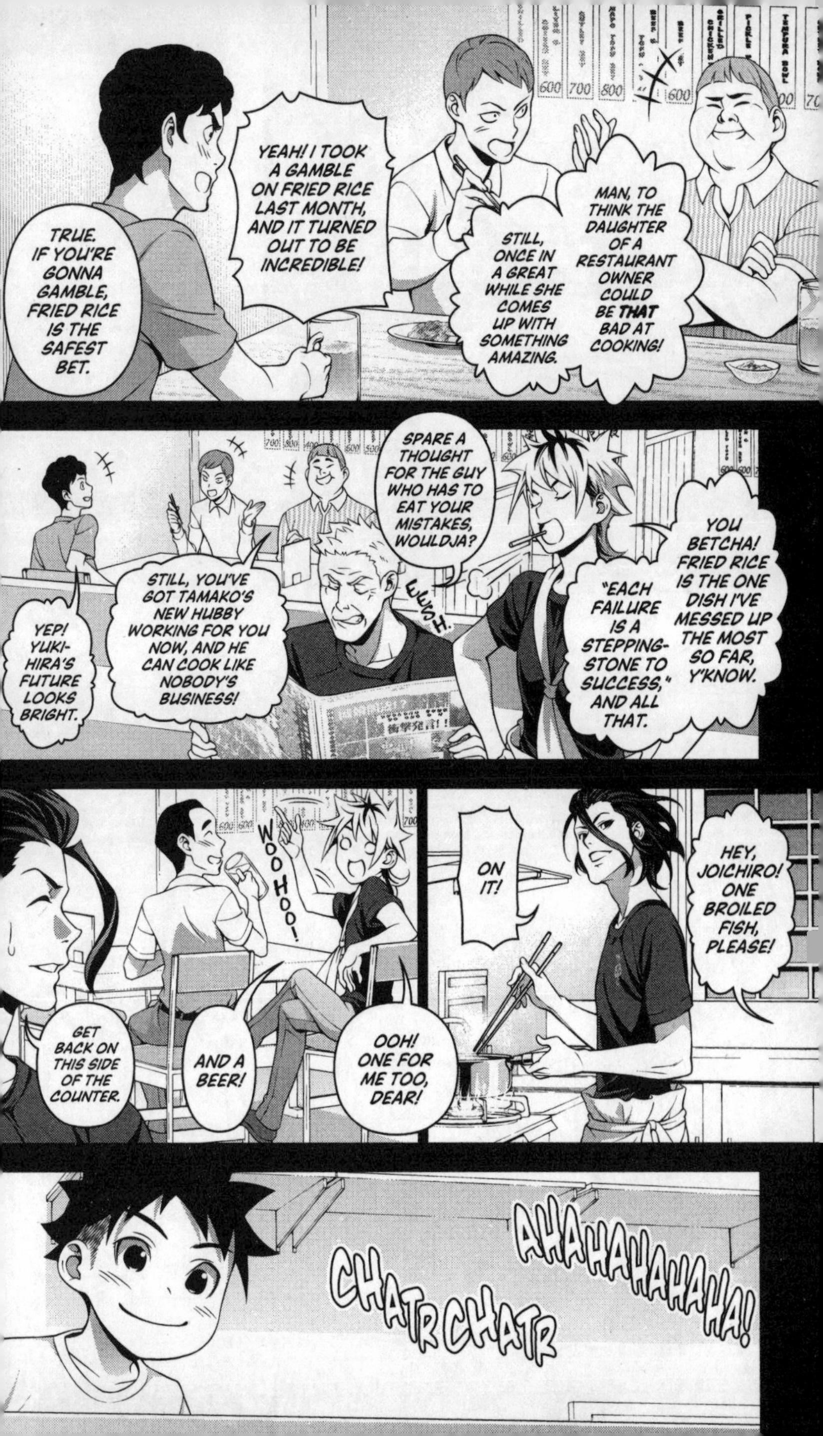
MAN, TO THINK THE DAUGHTER OF A RESTAURANT OWNER COULD BE THAT BAD AT COOKING!
STILL, ONCE IN A GREAT WHILE SHE COMES UP WITH SOMETHING AMAZING.
YEAH! I TOOK A GAMBLE ON FRIED RICE LAST MONTH, AND IT TURNED OUT TO BE INCREDIBLE!
TRUE. IF YOU'RE GONNA GAMBLE, FRIED RICE IS THE SAFEST BET.
YOU BETCHA! FRIED RICE IS THE ONE DISH I'VE MESSED UP THE MOST SO FAR, Y'KNOW.
"EACH FAILURE IS A STEPPING-STONE TO SUCCESS," AND ALL THAT.
SPARE A THOUGHT FOR THE GUY WHO HAS TO EAT YOUR MISTAKES, WOULDJA?
EESH.
STILL, YOU'VE GOT TAMAKO'S NEW HUBBY WORKING FOR YOU NOW, AND HE CAN COOK LIKE NOBODY'S BUSINESS!
YEP! YUKIHIRA'S FUTURE LOOKS BRIGHT.
HEY, JOICHIRO! ONE BROILED FISH, PLEASE!
ON IT!
WOO HOO!
OOH! ONE FOR ME TOO, DEAR!
AND A BEER!
GET BACK ON THIS SIDE OF THE COUNTER.
AHAHAHAHAHAHA!
CHATR CHATR

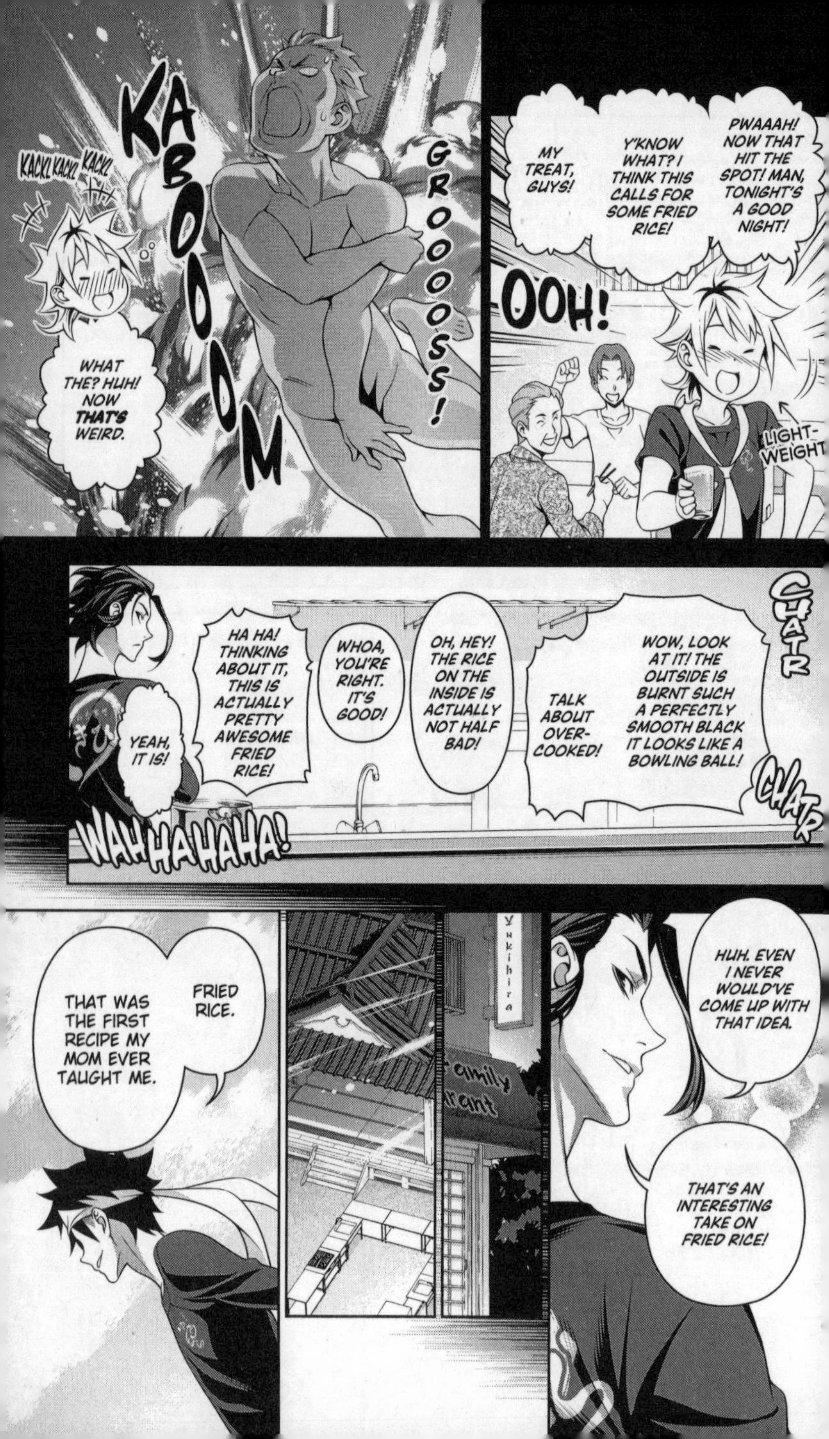
PWAAAH! NOW THAT HIT THE SPOT! MAN, TONIGHT'S A GOOD NIGHT!
Y'KNOW WHAT? I THINK THIS CALLS FOR SOME FRIED RICE!
MY TREAT, GUYS!
OOH!
LIGHT-WEIGHT
GROOOOOSS!
KABOOOOM
KACK! KACK! KACK!
WHAT THE? HUH! NOW **THAT'S** WEIRD.
CHATR
WOW, LOOK AT IT! THE OUTSIDE IS BURNT SUCH A PERFECTLY SMOOTH BLACK IT LOOKS LIKE A BOWLING BALL!
TALK ABOUT OVER-COOKED!
OH, HEY! THE RICE ON THE INSIDE IS ACTUALLY NOT HALF BAD!
WHOA, YOU'RE RIGHT. IT'S GOOD!
HA HA! THINKING ABOUT IT, THIS IS ACTUALLY PRETTY AWESOME FRIED RICE!
YEAH, IT IS!
CHATR
WAHHAHAHA!
HUH. EVEN I NEVER WOULD'VE COME UP WITH THAT IDEA.
THAT'S AN INTERESTING TAKE ON FRIED RICE!
Yukihira
FRIED RICE.
THAT WAS THE FIRST RECIPE MY MOM EVER TAUGHT ME.

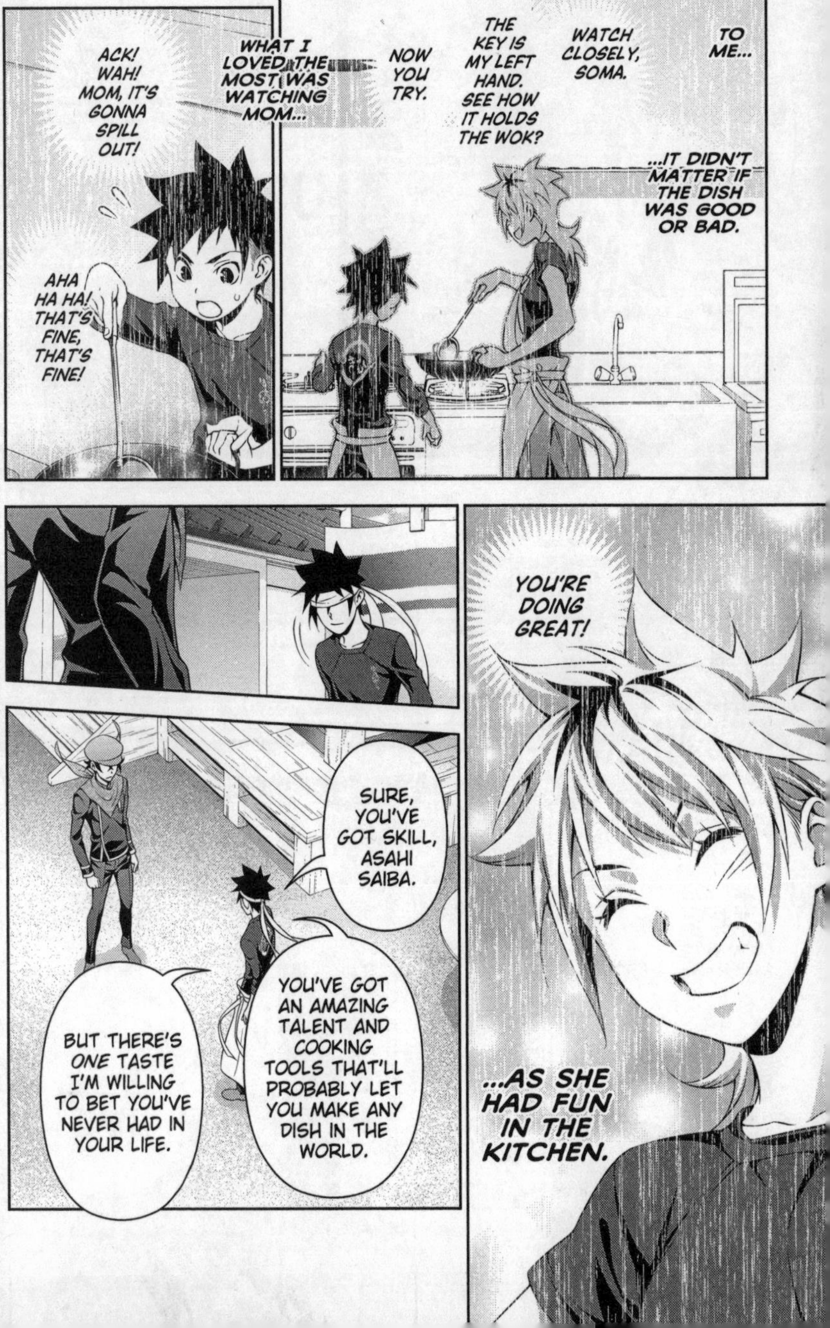
TO ME...
...IT DIDN'T MATTER IF THE DISH WAS GOOD OR BAD.
WATCH CLOSELY, SOMA.
THE KEY IS MY LEFT HAND. SEE HOW IT HOLDS THE WOK?
NOW YOU TRY.
WHAT I LOVED THE MOST WAS WATCHING MOM...
ACK! WAH! MOM, IT'S GONNA SPILL OUT!
AHA HA HA! THAT'S FINE, THAT'S FINE!
YOU'RE DOING GREAT!
...AS SHE HAD FUN IN THE KITCHEN.
SURE, YOU'VE GOT SKILL, ASAHI SAIBA.
YOU'VE GOT AN AMAZING TALENT AND COOKING TOOLS THAT'LL PROBABLY LET YOU MAKE ANY DISH IN THE WORLD.
BUT THERE'S ONE TASTE I'M WILLING TO BET YOU'VE NEVER HAD IN YOUR LIFE.

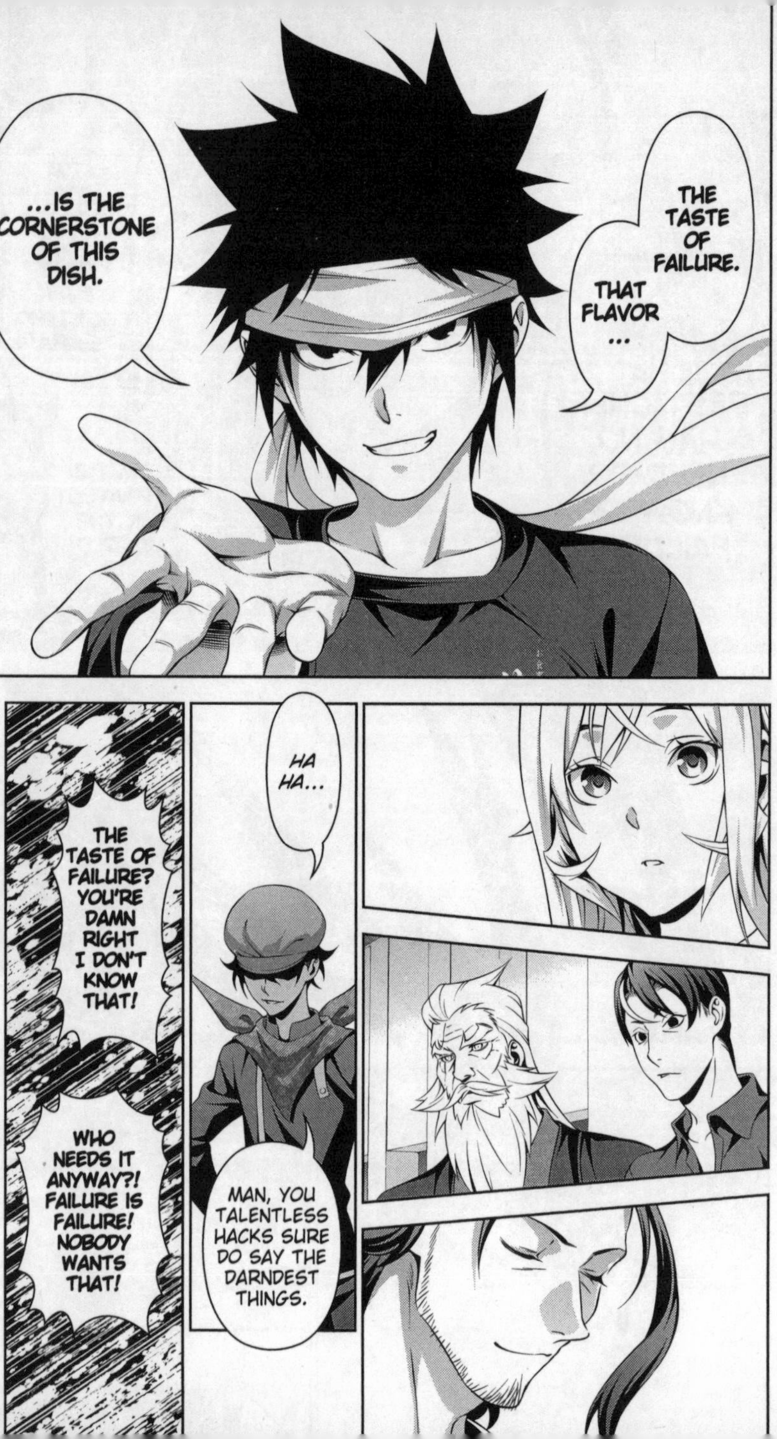
THE TASTE OF FAILURE.
THAT FLAVOR...
...IS THE CORNERSTONE OF THIS DISH.
HA HA...
MAN, YOU TALENTLESS HACKS SURE DO SAY THE DARNDEST THINGS.
THE TASTE OF FAILURE? YOU'RE DAMN RIGHT I DON'T KNOW THAT!
WHO NEEDS IT ANYWAY?! FAILURE IS FAILURE! NOBODY WANTS THAT!

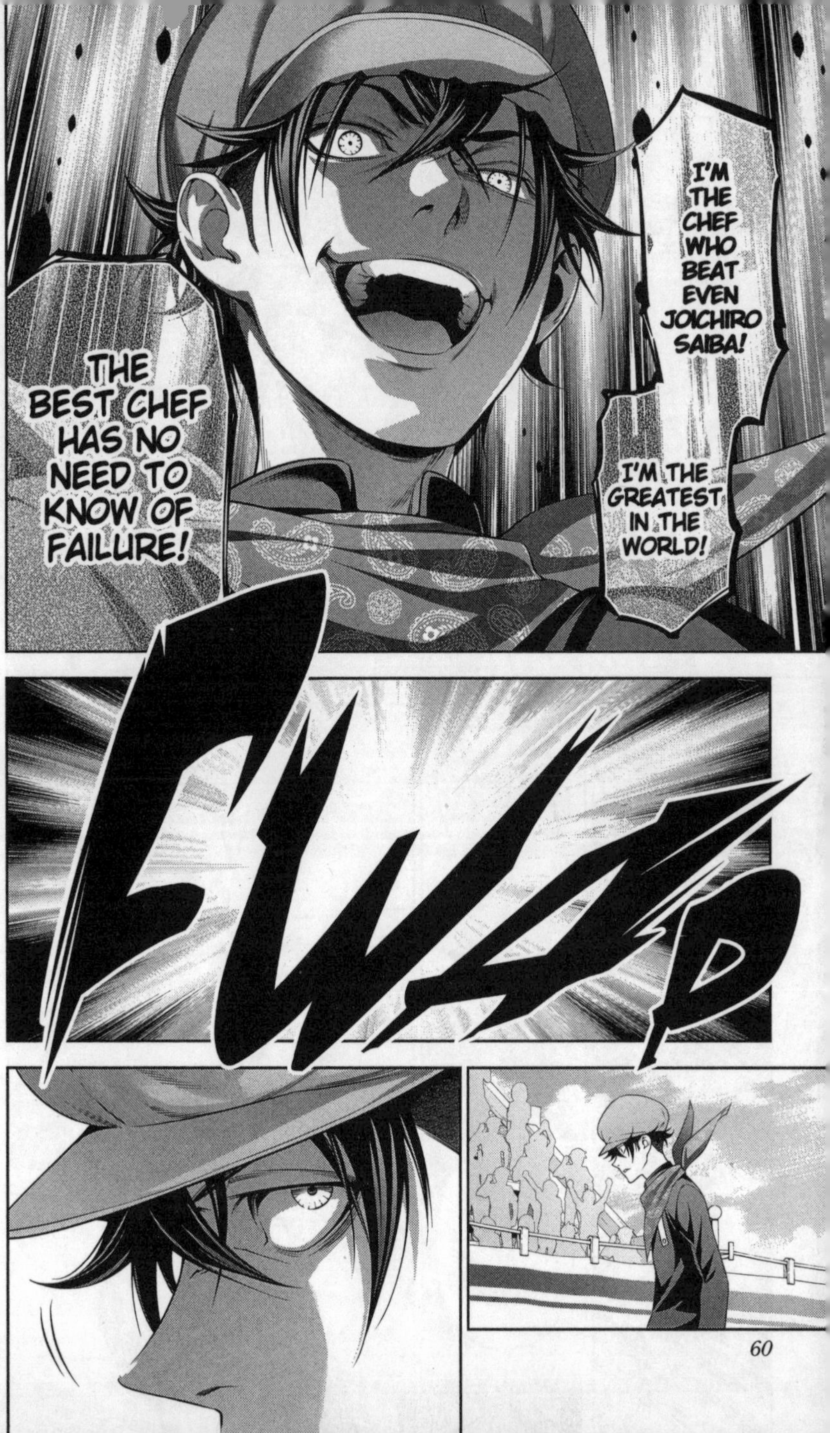
I'M THE CHEF WHO BEAT EVEN JOICHIRO SAIBA!
I'M THE GREATEST IN THE WORLD!
THE BEST CHEF HAS NO NEED TO KNOW OF FAILURE!
SWAP

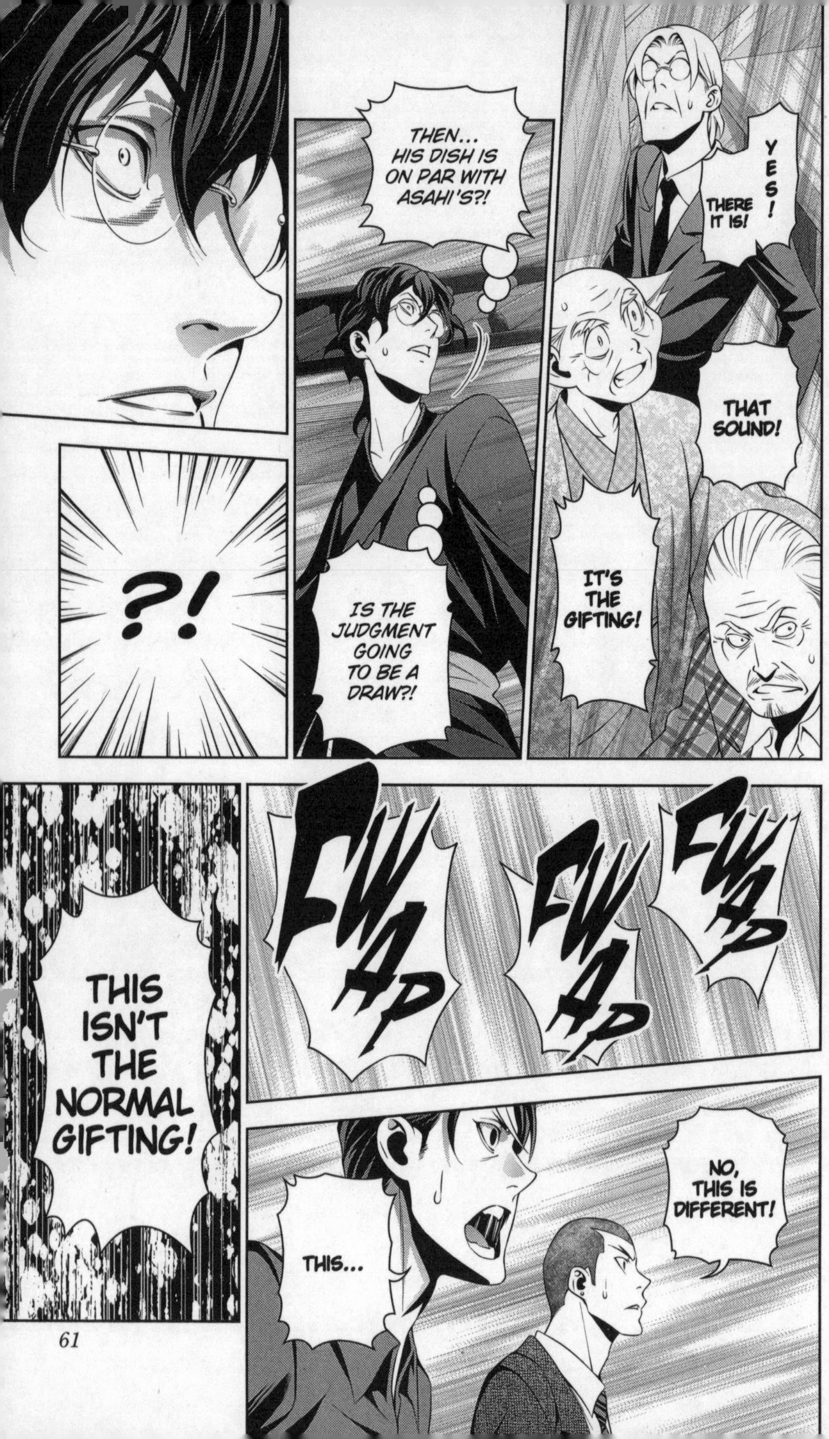
YES!
THERE IT IS!
THAT SOUND!
IT'S THE GIFTING!
THEN... HIS DISH IS ON PAR WITH ASAHI'S?!
IS THE JUDGMENT GOING TO BE A DRAW?!
?!
FWAP
FWAP
FWAP
NO, THIS IS DIFFERENT!
THIS...
THIS ISN'T THE NORMAL GIFTING!

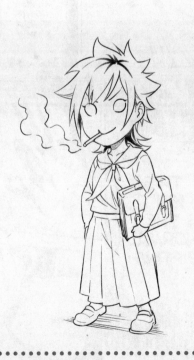

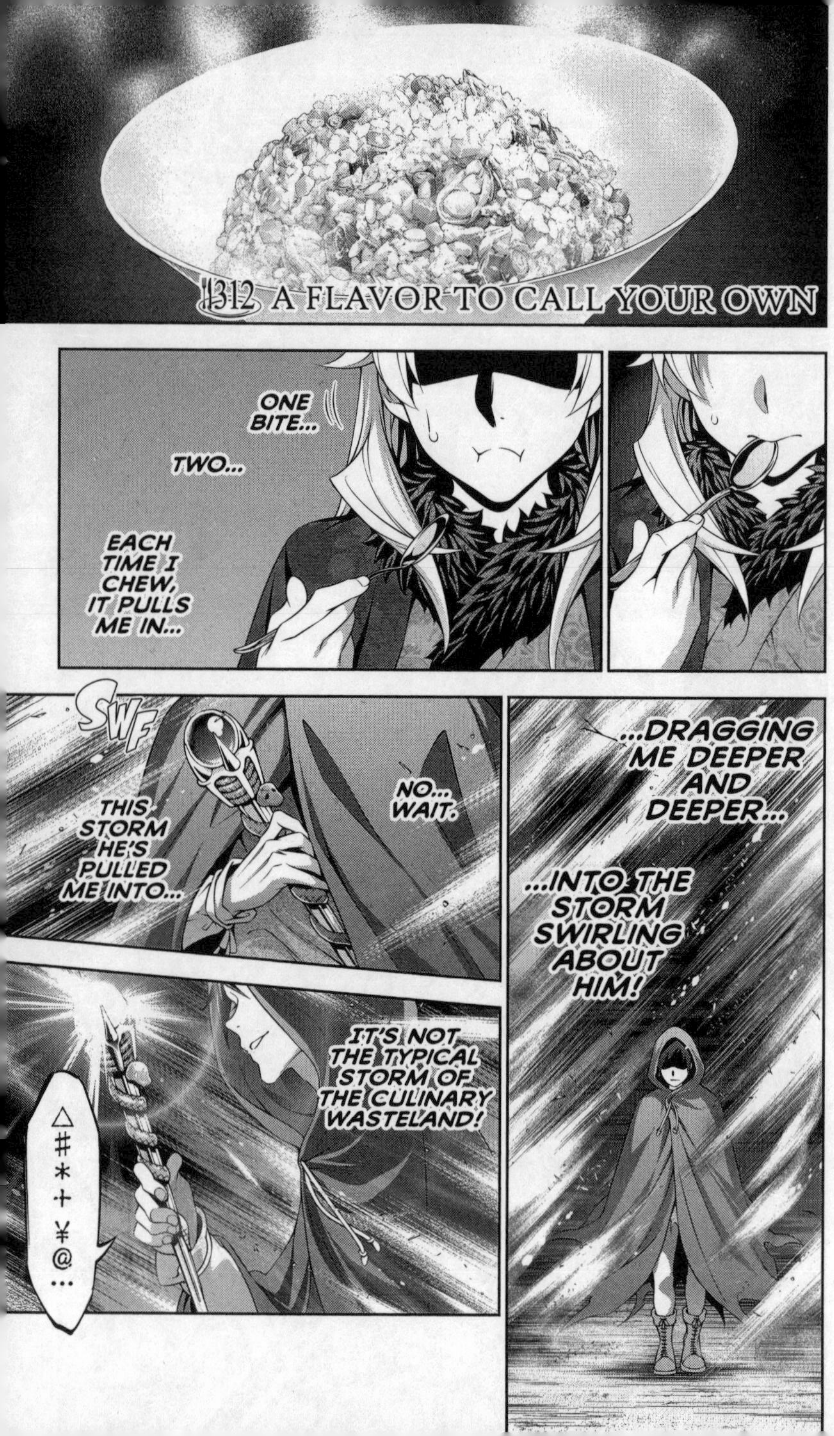
312 A FLAVOR TO CALL YOUR OWN
ONE BITE...
TWO...
EACH TIME I CHEW, IT PULLS ME IN...
...DRAGGING ME DEEPER AND DEEPER...
...INTO THE STORM SWIRLING ABOUT HIM!
SWF
NO... WAIT.
THIS STORM HE'S PULLED ME INTO...
IT'S NOT THE TYPICAL STORM OF THE CULINARY WASTELAND!
△#*+¥@...

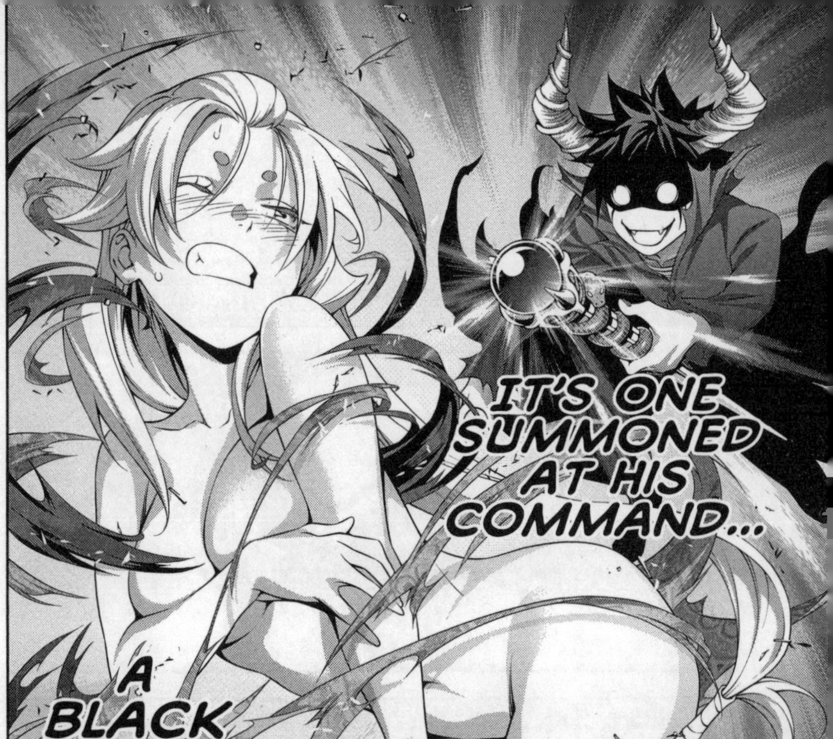
IT'S ONE SUMMONED AT HIS COMMAND...
A BLACK MAGIC SPELL!
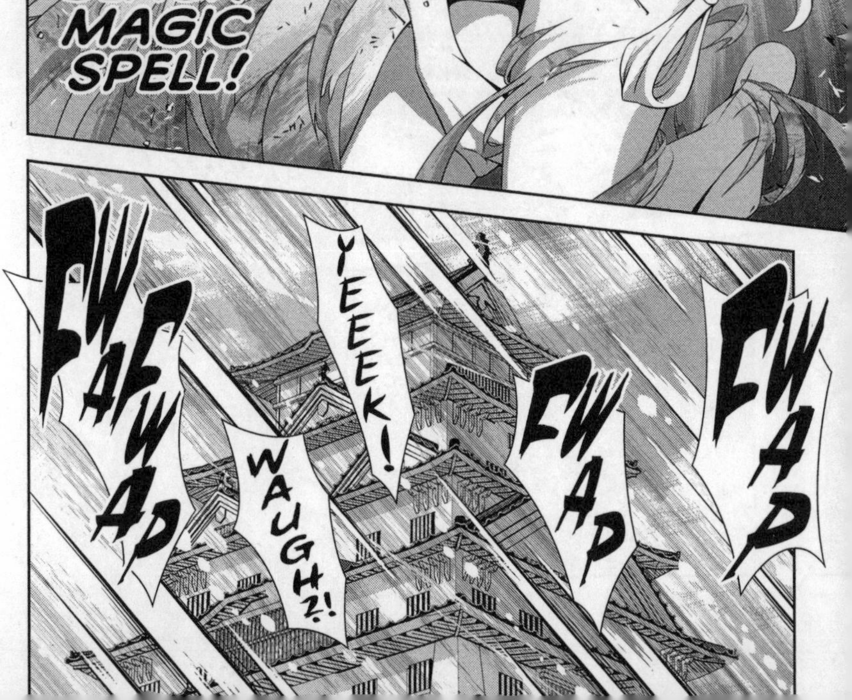
FWAP
FWAP
YEEEEK!
WAUGHZ!

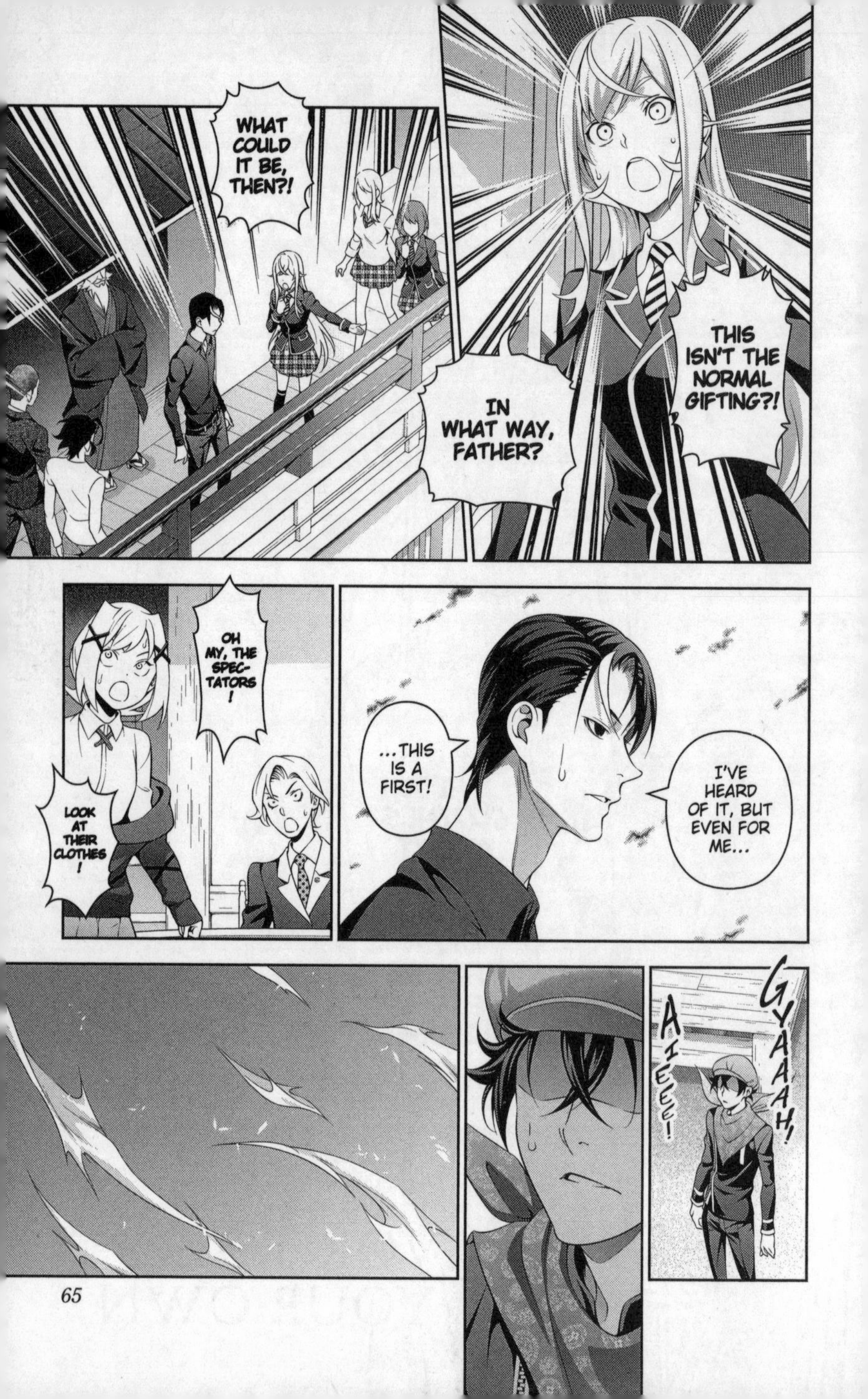
THIS ISN'T THE NORMAL GIFTING?!
IN WHAT WAY, FATHER?
WHAT COULD IT BE, THEN?!
I'VE HEARD OF IT, BUT EVEN FOR ME...
...THIS IS A FIRST!
OH MY, THE SPEC-TATORS!
LOOK AT THEIR CLOTHES!
GYAAAH!
AIEEE!

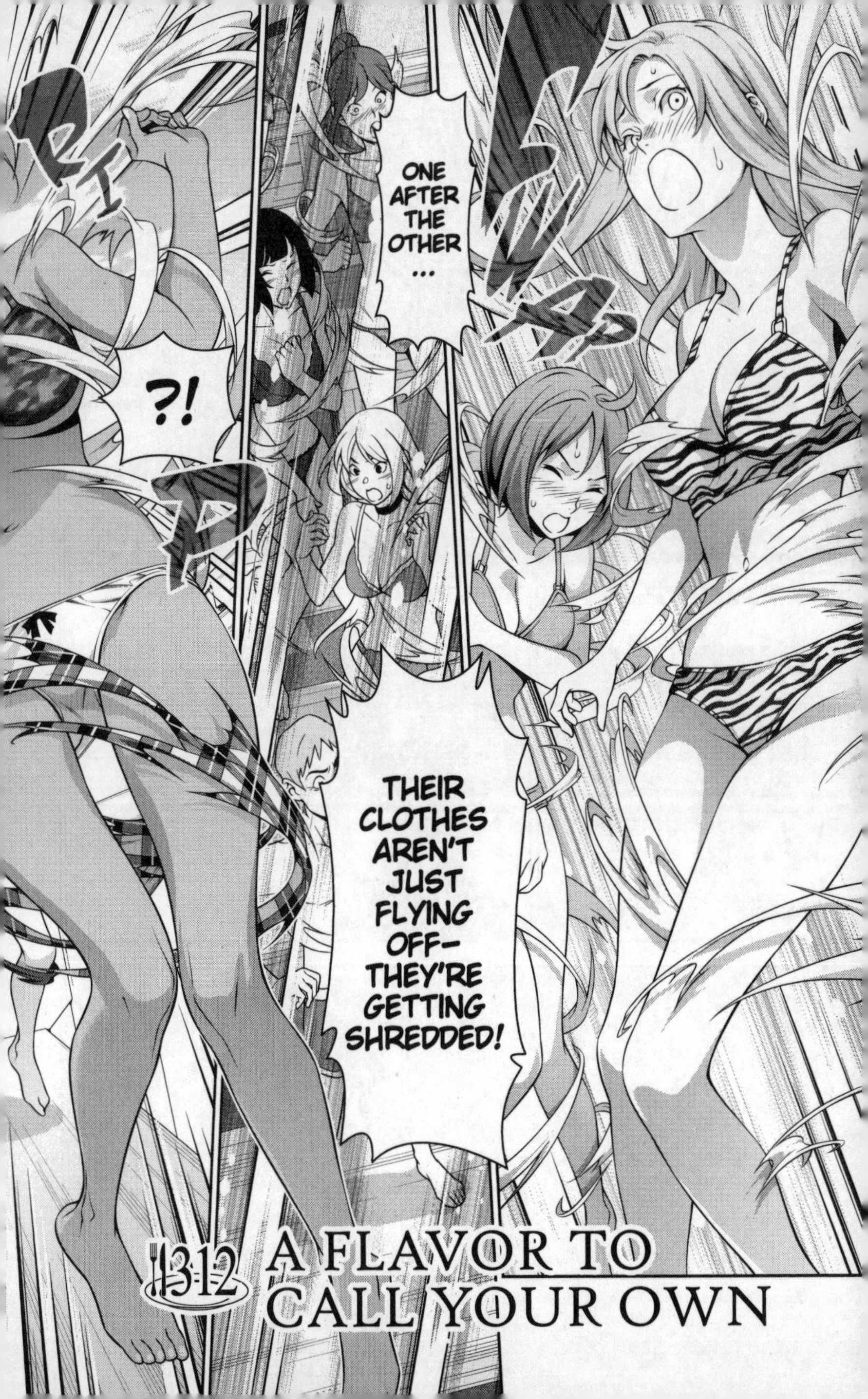
ONE AFTER THE OTHER...
?!
THEIR CLOTHES AREN'T JUST FLYING OFF— THEY'RE GETTING SHREDDED!
312 A FLAVOR TO CALL YOUR OWN

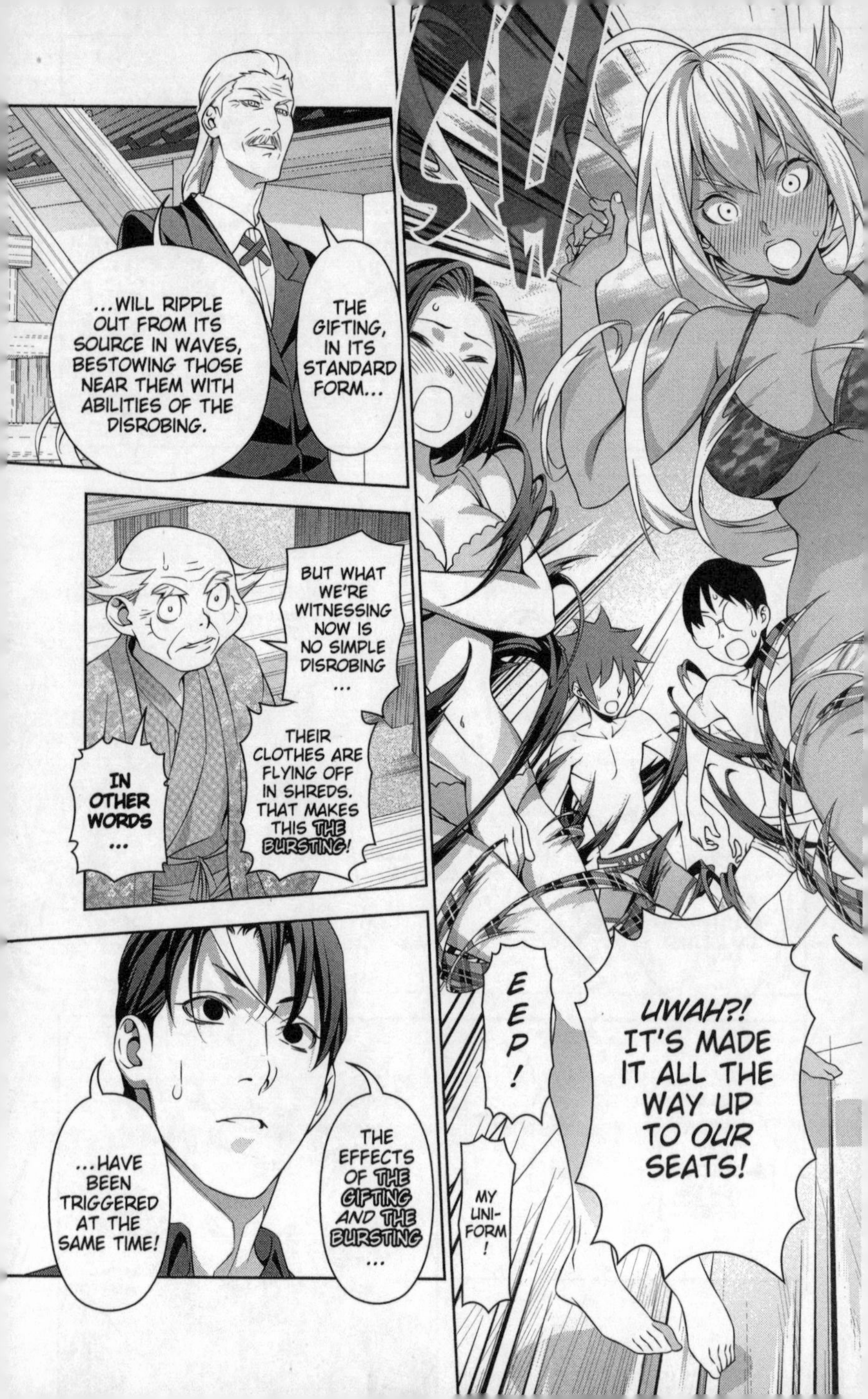
UWAH?! IT'S MADE IT ALL THE WAY UP TO OUR SEATS!
EEP!
MY UNI-FORM!
THE GIFTING, IN ITS STANDARD FORM...
...WILL RIPPLE OUT FROM ITS SOURCE IN WAVES, BESTOWING THOSE NEAR THEM WITH ABILITIES OF THE DISROBING.
BUT WHAT WE'RE WITNESSING NOW IS NO SIMPLE DISROBING...
THEIR CLOTHES ARE FLYING OFF IN SHREDS. THAT MAKES THIS THE BURSTING!
IN OTHER WORDS...
THE EFFECTS OF THE GIFTING AND THE BURSTING...
...HAVE BEEN TRIGGERED AT THE SAME TIME!

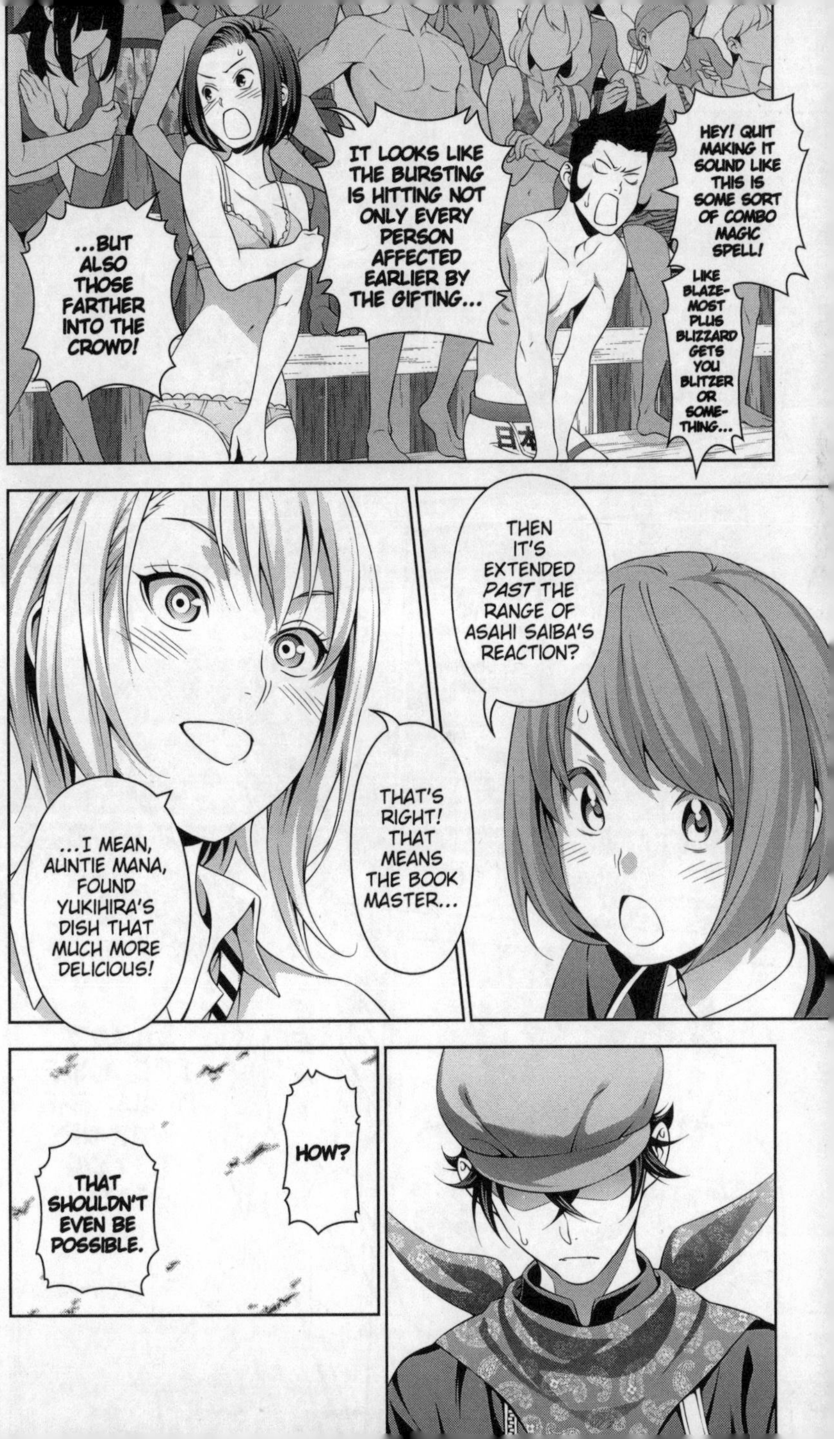
HEY! QUIT MAKING IT SOUND LIKE THIS IS SOME SORT OF COMBO MAGIC SPELL!
LIKE BLAZE-MOST PLUS BLIZZARD GETS YOU BLITZER OR SOME-THING...
IT LOOKS LIKE THE BURSTING IS HITTING NOT ONLY EVERY PERSON AFFECTED EARLIER BY THE GIFTING...
...BUT ALSO THOSE FARTHER INTO THE CROWD!
THEN IT'S EXTENDED *PAST* THE RANGE OF ASAHI SAIBA'S REACTION?
THAT'S RIGHT! THAT MEANS THE BOOK MASTER...
...I MEAN, AUNTIE MANA, FOUND YUKIHIRA'S DISH THAT MUCH MORE DELICIOUS!
HOW?
THAT SHOULDN'T EVEN BE POSSIBLE.

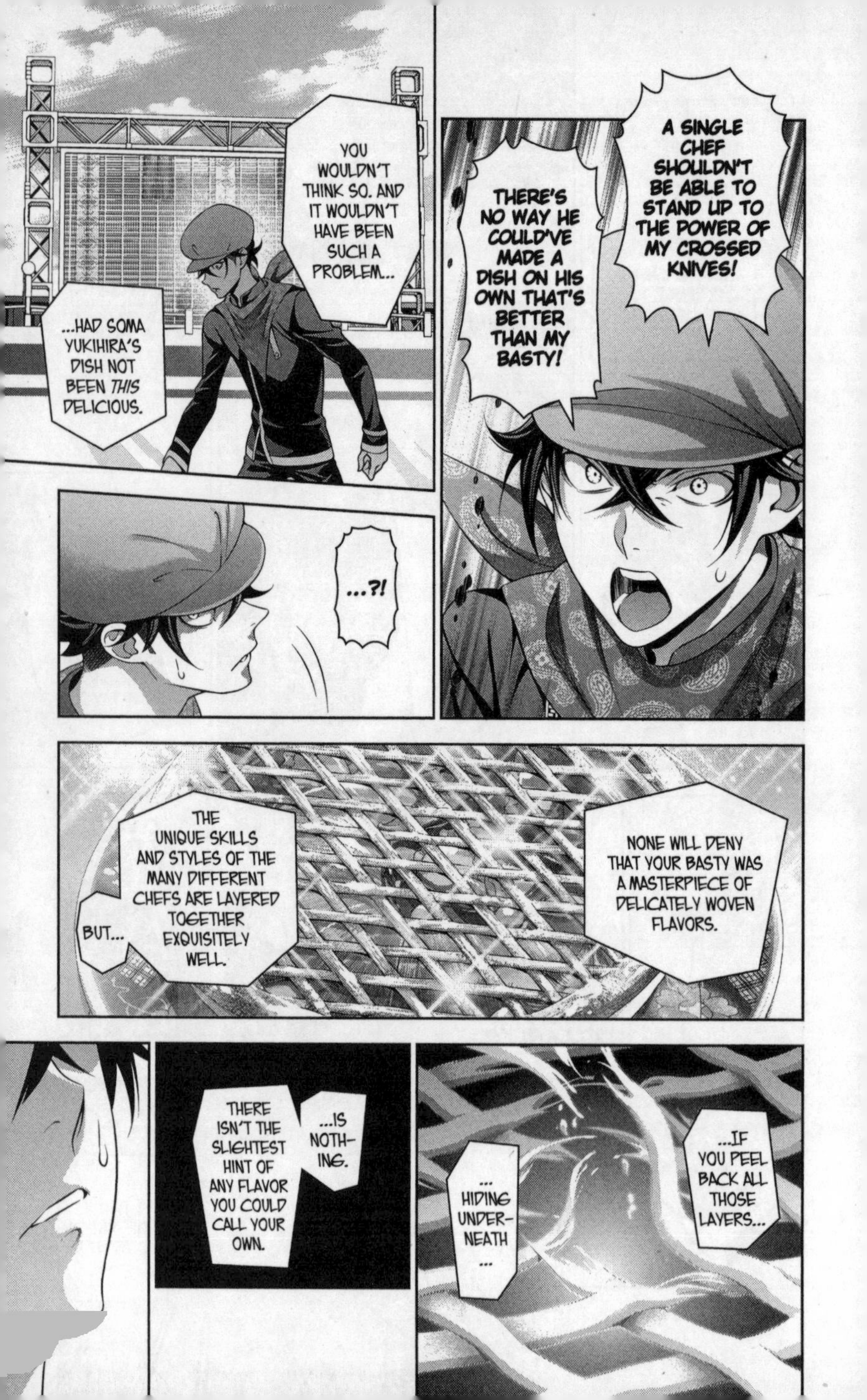
A SINGLE CHEF SHOULDN'T BE ABLE TO STAND UP TO THE POWER OF MY CROSSED KNIVES!
THERE'S NO WAY HE COULD'VE MADE A DISH ON HIS OWN THAT'S BETTER THAN MY BASTY!
YOU WOULDN'T THINK SO. AND IT WOULDN'T HAVE BEEN SUCH A PROBLEM...
...HAD SOMA YUKIHIRA'S DISH NOT BEEN *THIS* DELICIOUS.
...?!
NONE WILL DENY THAT YOUR BASTY WAS A MASTERPIECE OF DELICATELY WOVEN FLAVORS.
THE UNIQUE SKILLS AND STYLES OF THE MANY DIFFERENT CHEFS ARE LAYERED TOGETHER EXQUISITELY WELL.
BUT...
...IF YOU PEEL BACK ALL THOSE LAYERS...
...HIDING UNDER-NEATH...
...IS NOTH-ING.
THERE ISN'T THE SLIGHTEST HINT OF ANY FLAVOR YOU COULD CALL YOUR OWN.

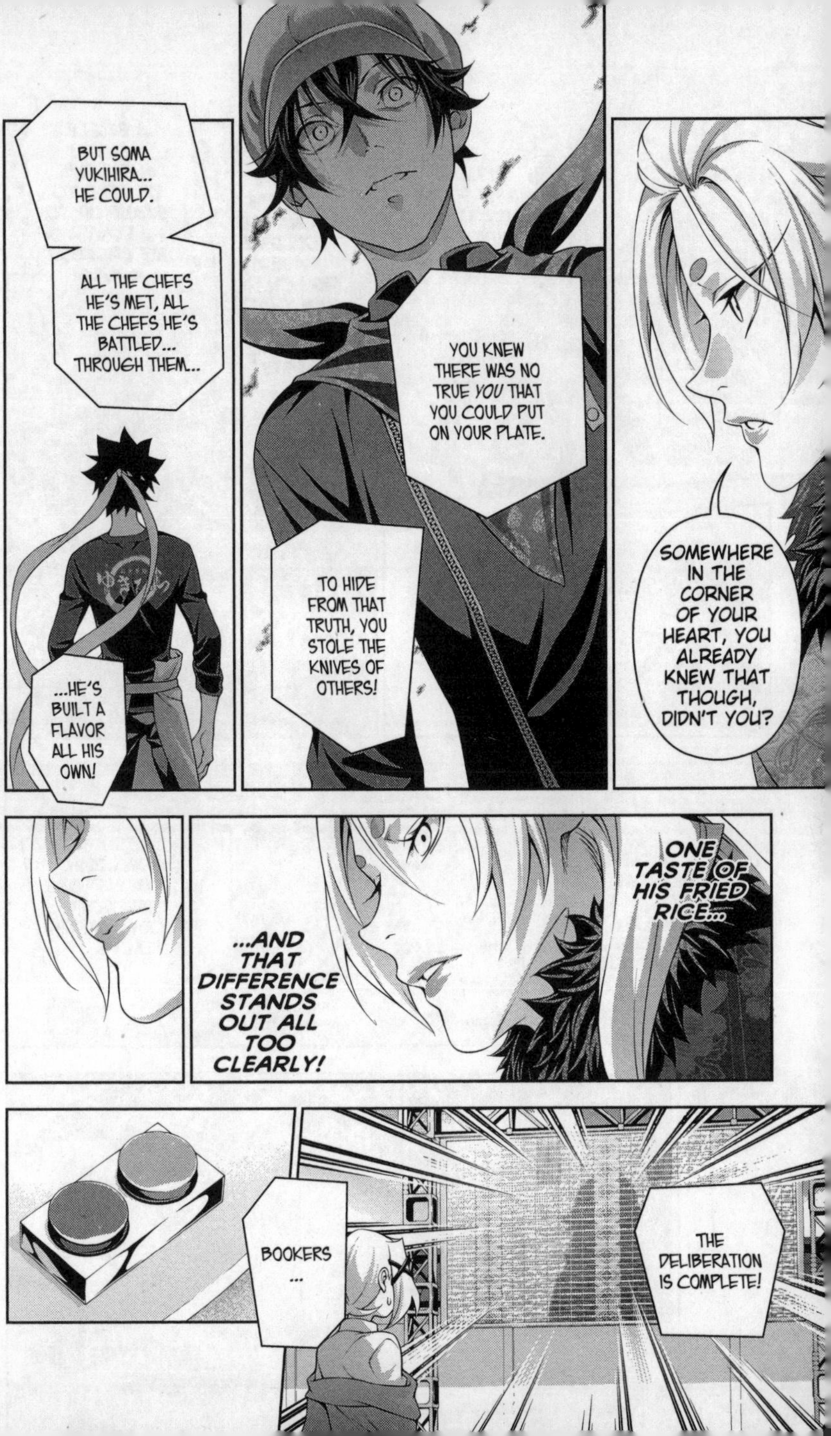
SOMEWHERE IN THE CORNER OF YOUR HEART, YOU ALREADY KNEW THAT THOUGH, DIDN'T YOU?
YOU KNEW THERE WAS NO TRUE *YOU* THAT YOU COULD PUT ON YOUR PLATE.
TO HIDE FROM THAT TRUTH, YOU STOLE THE KNIVES OF OTHERS!
BUT SOMA YUKIHIRA... HE COULD.
ALL THE CHEFS HE'S MET, ALL THE CHEFS HE'S BATTLED... THROUGH THEM...
...HE'S BUILT A FLAVOR ALL HIS OWN!
ONE TASTE OF HIS FRIED RICE...
...AND THAT DIFFERENCE STANDS OUT ALL TOO CLEARLY!
THE DELIBERATION IS COMPLETE!
BOOKERS ...

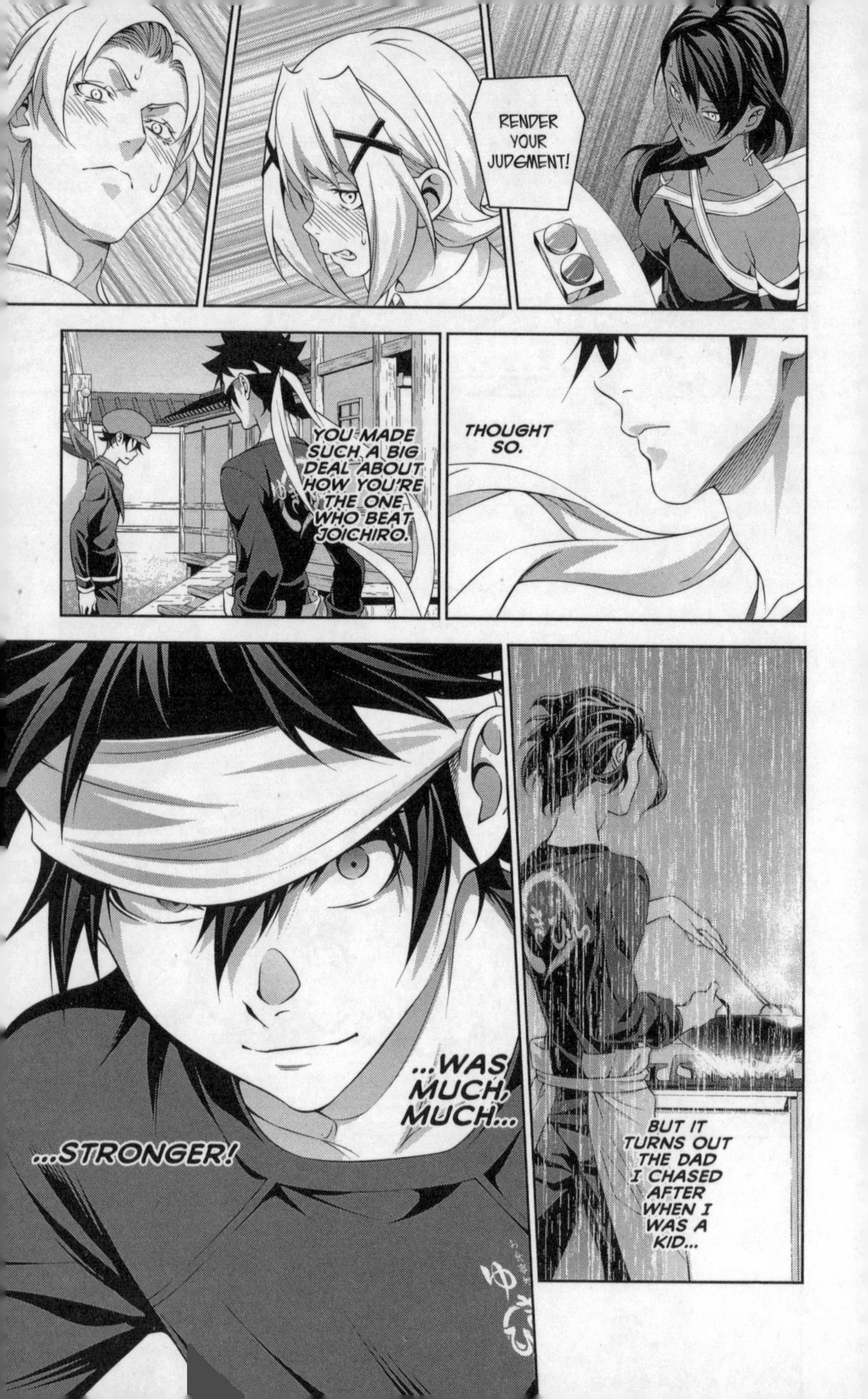
RENDER YOUR JUDGEMENT!
THOUGHT SO.
YOU MADE SUCH A BIG DEAL ABOUT HOW YOU'RE THE ONE WHO BEAT JOICHIRO.
BUT IT TURNS OUT THE DAD I CHASED AFTER WHEN I WAS A KID...
...WAS MUCH, MUCH...
...STRONGER!

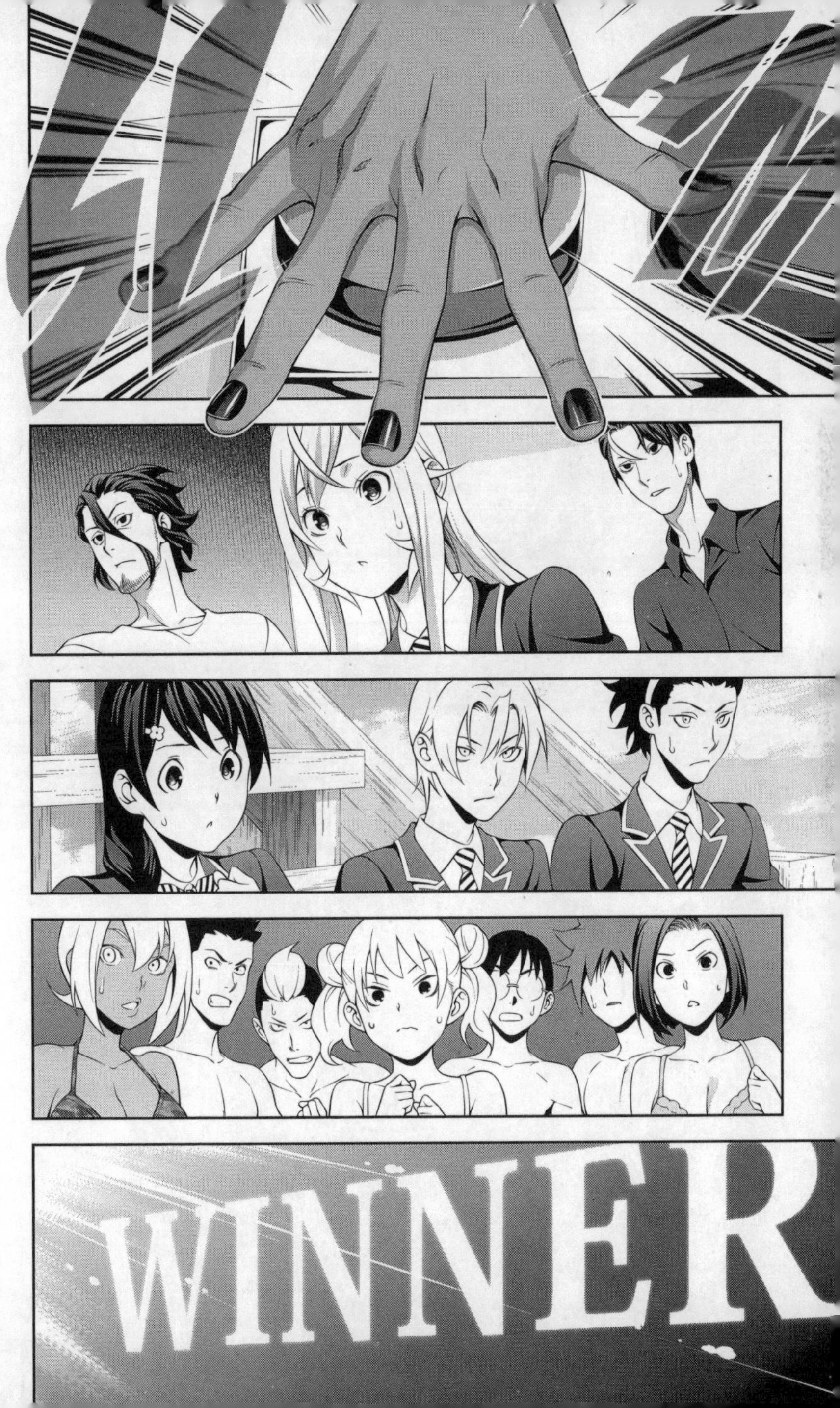
WINNER

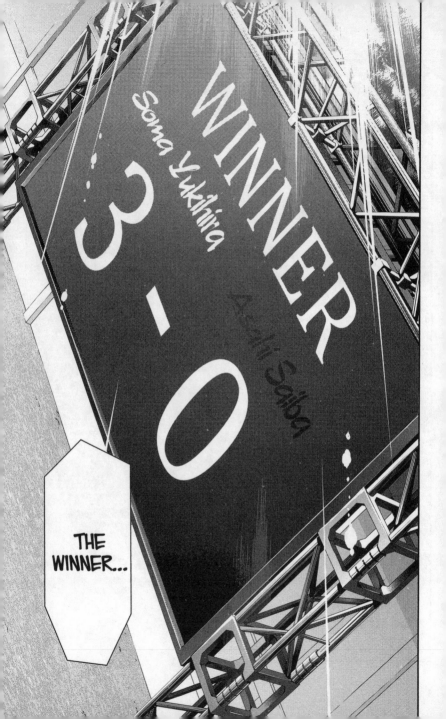

WINNER
Soma Yukihira
3 - 0
Asahi Saiba

THE
WINNER...

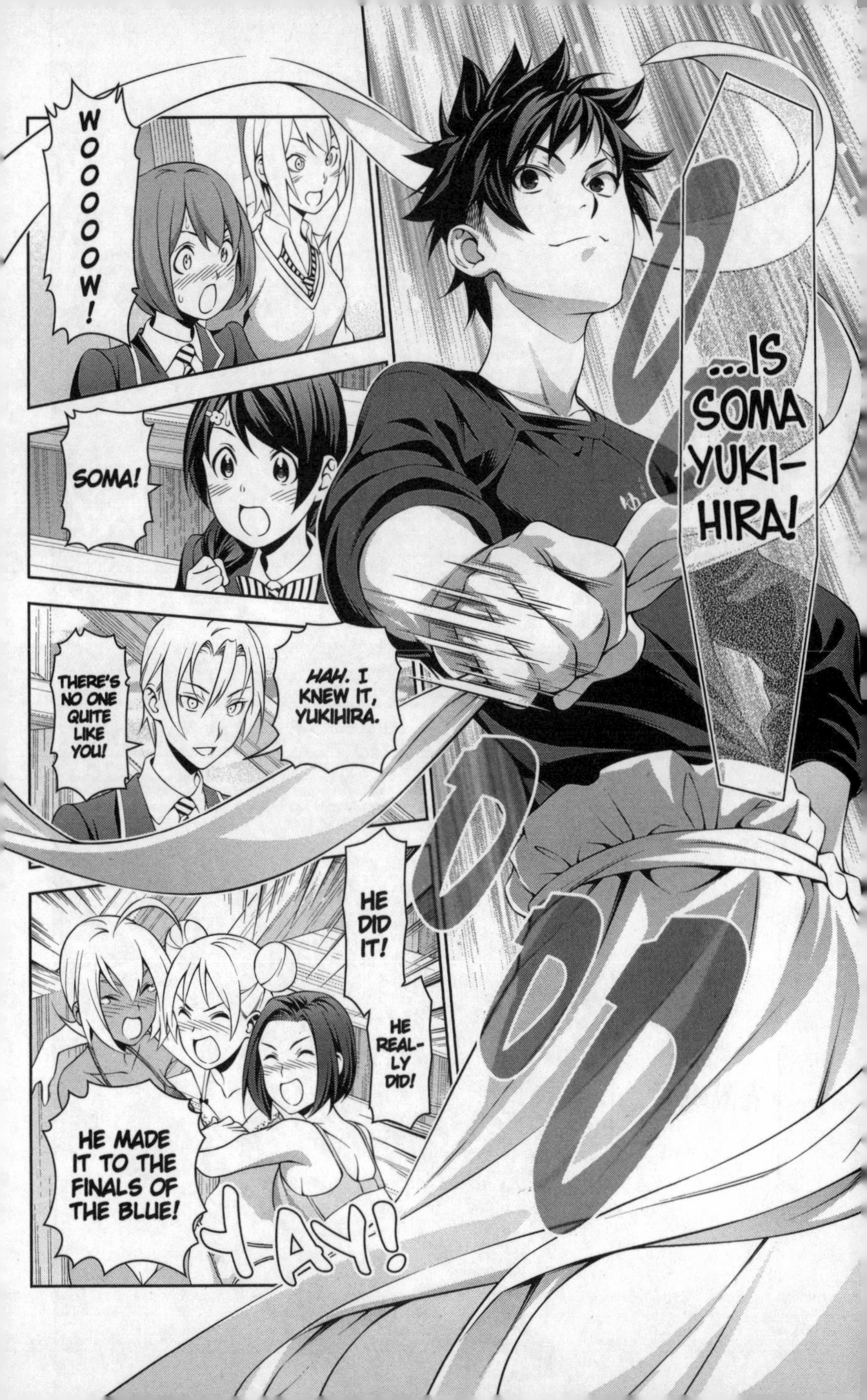
...IS SOMA YUKI-HIRA!
WOOOOOOW!
SOMA!
HAH. I KNEW IT, YUKIHIRA.
THERE'S NO ONE QUITE LIKE YOU!
HE DID IT!
HE REAL-LY DID!
HE MADE IT TO THE FINALS OF THE BLUE!
YAY!

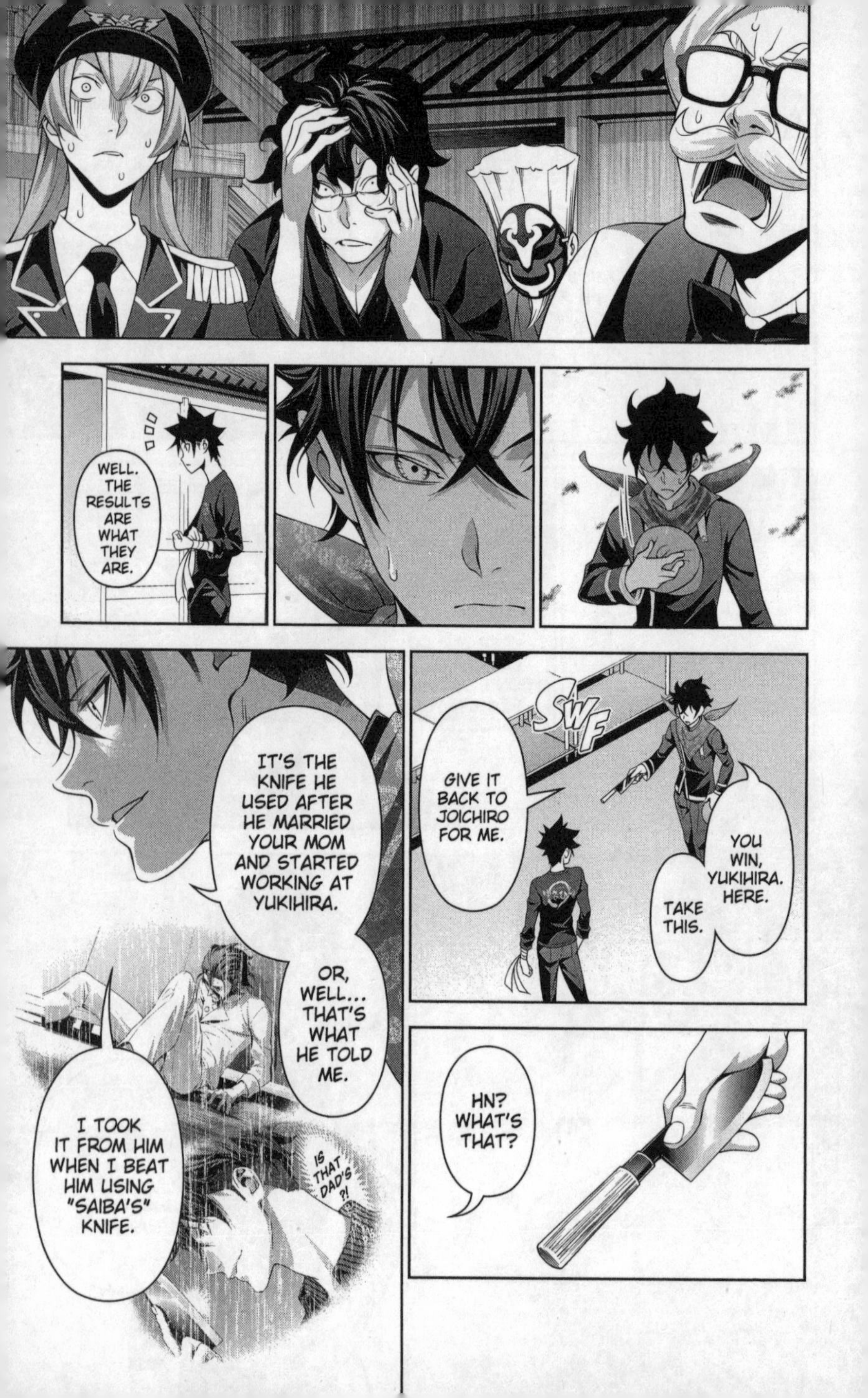
WELL. THE RESULTS ARE WHAT THEY ARE.
YOU WIN, YUKIHIRA. HERE.
TAKE THIS.
SWF
GIVE IT BACK TO JOICHIRO FOR ME.
HN? WHAT'S THAT?
IT'S THE KNIFE HE USED AFTER HE MARRIED YOUR MOM AND STARTED WORKING AT YUKIHIRA.
OR, WELL... THAT'S WHAT HE TOLD ME.
I TOOK IT FROM HIM WHEN I BEAT HIM USING "SAIBA'S" KNIFE.
IS THAT DAD'S?!

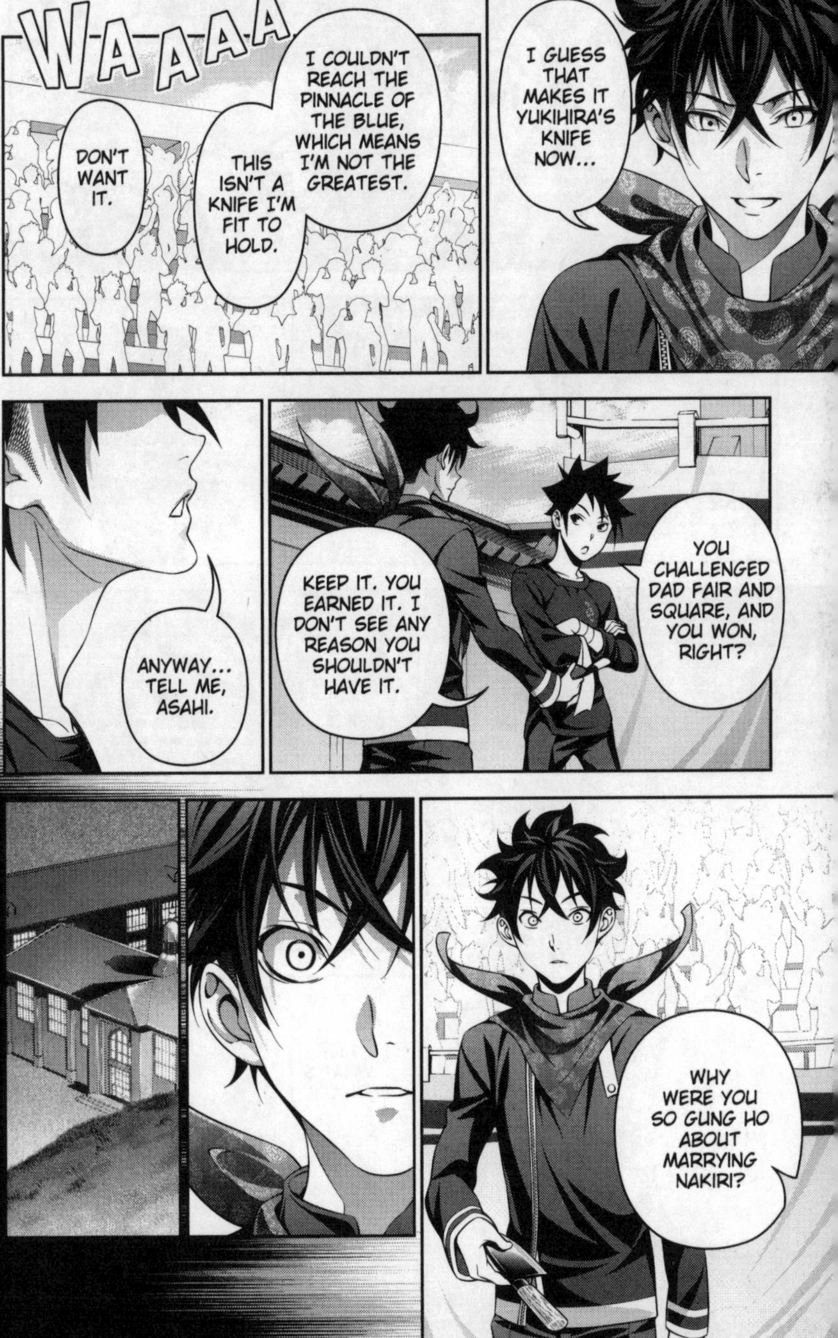
I GUESS THAT MAKES IT YUKIHIRA'S KNIFE NOW...
WAAAA
I COULDN'T REACH THE PINNACLE OF THE BLUE, WHICH MEANS I'M NOT THE GREATEST.
THIS ISN'T A KNIFE I'M FIT TO HOLD.
DON'T WANT IT.
YOU CHALLENGED DAD FAIR AND SQUARE, AND YOU WON, RIGHT?
KEEP IT. YOU EARNED IT. I DON'T SEE ANY REASON YOU SHOULDN'T HAVE IT.
ANYWAY... TELL ME, ASAHI.
WHY WERE YOU SO GUNG HO ABOUT MARRYING NAKIRI?

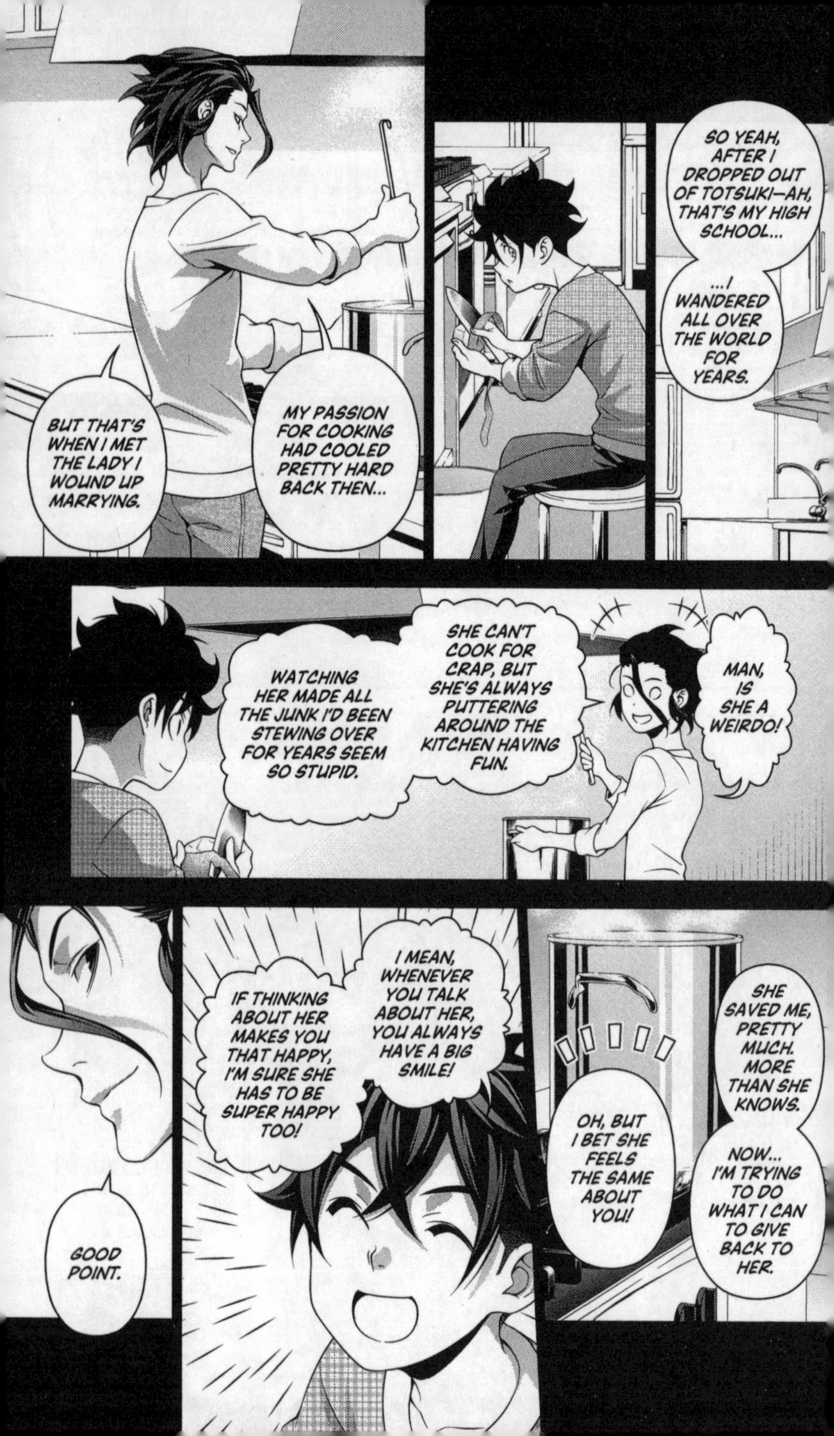
SO YEAH, AFTER I DROPPED OUT OF TOTSUKI—AH, THAT'S MY HIGH SCHOOL...
...I WANDERED ALL OVER THE WORLD FOR YEARS.
MY PASSION FOR COOKING HAD COOLED PRETTY HARD BACK THEN...
BUT THAT'S WHEN I MET THE LADY I WOUND UP MARRYING.
MAN, IS SHE A WEIRDO!
SHE CAN'T COOK FOR CRAP, BUT SHE'S ALWAYS PUTTERING AROUND THE KITCHEN HAVING FUN.
WATCHING HER MADE ALL THE JUNK I'D BEEN STEWING OVER FOR YEARS SEEM SO STUPID.
SHE SAVED ME, PRETTY MUCH. MORE THAN SHE KNOWS.
NOW... I'M TRYING TO DO WHAT I CAN TO GIVE BACK TO HER.
OH, BUT I BET SHE FEELS THE SAME ABOUT YOU!
I MEAN, WHENEVER YOU TALK ABOUT HER, YOU ALWAYS HAVE A BIG SMILE!
IF THINKING ABOUT HER MAKES YOU THAT HAPPY, I'M SURE SHE HAS TO BE SUPER HAPPY TOO!
GOOD POINT.

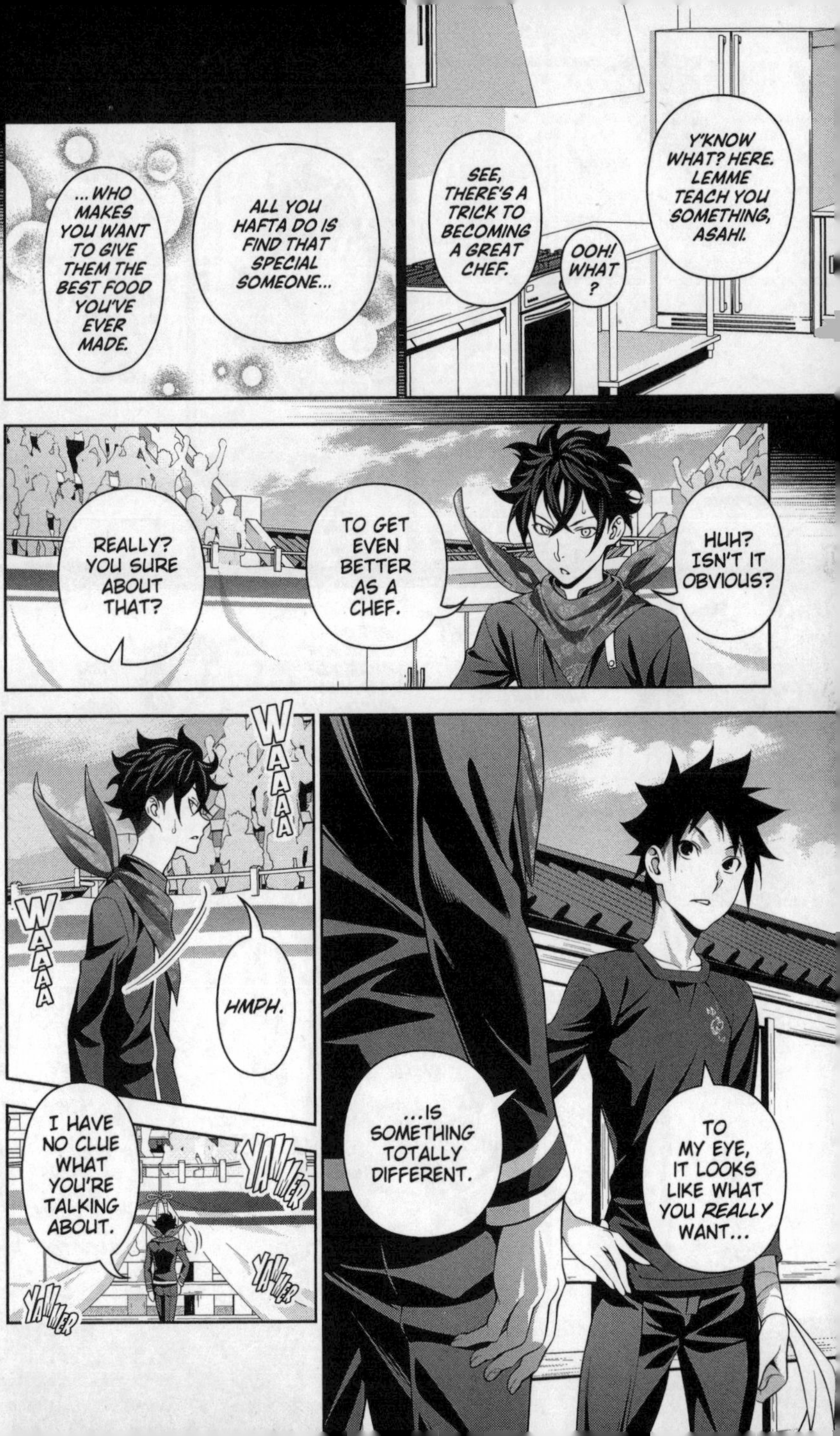
Y'KNOW WHAT? HERE. LEMME TEACH YOU SOMETHING, ASAHI.
OOH! WHAT?
SEE, THERE'S A TRICK TO BECOMING A GREAT CHEF.
ALL YOU HAFTA DO IS FIND THAT SPECIAL SOMEONE...
...WHO MAKES YOU WANT TO GIVE THEM THE BEST FOOD YOU'VE EVER MADE.
HUH? ISN'T IT OBVIOUS?
TO GET EVEN BETTER AS A CHEF.
REALLY? YOU SURE ABOUT THAT?
TO MY EYE, IT LOOKS LIKE WHAT YOU REALLY WANT...
...IS SOMETHING TOTALLY DIFFERENT.
WAAAA
HMPH.
WAAAA
YAMMER
YAMMER
YAMMER
I HAVE NO CLUE WHAT YOU'RE TALKING ABOUT.

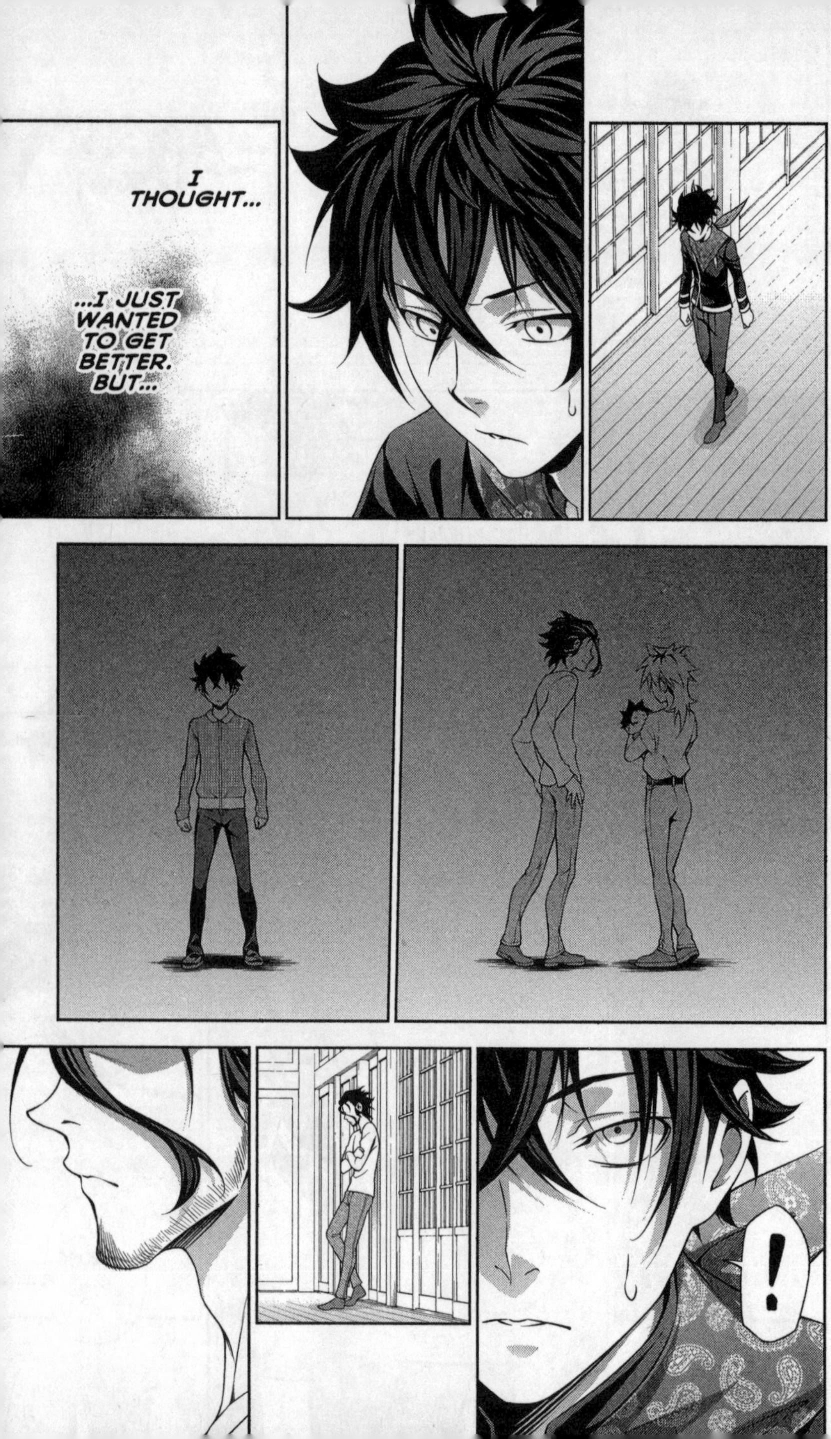
I THOUGHT...
...I JUST WANTED TO GET BETTER. BUT...
!

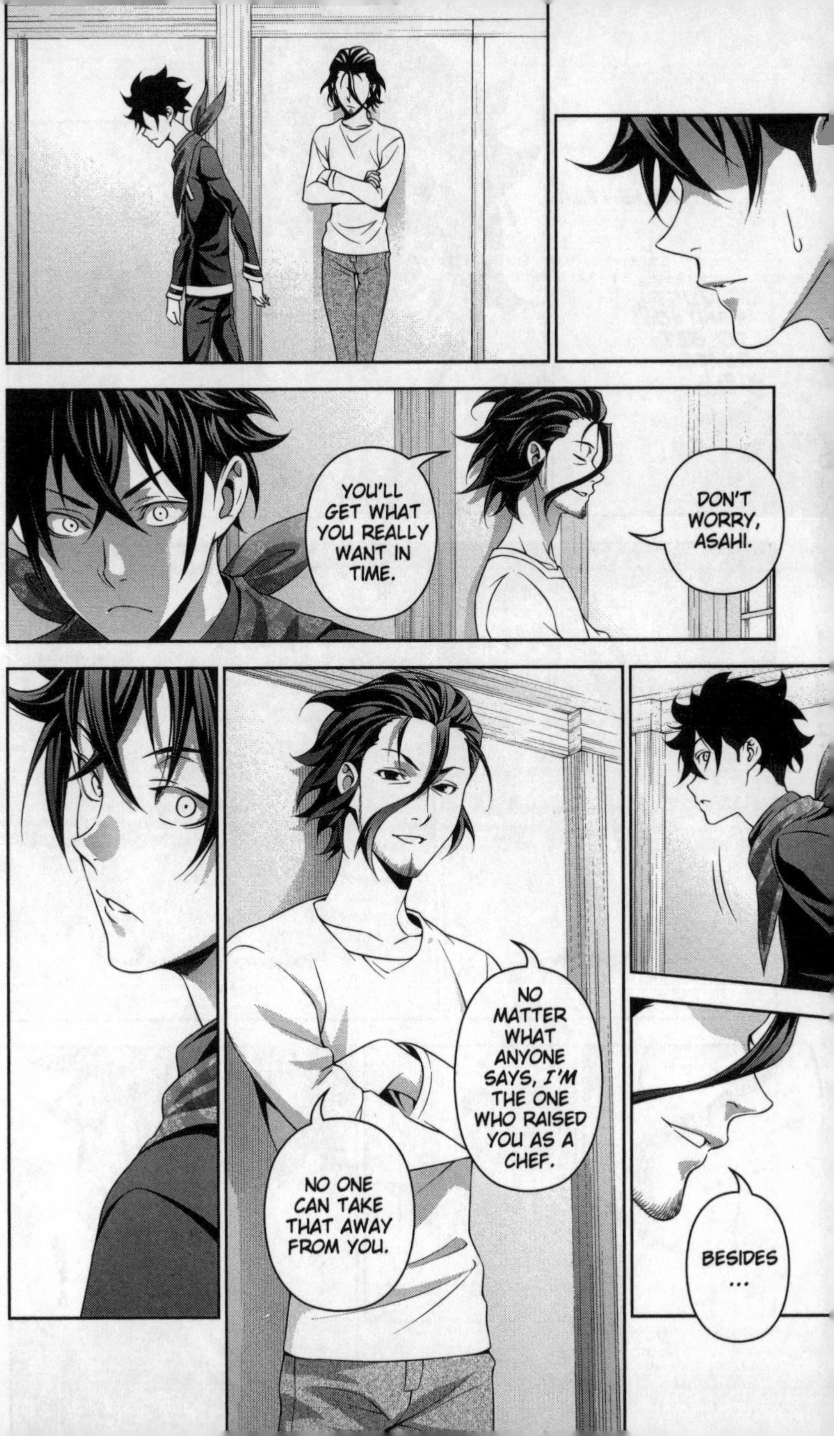
DON'T WORRY, ASAHI.
YOU'LL GET WHAT YOU REALLY WANT IN TIME.
BESIDES...
NO MATTER WHAT ANYONE SAYS, *I'M* THE ONE WHO RAISED YOU AS A CHEF.
NO ONE CAN TAKE THAT AWAY FROM YOU.

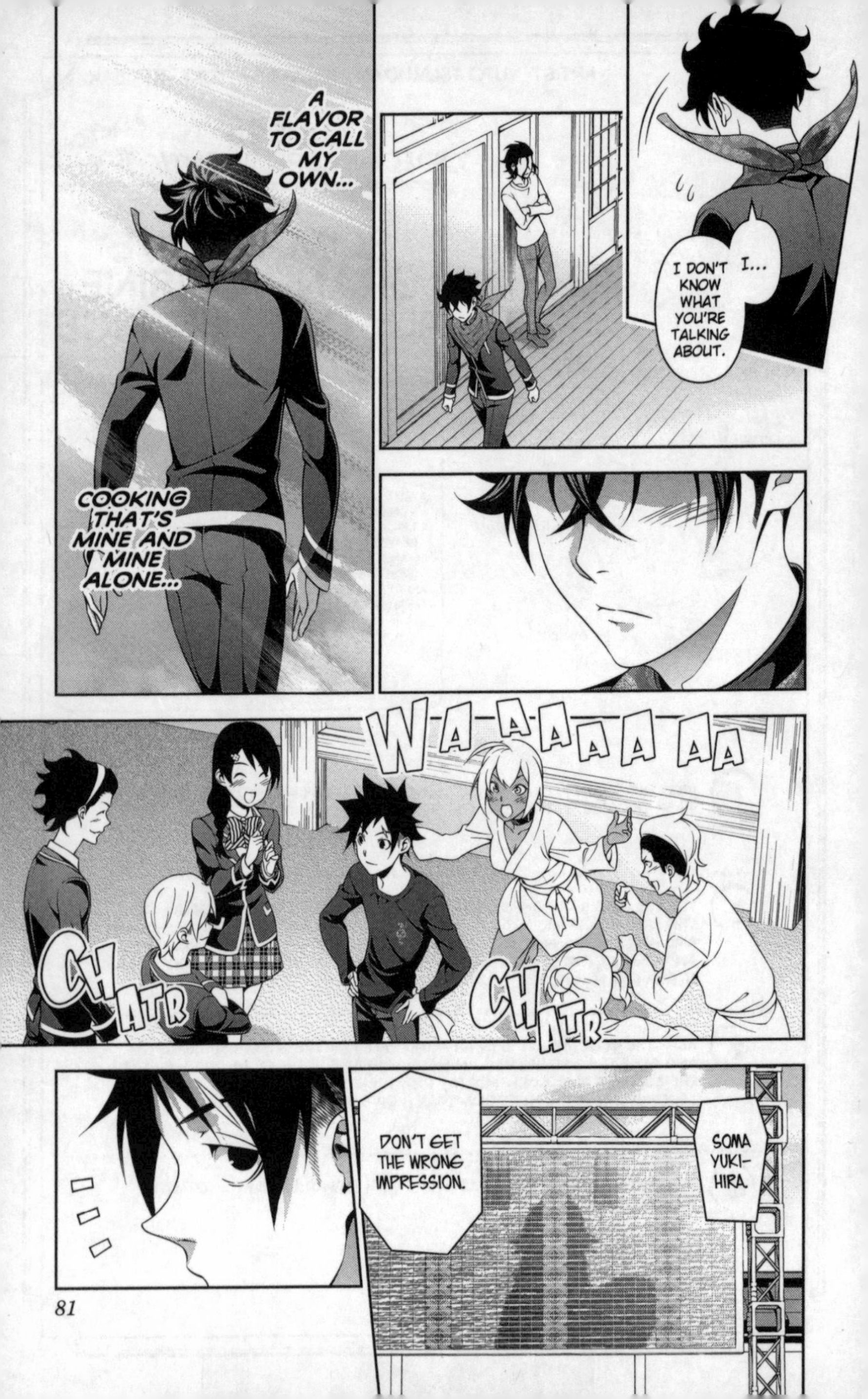

I... I DON'T KNOW WHAT YOU'RE TALKING ABOUT.
A FLAVOR TO CALL MY OWN...
COOKING THAT'S MINE AND MINE ALONE...
WAAAAAAA
CHATR
CHATR
SOMA YUKIHIRA.
DON'T GET THE WRONG IMPRESSION.

ARTIST: YUTO TSUKUDA RECIPE BY: YUKI MORISAKI

VOLUME 36 SPECIAL SUPPLEMENT!

PRACTICAL RECIPE

SOMA'S FIVE GRAND CUISINE ALL-IN FRIED RICE

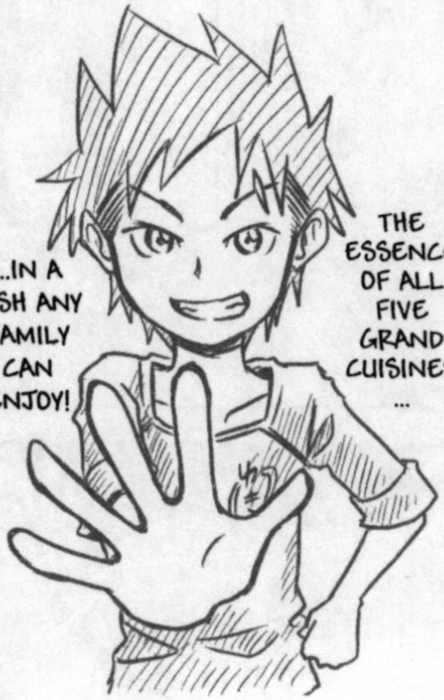

THE ESSENCE OF ALL FIVE GRAND CUISINES...
...IN A DISH ANY FAMILY CAN ENJOY!

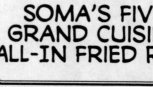

INGREDIENTS (SERVES 4)

2 CUPS UNCOOKED RICE
1/4 ONION
2 LARGE CABBAGE LEAVES
1 SMALL CAN CLAMS (RESERVE THE LIQUID)
200 GRAMS BRAISED PORK (OR GRILLED)

A
- 1 TABLESPOON GRANULATED CHICKEN STOCK
- 1 TEASPOON EACH SOY SAUCE, OYSTER SAUCE

B
- 2 EGGS
- 2 TABLESPOONS MAYONNAISE
- SALT, PEPPER

1 TABLESPOON EACH SHREDDED COCONUT, VEGETABLE OIL, PICKLED GINGER

1. DICE THE ONION AND CABBAGE LEAVES. CUT THE PORK INTO BITE-SIZE PIECES. WASH THE RICE, LET IT SOAK FOR 30 MINUTES, THEN DRAIN.

2. PUT THE RICE IN A DONABE POT. ADD TWO CUPS OF WATER, THE LIQUID FROM THE CANNED CLAMS, AND (A) AND STIR TO BLEND. PUT IN THE ONION, CLAMS AND PORK. COVER AND HEAT. ONCE IT COMES TO A BOIL, REDUCE HEAT TO LOW AND SIMMER FOR 12 MINUTES. THEN TURN OFF THE HEAT COMPLETELY AND LET STEAM FOR 15 MINUTES.

3. HEAT THE VEGETABLE OIL IN A FRYING PAN. ADD THE SHREDDED COCONUT AND CABBAGE AND SIMMER ON MEDIUM HEAT FOR THREE MINUTES, OR UNTIL THE COCONUT IS TENDER. MIX (B) TOGETHER AND THEN DRIZZLE OVER THE COCONUTS. SAUTÉ EVERYTHING TOGETHER INTO SCRAMBLED EGGS.

4. ADD (2) TO (3) AND ROUGHLY COMBINE WITH A SPATULA. PLATE, TOP WITH PICKLED GINGER AND DONE!

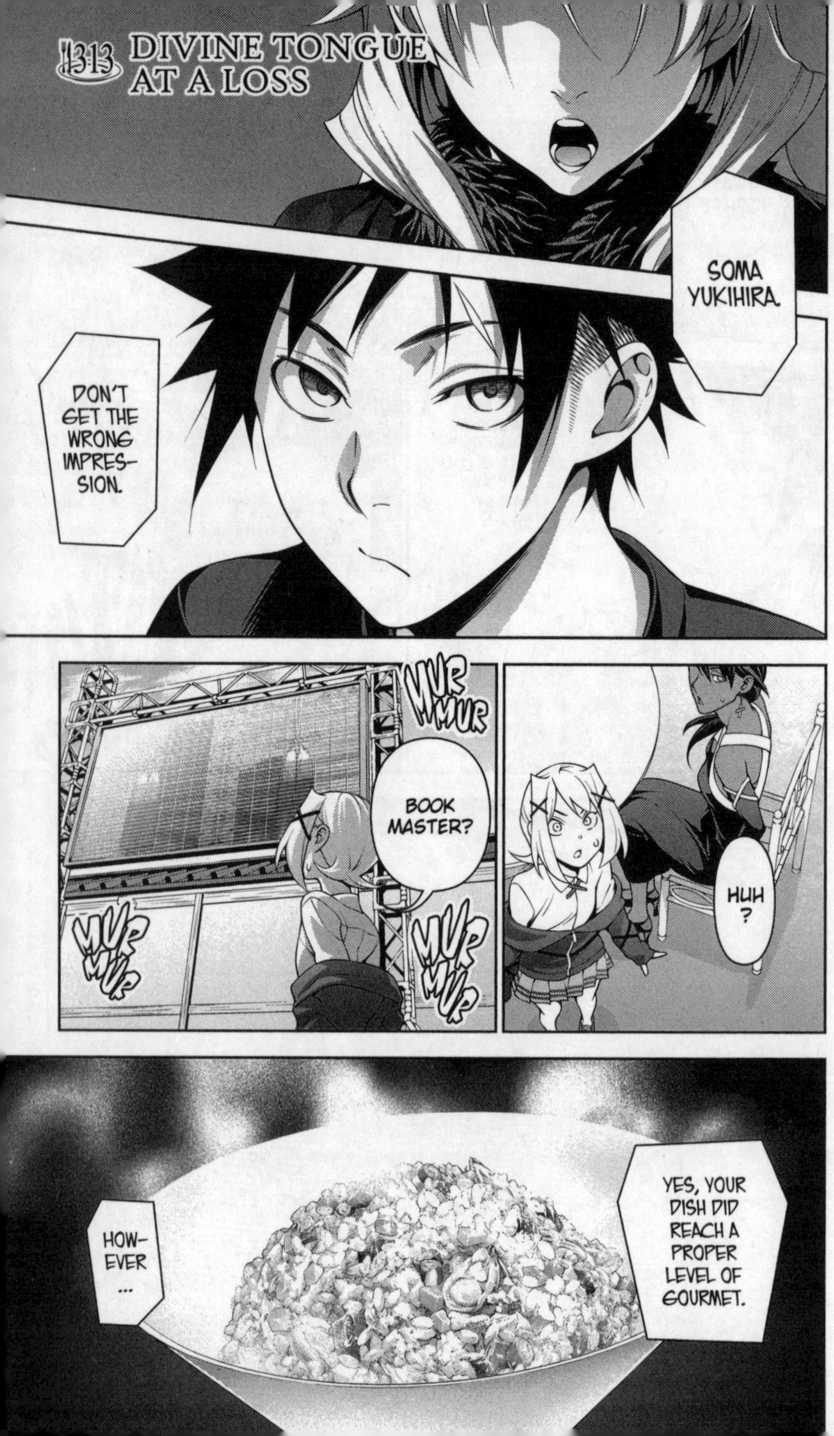
313 DIVINE TONGUE AT A LOSS
SOMA YUKIHIRA.
DON'T GET THE WRONG IMPRESSION.
HUH ?
MUR MUR
BOOK MASTER?
MUR MUR
MUR MUR
YES, YOUR DISH DID REACH A PROPER LEVEL OF GOURMET.
HOW-EVER ...

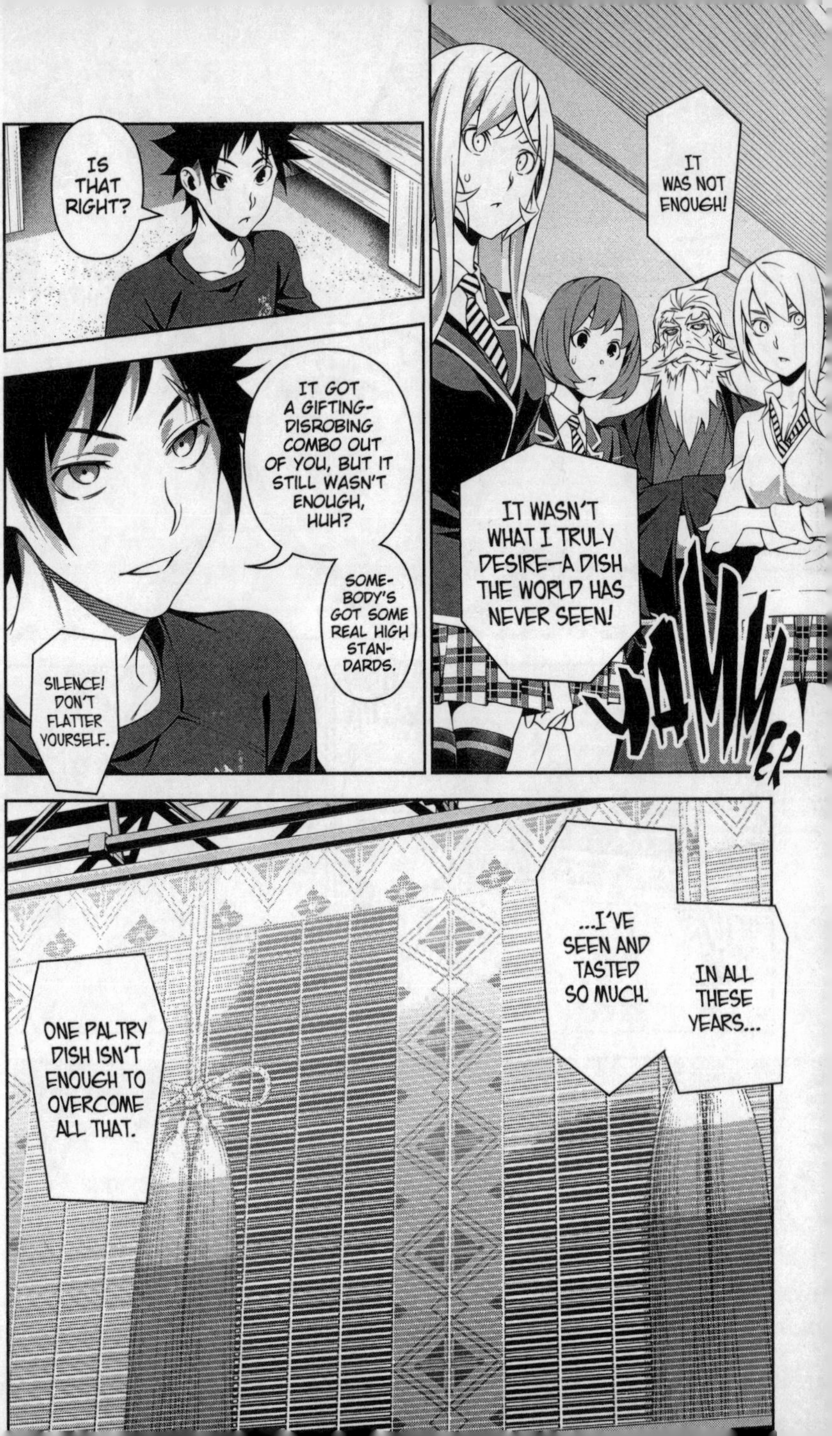
IT WAS NOT ENOUGH!
IT WASN'T WHAT I TRULY DESIRE—A DISH THE WORLD HAS NEVER SEEN!
IS THAT RIGHT?
IT GOT A GIFTING-DISROBING COMBO OUT OF YOU, BUT IT STILL WASN'T ENOUGH, HUH?
SOMEBODY'S GOT SOME REAL HIGH STANDARDS.
SILENCE! DON'T FLATTER YOURSELF.
IN ALL THESE YEARS...
...I'VE SEEN AND TASTED SO MUCH.
ONE PALTRY DISH ISN'T ENOUGH TO OVERCOME ALL THAT.

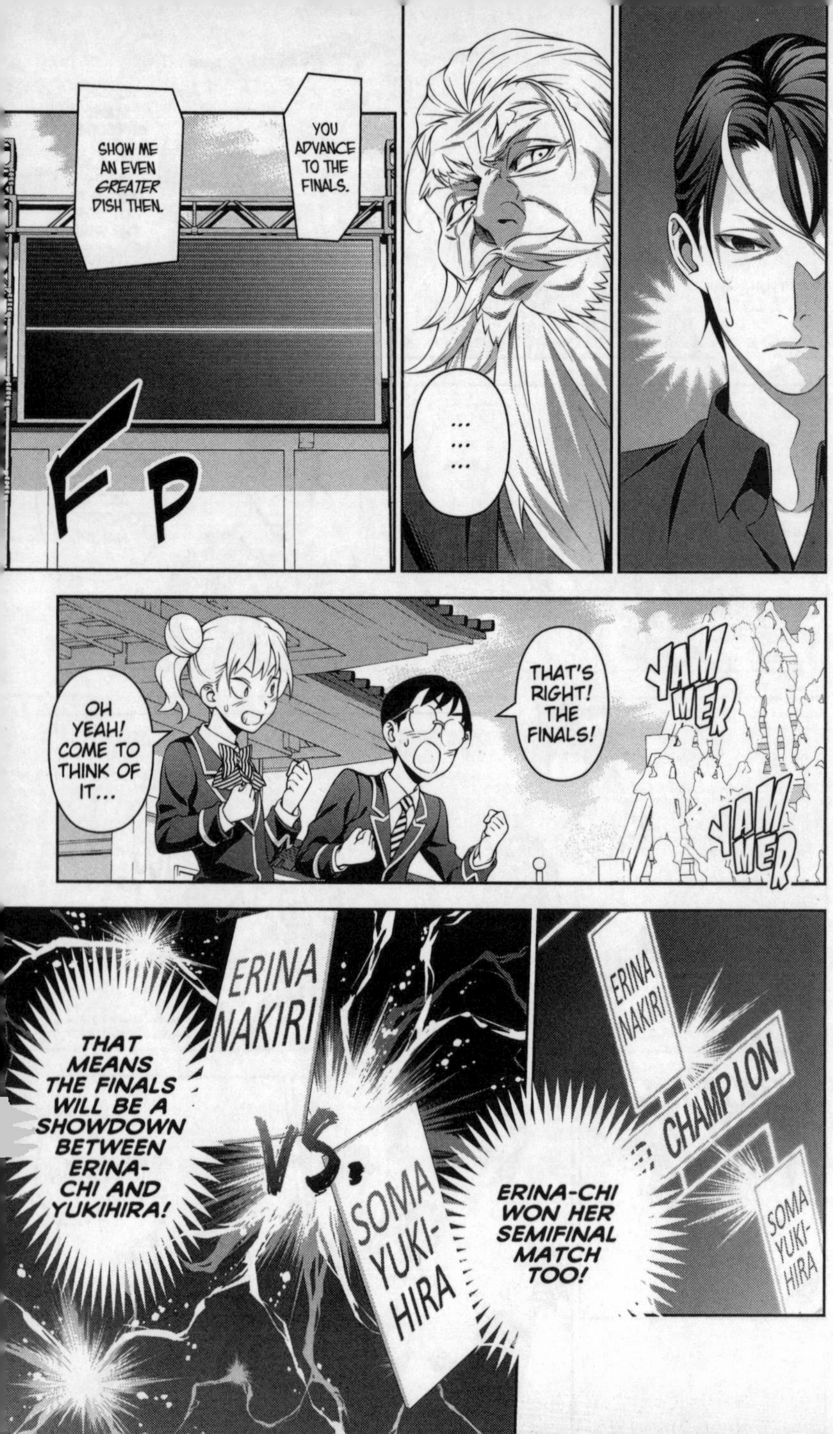
......
YOU ADVANCE TO THE FINALS.
SHOW ME AN EVEN *GREATER* DISH THEN.
FP
YAMMER
YAMMER
THAT'S RIGHT! THE FINALS!
OH YEAH! COME TO THINK OF IT...
ERINA NAKIRI
CHAMPION
SOMA YUKI-HIRA
ERINA-CHI WON HER SEMIFINAL MATCH TOO!
ERINA NAKIRI
VS.
SOMA YUKI-HIRA
THAT MEANS THE FINALS WILL BE A SHOWDOWN BETWEEN ERINA-CHI AND YUKIHIRA!

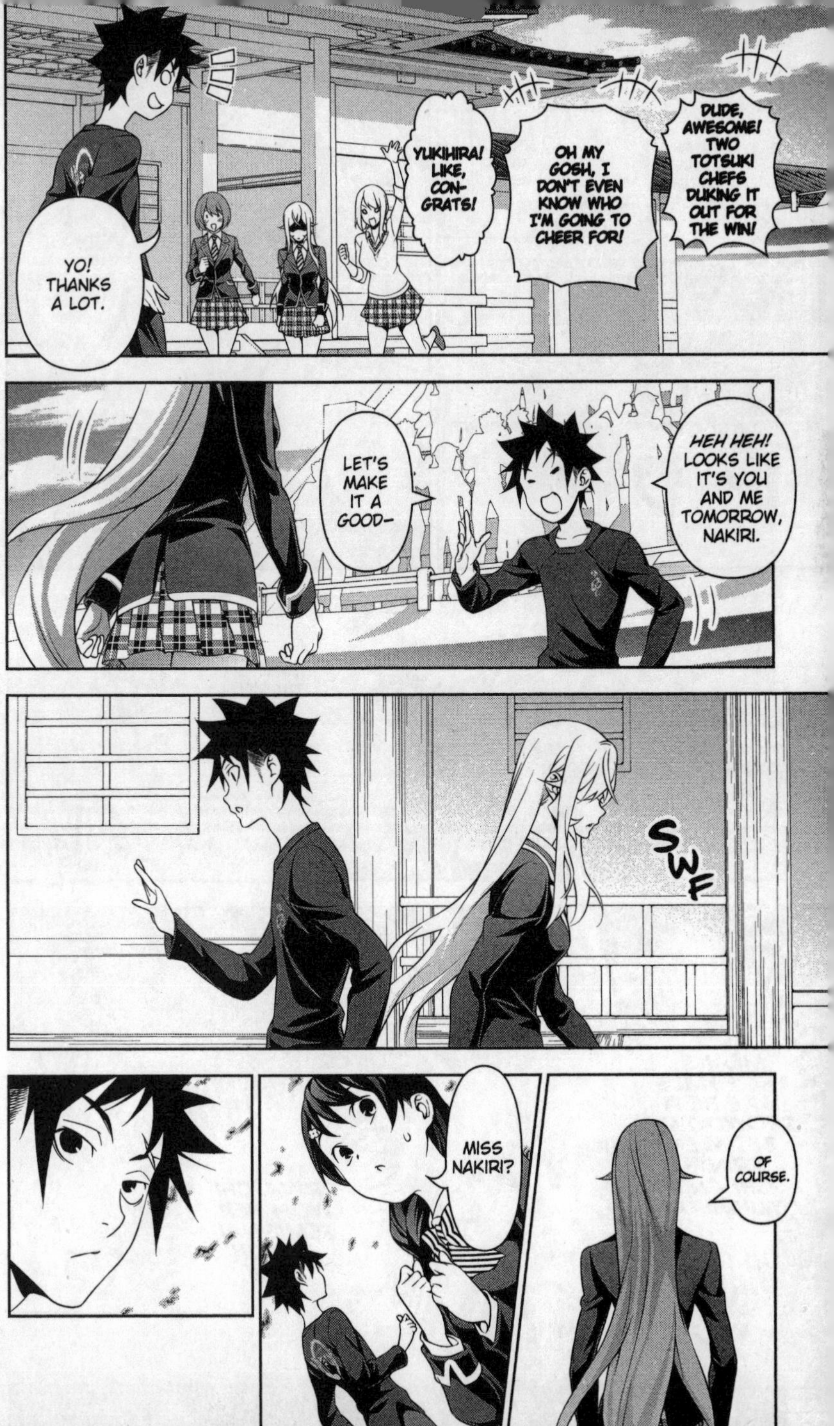
DUDE, AWESOME! TWO TOTSUKI CHEFS DUKING IT OUT FOR THE WIN!
OH MY GOSH, I DON'T EVEN KNOW WHO I'M GOING TO CHEER FOR!
YUKIHIRA! LIKE, CON-GRATS!
YO! THANKS A LOT.
HEH HEH! LOOKS LIKE IT'S YOU AND ME TOMORROW, NAKIRI.
LET'S MAKE IT A GOOD-
SWF
OF COURSE.
MISS NAKIRI?

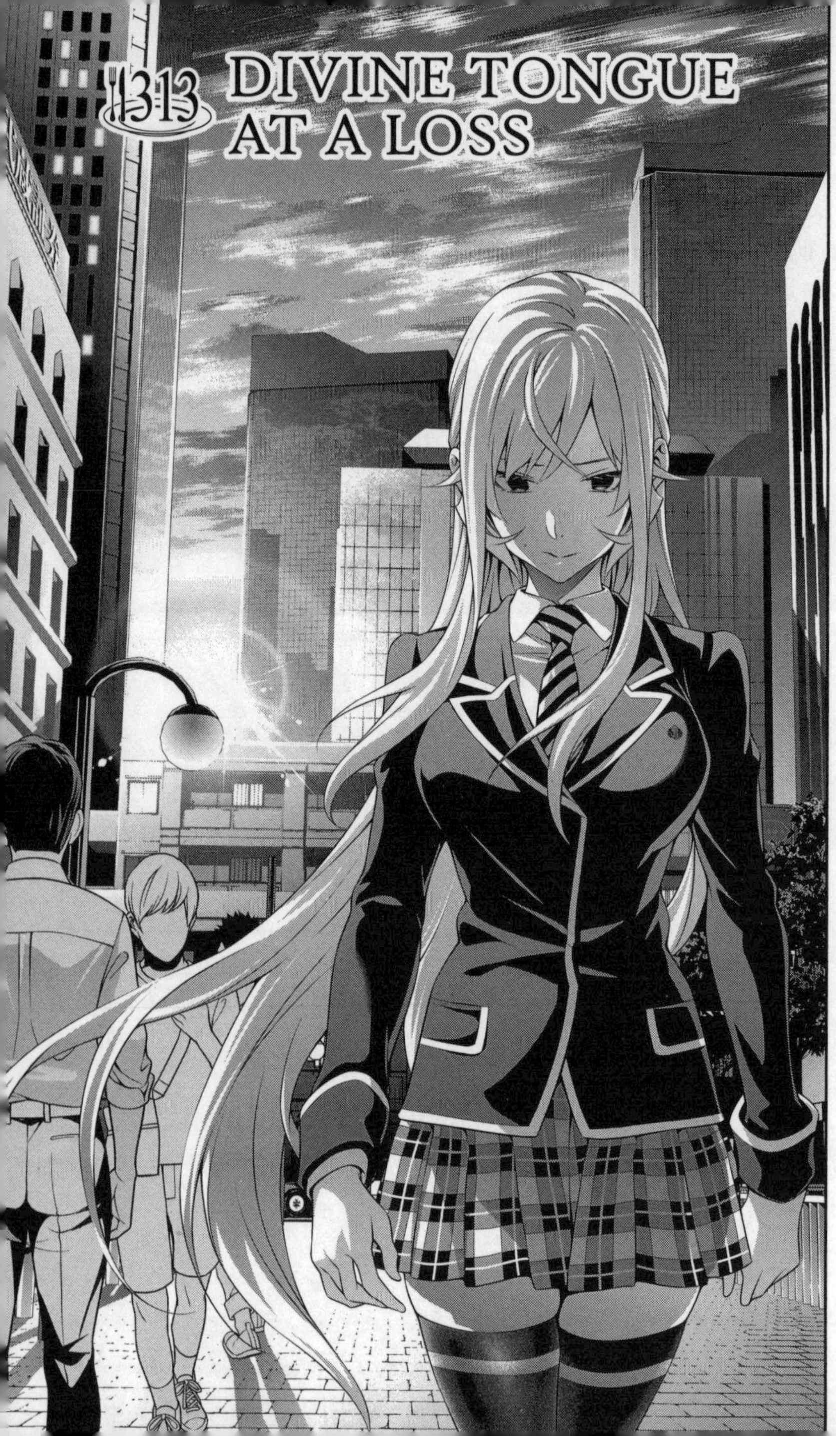
313
DIVINE TONGUE
AT A LOSS

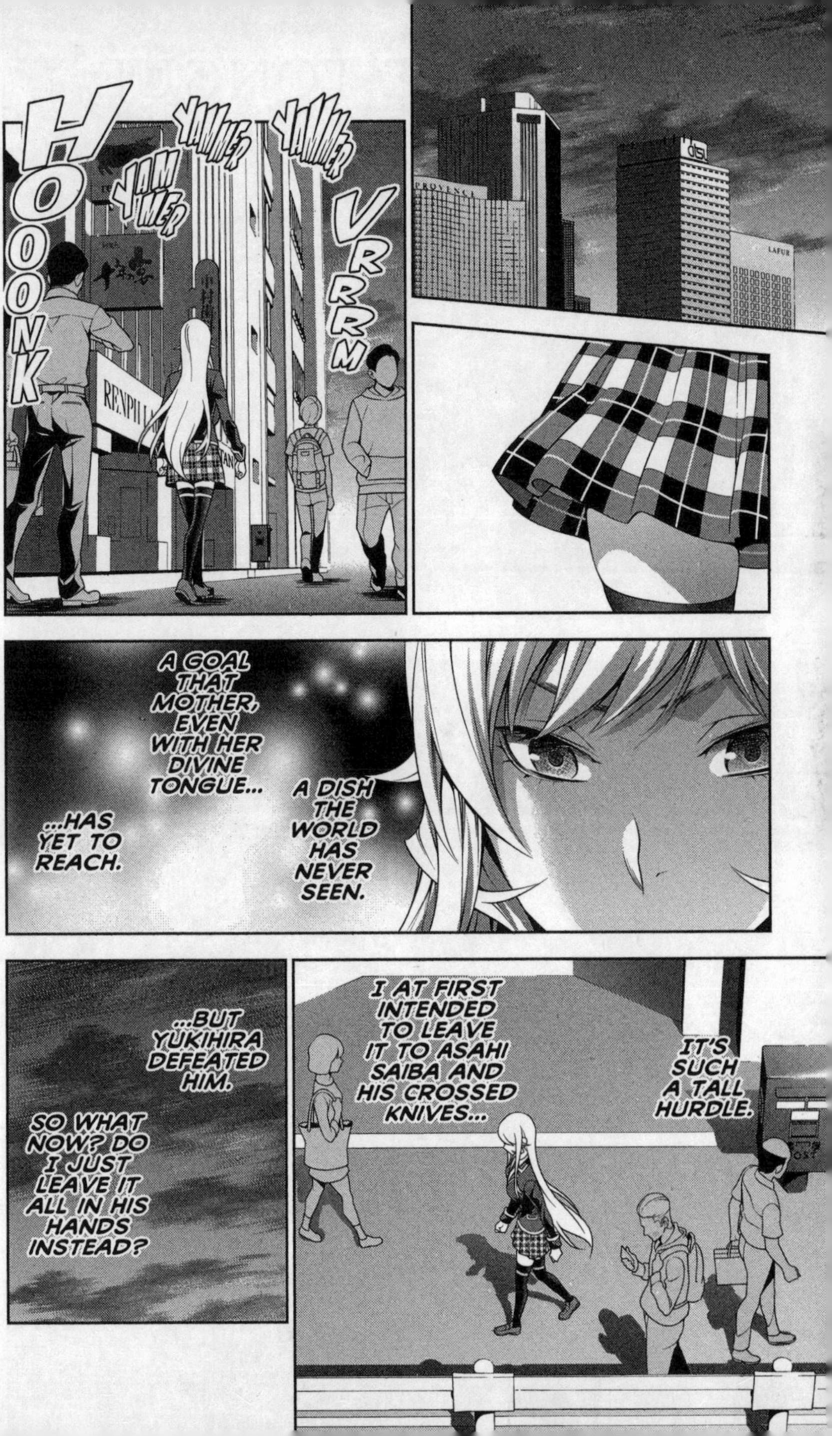
PROVENCE
LAFUR
HOOOONK
YAMMER YAMMER
YAM YAMMER
VRRRM
A DISH THE WORLD HAS NEVER SEEN.
A GOAL THAT MOTHER, EVEN WITH HER DIVINE TONGUE...
...HAS YET TO REACH.
IT'S SUCH A TALL HURDLE.
I AT FIRST INTENDED TO LEAVE IT TO ASAHI SAIBA AND HIS CROSSED KNIVES...
...BUT YUKIHIRA DEFEATED HIM.
SO WHAT NOW? DO I JUST LEAVE IT ALL IN HIS HANDS INSTEAD?

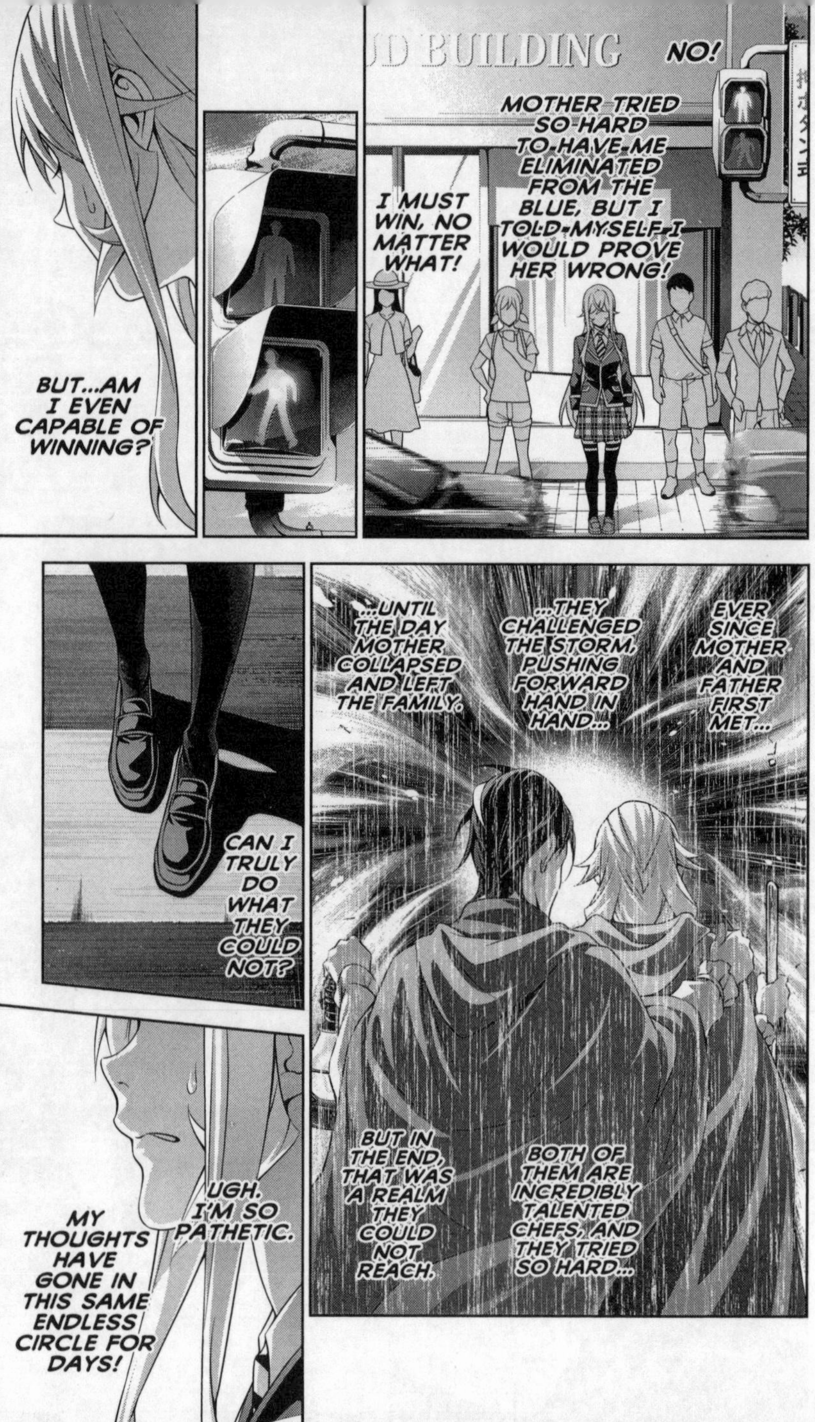
NO!
MOTHER TRIED SO HARD TO HAVE ME ELIMINATED FROM THE BLUE, BUT I TOLD MYSELF I WOULD PROVE HER WRONG!
I MUST WIN, NO MATTER WHAT!
BUT...AM I EVEN CAPABLE OF WINNING?
EVER SINCE MOTHER AND FATHER FIRST MET...
...THEY CHALLENGED THE STORM, PUSHING FORWARD HAND IN HAND...
...UNTIL THE DAY MOTHER COLLAPSED AND LEFT THE FAMILY.
BOTH OF THEM ARE INCREDIBLY TALENTED CHEFS, AND THEY TRIED SO HARD...
BUT IN THE END, THAT WAS A REALM THEY COULD NOT REACH.
CAN I TRULY DO WHAT THEY COULD NOT?
UGH. I'M SO PATHETIC.
MY THOUGHTS HAVE GONE IN THIS SAME ENDLESS CIRCLE FOR DAYS!

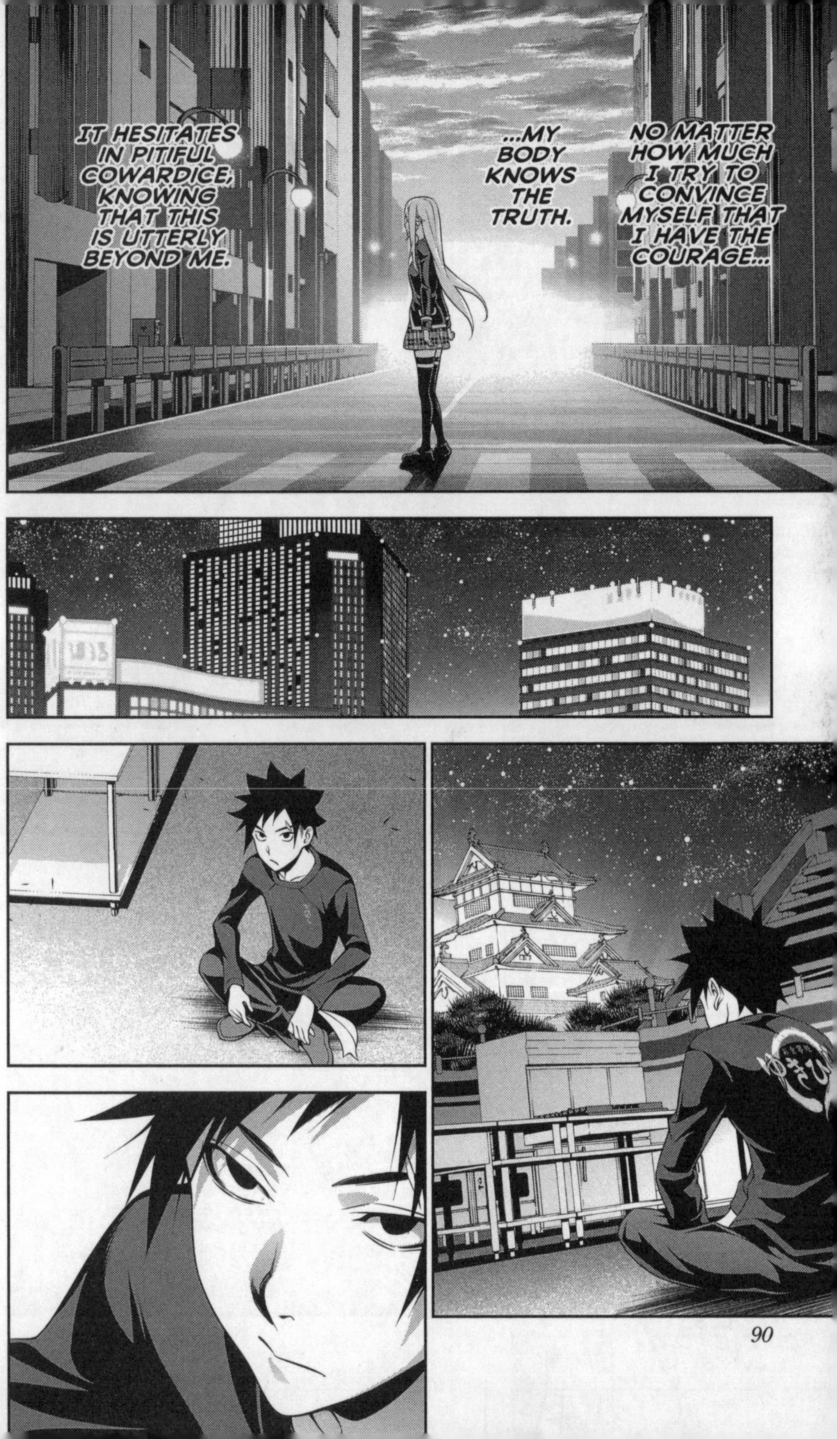
NO MATTER HOW MUCH I TRY TO CONVINCE MYSELF THAT I HAVE THE COURAGE...
...MY BODY KNOWS THE TRUTH.
IT HESITATES IN PITIFUL COWARDICE, KNOWING THAT THIS IS UTTERLY BEYOND ME.

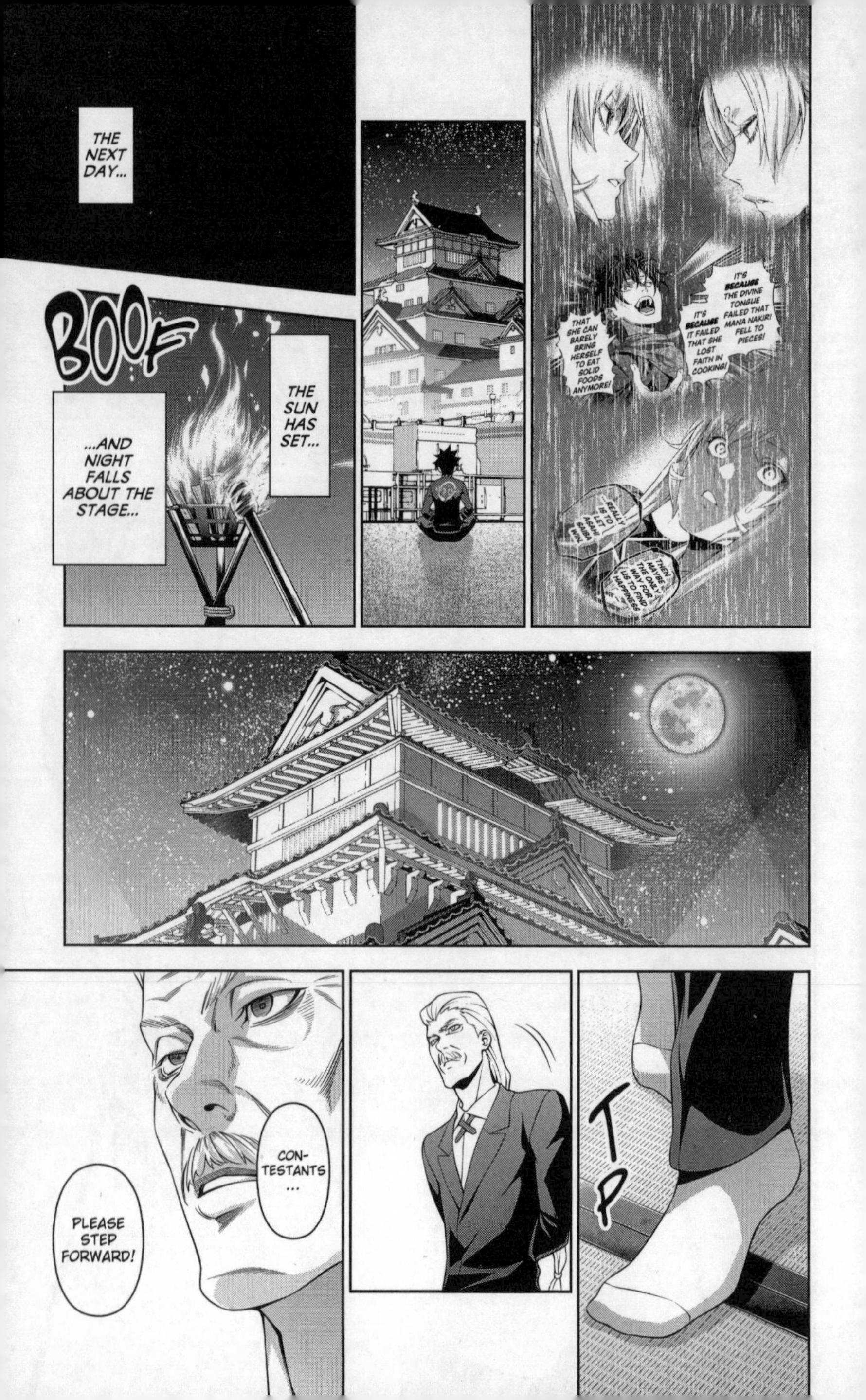
IT'S BECAUSE THE DIVINE TONGUE FAILED THAT MANA NAKIRI FELL TO PIECES!
IT'S BECAUSE IT FAILED THAT SHE LOST FAITH IN COOKING!
THAT SHE CAN BARELY BRING HERSELF TO EAT SOLID FOODS ANYMORE!
THEN MAYBE THE ONLY WAY FOR US TO FIND HAPPINESS
REALLY IS TO LET ASAHI WIN.
THE NEXT DAY...
BOOF
THE SUN HAS SET...
...AND NIGHT FALLS ABOUT THE STAGE...
TP
CON-TESTANTS...
PLEASE STEP FORWARD!

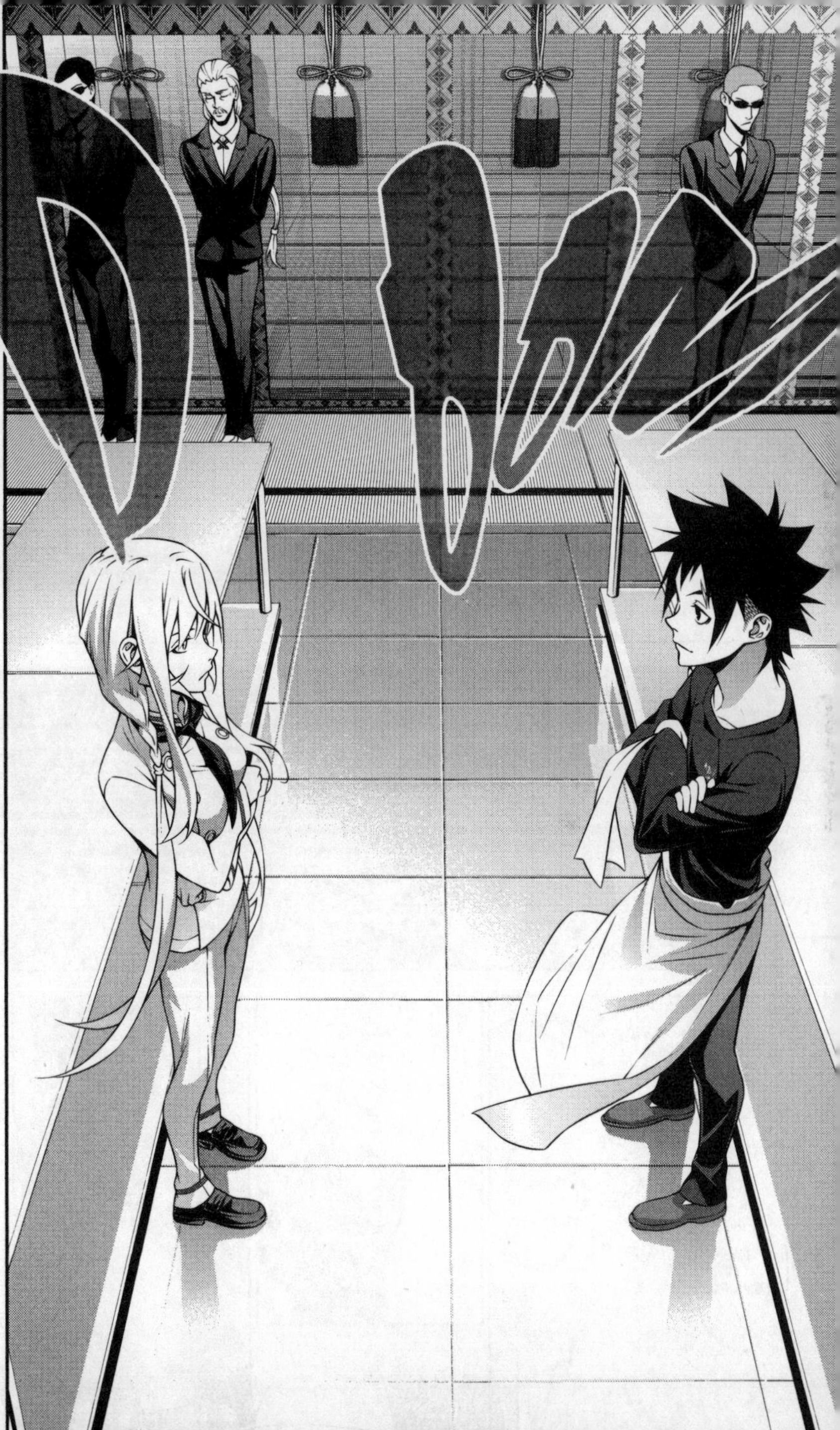

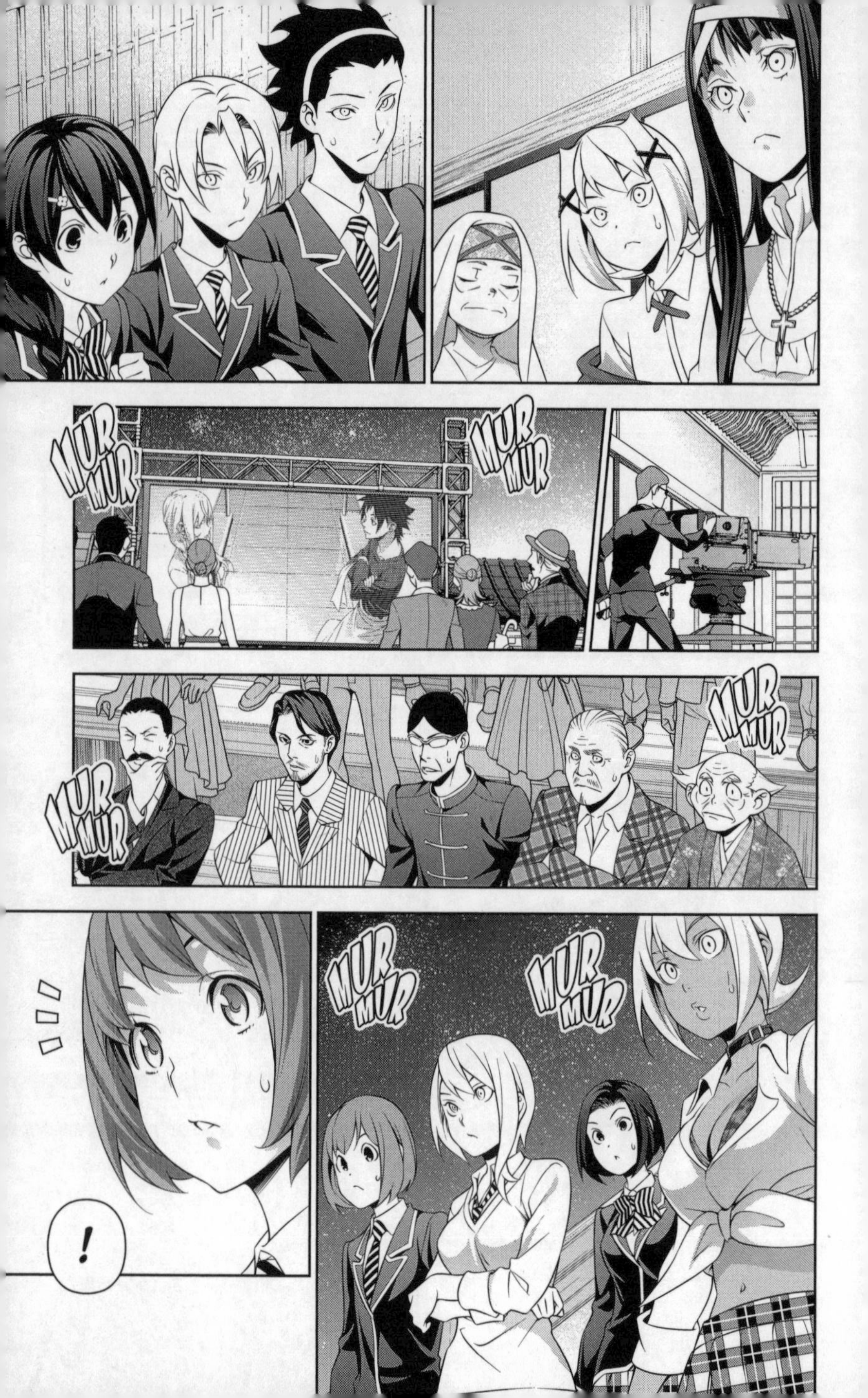

MUR MUR
MUR MUR
MUR MUR
MUR MUR
MUR MUR
MUR MUR
!

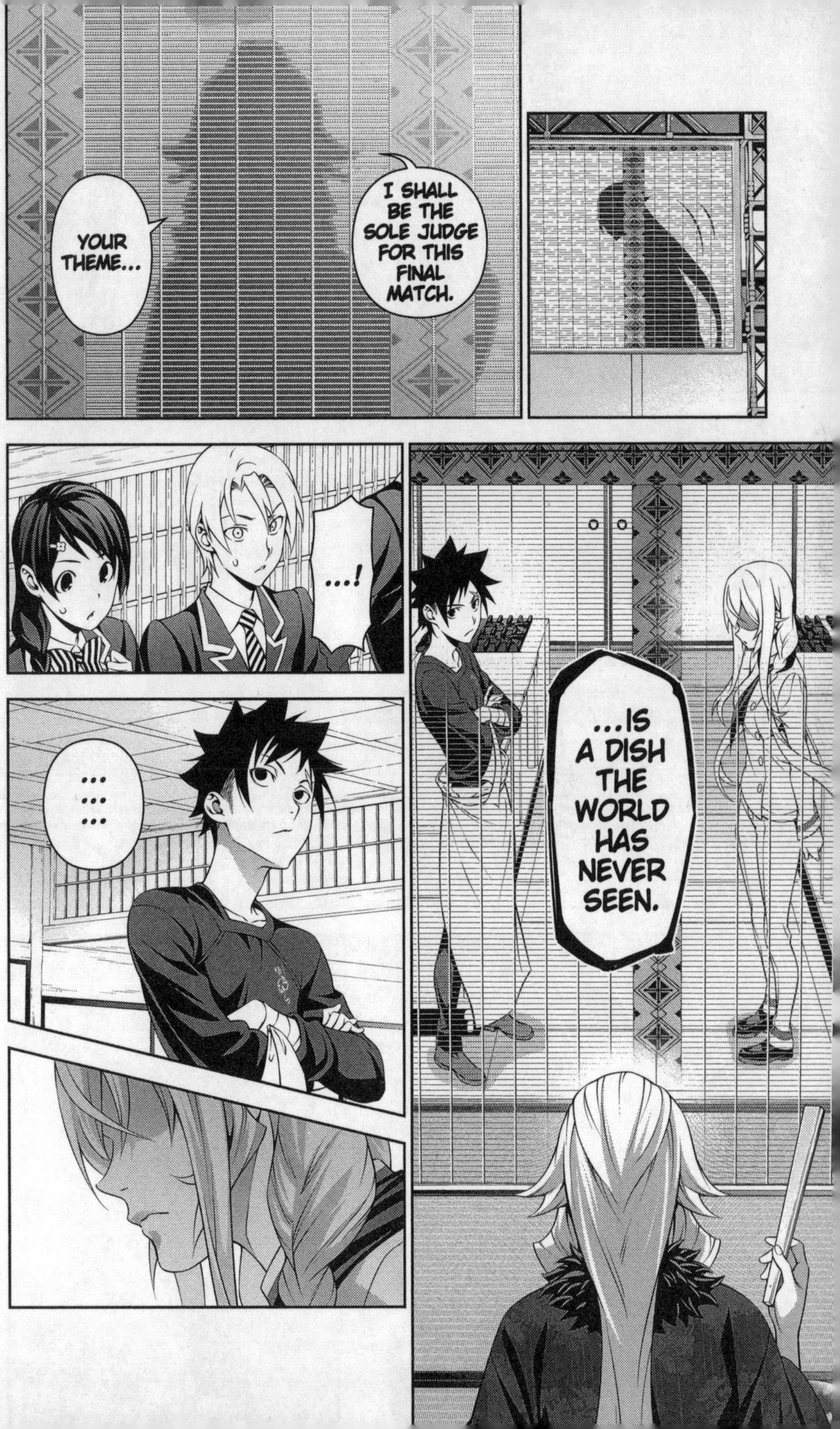
I SHALL BE THE SOLE JUDGE FOR THIS FINAL MATCH.
YOUR THEME...
...IS A DISH THE WORLD HAS NEVER SEEN.
...!
... ...

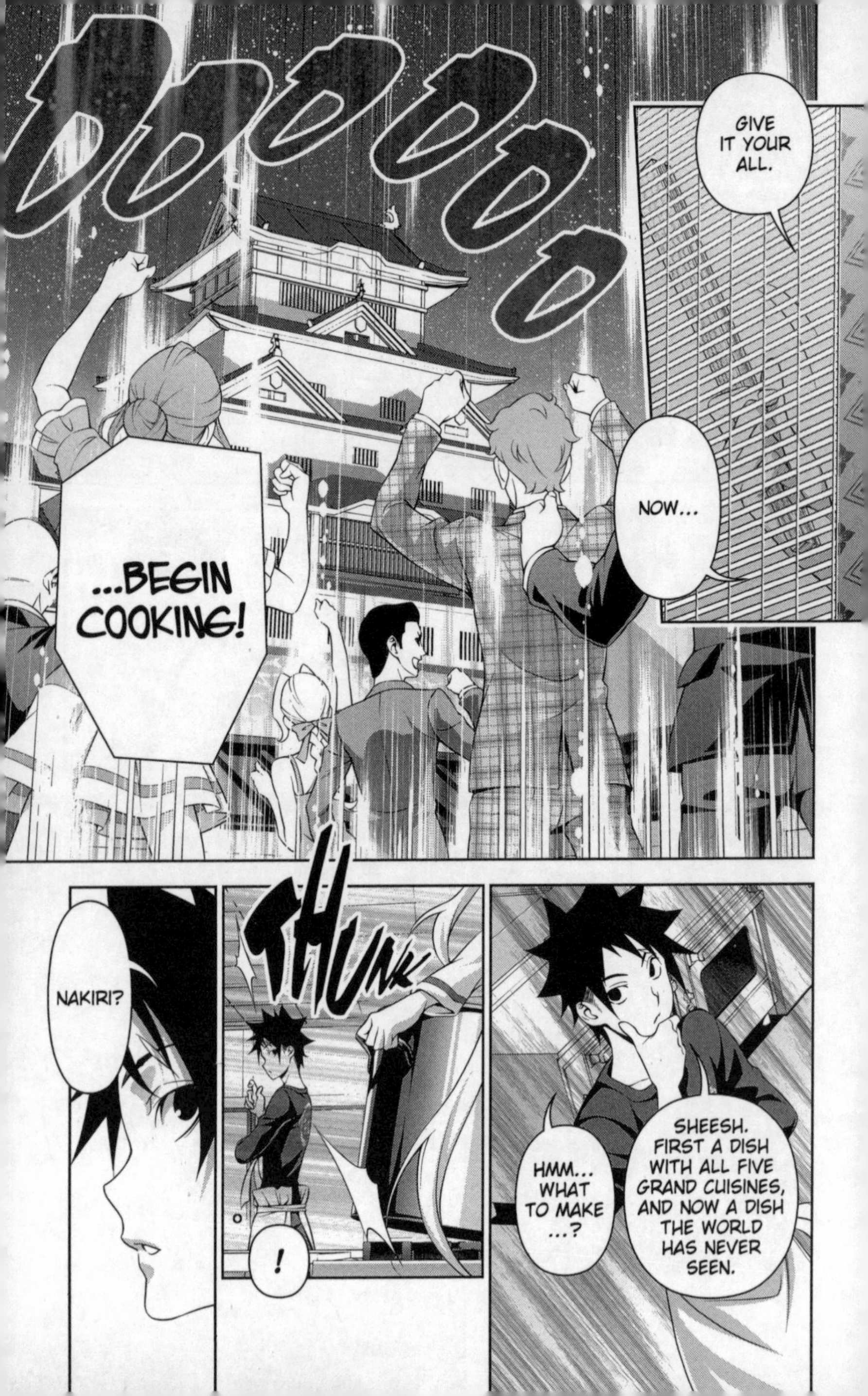
GIVE IT YOUR ALL.
DOOOOOO
NOW...
...BEGIN COOKING!
SHEESH. FIRST A DISH WITH ALL FIVE GRAND CUISINES, AND NOW A DISH THE WORLD HAS NEVER SEEN.
HMM... WHAT TO MAKE ...?
THUNK
!
NAKIRI?

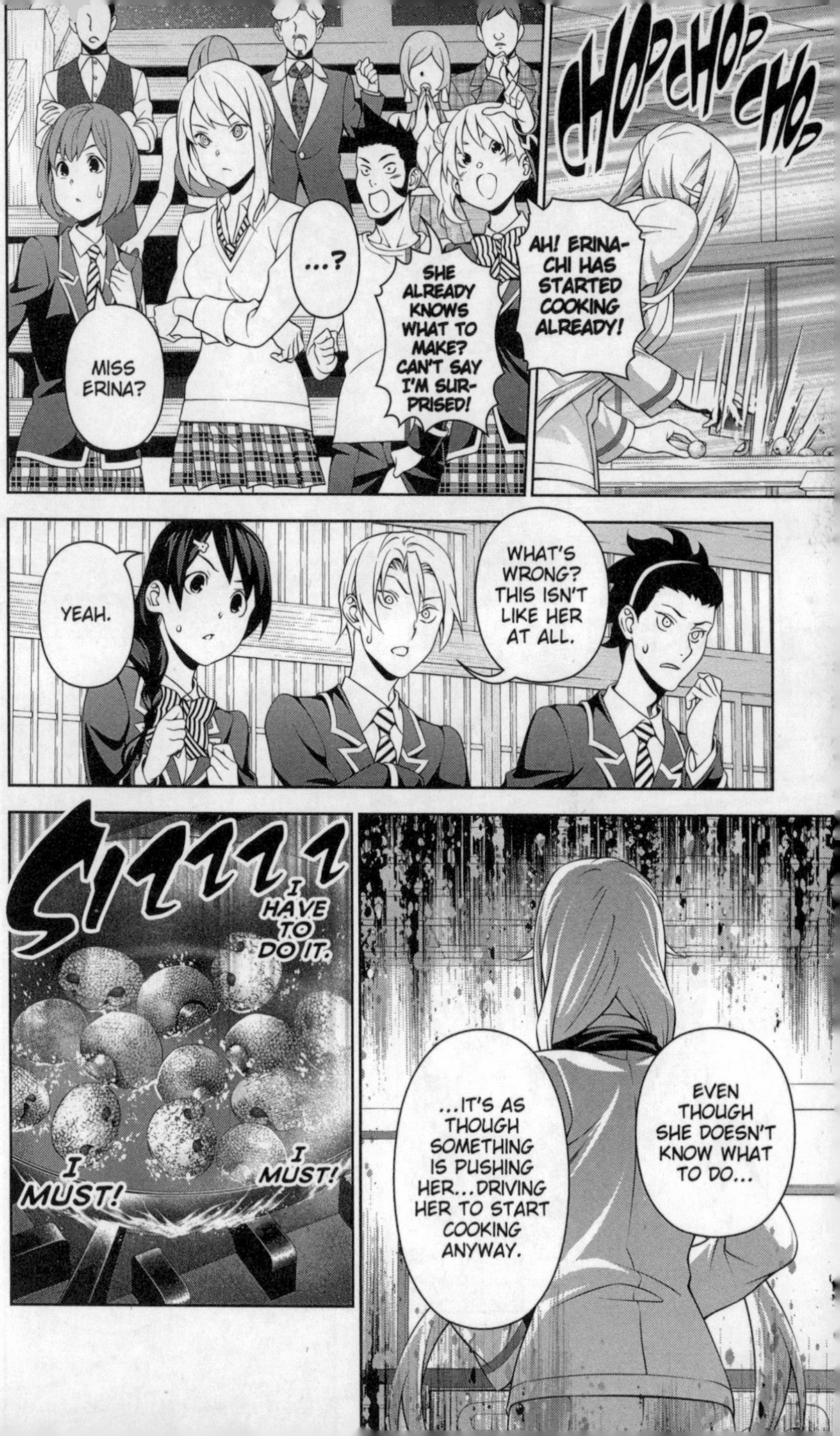
CHOP CHOP CHOP
AH! ERINA-CHI HAS STARTED COOKING ALREADY!
SHE ALREADY KNOWS WHAT TO MAKE? CAN'T SAY I'M SURPRISED!
...?
MISS ERINA?
WHAT'S WRONG? THIS ISN'T LIKE HER AT ALL.
YEAH.
EVEN THOUGH SHE DOESN'T KNOW WHAT TO DO...
...IT'S AS THOUGH SOMETHING IS PUSHING HER...DRIVING HER TO START COOKING ANYWAY.
SIZZZZZ
I HAVE TO DO IT.
I MUST!
I MUST!

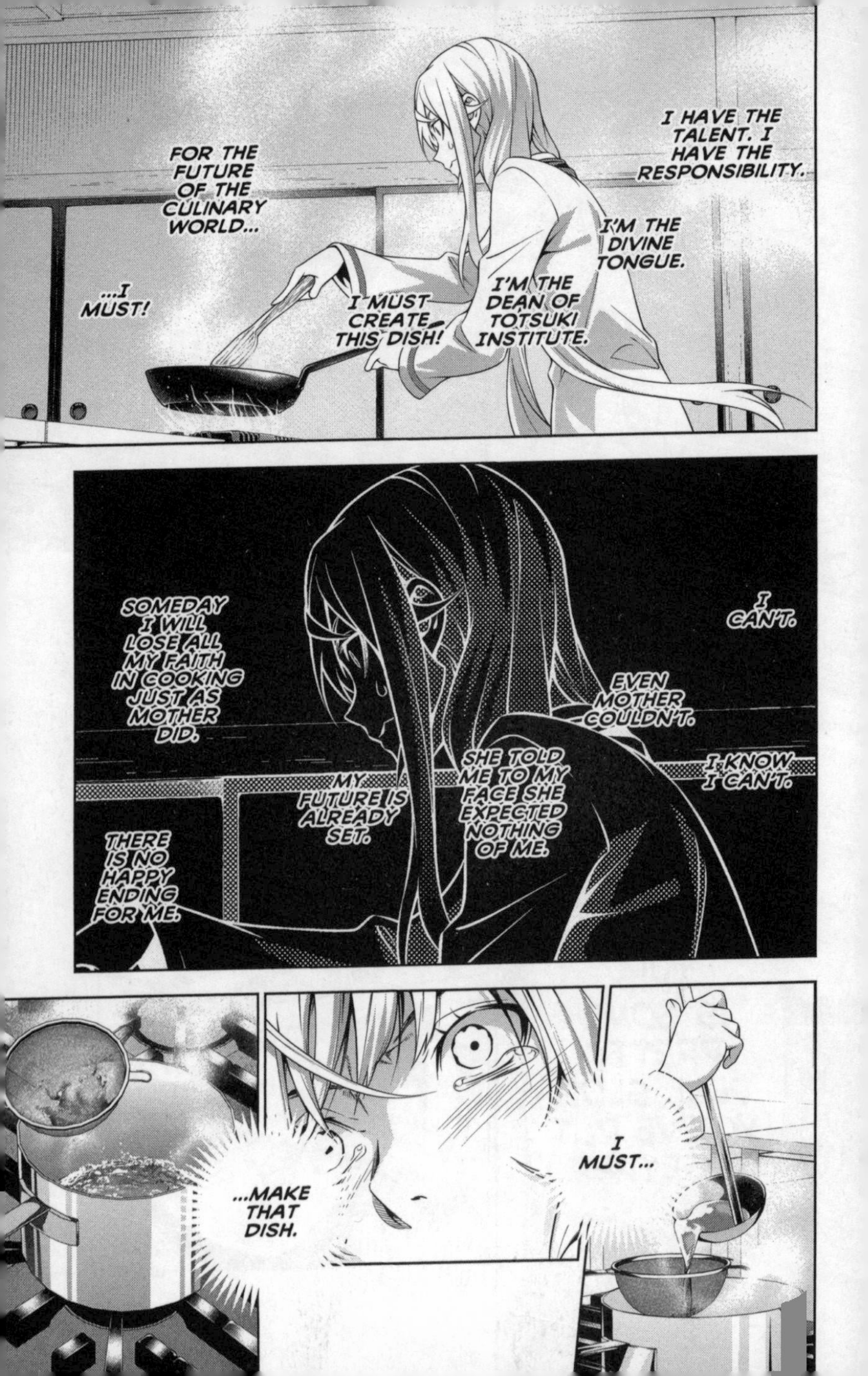
I HAVE THE TALENT. I HAVE THE RESPONSIBILITY.
I'M THE DIVINE TONGUE.
I'M THE DEAN OF TOTSUKI INSTITUTE.
I MUST CREATE THIS DISH!
FOR THE FUTURE OF THE CULINARY WORLD...
...I MUST!
I CAN'T.
EVEN MOTHER COULDN'T.
I KNOW I CAN'T.
SHE TOLD ME TO MY FACE SHE EXPECTED NOTHING OF ME.
SOMEDAY I WILL LOSE ALL MY FAITH IN COOKING JUST AS MOTHER DID.
MY FUTURE IS ALREADY SET.
THERE IS NO HAPPY ENDING FOR ME.
I MUST...
...MAKE THAT DISH.

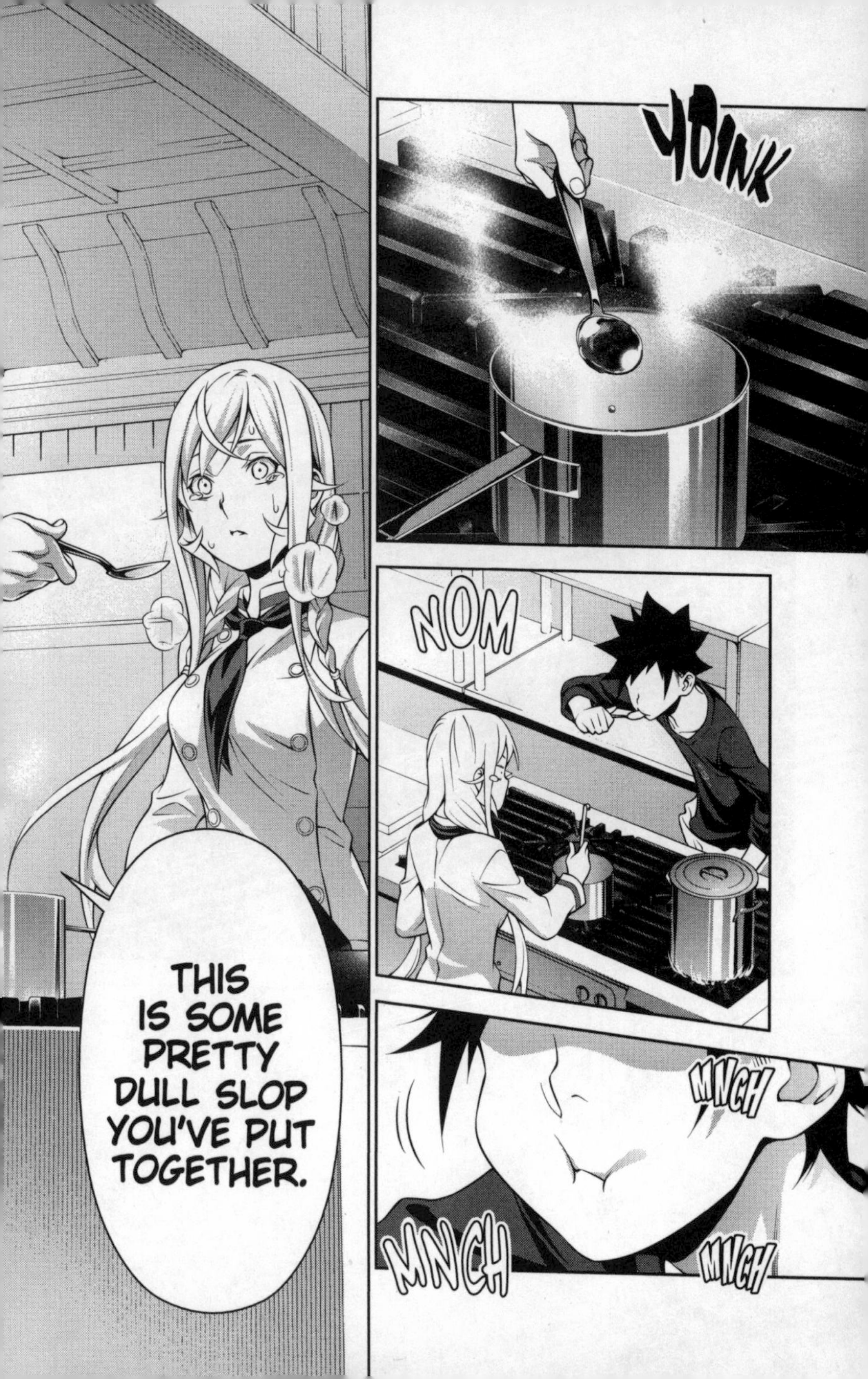
YOINK
NOM
MNCH
MNCH
MNCH
THIS IS SOME PRETTY DULL SLOP YOU'VE PUT TOGETHER.

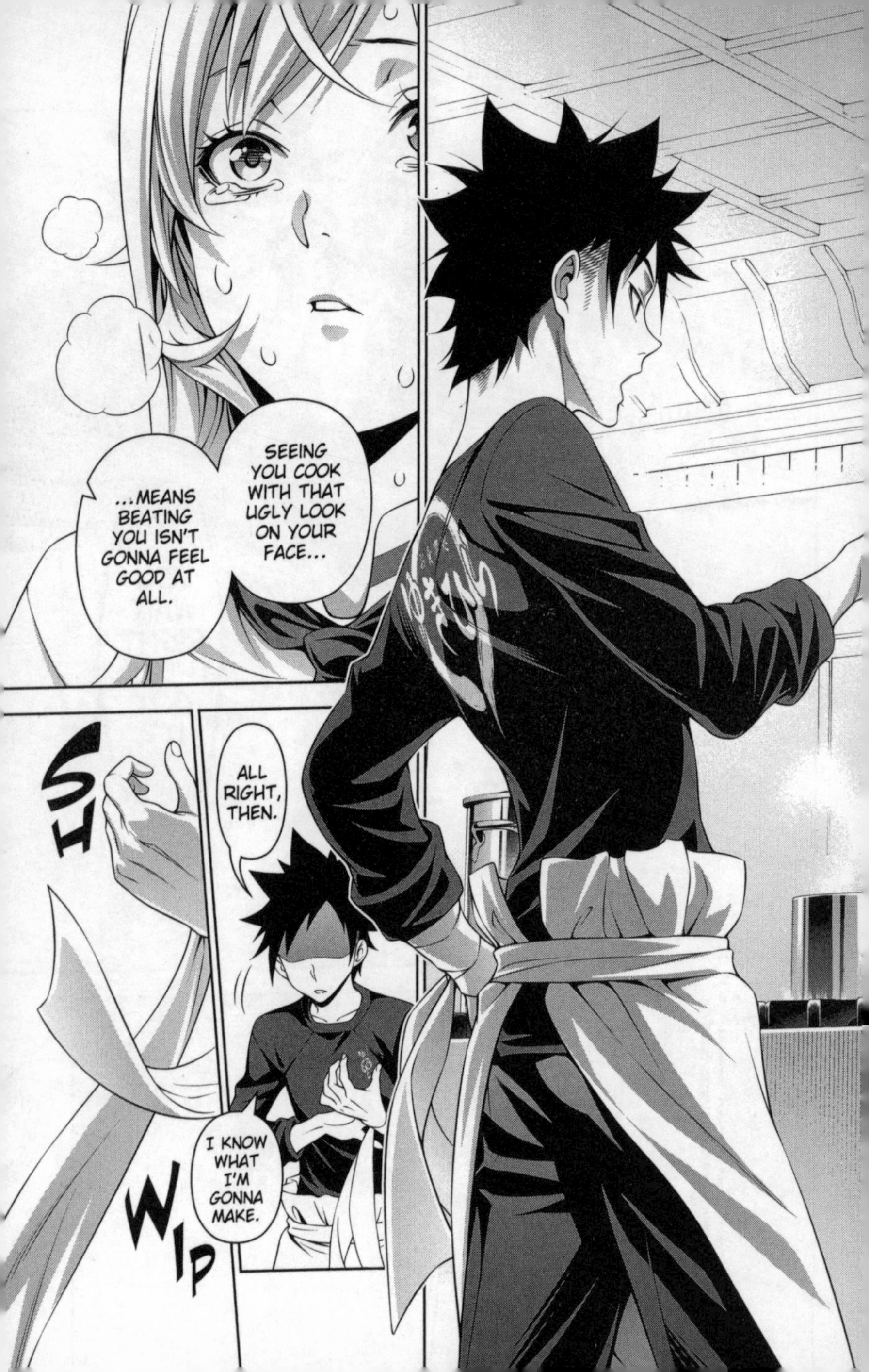
SEEING YOU COOK WITH THAT UGLY LOOK ON YOUR FACE...
...MEANS BEATING YOU ISN'T GONNA FEEL GOOD AT ALL.
ALL RIGHT, THEN.
SH
I KNOW WHAT I'M GONNA MAKE.
WIP

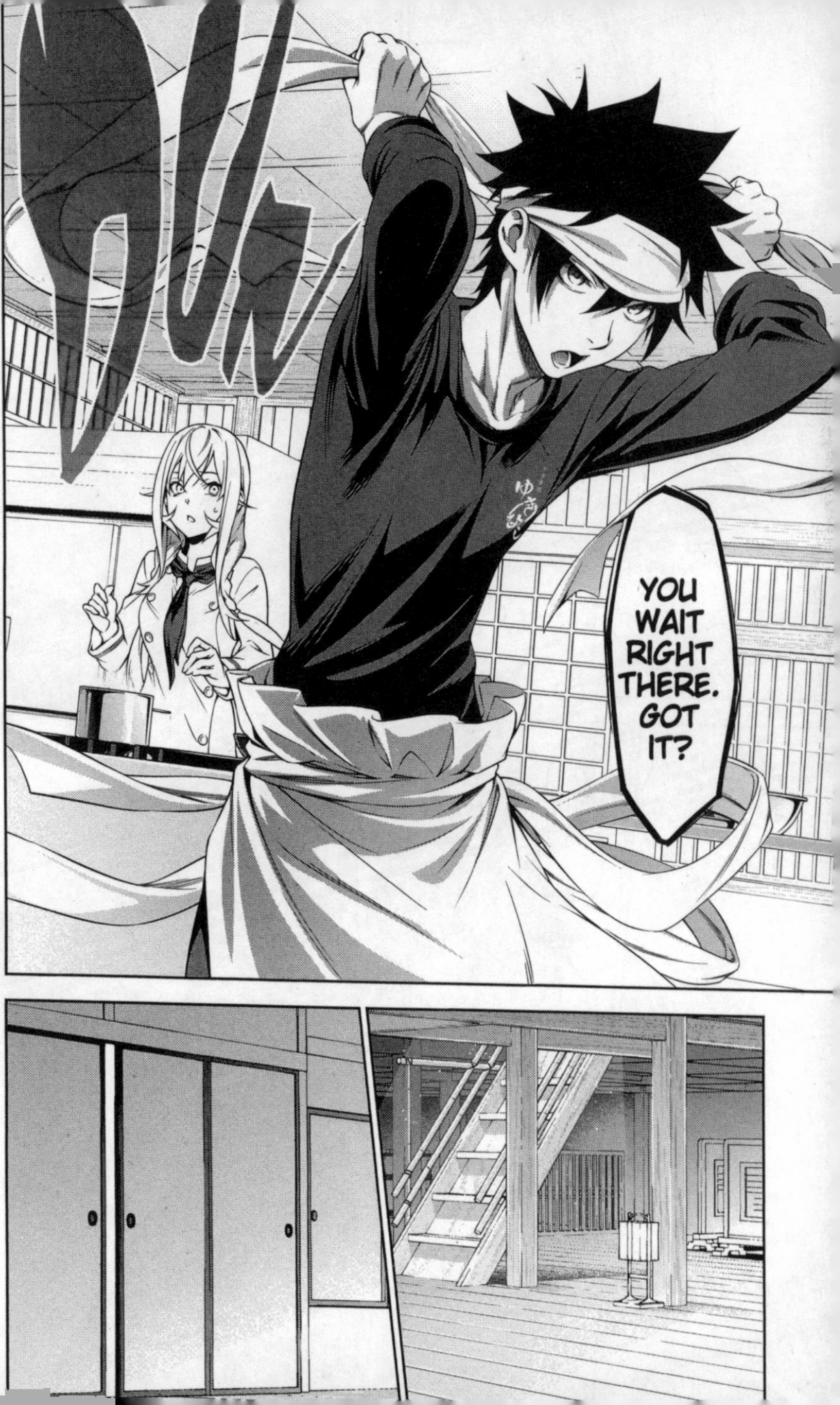
YOU WAIT RIGHT THERE. GOT IT?

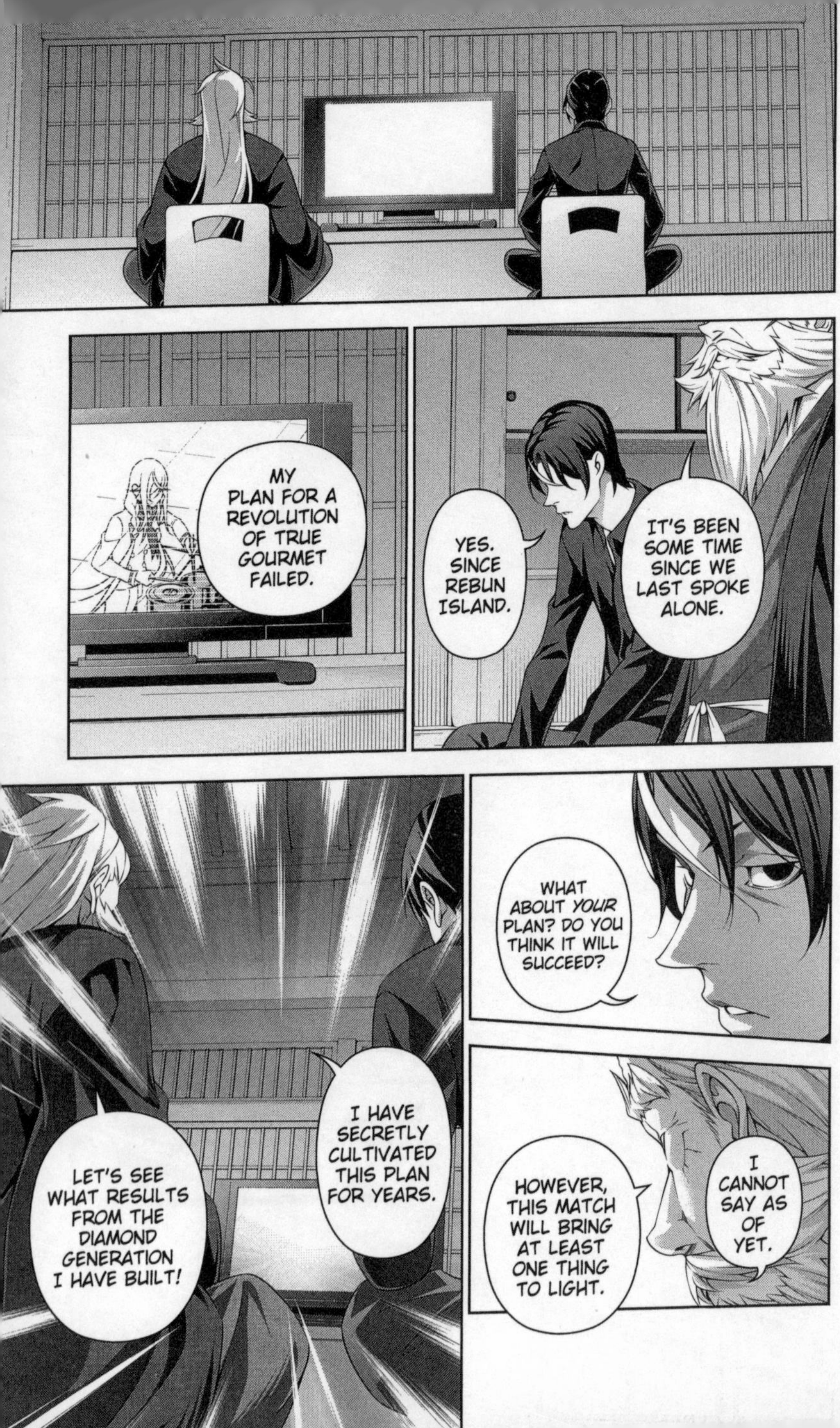
IT'S BEEN SOME TIME SINCE WE LAST SPOKE ALONE.
YES. SINCE REBUN ISLAND.
MY PLAN FOR A REVOLUTION OF TRUE GOURMET FAILED.
WHAT ABOUT *YOUR* PLAN? DO YOU THINK IT WILL SUCCEED?
I CANNOT SAY AS OF YET.
HOWEVER, THIS MATCH WILL BRING AT LEAST ONE THING TO LIGHT.
I HAVE SECRETLY CULTIVATED THIS PLAN FOR YEARS.
LET'S SEE WHAT RESULTS FROM THE DIAMOND GENERATION I HAVE BUILT!

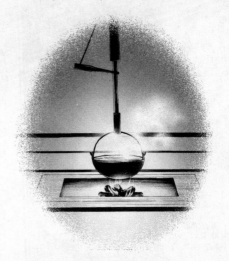

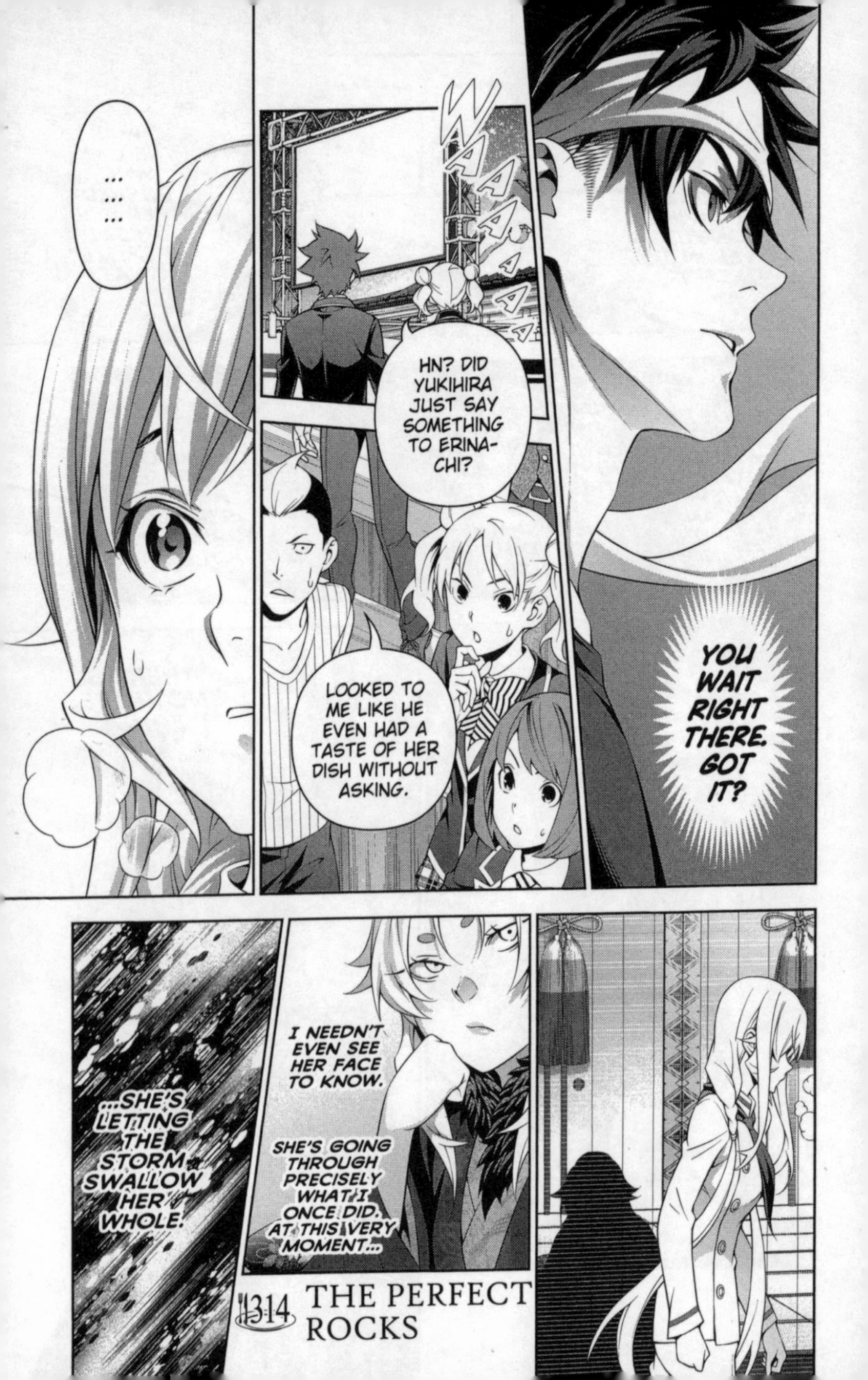
YOU WAIT RIGHT THERE. GOT IT?
WAAAAAAA
HN? DID YUKIHIRA JUST SAY SOMETHING TO ERINA-CHI?
LOOKED TO ME LIKE HE EVEN HAD A TASTE OF HER DISH WITHOUT ASKING.
......
I NEEDN'T EVEN SEE HER FACE TO KNOW.
SHE'S GOING THROUGH PRECISELY WHAT I ONCE DID. AT THIS VERY MOMENT...
...SHE'S LETTING THE STORM SWALLOW HER WHOLE.
314 THE PERFECT ROCKS

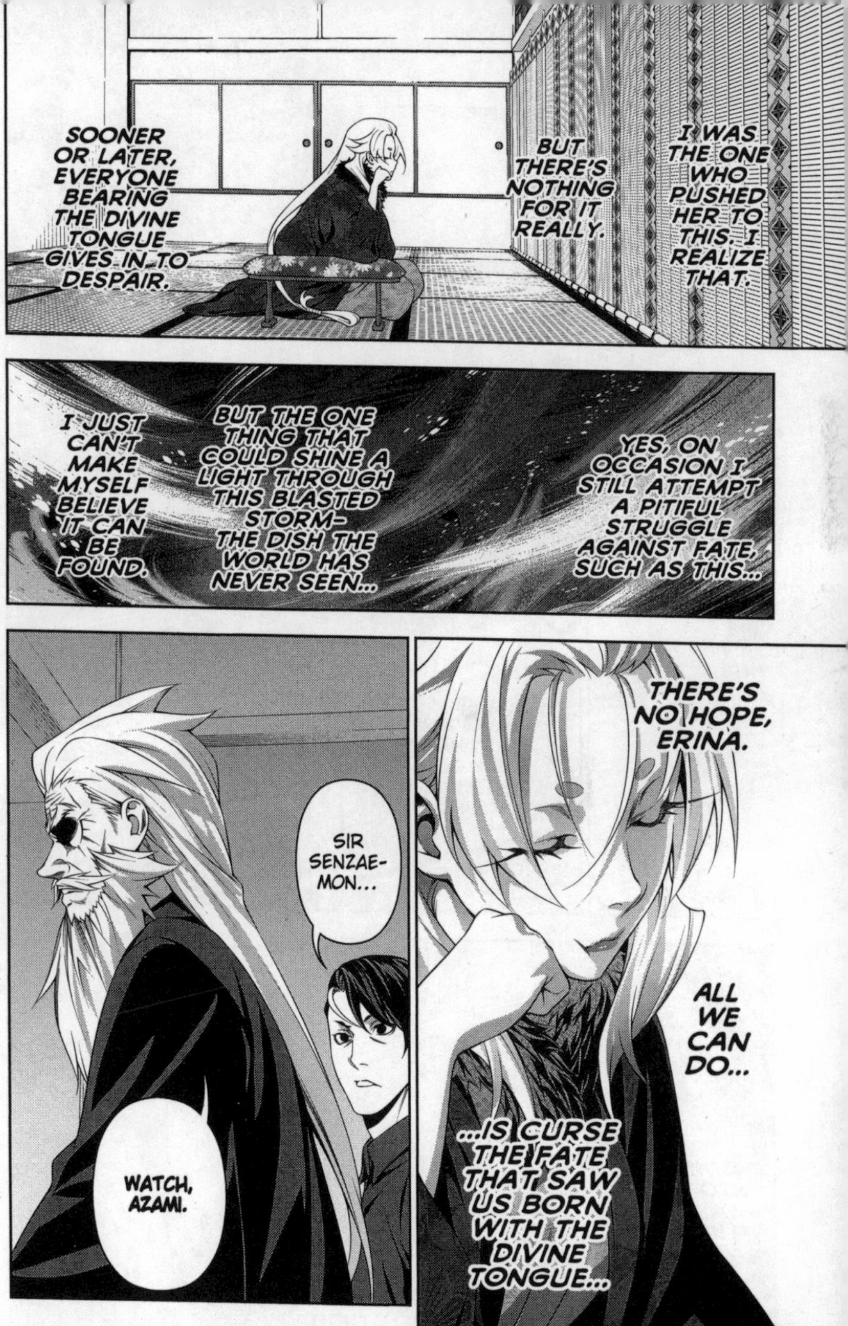
I WAS THE ONE WHO PUSHED HER TO THIS. I REALIZE THAT.
BUT THERE'S NOTHING FOR IT REALLY.
SOONER OR LATER, EVERYONE BEARING THE DIVINE TONGUE GIVES IN TO DESPAIR.
YES, ON OCCASION I STILL ATTEMPT A PITIFUL STRUGGLE AGAINST FATE, SUCH AS THIS...
BUT THE ONE THING THAT COULD SHINE A LIGHT THROUGH THIS BLASTED STORM— THE DISH THE WORLD HAS NEVER SEEN...
I JUST CAN'T MAKE MYSELF BELIEVE IT CAN BE FOUND.
THERE'S NO HOPE, ERINA.
ALL WE CAN DO...
...IS CURSE THE FATE THAT SAW US BORN WITH THE DIVINE TONGUE...
SIR SENZAEMON...
WATCH, AZAMI.

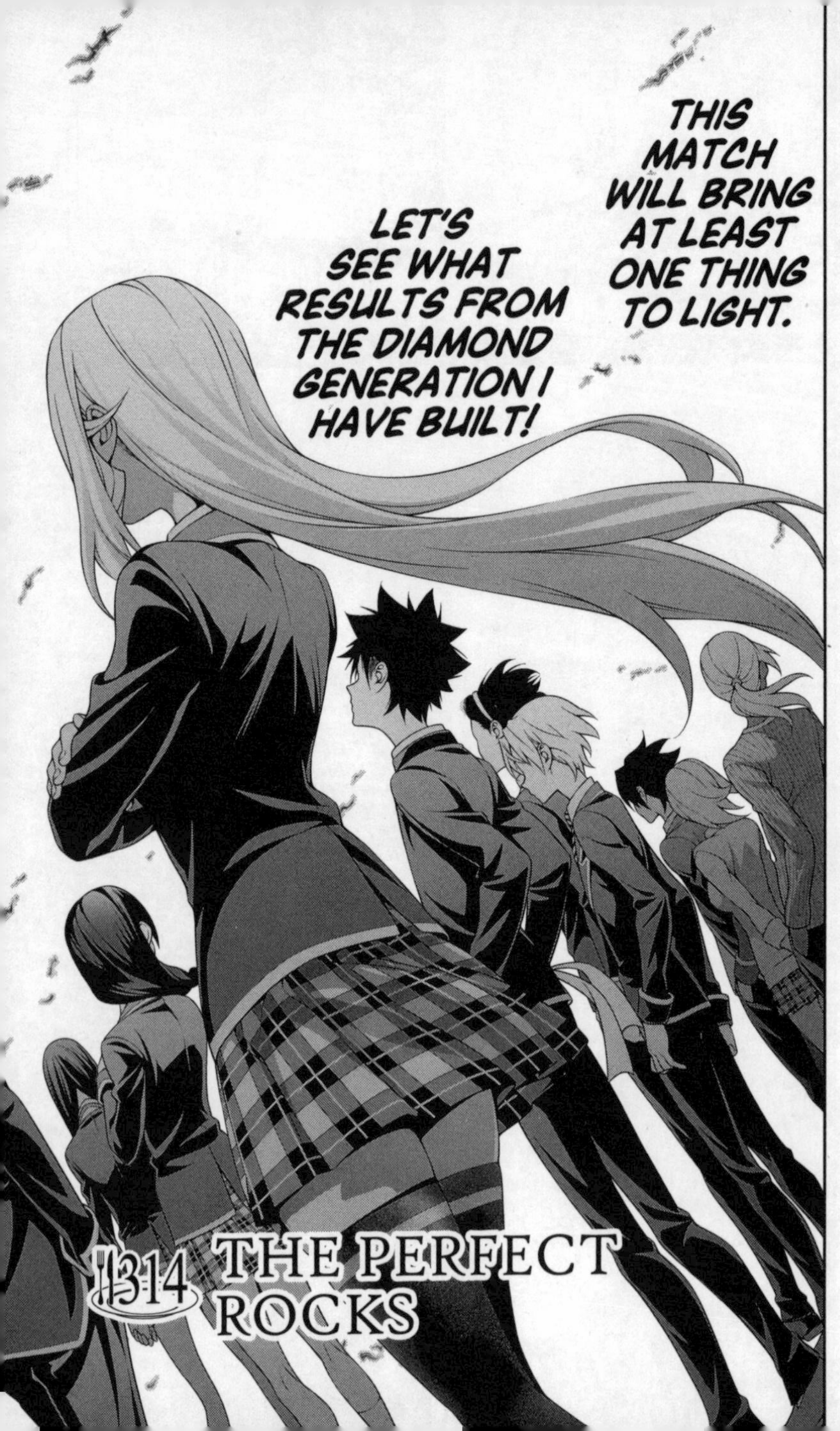
THIS MATCH WILL BRING AT LEAST ONE THING TO LIGHT.
LET'S SEE WHAT RESULTS FROM THE DIAMOND GENERATION I HAVE BUILT!
314 THE PERFECT ROCKS

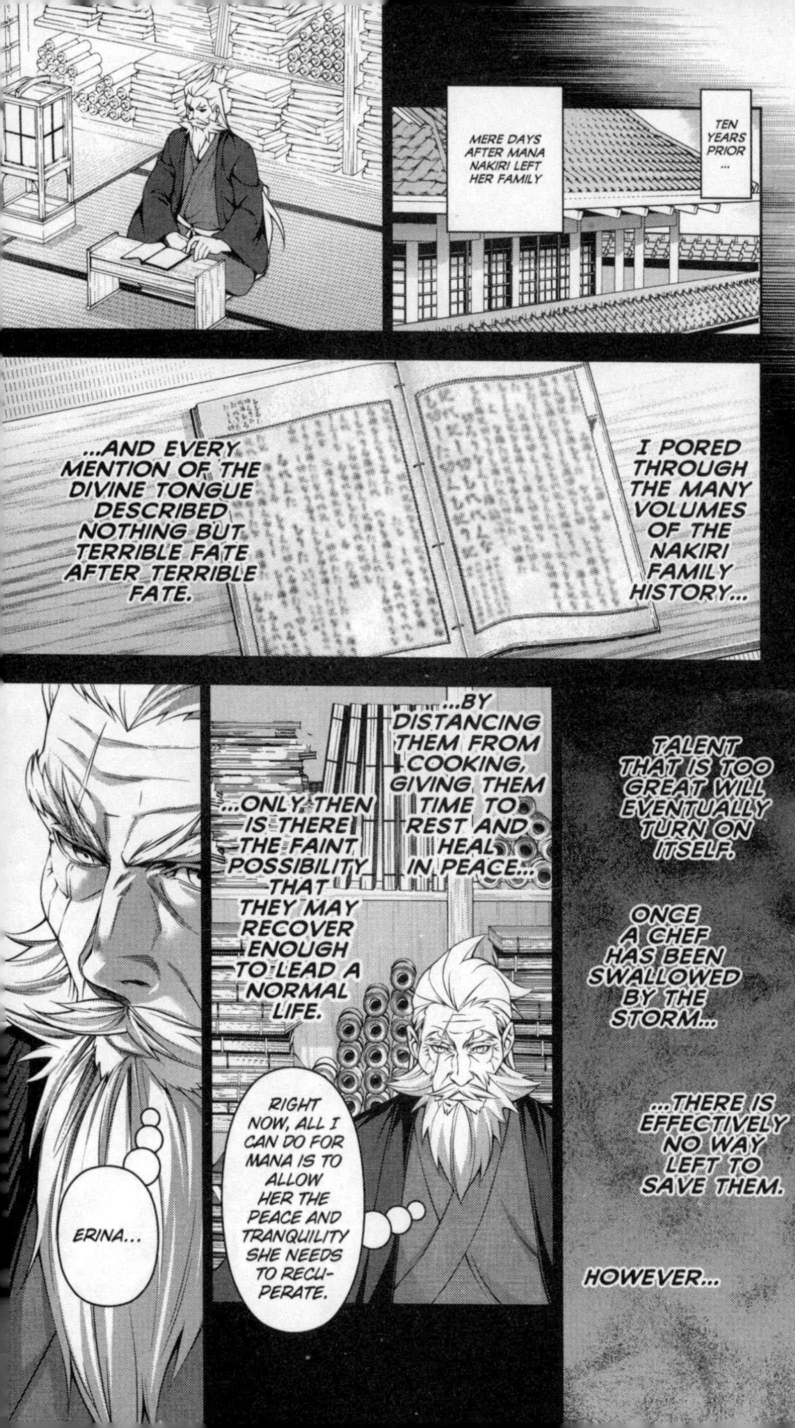
TEN YEARS PRIOR ...
MERE DAYS AFTER MANA NAKIRI LEFT HER FAMILY
I PORED THROUGH THE MANY VOLUMES OF THE NAKIRI FAMILY HISTORY...
...AND EVERY MENTION OF THE DIVINE TONGUE DESCRIBED NOTHING BUT TERRIBLE FATE AFTER TERRIBLE FATE.
TALENT THAT IS TOO GREAT WILL EVENTUALLY TURN ON ITSELF.
ONCE A CHEF HAS BEEN SWALLOWED BY THE STORM...
...THERE IS EFFECTIVELY NO WAY LEFT TO SAVE THEM.
HOWEVER...
...BY DISTANCING THEM FROM COOKING, GIVING THEM TIME TO REST AND HEAL IN PEACE...
...ONLY THEN IS THERE THE FAINT POSSIBILITY THAT THEY MAY RECOVER ENOUGH TO LEAD A NORMAL LIFE.
RIGHT NOW, ALL I CAN DO FOR MANA IS TO ALLOW HER THE PEACE AND TRANQUILITY SHE NEEDS TO RECU-PERATE.
ERINA...

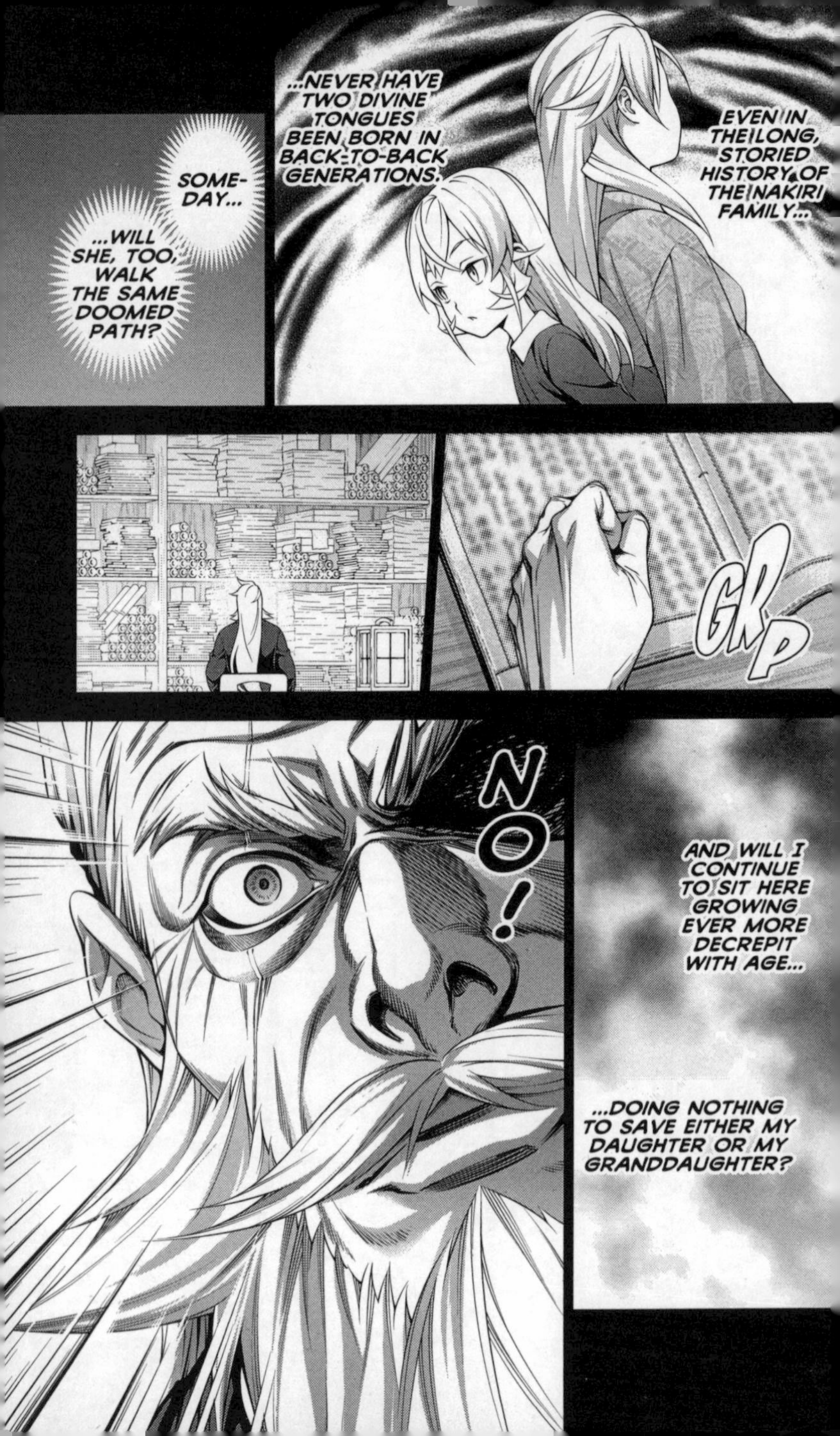
EVEN IN THE LONG, STORIED HISTORY OF THE NAKIRI FAMILY...
...NEVER HAVE TWO DIVINE TONGUES BEEN BORN IN BACK-TO-BACK GENERATIONS.
SOME-DAY...
...WILL SHE, TOO, WALK THE SAME DOOMED PATH?
GRP
AND WILL I CONTINUE TO SIT HERE GROWING EVER MORE DECREPIT WITH AGE...
...DOING NOTHING TO SAVE EITHER MY DAUGHTER OR MY GRANDDAUGHTER?
NO!

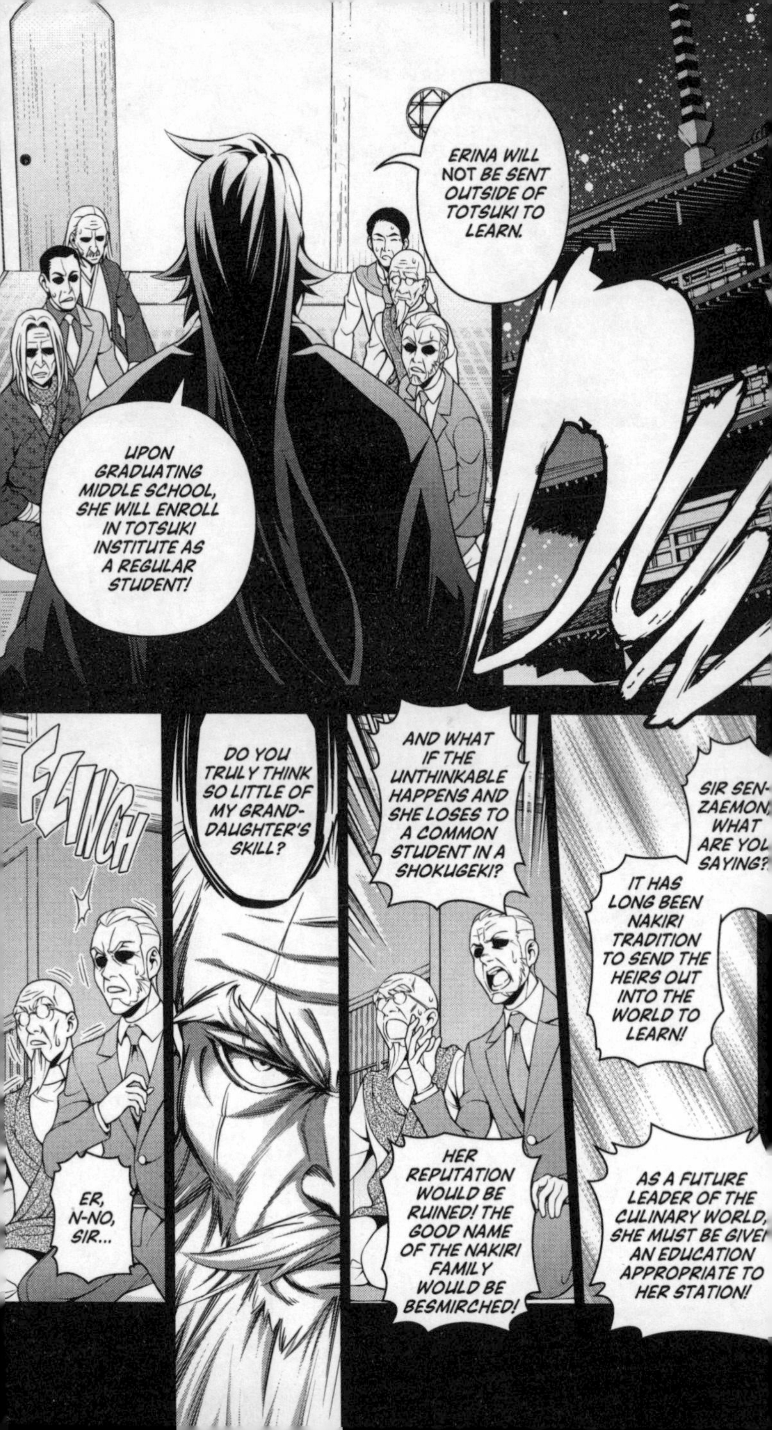
DUN
ERINA WILL NOT BE SENT OUTSIDE OF TOTSUKI TO LEARN.
UPON GRADUATING MIDDLE SCHOOL, SHE WILL ENROLL IN TOTSUKI INSTITUTE AS A REGULAR STUDENT!
SIR SEN-ZAEMON, WHAT ARE YOU SAYING?
IT HAS LONG BEEN NAKIRI TRADITION TO SEND THE HEIRS OUT INTO THE WORLD TO LEARN!
AS A FUTURE LEADER OF THE CULINARY WORLD, SHE MUST BE GIVEN AN EDUCATION APPROPRIATE TO HER STATION!
AND WHAT IF THE UNTHINKABLE HAPPENS AND SHE LOSES TO A COMMON STUDENT IN A SHOKUGEKI?
HER REPUTATION WOULD BE RUINED! THE GOOD NAME OF THE NAKIRI FAMILY WOULD BE BESMIRCHED!
DO YOU TRULY THINK SO LITTLE OF MY GRAND-DAUGHTER'S SKILL?
FLINCH
ER, N-NO, SIR...

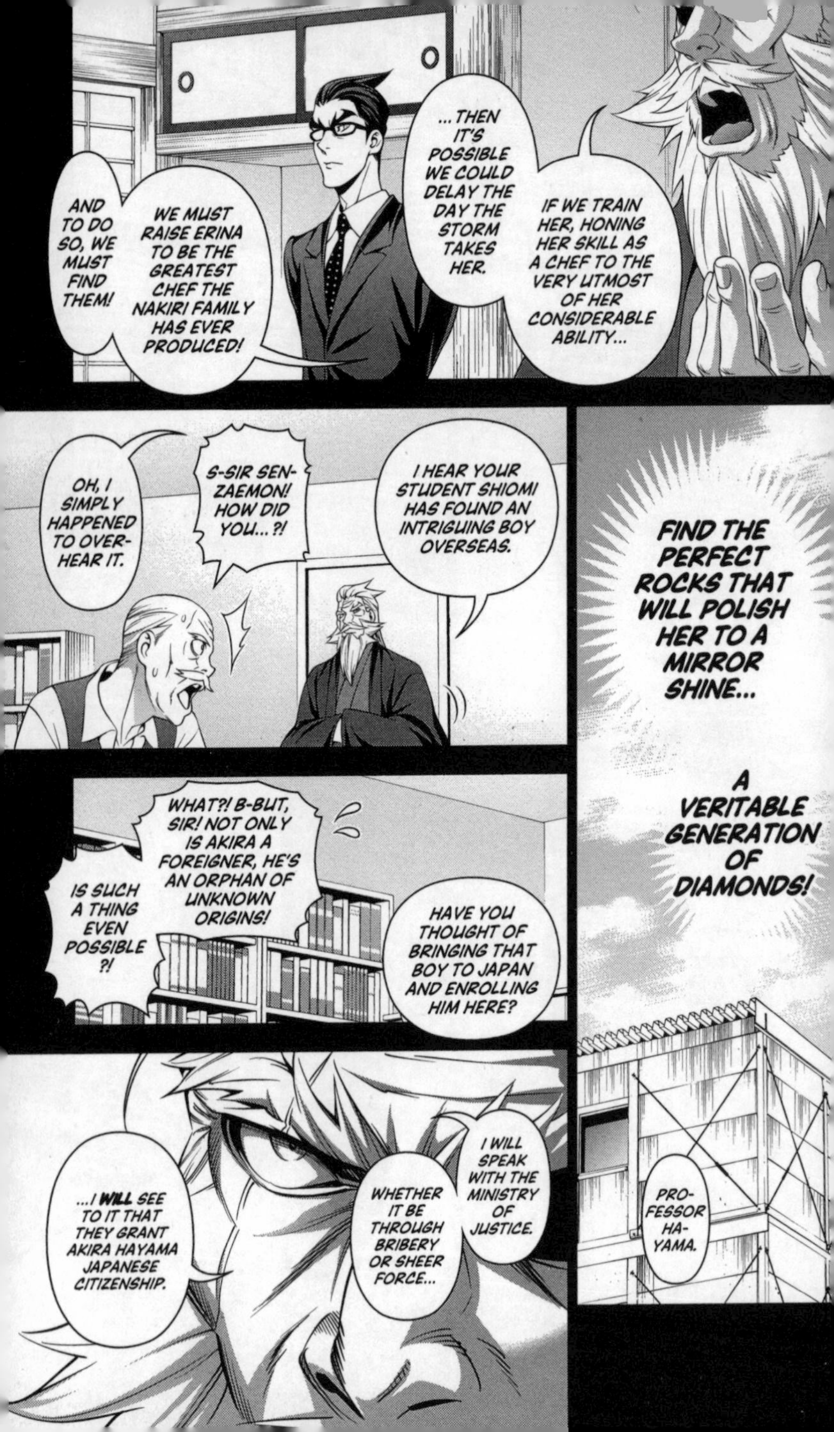
IF WE TRAIN HER, HONING HER SKILL AS A CHEF TO THE VERY UTMOST OF HER CONSIDERABLE ABILITY...
...THEN IT'S POSSIBLE WE COULD DELAY THE DAY THE STORM TAKES HER.
WE MUST RAISE ERINA TO BE THE GREATEST CHEF THE NAKIRI FAMILY HAS EVER PRODUCED!
AND TO DO SO, WE MUST FIND THEM!
FIND THE PERFECT ROCKS THAT WILL POLISH HER TO A MIRROR SHINE...
A VERITABLE GENERATION OF DIAMONDS!
PRO-FESSOR HA-YAMA.
I HEAR YOUR STUDENT SHIOMI HAS FOUND AN INTRIGUING BOY OVERSEAS.
S-SIR SEN-ZAEMON! HOW DID YOU...?!
OH, I SIMPLY HAPPENED TO OVER-HEAR IT.
HAVE YOU THOUGHT OF BRINGING THAT BOY TO JAPAN AND ENROLLING HIM HERE?
WHAT?! B-BUT, SIR! NOT ONLY IS AKIRA A FOREIGNER, HE'S AN ORPHAN OF UNKNOWN ORIGINS!
IS SUCH A THING EVEN POSSIBLE ?!
I WILL SPEAK WITH THE MINISTRY OF JUSTICE.
WHETHER IT BE THROUGH BRIBERY OR SHEER FORCE...
...I **WILL** SEE TO IT THAT THEY GRANT AKIRA HAYAMA JAPANESE CITIZENSHIP.

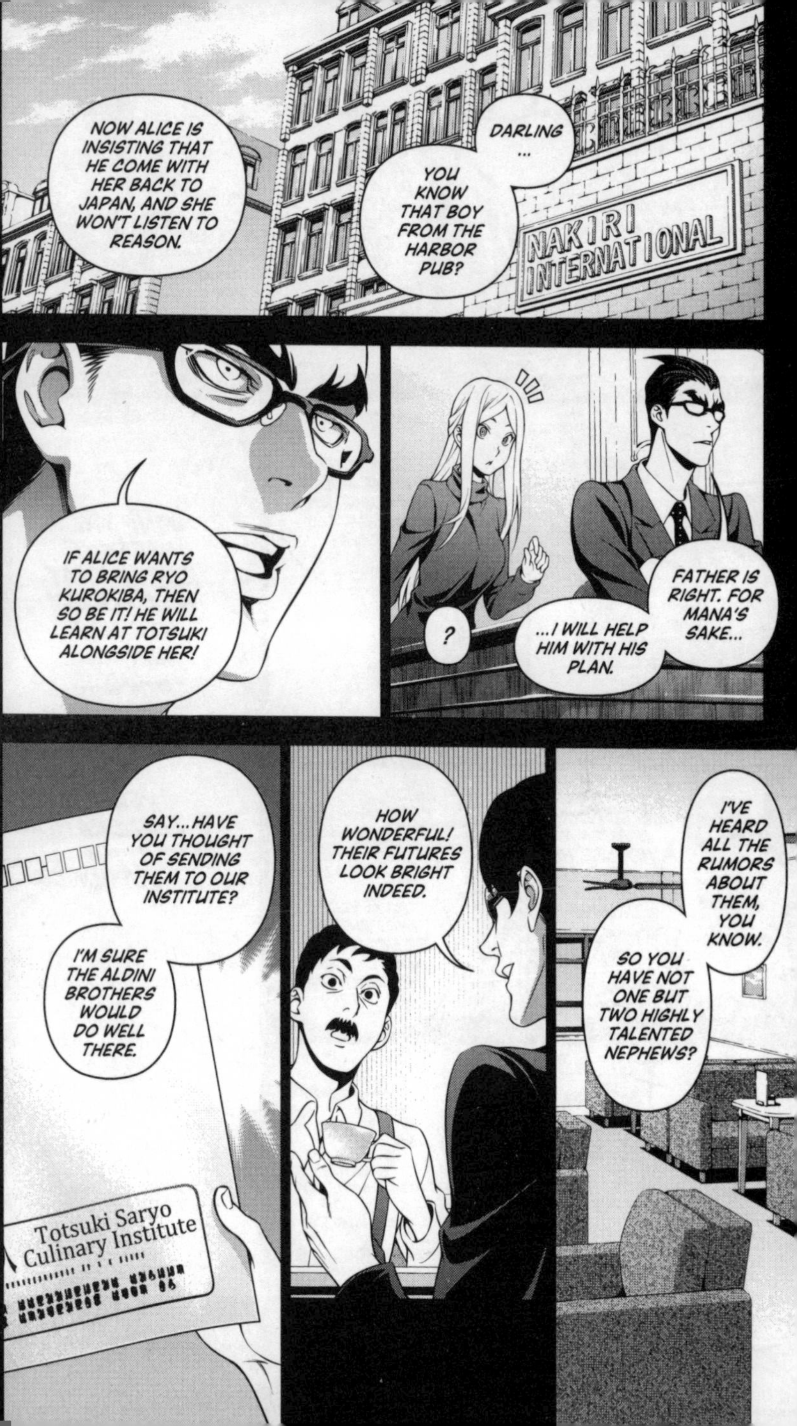
DARLING... YOU KNOW THAT BOY FROM THE HARBOR PUB?
NAKIRI INTERNATIONAL
NOW ALICE IS INSISTING THAT HE COME WITH HER BACK TO JAPAN, AND SHE WON'T LISTEN TO REASON.
FATHER IS RIGHT. FOR MANA'S SAKE...
...I WILL HELP HIM WITH HIS PLAN.
?
IF ALICE WANTS TO BRING RYO KUROKIBA, THEN SO BE IT! HE WILL LEARN AT TOTSUKI ALONGSIDE HER!
I'VE HEARD ALL THE RUMORS ABOUT THEM, YOU KNOW.
SO YOU HAVE NOT ONE BUT TWO HIGHLY TALENTED NEPHEWS?
HOW WONDERFUL! THEIR FUTURES LOOK BRIGHT INDEED.
SAY...HAVE YOU THOUGHT OF SENDING THEM TO OUR INSTITUTE?
I'M SURE THE ALDINI BROTHERS WOULD DO WELL THERE.
Totsuki Saryo Culinary Institute

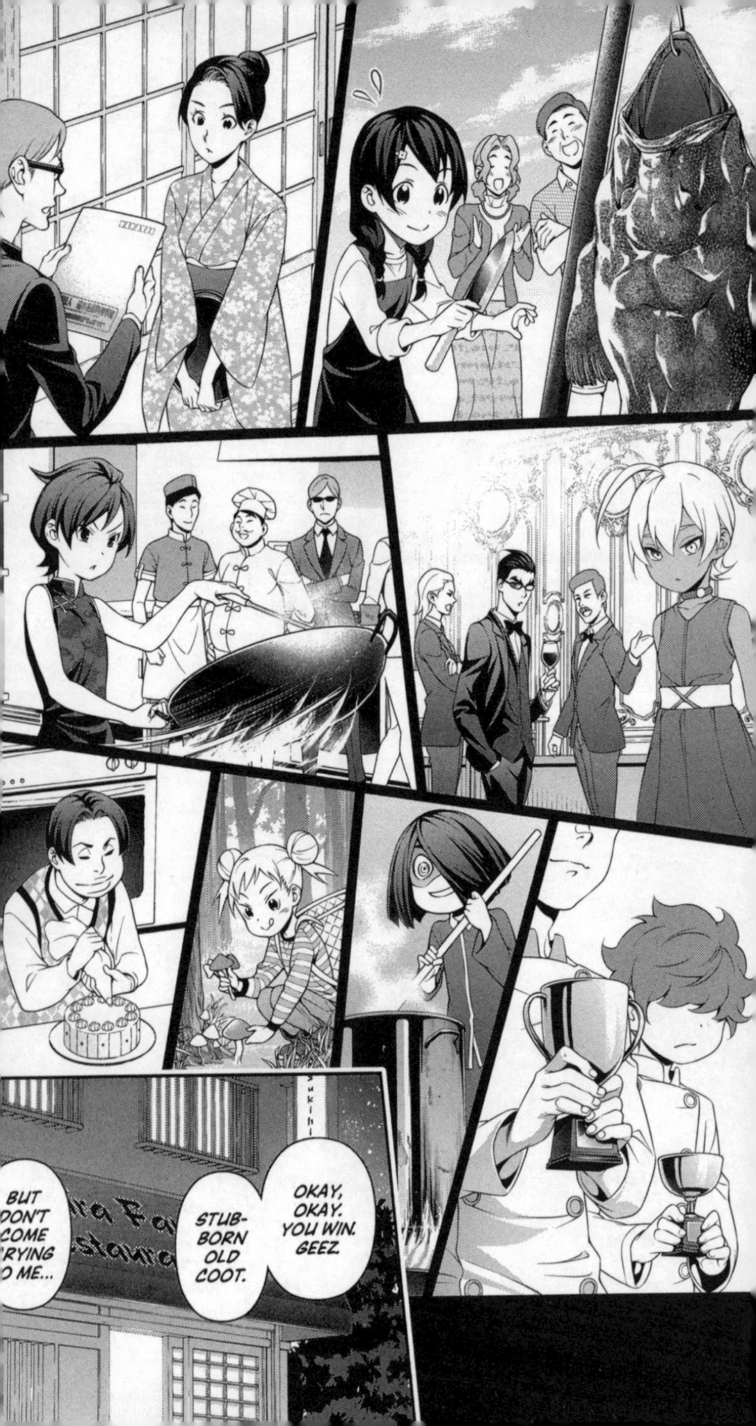
OKAY, OKAY. YOU WIN. GEEZ.
STUB-BORN OLD COOT.
BUT DON'T COME RYING O ME...

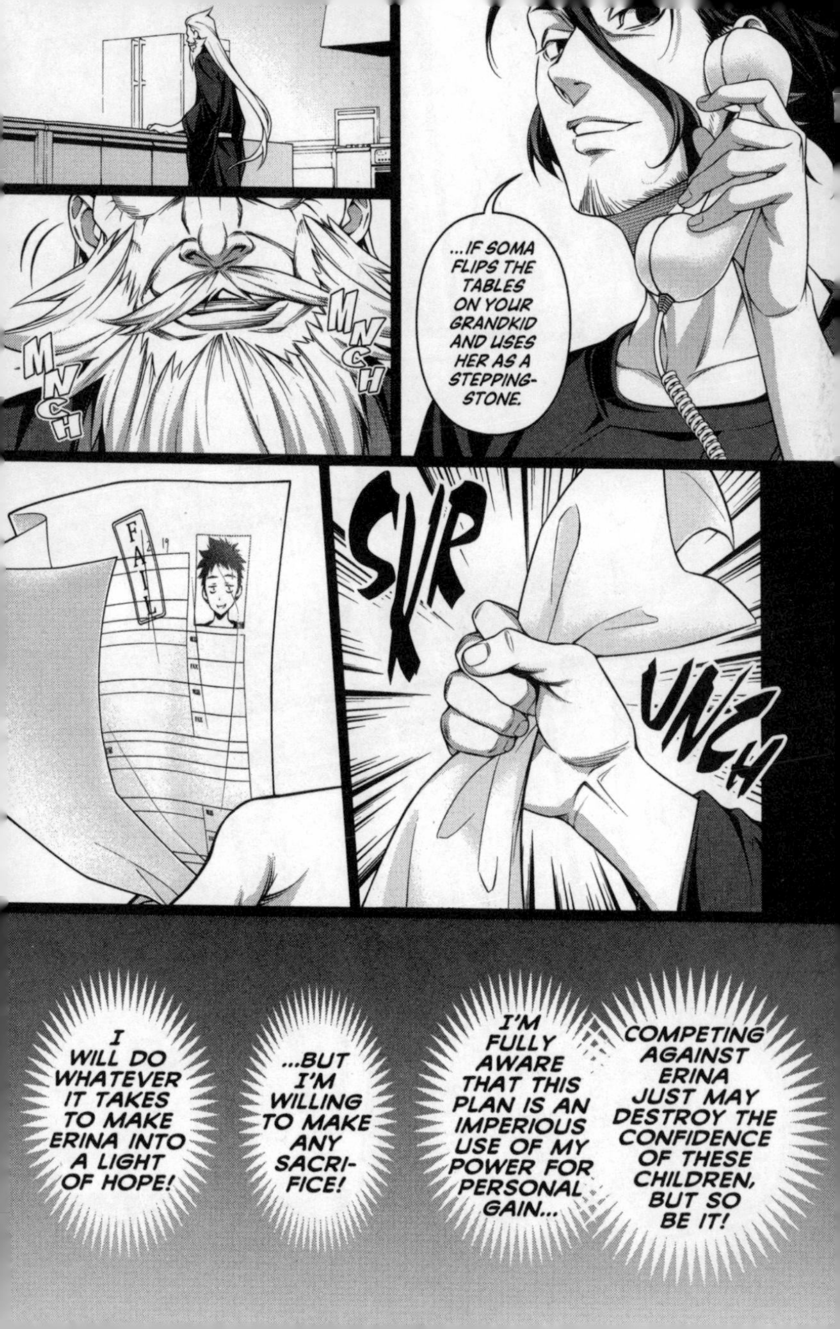
...IF SOMA FLIPS THE TABLES ON YOUR GRANDKID AND USES HER AS A STEPPING-STONE.
MNCH
MNCH
FAIL
SKR
UNCH
COMPETING AGAINST ERINA JUST MAY DESTROY THE CONFIDENCE OF THESE CHILDREN, BUT SO BE IT!
I'M FULLY AWARE THAT THIS PLAN IS AN IMPERIOUS USE OF MY POWER FOR PERSONAL GAIN...
...BUT I'M WILLING TO MAKE ANY SACRI-FICE!
I WILL DO WHATEVER IT TAKES TO MAKE ERINA INTO A LIGHT OF HOPE!

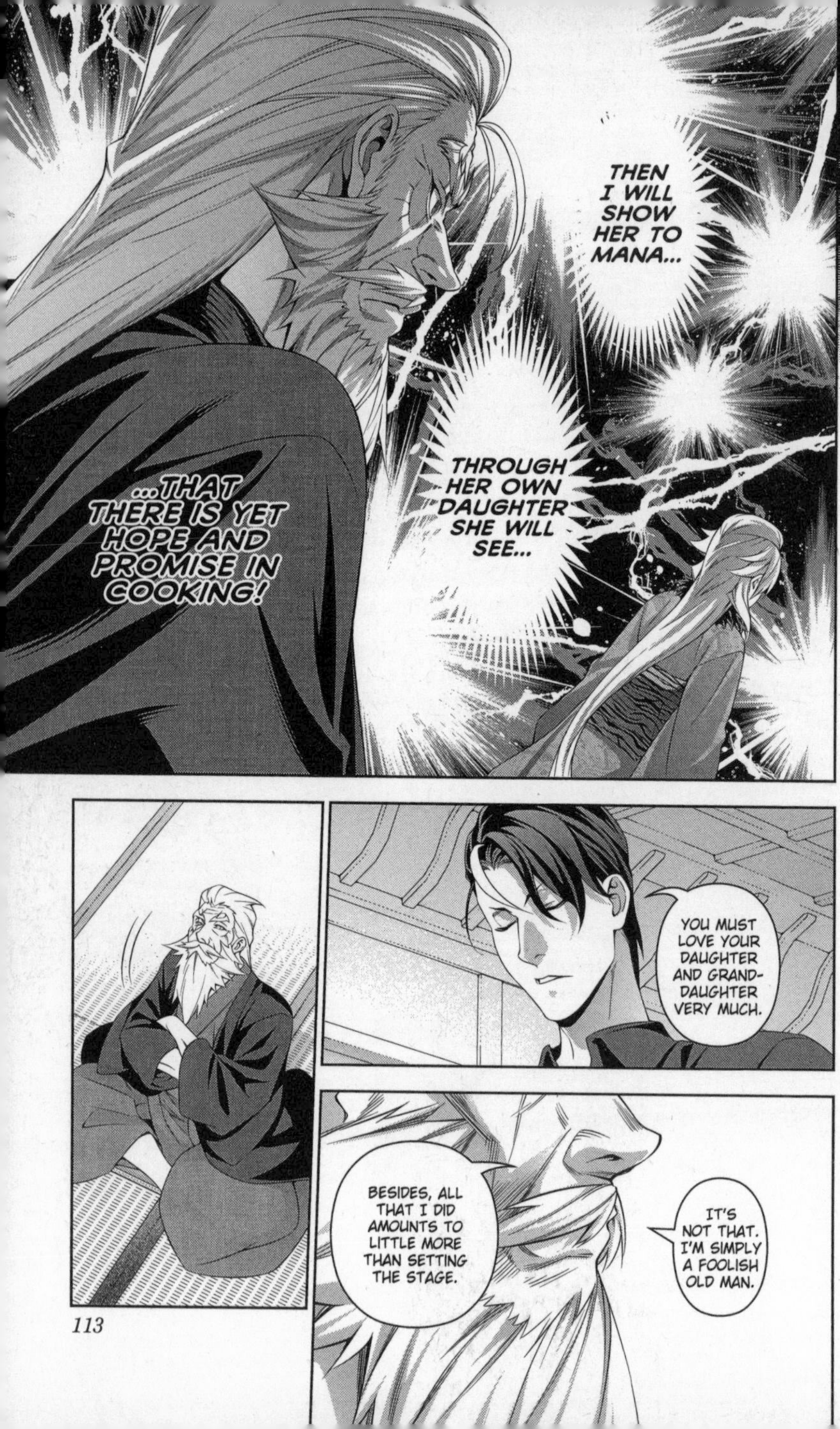
THEN I WILL SHOW HER TO MANA...
THROUGH HER OWN DAUGHTER SHE WILL SEE...
...THAT THERE IS YET HOPE AND PROMISE IN COOKING!
YOU MUST LOVE YOUR DAUGHTER AND GRAND-DAUGHTER VERY MUCH.
IT'S NOT THAT. I'M SIMPLY A FOOLISH OLD MAN.
BESIDES, ALL THAT I DID AMOUNTS TO LITTLE MORE THAN SETTING THE STAGE.

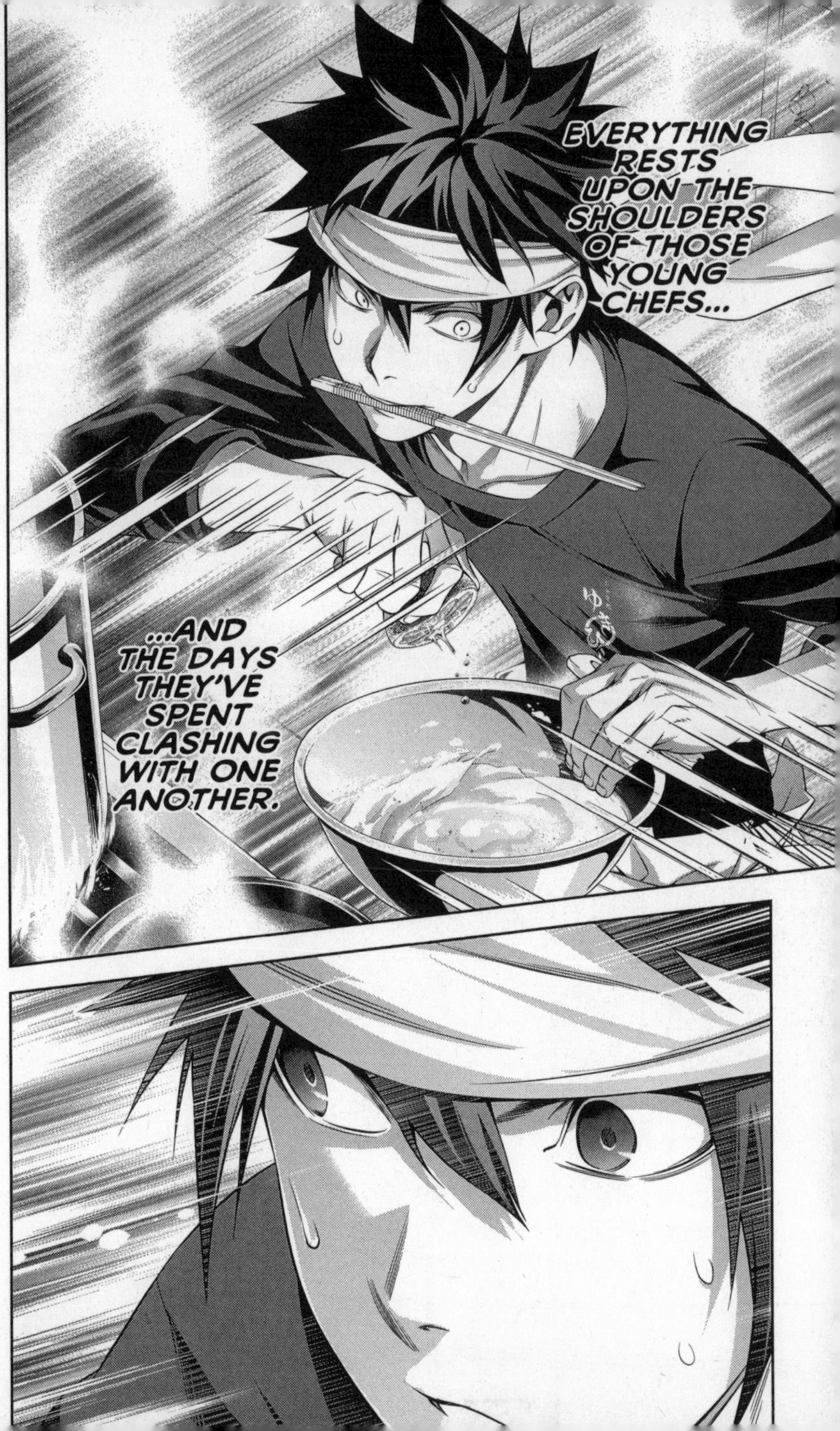
EVERYTHING RESTS UPON THE SHOULDERS OF THOSE YOUNG CHEFS...
...AND THE DAYS THEY'VE SPENT CLASHING WITH ONE ANOTHER.

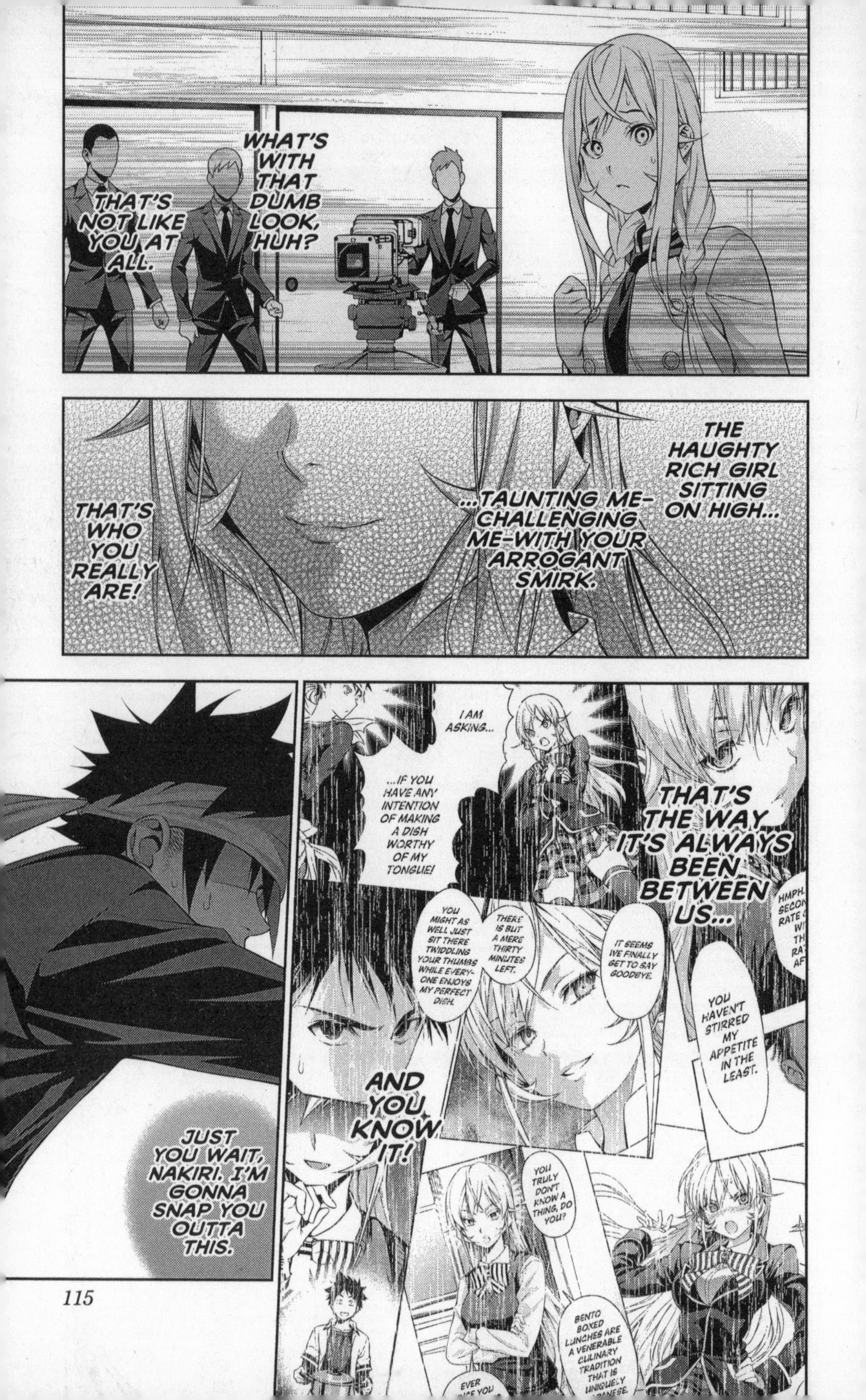
WHAT'S WITH THAT DUMB LOOK, HUH?
THAT'S NOT LIKE YOU AT ALL.
THE HAUGHTY RICH GIRL SITTING ON HIGH...
...TAUNTING ME—CHALLENGING ME—WITH YOUR ARROGANT SMIRK.
THAT'S WHO YOU REALLY ARE!
I AM ASKING...
...IF YOU HAVE ANY INTENTION OF MAKING A DISH WORTHY OF MY TONGUE!
THAT'S THE WAY IT'S ALWAYS BEEN BETWEEN US...
IT SEEMS WE FINALLY GET TO SAY GOODBYE.
THERE IS BUT A MERE THIRTY MINUTES LEFT.
YOU MIGHT AS WELL JUST SIT THERE TWIDDLING YOUR THUMBS WHILE EVERY-ONE ENJOYS MY PERFECT DISH.
YOU HAVEN'T STIRRED MY APPETITE IN THE LEAST.
AND YOU KNOW IT!
YOU TRULY DON'T KNOW A THING, DO YOU?
BENTO BOXED LUNCHES ARE A VENERABLE CULINARY TRADITION THAT IS UNIQUELY
JUST YOU WAIT, NAKIRI. I'M GONNA SNAP YOU OUTTA THIS.

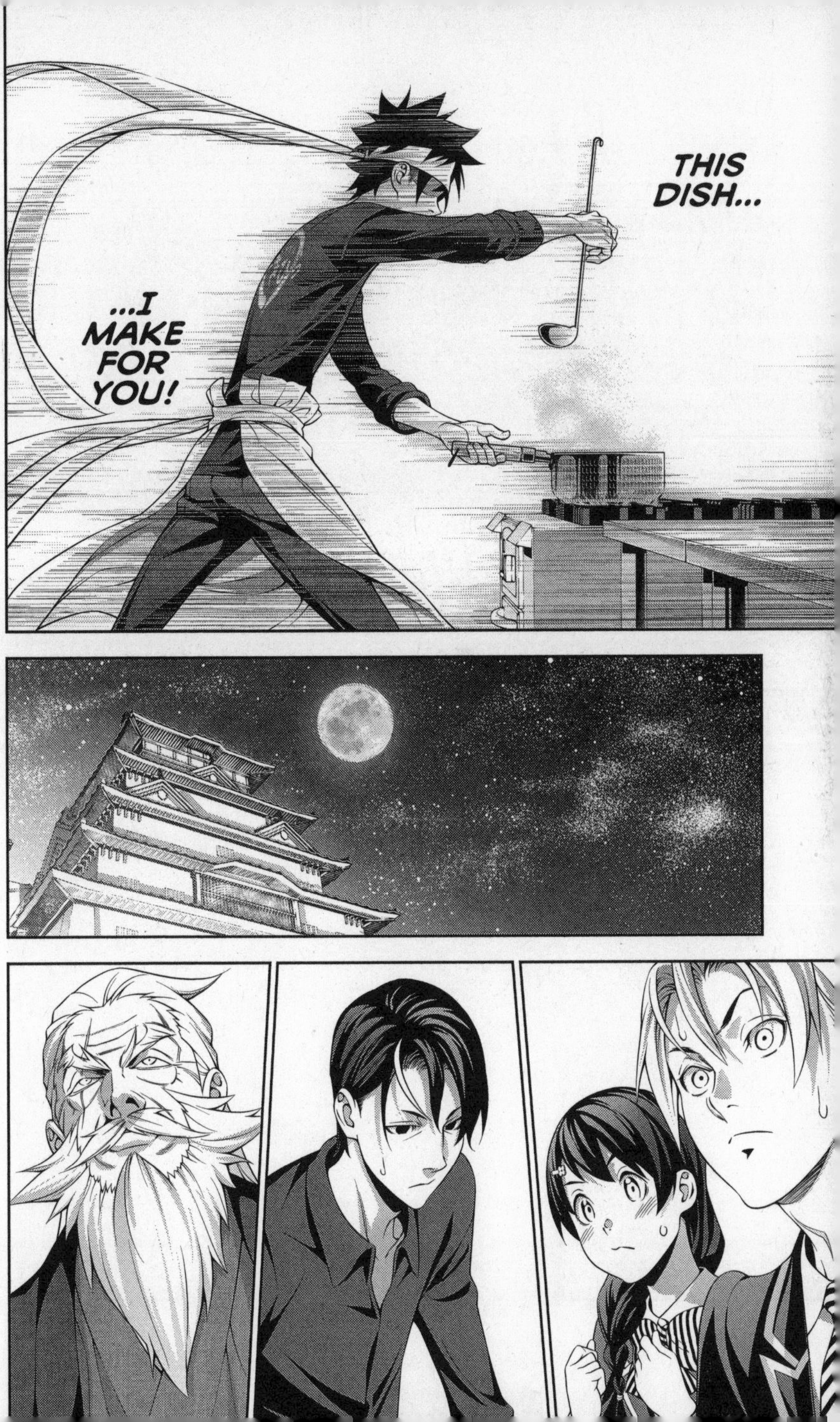
THIS DISH...
...I MAKE FOR YOU!

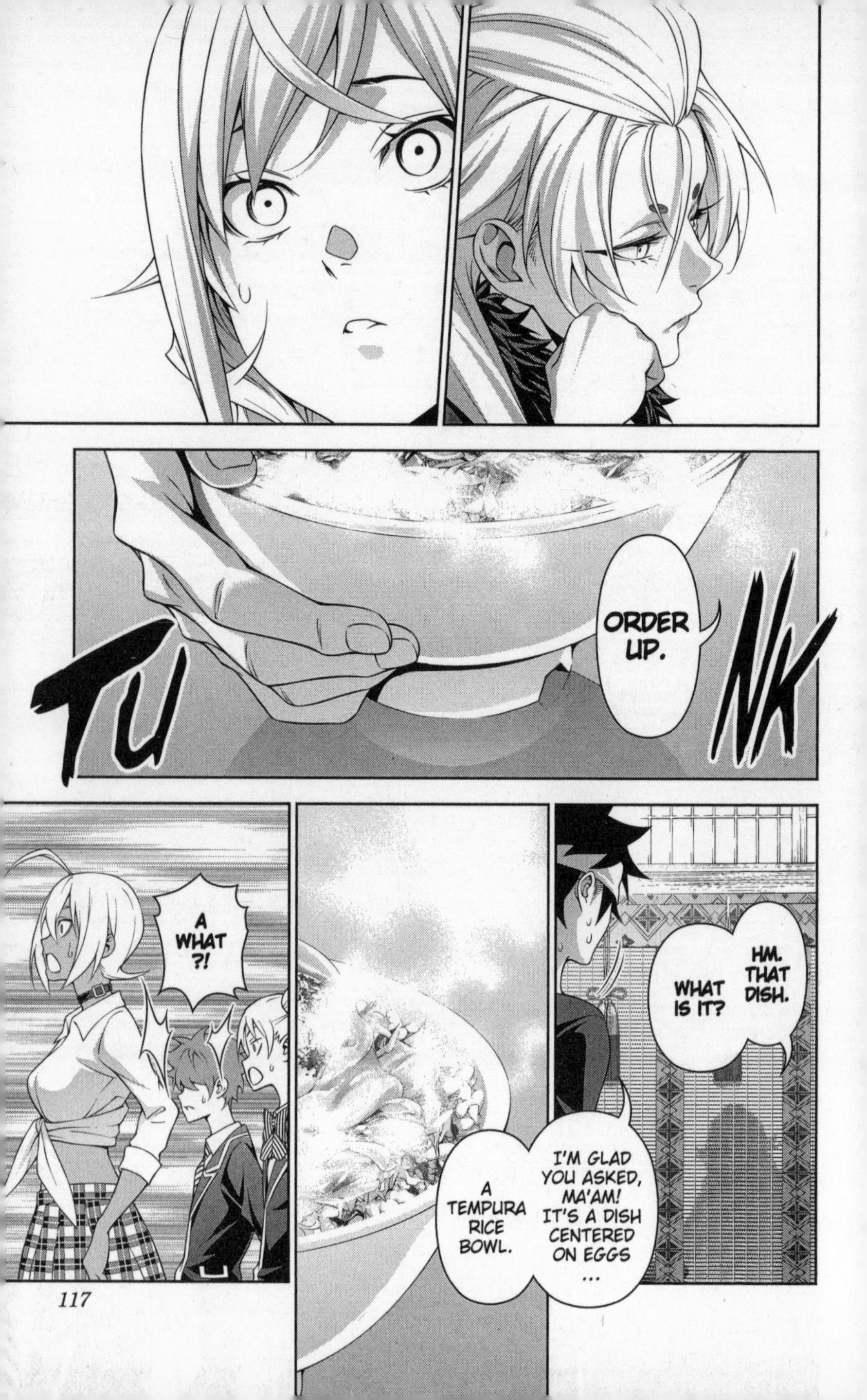
ORDER UP.
TUNK
HM. THAT DISH.
WHAT IS IT?
I'M GLAD YOU ASKED, MA'AM! IT'S A DISH CENTERED ON EGGS...
A TEMPURA RICE BOWL.
A WHAT?!

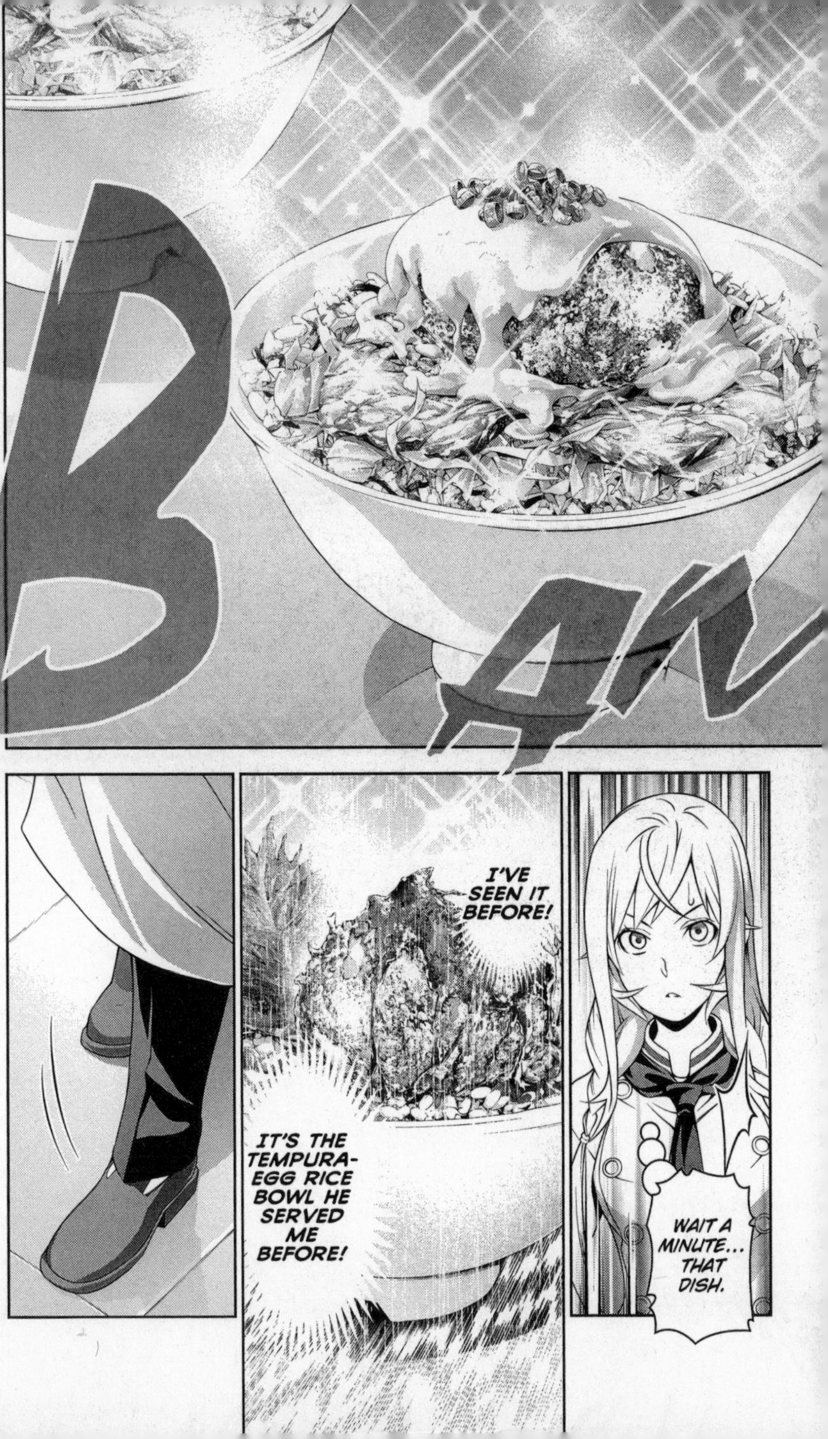
BAN
WAIT A MINUTE... THAT DISH.
I'VE SEEN IT BEFORE!
IT'S THE TEMPURA-EGG RICE BOWL HE SERVED ME BEFORE!

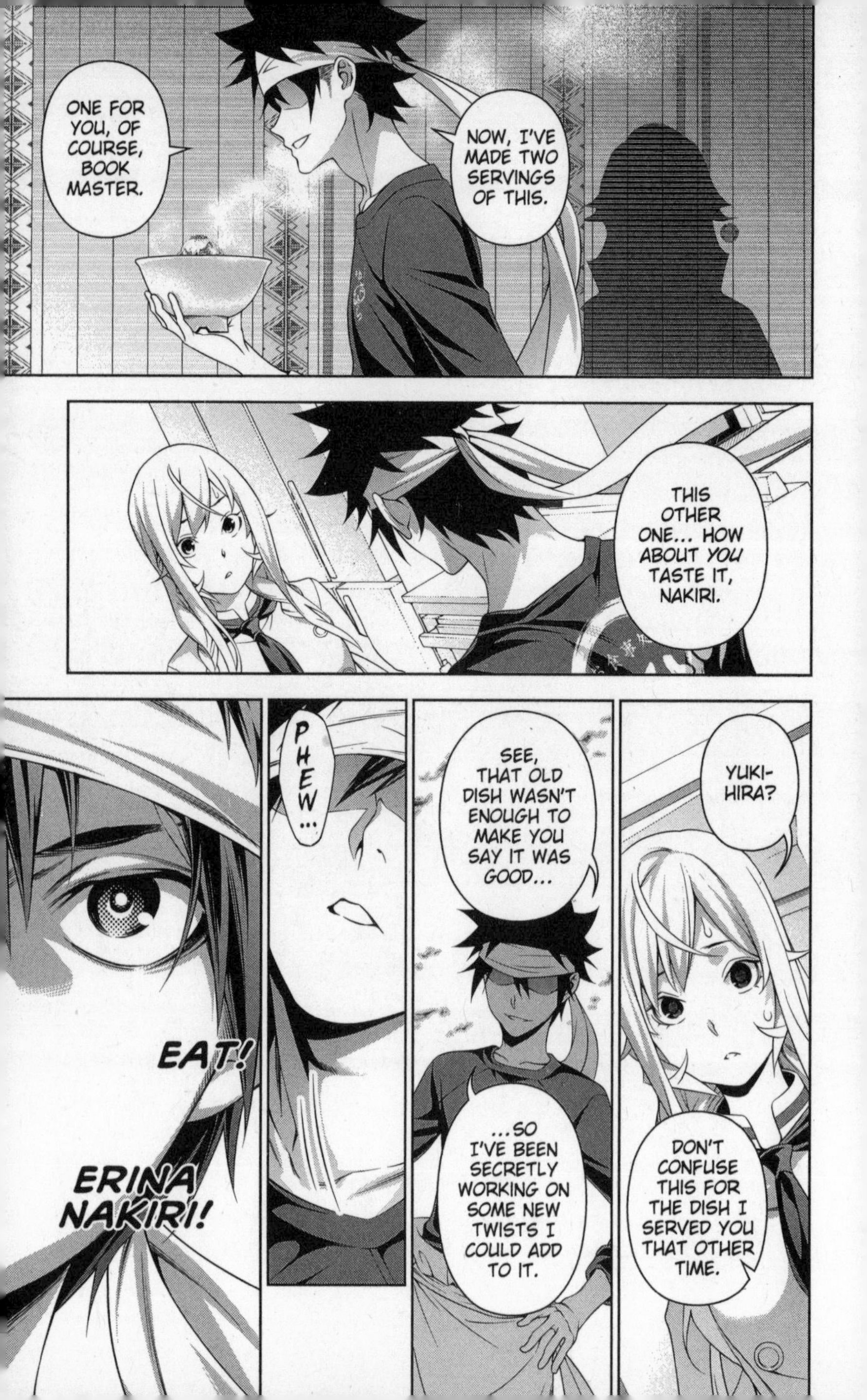
NOW, I'VE MADE TWO SERVINGS OF THIS.
ONE FOR YOU, OF COURSE, BOOK MASTER.
THIS OTHER ONE... HOW ABOUT *YOU* TASTE IT, NAKIRI.
YUKI-HIRA?
DON'T CONFUSE THIS FOR THE DISH I SERVED YOU THAT OTHER TIME.
SEE, THAT OLD DISH WASN'T ENOUGH TO MAKE YOU SAY IT WAS GOOD...
...SO I'VE BEEN SECRETLY WORKING ON SOME NEW TWISTS I COULD ADD TO IT.
PHEW...
EAT!
ERINA NAKIRI!

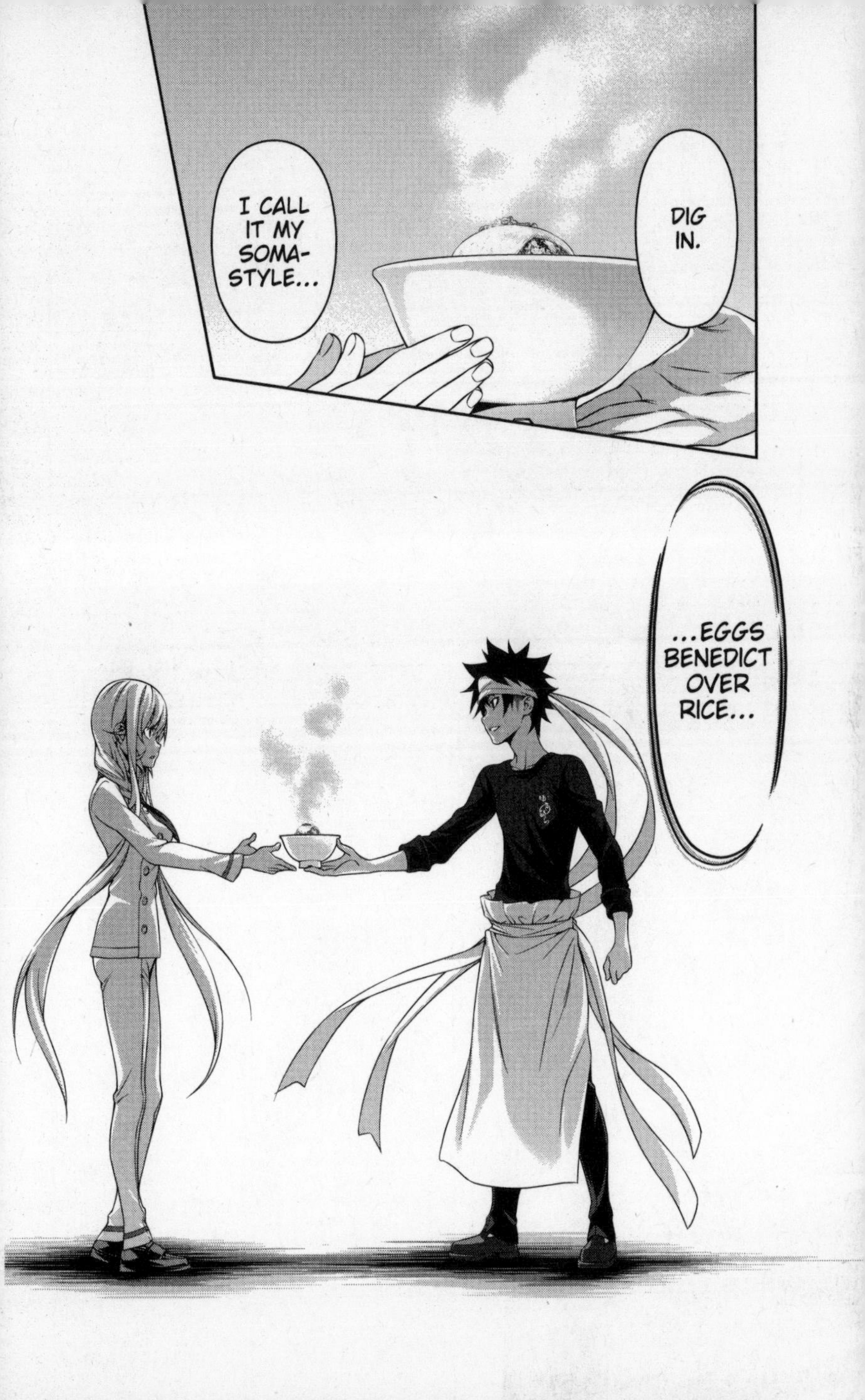
DIG IN.
I CALL IT MY SOMA-STYLE...
...EGGS BENEDICT OVER RICE...

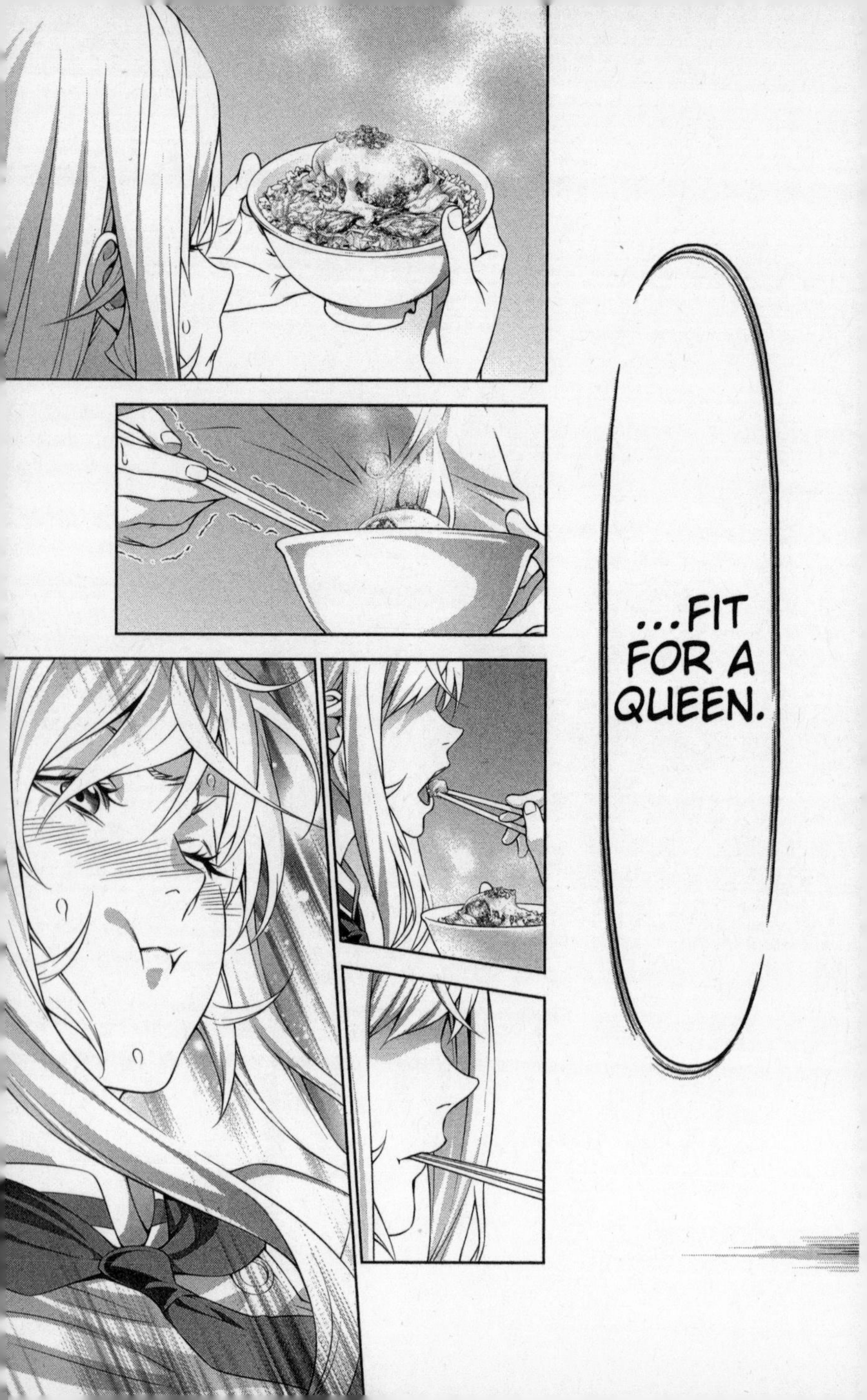
...FIT FOR A QUEEN.

315 SHOKUGEKI NO SOMA

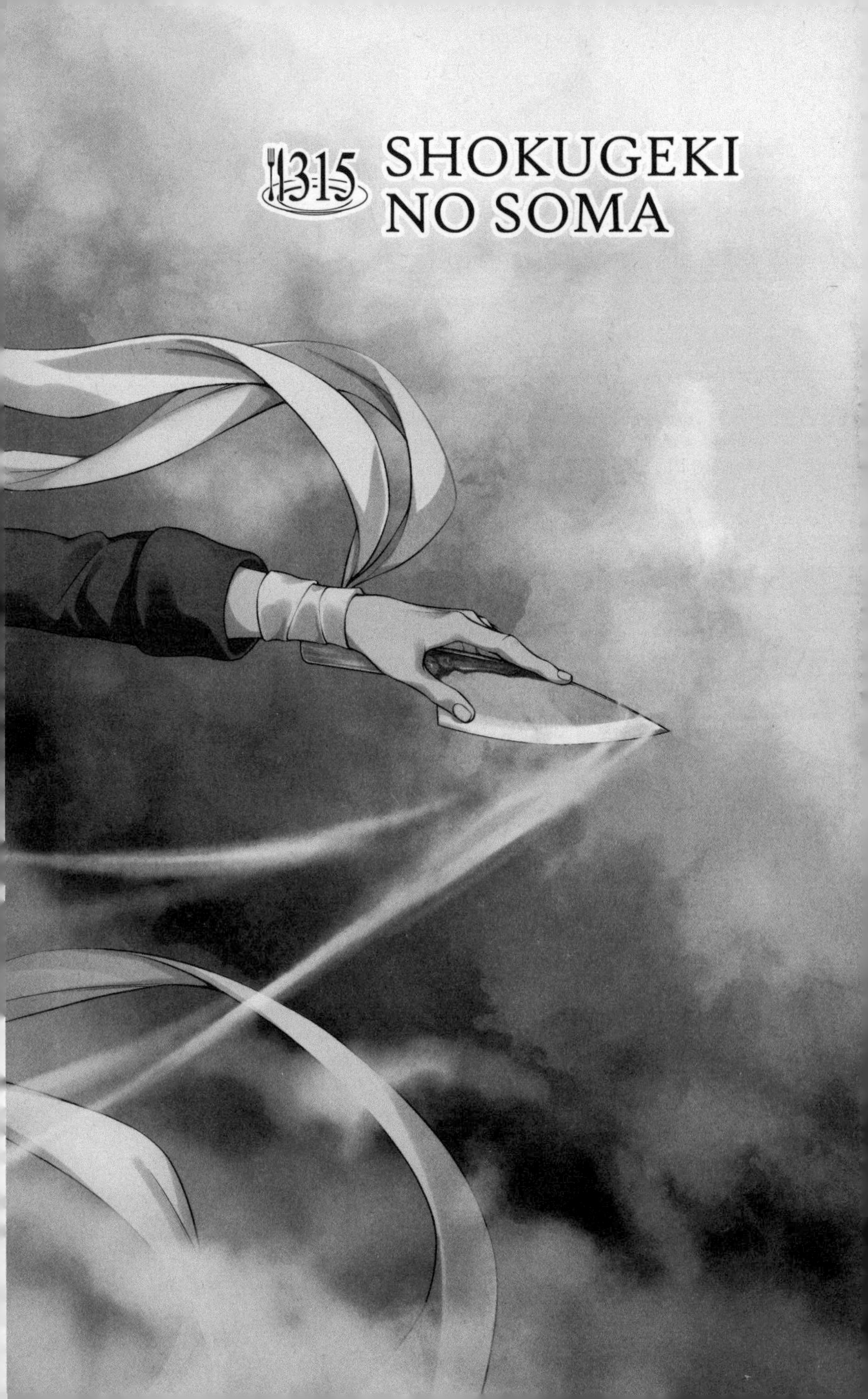

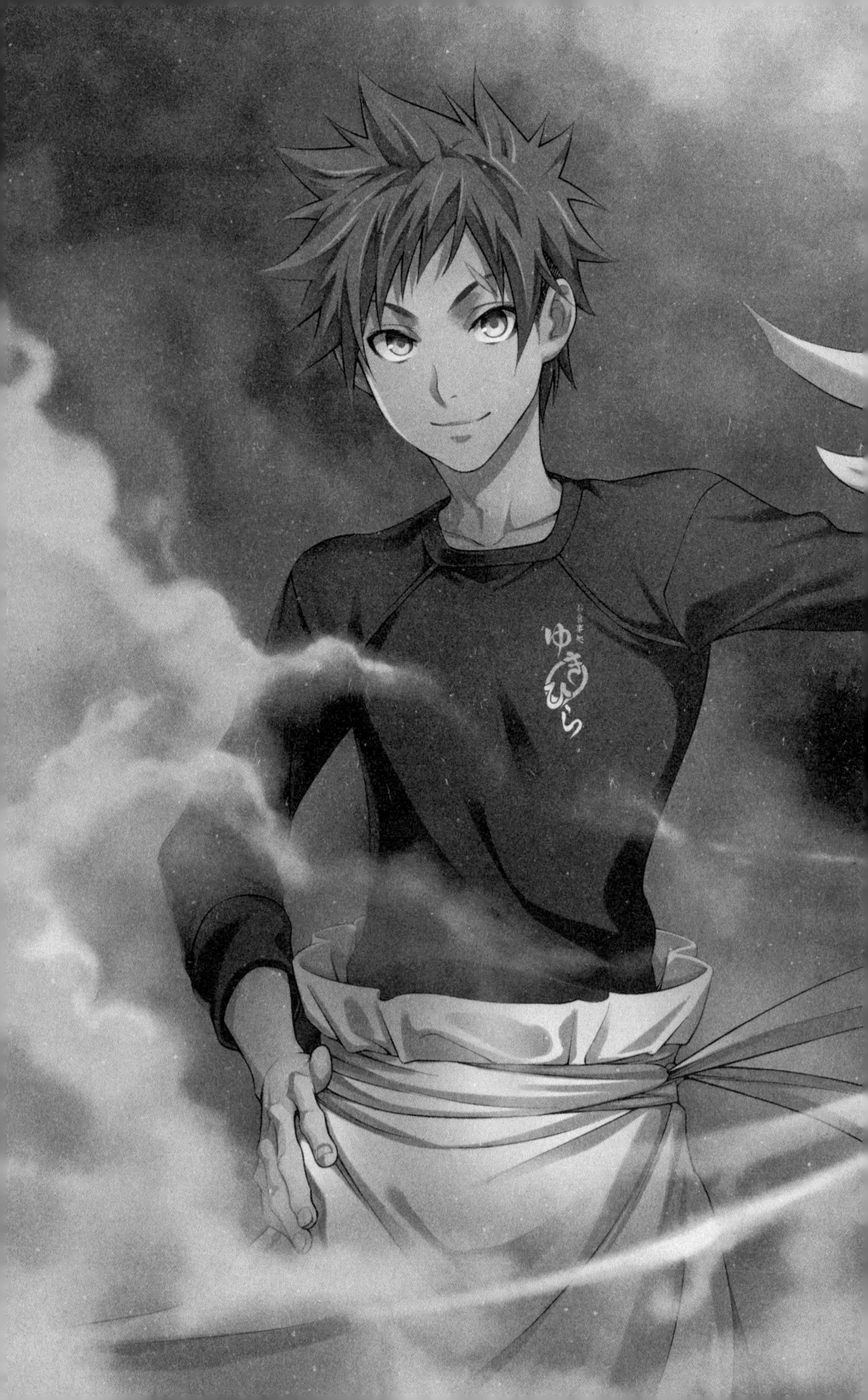
ゆきひら

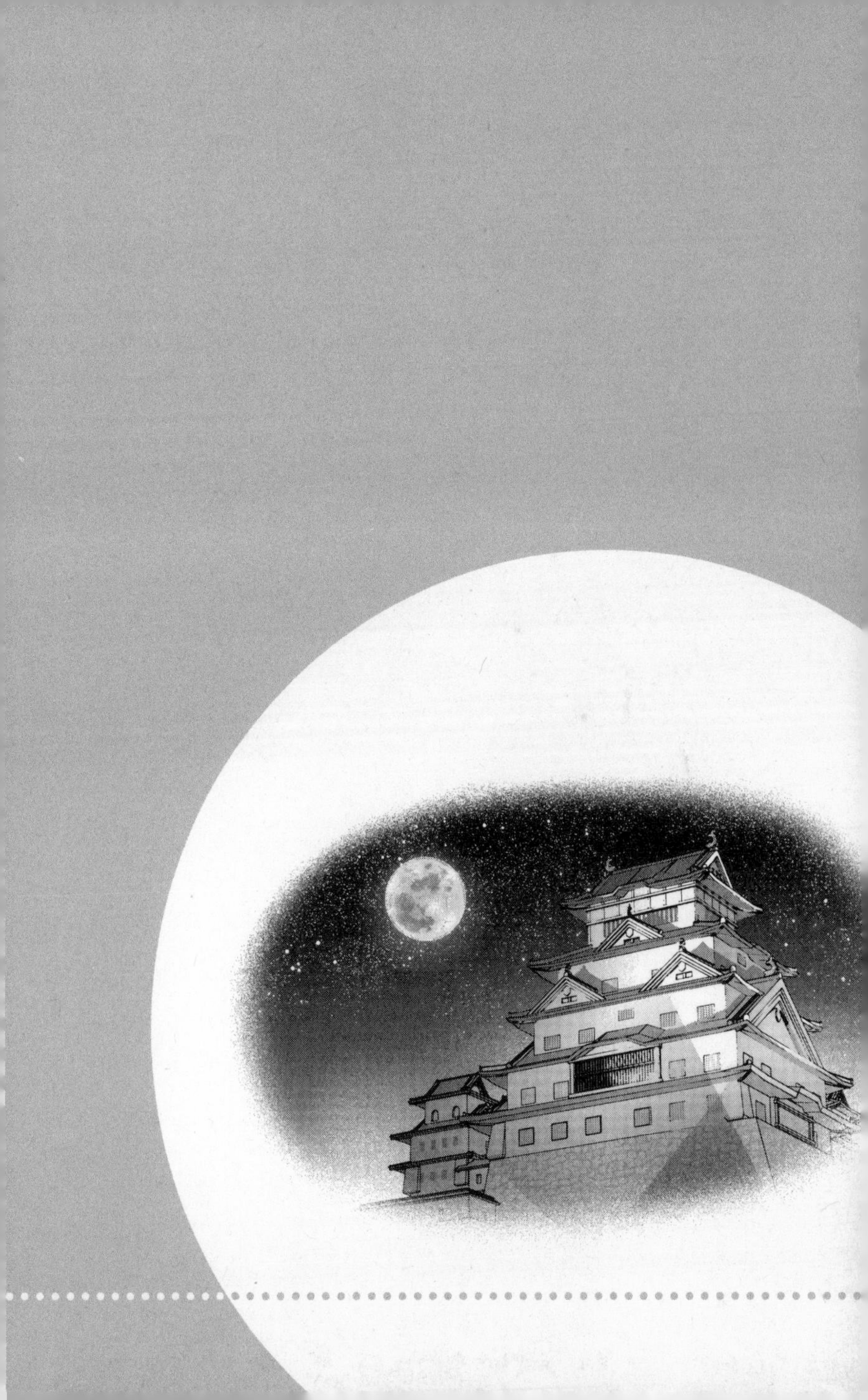

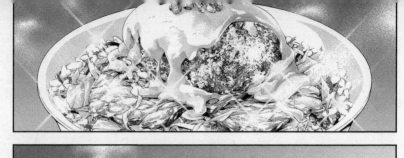

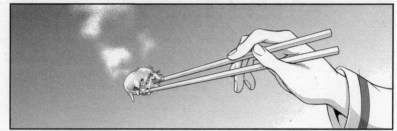

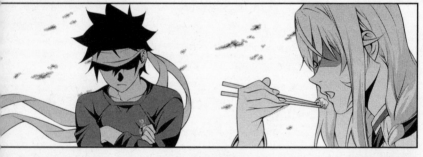

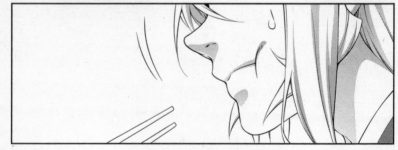

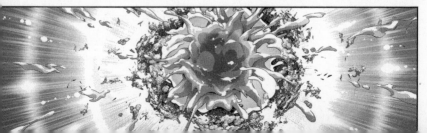

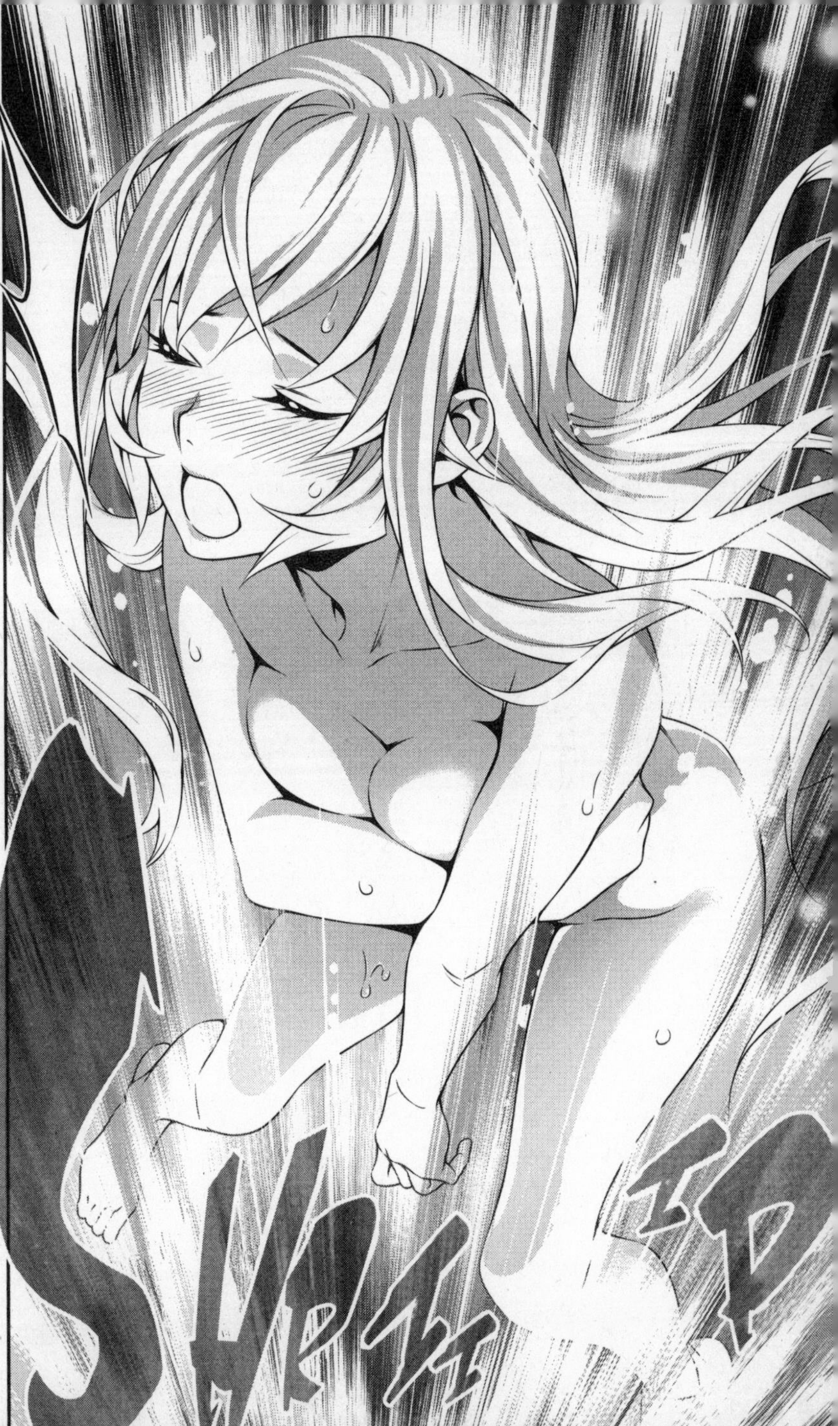

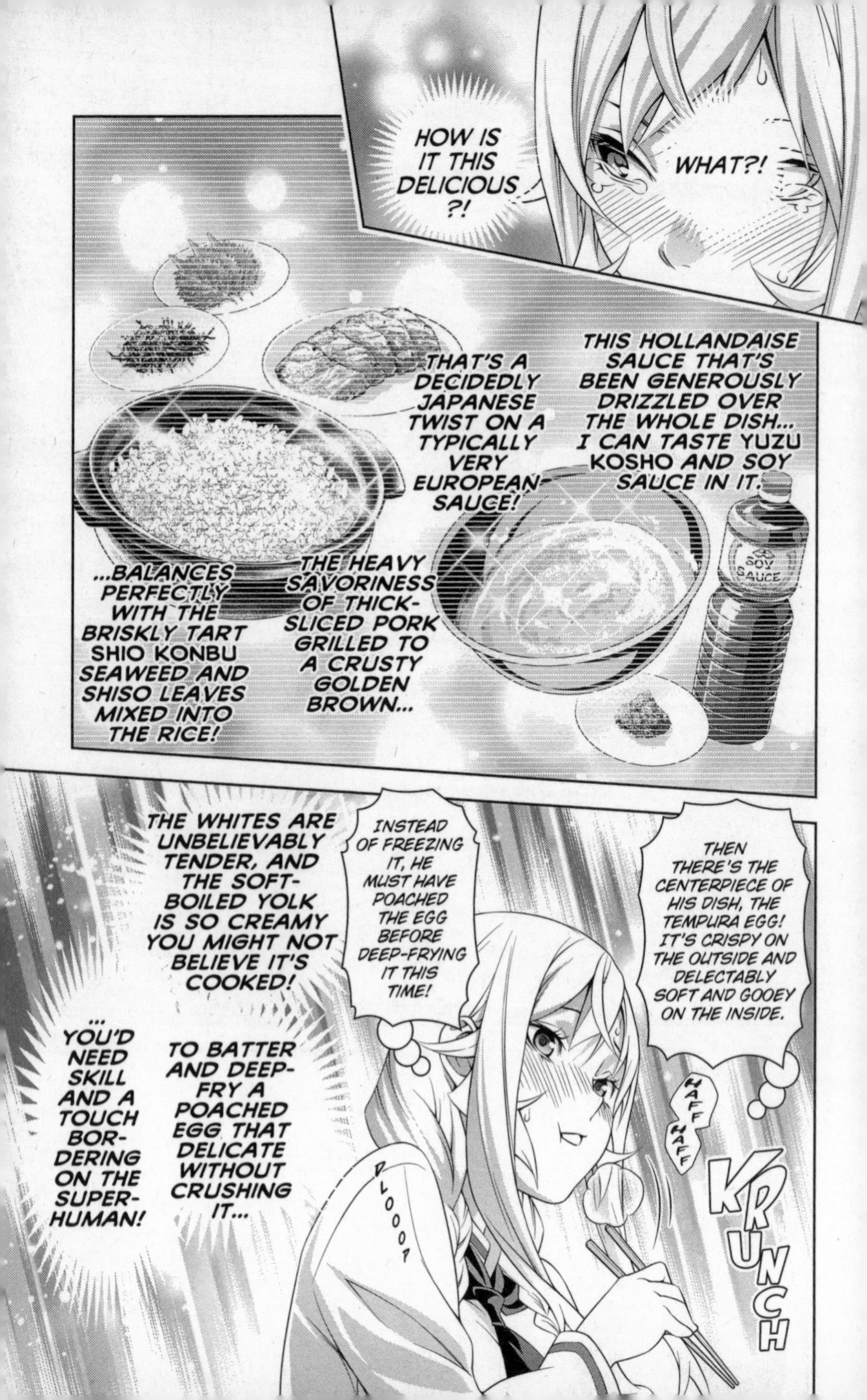
WHAT?!
HOW IS IT THIS DELICIOUS ?!
THIS HOLLANDAISE SAUCE THAT'S BEEN GENEROUSLY DRIZZLED OVER THE WHOLE DISH... I CAN TASTE YUZU KOSHO AND SOY SAUCE IN IT.
THAT'S A DECIDEDLY JAPANESE TWIST ON A TYPICALLY VERY EUROPEAN SAUCE!
SOY SAUCE
THE HEAVY SAVORINESS OF THICK-SLICED PORK GRILLED TO A CRUSTY GOLDEN BROWN...
...BALANCES PERFECTLY WITH THE BRISKLY TART SHIO KONBU SEAWEED AND SHISO LEAVES MIXED INTO THE RICE!
THEN THERE'S THE CENTERPIECE OF HIS DISH, THE TEMPURA EGG! IT'S CRISPY ON THE OUTSIDE AND DELECTABLY SOFT AND GOOEY ON THE INSIDE.
INSTEAD OF FREEZING IT, HE MUST HAVE POACHED THE EGG BEFORE DEEP-FRYING IT THIS TIME!
THE WHITES ARE UNBELIEVABLY TENDER, AND THE SOFT-BOILED YOLK IS SO CREAMY YOU MIGHT NOT BELIEVE IT'S COOKED!
HAFF HAFF
KRUNCH
TO BATTER AND DEEP-FRY A POACHED EGG THAT DELICATE WITHOUT CRUSHING IT...
...YOU'D NEED SKILL AND A TOUCH BOR-DERING ON THE SUPER-HUMAN!

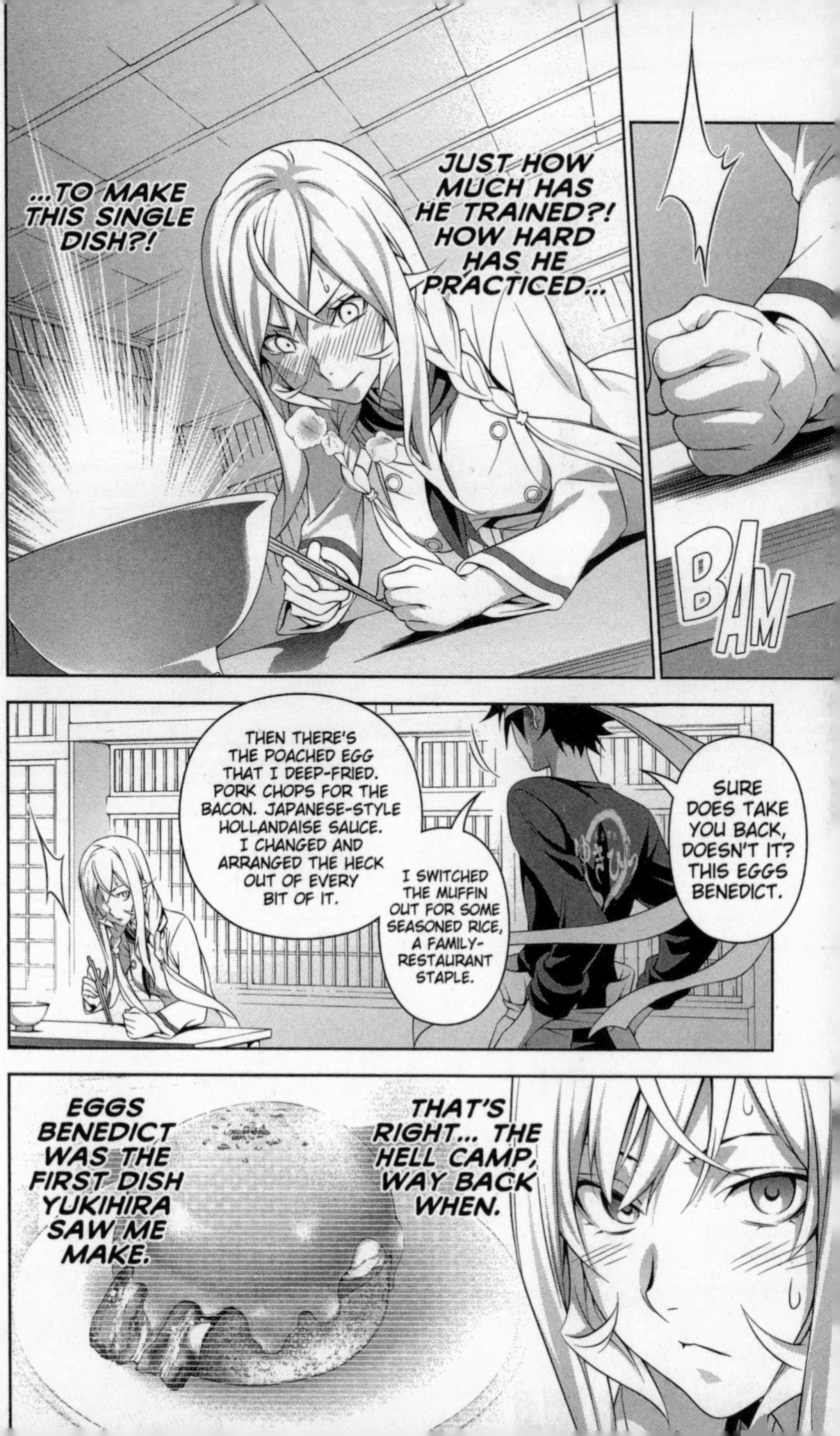
BAM
JUST HOW MUCH HAS HE TRAINED?! HOW HARD HAS HE PRACTICED...
...TO MAKE THIS SINGLE DISH?!
SURE DOES TAKE YOU BACK, DOESN'T IT? THIS EGGS BENEDICT.
I SWITCHED THE MUFFIN OUT FOR SOME SEASONED RICE, A FAMILY-RESTAURANT STAPLE.
THEN THERE'S THE POACHED EGG THAT I DEEP-FRIED. PORK CHOPS FOR THE BACON. JAPANESE-STYLE HOLLANDAISE SAUCE. I CHANGED AND ARRANGED THE HECK OUT OF EVERY BIT OF IT.
THAT'S RIGHT... THE HELL CAMP, WAY BACK WHEN.
EGGS BENEDICT WAS THE FIRST DISH YUKIHIRA SAW ME MAKE.

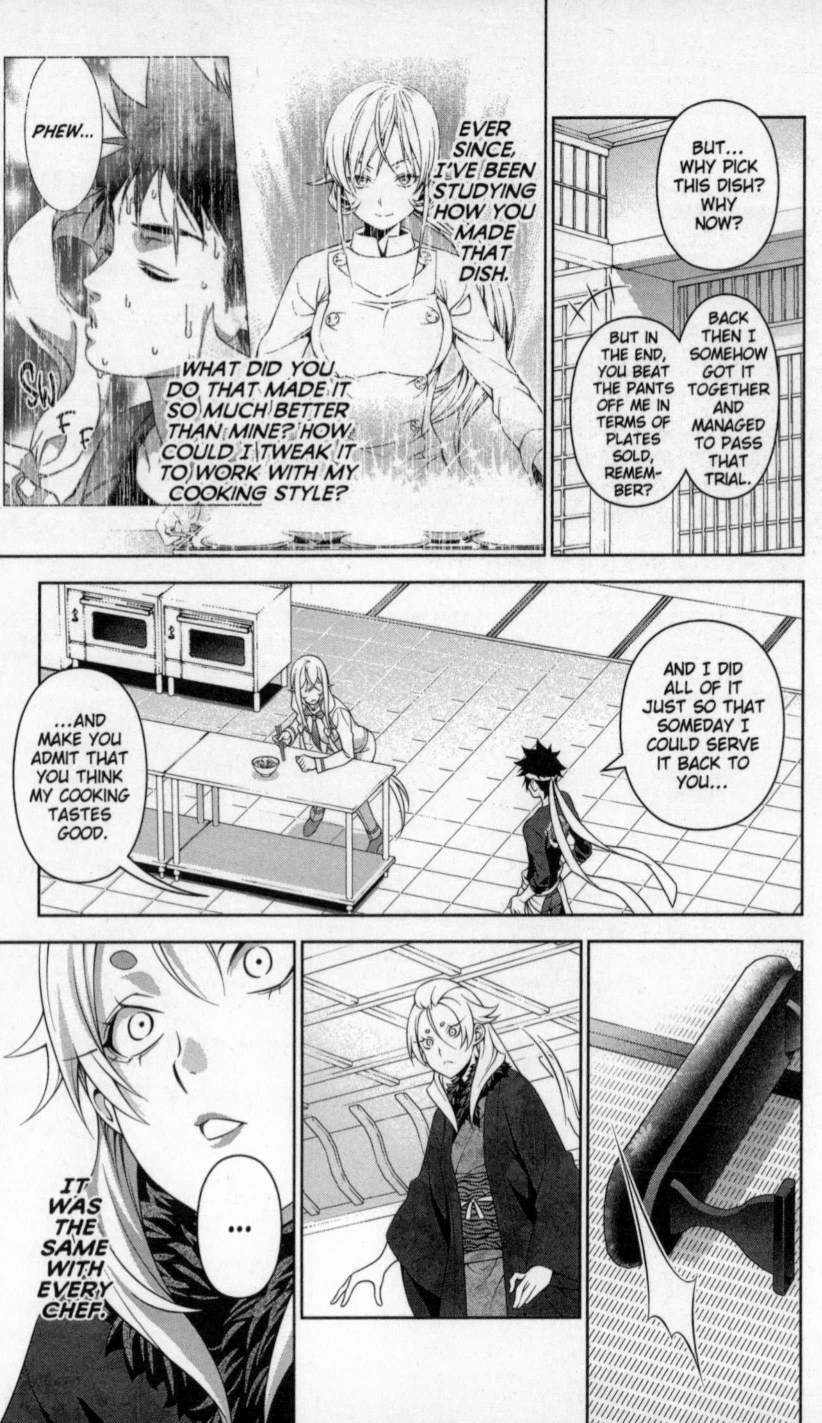
BUT... WHY PICK THIS DISH? WHY NOW?
BACK THEN I SOMEHOW GOT IT TOGETHER AND MANAGED TO PASS THAT TRIAL.
BUT IN THE END, YOU BEAT THE PANTS OFF ME IN TERMS OF PLATES SOLD, REMEMBER?
EVER SINCE, I'VE BEEN STUDYING HOW YOU MADE THAT DISH.
WHAT DID YOU DO THAT MADE IT SO MUCH BETTER THAN MINE? HOW COULD I TWEAK IT TO WORK WITH MY COOKING STYLE?
PHEW...
SWFF
AND I DID ALL OF IT JUST SO THAT SOMEDAY I COULD SERVE IT BACK TO YOU...
...AND MAKE YOU ADMIT THAT YOU THINK MY COOKING TASTES GOOD.
...
IT WAS THE SAME WITH EVERY CHEF.

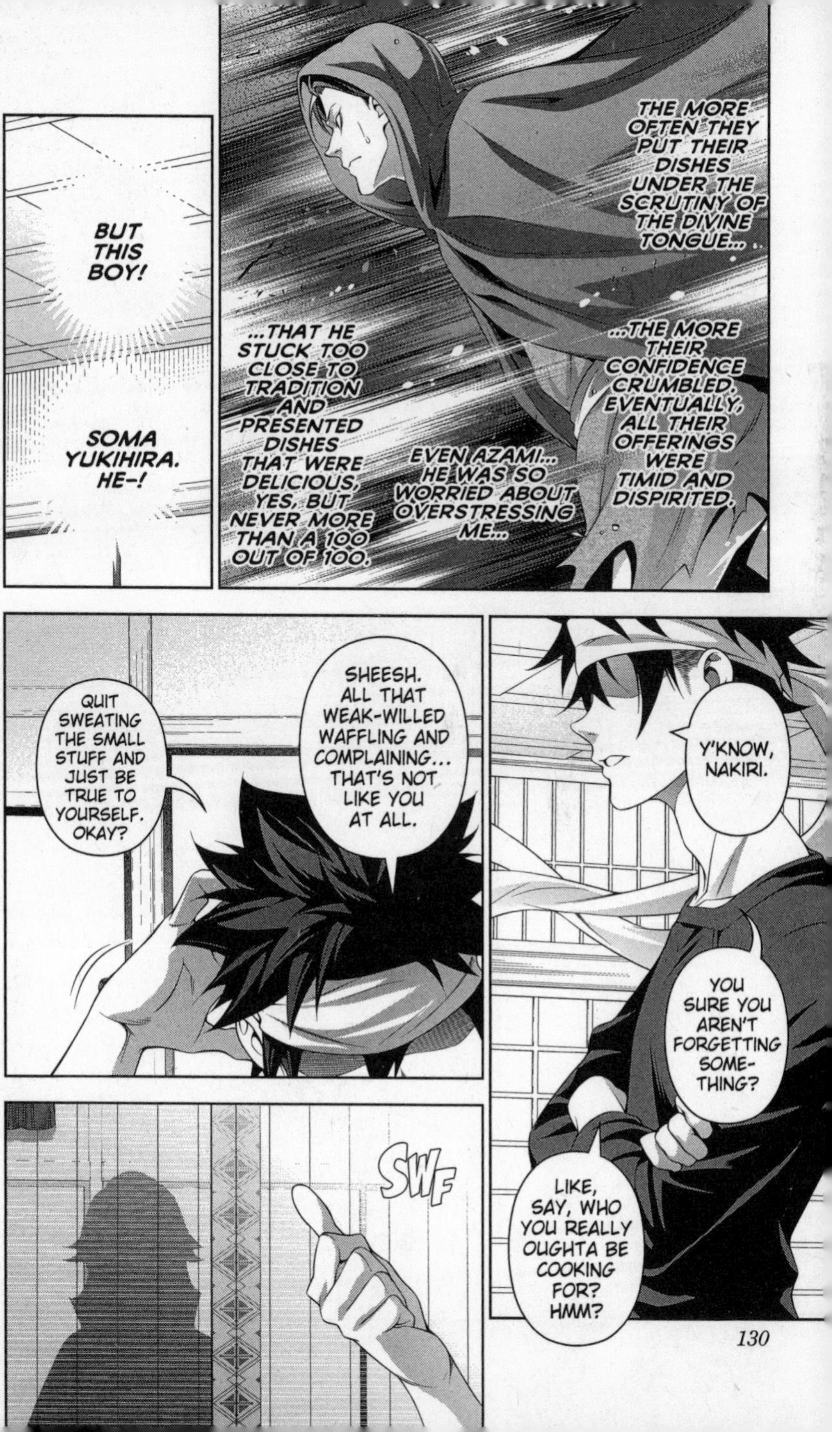
THE MORE OFTEN THEY PUT THEIR DISHES UNDER THE SCRUTINY OF THE DIVINE TONGUE...
...THE MORE THEIR CONFIDENCE CRUMBLED. EVENTUALLY, ALL THEIR OFFERINGS WERE TIMID AND DISPIRITED.
EVEN AZAMI... HE WAS SO WORRIED ABOUT OVERSTRESSING ME...
...THAT HE STUCK TOO CLOSE TO TRADITION AND PRESENTED DISHES THAT WERE DELICIOUS, YES, BUT NEVER MORE THAN A 100 OUT OF 100.
BUT THIS BOY!
SOMA YUKIHIRA. HE–!
Y'KNOW, NAKIRI.
YOU SURE YOU AREN'T FORGETTING SOME-THING?
LIKE, SAY, WHO YOU REALLY OUGHTA BE COOKING FOR? HMM?
SHEESH. ALL THAT WEAK-WILLED WAFFLING AND COMPLAINING... THAT'S NOT LIKE YOU AT ALL.
QUIT SWEATING THE SMALL STUFF AND JUST BE TRUE TO YOURSELF. OKAY?
SWF

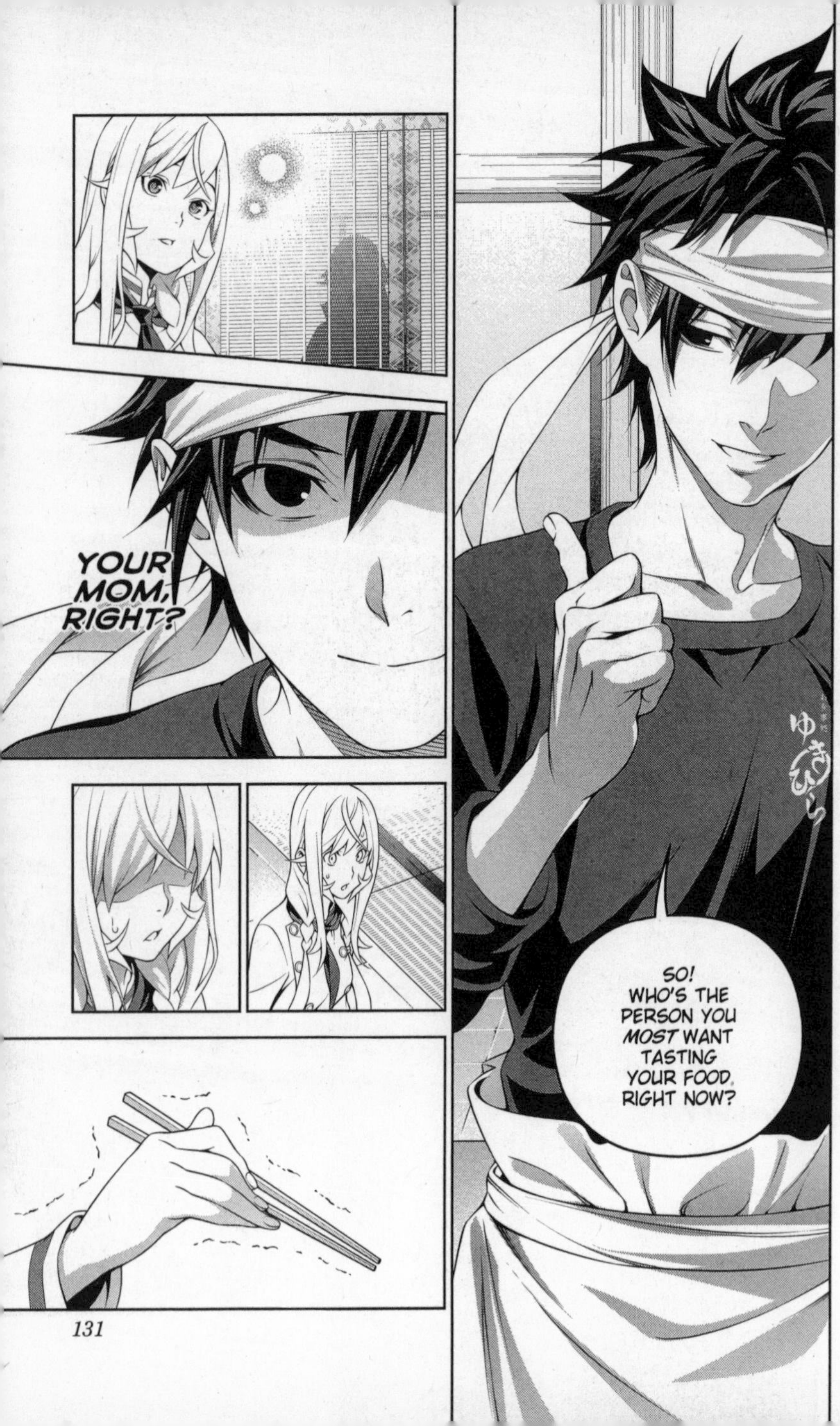
SO! WHO'S THE PERSON YOU *MOST* WANT TASTING YOUR FOOD RIGHT NOW?
YOUR MOM, RIGHT?

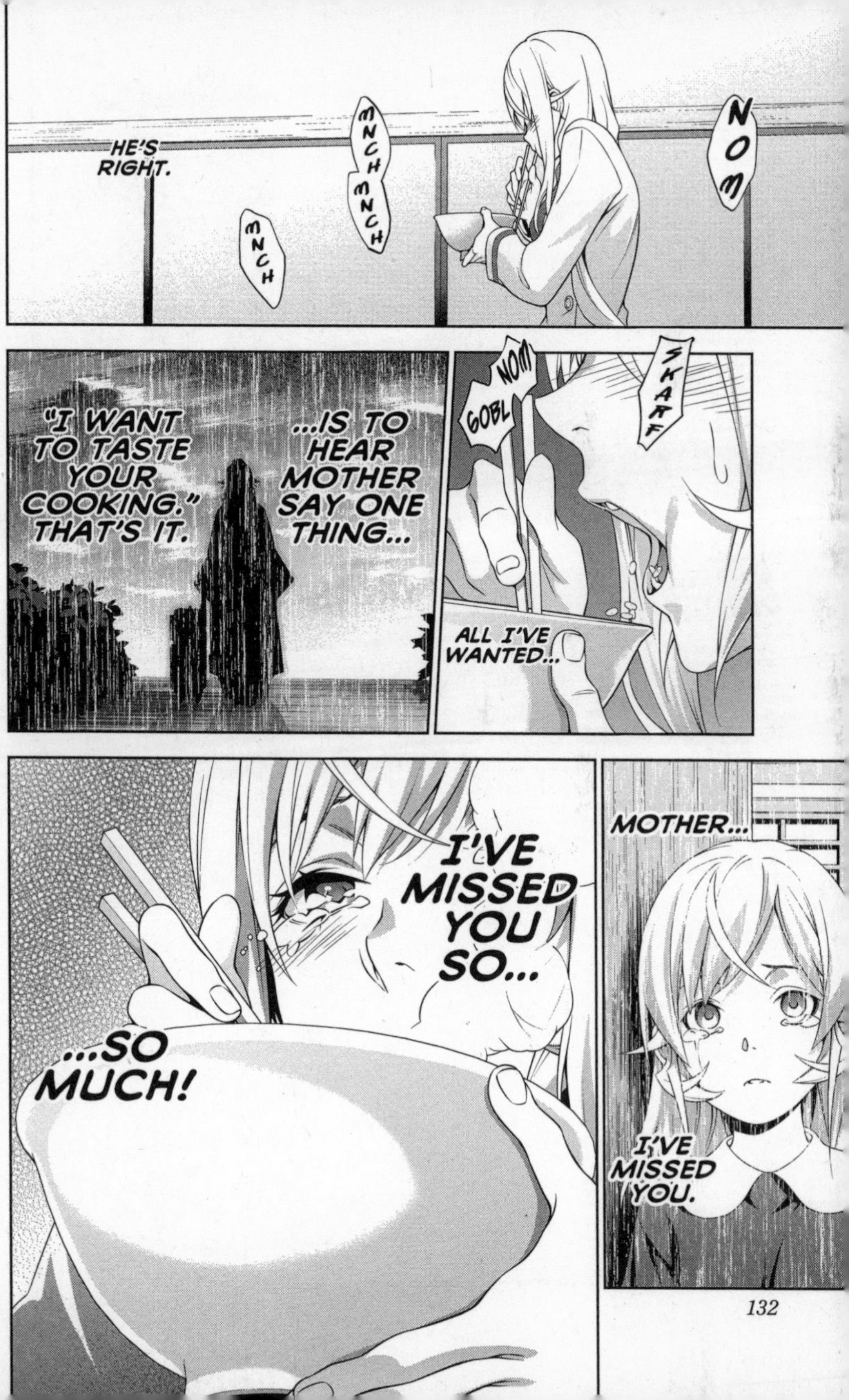
NOM
MNCH MNCH MNCH
MNCH
HE'S RIGHT.
SKARF
NOM
GOBL
ALL I'VE WANTED...
...IS TO HEAR MOTHER SAY ONE THING...
"I WANT TO TASTE YOUR COOKING." THAT'S IT.
MOTHER...
I'VE MISSED YOU.
I'VE MISSED YOU SO...
...SO MUCH!

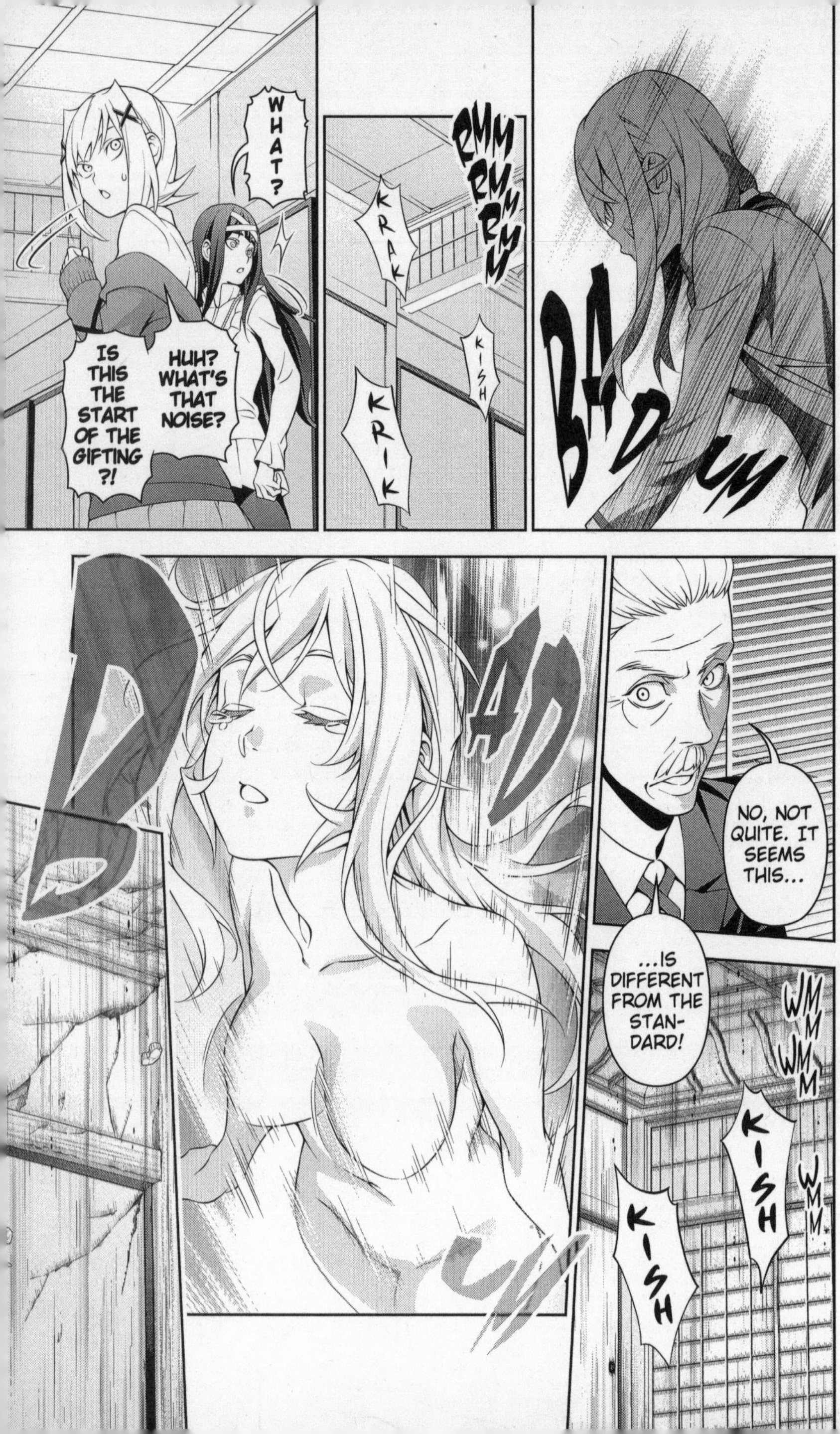
BADUM
RMM RUMM RUMM
KRAK
KISH
KRIK
WHAT?
HUH? WHAT'S THAT NOISE?
IS THIS THE START OF THE GIFTING?!
NO, NOT QUITE. IT SEEMS THIS...
...IS DIFFERENT FROM THE STAN-DARD!
WMM WMM WMM
KISH
KISH
WMM...

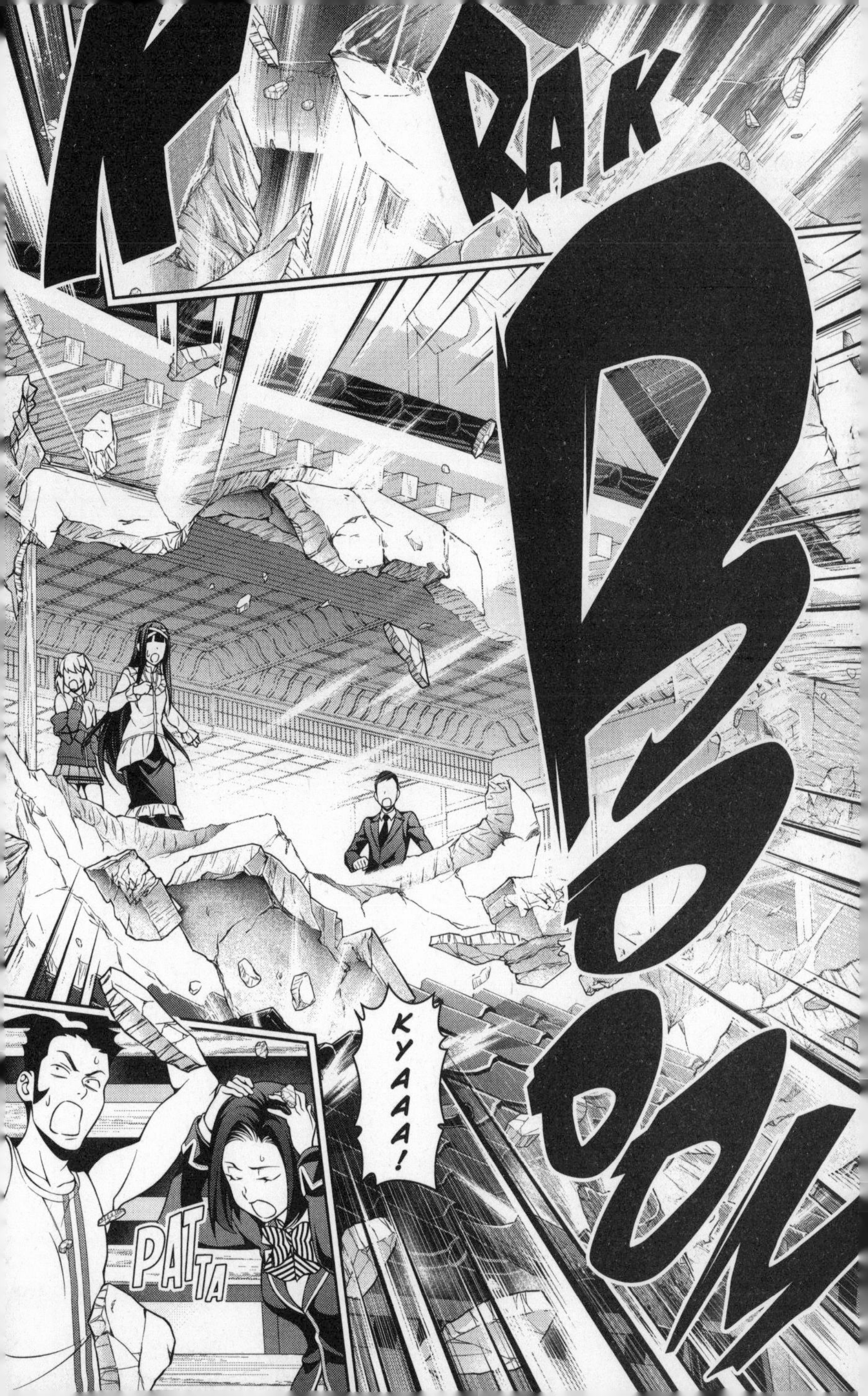
KRAK
KYAAAA!
PATTA

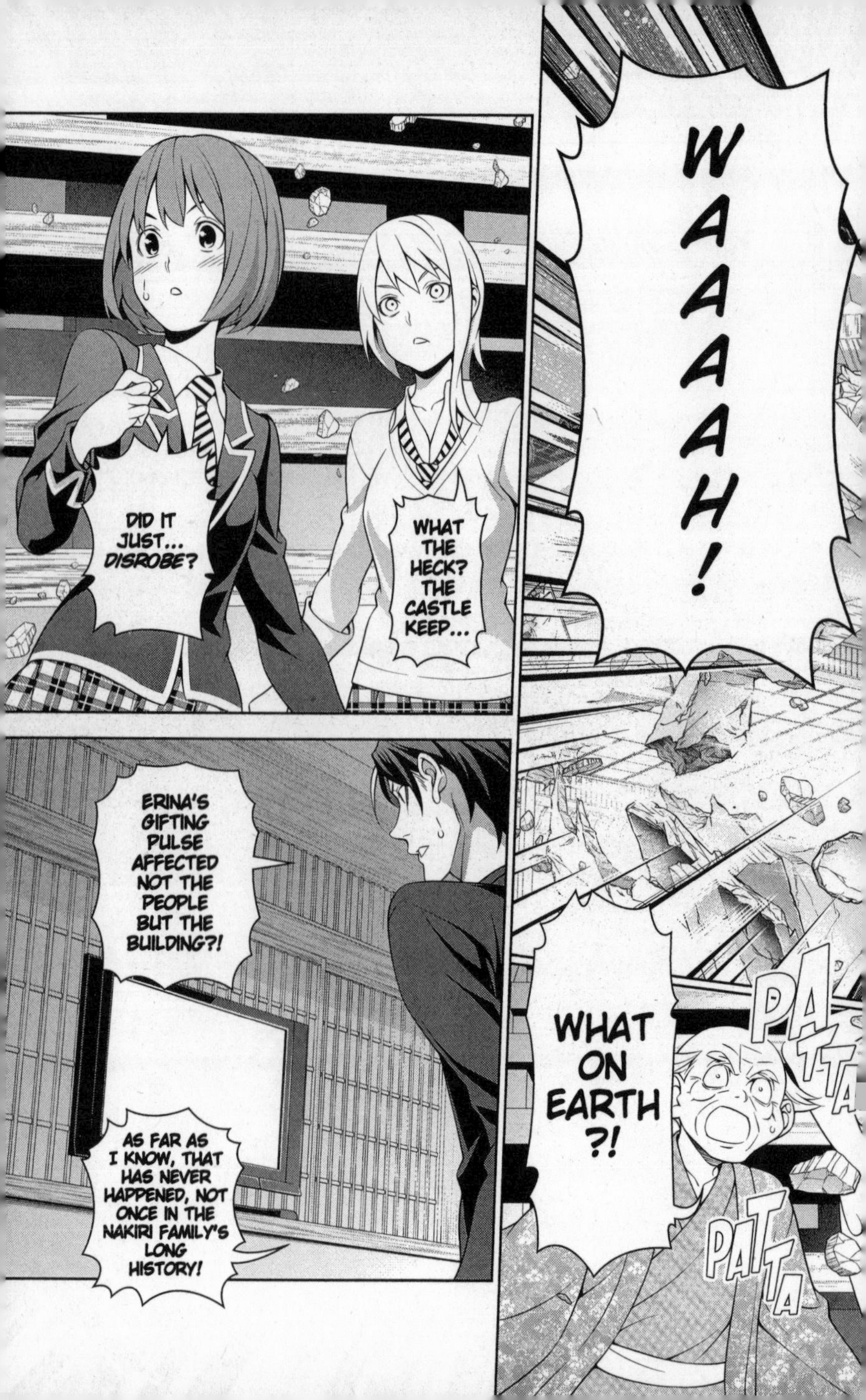
WAAAAAH!
WHAT THE HECK? THE CASTLE KEEP...
DID IT JUST... DISROBE?
WHAT ON EARTH?!
PA-TTA
PATTA
ERINA'S GIFTING PULSE AFFECTED NOT THE PEOPLE BUT THE BUILDING?!
AS FAR AS I KNOW, THAT HAS NEVER HAPPENED, NOT ONCE IN THE NAKIRI FAMILY'S LONG HISTORY!

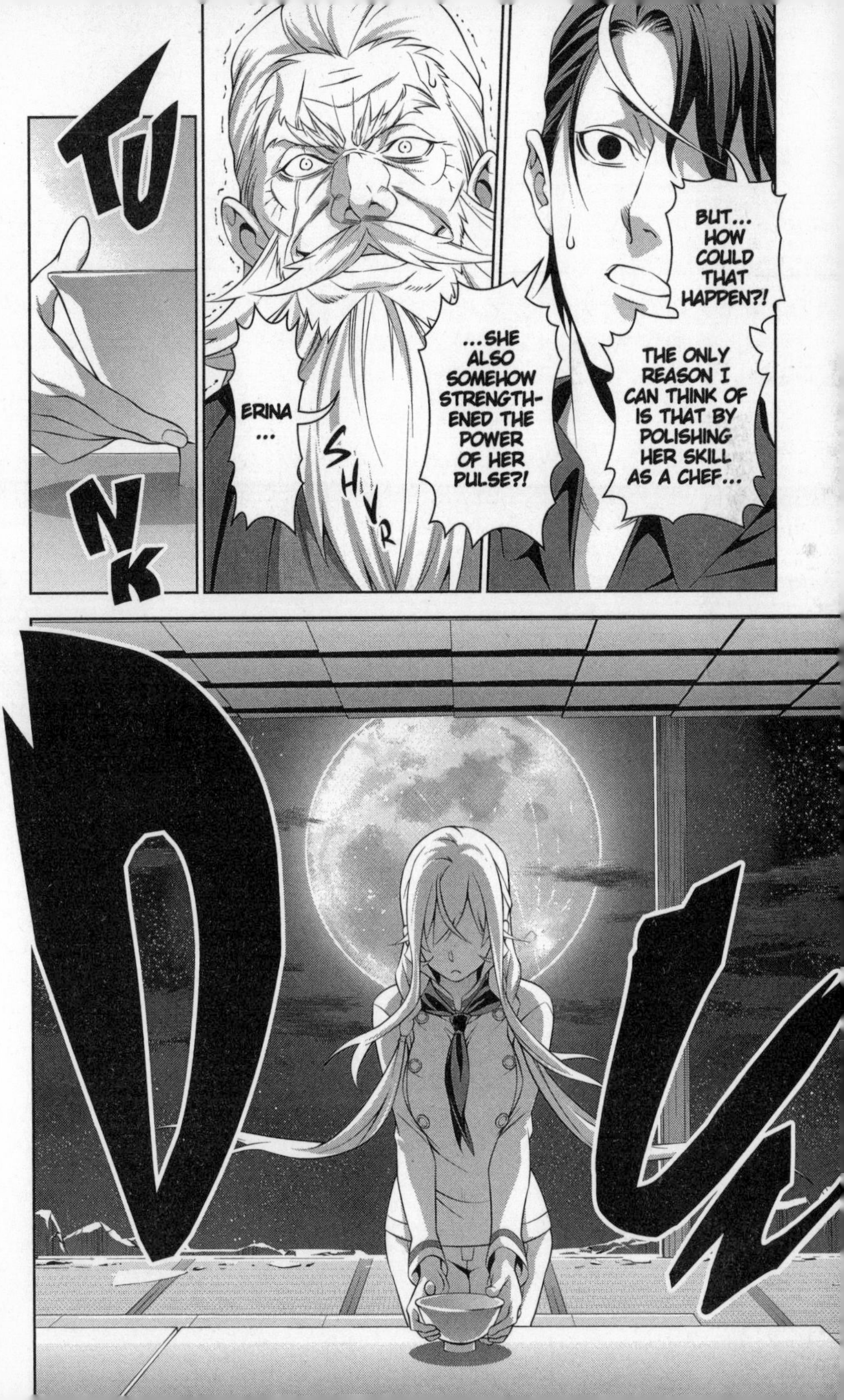
BUT... HOW COULD THAT HAPPEN?!
THE ONLY REASON I CAN THINK OF IS THAT BY POLISHING HER SKILL AS A CHEF...
...SHE ALSO SOMEHOW STRENGTHENED THE POWER OF HER PULSE?!
SHVR
ERINA...
TUNK

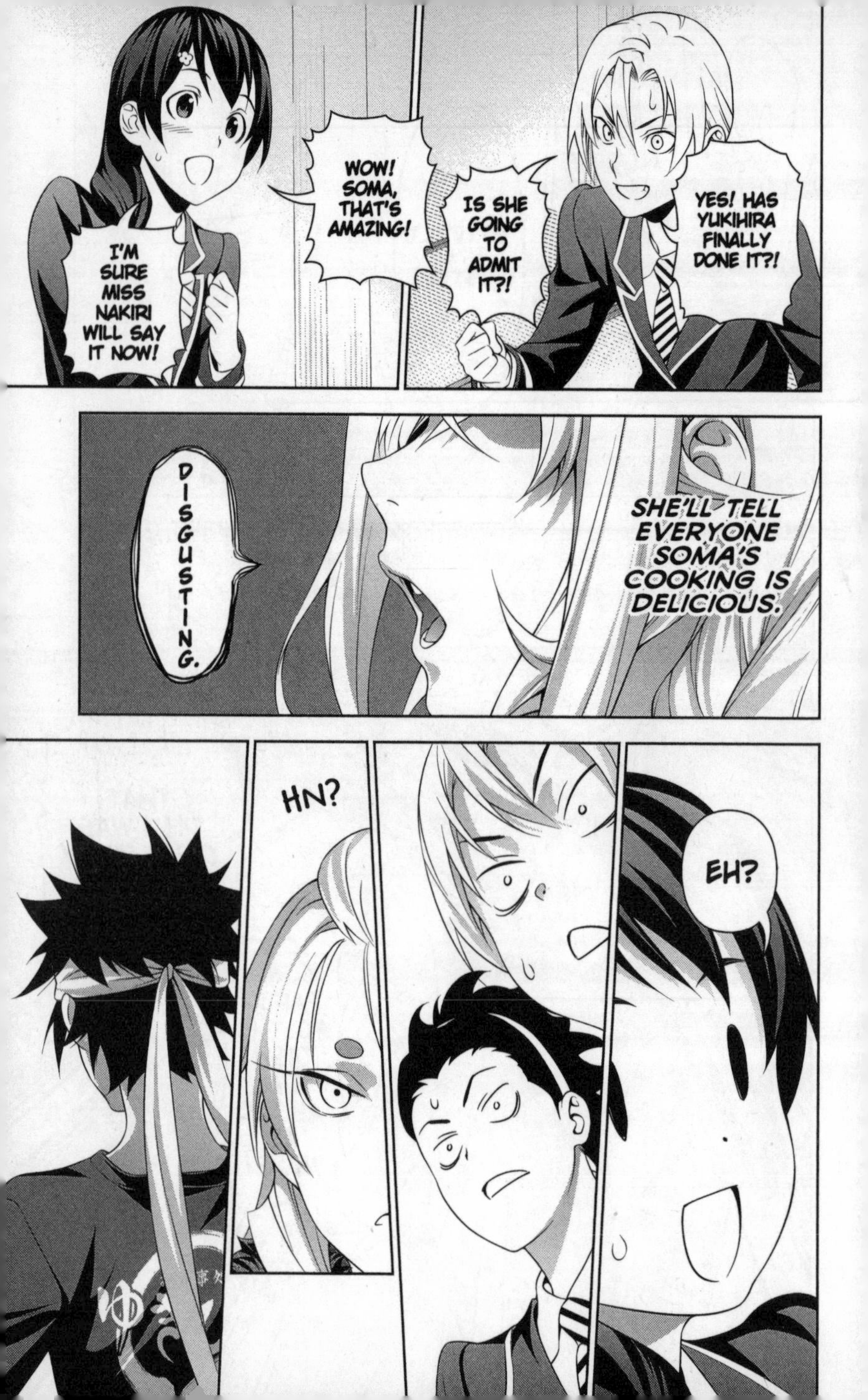
YES! HAS YUKIHIRA FINALLY DONE IT?!
IS SHE GOING TO ADMIT IT?!
WOW! SOMA, THAT'S AMAZING!
I'M SURE MISS NAKIRI WILL SAY IT NOW!
SHE'LL TELL EVERYONE SOMA'S COOKING IS DELICIOUS.
DISGUSTING.
EH?
HN?

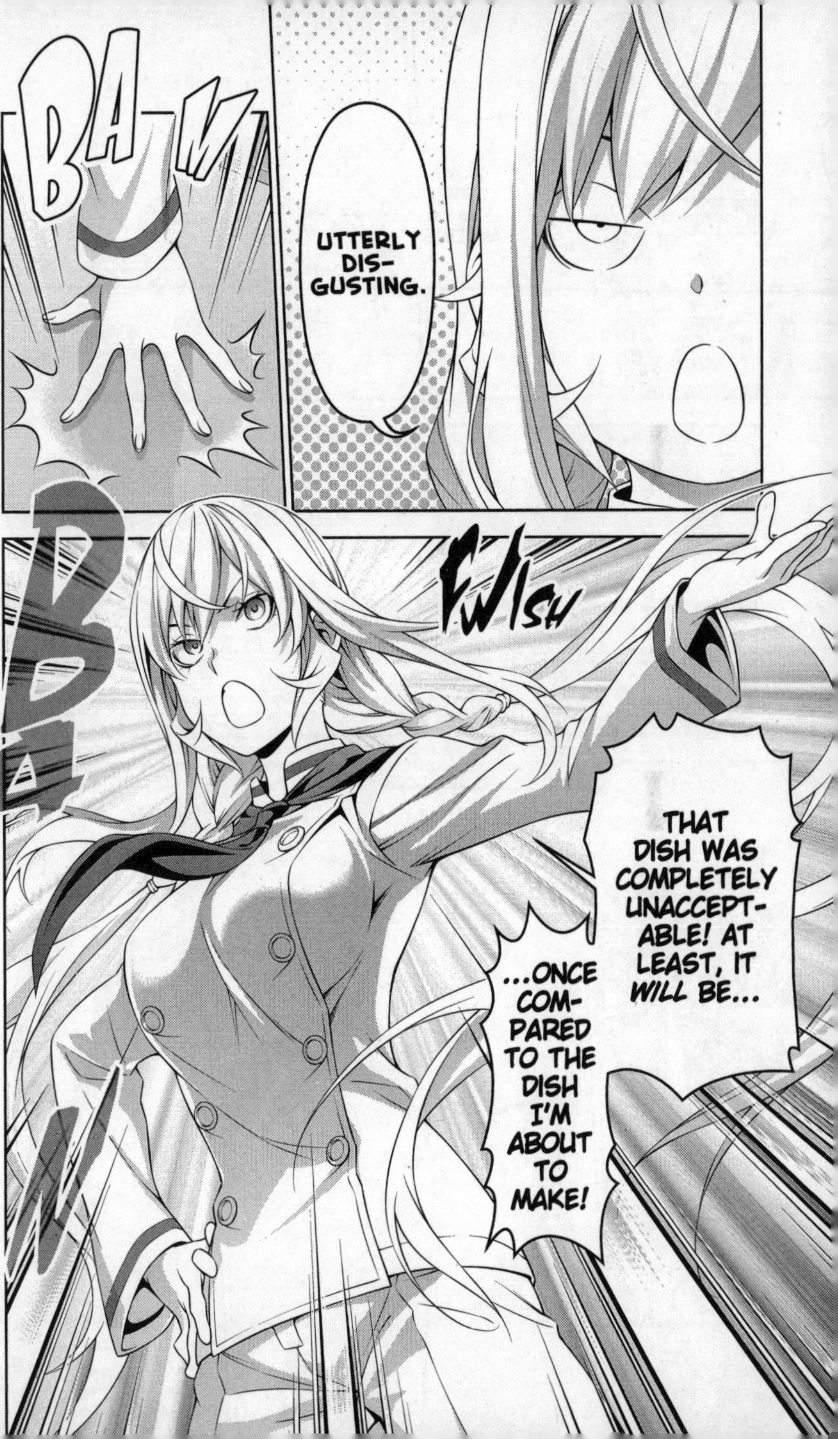
UTTERLY DIS-GUSTING.
BAM
FWISH
THAT DISH WAS COMPLETELY UNACCEPT-ABLE! AT LEAST, IT *WILL* BE...
...ONCE COM-PARED TO THE DISH I'M ABOUT TO MAKE!

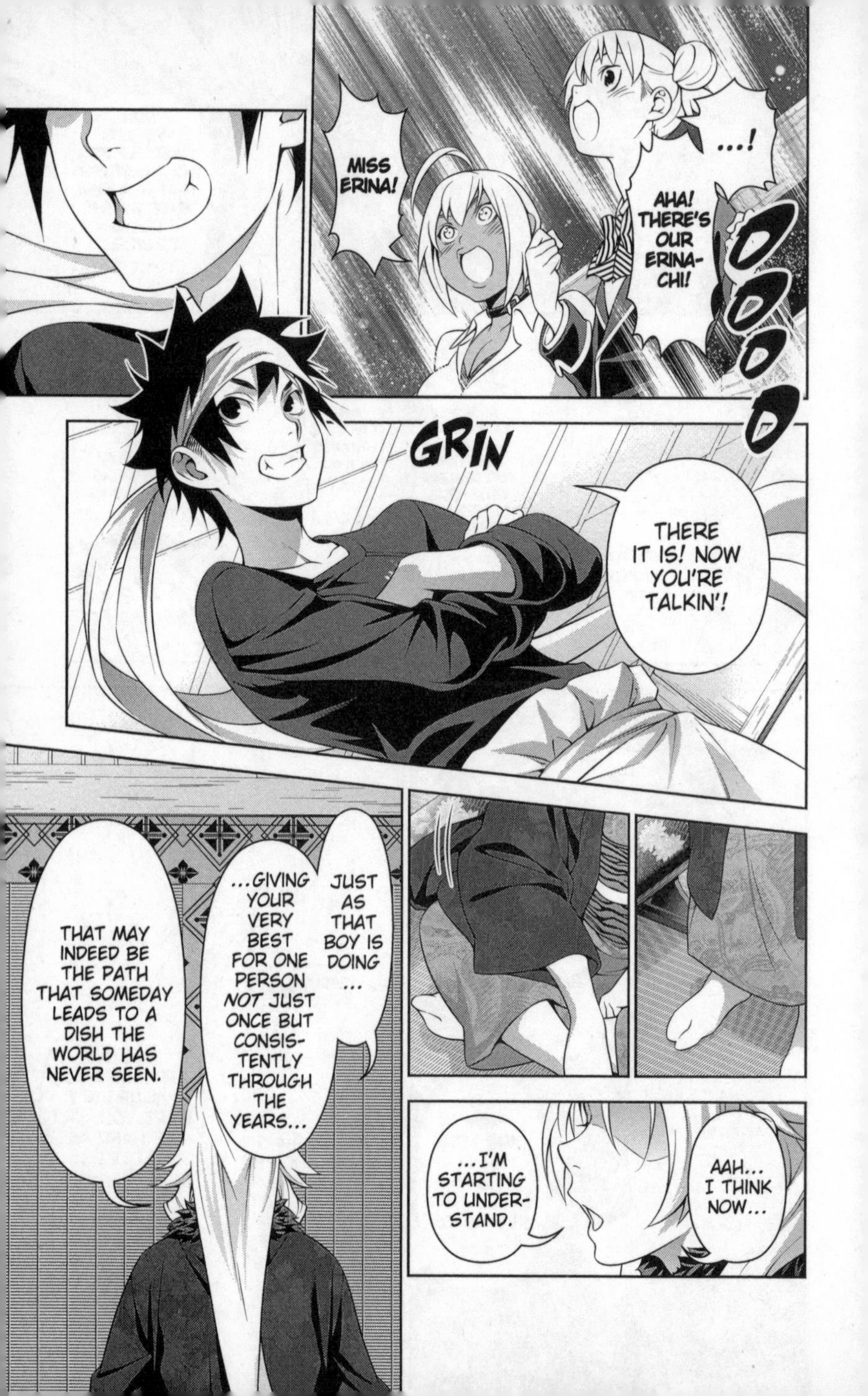

...!
AHA! THERE'S OUR ERINA-CHI!
MISS ERINA!
GRIN
THERE IT IS! NOW YOU'RE TALKIN'!
AAH... I THINK NOW...
...I'M STARTING TO UNDER-STAND.
JUST AS THAT BOY IS DOING...
...GIVING YOUR VERY BEST FOR ONE PERSON *NOT* JUST ONCE BUT CONSIS-TENTLY THROUGH THE YEARS...
THAT MAY INDEED BE THE PATH THAT SOMEDAY LEADS TO A DISH THE WORLD HAS NEVER SEEN.

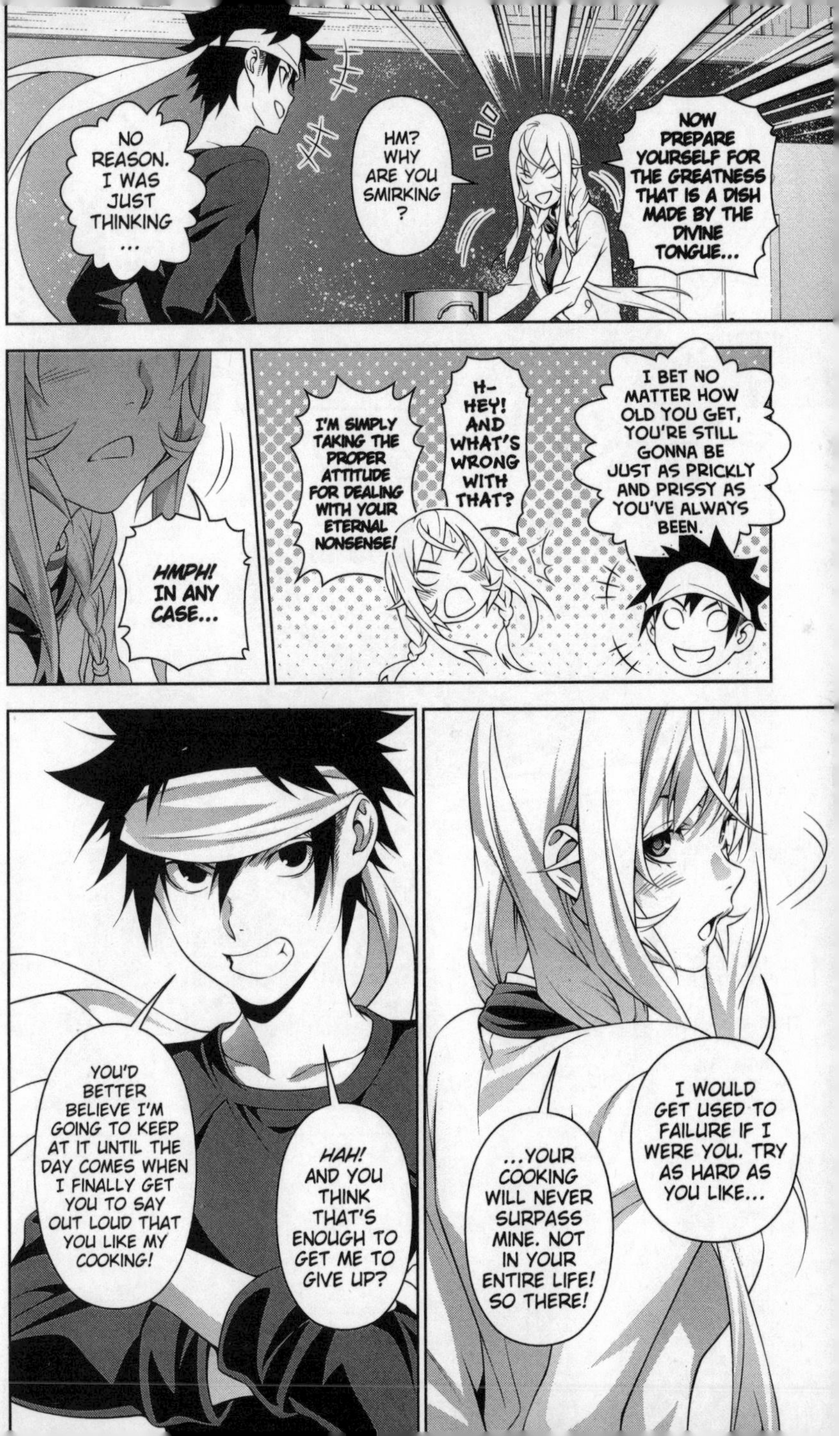
NOW PREPARE YOURSELF FOR THE GREATNESS THAT IS A DISH MADE BY THE DIVINE TONGUE...
HM? WHY ARE YOU SMIRKING?
NO REASON. I WAS JUST THINKING...
I BET NO MATTER HOW OLD YOU GET, YOU'RE STILL GONNA BE JUST AS PRICKLY AND PRISSY AS YOU'VE ALWAYS BEEN.
H-HEY! AND WHAT'S WRONG WITH THAT?
I'M SIMPLY TAKING THE PROPER ATTITUDE FOR DEALING WITH YOUR ETERNAL NONSENSE!
HMPH! IN ANY CASE...
I WOULD GET USED TO FAILURE IF I WERE YOU. TRY AS HARD AS YOU LIKE...
...YOUR COOKING WILL NEVER SURPASS MINE. NOT IN YOUR ENTIRE LIFE! SO THERE!
HAH! AND YOU THINK THAT'S ENOUGH TO GET ME TO GIVE UP?
YOU'D BETTER BELIEVE I'M GOING TO KEEP AT IT UNTIL THE DAY COMES WHEN I FINALLY GET YOU TO SAY OUT LOUD THAT YOU LIKE MY COOKING!

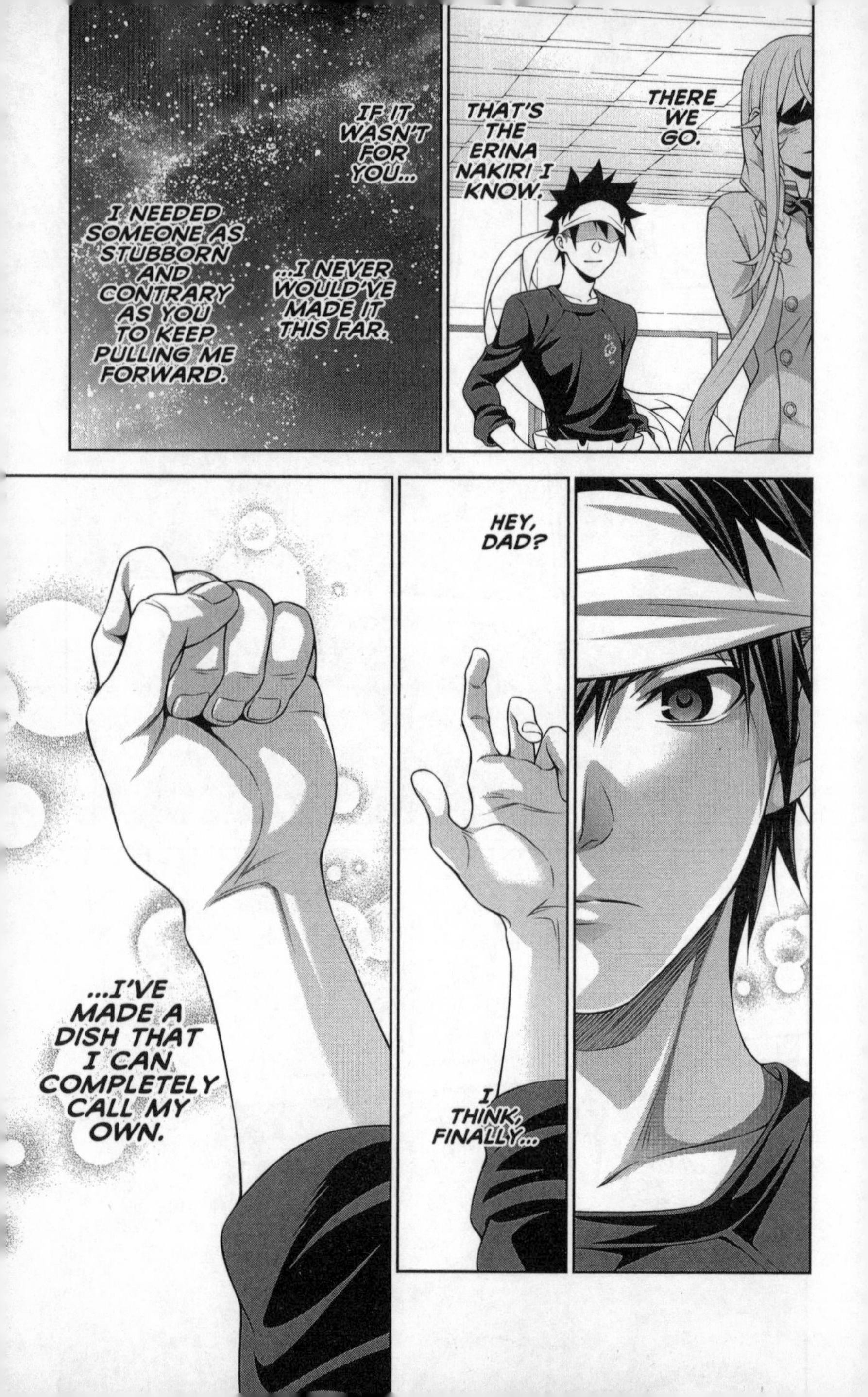
THERE WE GO.
THAT'S THE ERINA NAKIRI I KNOW.
IF IT WASN'T FOR YOU...
...I NEVER WOULD'VE MADE IT THIS FAR.
I NEEDED SOMEONE AS STUBBORN AND CONTRARY AS YOU TO KEEP PULLING ME FORWARD.
HEY, DAD?
I THINK, FINALLY...
...I'VE MADE A DISH THAT I CAN COMPLETELY CALL MY OWN.

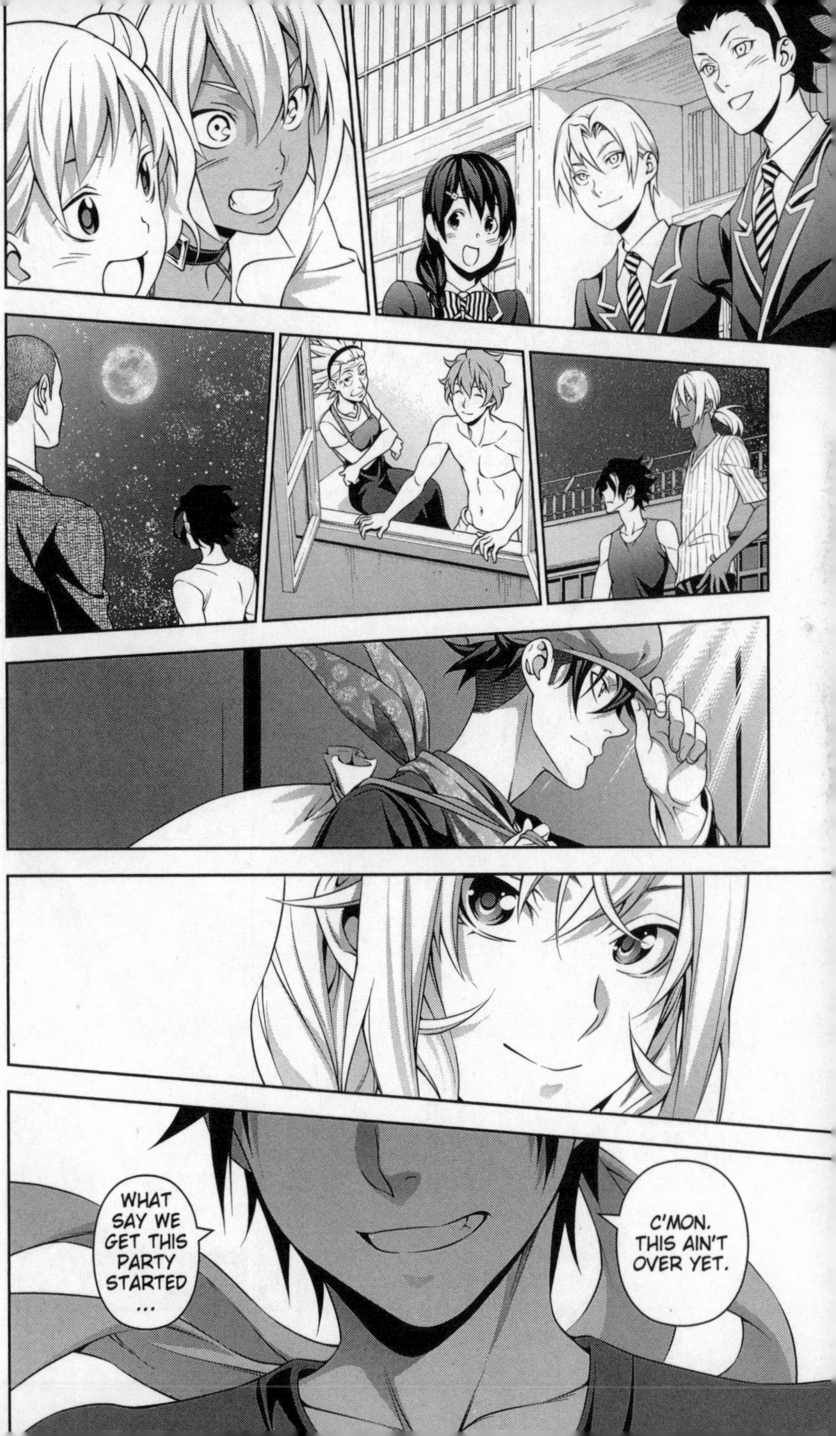
C'MON. THIS AIN'T OVER YET.
WHAT SAY WE GET THIS PARTY STARTED ...

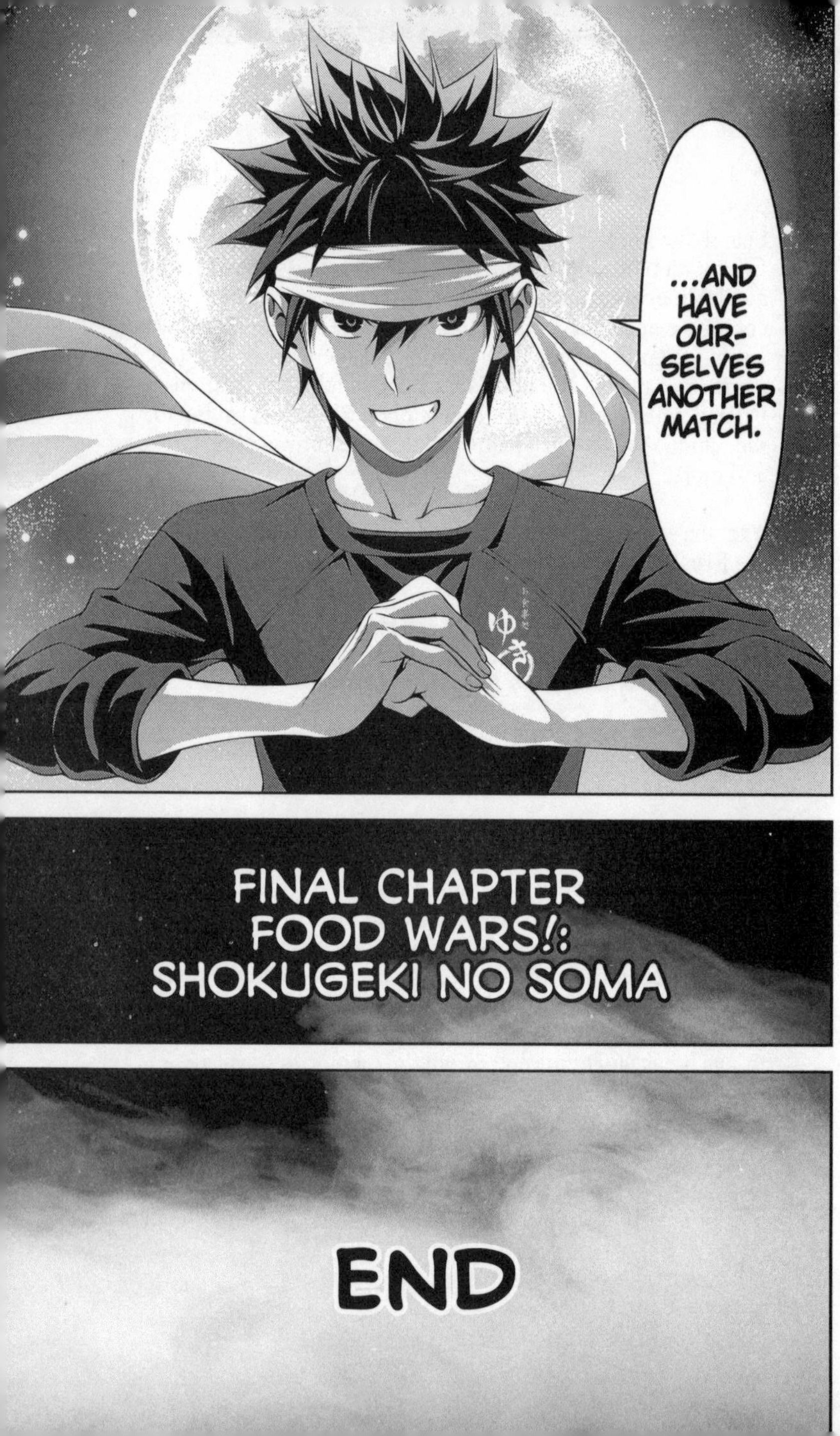
...AND HAVE OURSELVES ANOTHER MATCH.
FINAL CHAPTER FOOD WARS!: SHOKUGEKI NO SOMA
END

Search the internet and you'll find piles of recipes. Information on stuff like ingredients and spices is easily available in books and magazines. To create not just a cooking manga but one for the *shonen* demographic I feel was a pretty significant thing. Inspiration for the meat of the story came from manga and novels I'd read, dumb conversations I'd had with friends, things I remembered teachers saying to me, unique things I just happened to notice on vacations, and more.

Yes, the story of *Food Wars!* ends here, but I'd like to think the lives of the characters continue on somewhere we aren't watching. I'm sure every now and again I'll catch myself wondering what Soma and the gang are up to.

Thank you very much for reading. Happy to serve!

Yuto Tsukuda

The characters of *Food Wars!* may have different viewpoints and ideas, but it really feels like each of them has fully dedicated themselves to cooking. While I do want to make a living with my art, I occasionally find myself getting distracted by other things. Not only did the commitment of these characters inspire me to renew my own dedication, they have given me the courage to keep wandering the wasteland known as manga artistry. I'm grateful to this work for all the things it has taught me and for all the memories it has given me. I want to thank all our wonderful fans as well as everyone who helped to create this series every step of the way. Happy to serve!

Shun Saeki

Prior to this manga, I'd never had to think up recipes based on how they could win or lose. I would wait with both excitement and anxiousness for Tsukuda Sensei to contact me so I could finally discover who would be battling whom next. For each shokugeki, I built the recipes as I went through the battle in my mind. Then Saeki Sensei's art infused it with life before its publication in *Weekly Shonen Jump*. When I finally got to see the finished work, it was more than I'd ever hoped and brought tears to my eyes (*lol*).

In all my years as a culinary researcher, this was the first project of its kind. Since I decided to collaborate, I made certain every recipe had a home version readers could actually create. I thought giving the readers an opportunity to make and enjoy the dishes of their favorite characters might help them enjoy and experience *Food Wars!* on a deeper level. My personal recommendation is the canned mackerel burger. Try it! It's simple and tasty!

These last six and a half years have been an incredible experience for me, and I'm very grateful. Thank you.

Yuki Morisaki

Editorial

Seijiro Nakaji
Tomohiro Ueno
Yuya Namura

Volume Editor
Takefumi Ishii
(Publishing)

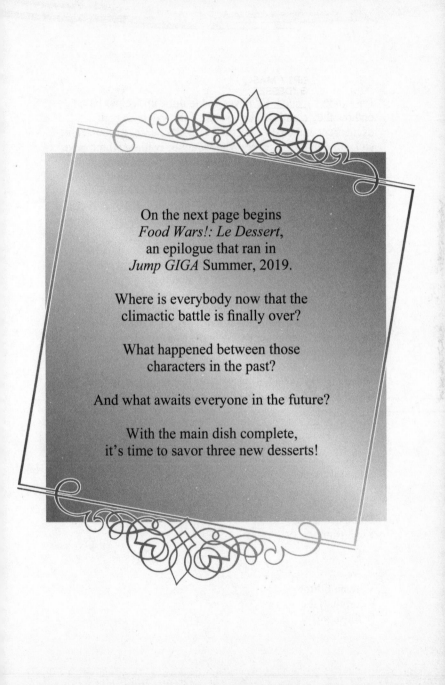

On the next page begins
Food Wars!: Le Dessert,
an epilogue that ran in
Jump GIGA Summer, 2019.

Where is everybody now that the
climactic battle is finally over?

What happened between those
characters in the past?

And what awaits everyone in the future?

With the main dish complete,
it's time to savor three new desserts!

DESSERT

PRONUNCIATION: [DE-SƐ:R] / MASCULINE NOUN
FRENCH WORD MEANING "DESSERT."

EXAMPLE

QU'EST-CE QUE VOUS PRENEZ COMME DESSERT?
(WHAT WILL YOU HAVE FOR DESSERT?)

SERVIR DES FRUITS AU DESSERT.
(I WILL SERVE FRUIT FOR DESSERT.)

1 LE PRÉSENT

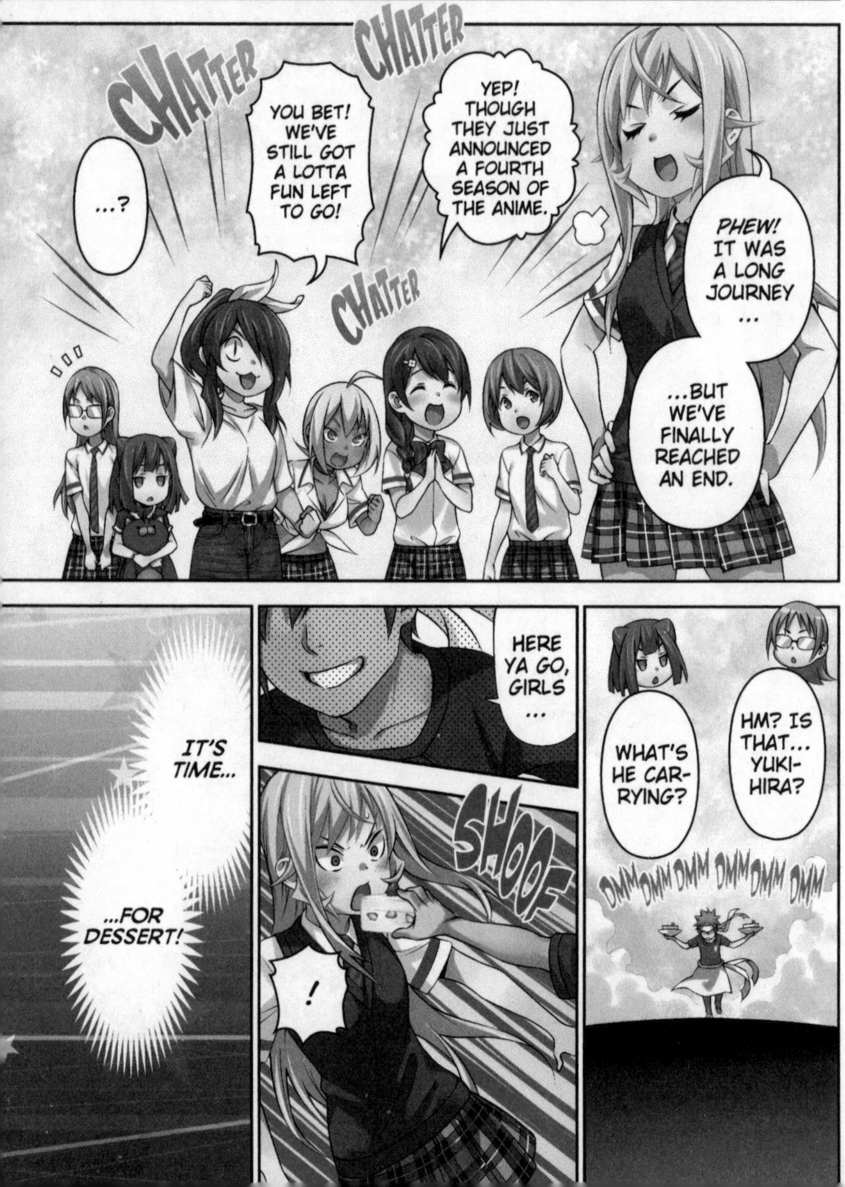

PHEW! IT WAS A LONG JOURNEY...
...BUT WE'VE FINALLY REACHED AN END.
YEP! THOUGH THEY JUST ANNOUNCED A FOURTH SEASON OF THE ANIME.
CHATTER
YOU BET! WE'VE STILL GOT A LOTTA FUN LEFT TO GO!
CHATTER
...?
CHATTER
DMM DMM DMM DMM DMM DMM
HM? IS THAT... YUKIHIRA?
WHAT'S HE CARRYING?
HERE YA GO, GIRLS...
SHOOF
!
IT'S TIME...
...FOR DESSERT!

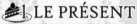

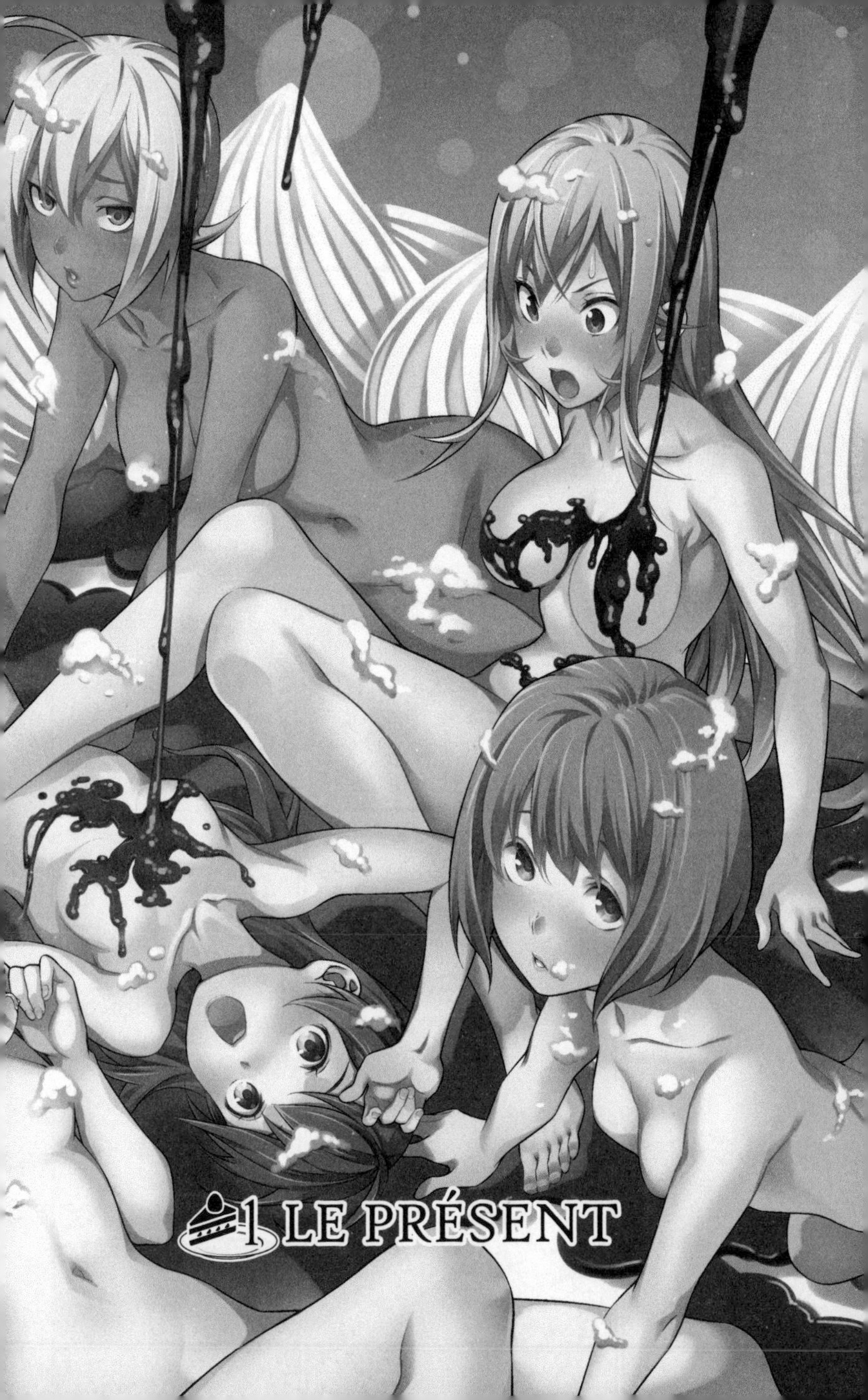
1 LE PRÉSENT

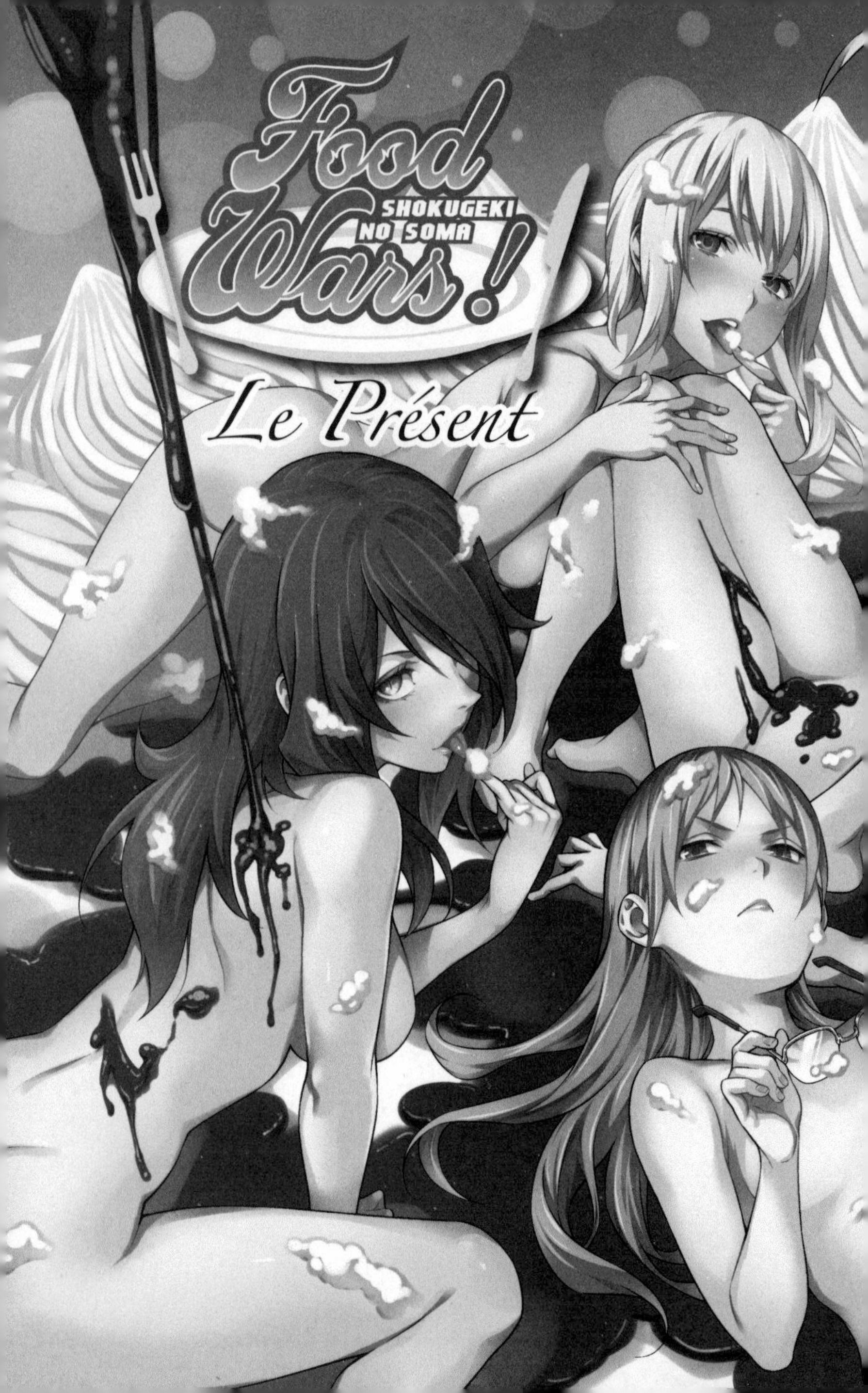
Food Wars!
SHOKUGEKI NO SOMA
Le Présent

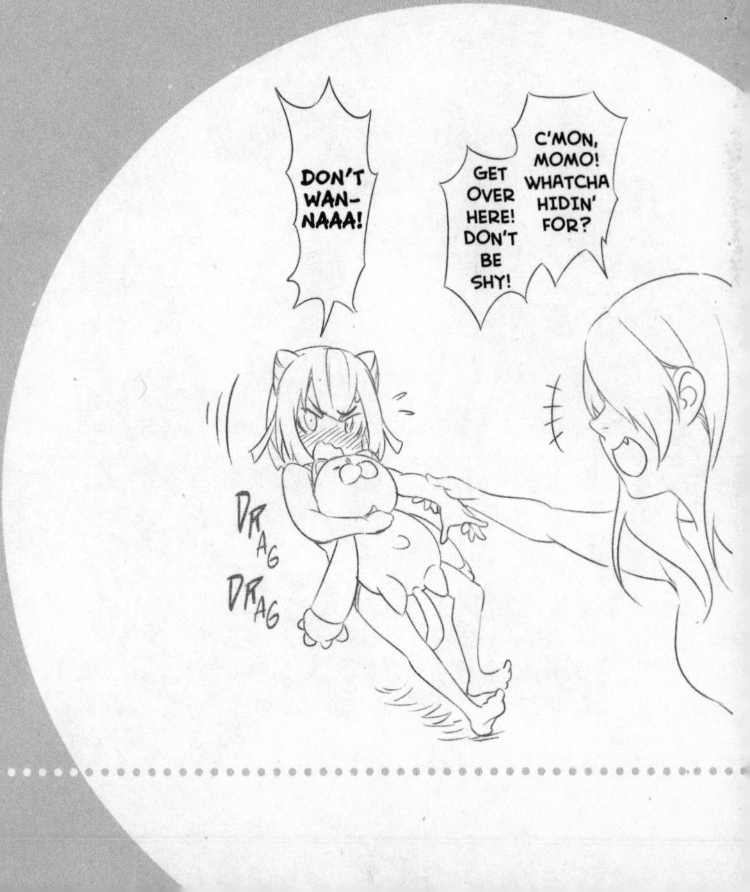
C'MON, MOMO! WHATCHA HIDIN' FOR?
GET OVER HERE! DON'T BE SHY!
DON'T WAN-NAAA!
DRAG
DRAG

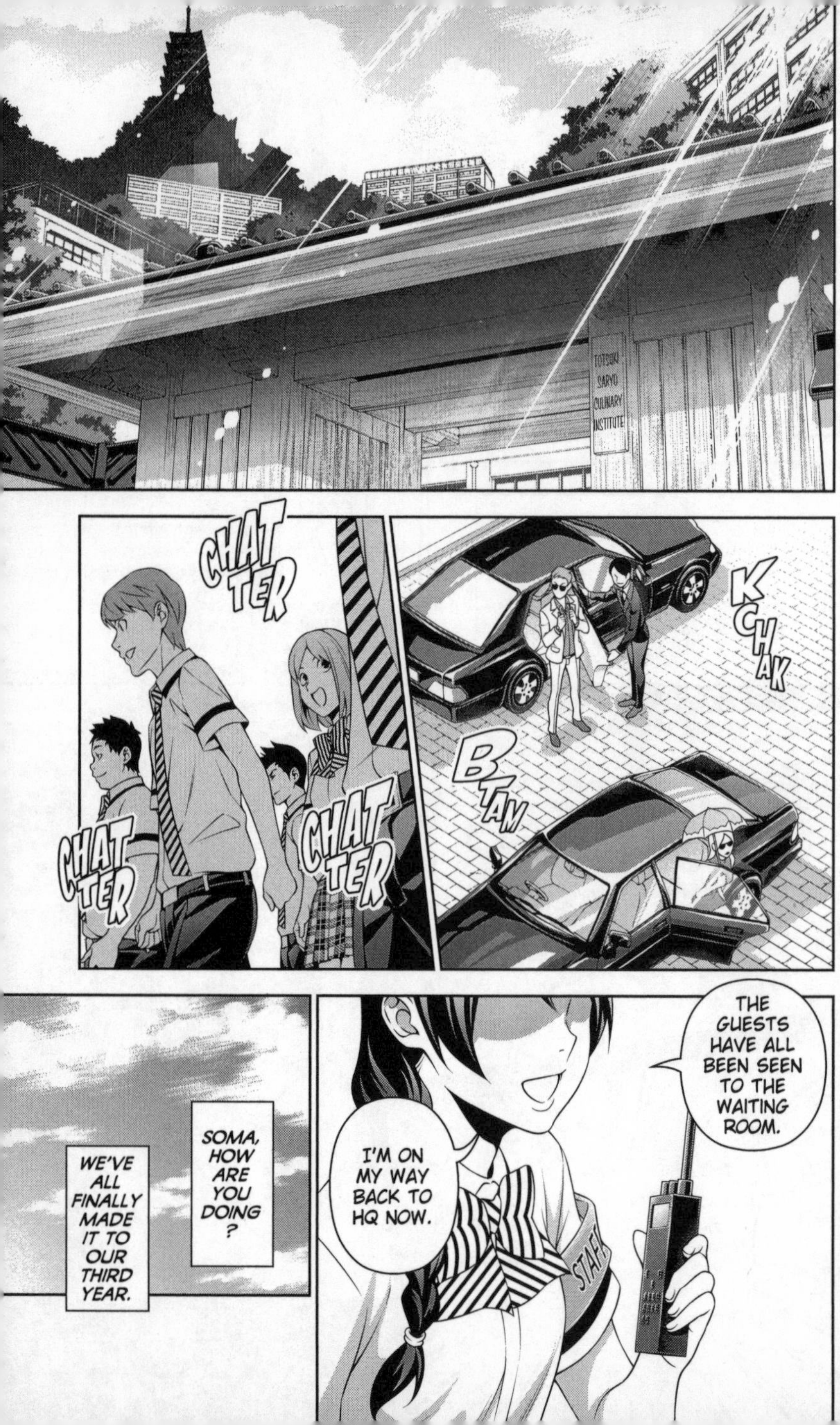
TOTSUKI SARYO CULINARY INSTITUTE
KCHAK
BTAM
CHATTER
CHATTER
CHATTER
THE GUESTS HAVE ALL BEEN SEEN TO THE WAITING ROOM.
I'M ON MY WAY BACK TO HQ NOW.
SOMA, HOW ARE YOU DOING?
WE'VE ALL FINALLY MADE IT TO OUR THIRD YEAR.

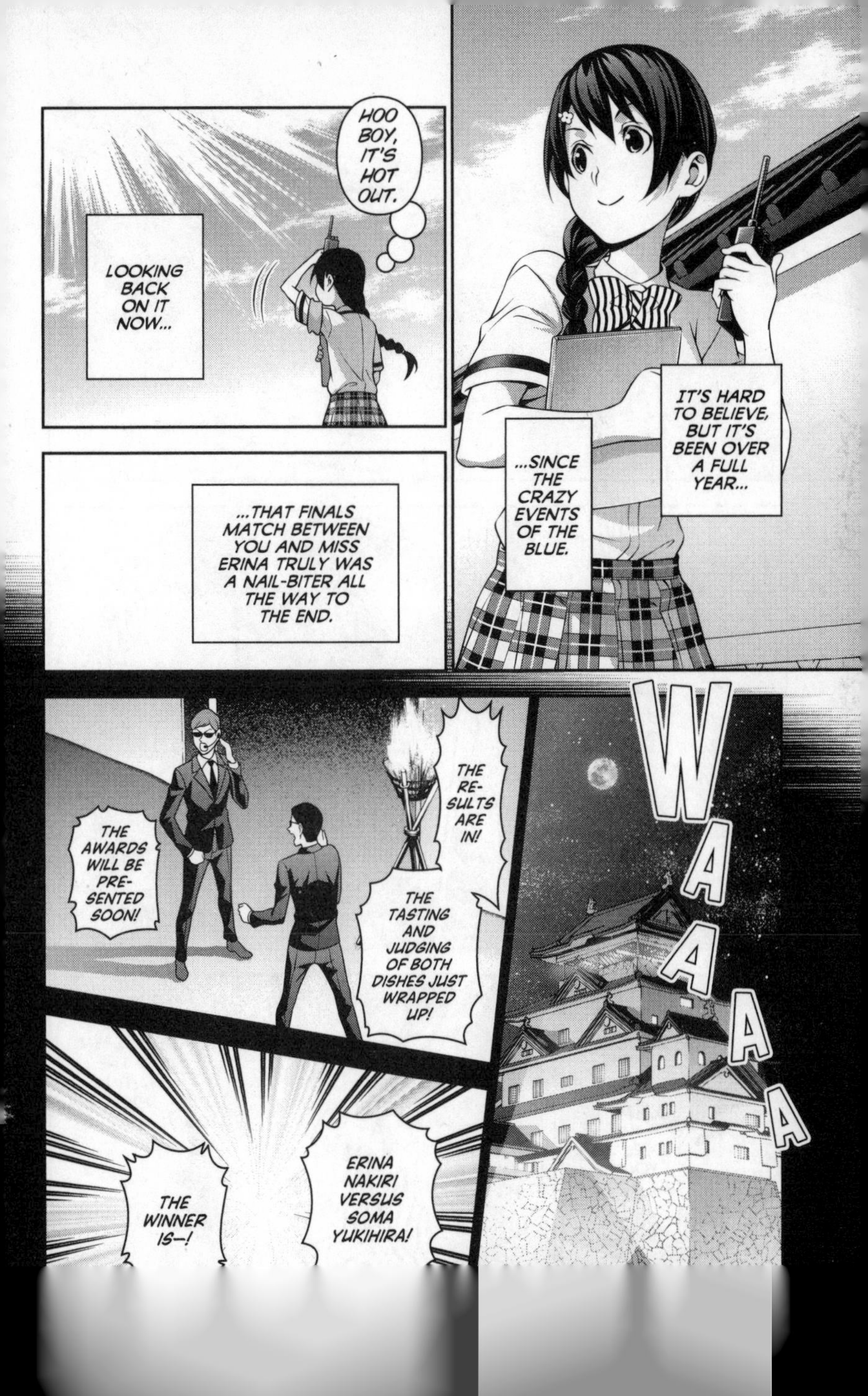
IT'S HARD TO BELIEVE, BUT IT'S BEEN OVER A FULL YEAR...
...SINCE THE CRAZY EVENTS OF THE BLUE.
HOO BOY, IT'S HOT OUT.
LOOKING BACK ON IT NOW...
...THAT FINALS MATCH BETWEEN YOU AND MISS ERINA TRULY WAS A NAIL-BITER ALL THE WAY TO THE END.
WAAAAA
THE RE-SULTS ARE IN!
THE TASTING AND JUDGING OF BOTH DISHES JUST WRAPPED UP!
THE AWARDS WILL BE PRE-SENTED SOON!
ERINA NAKIRI VERSUS SOMA YUKIHIRA!
THE WINNER IS—!

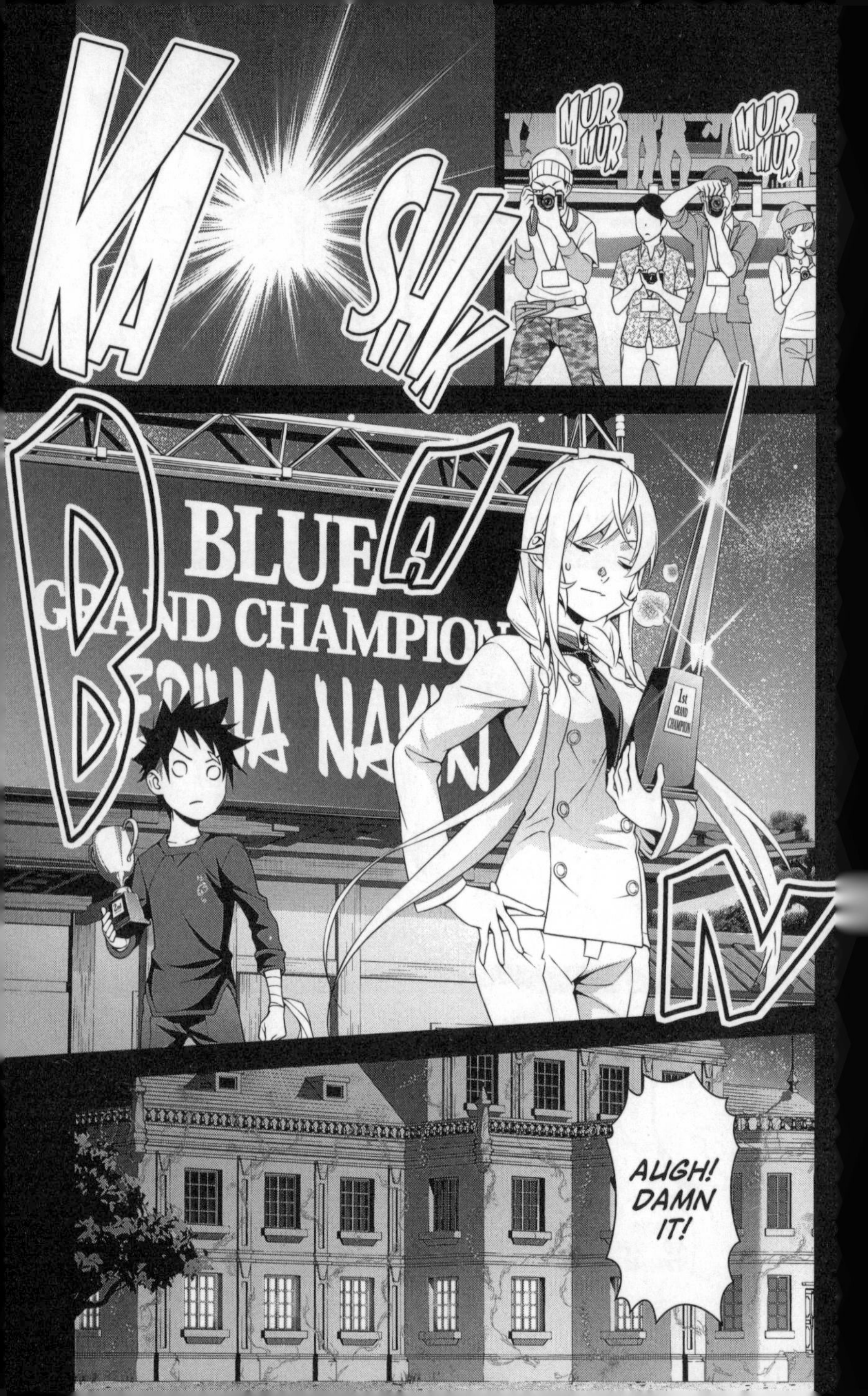
MUR MUR
MUR MUR
KA-SHIK
BLUE
GRAND CHAMPION
DAN
1st GRAND CHAMPION
AUGH! DAMN IT!

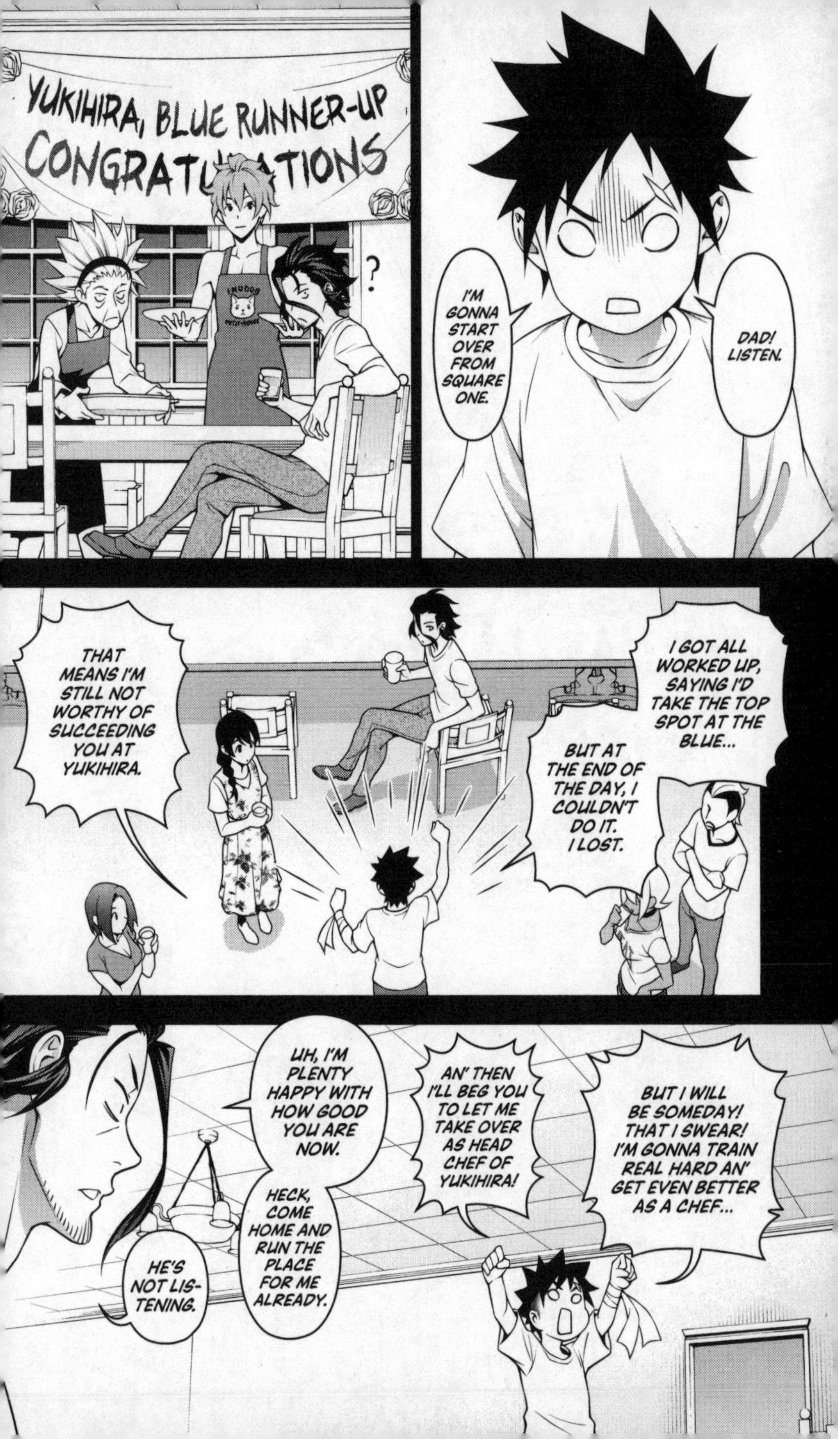
DAD! LISTEN.
I'M GONNA START OVER FROM SQUARE ONE.
YUKIHIRA, BLUE RUNNER-UP
CONGRATU ATIONS
?
I GOT ALL WORKED UP, SAYING I'D TAKE THE TOP SPOT AT THE BLUE...
BUT AT THE END OF THE DAY, I COULDN'T DO IT. I LOST.
THAT MEANS I'M STILL NOT WORTHY OF SUCCEEDING YOU AT YUKIHIRA.
BUT I WILL BE SOMEDAY! THAT I SWEAR! I'M GONNA TRAIN REAL HARD AN' GET EVEN BETTER AS A CHEF...
AN' THEN I'LL BEG YOU TO LET ME TAKE OVER AS HEAD CHEF OF YUKIHIRA!
UH, I'M PLENTY HAPPY WITH HOW GOOD YOU ARE NOW.
HECK, COME HOME AND RUN THE PLACE FOR ME ALREADY.
HE'S NOT LIS-TENING.

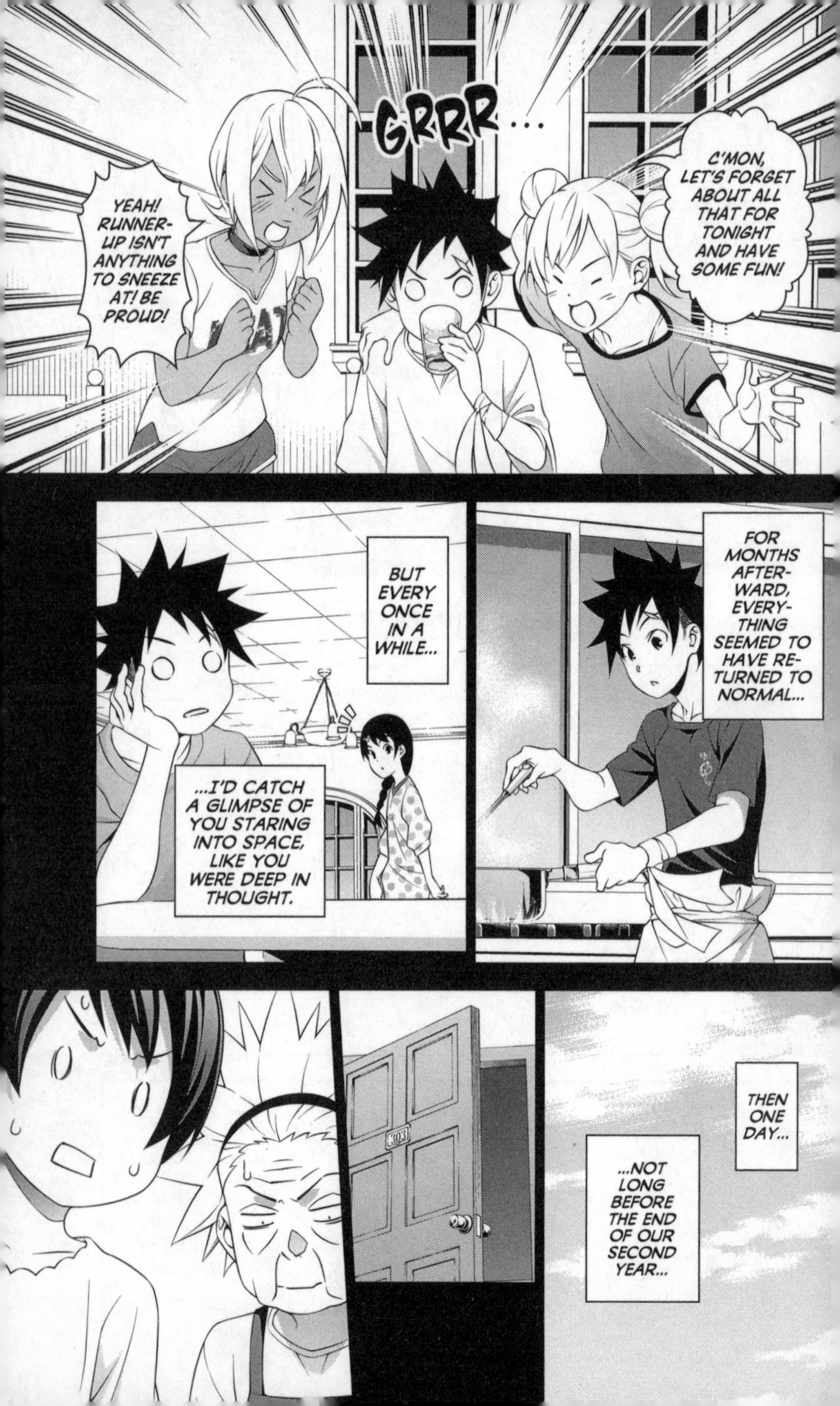
C'MON, LET'S FORGET ABOUT ALL THAT FOR TONIGHT AND HAVE SOME FUN!
GRRR...
YEAH! RUNNER-UP ISN'T ANYTHING TO SNEEZE AT! BE PROUD!
FOR MONTHS AFTER-WARD, EVERY-THING SEEMED TO HAVE RE-TURNED TO NORMAL...
BUT EVERY ONCE IN A WHILE...
...I'D CATCH A GLIMPSE OF YOU STARING INTO SPACE, LIKE YOU WERE DEEP IN THOUGHT.
THEN ONE DAY...
...NOT LONG BEFORE THE END OF OUR SECOND YEAR...
303

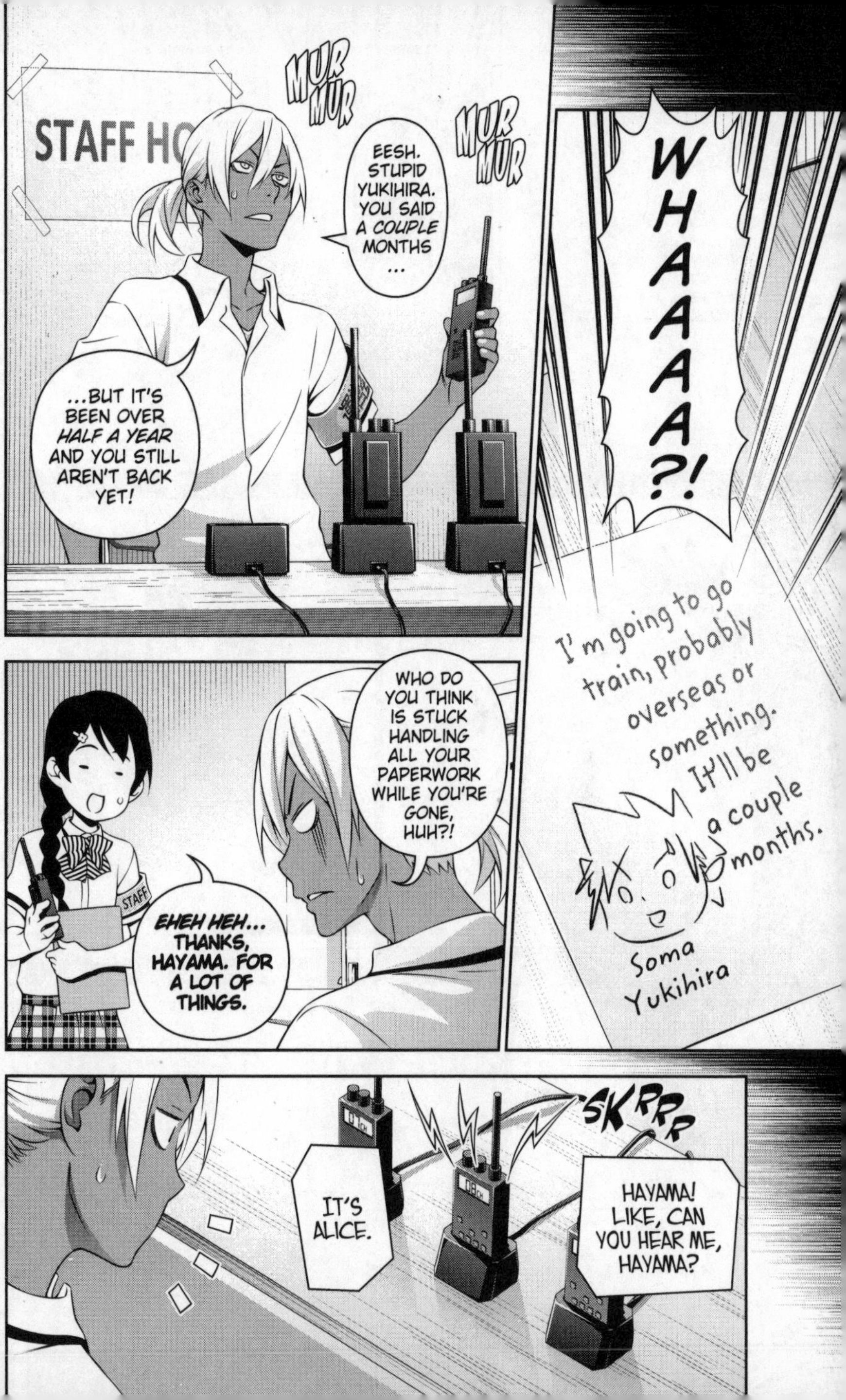
WHAAAAA?!
I'm going to go train, probably overseas or something. It'll be a couple months.
Soma Yukihira
STAFF HO
MUR MUR
MUR MUR
EESH. STUPID YUKIHIRA. YOU SAID A *COUPLE MONTHS* ...
...BUT IT'S BEEN OVER *HALF A YEAR* AND YOU STILL AREN'T BACK YET!
WHO DO YOU THINK IS STUCK HANDLING ALL YOUR PAPERWORK WHILE YOU'RE GONE, HUH?!
STAFF
EHEH HEH... THANKS, HAYAMA. FOR A LOT OF THINGS.
SKRRR
HAYAMA! LIKE, CAN YOU HEAR ME, HAYAMA?
IT'S ALICE.

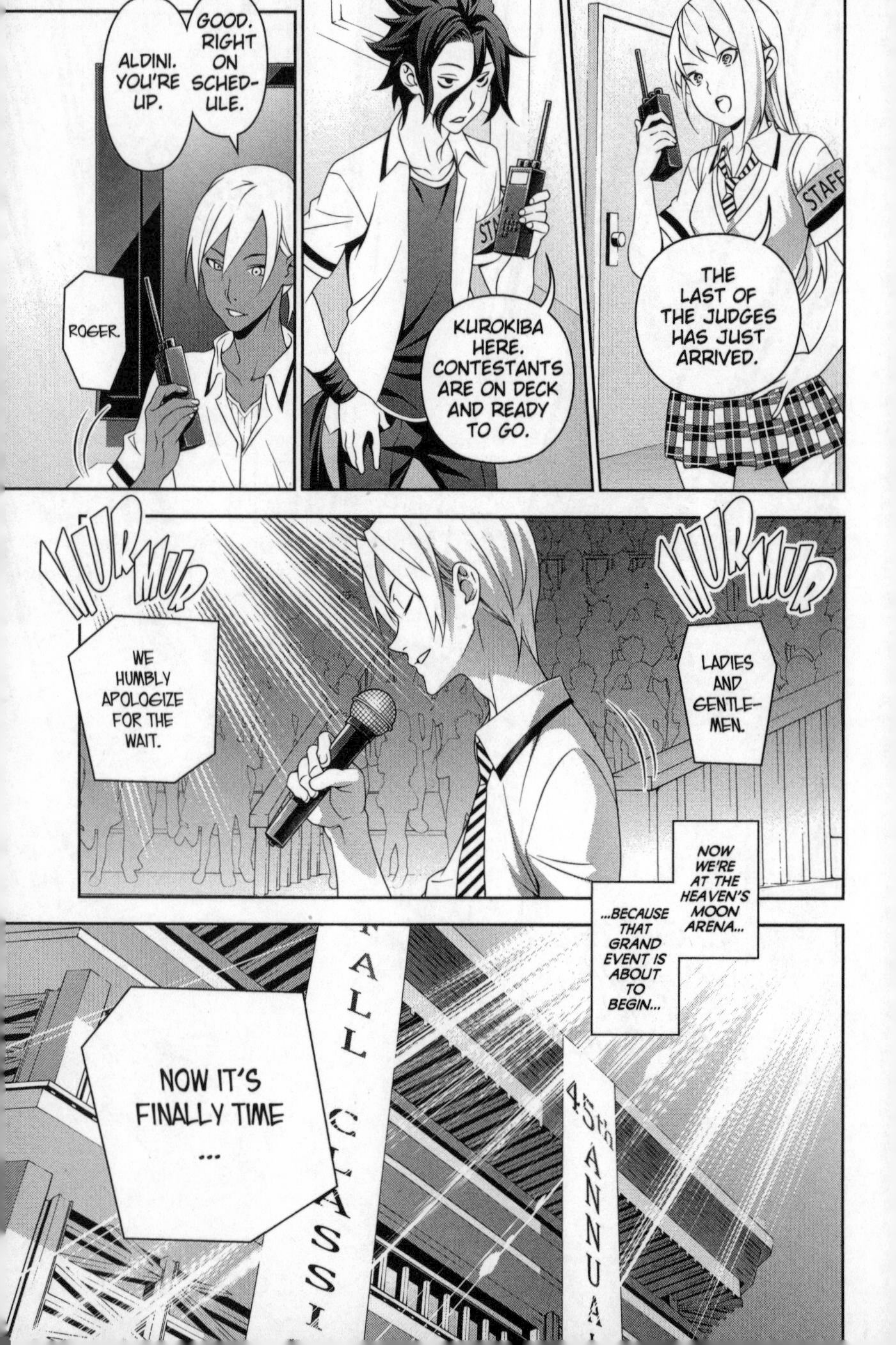
THE LAST OF THE JUDGES HAS JUST ARRIVED.
KUROKIBA HERE. CONTESTANTS ARE ON DECK AND READY TO GO.
GOOD. RIGHT ON SCHED-ULE.
ALDINI. YOU'RE UP.
ROGER.
MURMUR
LADIES AND GENTLE-MEN.
MURMUR
WE HUMBLY APOLOGIZE FOR THE WAIT.
NOW WE'RE AT THE HEAVEN'S MOON ARENA...
...BECAUSE THAT GRAND EVENT IS ABOUT TO BEGIN...
45th ANNUA
ALL CLASS
NOW IT'S FINALLY TIME ...

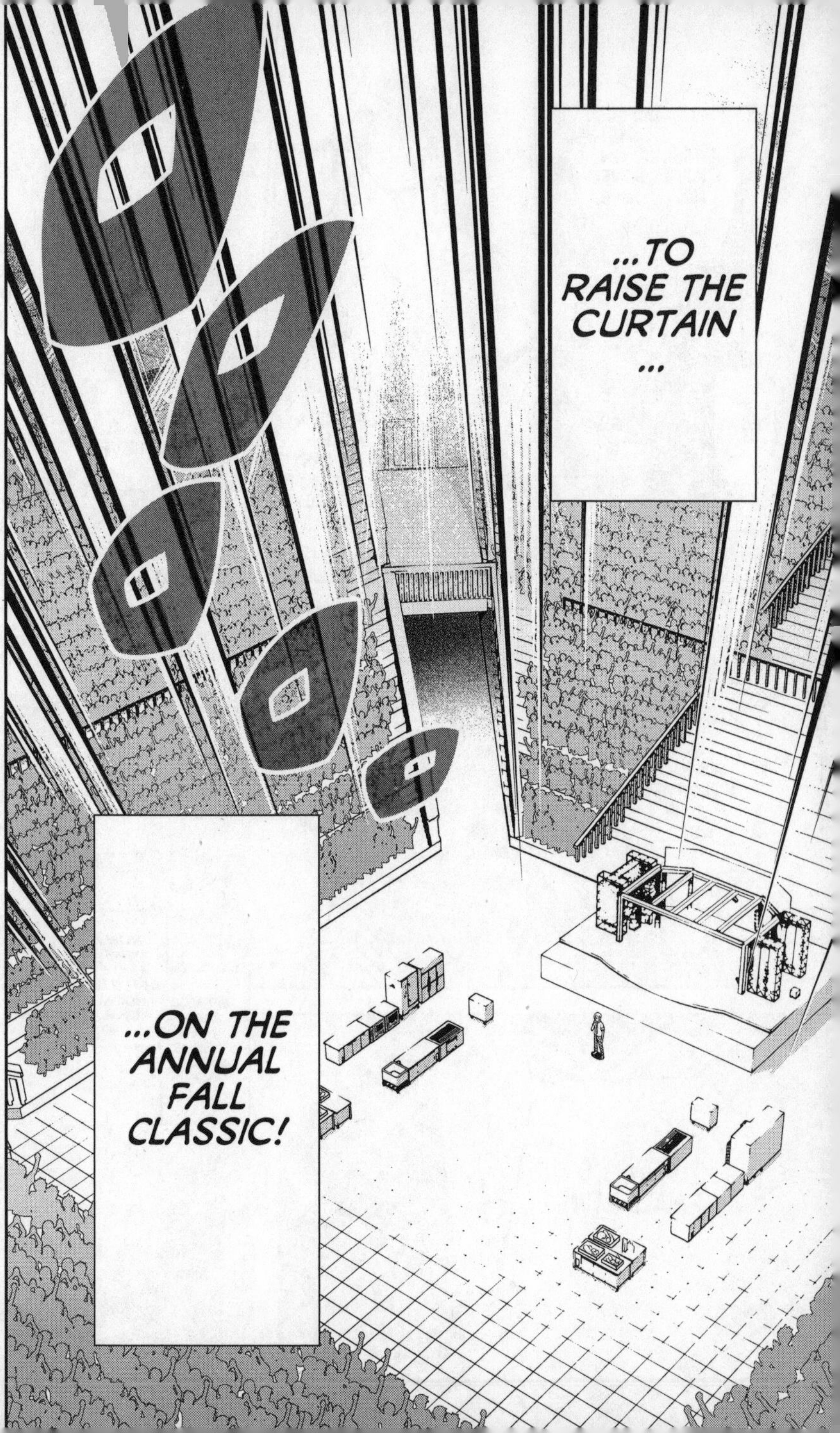
...TO RAISE THE CURTAIN ...
...ON THE ANNUAL FALL CLASSIC!

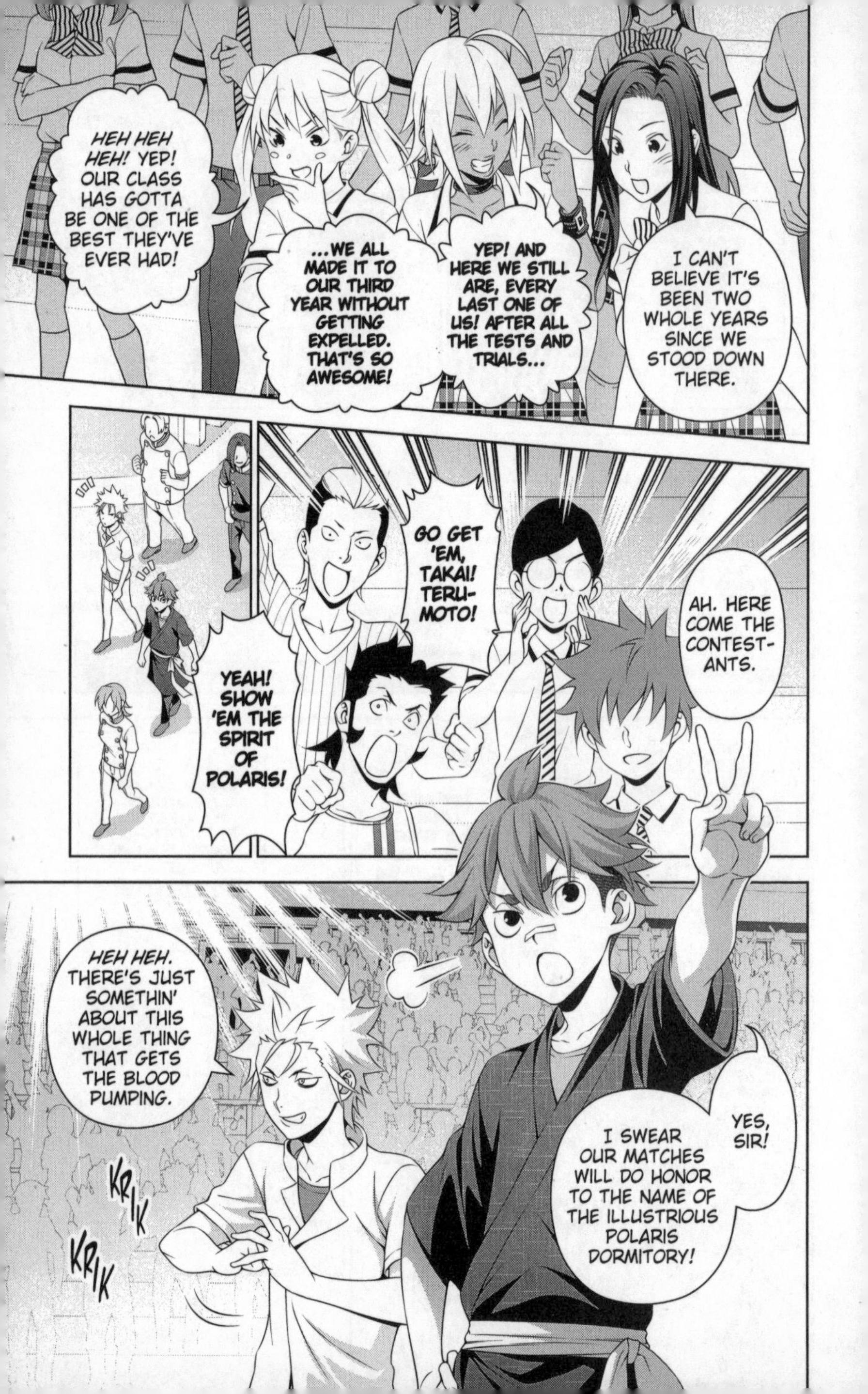
I CAN'T BELIEVE IT'S BEEN TWO WHOLE YEARS SINCE WE STOOD DOWN THERE.
YEP! AND HERE WE STILL ARE, EVERY LAST ONE OF US! AFTER ALL THE TESTS AND TRIALS...
...WE ALL MADE IT TO OUR THIRD YEAR WITHOUT GETTING EXPELLED. THAT'S SO AWESOME!
HEH HEH HEH! YEP! OUR CLASS HAS GOTTA BE ONE OF THE BEST THEY'VE EVER HAD!
AH. HERE COME THE CONTEST-ANTS.
GO GET 'EM, TAKAI! TERU-MOTO!
YEAH! SHOW 'EM THE SPIRIT OF POLARIS!
YES, SIR!
I SWEAR OUR MATCHES WILL DO HONOR TO THE NAME OF THE ILLUSTRIOUS POLARIS DORMITORY!
HEH HEH. THERE'S JUST SOMETHIN' ABOUT THIS WHOLE THING THAT GETS THE BLOOD PUMPING.
KRIK
KRIK

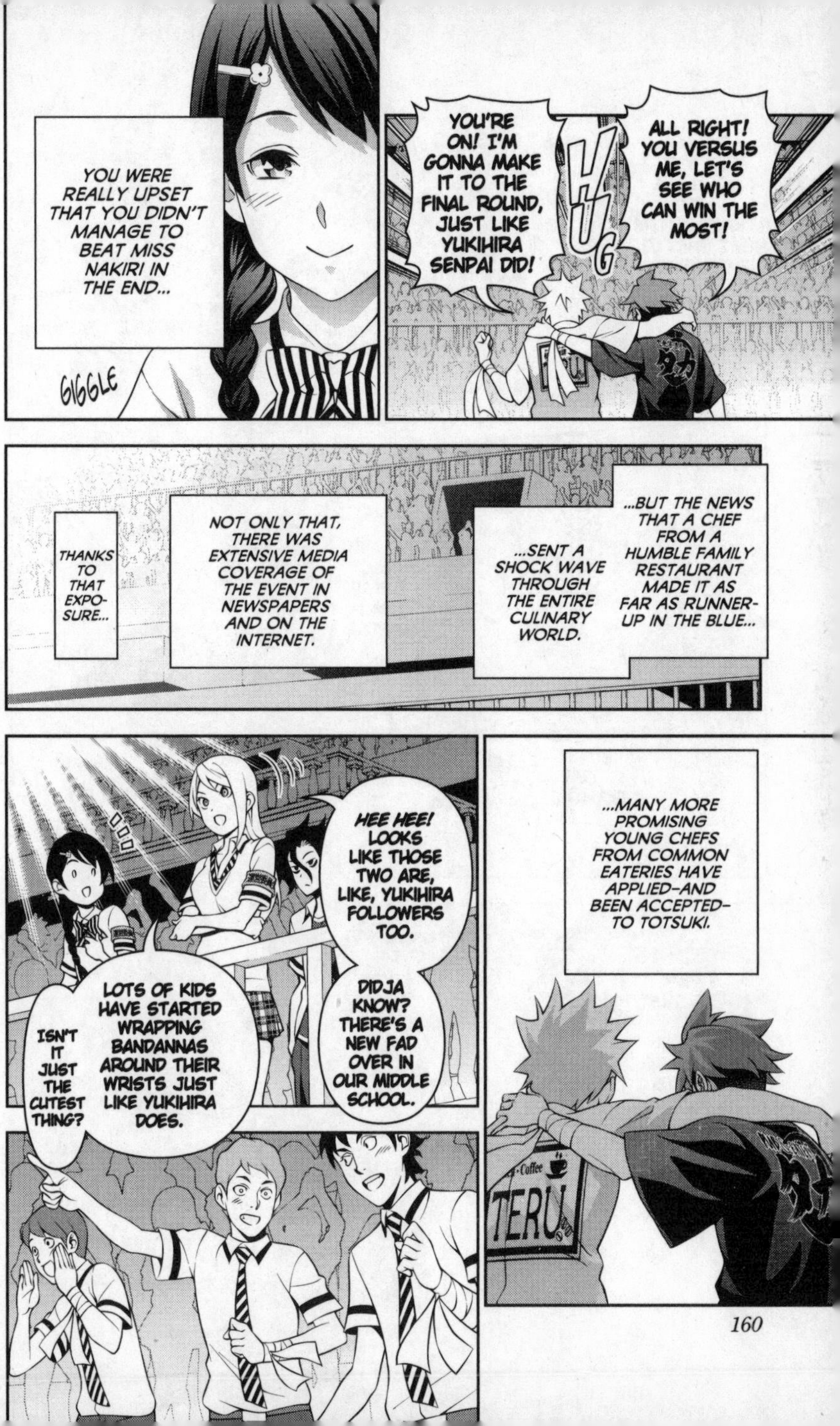
ALL RIGHT! YOU VERSUS ME, LET'S SEE WHO CAN WIN THE MOST!
HUG
YOU'RE ON! I'M GONNA MAKE IT TO THE FINAL ROUND, JUST LIKE YUKIHIRA SENPAI DID!
YOU WERE REALLY UPSET THAT YOU DIDN'T MANAGE TO BEAT MISS NAKIRI IN THE END...
GIGGLE
...BUT THE NEWS THAT A CHEF FROM A HUMBLE FAMILY RESTAURANT MADE IT AS FAR AS RUNNER-UP IN THE BLUE...
...SENT A SHOCK WAVE THROUGH THE ENTIRE CULINARY WORLD.
NOT ONLY THAT, THERE WAS EXTENSIVE MEDIA COVERAGE OF THE EVENT IN NEWSPAPERS AND ON THE INTERNET.
THANKS TO THAT EXPOSURE...
...MANY MORE PROMISING YOUNG CHEFS FROM COMMON EATERIES HAVE APPLIED—AND BEEN ACCEPTED—TO TOTSUKI.
Coffee
TERU
HEE HEE! LOOKS LIKE THOSE TWO ARE, LIKE, YUKIHIRA FOLLOWERS TOO.
DIDJA KNOW? THERE'S A NEW FAD OVER IN OUR MIDDLE SCHOOL.
LOTS OF KIDS HAVE STARTED WRAPPING BANDANNAS AROUND THEIR WRISTS JUST LIKE YUKIHIRA DOES.
ISN'T IT JUST THE CUTEST THING?

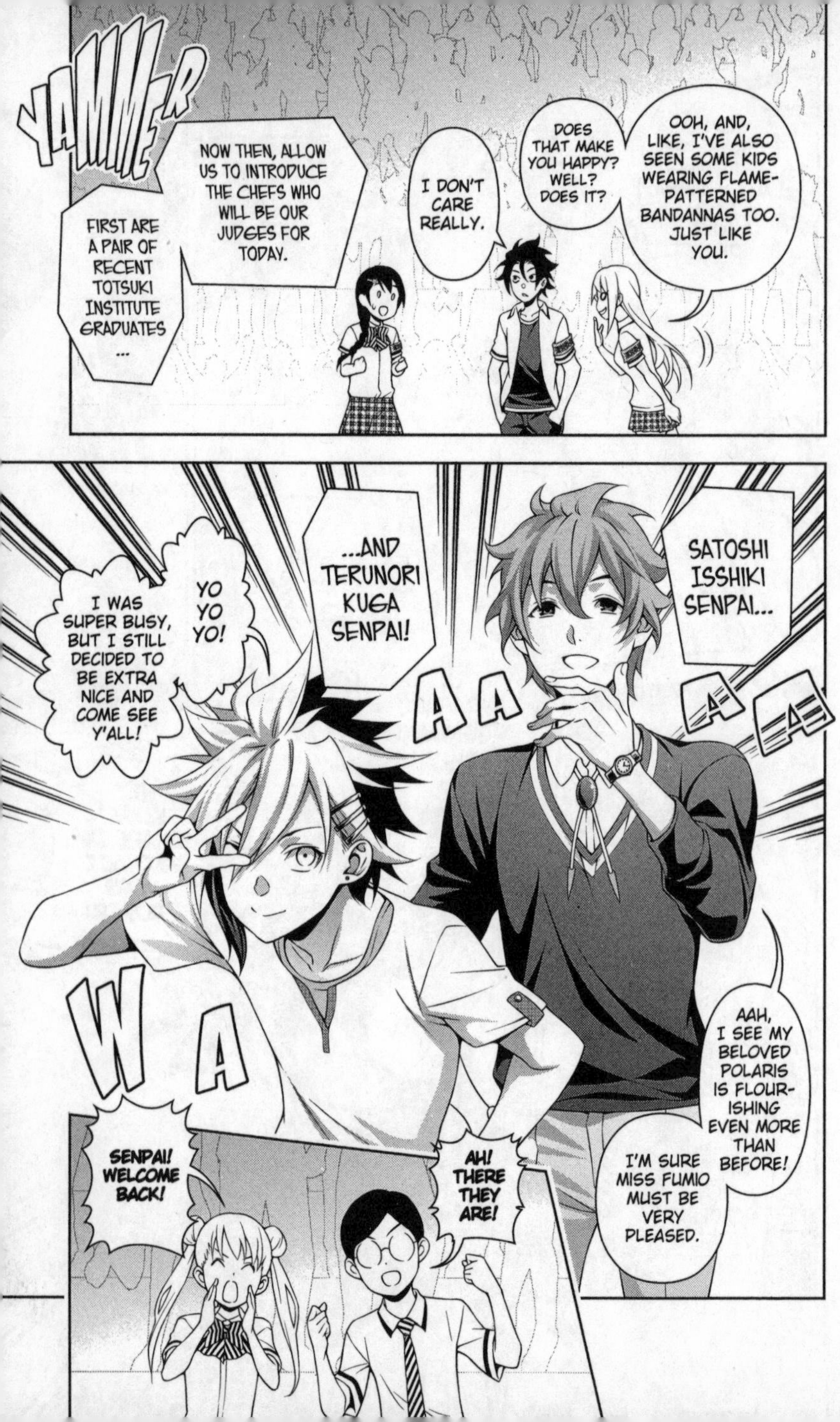
OOH, AND, LIKE, I'VE ALSO SEEN SOME KIDS WEARING FLAME-PATTERNED BANDANNAS TOO. JUST LIKE YOU.
DOES THAT MAKE YOU HAPPY? WELL? DOES IT?
I DON'T CARE REALLY.
NOW THEN, ALLOW US TO INTRODUCE THE CHEFS WHO WILL BE OUR JUDGES FOR TODAY.
FIRST ARE A PAIR OF RECENT TOTSUKI INSTITUTE GRADUATES ...
YAMMER
SATOSHI ISSHIKI SENPAI...
...AND TERUNORI KUGA SENPAI!
YO YO YO!
I WAS SUPER BUSY, BUT I STILL DECIDED TO BE EXTRA NICE AND COME SEE Y'ALL!
AAAA
WA
AAH, I SEE MY BELOVED POLARIS IS FLOURISHING EVEN MORE THAN BEFORE!
I'M SURE MISS FUMIO MUST BE VERY PLEASED.
AH! THERE THEY ARE!
SENPAI! WELCOME BACK!

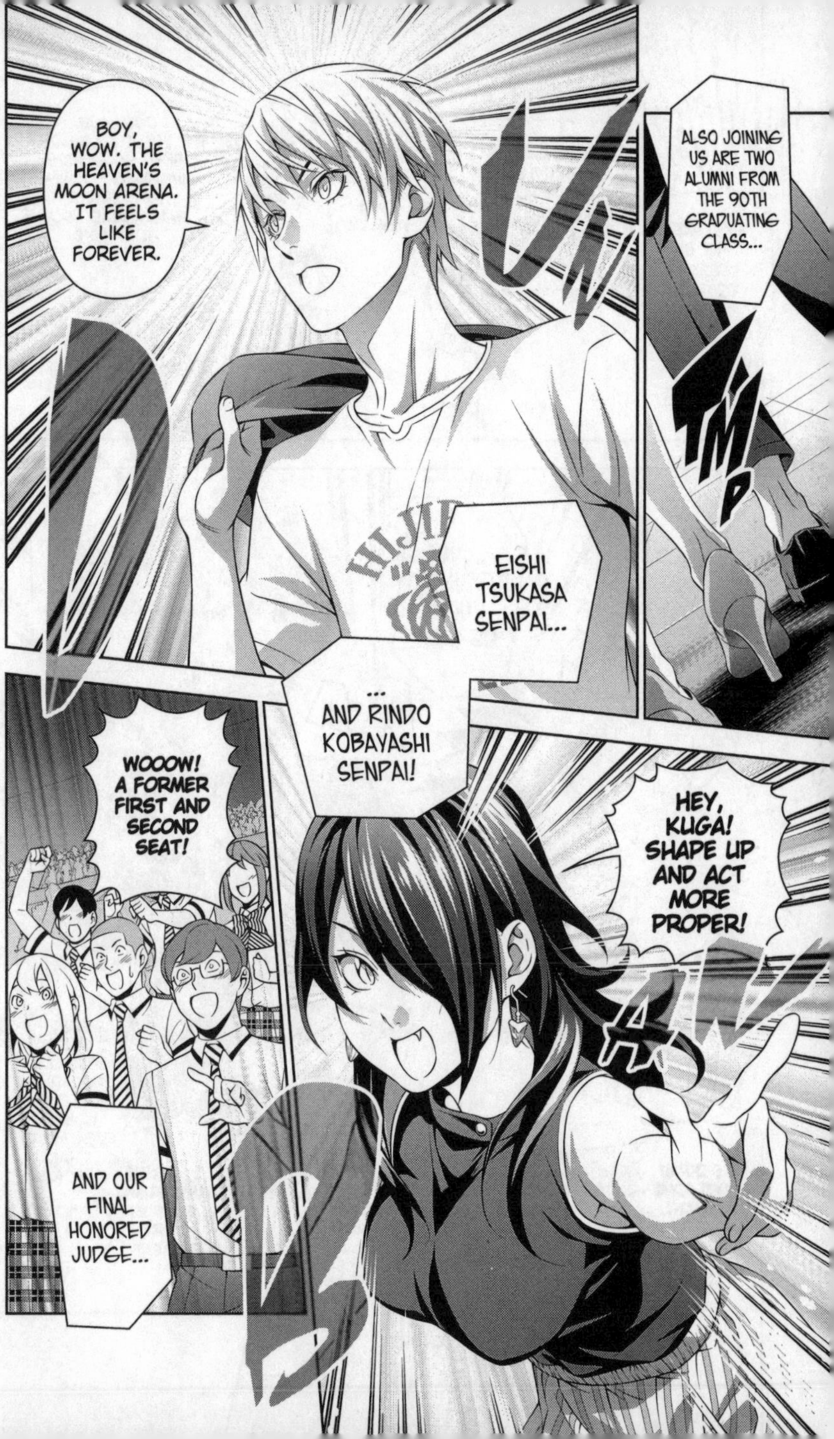
ALSO JOINING US ARE TWO ALUMNI FROM THE 90TH GRADUATING CLASS...
TMP
BOY, WOW. THE HEAVEN'S MOON ARENA. IT FEELS LIKE FOREVER.
EISHI TSUKASA SENPAI...
... AND RINDO KOBAYASHI SENPAI!
HEY, KUGA! SHAPE UP AND ACT MORE PROPER!
WOOOW! A FORMER FIRST AND SECOND SEAT!
AND OUR FINAL HONORED JUDGE...

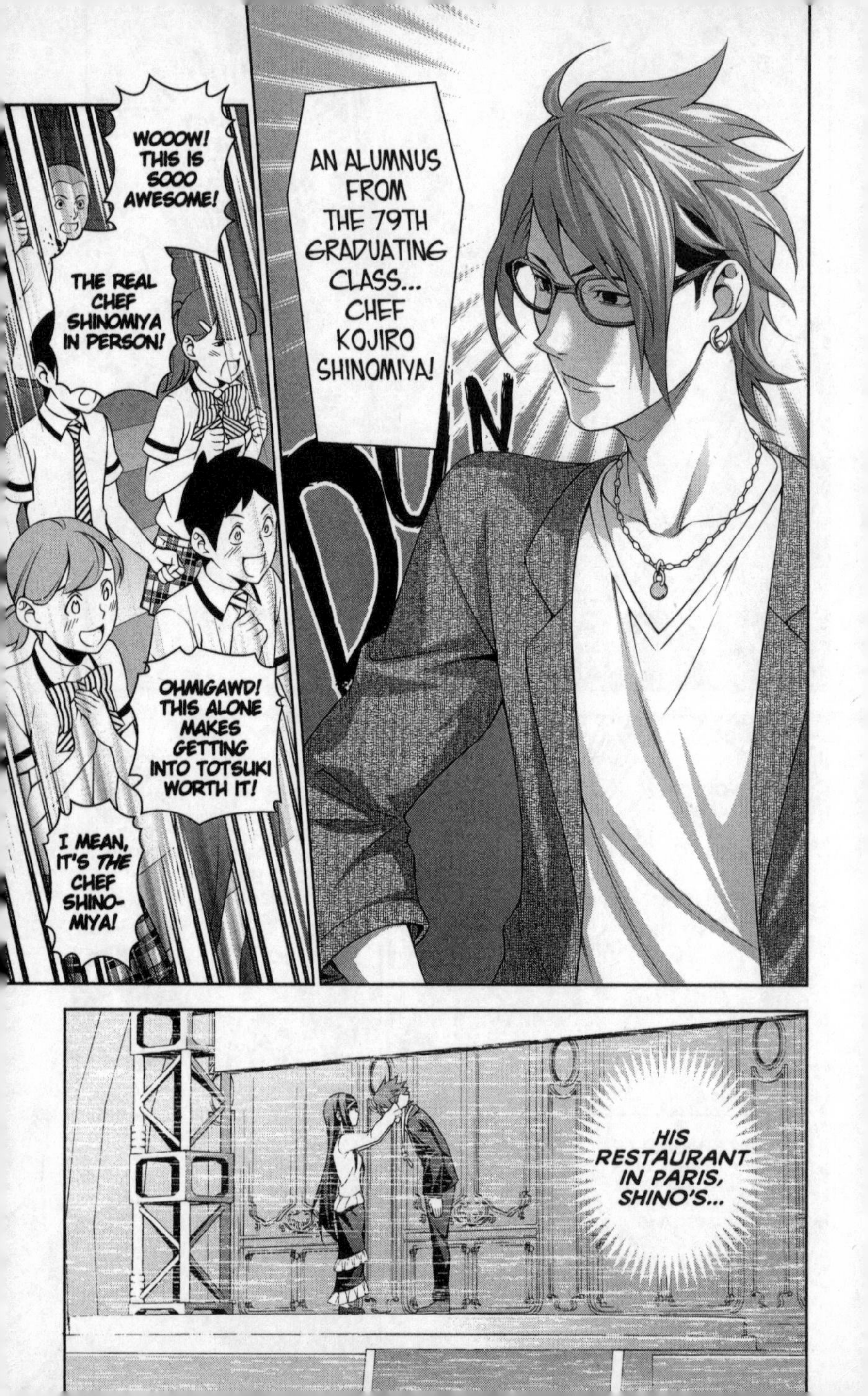

AN ALUMNUS FROM THE 79TH GRADUATING CLASS... CHEF KOJIRO SHINOMIYA!
WOOOW! THIS IS SOOO AWESOME!
THE REAL CHEF SHINOMIYA IN PERSON!
OHMIGAWD! THIS ALONE MAKES GETTING INTO TOTSUKI WORTH IT!
I MEAN, IT'S *THE* CHEF SHINO-MIYA!
HIS RESTAURANT IN PARIS, SHINO'S...

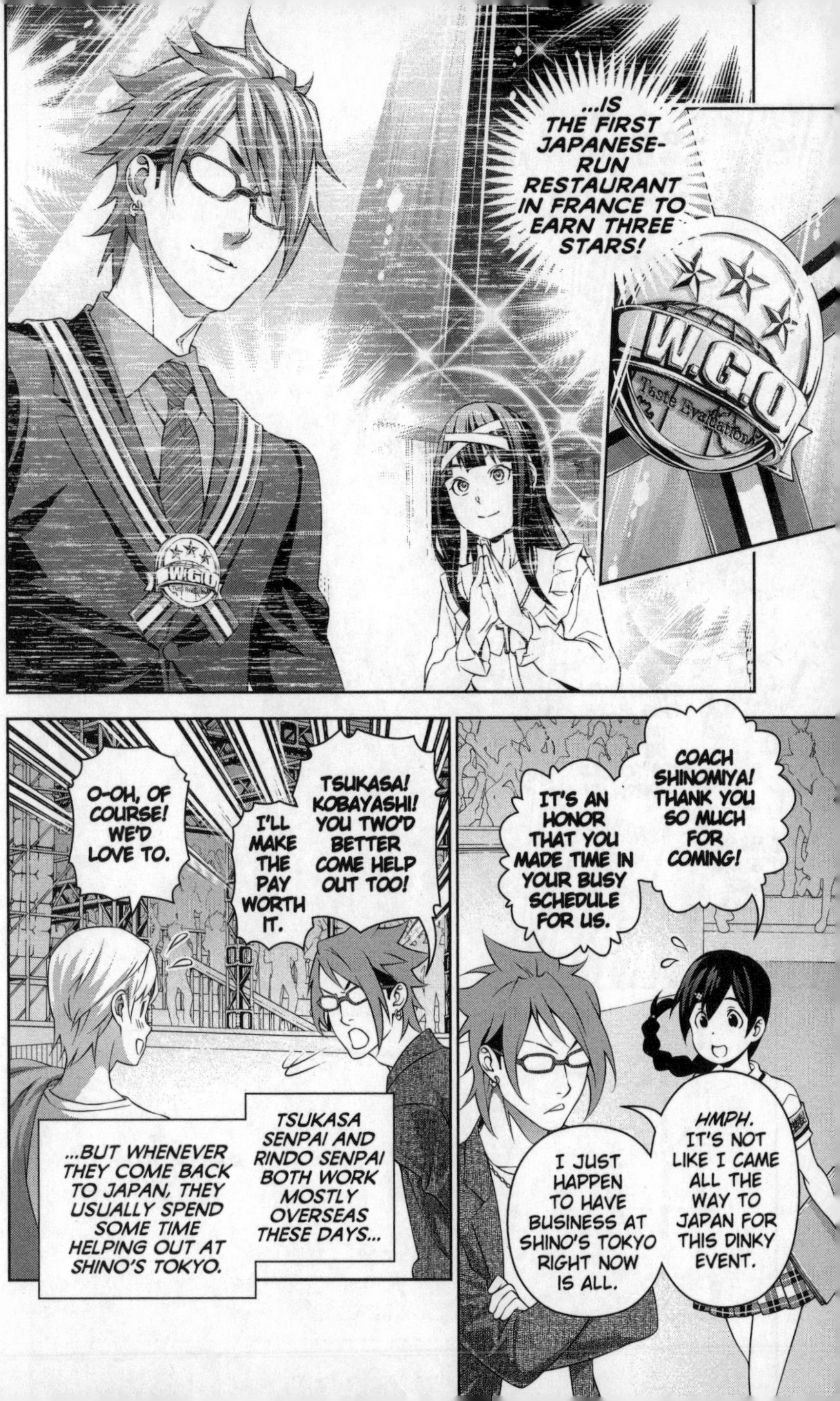
...IS THE FIRST JAPANESE-RUN RESTAURANT IN FRANCE TO EARN THREE STARS!
W.G.O
Taste Evaluation
COACH SHINOMIYA! THANK YOU SO MUCH FOR COMING!
IT'S AN HONOR THAT YOU MADE TIME IN YOUR BUSY SCHEDULE FOR US.
HMPH. IT'S NOT LIKE I CAME ALL THE WAY TO JAPAN FOR THIS DINKY EVENT.
I JUST HAPPEN TO HAVE BUSINESS AT SHINO'S TOKYO RIGHT NOW IS ALL.
TSUKASA! KOBAYASHI! YOU TWO'D BETTER COME HELP OUT TOO!
I'LL MAKE THE PAY WORTH IT.
O-OH, OF COURSE! WE'D LOVE TO.
TSUKASA SENPAI AND RINDO SENPAI BOTH WORK MOSTLY OVERSEAS THESE DAYS...
...BUT WHENEVER THEY COME BACK TO JAPAN, THEY USUALLY SPEND SOME TIME HELPING OUT AT SHINO'S TOKYO.

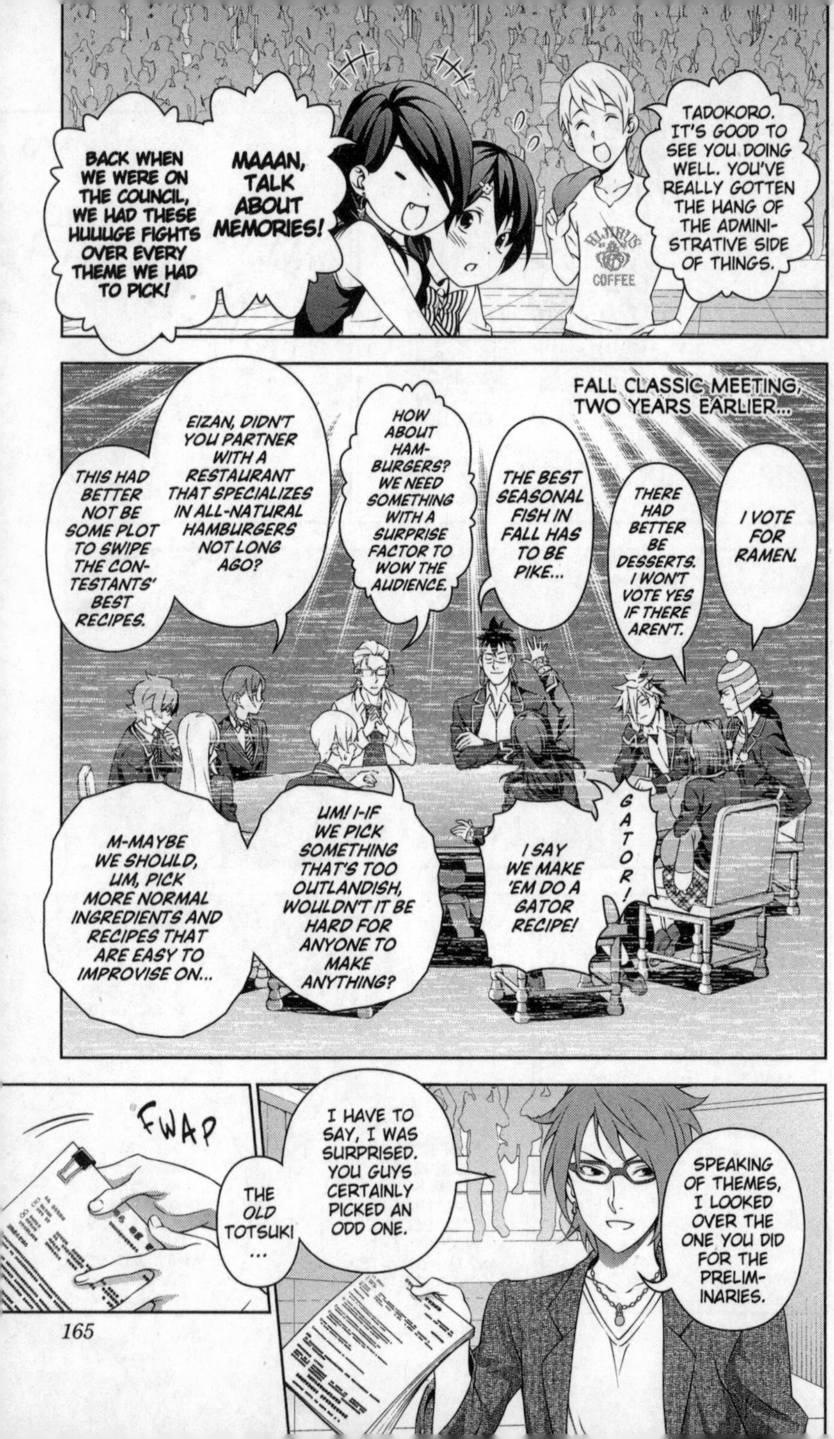

TADOKORO. IT'S GOOD TO SEE YOU DOING WELL. YOU'VE REALLY GOTTEN THE HANG OF THE ADMINISTRATIVE SIDE OF THINGS.
MAAAN, TALK ABOUT MEMORIES!
BACK WHEN WE WERE ON THE COUNCIL, WE HAD THESE HUUUGE FIGHTS OVER EVERY THEME WE HAD TO PICK!
FALL CLASSIC MEETING, TWO YEARS EARLIER...
I VOTE FOR RAMEN.
THERE HAD BETTER BE DESSERTS. I WON'T VOTE YES IF THERE AREN'T.
THE BEST SEASONAL FISH IN FALL HAS TO BE PIKE...
HOW ABOUT HAMBURGERS? WE NEED SOMETHING WITH A SURPRISE FACTOR TO WOW THE AUDIENCE.
EIZAN, DIDN'T YOU PARTNER WITH A RESTAURANT THAT SPECIALIZES IN ALL-NATURAL HAMBURGERS NOT LONG AGO?
THIS HAD BETTER NOT BE SOME PLOT TO SWIPE THE CONTESTANTS' BEST RECIPES.
GATOR!
I SAY WE MAKE 'EM DO A GATOR RECIPE!
UM! I-IF WE PICK SOMETHING THAT'S TOO OUTLANDISH, WOULDN'T IT BE HARD FOR ANYONE TO MAKE ANYTHING?
M-MAYBE WE SHOULD, UM, PICK MORE NORMAL INGREDIENTS AND RECIPES THAT ARE EASY TO IMPROVISE ON...
SPEAKING OF THEMES, I LOOKED OVER THE ONE YOU DID FOR THE PRELIMINARIES.
I HAVE TO SAY, I WAS SURPRISED. YOU GUYS CERTAINLY PICKED AN ODD ONE.
THE OLD TOTSUKI ...
FWAP

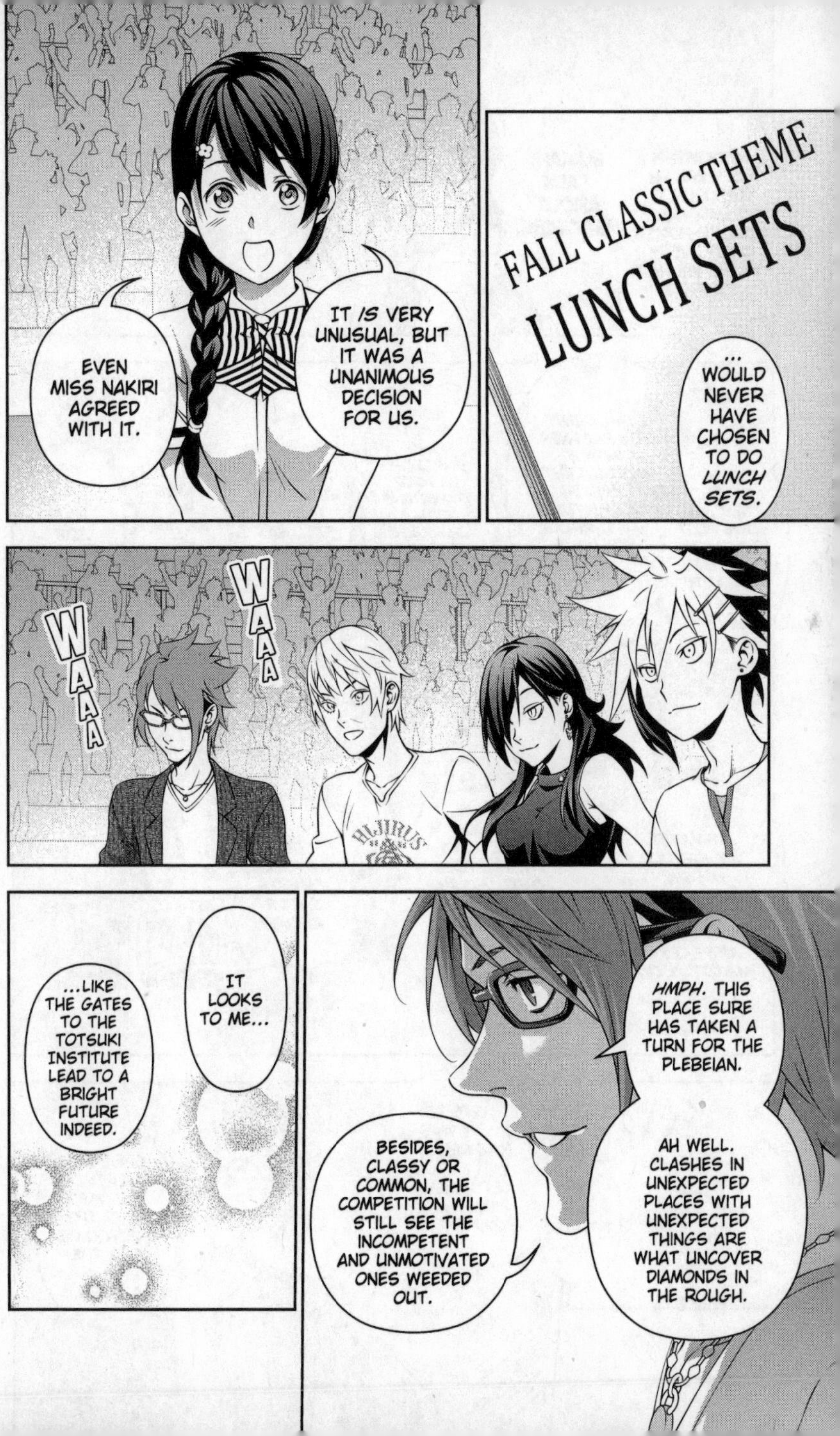

FALL CLASSIC THEME
LUNCH SETS
... WOULD NEVER HAVE CHOSEN TO DO *LUNCH SETS.*
IT *IS* VERY UNUSUAL, BUT IT WAS A UNANIMOUS DECISION FOR US.
EVEN MISS NAKIRI AGREED WITH IT.
WAAA
WAAA
HMPH. THIS PLACE SURE HAS TAKEN A TURN FOR THE PLEBEIAN.
AH WELL. CLASHES IN UNEXPECTED PLACES WITH UNEXPECTED THINGS ARE WHAT UNCOVER DIAMONDS IN THE ROUGH.
BESIDES, CLASSY OR COMMON, THE COMPETITION WILL STILL SEE THE INCOMPETENT AND UNMOTIVATED ONES WEEDED OUT.
IT LOOKS TO ME...
...LIKE THE GATES TO THE TOTSUKI INSTITUTE LEAD TO A BRIGHT FUTURE INDEED.

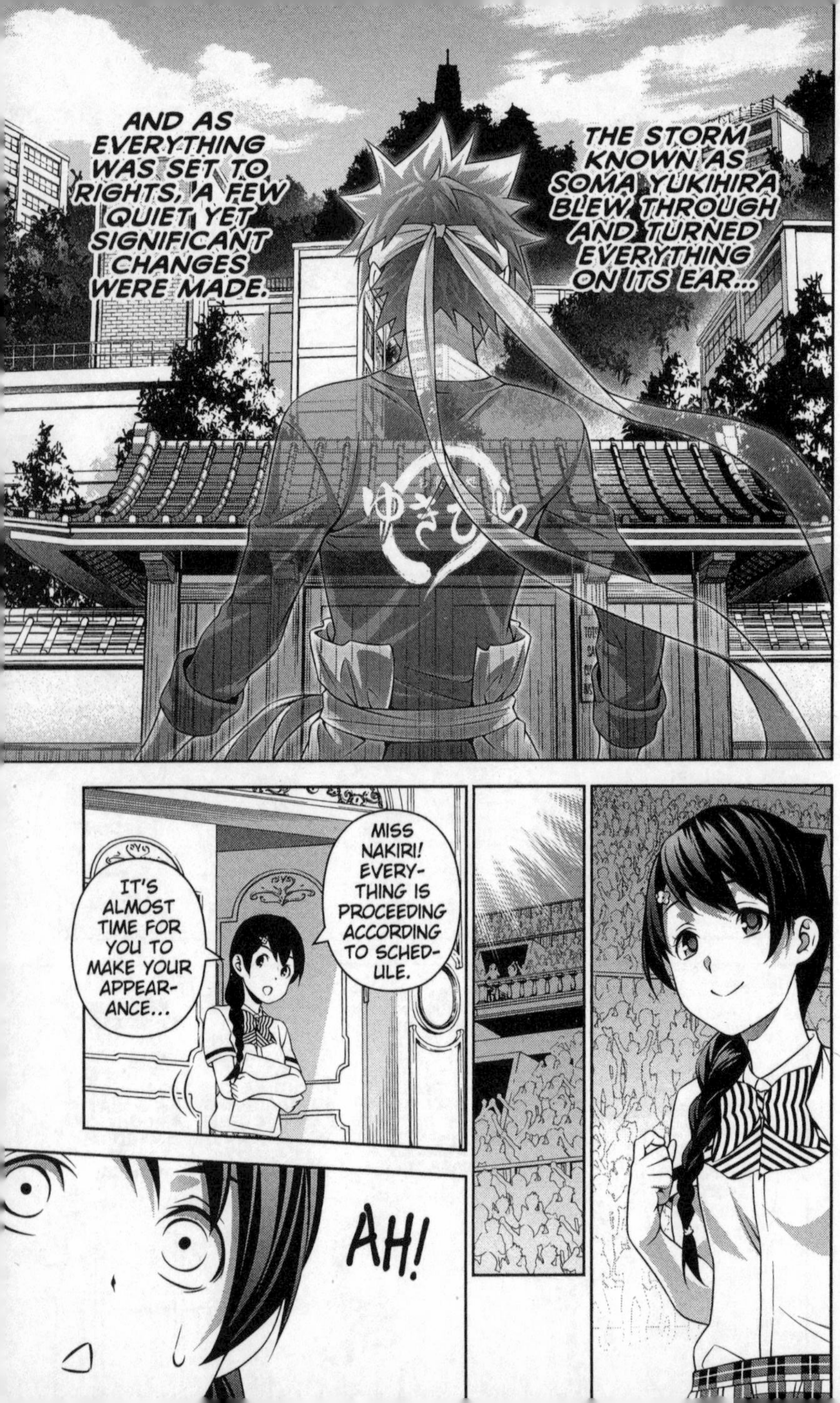
THE STORM KNOWN AS SOMA YUKIHIRA BLEW THROUGH AND TURNED EVERYTHING ON ITS EAR...
AND AS EVERYTHING WAS SET TO RIGHTS, A FEW QUIET YET SIGNIFICANT CHANGES WERE MADE.
MISS NAKIRI! EVERY-THING IS PROCEEDING ACCORDING TO SCHED-ULE.
IT'S ALMOST TIME FOR YOU TO MAKE YOUR APPEAR-ANCE...
AH!

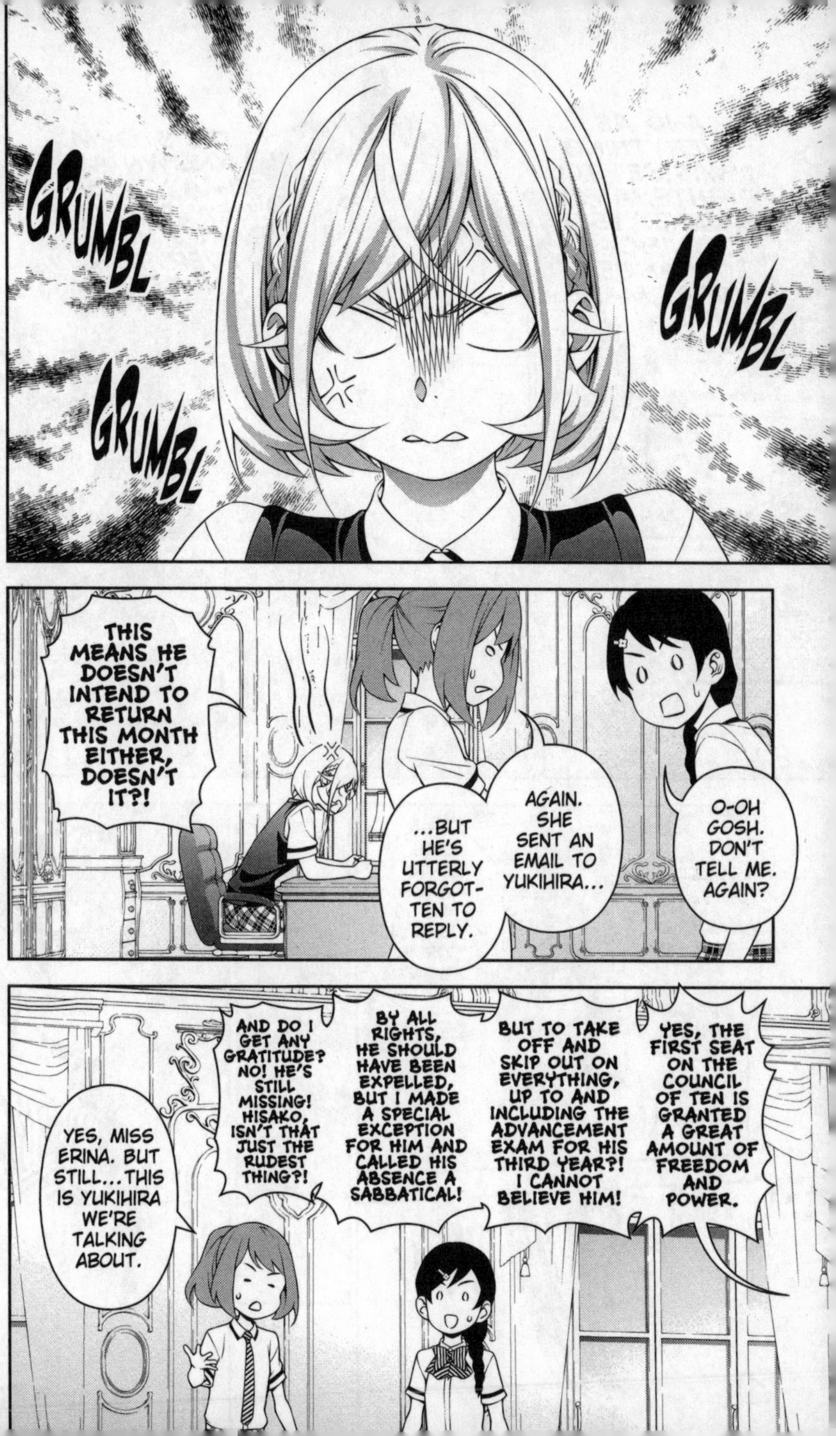
GRUMBL
GRUMBL
GRUMBL
O-OH GOSH. DON'T TELL ME. AGAIN?
AGAIN. SHE SENT AN EMAIL TO YUKIHIRA...
...BUT HE'S UTTERLY FORGOT-TEN TO REPLY.
THIS MEANS HE DOESN'T INTEND TO RETURN THIS MONTH EITHER, DOESN'T IT?!
YES, THE FIRST SEAT ON THE COUNCIL OF TEN IS GRANTED A GREAT AMOUNT OF FREEDOM AND POWER.
BUT TO TAKE OFF AND SKIP OUT ON EVERYTHING, UP TO AND INCLUDING THE ADVANCEMENT EXAM FOR HIS THIRD YEAR?! I CANNOT BELIEVE HIM!
BY ALL RIGHTS, HE SHOULD HAVE BEEN EXPELLED, BUT I MADE A SPECIAL EXCEPTION FOR HIM AND CALLED HIS ABSENCE A SABBATICAL!
AND DO I GET ANY GRATITUDE? NO! HE'S STILL MISSING! HISAKO, ISN'T THAT JUST THE RUDEST THING?!
YES, MISS ERINA. BUT STILL...THIS IS YUKIHIRA WE'RE TALKING ABOUT.

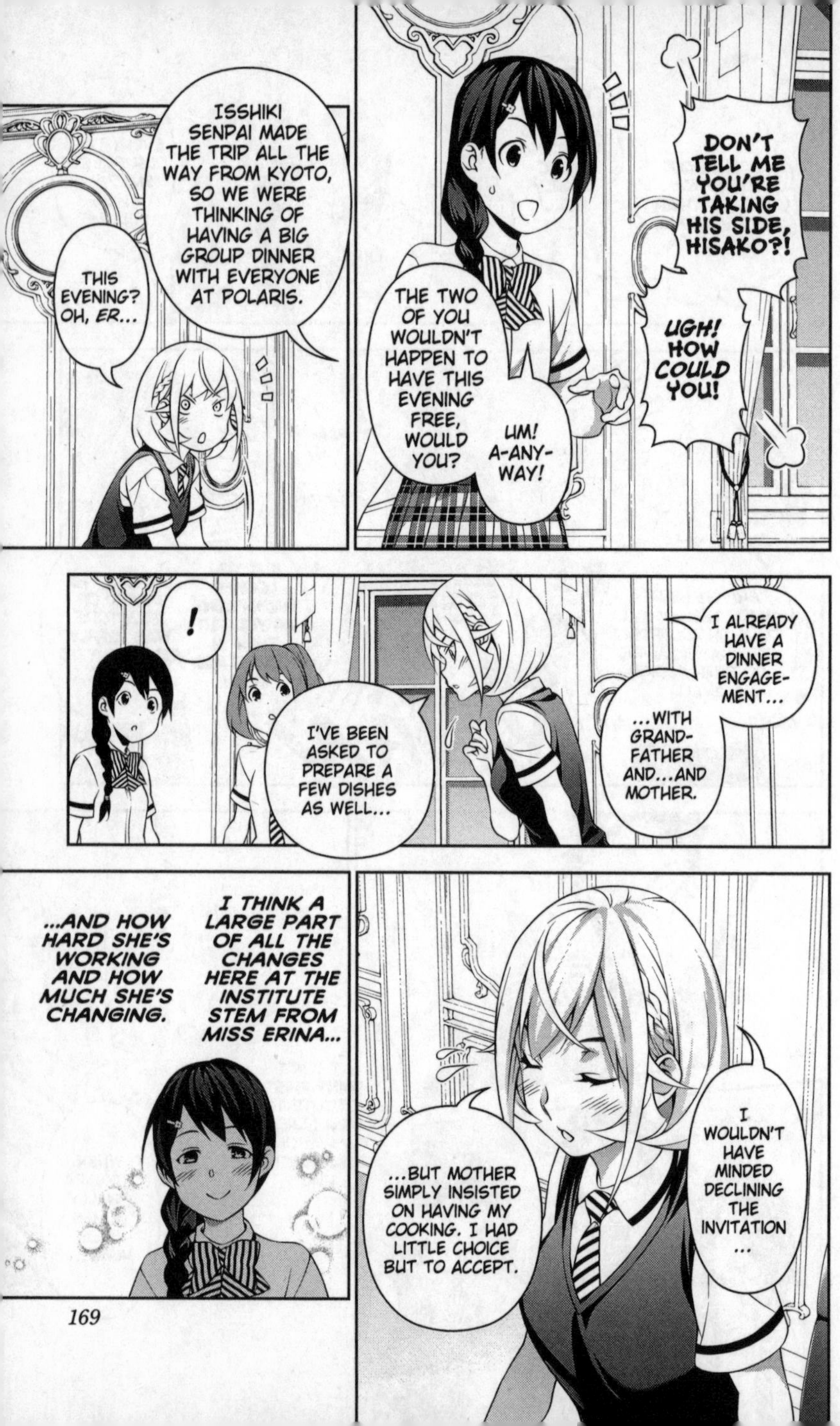
DON'T TELL ME YOU'RE TAKING HIS SIDE, HISAKO?!
UGH! HOW COULD YOU!
UM! A-ANYWAY!
THE TWO OF YOU WOULDN'T HAPPEN TO HAVE THIS EVENING FREE, WOULD YOU?
ISSHIKI SENPAI MADE THE TRIP ALL THE WAY FROM KYOTO, SO WE WERE THINKING OF HAVING A BIG GROUP DINNER WITH EVERYONE AT POLARIS.
THIS EVENING? OH, *ER*...
I ALREADY HAVE A DINNER ENGAGEMENT...
...WITH GRANDFATHER AND...AND MOTHER.
I'VE BEEN ASKED TO PREPARE A FEW DISHES AS WELL...
!
I WOULDN'T HAVE MINDED DECLINING THE INVITATION...
...BUT MOTHER SIMPLY INSISTED ON HAVING MY COOKING. I HAD LITTLE CHOICE BUT TO ACCEPT.
I THINK A LARGE PART OF ALL THE CHANGES HERE AT THE INSTITUTE STEM FROM MISS ERINA...
...AND HOW HARD SHE'S WORKING AND HOW MUCH SHE'S CHANGING.

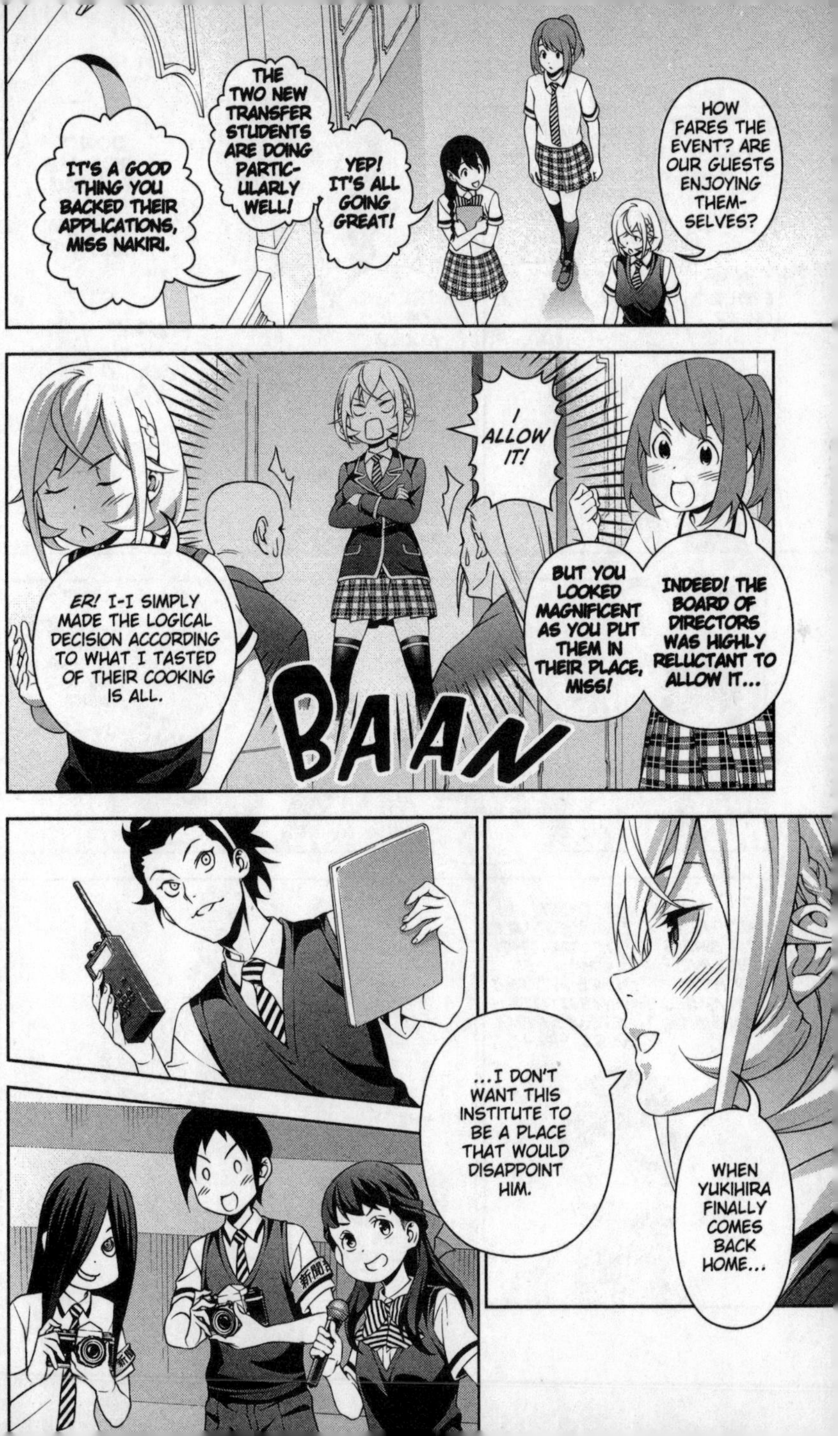
HOW FARES THE EVENT? ARE OUR GUESTS ENJOYING THEM-SELVES?
YEP! IT'S ALL GOING GREAT!
THE TWO NEW TRANSFER STUDENTS ARE DOING PARTIC-ULARLY WELL!
IT'S A GOOD THING YOU BACKED THEIR APPLICATIONS, MISS NAKIRI.
INDEED! THE BOARD OF DIRECTORS WAS HIGHLY RELUCTANT TO ALLOW IT...
I ALLOW IT!
BUT YOU LOOKED MAGNIFICENT AS YOU PUT THEM IN THEIR PLACE, MISS!
BAAN
ER! I-I SIMPLY MADE THE LOGICAL DECISION ACCORDING TO WHAT I TASTED OF THEIR COOKING IS ALL.
WHEN YUKIHIRA FINALLY COMES BACK HOME...
...I DON'T WANT THIS INSTITUTE TO BE A PLACE THAT WOULD DISAPPOINT HIM.

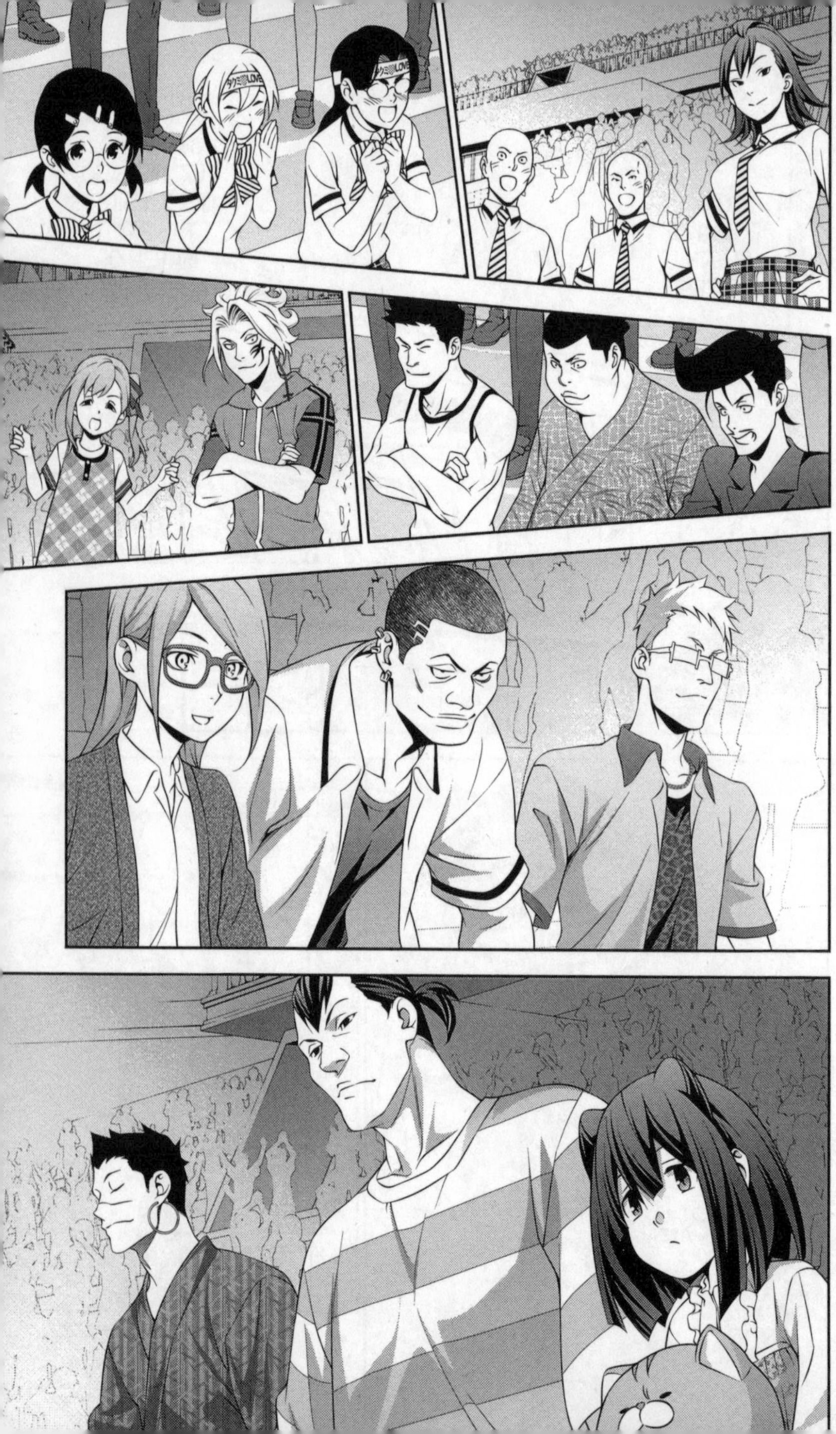
タクミ LOVE
タクミ LOVE

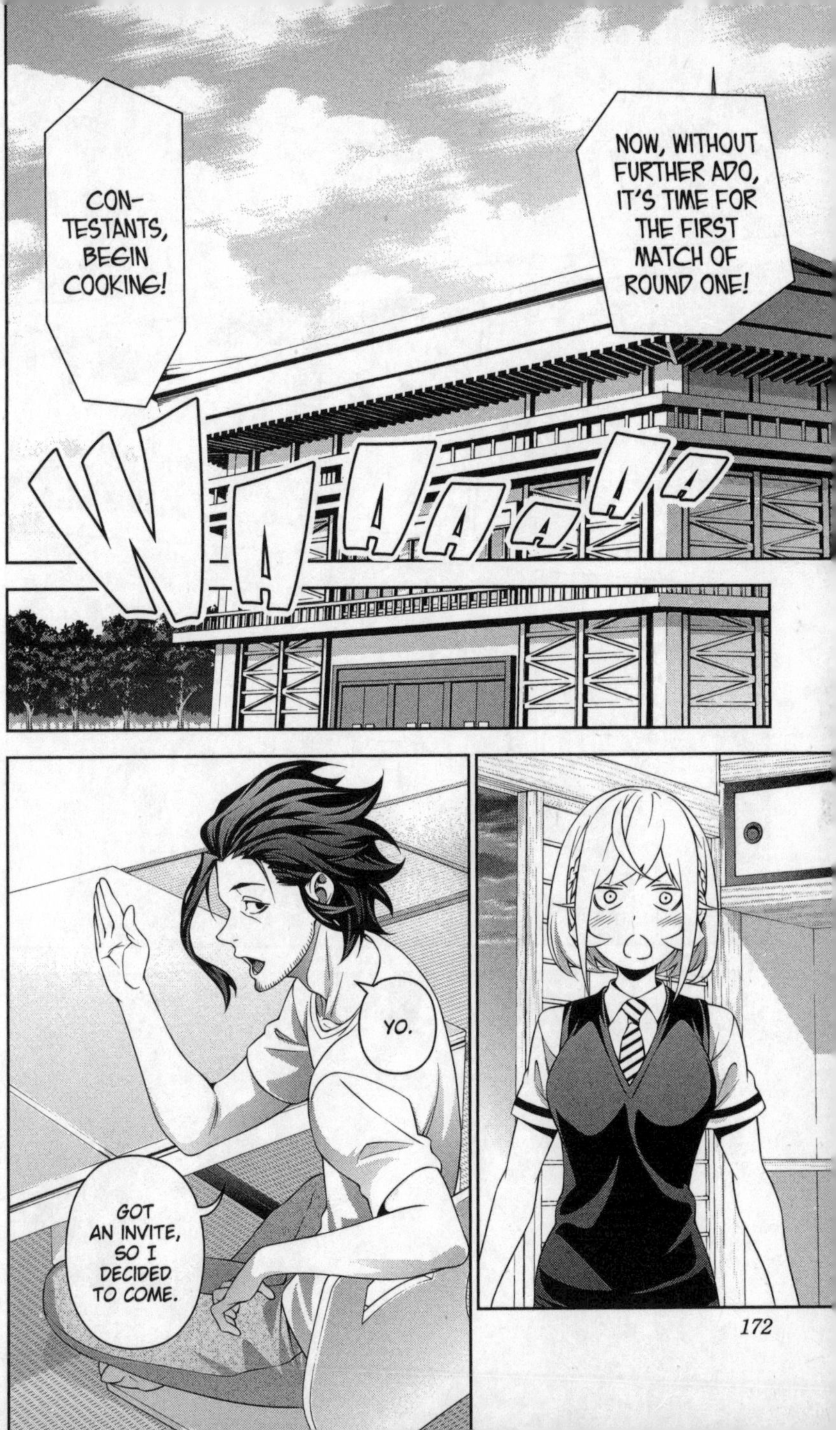
NOW, WITHOUT FURTHER ADO, IT'S TIME FOR THE FIRST MATCH OF ROUND ONE!
CON-TESTANTS, BEGIN COOKING!
WAAAAAA
YO.
GOT AN INVITE, SO I DECIDED TO COME.

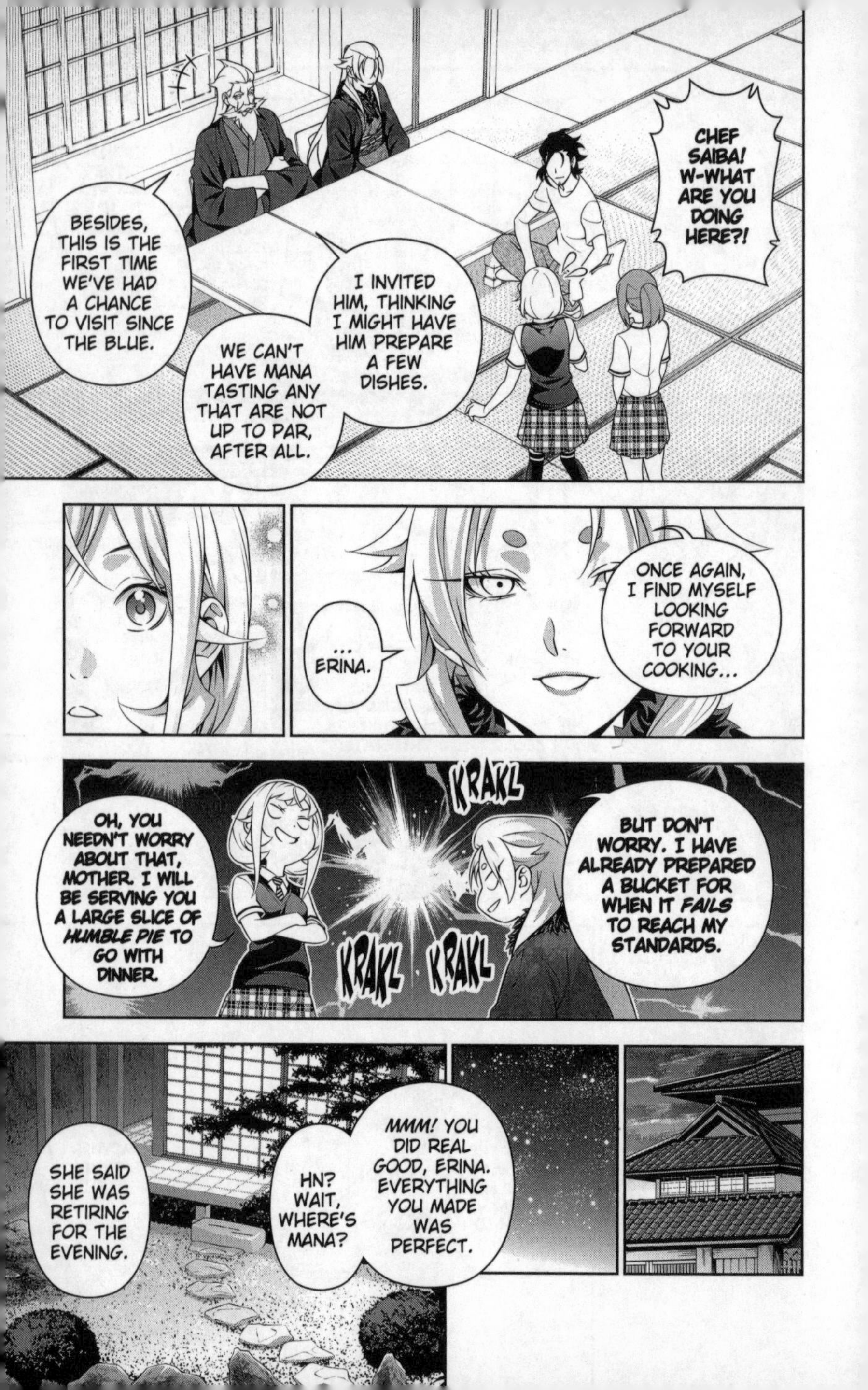
CHEF SAIBA! W-WHAT ARE YOU DOING HERE?!
I INVITED HIM, THINKING I MIGHT HAVE HIM PREPARE A FEW DISHES.
WE CAN'T HAVE MANA TASTING ANY THAT ARE NOT UP TO PAR, AFTER ALL.
BESIDES, THIS IS THE FIRST TIME WE'VE HAD A CHANCE TO VISIT SINCE THE BLUE.
ONCE AGAIN, I FIND MYSELF LOOKING FORWARD TO YOUR COOKING...
... ERINA.
BUT DON'T WORRY. I HAVE ALREADY PREPARED A BUCKET FOR WHEN IT *FAILS* TO REACH MY STANDARDS.
KRAKL
OH, YOU NEEDN'T WORRY ABOUT THAT, MOTHER. I WILL BE SERVING YOU A LARGE SLICE OF *HUMBLE PIE* TO GO WITH DINNER.
KRAKL KRAKL
MMM! YOU DID REAL GOOD, ERINA. EVERYTHING YOU MADE WAS PERFECT.
HN? WAIT, WHERE'S MANA?
SHE SAID SHE WAS RETIRING FOR THE EVENING.

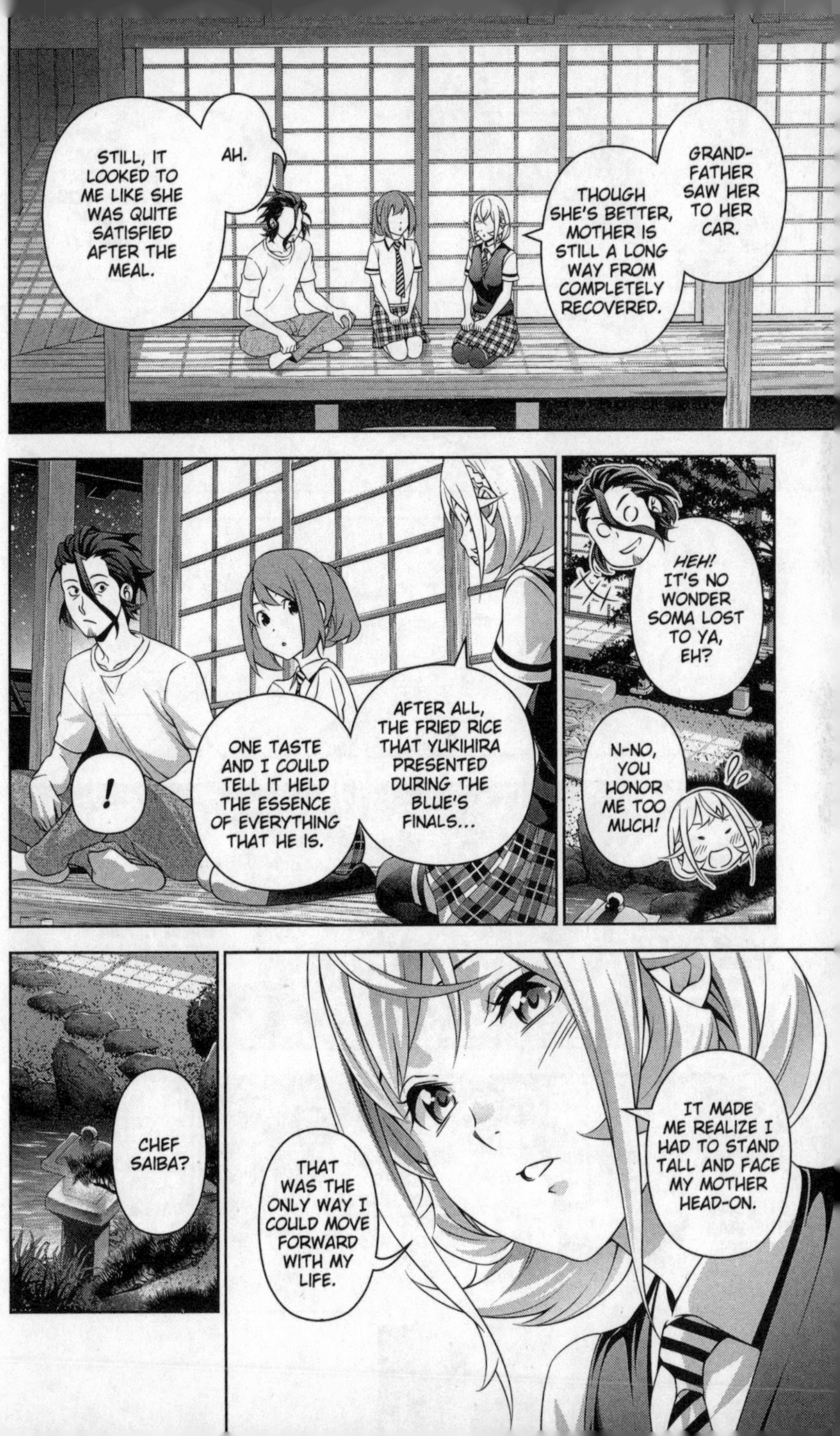
GRAND-FATHER SAW HER TO HER CAR.
THOUGH SHE'S BETTER, MOTHER IS STILL A LONG WAY FROM COMPLETELY RECOVERED.
AH.
STILL, IT LOOKED TO ME LIKE SHE WAS QUITE SATISFIED AFTER THE MEAL.
HEH! IT'S NO WONDER SOMA LOST TO YA, EH?
N-NO, YOU HONOR ME TOO MUCH!
AFTER ALL, THE FRIED RICE THAT YUKIHIRA PRESENTED DURING THE BLUE'S FINALS...
ONE TASTE AND I COULD TELL IT HELD THE ESSENCE OF EVERYTHING THAT HE IS.
!
IT MADE ME REALIZE I HAD TO STAND TALL AND FACE MY MOTHER HEAD-ON.
THAT WAS THE ONLY WAY I COULD MOVE FORWARD WITH MY LIFE.
CHEF SAIBA?

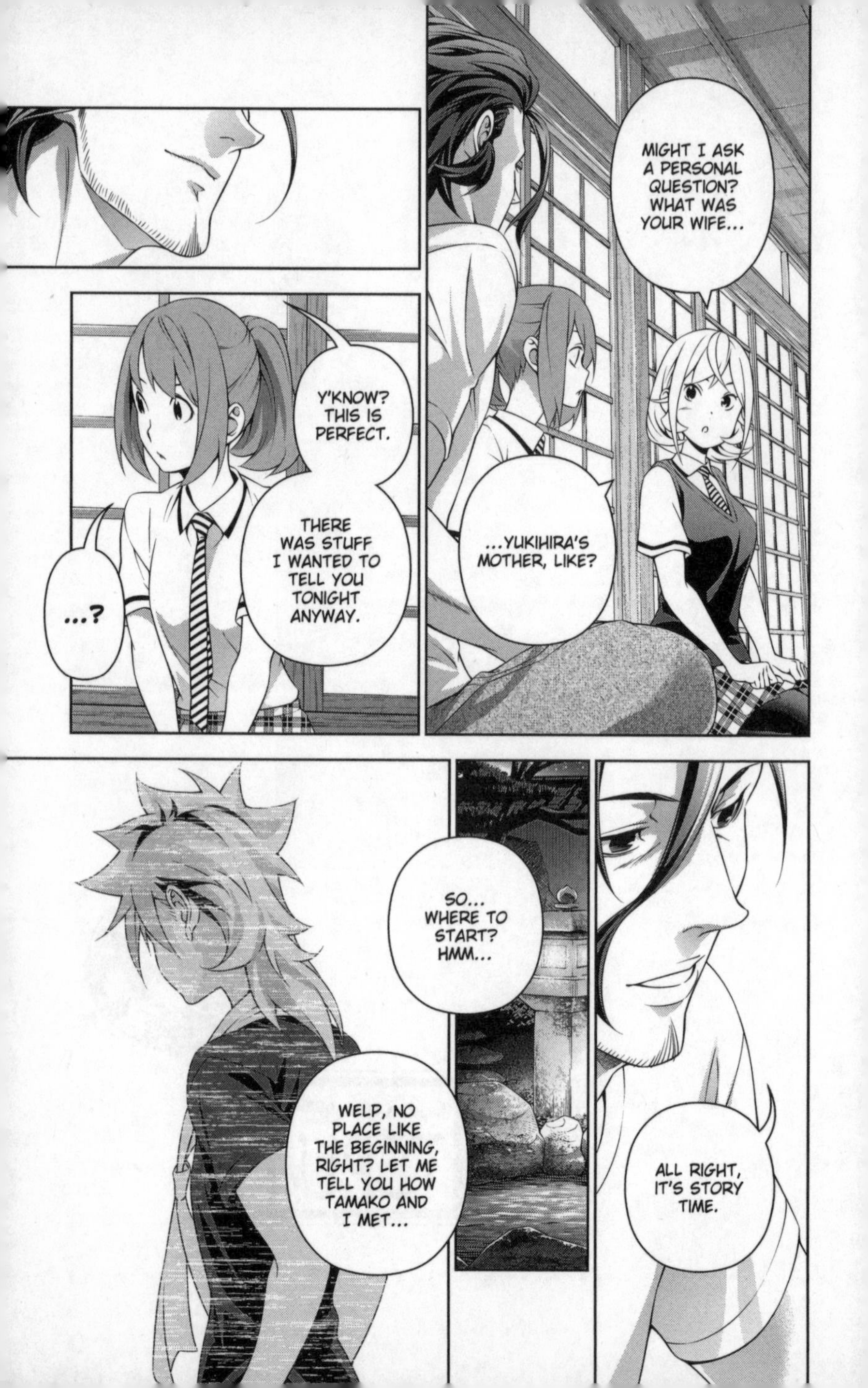
MIGHT I ASK A PERSONAL QUESTION? WHAT WAS YOUR WIFE...
...YUKIHIRA'S MOTHER, LIKE?
Y'KNOW? THIS IS PERFECT.
THERE WAS STUFF I WANTED TO TELL YOU TONIGHT ANYWAY.
...?
ALL RIGHT, IT'S STORY TIME.
SO... WHERE TO START? HMM...
WELP, NO PLACE LIKE THE BEGINNING, RIGHT? LET ME TELL YOU HOW TAMAKO AND I MET...

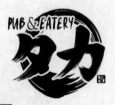

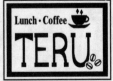

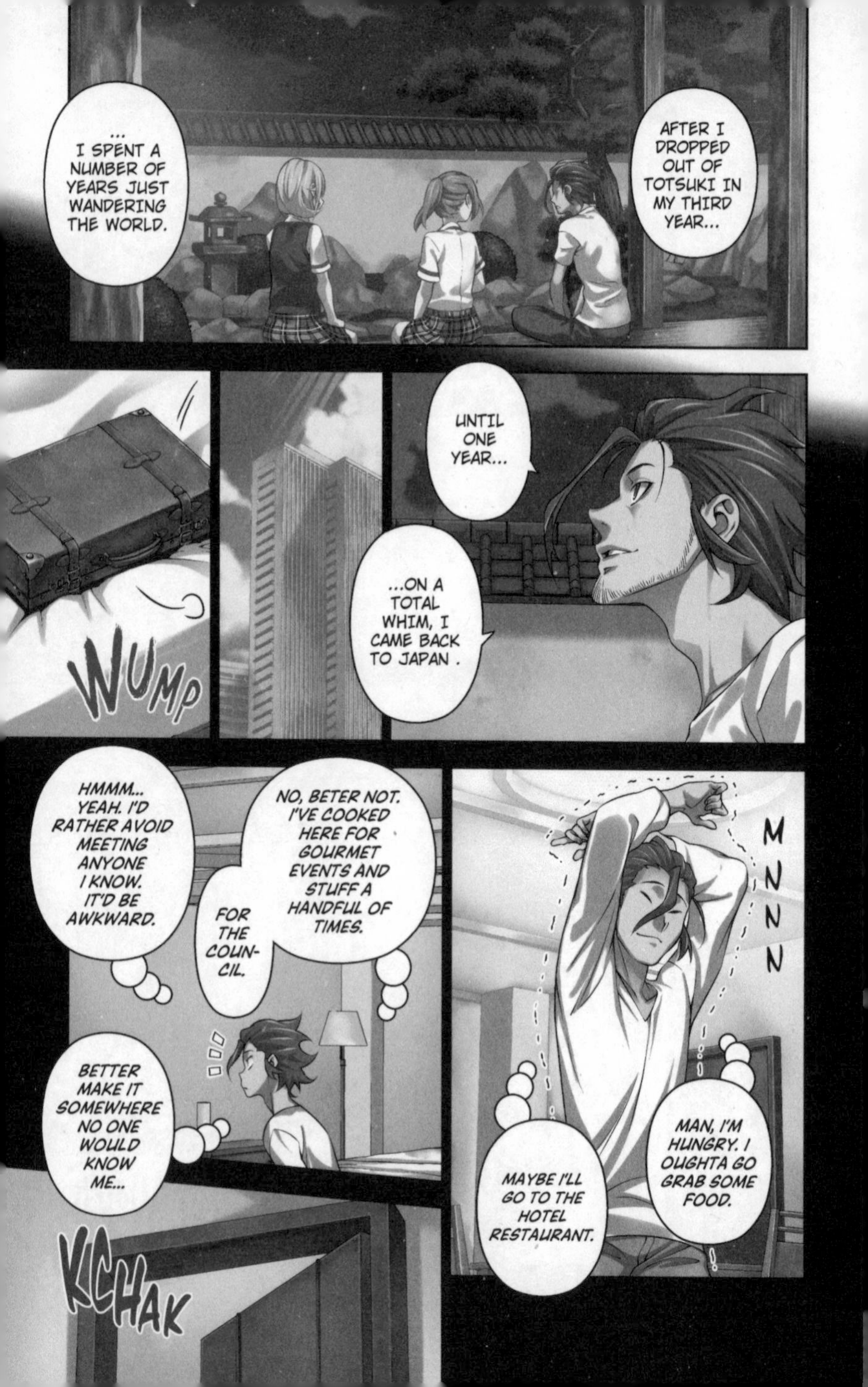
AFTER I DROPPED OUT OF TOTSUKI IN MY THIRD YEAR...
... I SPENT A NUMBER OF YEARS JUST WANDERING THE WORLD.
UNTIL ONE YEAR...
...ON A TOTAL WHIM, I CAME BACK TO JAPAN .
WUMP
MNNN
MAN, I'M HUNGRY. I OUGHTA GO GRAB SOME FOOD.
MAYBE I'LL GO TO THE HOTEL RESTAURANT.
NO, BETER NOT. I'VE COOKED HERE FOR GOURMET EVENTS AND STUFF A HANDFUL OF TIMES.
FOR THE COUN-CIL.
HMMM... YEAH. I'D RATHER AVOID MEETING ANYONE I KNOW. IT'D BE AWKWARD.
BETTER MAKE IT SOMEWHERE NO ONE WOULD KNOW ME...
KCHAK

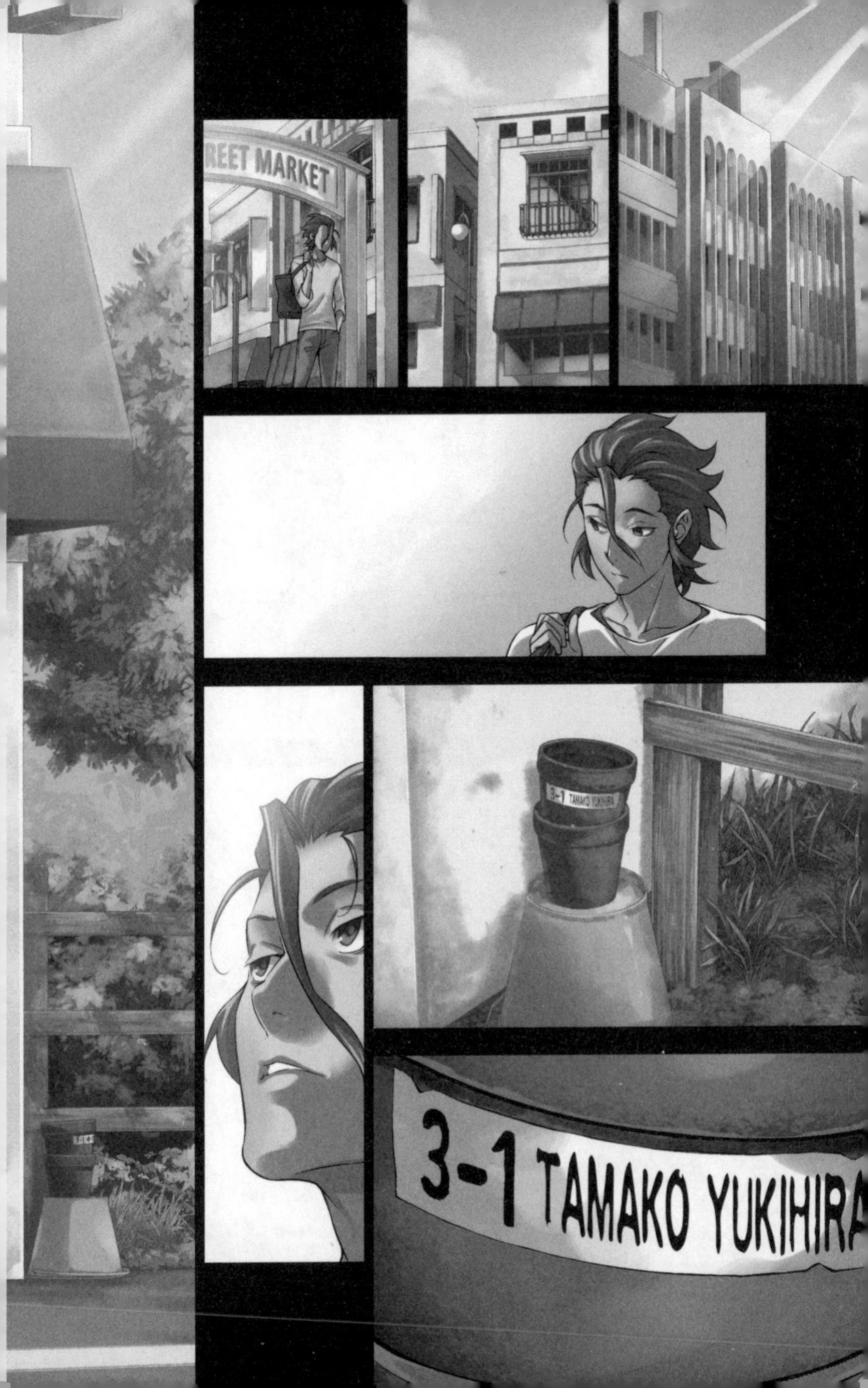
REET MARKET
3-1 TAMAKO YUKIHIRA
3-1 TAMAKO YUKIHIRA

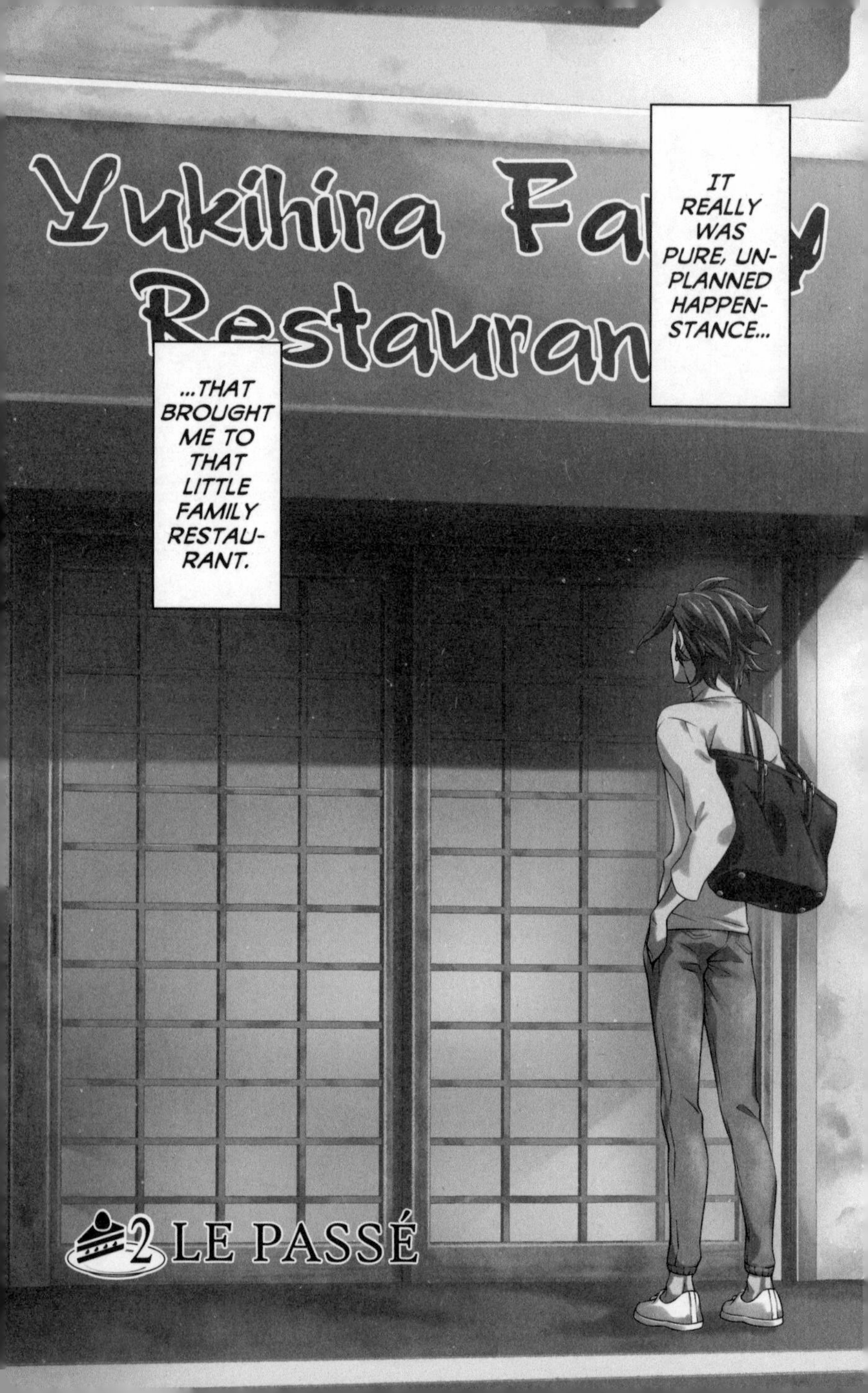
Yukihira Family Restaurant
IT REALLY WAS PURE, UN-PLANNED HAPPEN-STANCE...
...THAT BROUGHT ME TO THAT LITTLE FAMILY RESTAU-RANT.
2 LE PASSÉ

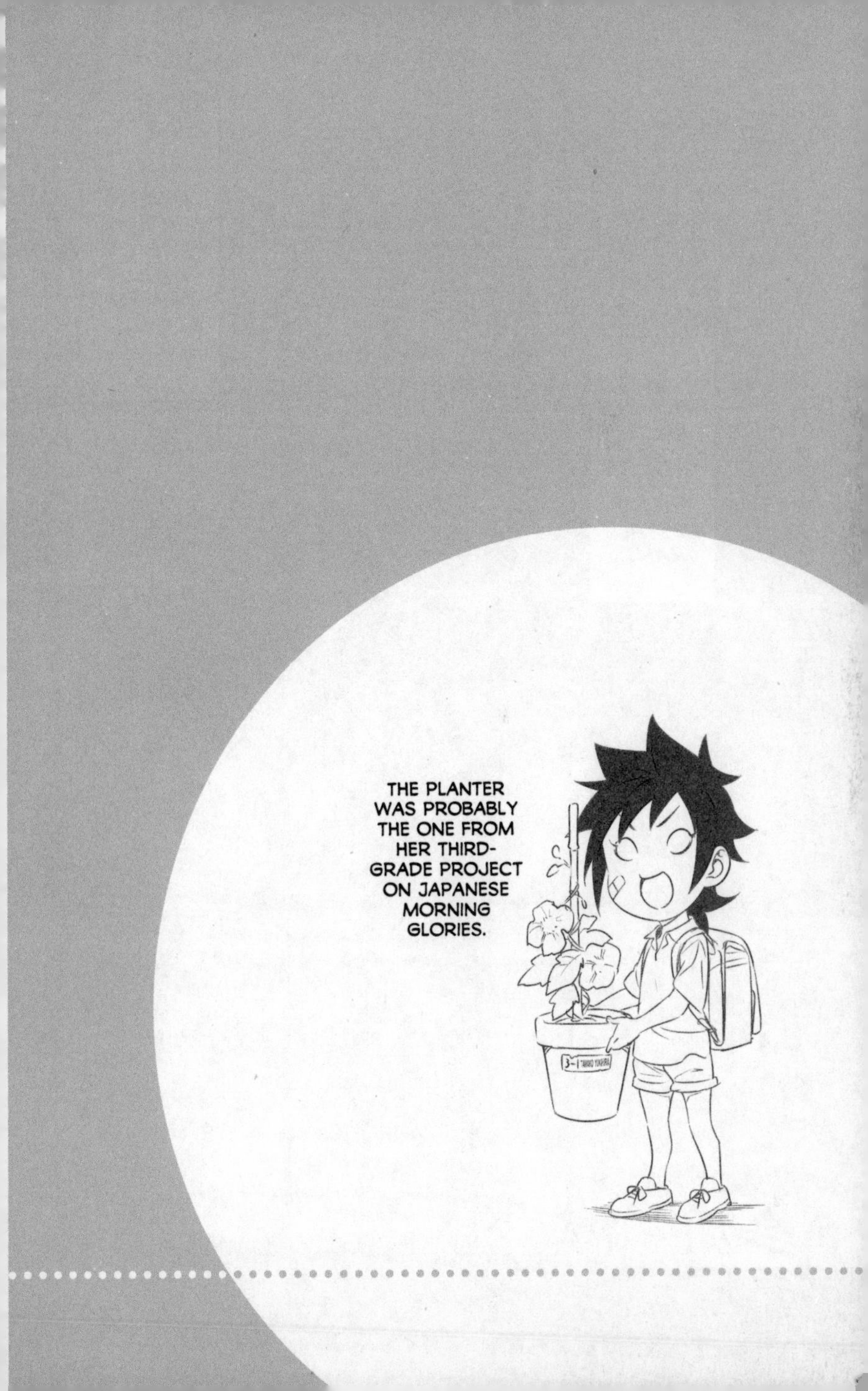
THE PLANTER WAS PROBABLY THE ONE FROM HER THIRD-GRADE PROJECT ON JAPANESE MORNING GLORIES.

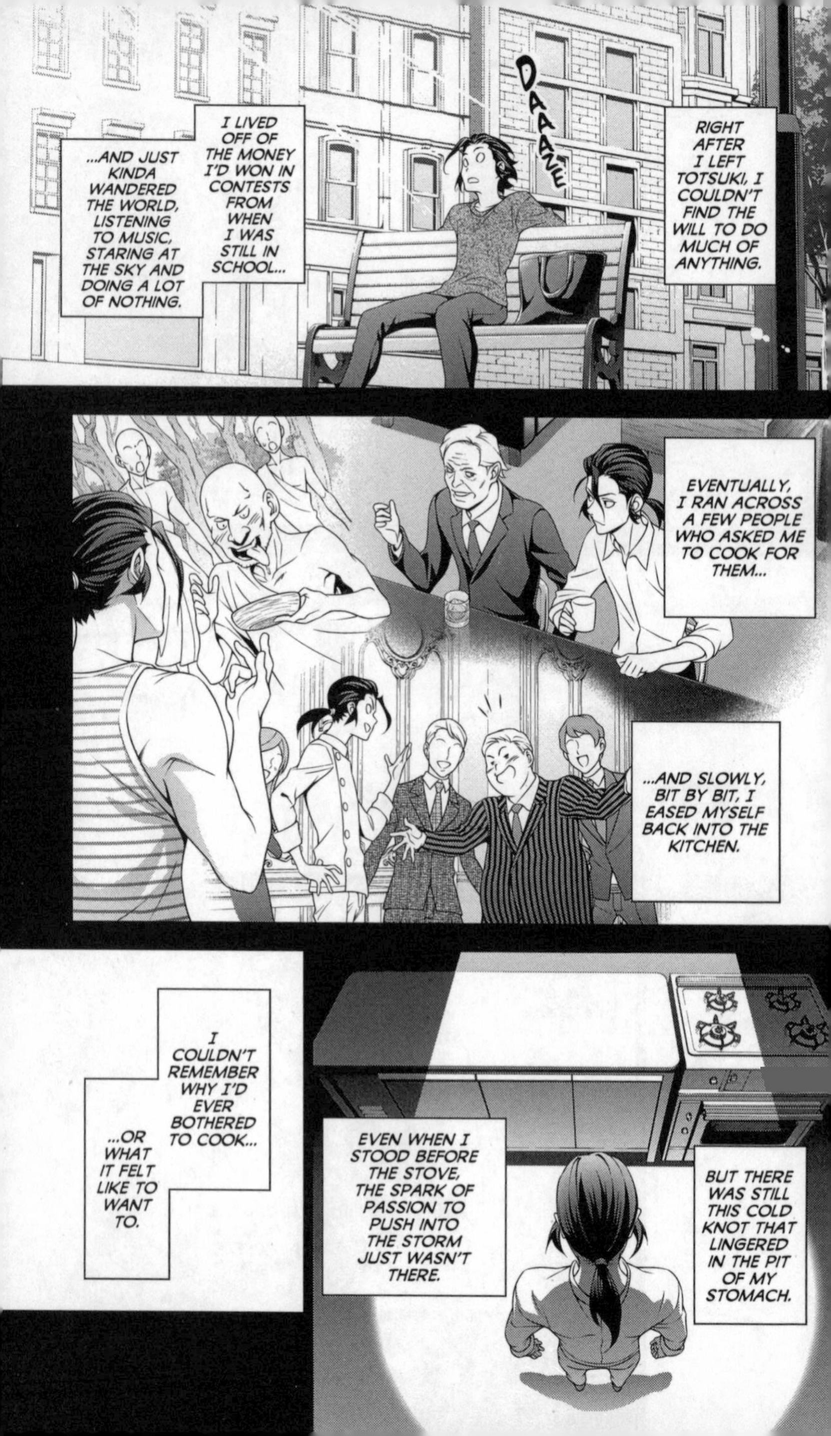
RIGHT AFTER I LEFT TOTSUKI, I COULDN'T FIND THE WILL TO DO MUCH OF ANYTHING.
DAAAZE
I LIVED OFF OF THE MONEY I'D WON IN CONTESTS FROM WHEN I WAS STILL IN SCHOOL...
...AND JUST KINDA WANDERED THE WORLD, LISTENING TO MUSIC, STARING AT THE SKY AND DOING A LOT OF NOTHING.
EVENTUALLY, I RAN ACROSS A FEW PEOPLE WHO ASKED ME TO COOK FOR THEM...
...AND SLOWLY, BIT BY BIT, I EASED MYSELF BACK INTO THE KITCHEN.
EVEN WHEN I STOOD BEFORE THE STOVE, THE SPARK OF PASSION TO PUSH INTO THE STORM JUST WASN'T THERE.
BUT THERE WAS STILL THIS COLD KNOT THAT LINGERED IN THE PIT OF MY STOMACH.
I COULDN'T REMEMBER WHY I'D EVER BOTHERED TO COOK...
...OR WHAT IT FELT LIKE TO WANT TO.

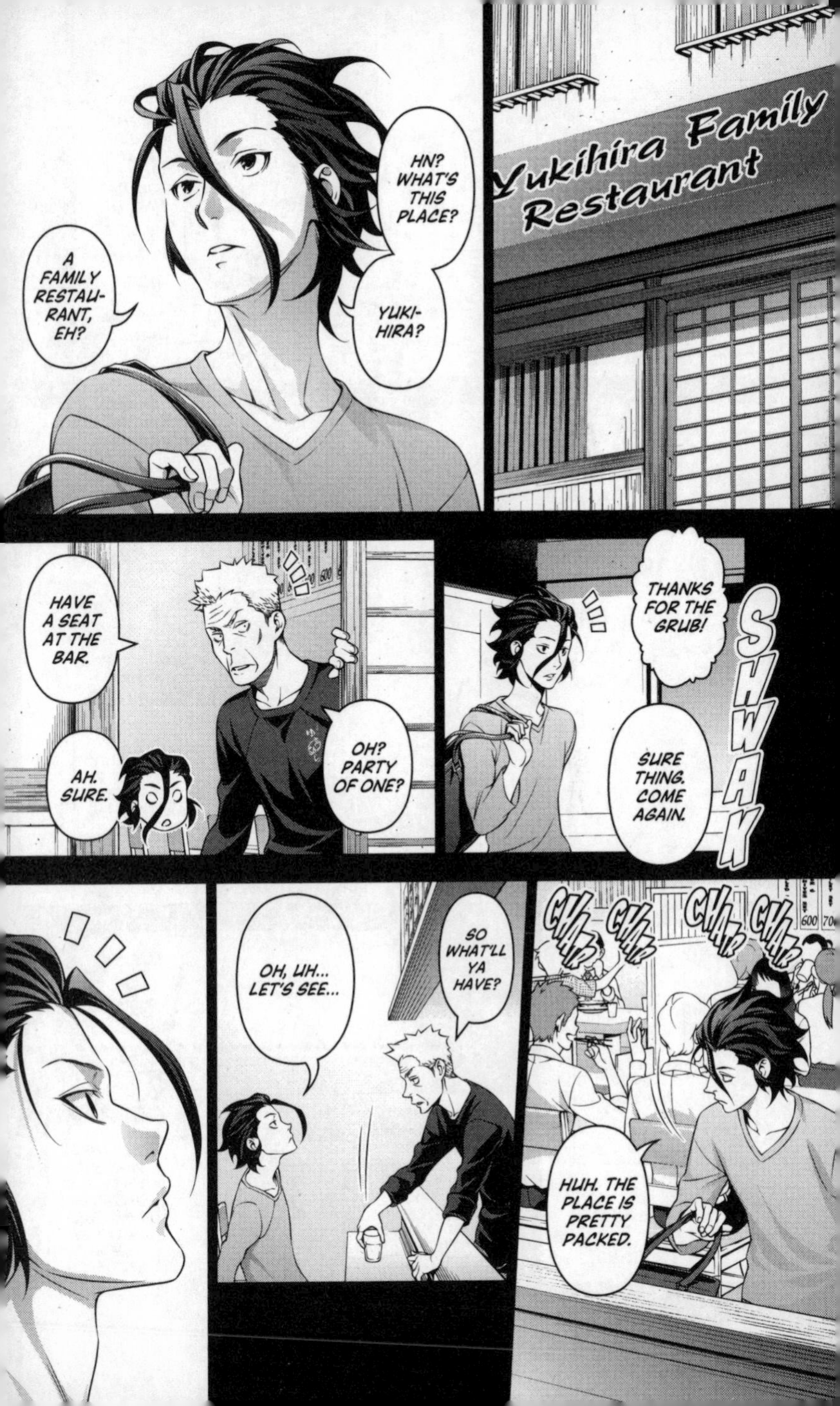
Yukihira Family Restaurant
HN? WHAT'S THIS PLACE?
YUKI-HIRA?
A FAMILY RESTAU-RANT, EH?
THANKS FOR THE GRUB!
SHWAK
SURE THING. COME AGAIN.
OH? PARTY OF ONE?
AH. SURE.
HAVE A SEAT AT THE BAR.
CHAK CHAK CHAK CHAK
HUH. THE PLACE IS PRETTY PACKED.
SO WHAT'LL YA HAVE?
OH, UH... LET'S SEE...

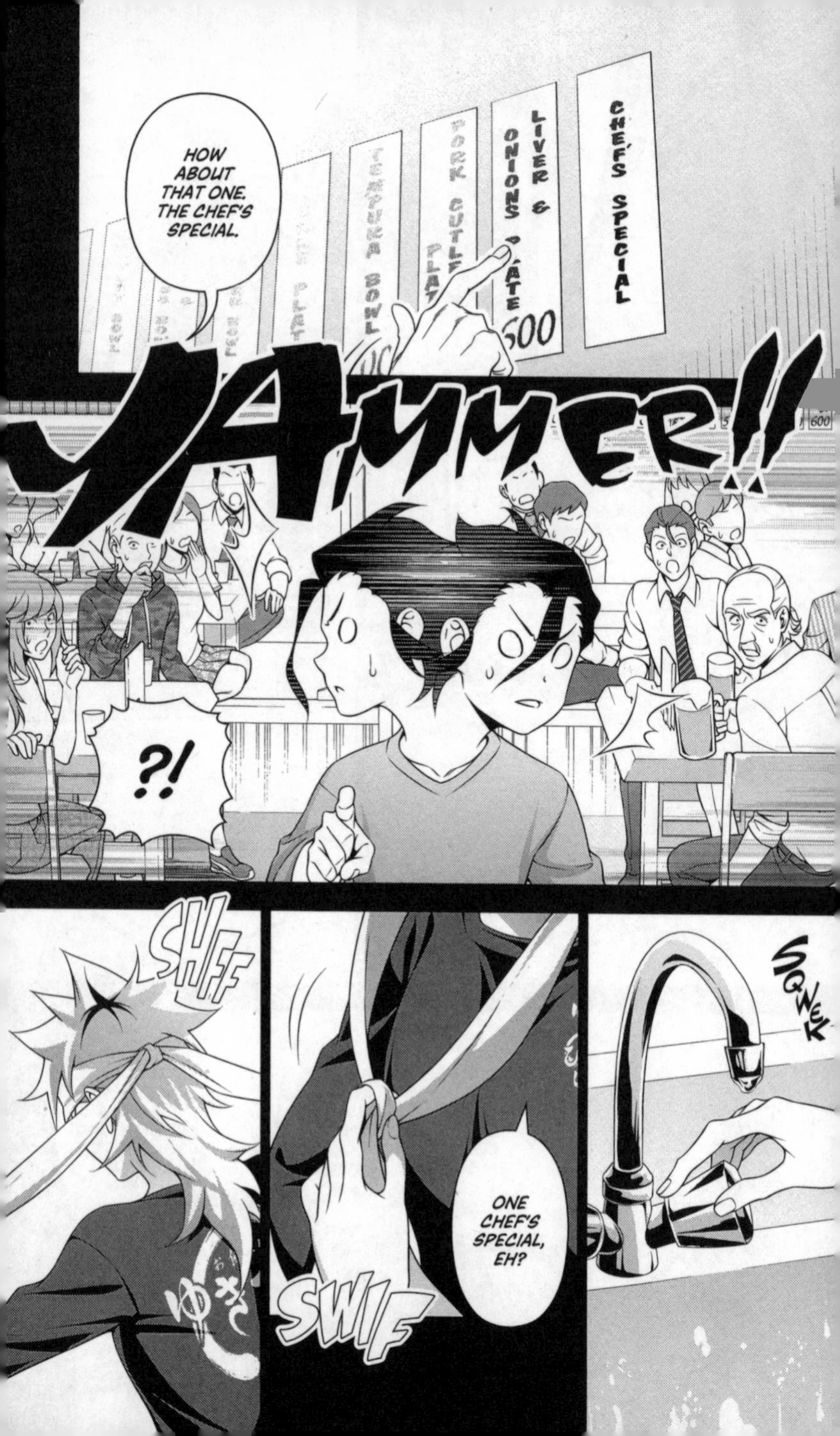
CHEF'S SPECIAL
LIVER & ONIONS PLATE 600
PORK CUTLE
TEMPURA BOWL
HOW ABOUT THAT ONE. THE CHEF'S SPECIAL.
YAMMER!!
?!
SQWEK
ONE CHEF'S SPECIAL, EH?
SWIF
SHFF

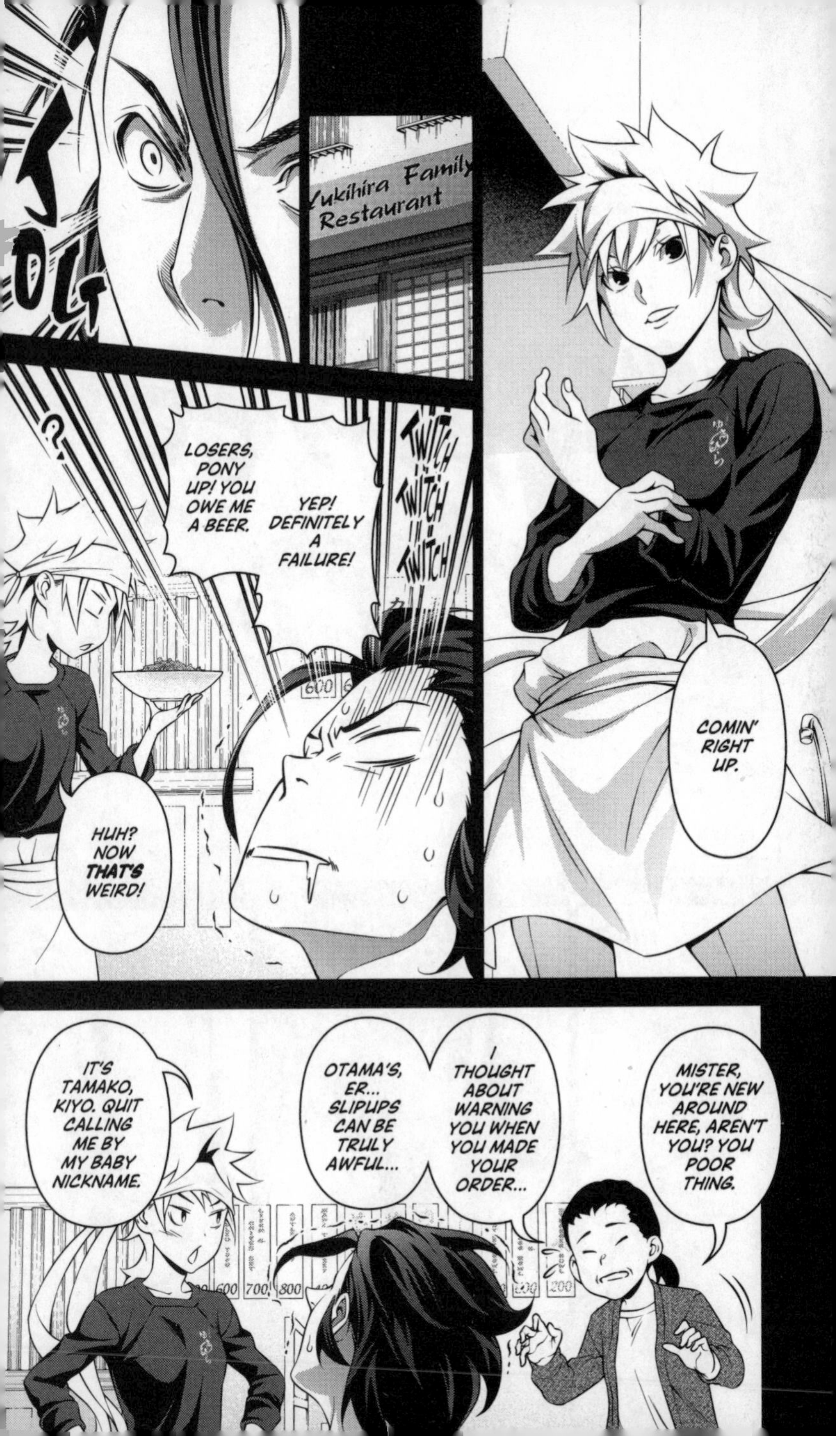
COMIN' RIGHT UP.
Yukihira Family Restaurant
TWITCH TWITCH TWITCH
YEP! DEFINITELY A FAILURE!
LOSERS, PONY UP! YOU OWE ME A BEER.
HUH? NOW THAT'S WEIRD!
MISTER, YOU'RE NEW AROUND HERE, AREN'T YOU? YOU POOR THING.
I THOUGHT ABOUT WARNING YOU WHEN YOU MADE YOUR ORDER...
OTAMA'S, ER... SLIPUPS CAN BE TRULY AWFUL...
IT'S TAMAKO, KIYO. QUIT CALLING ME BY MY BABY NICKNAME.

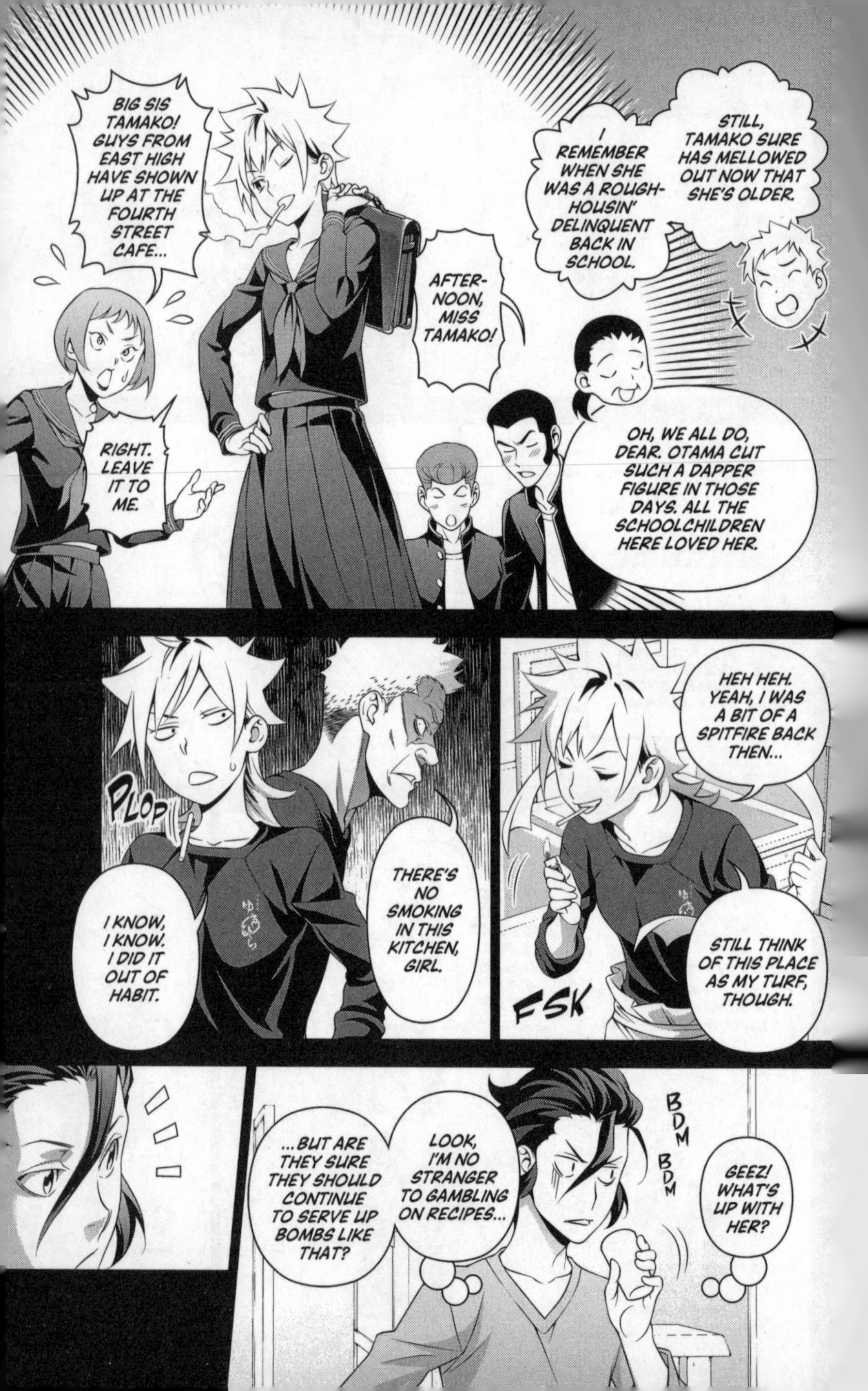
STILL, TAMAKO SURE HAS MELLOWED OUT NOW THAT SHE'S OLDER.
I REMEMBER WHEN SHE WAS A ROUGH-HOUSIN' DELINQUENT BACK IN SCHOOL.
BIG SIS TAMAKO! GUYS FROM EAST HIGH HAVE SHOWN UP AT THE FOURTH STREET CAFE...
AFTER-NOON, MISS TAMAKO!
OH, WE ALL DO, DEAR. OTAMA CUT SUCH A DAPPER FIGURE IN THOSE DAYS. ALL THE SCHOOLCHILDREN HERE LOVED HER.
RIGHT. LEAVE IT TO ME.
HEH HEH. YEAH, I WAS A BIT OF A SPITFIRE BACK THEN...
STILL THINK OF THIS PLACE AS MY TURF, THOUGH.
FSK
PLOP
THERE'S NO SMOKING IN THIS KITCHEN, GIRL.
I KNOW, I KNOW. I DID IT OUT OF HABIT.
BDM
BDM
GEEZ! WHAT'S UP WITH HER?
LOOK, I'M NO STRANGER TO GAMBLING ON RECIPES...
...BUT ARE THEY SURE THEY SHOULD CONTINUE TO SERVE UP BOMBS LIKE THAT?

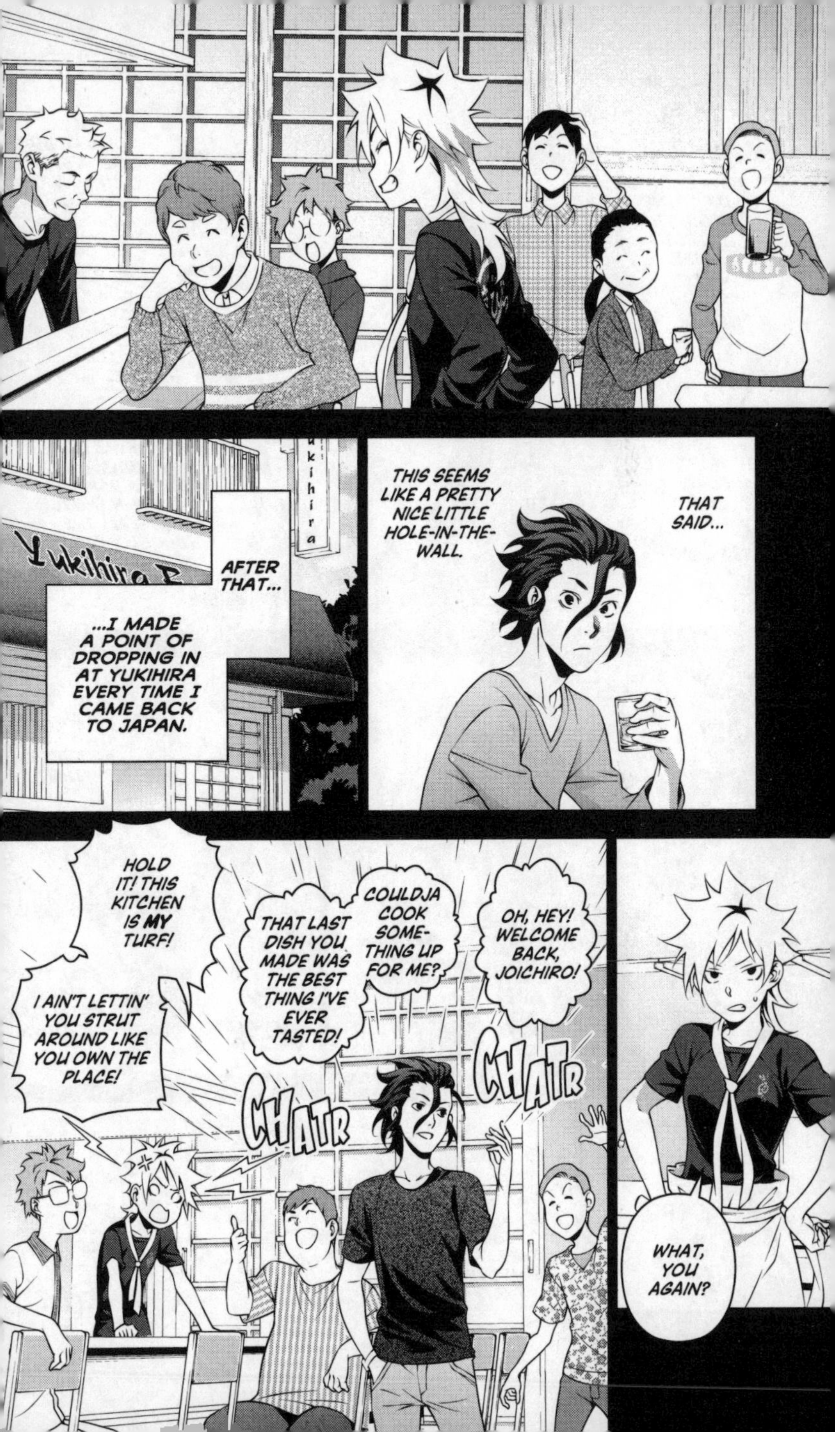
THIS SEEMS LIKE A PRETTY NICE LITTLE HOLE-IN-THE-WALL.
THAT SAID...
AFTER THAT...
...I MADE A POINT OF DROPPING IN AT YUKIHIRA EVERY TIME I CAME BACK TO JAPAN.
Yukihira
WHAT, YOU AGAIN?
OH, HEY! WELCOME BACK, JOICHIRO!
COULDJA COOK SOME-THING UP FOR ME?
THAT LAST DISH YOU MADE WAS THE BEST THING I'VE EVER TASTED!
CHATR
HOLD IT! THIS KITCHEN IS **MY** TURF!
I AIN'T LETTIN' YOU STRUT AROUND LIKE YOU OWN THE PLACE!
CHATR

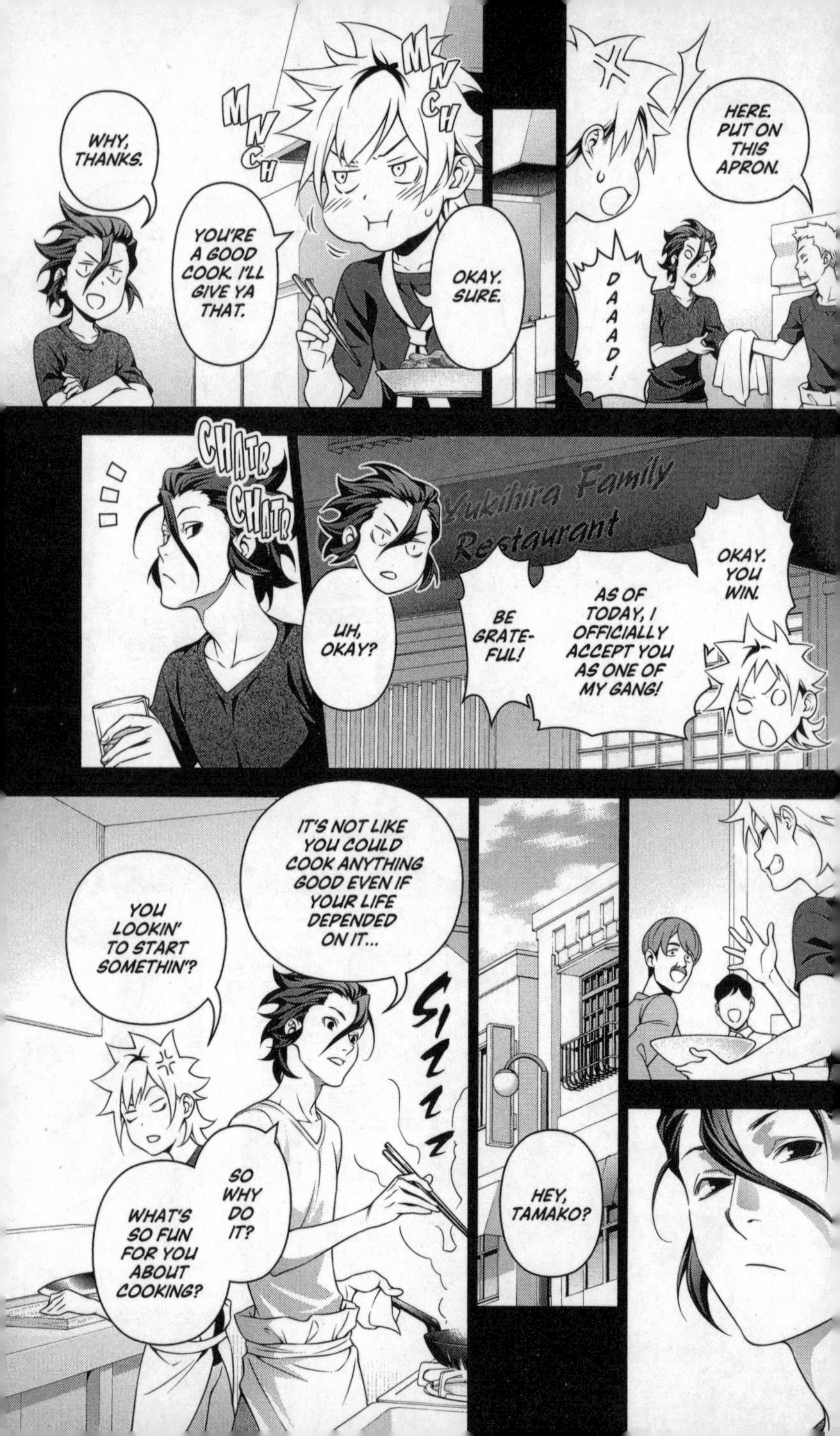
HERE. PUT ON THIS APRON.
DAAAAD!
MNCH
MNCH
OKAY. SURE.
YOU'RE A GOOD COOK. I'LL GIVE YA THAT.
WHY, THANKS.
OKAY. YOU WIN.
AS OF TODAY, I OFFICIALLY ACCEPT YOU AS ONE OF MY GANG!
BE GRATE-FUL!
Yukihira Family Restaurant
UH, OKAY?
CHATR
CHATR
HEY, TAMAKO?
IT'S NOT LIKE YOU COULD COOK ANYTHING GOOD EVEN IF YOUR LIFE DEPENDED ON IT...
YOU LOOKIN' TO START SOMETHIN'?
SIZZZZ
SO WHY DO IT?
WHAT'S SO FUN FOR YOU ABOUT COOKING?

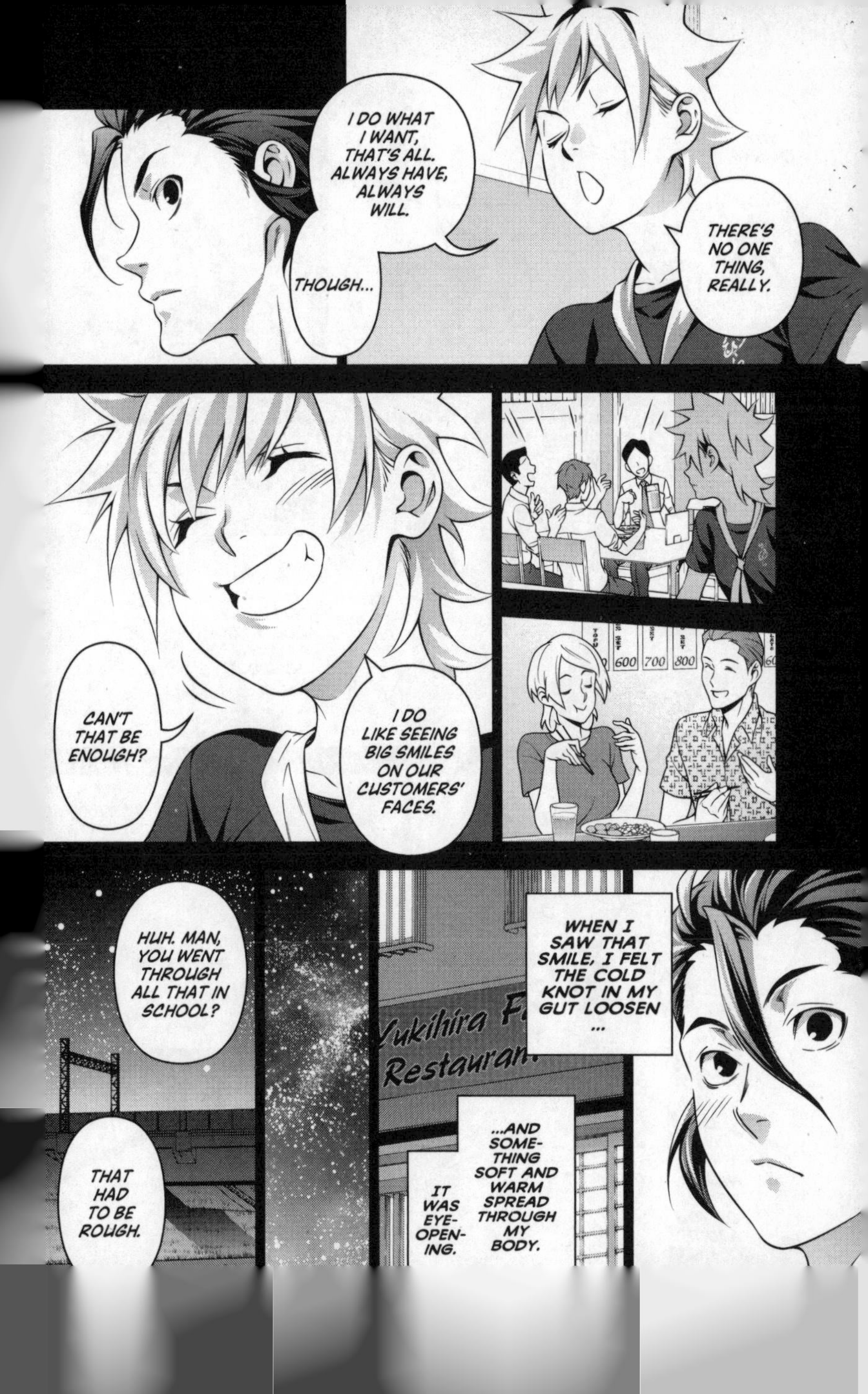
THERE'S NO ONE THING, REALLY.
I DO WHAT I WANT, THAT'S ALL. ALWAYS HAVE, ALWAYS WILL.
THOUGH...
600 700 800
I DO LIKE SEEING BIG SMILES ON OUR CUSTOMERS' FACES.
CAN'T THAT BE ENOUGH?
WHEN I SAW THAT SMILE, I FELT THE COLD KNOT IN MY GUT LOOSEN ...
...AND SOMETHING SOFT AND WARM SPREAD THROUGH MY BODY.
IT WAS EYE-OPENING.
Yukihira
HUH. MAN, YOU WENT THROUGH ALL THAT IN SCHOOL?
THAT HAD TO BE ROUGH.

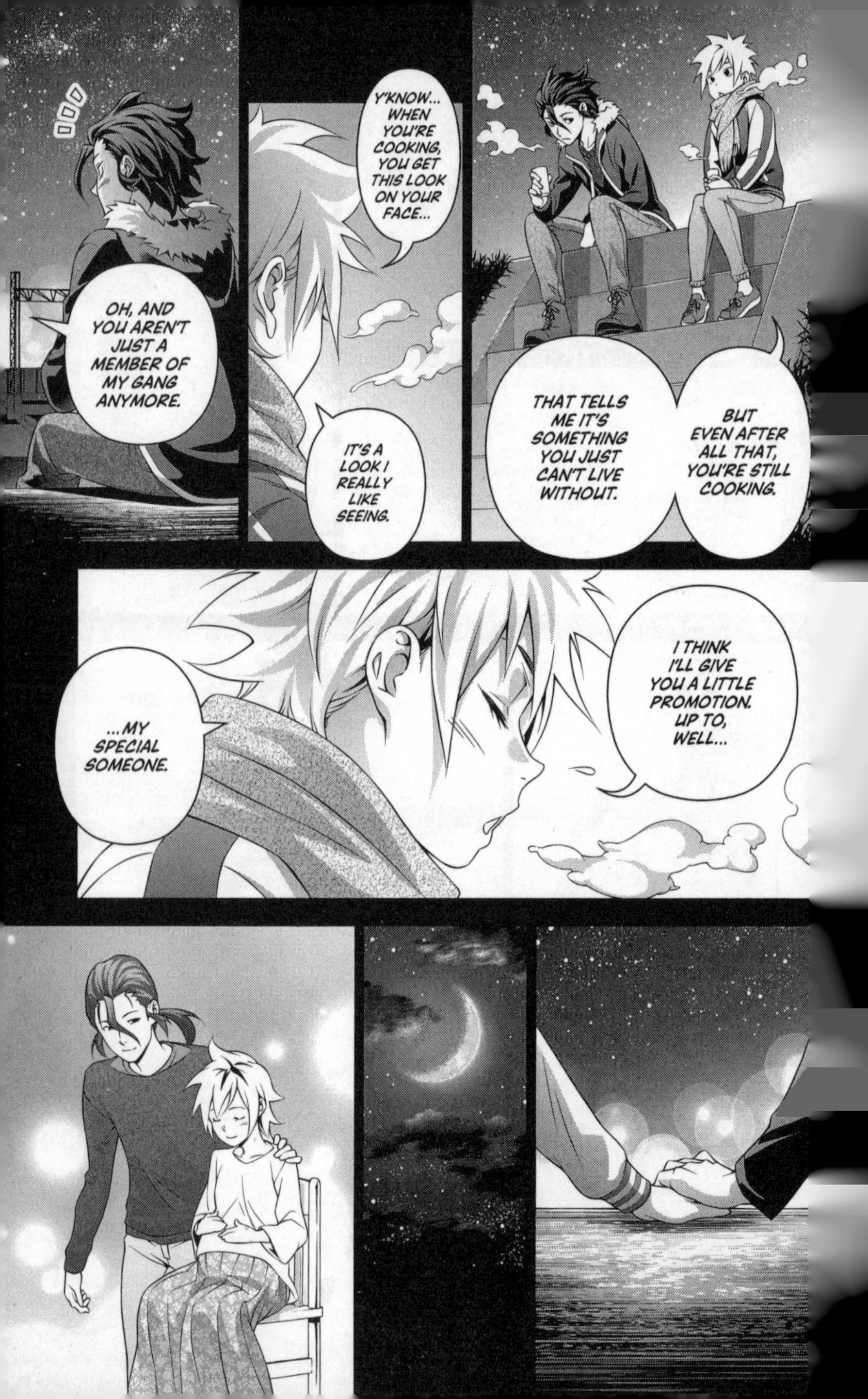
BUT EVEN AFTER ALL THAT, YOU'RE STILL COOKING.
THAT TELLS ME IT'S SOMETHING YOU JUST CAN'T LIVE WITHOUT.
Y'KNOW... WHEN YOU'RE COOKING, YOU GET THIS LOOK ON YOUR FACE...
IT'S A LOOK I REALLY LIKE SEEING.
OH, AND YOU AREN'T JUST A MEMBER OF MY GANG ANYMORE.
I THINK I'LL GIVE YOU A LITTLE PROMOTION. UP TO, WELL...
...MY SPECIAL SOMEONE.

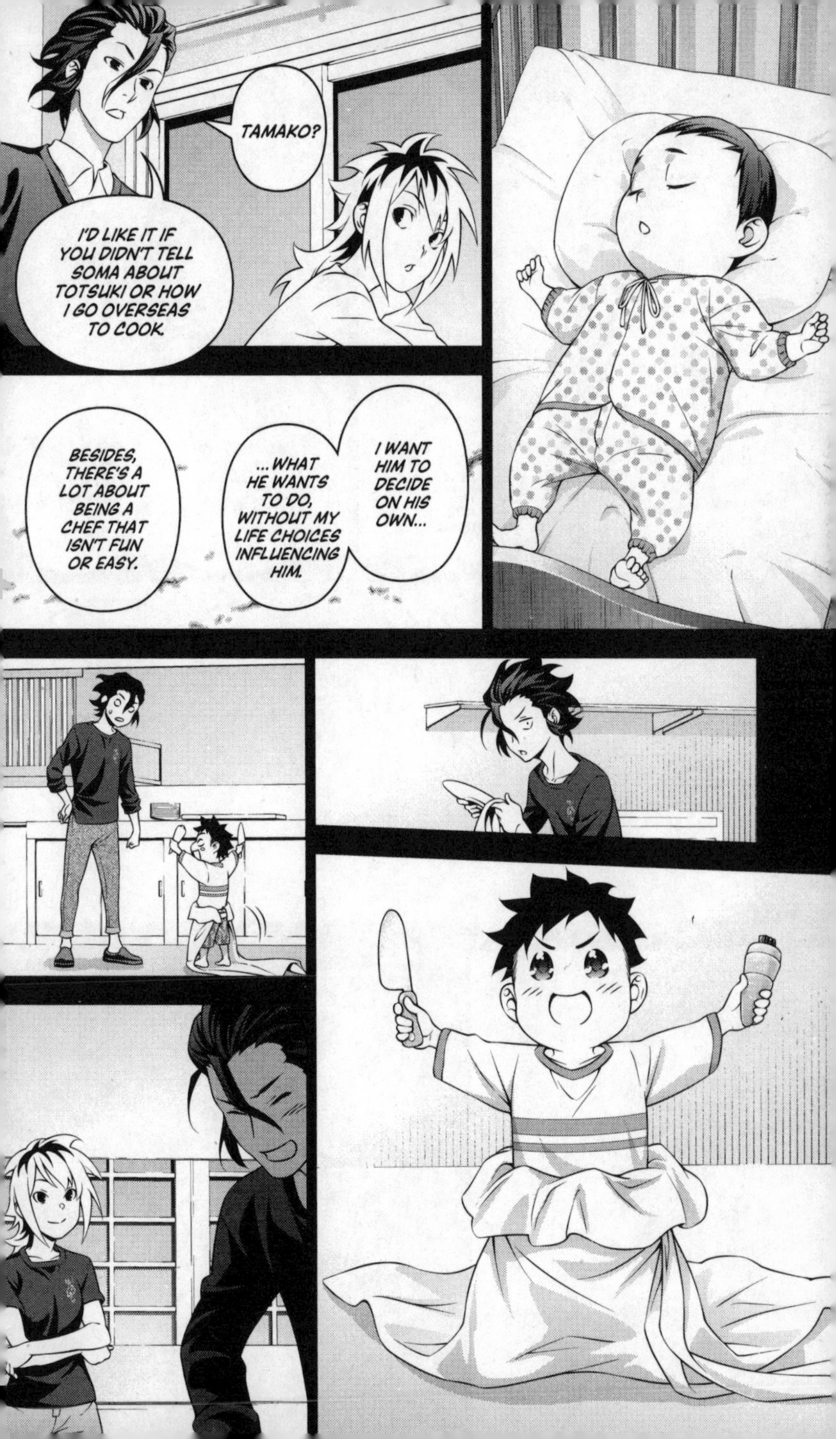
TAMAKO?
I'D LIKE IT IF YOU DIDN'T TELL SOMA ABOUT TOTSUKI OR HOW I GO OVERSEAS TO COOK.
I WANT HIM TO DECIDE ON HIS OWN...
...WHAT HE WANTS TO DO, WITHOUT MY LIFE CHOICES INFLUENCING HIM.
BESIDES, THERE'S A LOT ABOUT BEING A CHEF THAT ISN'T FUN OR EASY.

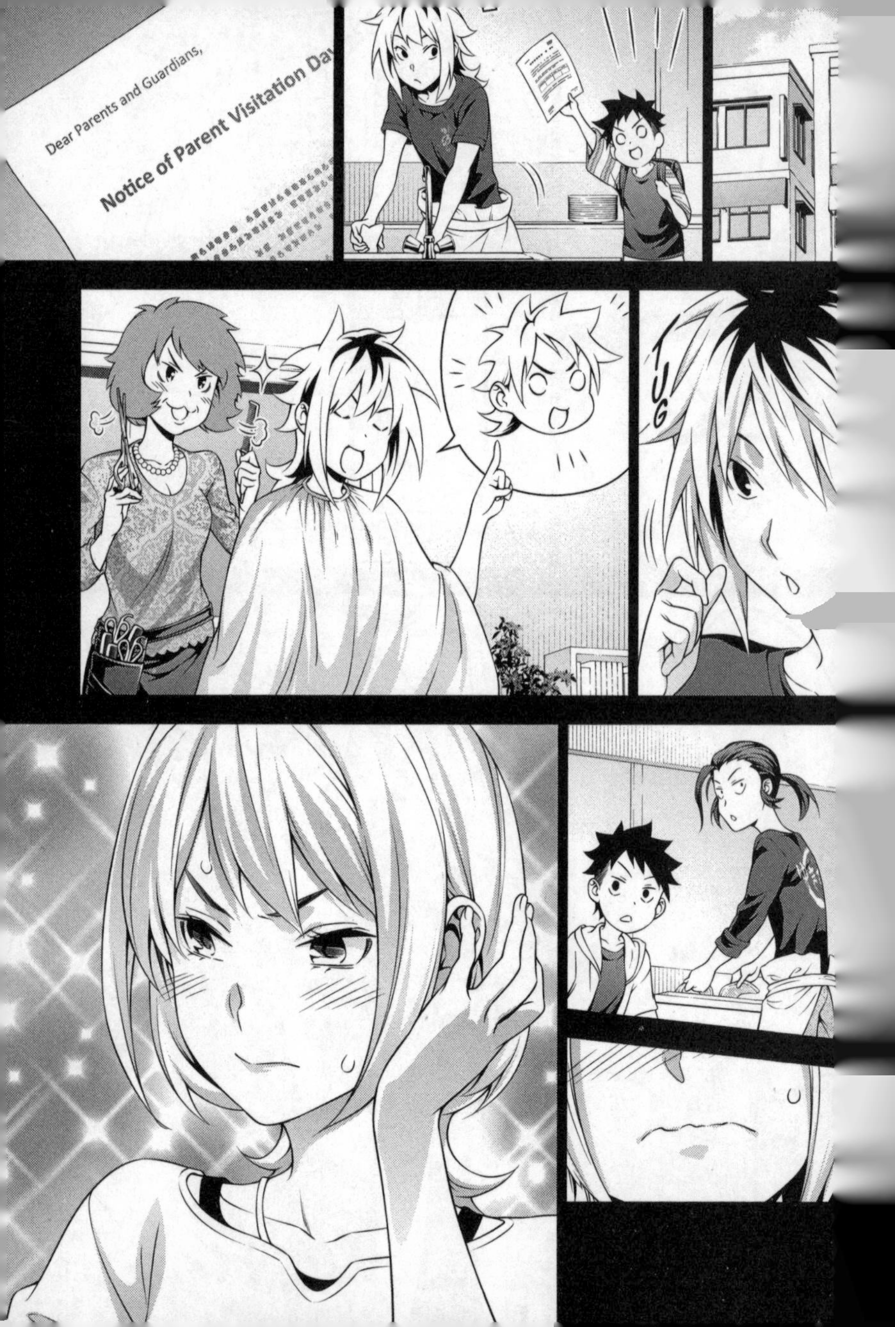

Dear Parents and Guardians,
Notice of Parent Visitation Day
TUG

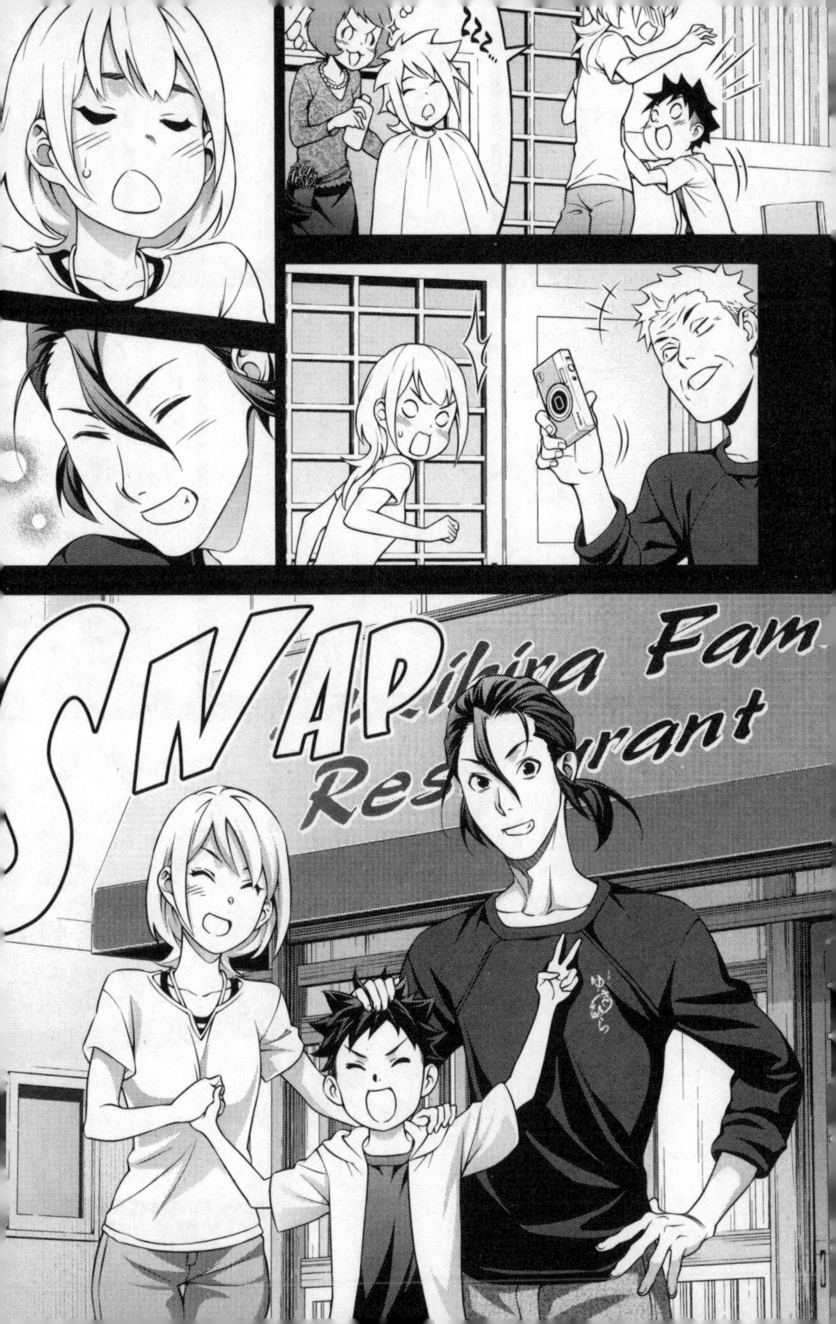
zzz...
SNAP

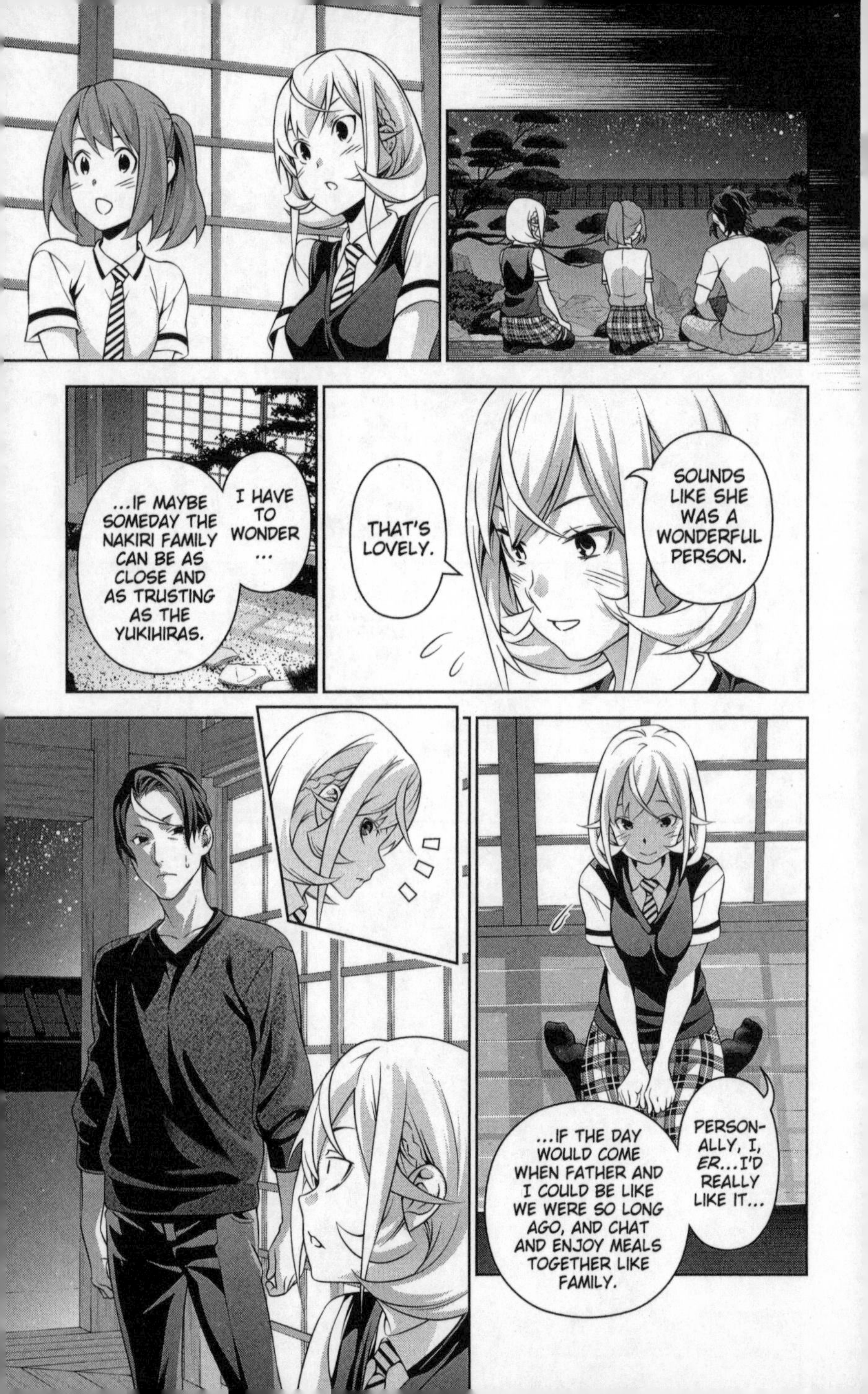
SOUNDS LIKE SHE WAS A WONDERFUL PERSON.
THAT'S LOVELY.
I HAVE TO WONDER...
...IF MAYBE SOMEDAY THE NAKIRI FAMILY CAN BE AS CLOSE AND AS TRUSTING AS THE YUKIHIRAS.
PERSON-ALLY, I, ER...I'D REALLY LIKE IT...
...IF THE DAY WOULD COME WHEN FATHER AND I COULD BE LIKE WE WERE SO LONG AGO, AND CHAT AND ENJOY MEALS TOGETHER LIKE FAMILY.

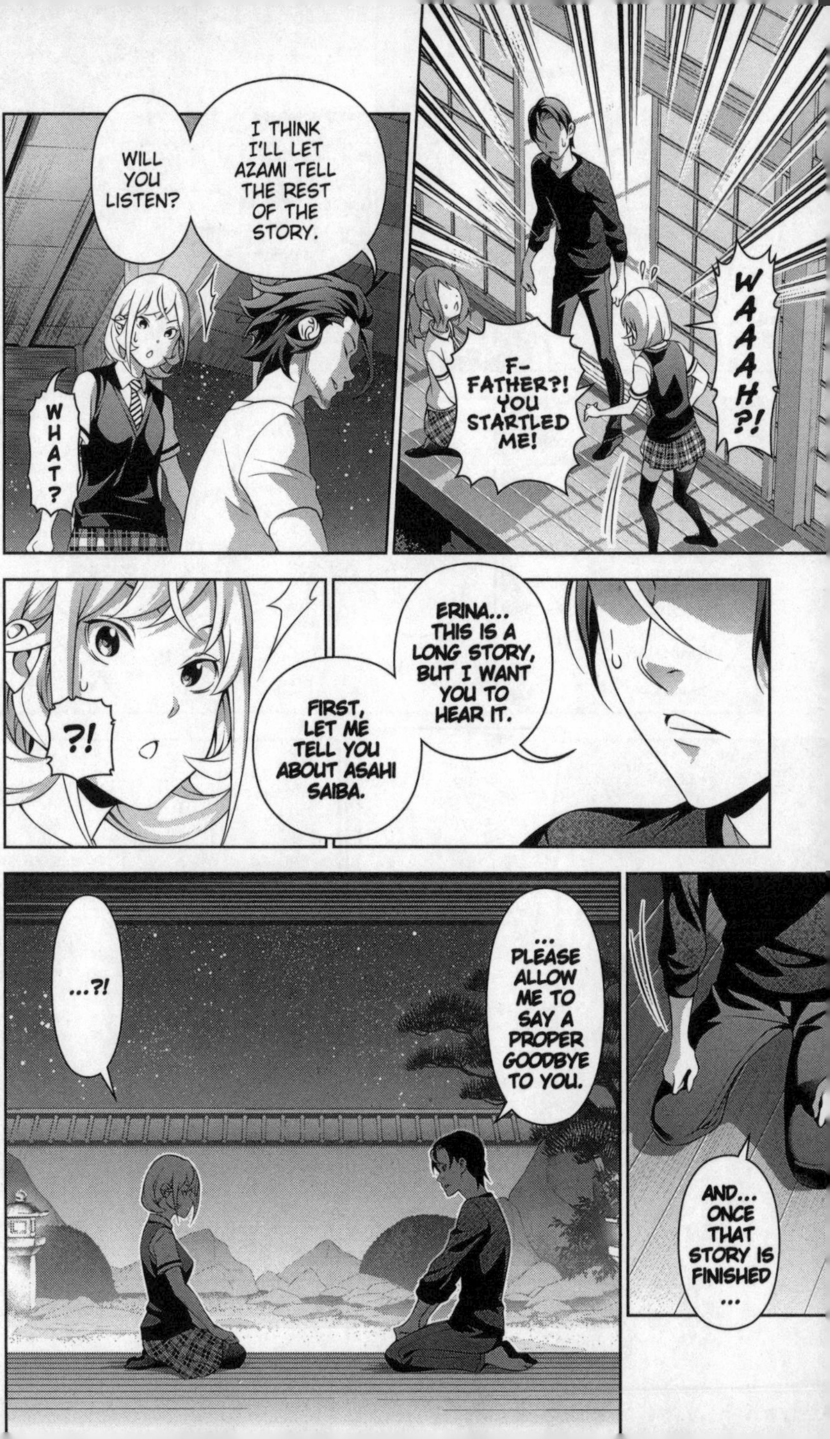
WAAAAH?!
F-FATHER?! YOU STARTLED ME!
I THINK I'LL LET AZAMI TELL THE REST OF THE STORY.
WILL YOU LISTEN?
WHAT?
ERINA... THIS IS A LONG STORY, BUT I WANT YOU TO HEAR IT.
FIRST, LET ME TELL YOU ABOUT ASAHI SAIBA.
?!
AND... ONCE THAT STORY IS FINISHED ...
... PLEASE ALLOW ME TO SAY A PROPER GOODBYE TO YOU.
...?!

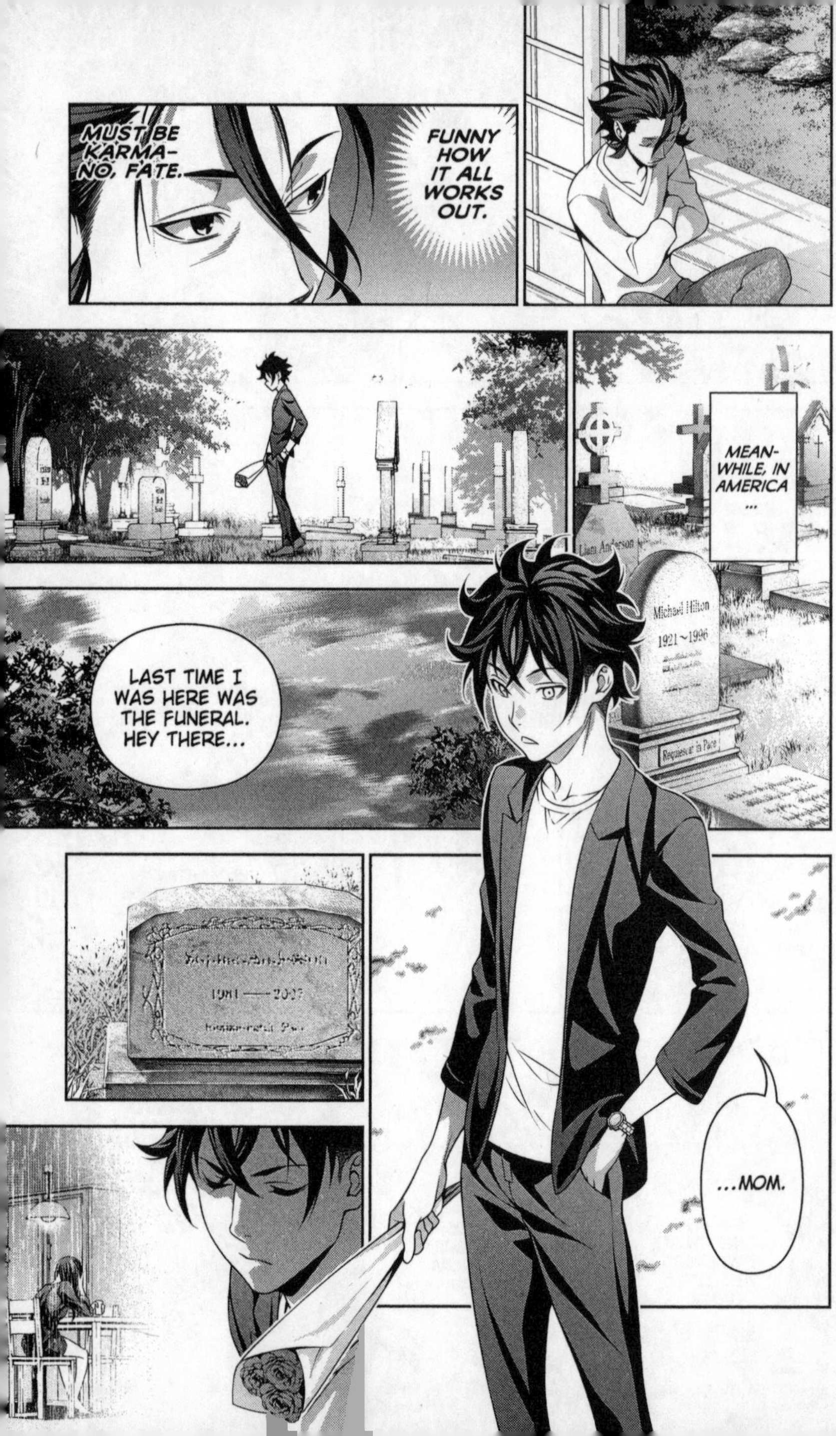
FUNNY HOW IT ALL WORKS OUT.
MUST BE KARMA—NO, FATE.
MEAN-WHILE, IN AMERICA ...
Liam Anderson
Michael Hilton
1921~1996
Requiescat in Pace
LAST TIME I WAS HERE WAS THE FUNERAL. HEY THERE...
...MOM.

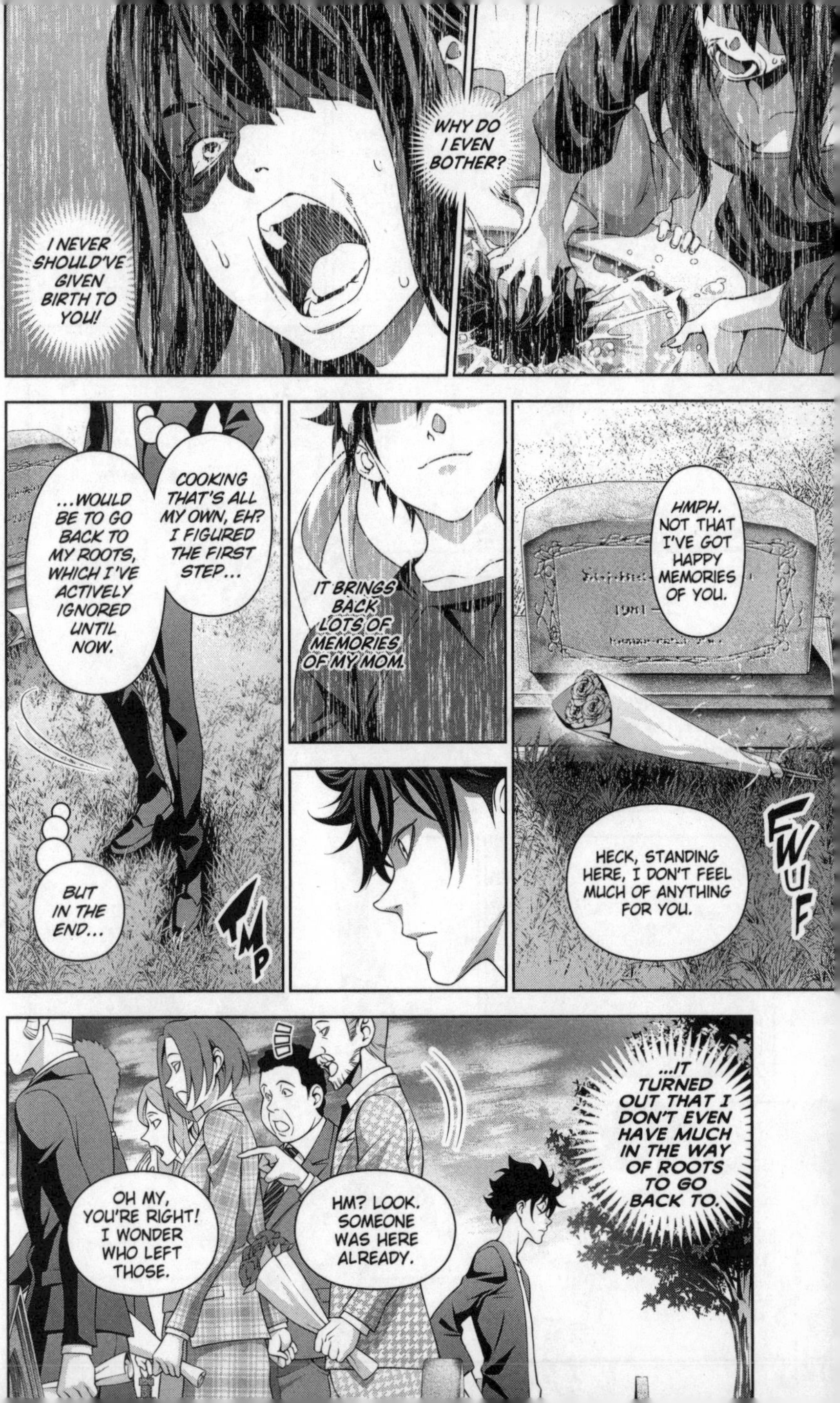
WHY DO I EVEN BOTHER?
I NEVER SHOULD'VE GIVEN BIRTH TO YOU!
HMPH. NOT THAT I'VE GOT HAPPY MEMORIES OF YOU.
HECK, STANDING HERE, I DON'T FEEL MUCH OF ANYTHING FOR YOU.
FWUF
IT BRINGS BACK LOTS OF MEMORIES OF MY MOM.
COOKING THAT'S ALL MY OWN, EH? I FIGURED THE FIRST STEP...
...WOULD BE TO GO BACK TO MY ROOTS, WHICH I'VE ACTIVELY IGNORED UNTIL NOW.
BUT IN THE END...
TMP
...IT TURNED OUT THAT I DON'T EVEN HAVE MUCH IN THE WAY OF ROOTS TO GO BACK TO.
HM? LOOK. SOMEONE WAS HERE ALREADY.
OH MY, YOU'RE RIGHT! I WONDER WHO LEFT THOSE.

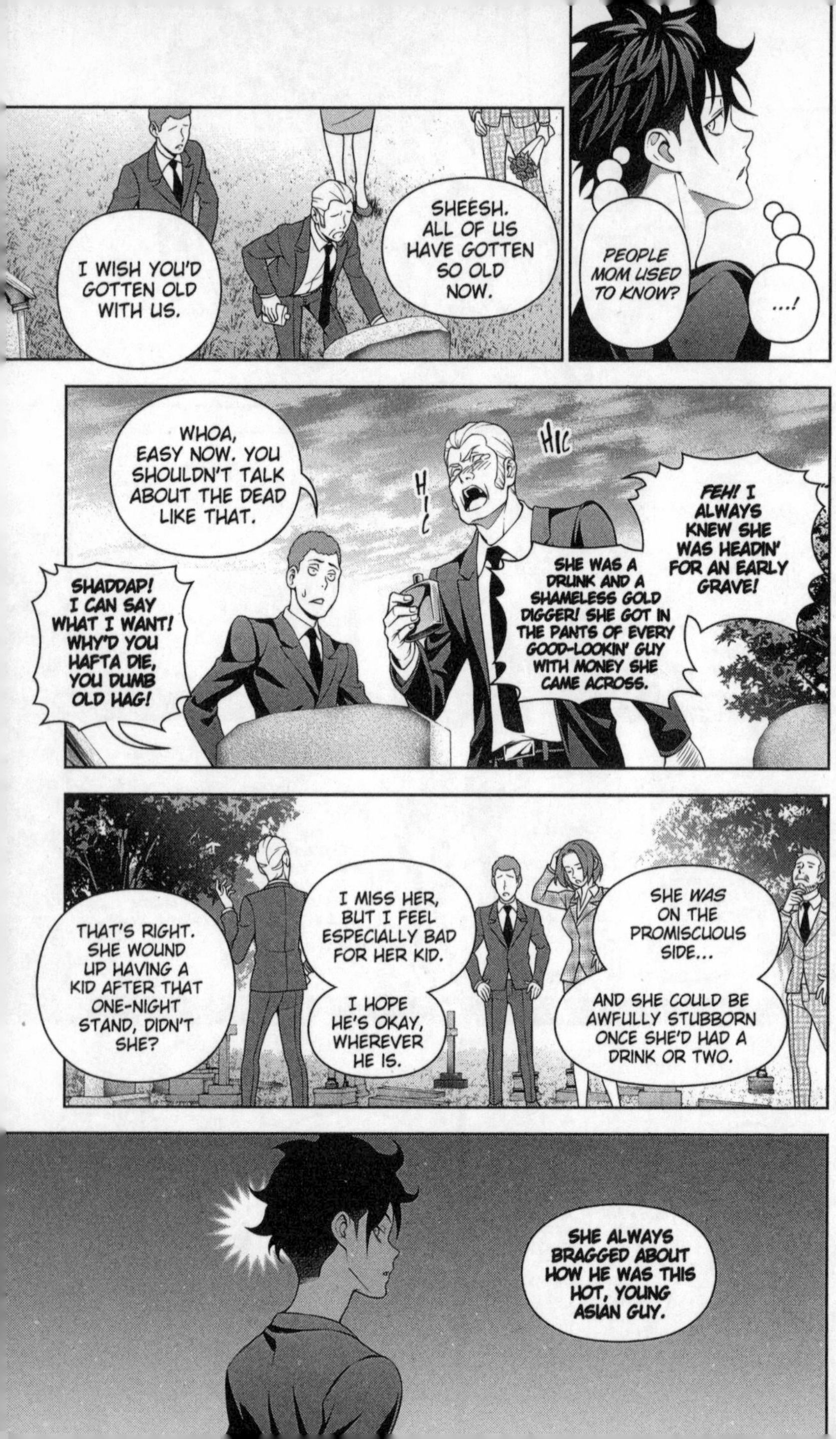
PEOPLE MOM USED TO KNOW?
...!
SHEESH. ALL OF US HAVE GOTTEN SO OLD NOW.
I WISH YOU'D GOTTEN OLD WITH US.
FEH! I ALWAYS KNEW SHE WAS HEADIN' FOR AN EARLY GRAVE!
SHE WAS A DRUNK AND A SHAMELESS GOLD DIGGER! SHE GOT IN THE PANTS OF EVERY GOOD-LOOKIN' GUY WITH MONEY SHE CAME ACROSS.
HIC
HIC
WHOA, EASY NOW. YOU SHOULDN'T TALK ABOUT THE DEAD LIKE THAT.
SHADDAP! I CAN SAY WHAT I WANT! WHY'D YOU HAFTA DIE, YOU DUMB OLD HAG!
SHE *WAS* ON THE PROMISCUOUS SIDE...
AND SHE COULD BE AWFULLY STUBBORN ONCE SHE'D HAD A DRINK OR TWO.
I MISS HER, BUT I FEEL ESPECIALLY BAD FOR HER KID.
I HOPE HE'S OKAY, WHEREVER HE IS.
THAT'S RIGHT. SHE WOUND UP HAVING A KID AFTER THAT ONE-NIGHT STAND, DIDN'T SHE?
SHE ALWAYS BRAGGED ABOUT HOW HE WAS THIS HOT, YOUNG ASIAN GUY.

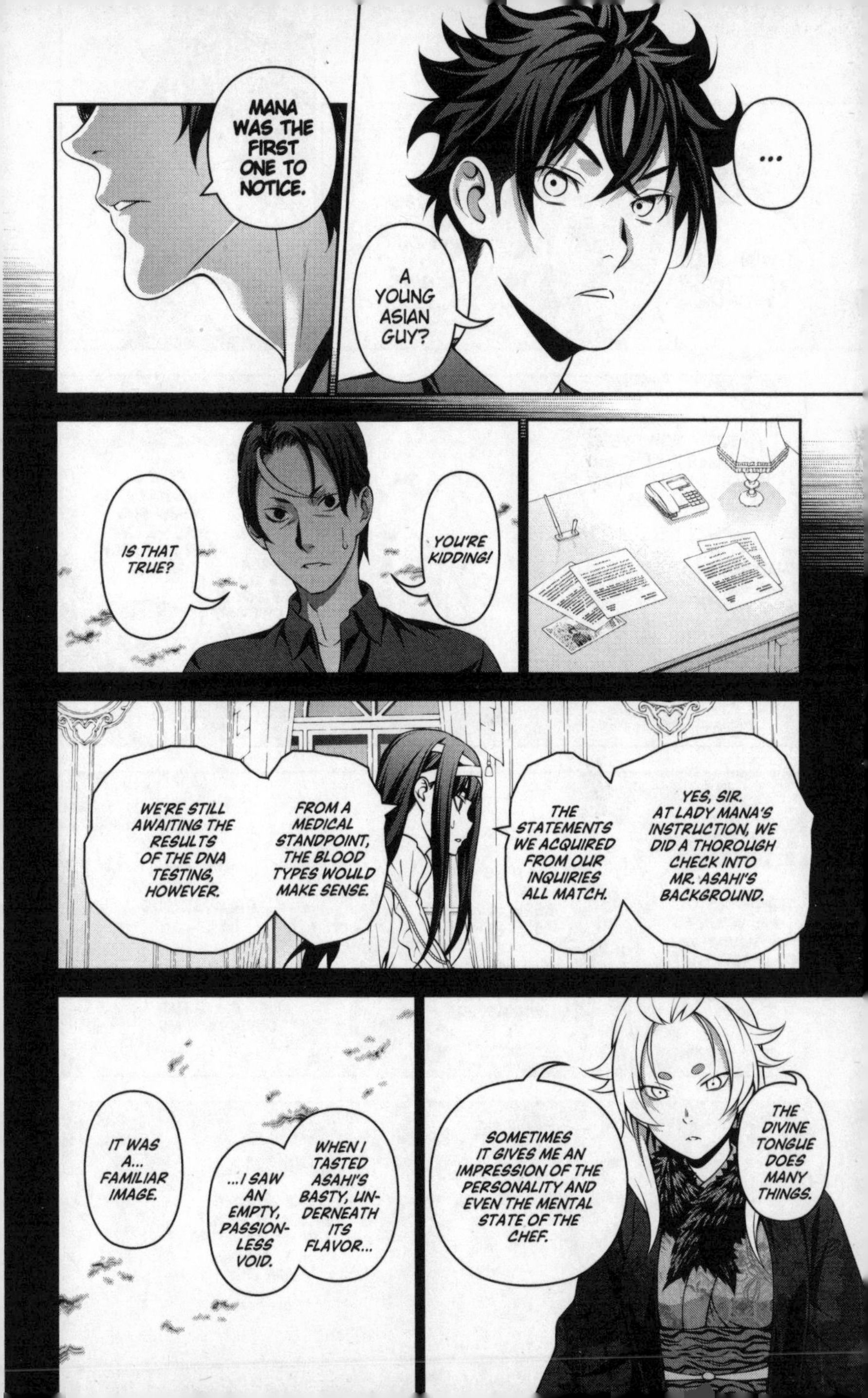
...
A YOUNG ASIAN GUY?
MANA WAS THE FIRST ONE TO NOTICE.
YOU'RE KIDDING!
IS THAT TRUE?
YES, SIR. AT LADY MANA'S INSTRUCTION, WE DID A THOROUGH CHECK INTO MR. ASAHI'S BACKGROUND.
THE STATEMENTS WE ACQUIRED FROM OUR INQUIRIES ALL MATCH.
FROM A MEDICAL STANDPOINT, THE BLOOD TYPES WOULD MAKE SENSE.
WE'RE STILL AWAITING THE RESULTS OF THE DNA TESTING, HOWEVER.
THE DIVINE TONGUE DOES MANY THINGS.
SOMETIMES IT GIVES ME AN IMPRESSION OF THE PERSONALITY AND EVEN THE MENTAL STATE OF THE CHEF.
WHEN I TASTED ASAHI'S BASTY, UNDERNEATH ITS FLAVOR...
...I SAW AN EMPTY, PASSIONLESS VOID.
IT WAS A... FAMILIAR IMAGE.

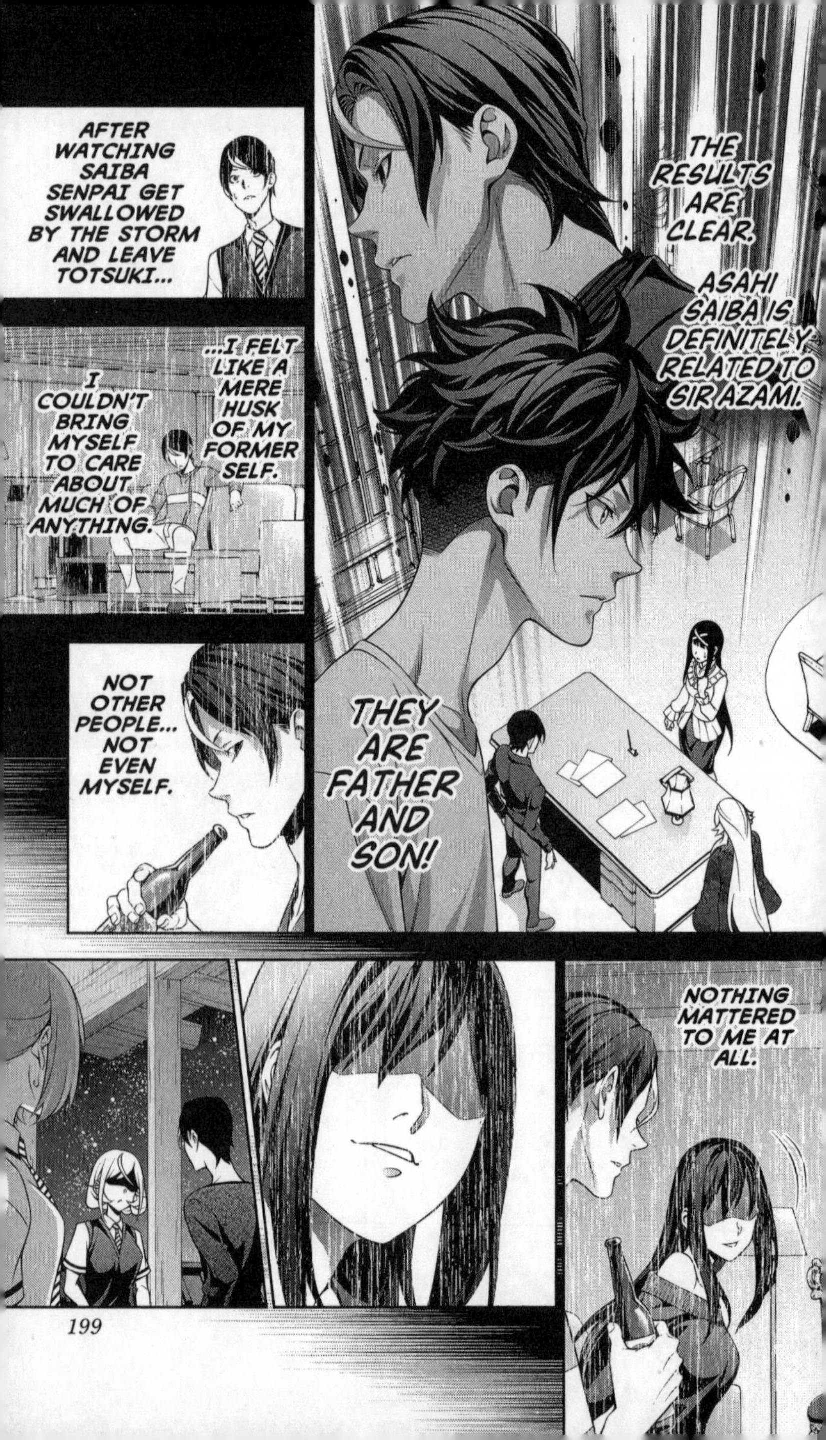
THE RESULTS ARE CLEAR.
ASAHI SAIBA IS DEFINITELY RELATED TO SIR AZAMI.
THEY ARE FATHER AND SON!
AFTER WATCHING SAIBA SENPAI GET SWALLOWED BY THE STORM AND LEAVE TOTSUKI...
...I FELT LIKE A MERE HUSK OF MY FORMER SELF.
I COULDN'T BRING MYSELF TO CARE ABOUT MUCH OF ANYTHING.
NOT OTHER PEOPLE... NOT EVEN MYSELF.
NOTHING MATTERED TO ME AT ALL.

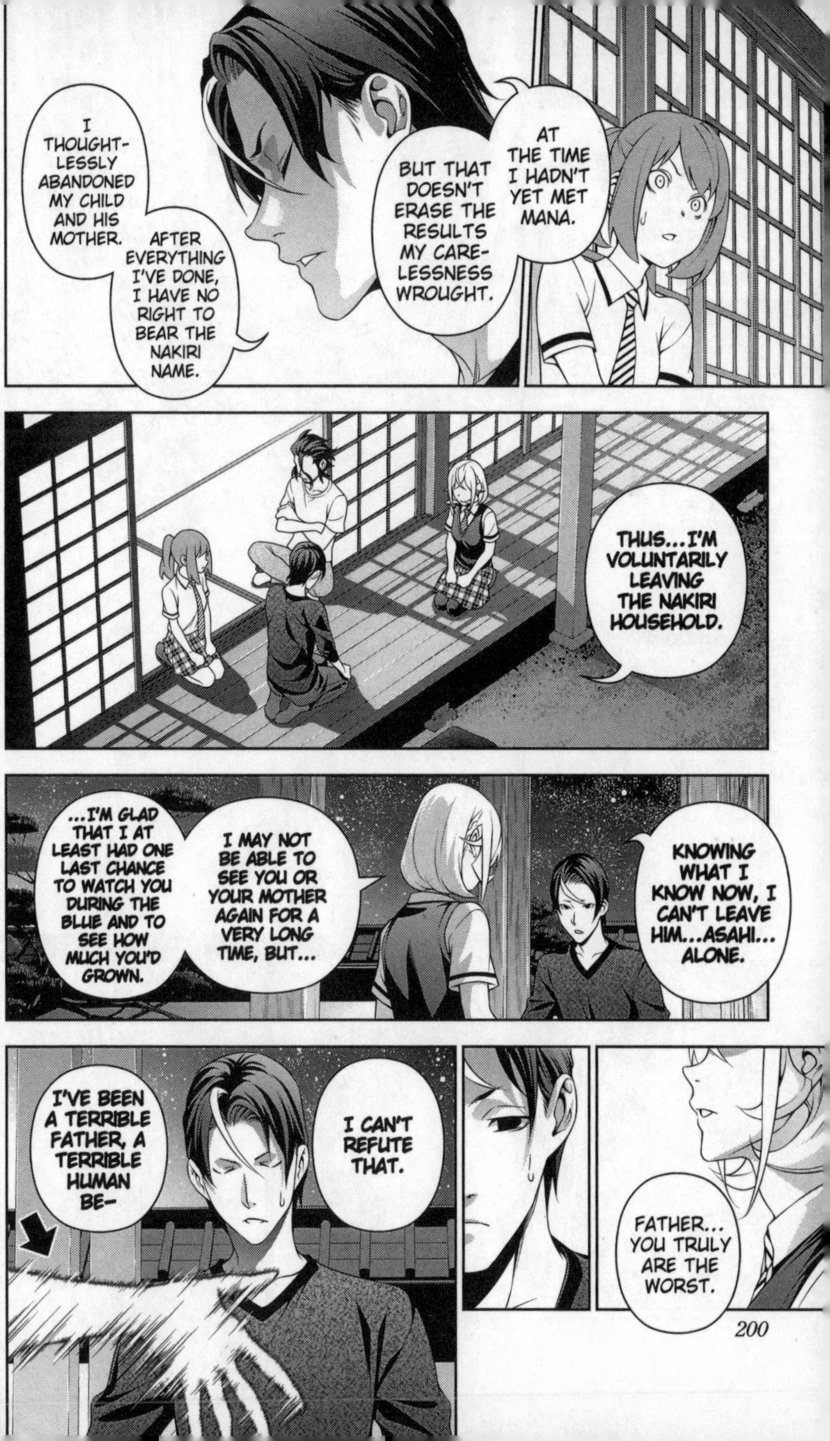
AT THE TIME I HADN'T YET MET MANA.
BUT THAT DOESN'T ERASE THE RESULTS MY CARE-LESSNESS WROUGHT.
I THOUGHT-LESSLY ABANDONED MY CHILD AND HIS MOTHER.
AFTER EVERYTHING I'VE DONE, I HAVE NO RIGHT TO BEAR THE NAKIRI NAME.
THUS...I'M VOLUNTARILY LEAVING THE NAKIRI HOUSEHOLD.
KNOWING WHAT I KNOW NOW, I CAN'T LEAVE HIM...ASAHI... ALONE.
I MAY NOT BE ABLE TO SEE YOU OR YOUR MOTHER AGAIN FOR A VERY LONG TIME, BUT...
...I'M GLAD THAT I AT LEAST HAD ONE LAST CHANCE TO WATCH YOU DURING THE BLUE AND TO SEE HOW MUCH YOU'D GROWN.
FATHER... YOU TRULY ARE THE WORST.
I CAN'T REFUTE THAT.
I'VE BEEN A TERRIBLE FATHER, A TERRIBLE HUMAN BE-

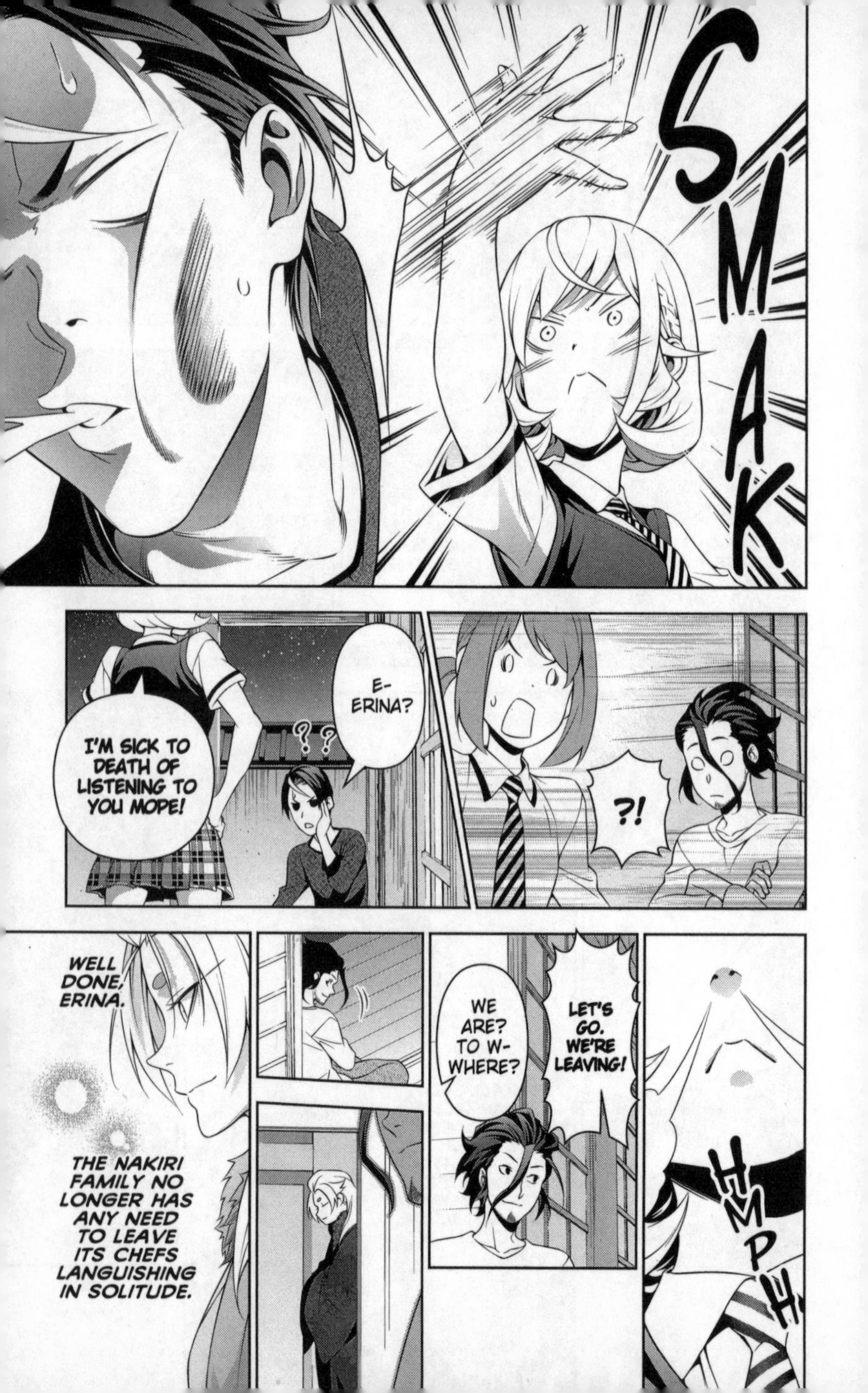
SMAK
?!
E-ERINA?
??
I'M SICK TO DEATH OF LISTENING TO YOU MOPE!
HMPH
LET'S GO. WE'RE LEAVING!
WE ARE? TO W-WHERE?
WELL DONE, ERINA.
THE NAKIRI FAMILY NO LONGER HAS ANY NEED TO LEAVE ITS CHEFS LANGUISHING IN SOLITUDE.

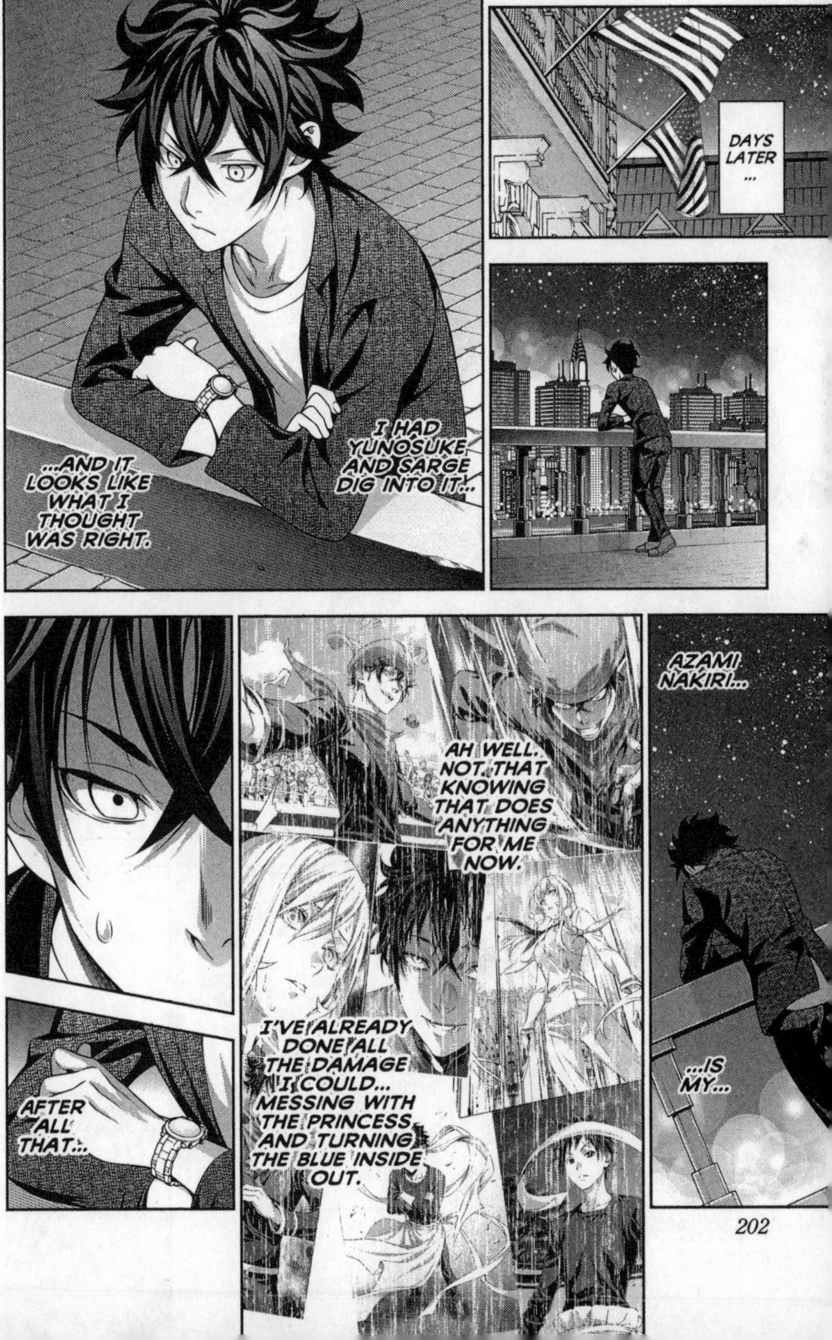
DAYS LATER ...
I HAD YUNOSUKE AND SARGE DIG INTO IT...
...AND IT LOOKS LIKE WHAT I THOUGHT WAS RIGHT.
AZAMI NAKIRI...
...IS MY...
AH WELL. NOT THAT KNOWING THAT DOES ANYTHING FOR ME NOW.
I'VE ALREADY DONE ALL THE DAMAGE I COULD... MESSING WITH THE PRINCESS AND TURNING THE BLUE INSIDE OUT.
AFTER ALL THAT...

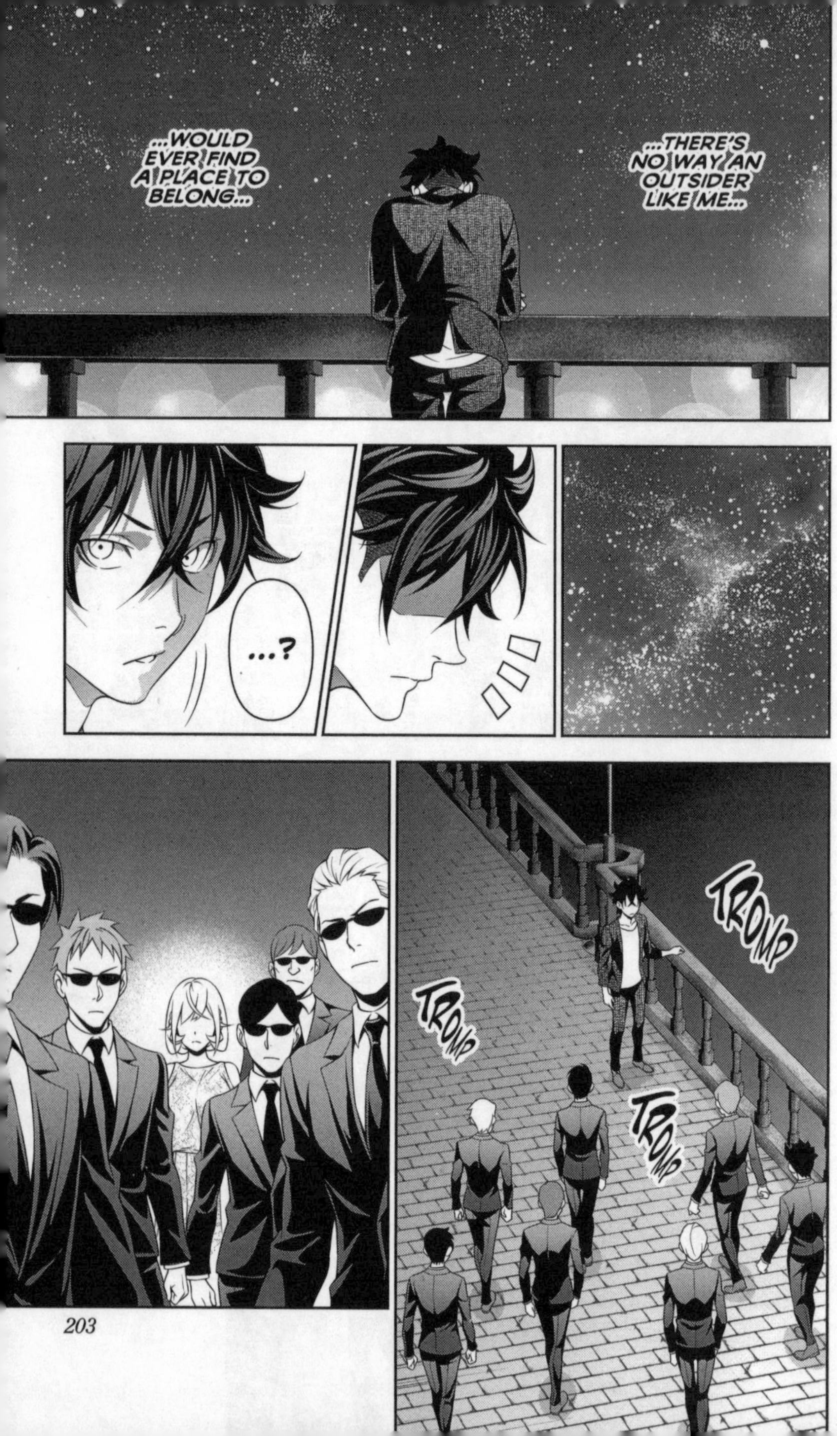
...THERE'S NO WAY AN OUTSIDER LIKE ME...
...WOULD EVER FIND A PLACE TO BELONG...
...?
TROMP
TROMP
TROMP

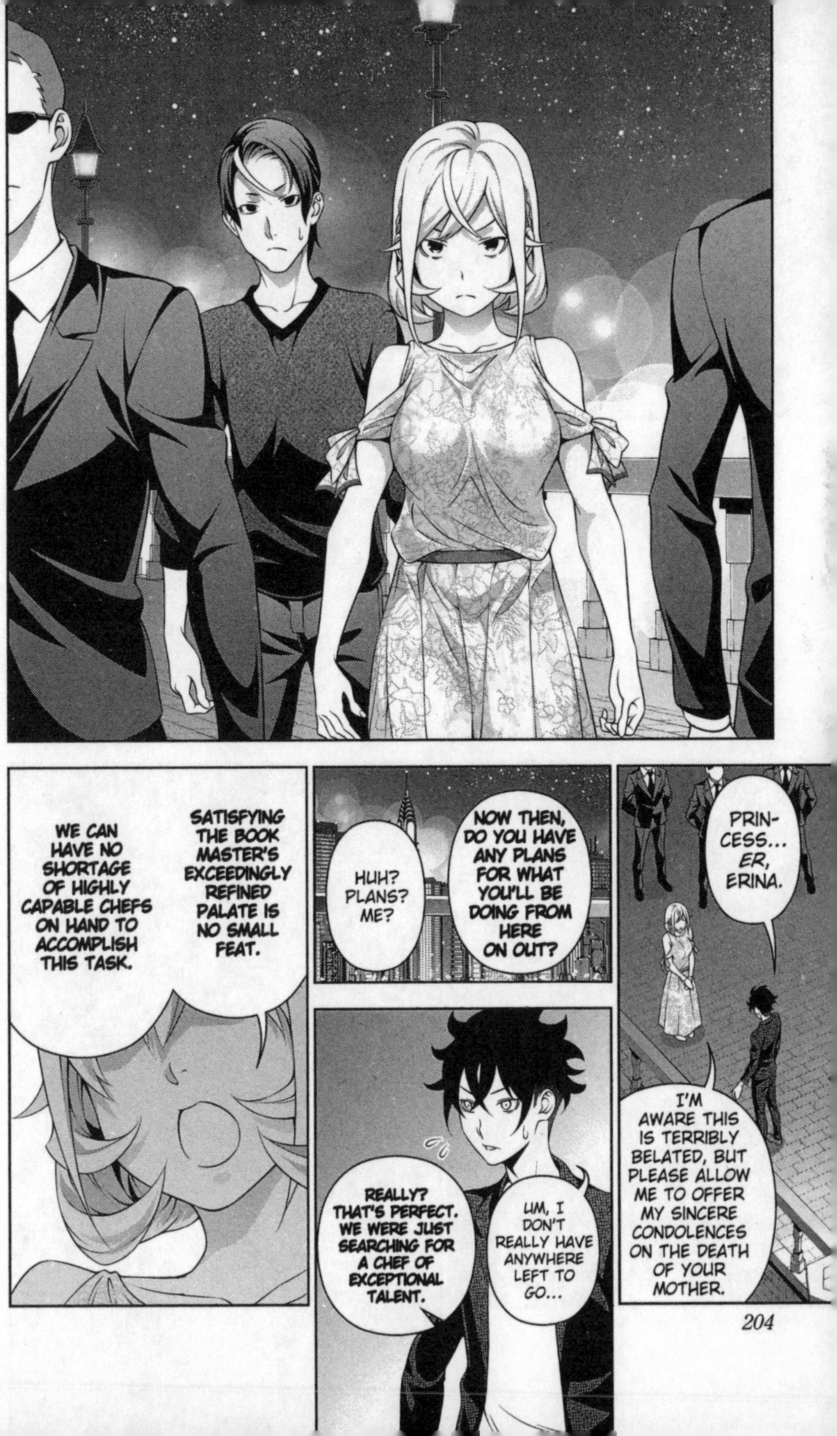
PRIN-CESS... ER, ERINA.
I'M AWARE THIS IS TERRIBLY BELATED, BUT PLEASE ALLOW ME TO OFFER MY SINCERE CONDOLENCES ON THE DEATH OF YOUR MOTHER.
NOW THEN, DO YOU HAVE ANY PLANS FOR WHAT YOU'LL BE DOING FROM HERE ON OUT?
HUH? PLANS? ME?
UM, I DON'T REALLY HAVE ANYWHERE LEFT TO GO...
REALLY? THAT'S PERFECT. WE WERE JUST SEARCHING FOR A CHEF OF EXCEPTIONAL TALENT.
SATISFYING THE BOOK MASTER'S EXCEEDINGLY REFINED PALATE IS NO SMALL FEAT.
WE CAN HAVE NO SHORTAGE OF HIGHLY CAPABLE CHEFS ON HAND TO ACCOMPLISH THIS TASK.

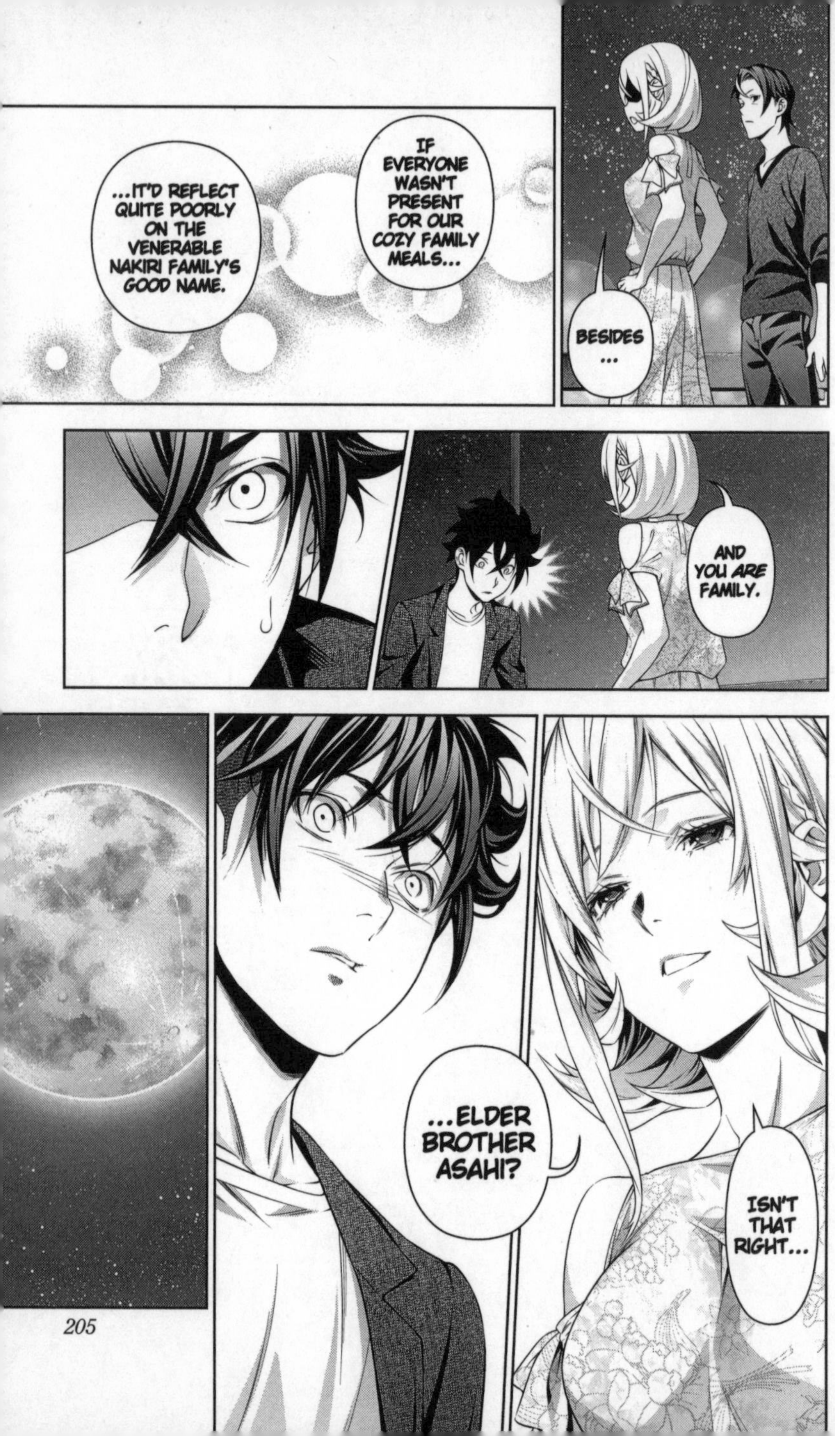
BESIDES...
IF EVERYONE WASN'T PRESENT FOR OUR COZY FAMILY MEALS...
...IT'D REFLECT QUITE POORLY ON THE VENERABLE NAKIRI FAMILY'S GOOD NAME.
AND YOU *ARE* FAMILY.
ISN'T THAT RIGHT...
...ELDER BROTHER ASAHI?

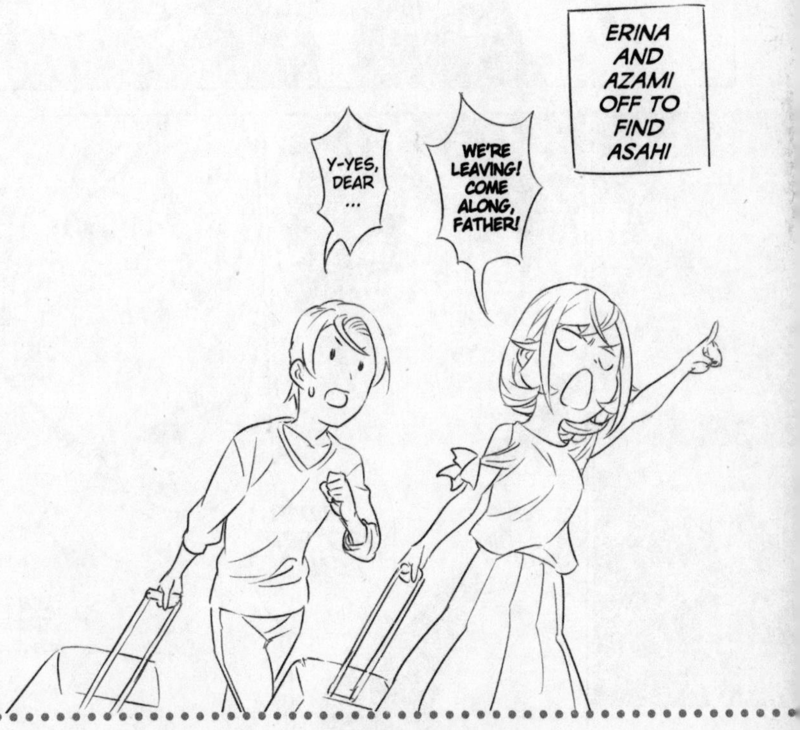
ERINA AND AZAMI OFF TO FIND ASAHI
WE'RE LEAVING! COME ALONG, FATHER!
Y-YES, DEAR ...

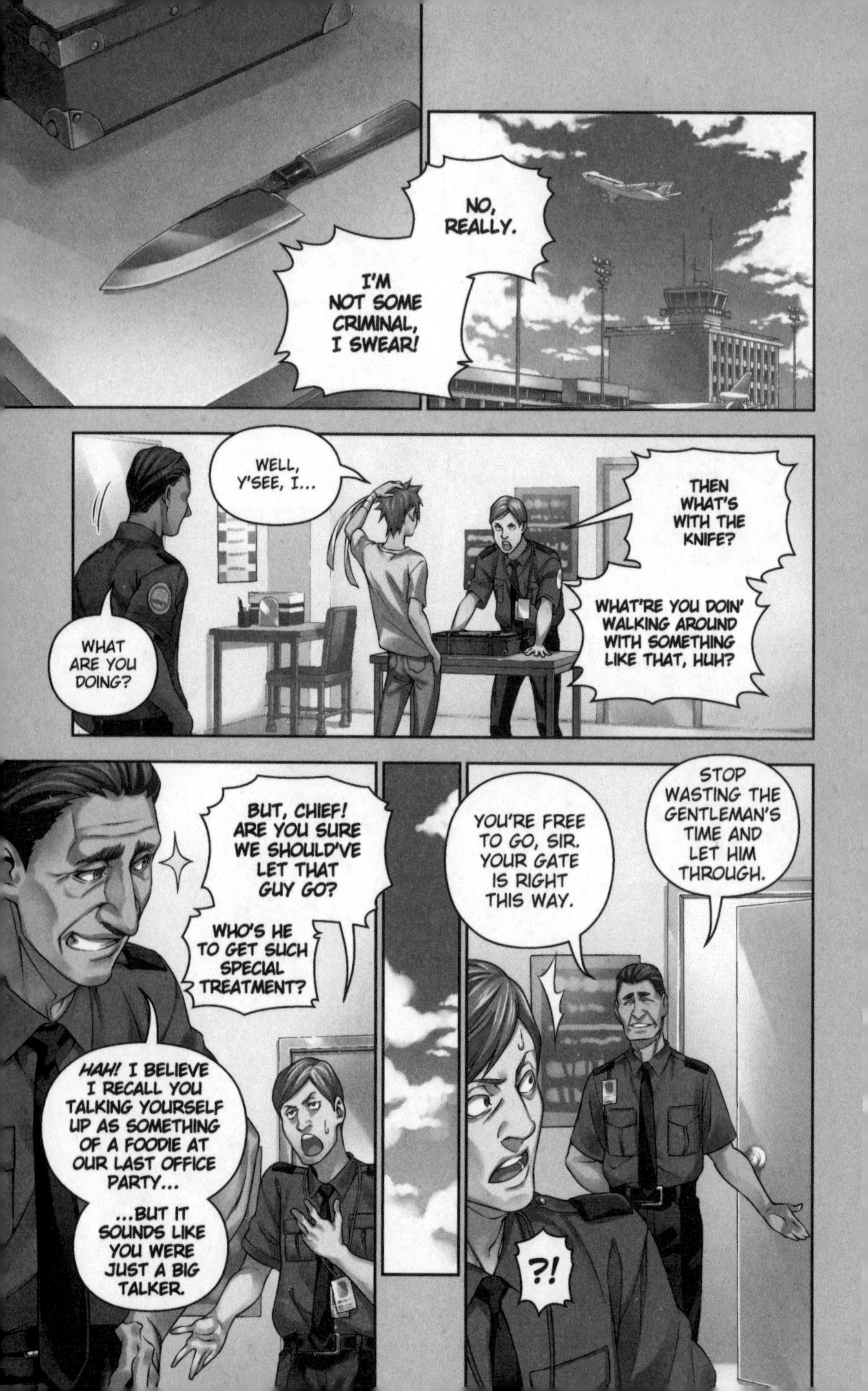
NO, REALLY.
I'M NOT SOME CRIMINAL, I SWEAR!
THEN WHAT'S WITH THE KNIFE?
WHAT'RE YOU DOIN' WALKING AROUND WITH SOMETHING LIKE THAT, HUH?
WELL, Y'SEE, I...
WHAT ARE YOU DOING?
STOP WASTING THE GENTLEMAN'S TIME AND LET HIM THROUGH.
YOU'RE FREE TO GO, SIR. YOUR GATE IS RIGHT THIS WAY.
?!
BUT, CHIEF! ARE YOU SURE WE SHOULD'VE LET THAT GUY GO?
WHO'S HE TO GET SUCH SPECIAL TREATMENT?
HAH! I BELIEVE I RECALL YOU TALKING YOURSELF UP AS SOMETHING OF A FOODIE AT OUR LAST OFFICE PARTY...
...BUT IT SOUNDS LIKE YOU WERE JUST A BIG TALKER.

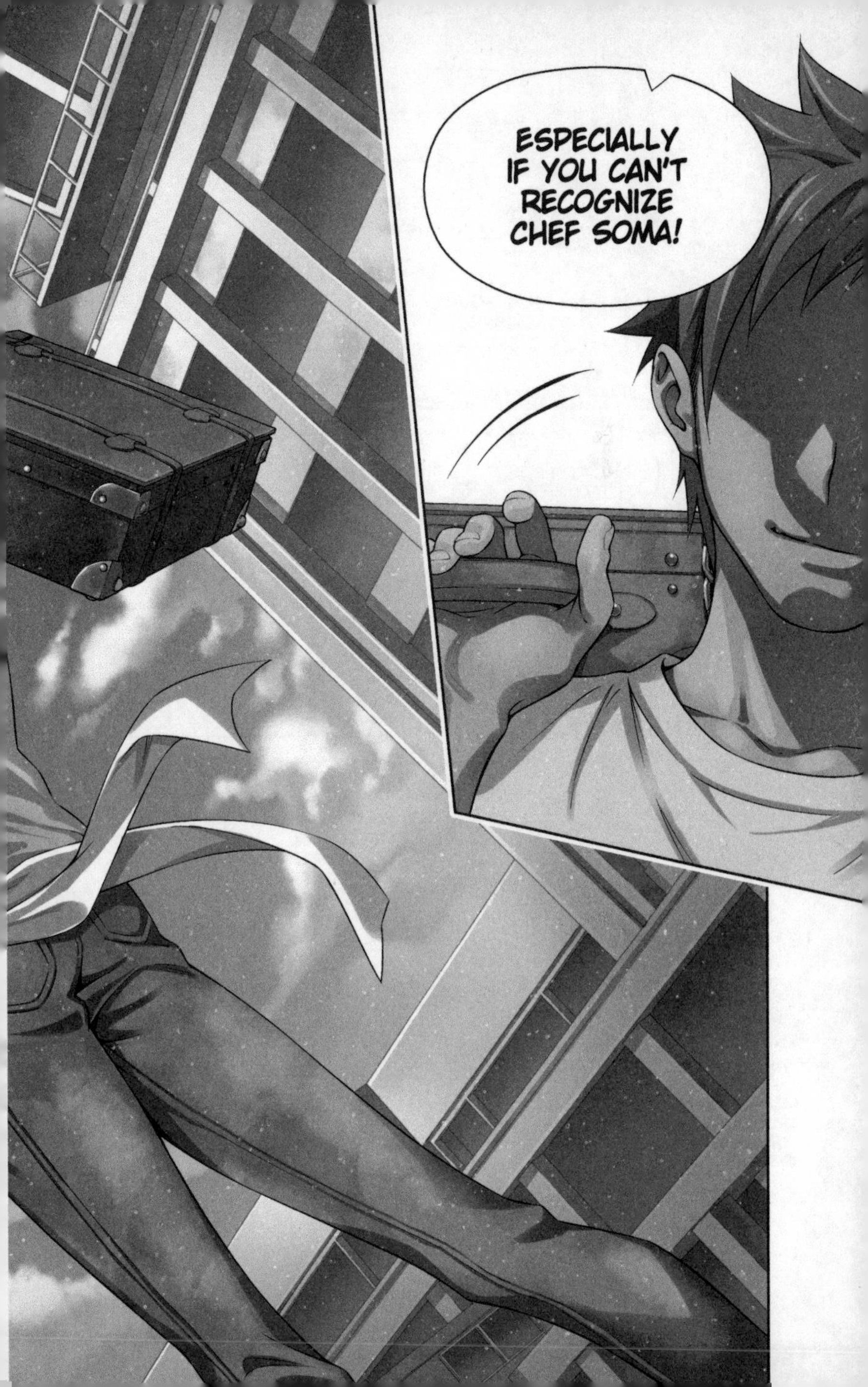
ESPECIALLY IF YOU CAN'T RECOGNIZE CHEF SOMA!

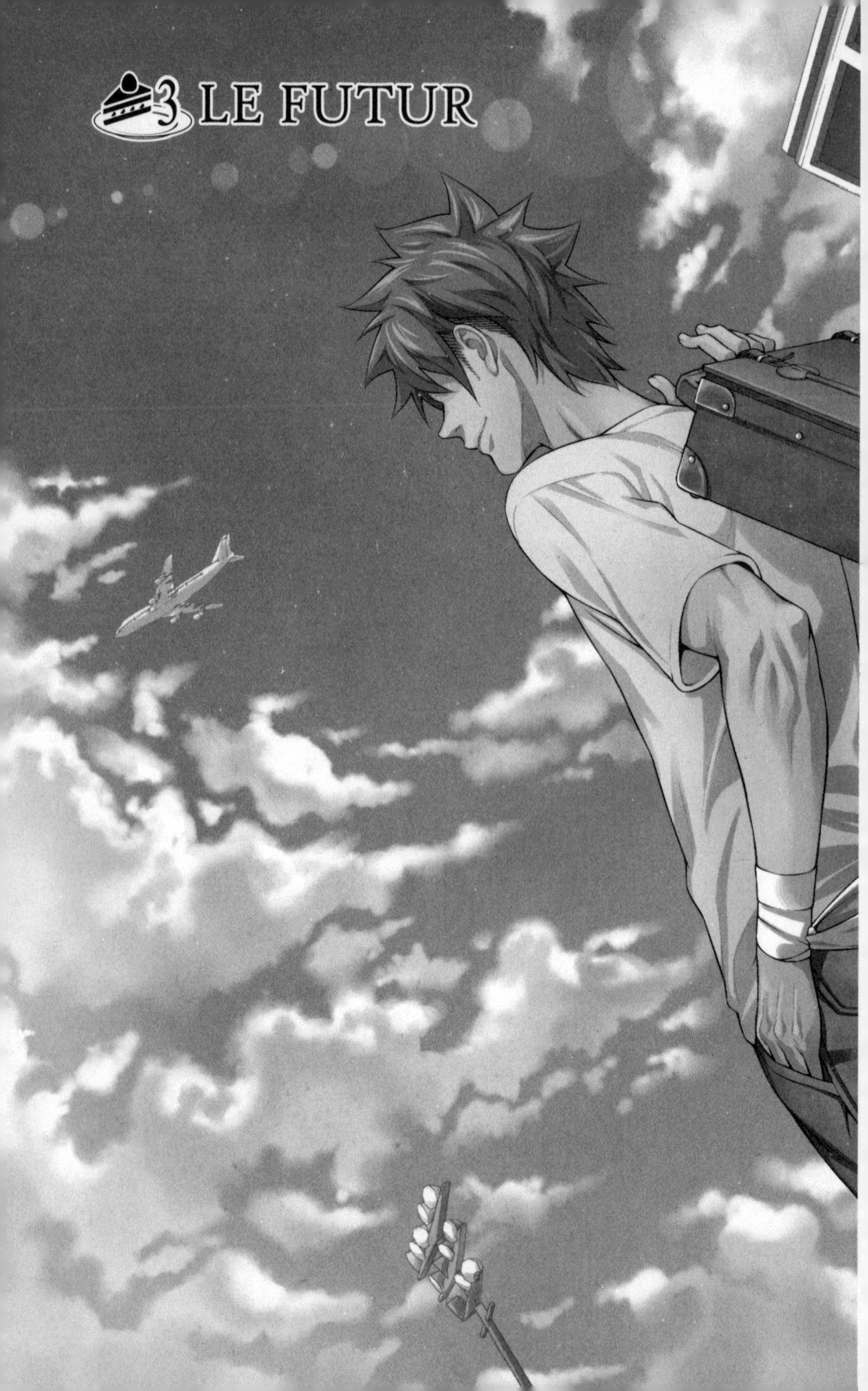
3 LE FUTUR

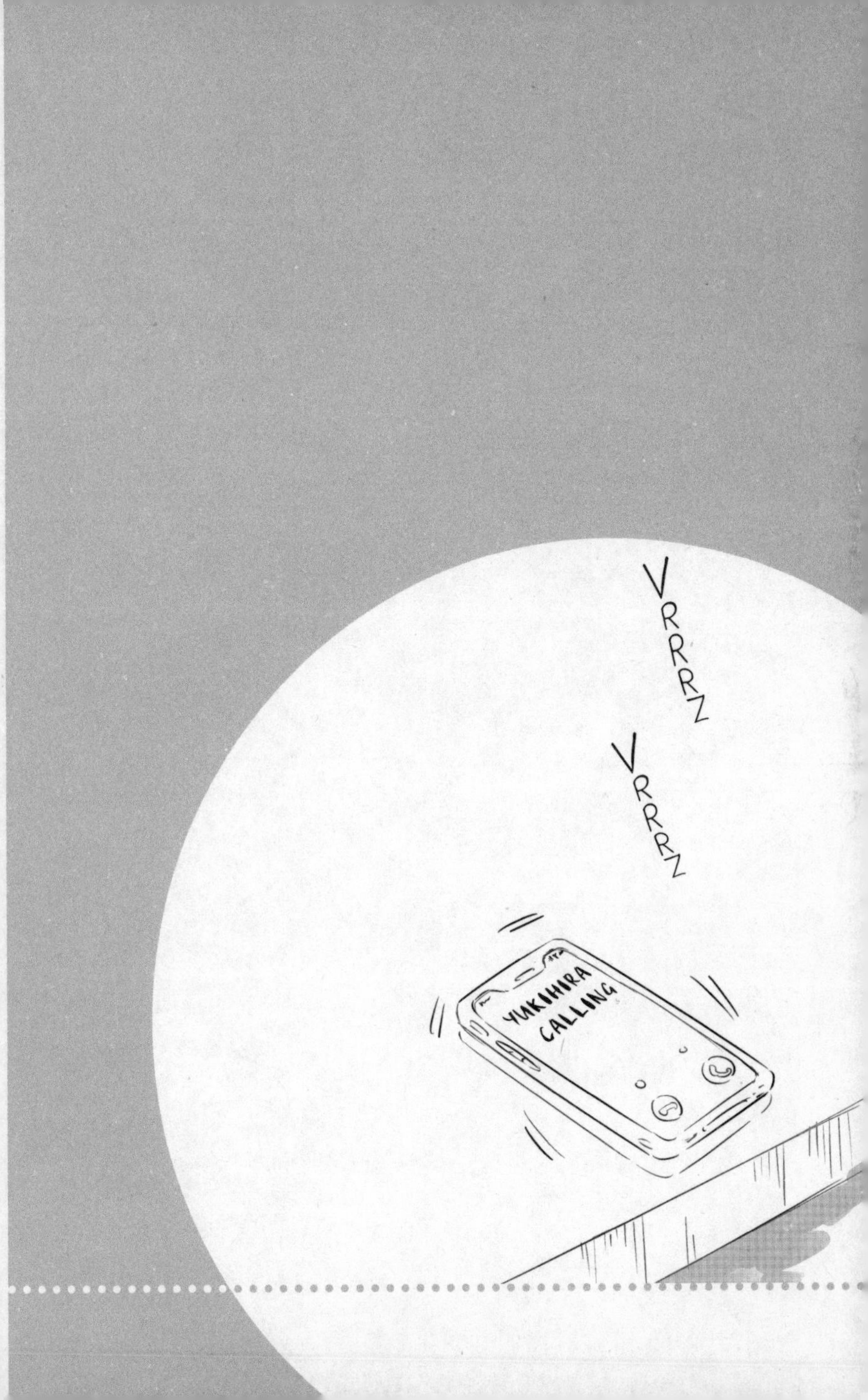
VRRRZ
VRRRZ
YUKIHIRA CALLING

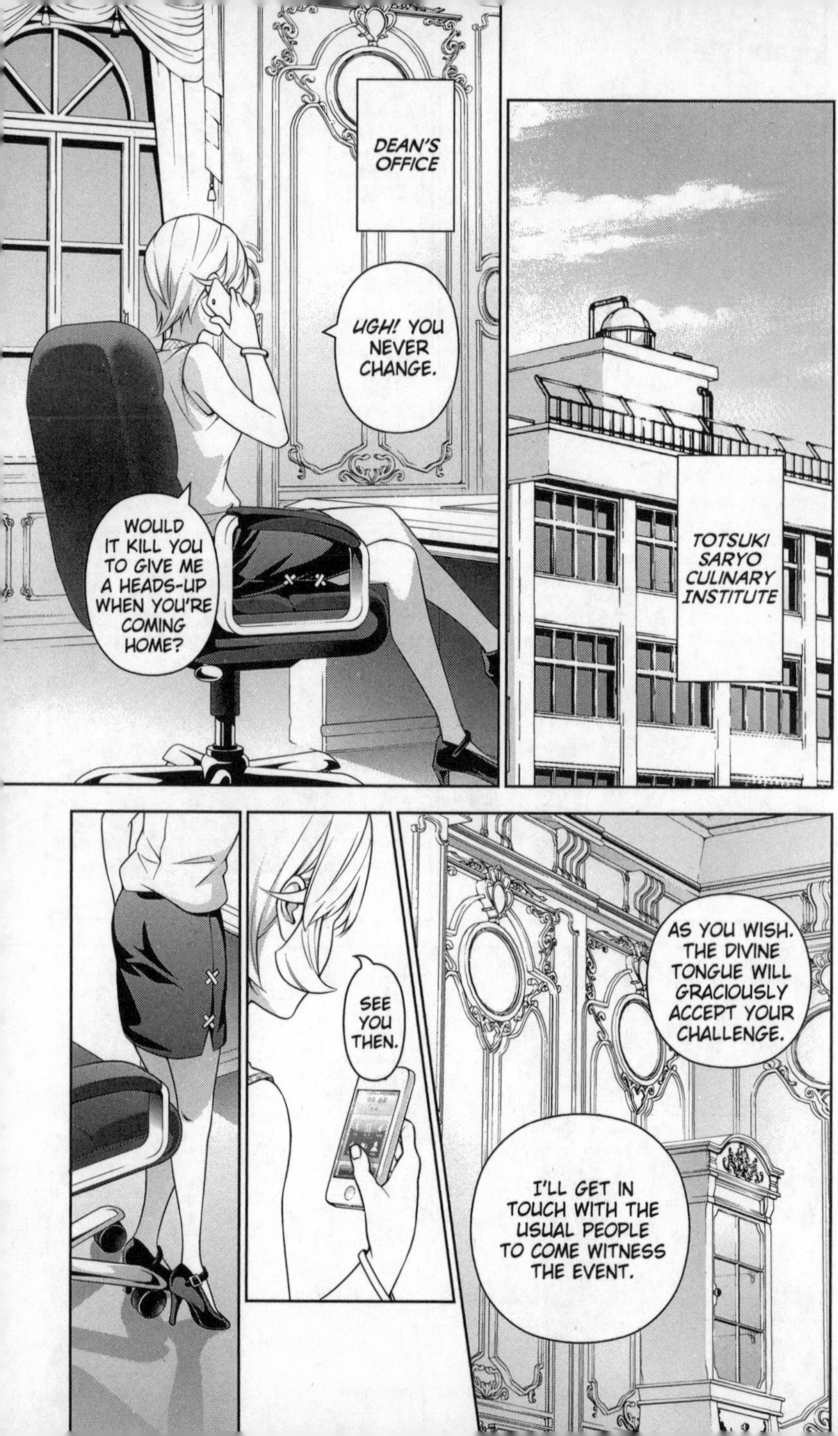
TOTSUKI SARYO CULINARY INSTITUTE
DEAN'S OFFICE
UGH! YOU NEVER CHANGE.
WOULD IT KILL YOU TO GIVE ME A HEADS-UP WHEN YOU'RE COMING HOME?
AS YOU WISH. THE DIVINE TONGUE WILL GRACIOUSLY ACCEPT YOUR CHALLENGE.
I'LL GET IN TOUCH WITH THE USUAL PEOPLE TO COME WITNESS THE EVENT.
SEE YOU THEN.

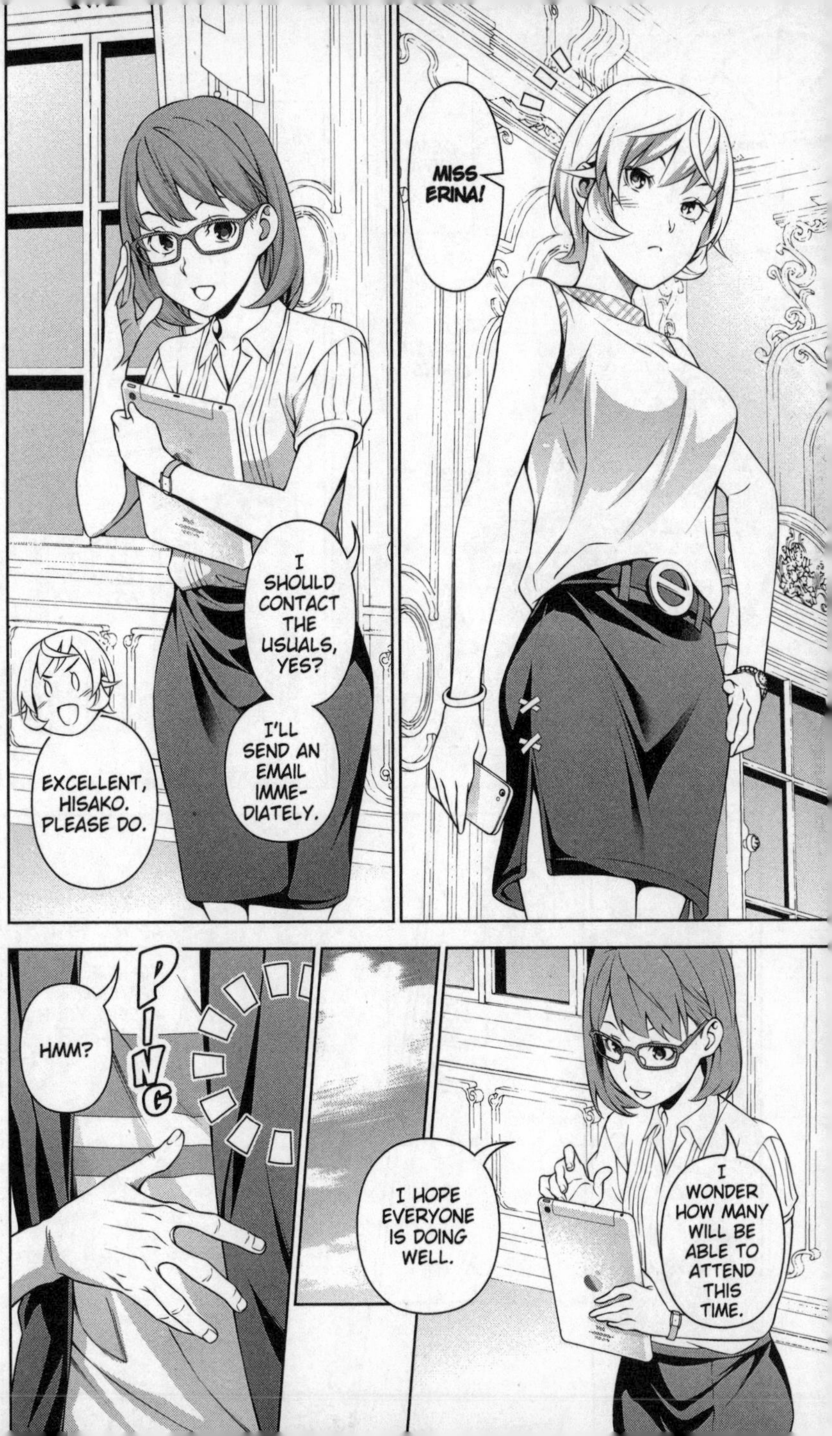
MISS ERINA!
I SHOULD CONTACT THE USUALS, YES?
I'LL SEND AN EMAIL IMMEDIATELY.
EXCELLENT, HISAKO. PLEASE DO.
I WONDER HOW MANY WILL BE ABLE TO ATTEND THIS TIME.
I HOPE EVERYONE IS DOING WELL.
PING
HMM?

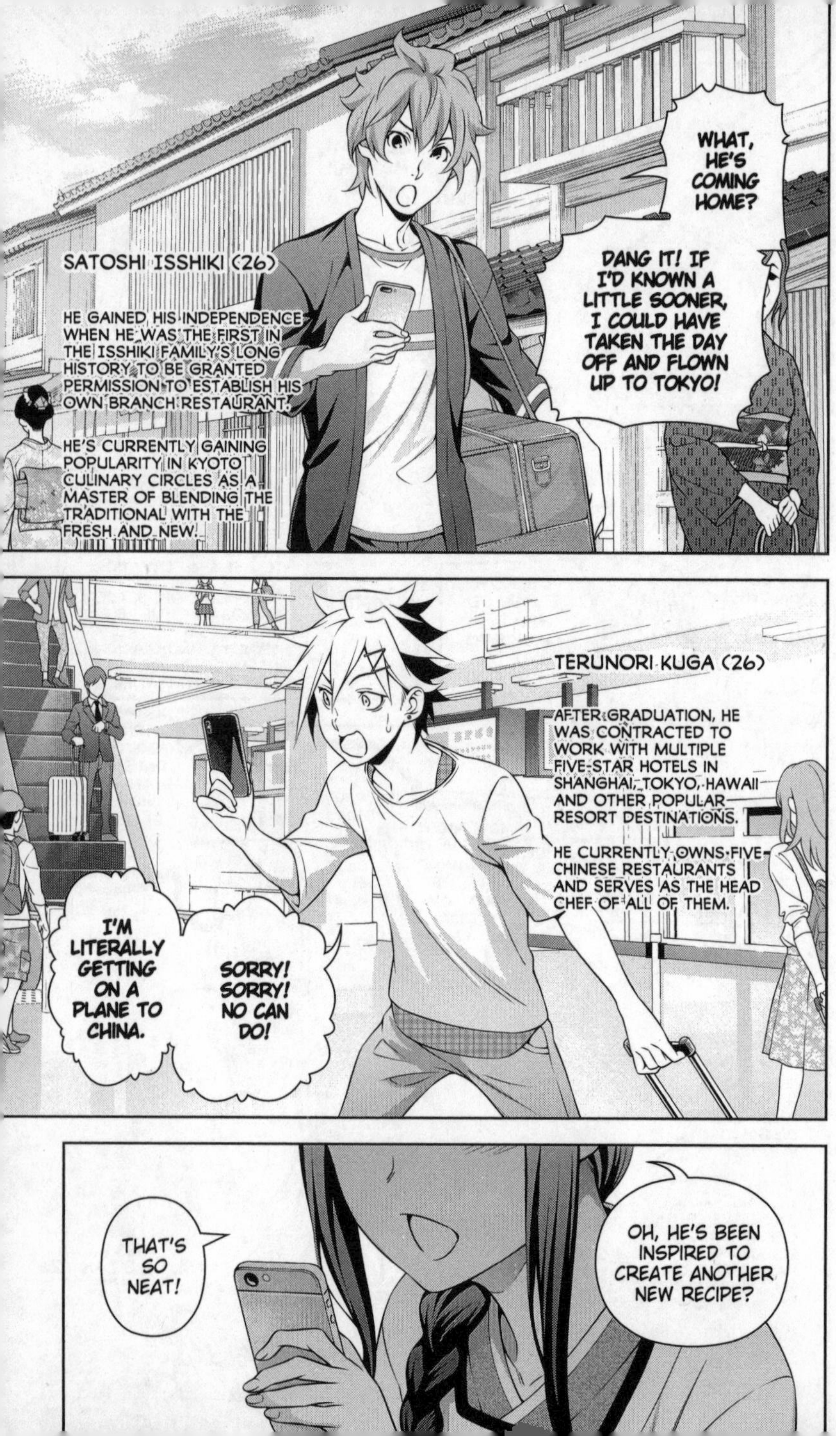
WHAT, HE'S COMING HOME?
DANG IT! IF I'D KNOWN A LITTLE SOONER, I COULD HAVE TAKEN THE DAY OFF AND FLOWN UP TO TOKYO!
SATOSHI ISSHIKI (26)
HE GAINED HIS INDEPENDENCE WHEN HE WAS THE FIRST IN THE ISSHIKI FAMILY'S LONG HISTORY TO BE GRANTED PERMISSION TO ESTABLISH HIS OWN BRANCH RESTAURANT.
HE'S CURRENTLY GAINING POPULARITY IN KYOTO CULINARY CIRCLES AS A MASTER OF BLENDING THE TRADITIONAL WITH THE FRESH AND NEW.
TERUNORI KUGA (26)
AFTER GRADUATION, HE WAS CONTRACTED TO WORK WITH MULTIPLE FIVE-STAR HOTELS IN SHANGHAI, TOKYO, HAWAII AND OTHER POPULAR RESORT DESTINATIONS.
HE CURRENTLY OWNS FIVE CHINESE RESTAURANTS AND SERVES AS THE HEAD CHEF OF ALL OF THEM.
SORRY! SORRY! NO CAN DO!
I'M LITERALLY GETTING ON A PLANE TO CHINA.
OH, HE'S BEEN INSPIRED TO CREATE ANOTHER NEW RECIPE?
THAT'S SO NEAT!

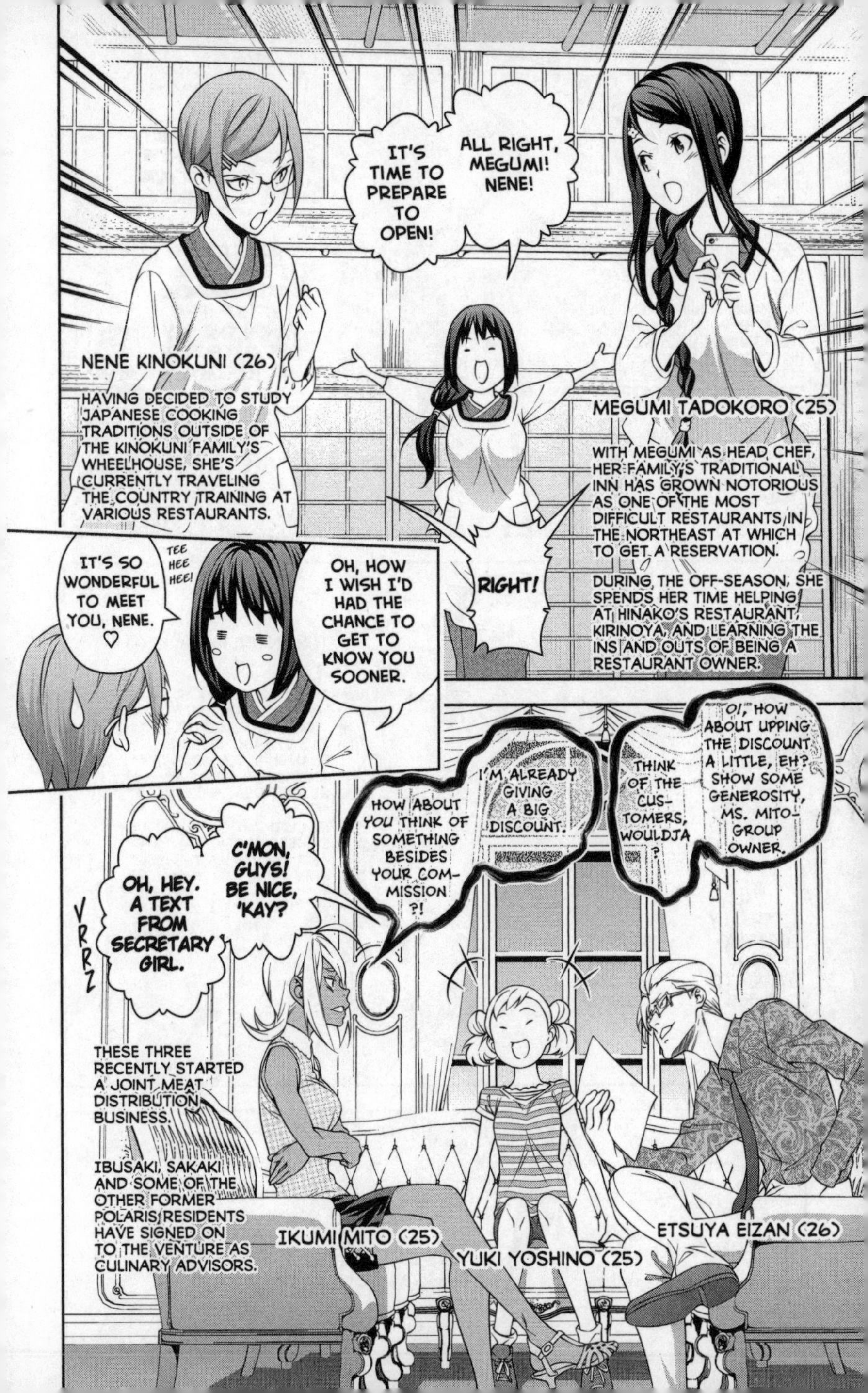
ALL RIGHT, MEGUMI! NENE!
IT'S TIME TO PREPARE TO OPEN!
MEGUMI TADOKORO (25)
WITH MEGUMI AS HEAD CHEF, HER FAMILY'S TRADITIONAL INN HAS GROWN NOTORIOUS AS ONE OF THE MOST DIFFICULT RESTAURANTS IN THE NORTHEAST AT WHICH TO GET A RESERVATION.
DURING THE OFF-SEASON, SHE SPENDS HER TIME HELPING AT HINAKO'S RESTAURANT, KIRINOYA, AND LEARNING THE INS AND OUTS OF BEING A RESTAURANT OWNER.
NENE KINOKUNI (26)
HAVING DECIDED TO STUDY JAPANESE COOKING TRADITIONS OUTSIDE OF THE KINOKUNI FAMILY'S WHEELHOUSE, SHE'S CURRENTLY TRAVELING THE COUNTRY TRAINING AT VARIOUS RESTAURANTS.
RIGHT!
OH, HOW I WISH I'D HAD THE CHANCE TO GET TO KNOW YOU SOONER.
TEE HEE HEE!
IT'S SO WONDERFUL TO MEET YOU, NENE. ♡
OI, HOW ABOUT UPPING THE DISCOUNT A LITTLE, EH? SHOW SOME GENEROSITY, MS. MITO GROUP OWNER.
THINK OF THE CUS- TOMERS, WOULDJA ?
I'M ALREADY GIVING A BIG DISCOUNT.
HOW ABOUT YOU THINK OF SOMETHING BESIDES YOUR COM- MISSION ?!
C'MON, GUYS! BE NICE, 'KAY?
OH, HEY. A TEXT FROM SECRETARY GIRL.
VRRZ
ETSUYA EIZAN (26)
YUKI YOSHINO (25)
IKUMI MITO (25)
THESE THREE RECENTLY STARTED A JOINT MEAT DISTRIBUTION BUSINESS.
IBUSAKI, SAKAKI AND SOME OF THE OTHER FORMER POLARIS RESIDENTS HAVE SIGNED ON TO THE VENTURE AS CULINARY ADVISORS.

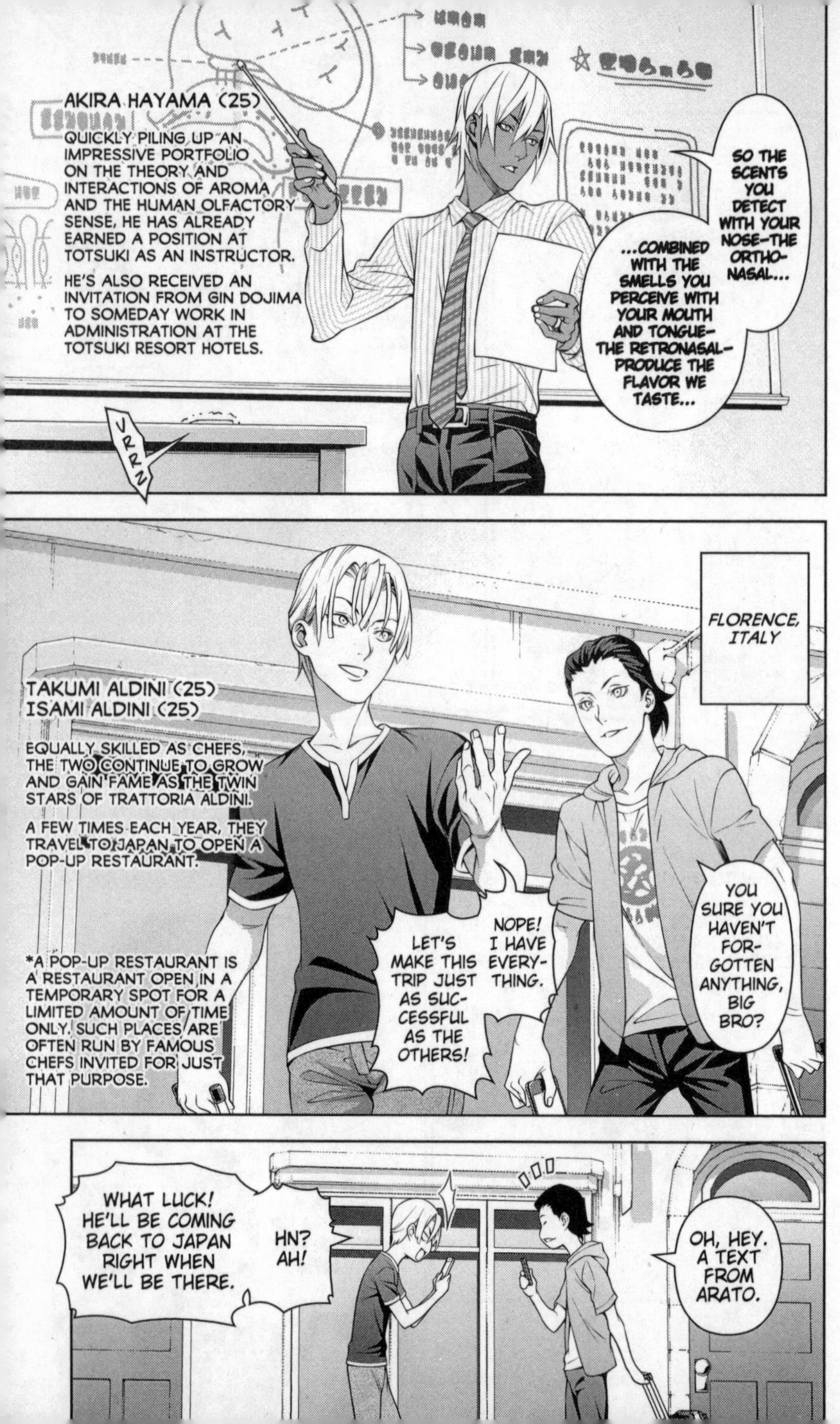
SO THE SCENTS YOU DETECT WITH YOUR NOSE—THE ORTHONASAL...
...COMBINED WITH THE SMELLS YOU PERCEIVE WITH YOUR MOUTH AND TONGUE—THE RETRONASAL—PRODUCE THE FLAVOR WE TASTE...
AKIRA HAYAMA (25)
QUICKLY PILING UP AN IMPRESSIVE PORTFOLIO ON THE THEORY AND INTERACTIONS OF AROMA AND THE HUMAN OLFACTORY SENSE, HE HAS ALREADY EARNED A POSITION AT TOTSUKI AS AN INSTRUCTOR.
HE'S ALSO RECEIVED AN INVITATION FROM GIN DOJIMA TO SOMEDAY WORK IN ADMINISTRATION AT THE TOTSUKI RESORT HOTELS.
VRRZ
FLORENCE, ITALY
YOU SURE YOU HAVEN'T FORGOTTEN ANYTHING, BIG BRO?
NOPE! I HAVE EVERYTHING.
LET'S MAKE THIS TRIP JUST AS SUCCESSFUL AS THE OTHERS!
TAKUMI ALDINI (25)
ISAMI ALDINI (25)
EQUALLY SKILLED AS CHEFS, THE TWO CONTINUE TO GROW AND GAIN FAME AS THE TWIN STARS OF TRATTORIA ALDINI.
A FEW TIMES EACH YEAR, THEY TRAVEL TO JAPAN TO OPEN A POP-UP RESTAURANT.
*A POP-UP RESTAURANT IS A RESTAURANT OPEN IN A TEMPORARY SPOT FOR A LIMITED AMOUNT OF TIME ONLY. SUCH PLACES ARE OFTEN RUN BY FAMOUS CHEFS INVITED FOR JUST THAT PURPOSE.
OH, HEY. A TEXT FROM ARATO.
HN? AH!
WHAT LUCK! HE'LL BE COMING BACK TO JAPAN RIGHT WHEN WE'LL BE THERE.

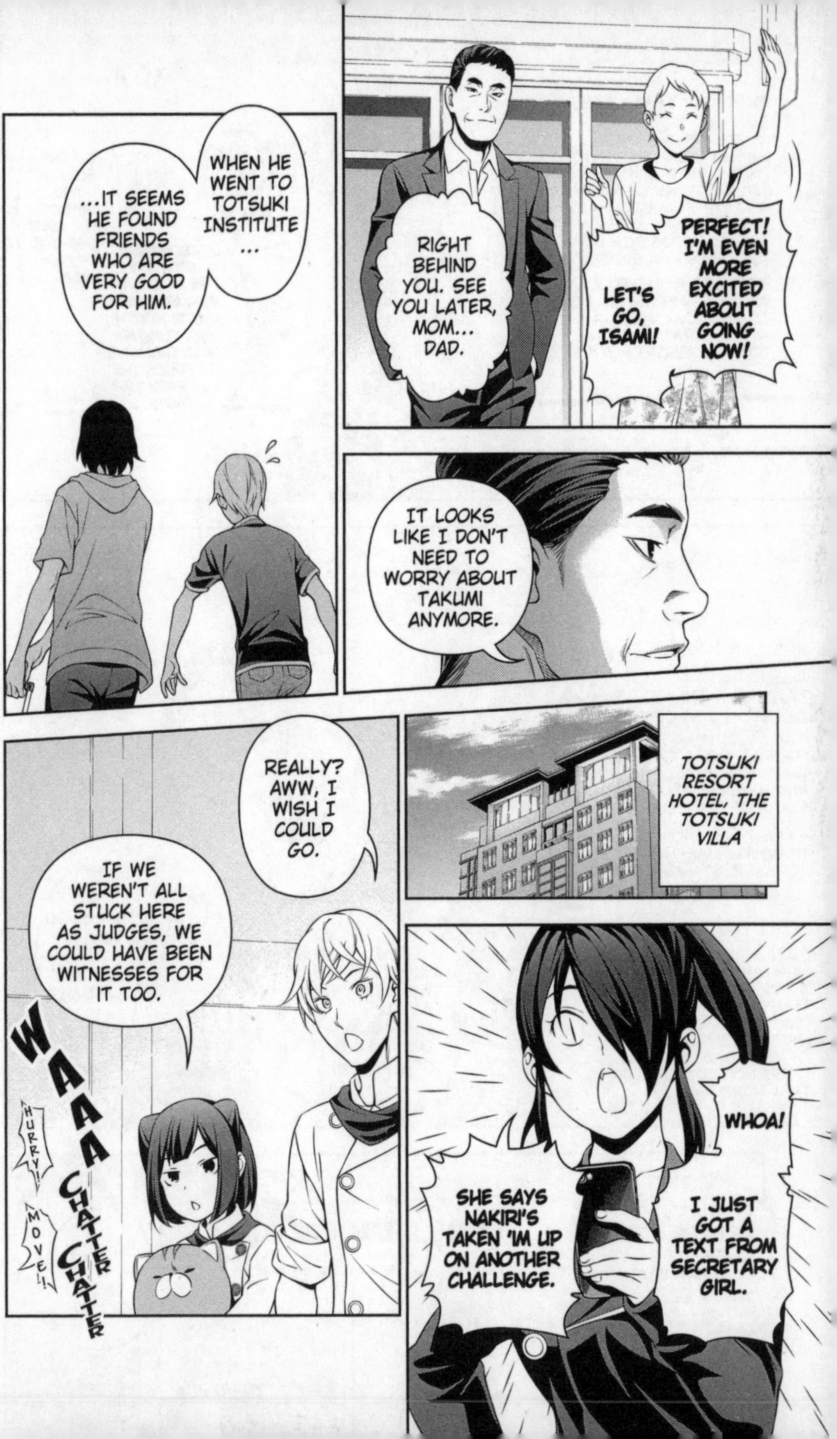
PERFECT! I'M EVEN MORE EXCITED ABOUT GOING NOW!
LET'S GO, ISAMI!
RIGHT BEHIND YOU. SEE YOU LATER, MOM... DAD.
IT LOOKS LIKE I DON'T NEED TO WORRY ABOUT TAKUMI ANYMORE.
WHEN HE WENT TO TOTSUKI INSTITUTE...
...IT SEEMS HE FOUND FRIENDS WHO ARE VERY GOOD FOR HIM.
TOTSUKI RESORT HOTEL, THE TOTSUKI VILLA
WHOA!
I JUST GOT A TEXT FROM SECRETARY GIRL.
SHE SAYS NAKIRI'S TAKEN 'IM UP ON ANOTHER CHALLENGE.
REALLY? AWW, I WISH I COULD GO.
IF WE WEREN'T ALL STUCK HERE AS JUDGES, WE COULD HAVE BEEN WITNESSES FOR IT TOO.
WAAA
CHATTER CHATTER
HURRY!
MOVE!

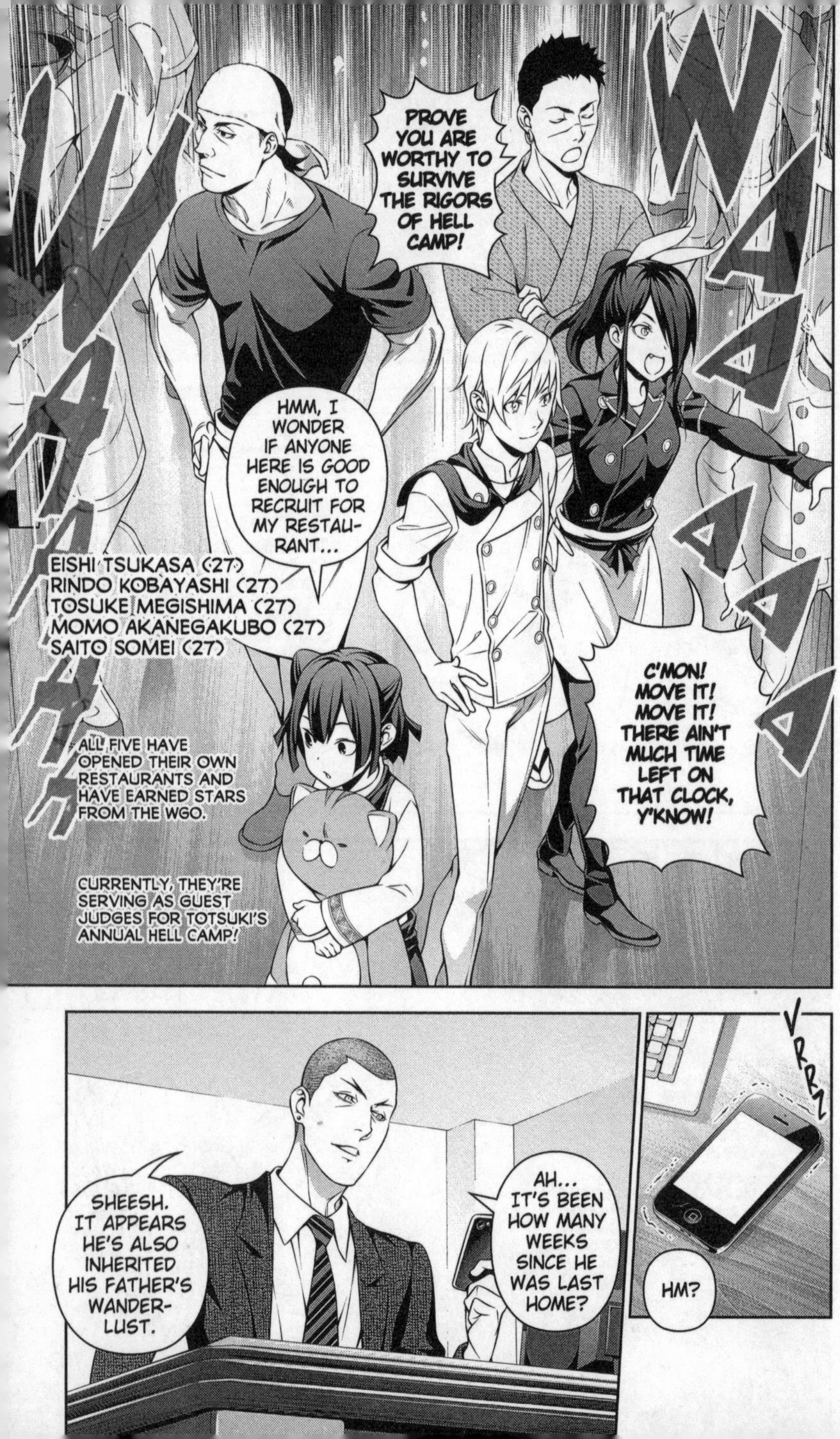
PROVE YOU ARE WORTHY TO SURVIVE THE RIGORS OF HELL CAMP!
C'MON! MOVE IT! MOVE IT! THERE AIN'T MUCH TIME LEFT ON THAT CLOCK, Y'KNOW!
HMM, I WONDER IF ANYONE HERE IS GOOD ENOUGH TO RECRUIT FOR MY RESTAURANT...
EISHI TSUKASA (27)
RINDO KOBAYASHI (27)
TOSUKE MEGISHIMA (27)
MOMO AKANEGAKUBO (27)
SAITO SOMEI (27)
ALL FIVE HAVE OPENED THEIR OWN RESTAURANTS AND HAVE EARNED STARS FROM THE WGO.
CURRENTLY, THEY'RE SERVING AS GUEST JUDGES FOR TOTSUKI'S ANNUAL HELL CAMP!
HM?
AH... IT'S BEEN HOW MANY WEEKS SINCE HE WAS LAST HOME?
SHEESH. IT APPEARS HE'S ALSO INHERITED HIS FATHER'S WANDERLUST.

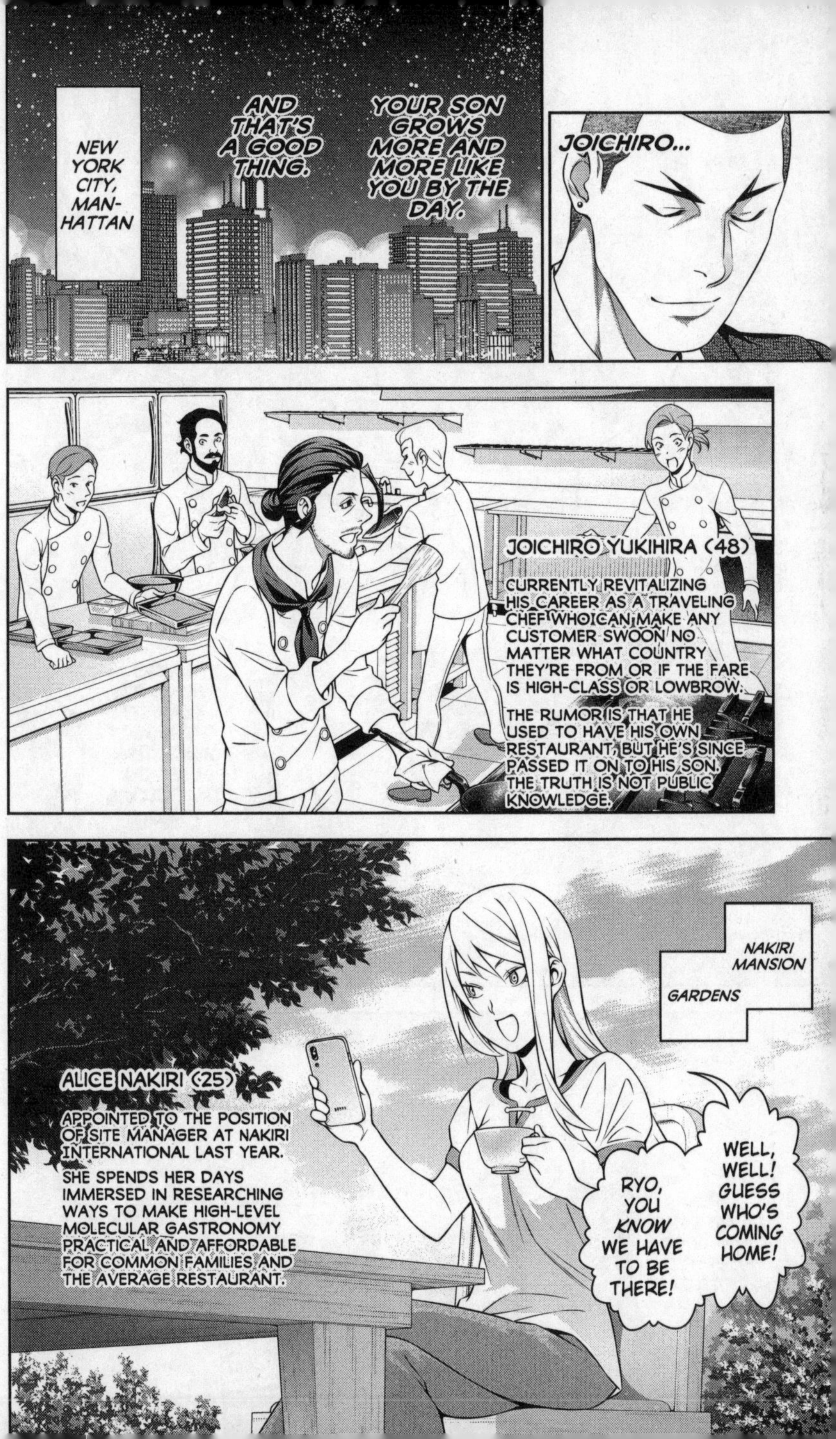
JOICHIRO...
YOUR SON GROWS MORE AND MORE LIKE YOU BY THE DAY.
AND THAT'S A GOOD THING.
NEW YORK CITY, MAN-HATTAN
JOICHIRO YUKIHIRA (48)
CURRENTLY REVITALIZING HIS CAREER AS A TRAVELING CHEF WHO CAN MAKE ANY CUSTOMER SWOON NO MATTER WHAT COUNTRY THEY'RE FROM OR IF THE FARE IS HIGH-CLASS OR LOWBROW.
THE RUMOR IS THAT HE USED TO HAVE HIS OWN RESTAURANT, BUT HE'S SINCE PASSED IT ON TO HIS SON. THE TRUTH IS NOT PUBLIC KNOWLEDGE.
NAKIRI MANSION
GARDENS
WELL, WELL! GUESS WHO'S COMING HOME!
RYO, YOU *KNOW* WE HAVE TO BE THERE!
ALICE NAKIRI (25)
APPOINTED TO THE POSITION OF SITE MANAGER AT NAKIRI INTERNATIONAL LAST YEAR.
SHE SPENDS HER DAYS IMMERSED IN RESEARCHING WAYS TO MAKE HIGH-LEVEL MOLECULAR GASTRONOMY PRACTICAL AND AFFORDABLE FOR COMMON FAMILIES AND THE AVERAGE RESTAURANT.

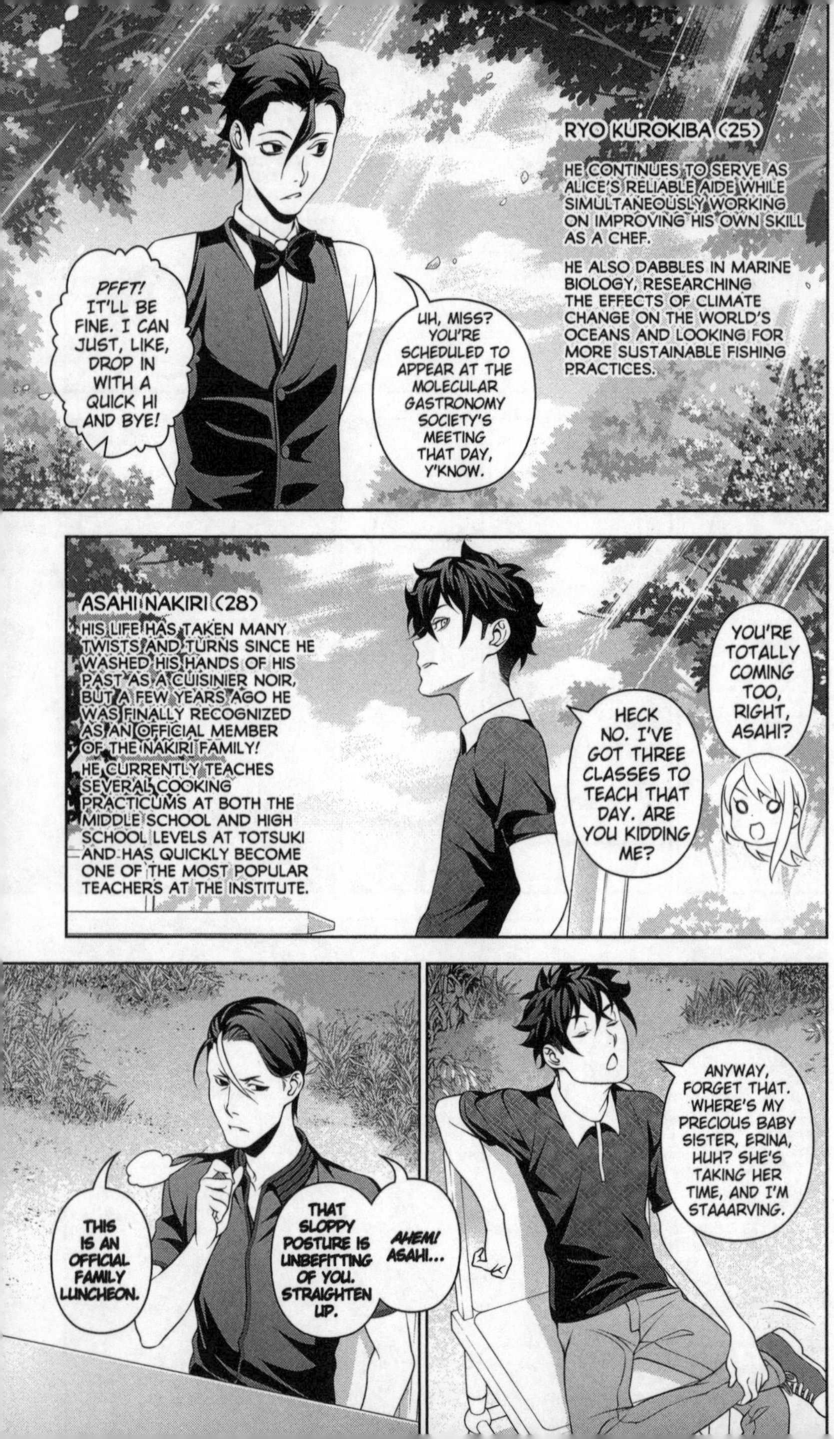
RYO KUROKIBA (25)
HE CONTINUES TO SERVE AS ALICE'S RELIABLE AIDE WHILE SIMULTANEOUSLY WORKING ON IMPROVING HIS OWN SKILL AS A CHEF.
HE ALSO DABBLES IN MARINE BIOLOGY, RESEARCHING THE EFFECTS OF CLIMATE CHANGE ON THE WORLD'S OCEANS AND LOOKING FOR MORE SUSTAINABLE FISHING PRACTICES.
UH, MISS? YOU'RE SCHEDULED TO APPEAR AT THE MOLECULAR GASTRONOMY SOCIETY'S MEETING THAT DAY, Y'KNOW.
PFFT! IT'LL BE FINE. I CAN JUST, LIKE, DROP IN WITH A QUICK HI AND BYE!
YOU'RE TOTALLY COMING TOO, RIGHT, ASAHI?
HECK NO. I'VE GOT THREE CLASSES TO TEACH THAT DAY. ARE YOU KIDDING ME?
ASAHI NAKIRI (28)
HIS LIFE HAS TAKEN MANY TWISTS AND TURNS SINCE HE WASHED HIS HANDS OF HIS PAST AS A CUISINIER NOIR, BUT A FEW YEARS AGO HE WAS FINALLY RECOGNIZED AS AN OFFICIAL MEMBER OF THE NAKIRI FAMILY!
HE CURRENTLY TEACHES SEVERAL COOKING PRACTICUMS AT BOTH THE MIDDLE SCHOOL AND HIGH SCHOOL LEVELS AT TOTSUKI AND HAS QUICKLY BECOME ONE OF THE MOST POPULAR TEACHERS AT THE INSTITUTE.
ANYWAY, FORGET THAT. WHERE'S MY PRECIOUS BABY SISTER, ERINA, HUH? SHE'S TAKING HER TIME, AND I'M STAAARVING.
AHEM! ASAHI...
THAT SLOPPY POSTURE IS UNBEFITTING OF YOU. STRAIGHTEN UP.
THIS IS AN OFFICIAL FAMILY LUNCHEON.

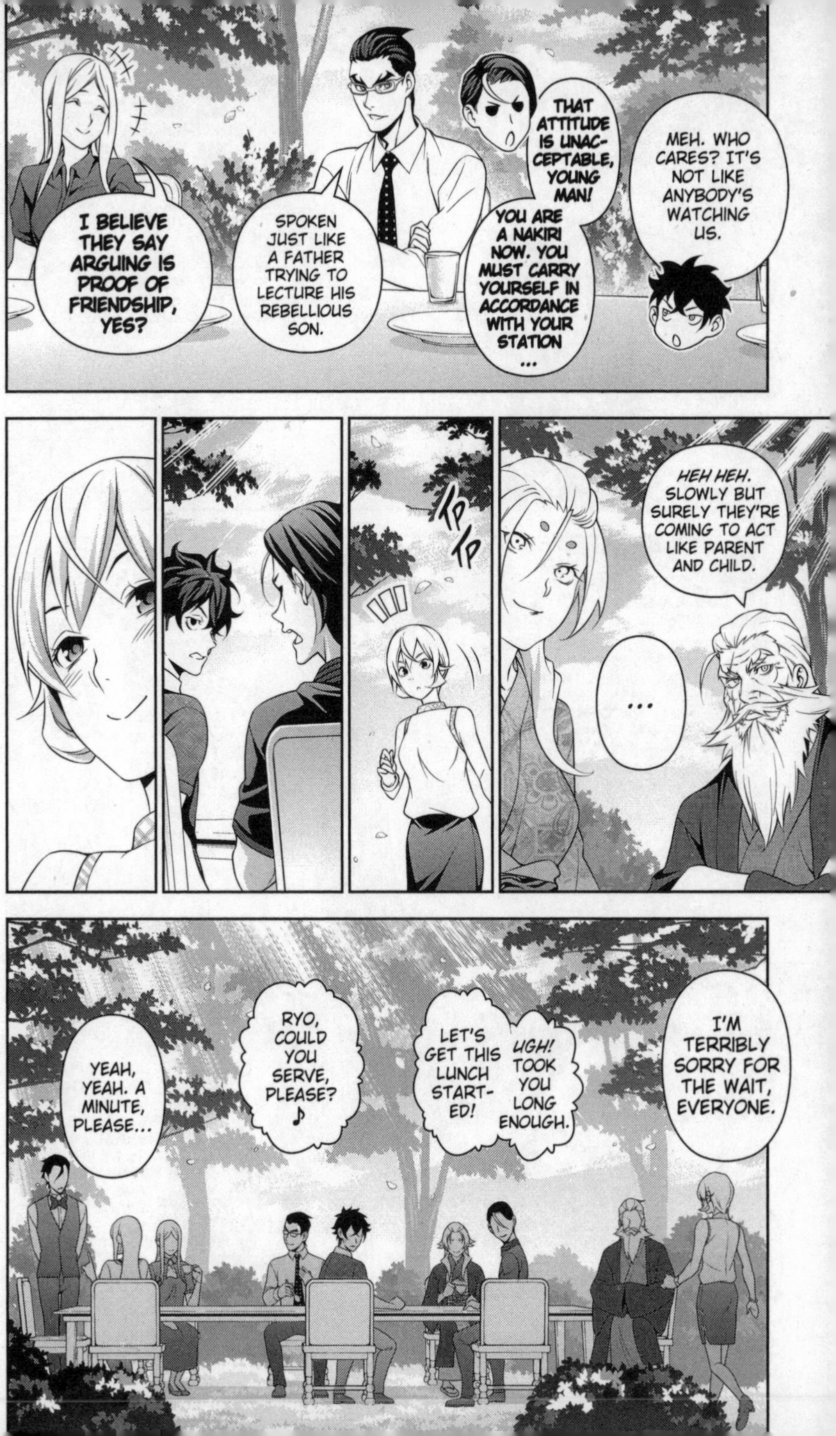
MEH. WHO CARES? IT'S NOT LIKE ANYBODY'S WATCHING US.
THAT ATTITUDE IS UNACCEPTABLE, YOUNG MAN!
YOU ARE A NAKIRI NOW. YOU MUST CARRY YOURSELF IN ACCORDANCE WITH YOUR STATION...
SPOKEN JUST LIKE A FATHER TRYING TO LECTURE HIS REBELLIOUS SON.
I BELIEVE THEY SAY ARGUING IS PROOF OF FRIENDSHIP, YES?
HEH HEH. SLOWLY BUT SURELY THEY'RE COMING TO ACT LIKE PARENT AND CHILD.
...
TP TP
I'M TERRIBLY SORRY FOR THE WAIT, EVERYONE.
UGH! TOOK YOU LONG ENOUGH.
LET'S GET THIS LUNCH START-ED!
RYO, COULD YOU SERVE, PLEASE? ♪
YEAH, YEAH. A MINUTE, PLEASE...

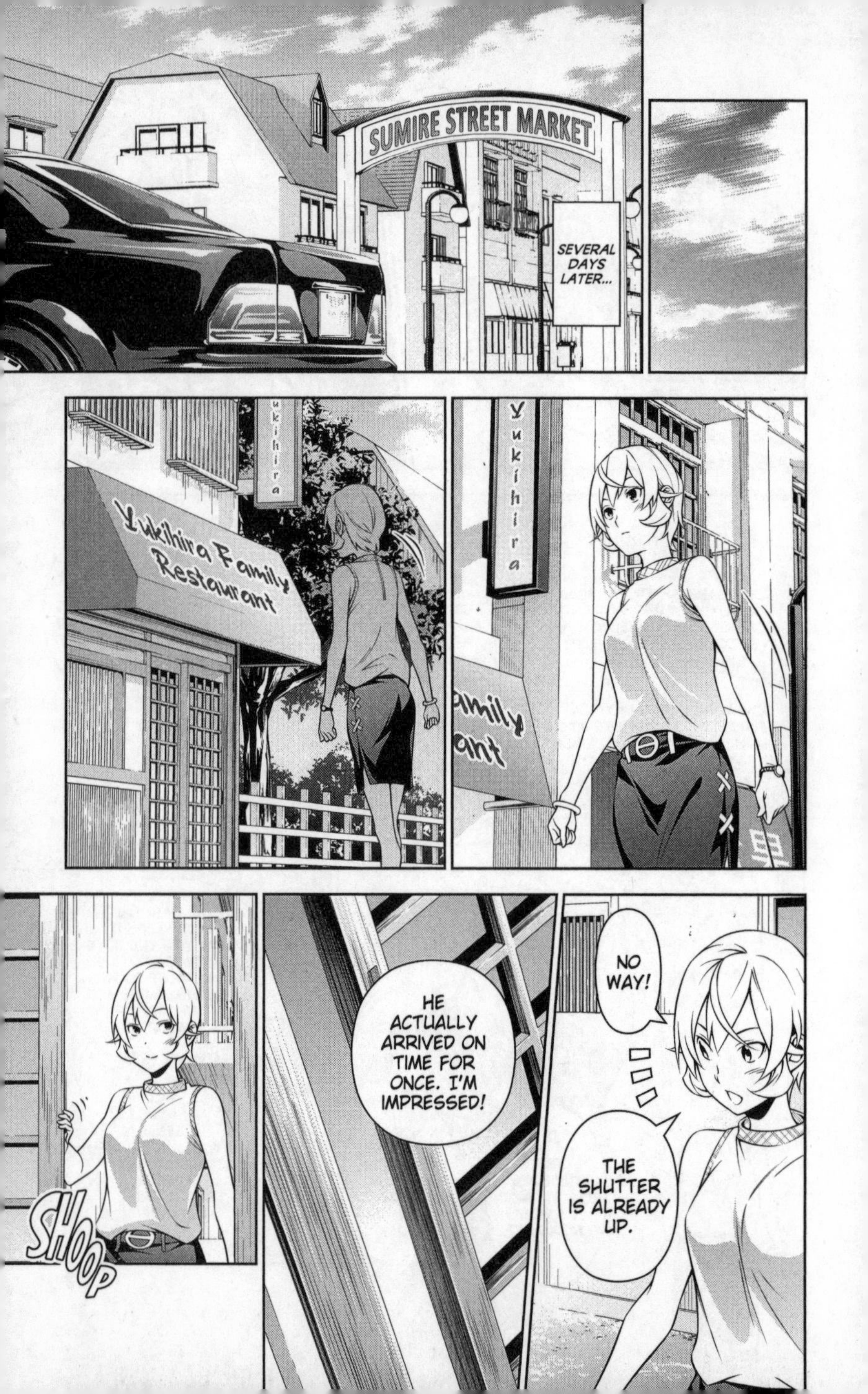
SUMIRE STREET MARKET
SEVERAL DAYS LATER...
Yukihira
Yukihira Family Restaurant
Yukihira
NO WAY!
...
THE SHUTTER IS ALREADY UP.
HE ACTUALLY ARRIVED ON TIME FOR ONCE. I'M IMPRESSED!
SHOOP

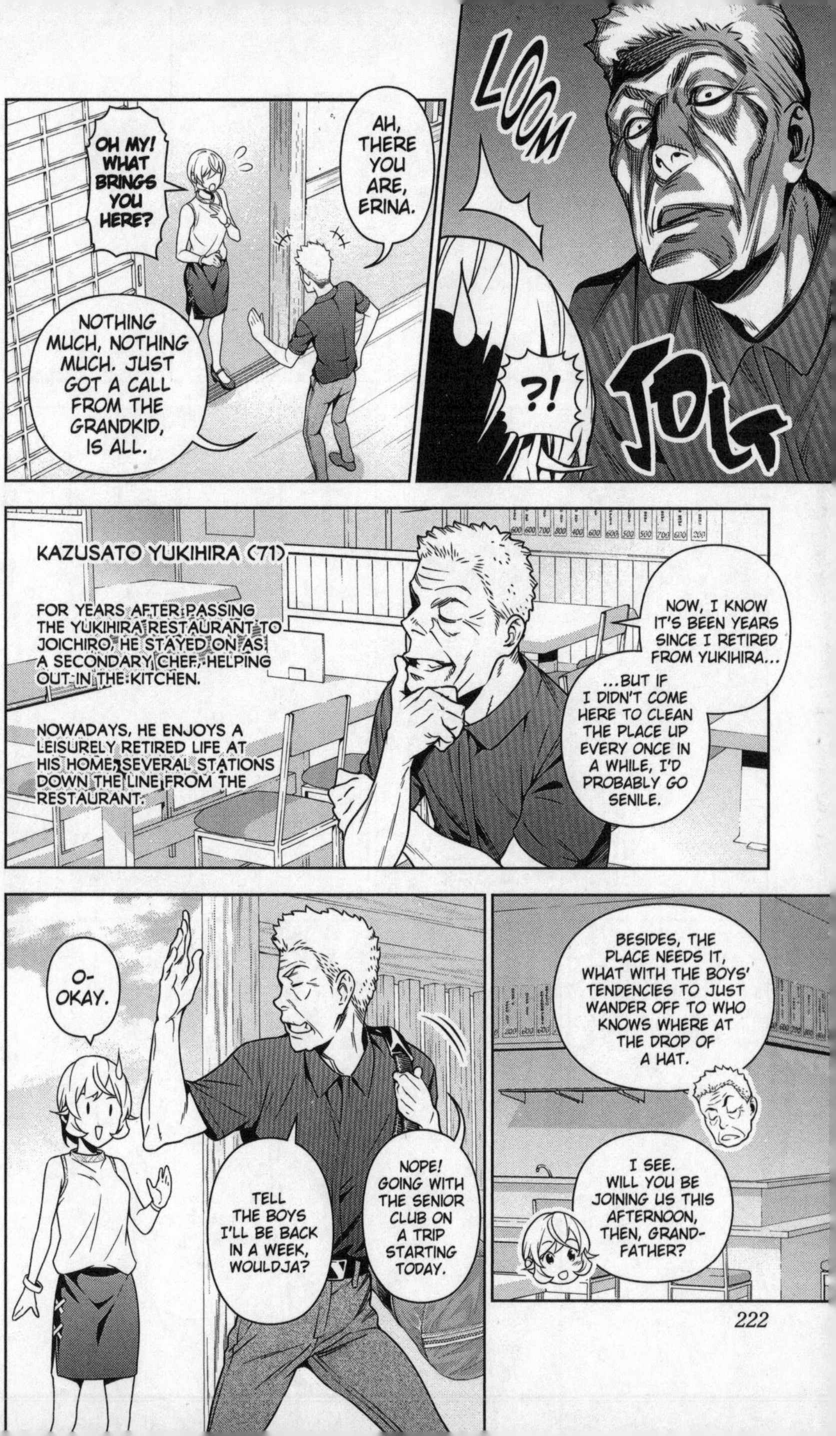
LOOM
?!
JOLT
AH, THERE YOU ARE, ERINA.
OH MY! WHAT BRINGS YOU HERE?
NOTHING MUCH, NOTHING MUCH. JUST GOT A CALL FROM THE GRANDKID, IS ALL.
NOW, I KNOW IT'S BEEN YEARS SINCE I RETIRED FROM YUKIHIRA...
...BUT IF I DIDN'T COME HERE TO CLEAN THE PLACE UP EVERY ONCE IN A WHILE, I'D PROBABLY GO SENILE.
KAZUSATO YUKIHIRA (71)
FOR YEARS AFTER PASSING THE YUKIHIRA RESTAURANT TO JOICHIRO, HE STAYED ON AS A SECONDARY CHEF, HELPING OUT IN THE KITCHEN.
NOWADAYS, HE ENJOYS A LEISURELY RETIRED LIFE AT HIS HOME SEVERAL STATIONS DOWN THE LINE FROM THE RESTAURANT.
BESIDES, THE PLACE NEEDS IT, WHAT WITH THE BOYS' TENDENCIES TO JUST WANDER OFF TO WHO KNOWS WHERE AT THE DROP OF A HAT.
I SEE. WILL YOU BE JOINING US THIS AFTERNOON, THEN, GRAND-FATHER?
NOPE! GOING WITH THE SENIOR CLUB ON A TRIP STARTING TODAY.
TELL THE BOYS I'LL BE BACK IN A WEEK, WOULDJA?
O-OKAY.

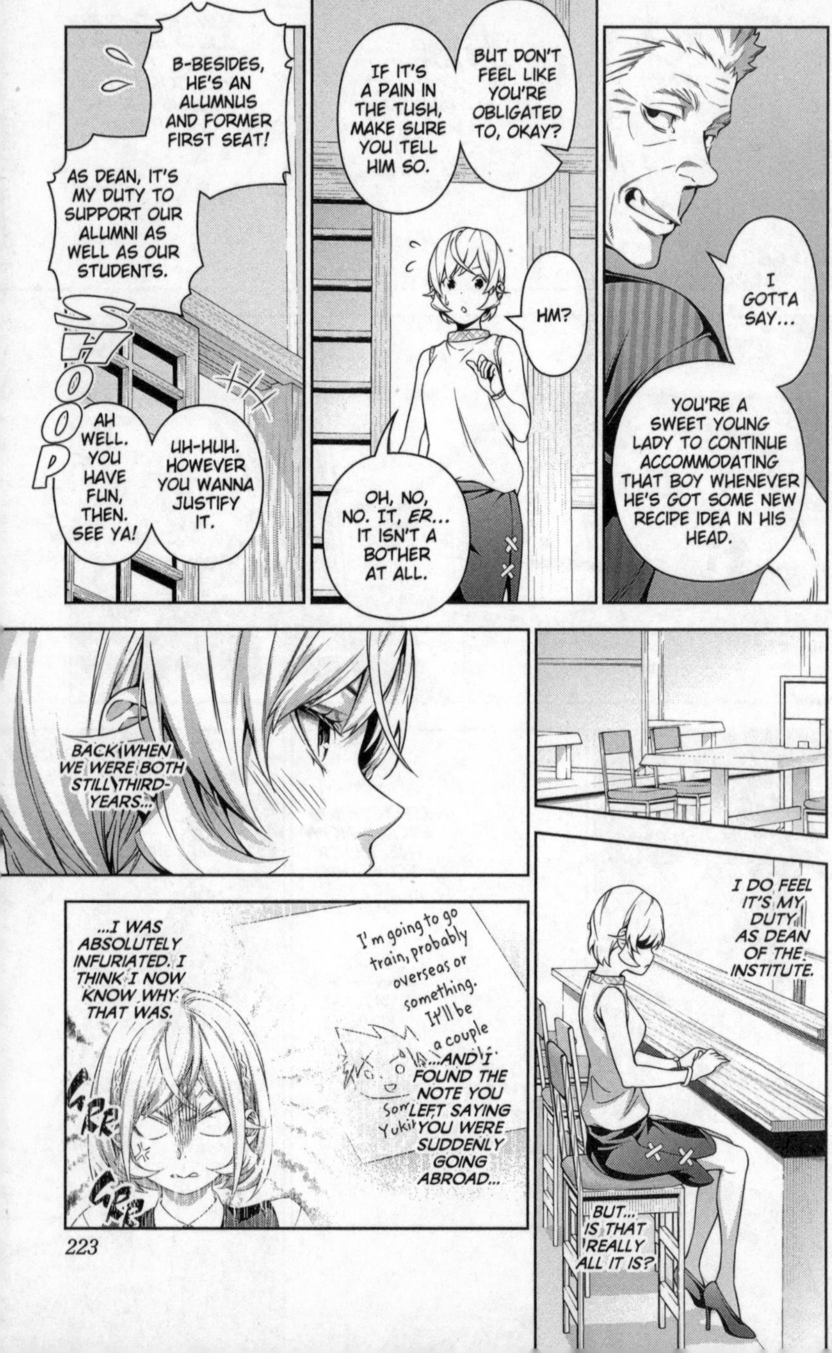
I GOTTA SAY...
YOU'RE A SWEET YOUNG LADY TO CONTINUE ACCOMMODATING THAT BOY WHENEVER HE'S GOT SOME NEW RECIPE IDEA IN HIS HEAD.
HM?
OH, NO, NO. IT, *ER*... IT ISN'T A BOTHER AT ALL.
BUT DON'T FEEL LIKE YOU'RE OBLIGATED TO, OKAY?
IF IT'S A PAIN IN THE TUSH, MAKE SURE YOU TELL HIM SO.
B-BESIDES, HE'S AN ALUMNUS AND FORMER FIRST SEAT!
AS DEAN, IT'S MY DUTY TO SUPPORT OUR ALUMNI AS WELL AS OUR STUDENTS.
UH-HUH. HOWEVER YOU WANNA JUSTIFY IT.
AH WELL. YOU HAVE FUN, THEN. SEE YA!
SHOOP
BACK WHEN WE WERE BOTH STILL THIRD-YEARS...
I DO FEEL IT'S MY DUTY AS DEAN OF THE INSTITUTE.
BUT... IS THAT REALLY ALL IT IS?
I'm going to go train, probably overseas or something. It'll be a couple
...AND I FOUND THE NOTE YOU LEFT SAYING YOU WERE SUDDENLY GOING ABROAD...
...I WAS ABSOLUTELY INFURIATED. I THINK I NOW KNOW WHY THAT WAS.
GRR
GRR

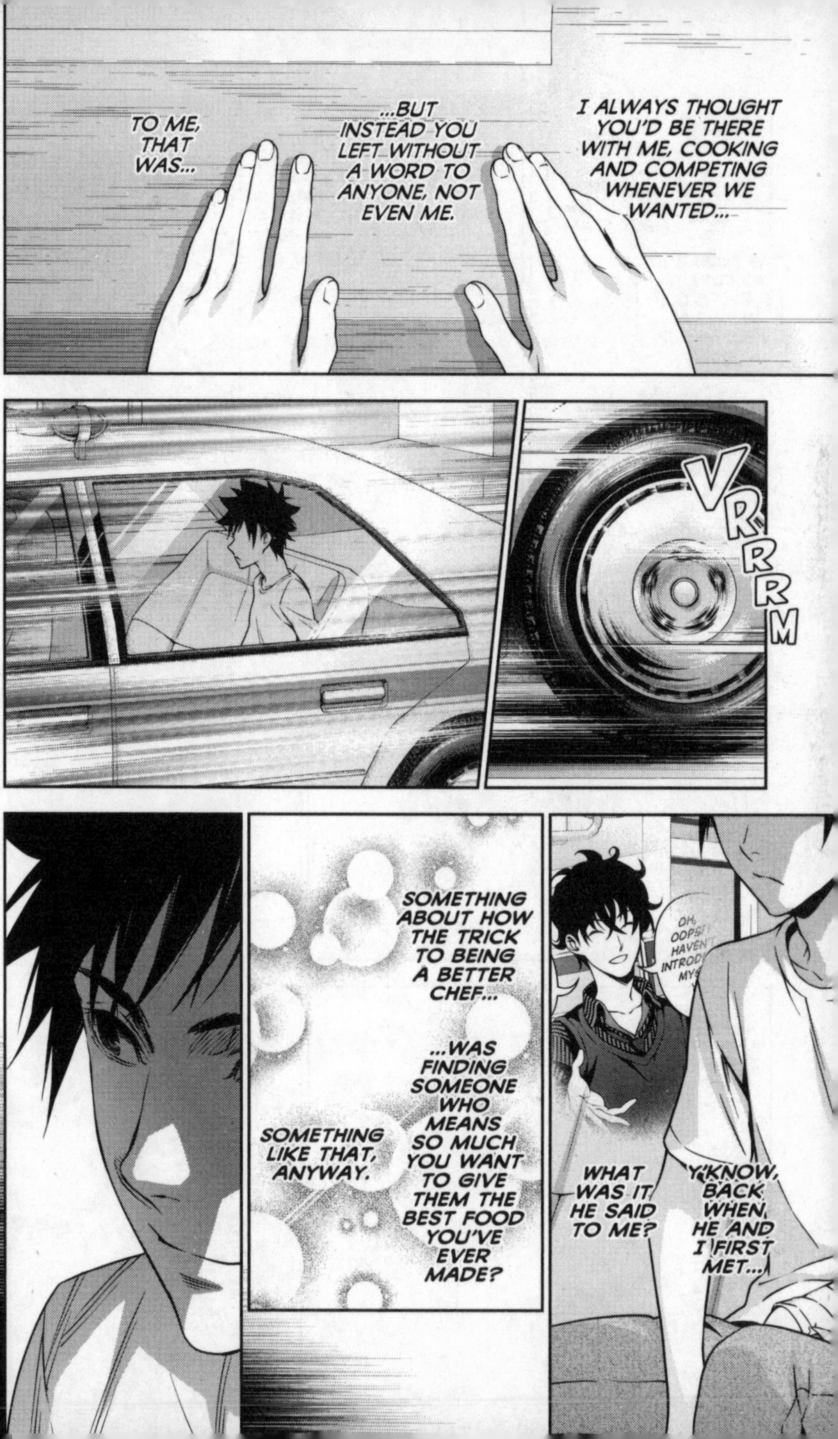
I ALWAYS THOUGHT YOU'D BE THERE WITH ME, COOKING AND COMPETING WHENEVER WE WANTED...
...BUT INSTEAD YOU LEFT WITHOUT A WORD TO ANYONE, NOT EVEN ME.
TO ME, THAT WAS...
VRRRM
Y'KNOW, BACK WHEN HE AND I FIRST MET...
WHAT WAS IT HE SAID TO ME?
SOMETHING ABOUT HOW THE TRICK TO BEING A BETTER CHEF...
...WAS FINDING SOMEONE WHO MEANS SO MUCH YOU WANT TO GIVE THEM THE BEST FOOD YOU'VE EVER MADE?
SOMETHING LIKE THAT, ANYWAY.

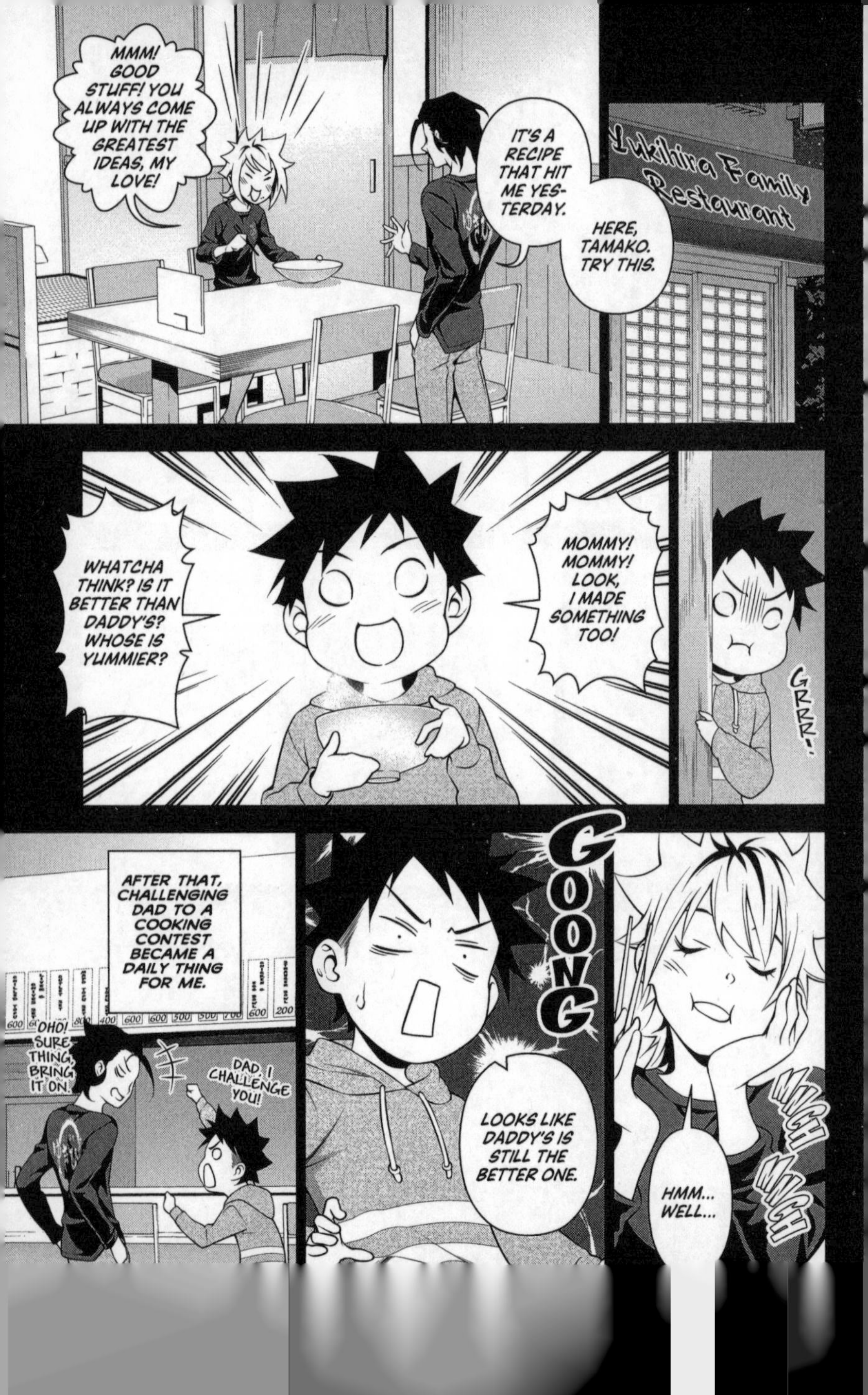
Yukihira Family Restaurant
IT'S A RECIPE THAT HIT ME YESTERDAY.
HERE, TAMAKO. TRY THIS.
MMM! GOOD STUFF! YOU ALWAYS COME UP WITH THE GREATEST IDEAS, MY LOVE!
GRRR!
MOMMY! MOMMY! LOOK, I MADE SOMETHING TOO!
WHATCHA THINK? IS IT BETTER THAN DADDY'S? WHOSE IS YUMMIER?
MNCH MNCH
HMM... WELL...
GOOONG
LOOKS LIKE DADDY'S IS STILL THE BETTER ONE.
AFTER THAT, CHALLENGING DAD TO A COOKING CONTEST BECAME A DAILY THING FOR ME.
DAD, I CHALLENGE YOU!
OHO! SURE THING, BRING IT ON.

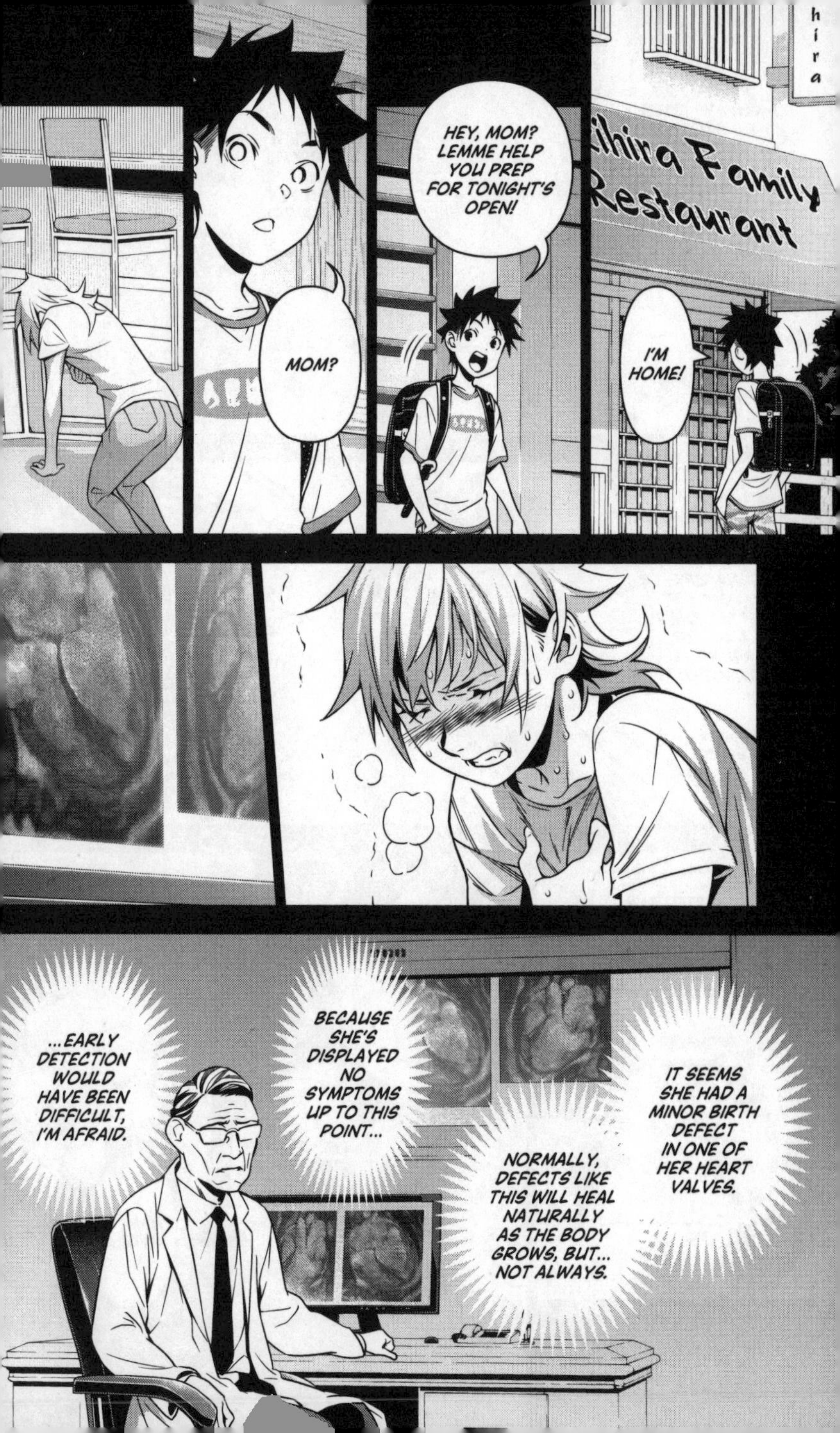
hira
hira Family Restaurant
I'M HOME!
HEY, MOM? LEMME HELP YOU PREP FOR TONIGHT'S OPEN!
MOM?
IT SEEMS SHE HAD A MINOR BIRTH DEFECT IN ONE OF HER HEART VALVES.
NORMALLY, DEFECTS LIKE THIS WILL HEAL NATURALLY AS THE BODY GROWS, BUT... NOT ALWAYS.
BECAUSE SHE'S DISPLAYED NO SYMPTOMS UP TO THIS POINT...
...EARLY DETECTION WOULD HAVE BEEN DIFFICULT, I'M AFRAID.

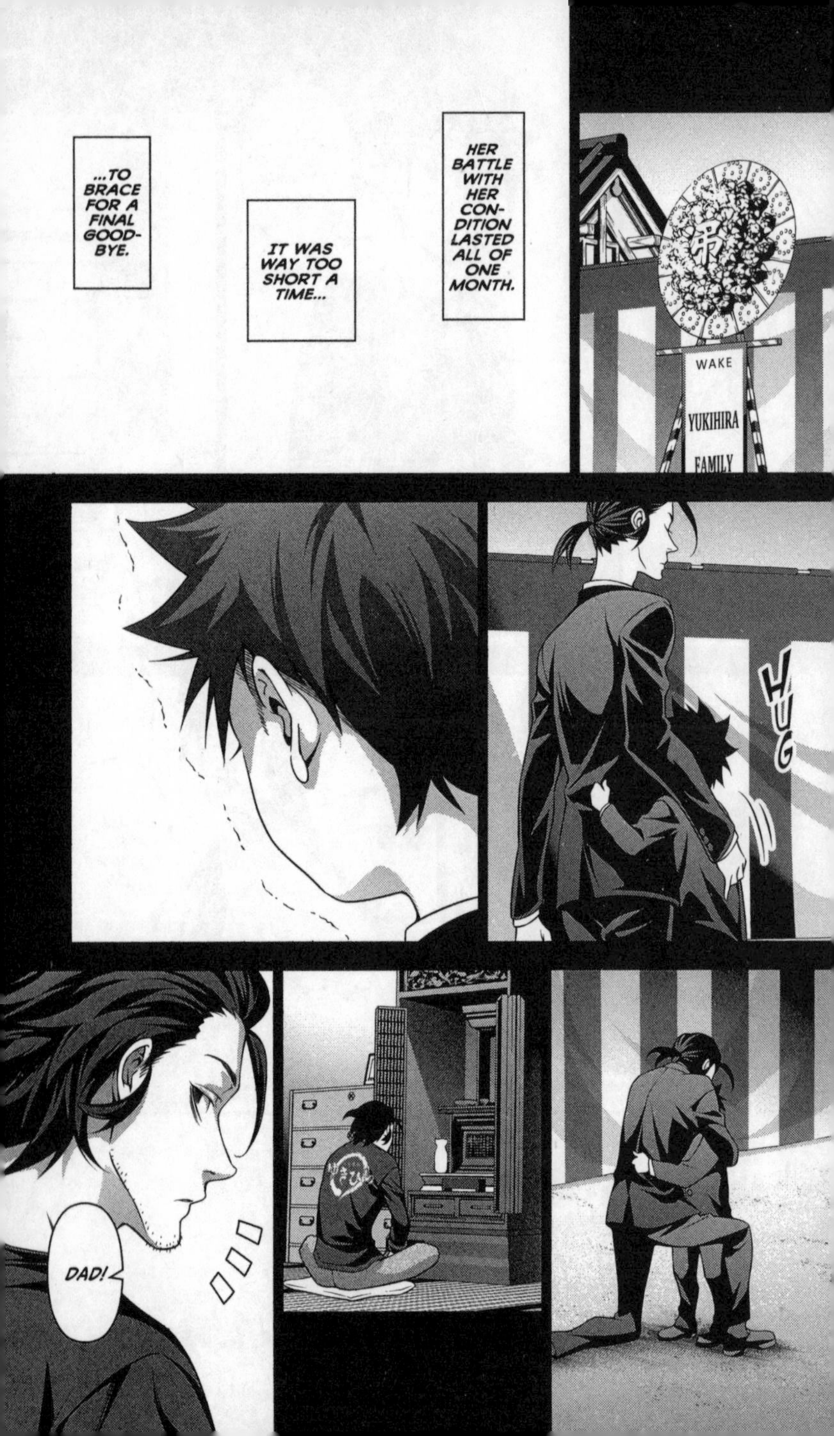

HER BATTLE WITH HER CON-DITION LASTED ALL OF ONE MONTH.
IT WAS WAY TOO SHORT A TIME...
...TO BRACE FOR A FINAL GOOD-BYE.
弔
WAKE
YUKIHIRA
FAMILY
HUG
DAD!

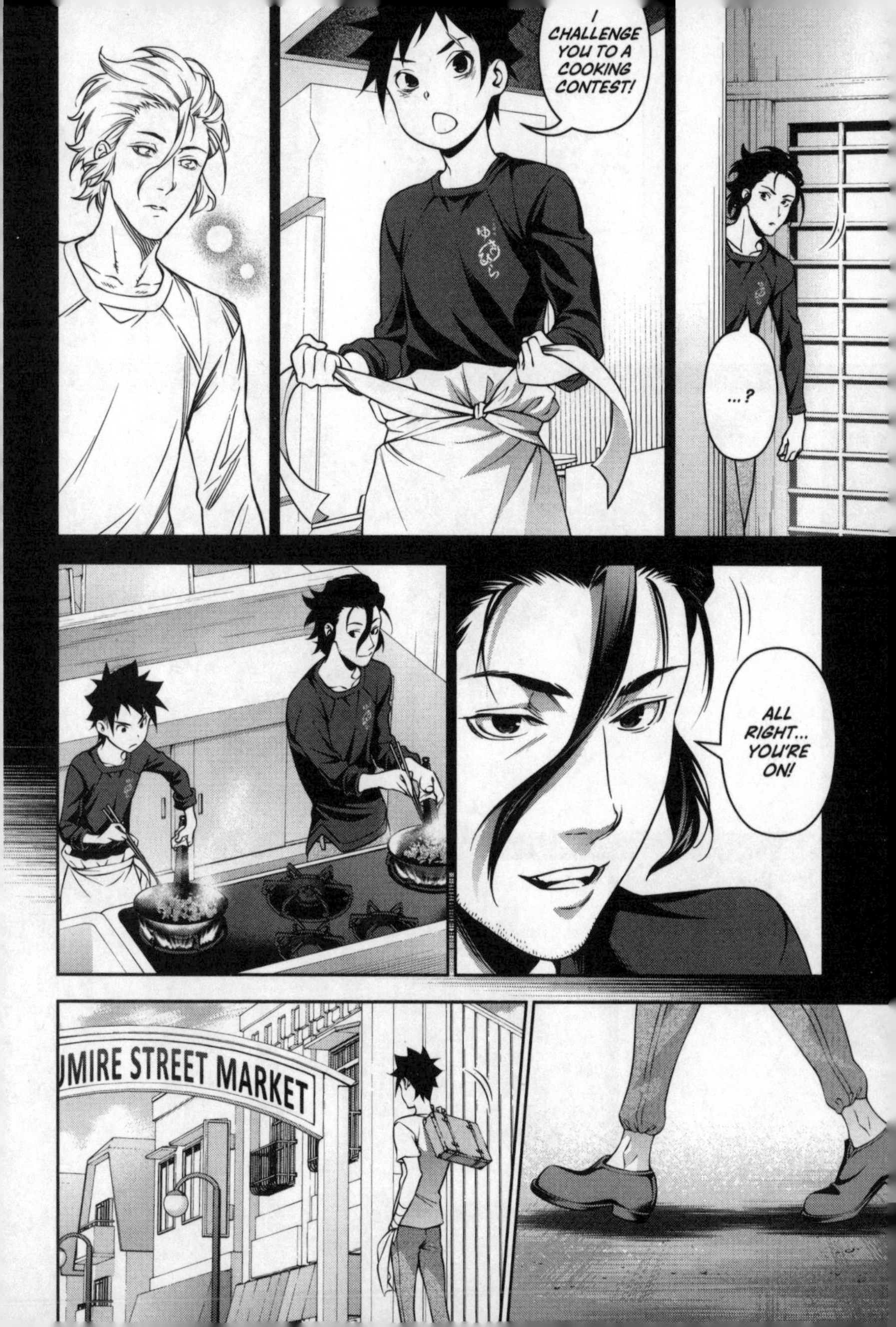
...?
I CHALLENGE YOU TO A COOKING CONTEST!
ALL RIGHT... YOU'RE ON!
UMIRE STREET MARKET

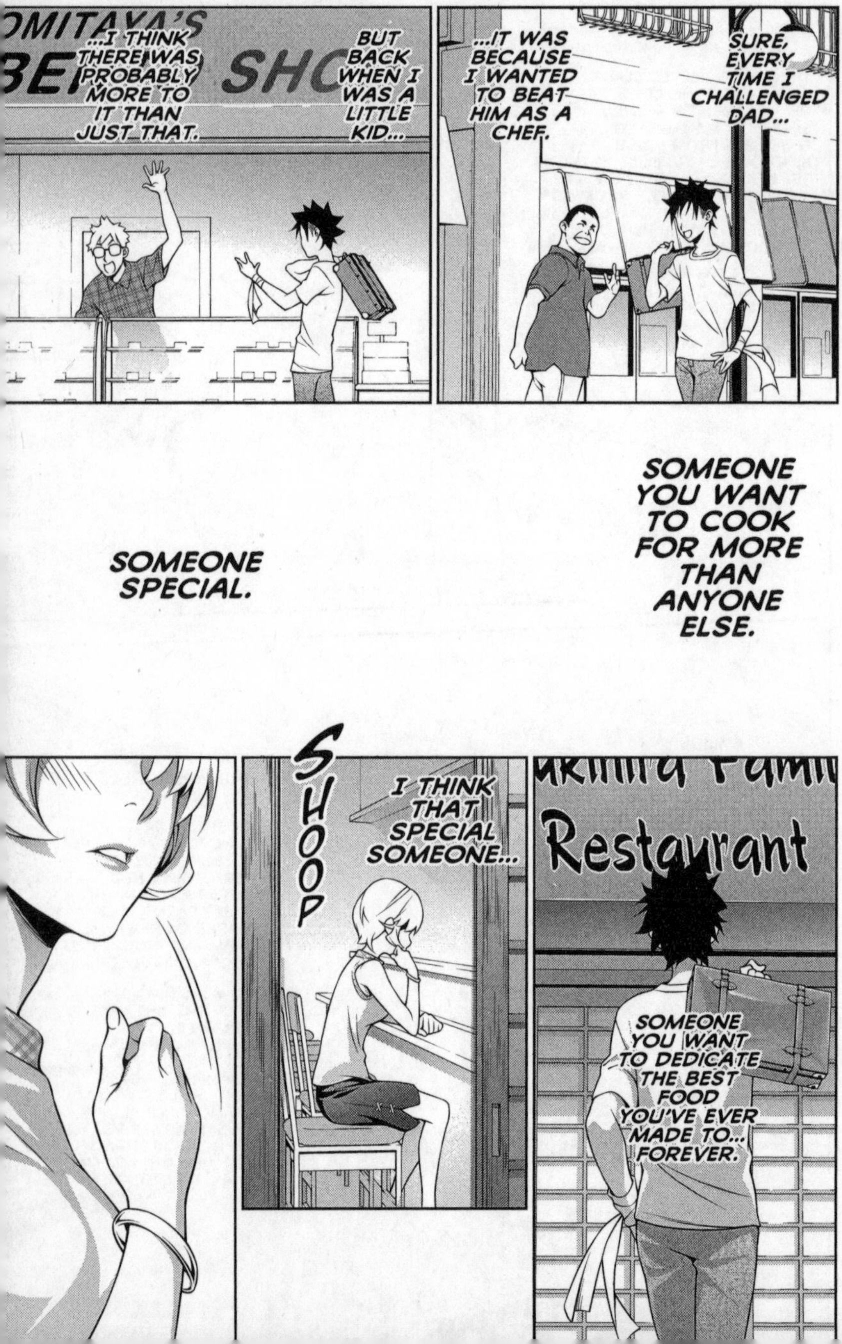
SURE, EVERY TIME I CHALLENGED DAD...
...IT WAS BECAUSE I WANTED TO BEAT HIM AS A CHEF.
BUT BACK WHEN I WAS A LITTLE KID...
...I THINK THERE WAS PROBABLY MORE TO IT THAN JUST THAT.
SOMEONE YOU WANT TO COOK FOR MORE THAN ANYONE ELSE.
SOMEONE SPECIAL.
Restaurant
SOMEONE YOU WANT TO DEDICATE THE BEST FOOD YOU'VE EVER MADE TO... FOREVER.
SHOOP
I THINK THAT SPECIAL SOMEONE...

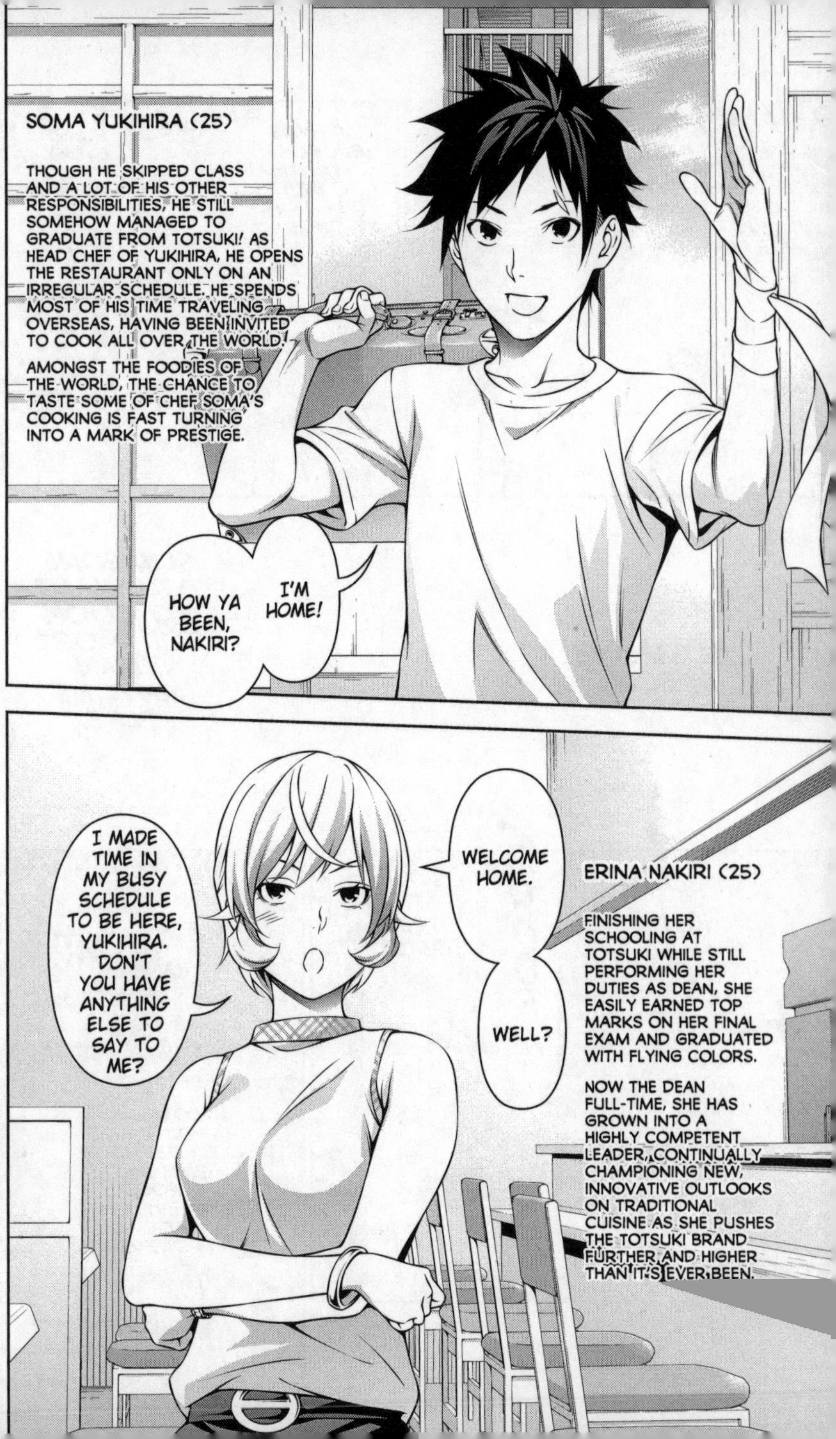
SOMA YUKIHIRA (25)
THOUGH HE SKIPPED CLASS AND A LOT OF HIS OTHER RESPONSIBILITIES, HE STILL SOMEHOW MANAGED TO GRADUATE FROM TOTSUKI! AS HEAD CHEF OF YUKIHIRA, HE OPENS THE RESTAURANT ONLY ON AN IRREGULAR SCHEDULE. HE SPENDS MOST OF HIS TIME TRAVELING OVERSEAS, HAVING BEEN INVITED TO COOK ALL OVER THE WORLD!
AMONGST THE FOODIES OF THE WORLD, THE CHANCE TO TASTE SOME OF CHEF SOMA'S COOKING IS FAST TURNING INTO A MARK OF PRESTIGE.
I'M HOME!
HOW YA BEEN, NAKIRI?
ERINA NAKIRI (25)
FINISHING HER SCHOOLING AT TOTSUKI WHILE STILL PERFORMING HER DUTIES AS DEAN, SHE EASILY EARNED TOP MARKS ON HER FINAL EXAM AND GRADUATED WITH FLYING COLORS.
NOW THE DEAN FULL-TIME, SHE HAS GROWN INTO A HIGHLY COMPETENT LEADER, CONTINUALLY CHAMPIONING NEW, INNOVATIVE OUTLOOKS ON TRADITIONAL CUISINE AS SHE PUSHES THE TOTSUKI BRAND FURTHER AND HIGHER THAN IT'S EVER BEEN.
WELCOME HOME.
WELL?
I MADE TIME IN MY BUSY SCHEDULE TO BE HERE, YUKIHIRA. DON'T YOU HAVE ANYTHING ELSE TO SAY TO ME?

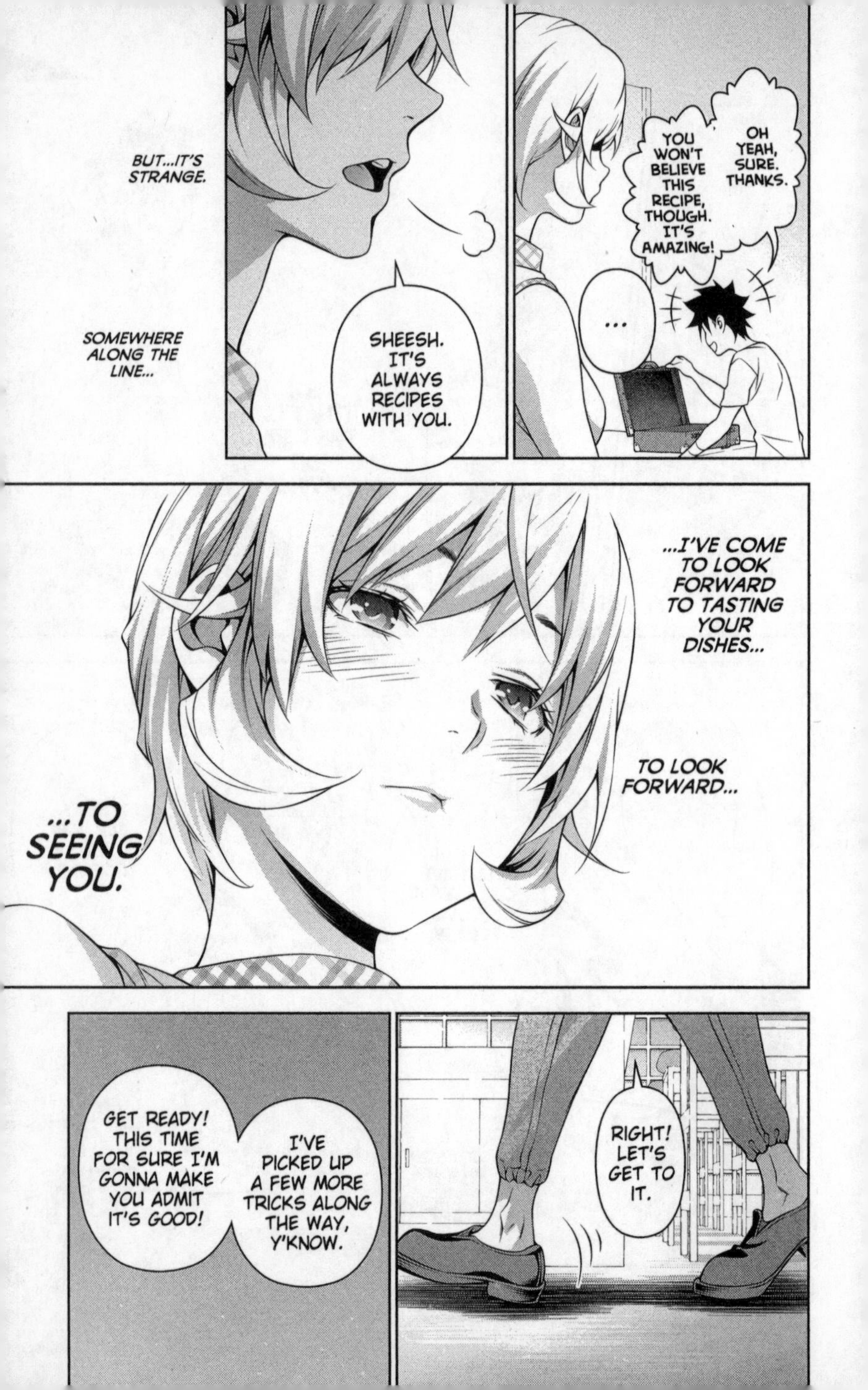
OH YEAH, SURE. THANKS.
YOU WON'T BELIEVE THIS RECIPE, THOUGH. IT'S AMAZING!
...
SHEESH. IT'S ALWAYS RECIPES WITH YOU.
BUT...IT'S STRANGE.
SOMEWHERE ALONG THE LINE...
...I'VE COME TO LOOK FORWARD TO TASTING YOUR DISHES...
TO LOOK FORWARD...
...TO SEEING YOU.
RIGHT! LET'S GET TO IT.
I'VE PICKED UP A FEW MORE TRICKS ALONG THE WAY, Y'KNOW.
GET READY! THIS TIME FOR SURE I'M GONNA MAKE YOU ADMIT IT'S GOOD!

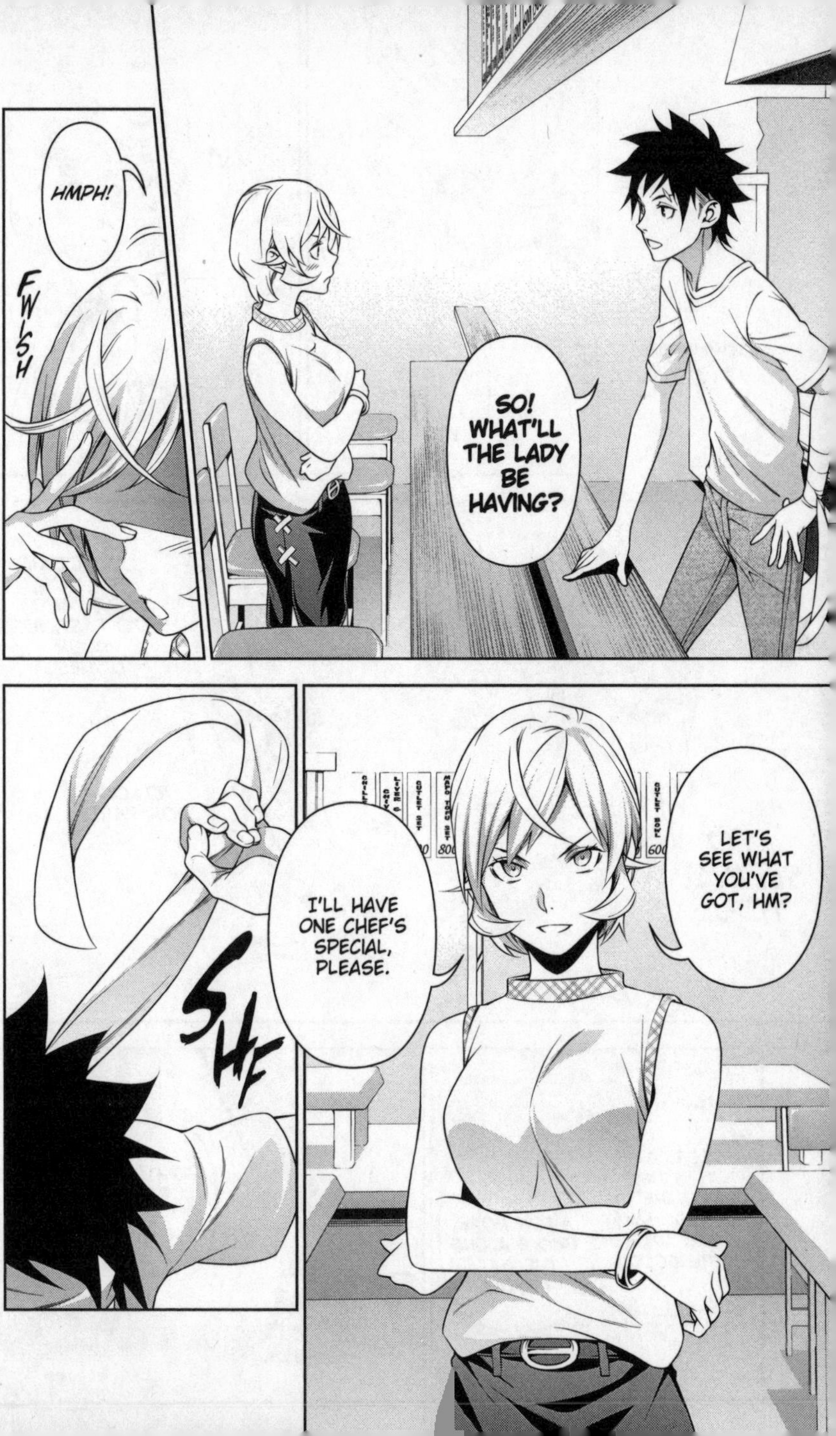
SO! WHAT'LL THE LADY BE HAVING?
HMPH!
FWISH
LET'S SEE WHAT YOU'VE GOT, HM?
I'LL HAVE ONE CHEF'S SPECIAL, PLEASE.
SHF

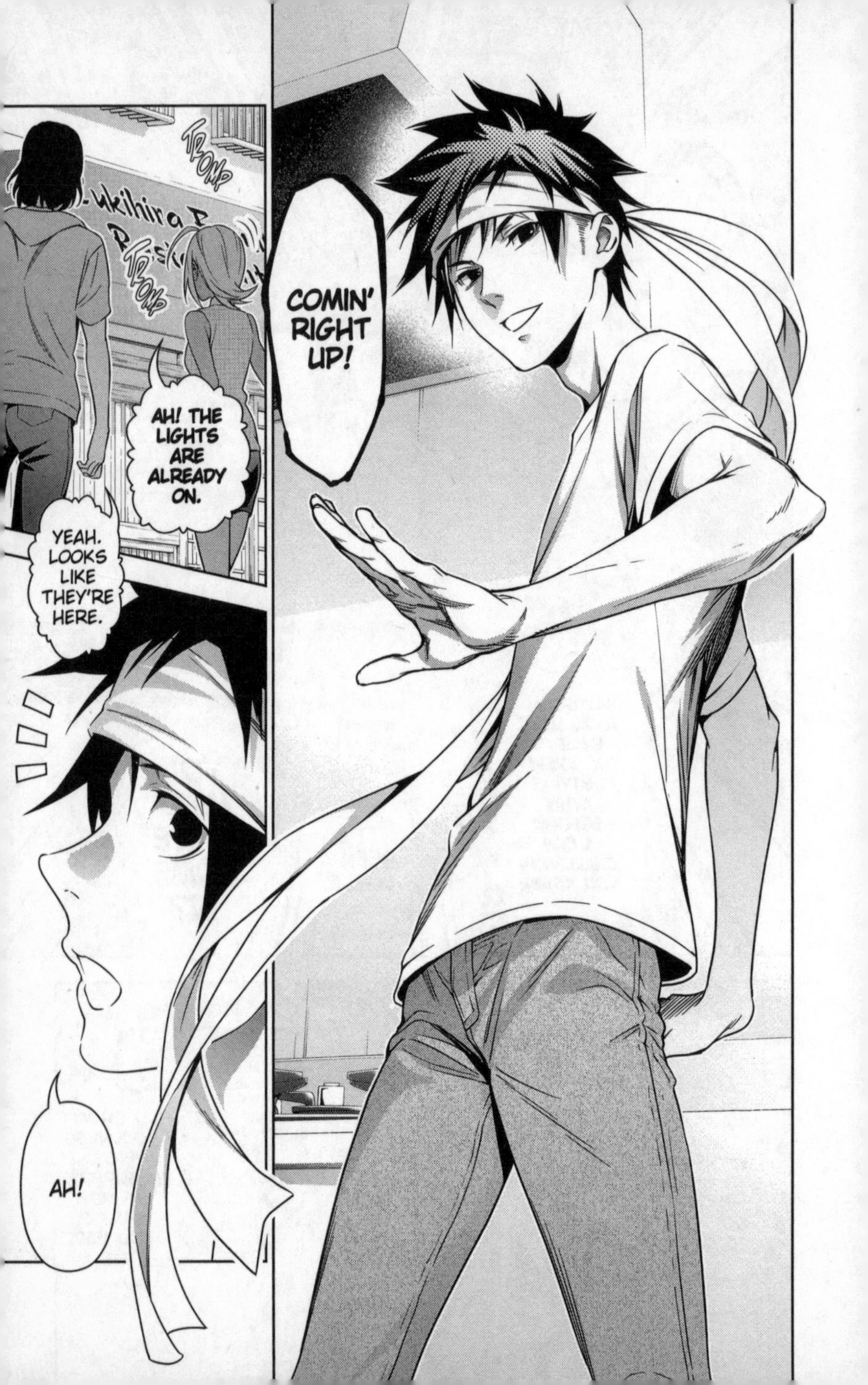
COMIN' RIGHT UP!
TROMP
TROMP
AH! THE LIGHTS ARE ALREADY ON.
YEAH. LOOKS LIKE THEY'RE HERE.
AH!

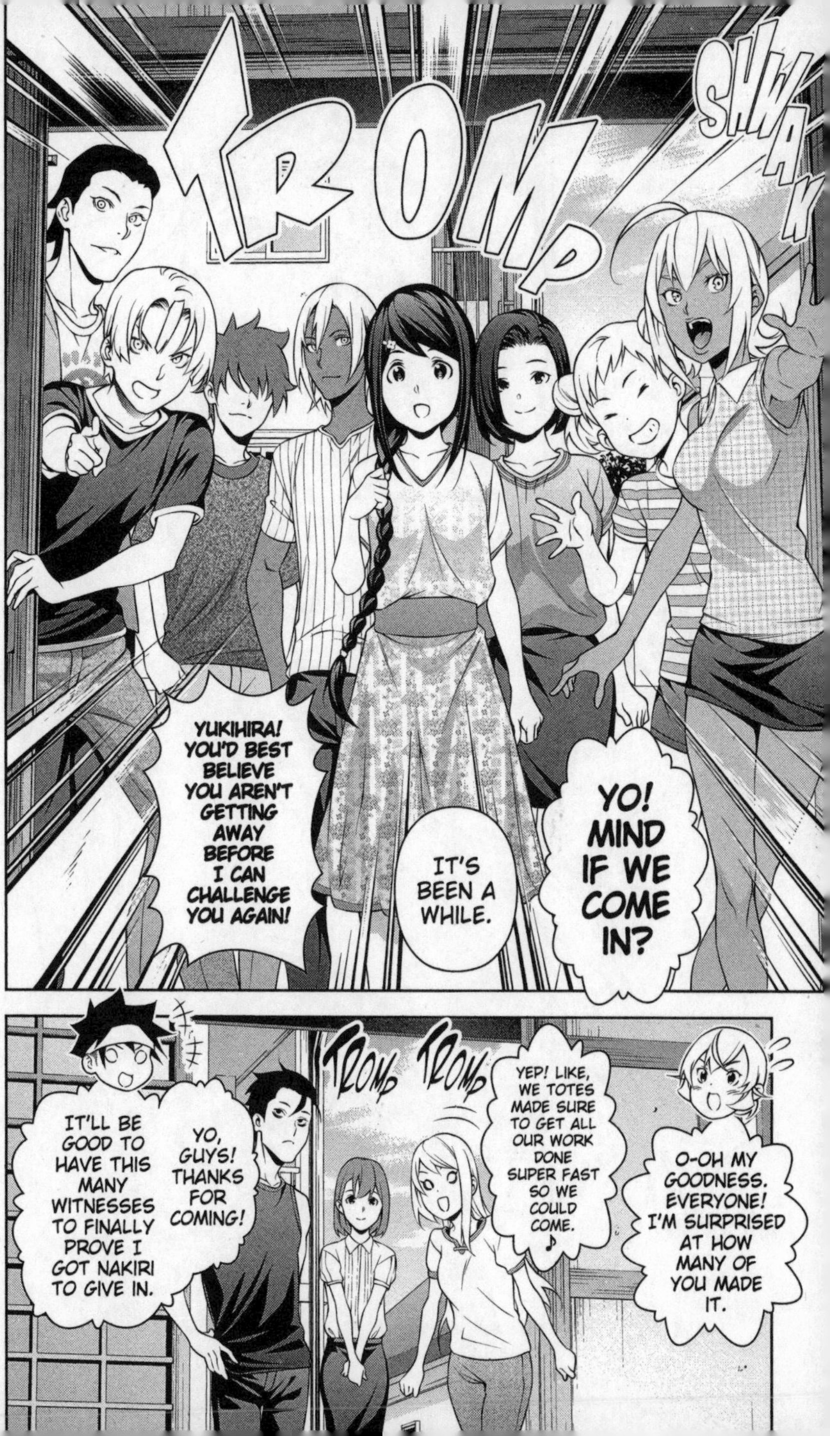
SHWAK
TROMP
YO! MIND IF WE COME IN?
IT'S BEEN A WHILE.
YUKIHIRA! YOU'D BEST BELIEVE YOU AREN'T GETTING AWAY BEFORE I CAN CHALLENGE YOU AGAIN!
O-OH MY GOODNESS. EVERYONE! I'M SURPRISED AT HOW MANY OF YOU MADE IT.
YEP! LIKE, WE TOTES MADE SURE TO GET ALL OUR WORK DONE SUPER FAST SO WE COULD COME. ♪
TROMP TROMP
YO, GUYS! THANKS FOR COMING!
IT'LL BE GOOD TO HAVE THIS MANY WITNESSES TO FINALLY PROVE I GOT NAKIRI TO GIVE IN.

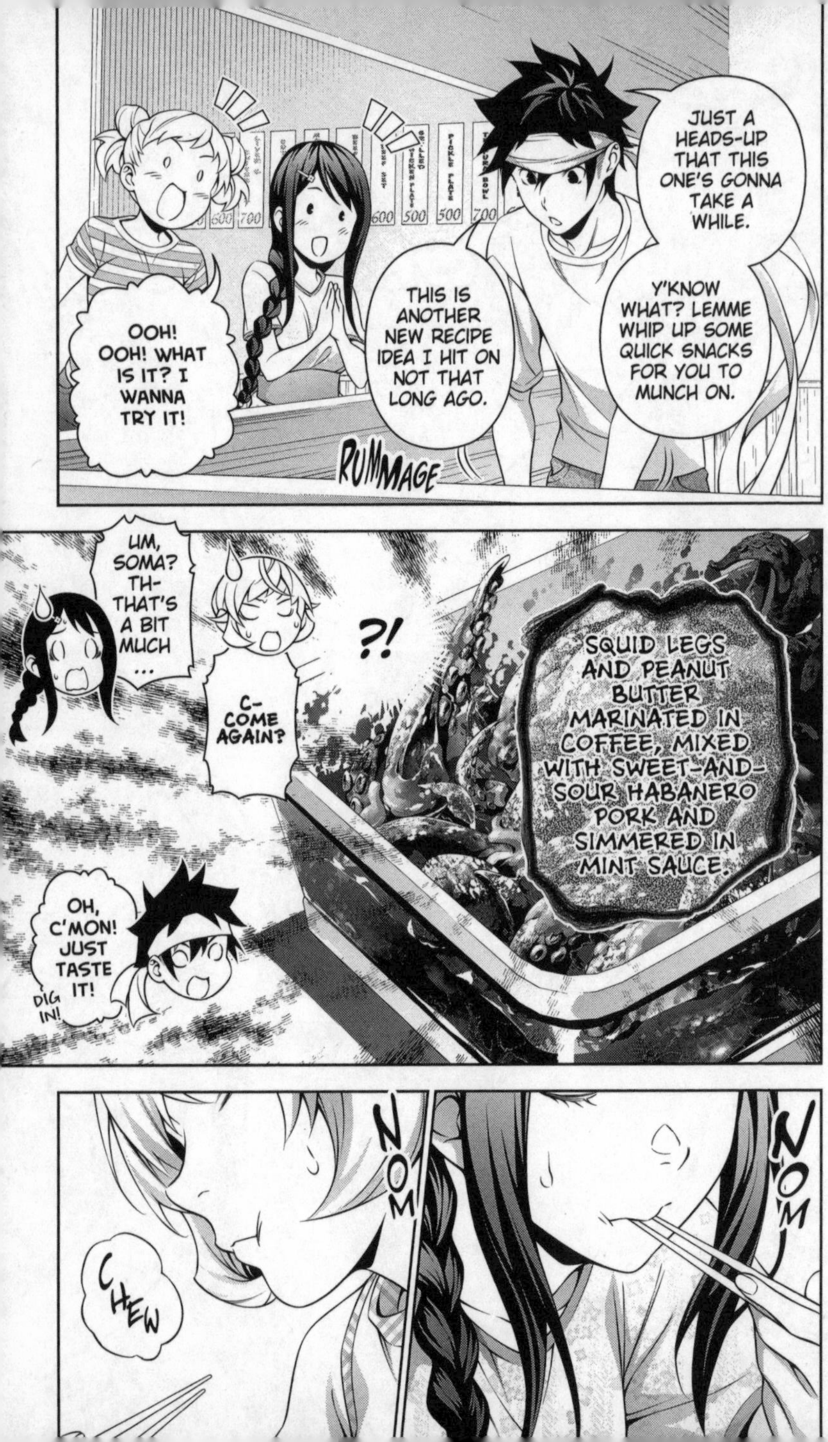
JUST A HEADS-UP THAT THIS ONE'S GONNA TAKE A WHILE.
Y'KNOW WHAT? LEMME WHIP UP SOME QUICK SNACKS FOR YOU TO MUNCH ON.
THIS IS ANOTHER NEW RECIPE IDEA I HIT ON NOT THAT LONG AGO.
OOH! OOH! WHAT IS IT? I WANNA TRY IT!
RUMMAGE
SQUID LEGS AND PEANUT BUTTER MARINATED IN COFFEE, MIXED WITH SWEET-AND-SOUR HABANERO PORK AND SIMMERED IN MINT SAUCE.
?!
C-COME AGAIN?
UM, SOMA? TH-THAT'S A BIT MUCH...
OH, C'MON! JUST TASTE IT!
DIG IN!
NOM
NOM
CHEW

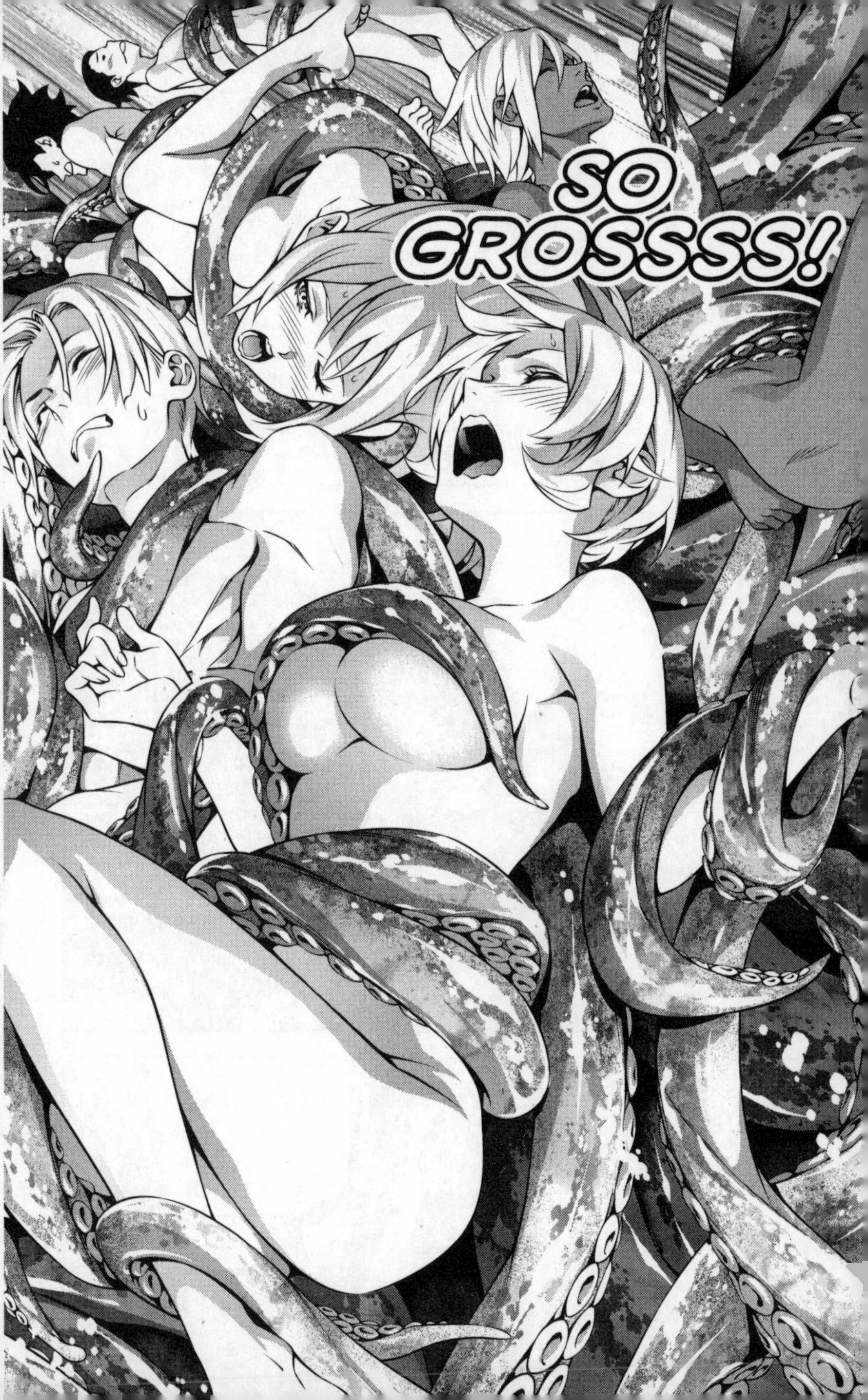
SO GROSSSS!

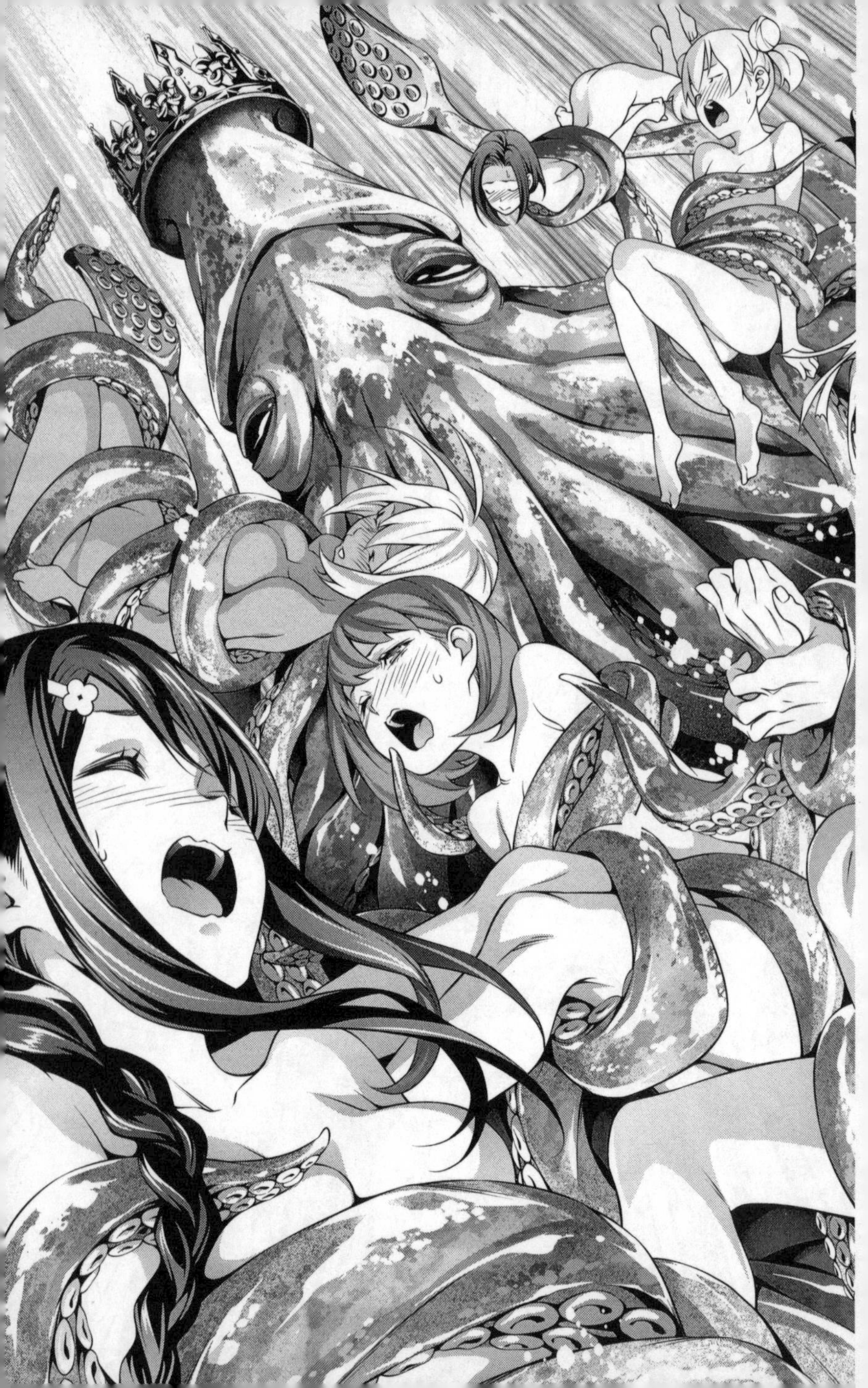

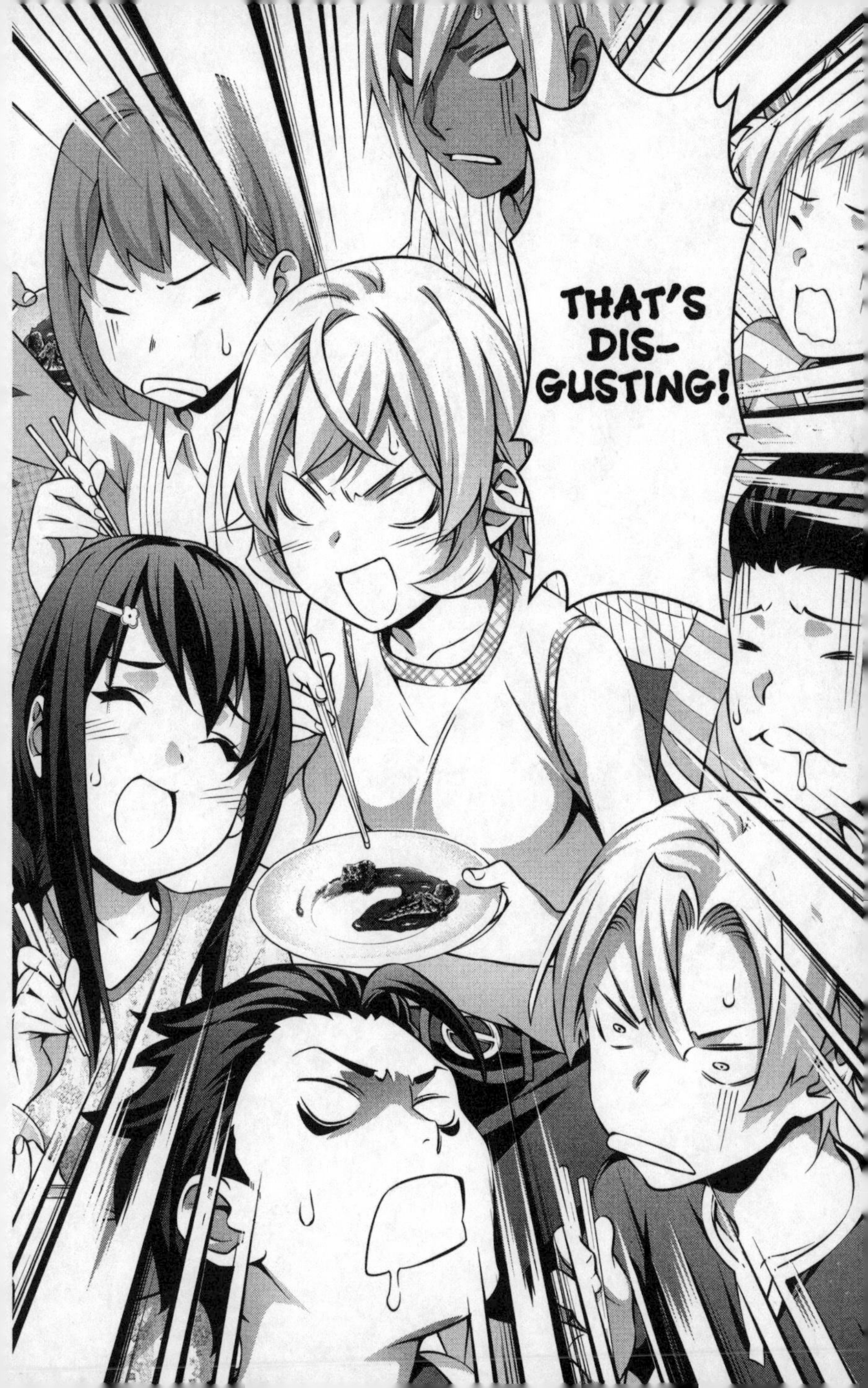
THAT'S DIS-GUSTING!

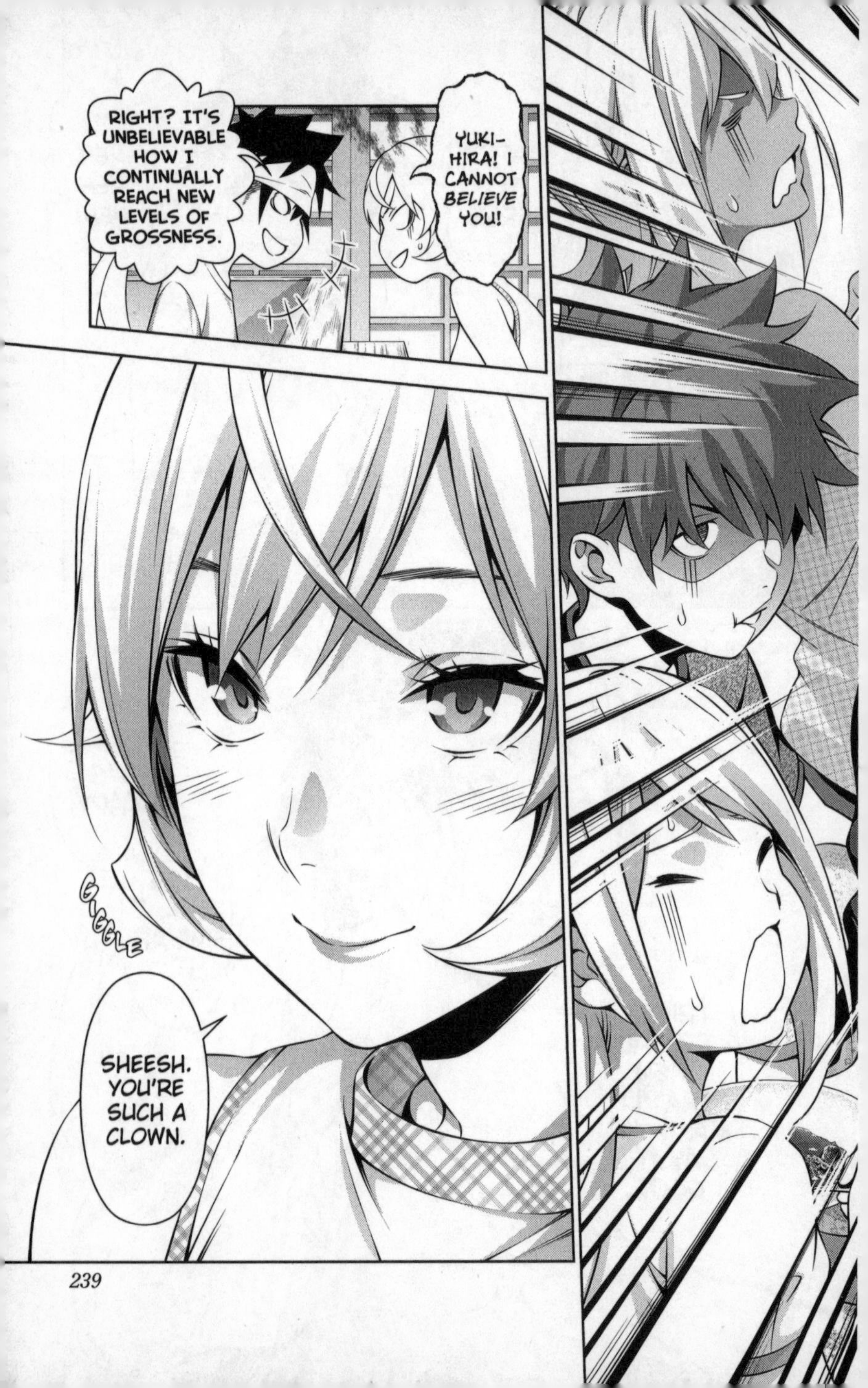
YUKI-HIRA! I CANNOT BELIEVE YOU!
RIGHT? IT'S UNBELIEVABLE HOW I CONTINUALLY REACH NEW LEVELS OF GROSSNESS.
GIGGLE
SHEESH. YOU'RE SUCH A CLOWN.

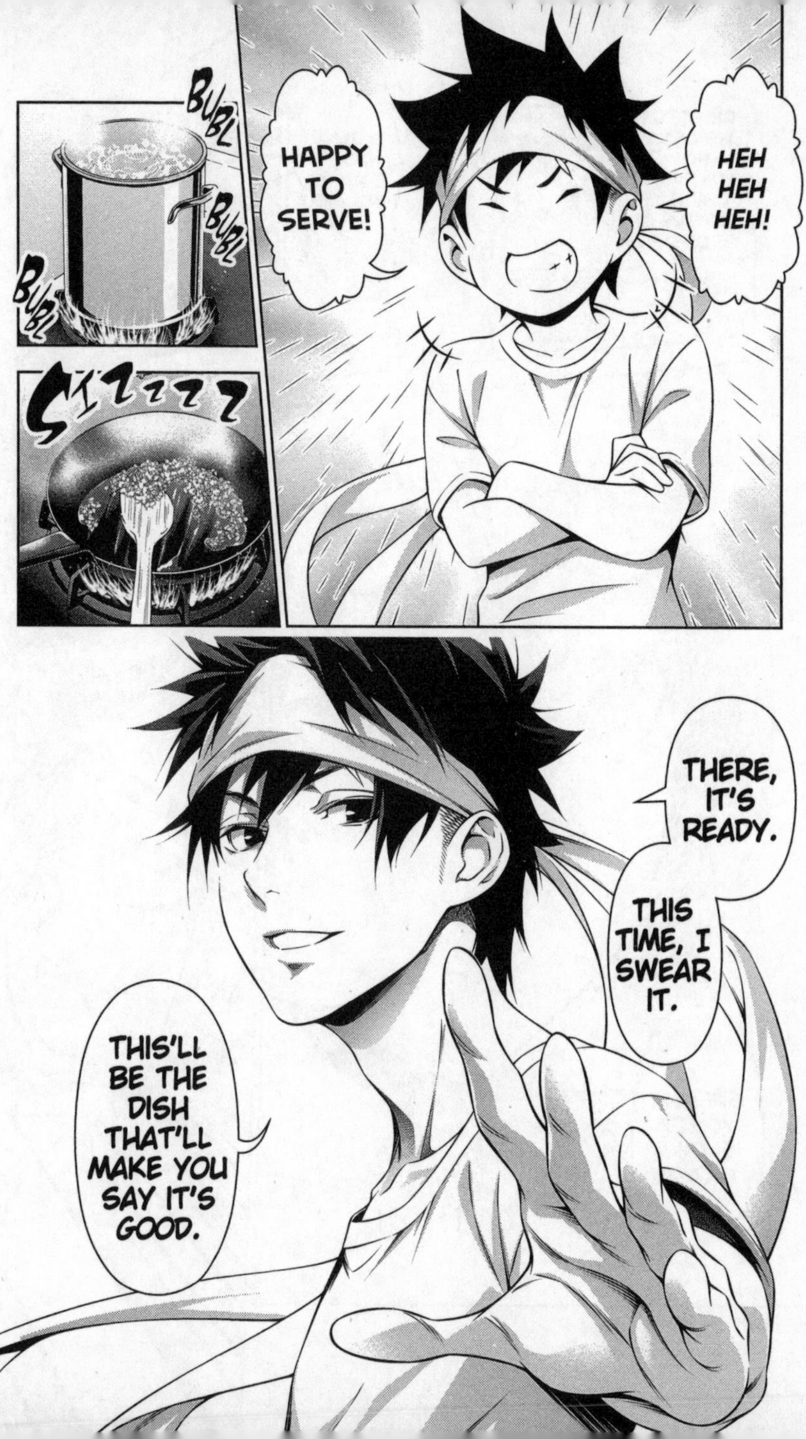
HEH HEH HEH!
HAPPY TO SERVE!
BUBL
BUBL
BUBL
SIZZZZZ
THERE, IT'S READY.
THIS TIME, I SWEAR IT.
THIS'LL BE THE DISH THAT'LL MAKE YOU SAY IT'S GOOD.

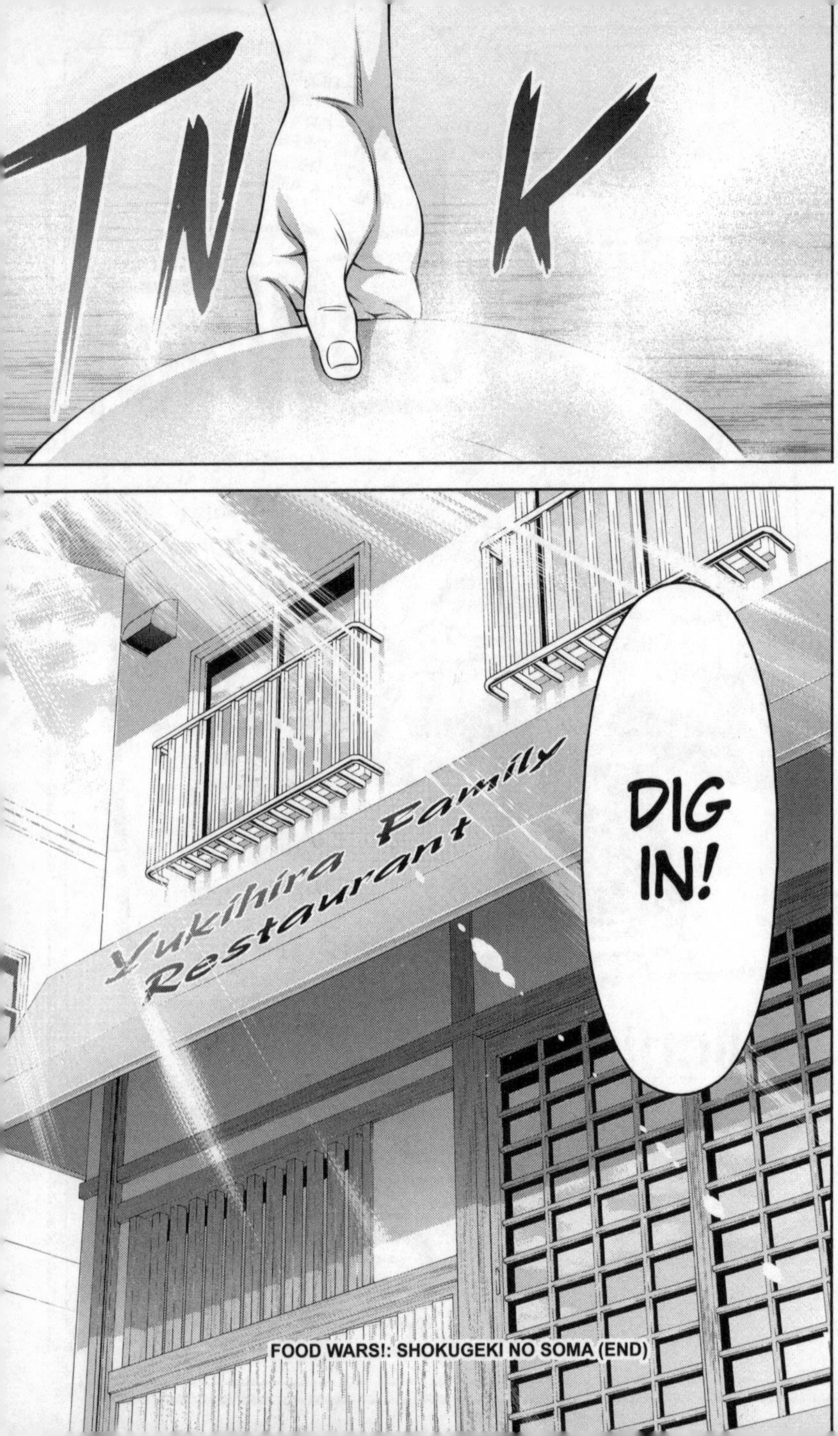
TNK
Yukihira Family Restaurant
DIG IN!
FOOD WARS!: SHOKUGEKI NO SOMA (END)

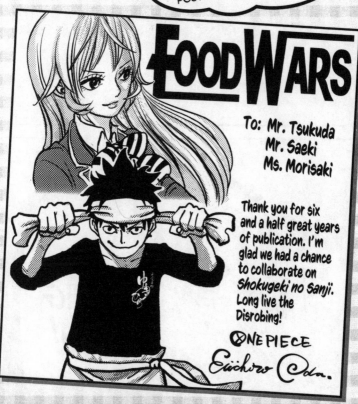

WOW! WE RECEIVED SOME INCREDIBLE SPECIAL ILLUSTRATIONS FROM SOME OTHER *JUMP* MANGA CREATORS (HAPPY TEARS & GRATITUDE)! TALK ABOUT AN AFTER-DESSERT SPECIAL! PLEASE ENJOY THIS ROUND OF POST-MEAL TEA AND COFFEE!

FOOD WARS

To: Mr. Tsukuda
Mr. Saeki
Ms. Morisaki

Thank you for six and a half great years of publication. I'm glad we had a chance to collaborate on *Shokugeki no Sanji*. Long live the Disrobing!

ONE PIECE
Eiichiro Oda.

Eiichiro Oda

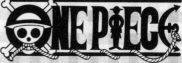

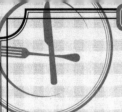

Kohei Horikoshi

MY HERO ACADEMIA

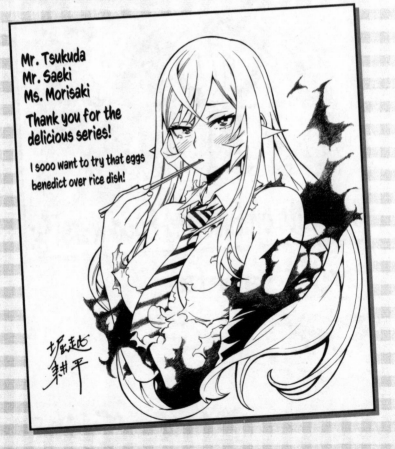

Mr. Tsukuda
Mr. Saeki
Ms. Morisaki

Thank you for the delicious series!

I sooo want to try that eggs benedict over rice dish!

Congrats on finishing Food Wars!

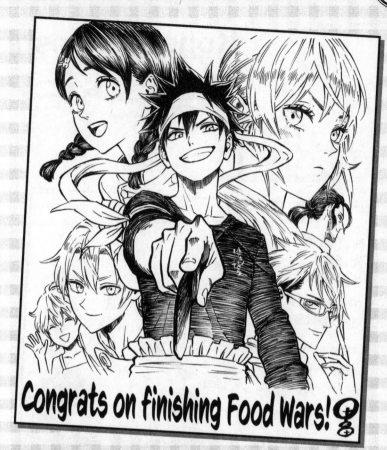

Yuki Tabata

Black Clover

SPECIAL COMMEMORATIVE ILLUSTRATIONS ON THE END OF FOOD WARS!

Tadahiro Miura

ゆらぎ荘の幽奈さん
Yuna of the Haunted Hot Springs

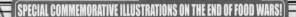

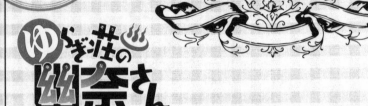

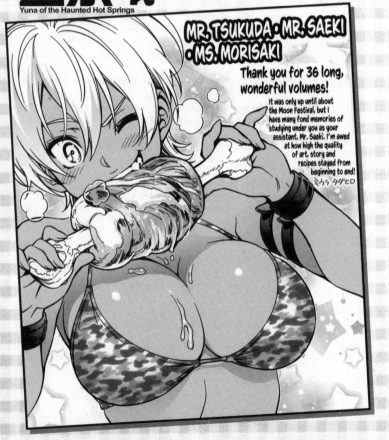

MR. TSUKUDA • MR. SAEKI • MS. MORISAKI
Thank you for 36 long, wonderful volumes!
It was only up until about the Moon Festival, but I have many fond memories of studying under you as your assistant, Mr. Saeki. I'm awed at how high the quality of art, story and recipes stayed from beginning to end!
ミウラタダヒロ

●THANK YOU TO EVERYONE WHO SENT AN ILLUSTRATION!●

Food Wars!
SHOKUGEKI NO SOMA

Volume 36
Shonen Jump Manga Edition
Story by Yuto Tsukuda, Art by Shun Saeki
Contributor Yuki Morisaki

Translation: Adrienne Beck
Touch-Up Art & Lettering: James Gaubatz, Mara Coman
Design: Alice Lewis
Editor: Jennifer LeBlanc

SHOKUGEKI NO SOMA © 2012 by Yuto Tsukuda, Shun Saeki
All rights reserved.
First published in Japan in 2012 by SHUEISHA Inc., Tokyo.
English translation rights arranged by SHUEISHA Inc.

The stories, characters and incidents mentioned in this publication
are entirely fictional.

Printed in the U.S.A.

Published by VIZ Media, LLC
P.O. Box 77010
San Francisco, CA 94107

10 9 8 7 6 5 4 3 2 1
First printing, June 2020

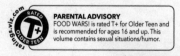

PARENTAL ADVISORY
FOOD WARS! is rated T+ for Older Teen and
is recommended for ages 16 and up. This
volume contains sexual situations/humor.

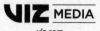

viz.com

shonenjump.com

JoJo's
BIZARRE ADVENTURE

★ PART 4 ★
DIAMOND IS UNBREAKABLE

Story & Art by
HIROHIKO ARAKI

A MULTIGENERATIONAL TALE OF THE HEROIC JOESTAR
FAMILY AND THEIR NEVER-ENDING BATTLE AGAINST EVIL!

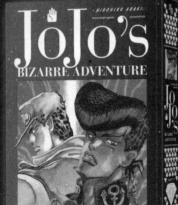

In April 1999, Jotaro Kujo travels to a town in Japan called Morioh to find a young man named Josuke Higashikata, the secret love child of his grandfather, Joseph Joestar. Upon finding him, Jotaro is surprised to learn that Josuke also possesses a Stand. After their strange meeting, the pair team up to investigate the town's proliferation of unusual Stands!

You're Reading in the Wrong Direction!!

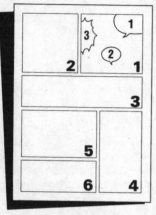

Whoops! Guess what? You're starting at the wrong end of the comic!

...It's true! In keeping with the original Japanese format, **Food Wars!** is meant to be read from right to left, starting in the upper-right corner.

Unlike English, which is read from left to right, Japanese is read from right to left, meaning that action, sound effects and word-balloon order are completely reversed... something which can make readers unfamiliar with Japanese feel pretty backwards themselves. For this reason, manga or Japanese comics published in the U.S. in English have sometimes been published "flopped"—that is, printed in exact reverse order, as though seen from the other side of a mirror.

By flopping pages, U.S. publishers can avoid confusing readers, but the compromise is not without its downside. For one thing, a character in a flopped manga series who once wore in the original Japanese version a T-shirt emblazoned with "M A Y" (as in "the merry month of") now wears one which reads "Y A M"! Additionally, many manga creators in Japan are themselves unhappy with the process, as some feel the mirror-imaging of their art skews their original intentions.

We are proud to bring you Yuto Tsukuda and Shun Saeki's **Food Wars!** in the original un-flopped format.

For now, though, turn to the other side of the book and let the adventure begin...!

—Editor

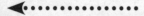

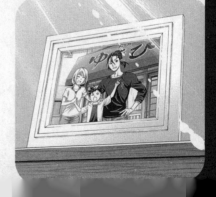